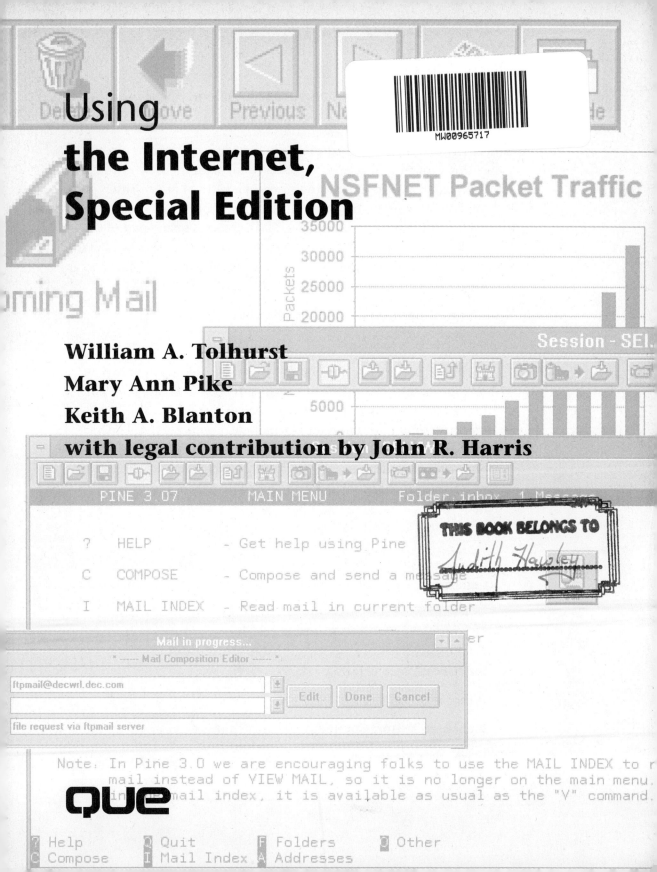

Using
the Internet,
Special Edition

William A. Tolhurst

Mary Ann Pike

Keith A. Blanton

with legal contribution by John R. Harris

NSFNET Packet Traffic

PINE 3.07   MAIN MENU   Folder inbox 1 Message

?   HELP   - Get help using Pine

C   COMPOSE   - Compose and send a message

I   MAIL INDEX   - Read mail in current folder

Mail in progress...
" ----- Mail Composition Editor ----- "

ftpmail@decwrl.dec.com

Edit   Done   Cancel

file request via ftpmail server

Note: In Pine 3.0 we are encouraging folks to use the MAIL INDEX to r
      mail instead of VIEW MAIL, so it is no longer on the main menu.
      mail index, it is available as usual as the "V" command.

que

? Help   Q Quit   F Folders   O Other
C Compose   I Mail Index A Addresses

Using the Internet, Special Edition

Library of Congress Catalog No.: 93-86861

ISBN: 1-56529-353-3

96   95   94   4   3   2   1

Interpretation of the printing code: the rightmost double-digit number is the year of the book's printing; the rightmost single-digit number, the number of the book's printing. For example, a printing code of 94-1 shows that the first printing of the book occurred in 1994.

Publisher: David P. Ewing

Director of Publishing: Mike Miller

Managing Editor: Corinne Walls

Marketing Manager: Ray Robinson

Credits

Publishing Managers
Don Roche Jr.
Lisa A. Bucki

Acquisitions Editor
Nancy Stevenson

Product Development Specialist
Steven M. Schafer

Production Editors
Susan Shaw Dunn
J. Christopher Nelson

Editors
William A. Barton
Elsa Bell
Lorna Gentry
Thomas F. Hayes
Patrick Kanouse
Heather Kaufman
Susan Ross Moore
Anne Owen
Brad Sullivan

Technical Editor
Steve Berger

Technical Support
Rolf A. Crozier

Book Designer
Amy Peppler-Adams

Cover Designer
Jay Corpus

Production Team
Angela Bannan
Claudia Bell
Danielle Bird
Paula Carroll
Charlotte Clapp
Ann Dickerson
Karen Dodson
Teresa Forrester
Joelynn Gifford
Carla Hall
Jenny Kucera
Bob LaRoche
Elizabeth Lewis
Tim Montgomery
Nanci Sears Perry
Dennis Sheehan
Amy Steed
Marcella Thompson
Sue VandeWalle
Mary Beth Wakefield
Donna Winter
Michelle Worthington
Lillian Yates

Indexers
Johnna VanHoose
Joy Dean Lee

Editorial Assistant
Jill Stanley

Composed in *Stone Serif* and *MCPdigital* by Que Corporation.

Dedication

To those who touch our lives, not knowing that they do.

About the Authors

William A. Tolhurst is co-founder and vice president of engineering for Atlanta Innovation, Inc., a firm that provides engineering services for new product development. His professional specialties include environment simulation, hardware design, signal processing, computer graphics, software development, and project management. Mr. Tolhurst received his B.S. in electrical engineering from the University of Texas at San Antonio.

Keith Blanton is co-founder and vice president of research and development for Atlanta Innovation, Inc., a firm that provides engineering services for new product development. His professional specialties include digital signal processing, computer graphics, advanced algorithm and software development, and evaluation of new technologies. He holds six patents for his work in computer speech synthesis, optical character recognition, and flight simulator image generation. He received his S.M. and S.B. degrees in electrical engineering from the Massachusetts Institute of Technology.

Mary Ann Pike is a technical writing consultant in southwestern Pennsylvania. She has a B.S. in electrical engineering and an M.A. in professional writing from Carnegie Mellon University. She has been on the Internet for at least 10 of the last 16 years, and hopes that everyone will have an Internet connection at home eventually.

Special Contribution

John R. Harris is a partner in the Atlanta, Georgia, intellectual property law firm of Jones & Askew. He practices patent, trademark, and copyright law, with special emphasis in the computer and electrical arts. Mr. Harris received a J.D. and M.B.A. from Emory University, and a bachelor's in electrical engineering from the Georgia Institute of Technology. During the mid 1970s, Mr. Harris was a special-purpose computer system design engineer at Harris Corporation, Melbourne, Florida.

Contributing Authors

Richard Phillips is the hardware engineering manager for IVEX Corporation in Atlanta, Georgia. He is responsible for the development of real-time computer graphics systems for training and simulation applications. Previously, he has worked on a variety of graphics, imaging, audio, and medical electronics products. Mr. Phillips received his bachelor of engineering in electrical engineering and computer science from Stevens Institute of Technology in New Jersey, and is now pursuing graduate studies at the Georgia Institute of Technology.

K. Mitchell Thompson has enjoyed a 10-year career as a software generalist in an age of specialization. His software development projects have spanned real-time embedded systems, operating system internals, computer graphics, and distributed applications. His current interests are high-performance distributed applications and software engineering techniques for software maintenance.

Acknowledgments

A project of this magnitude is possible only if the authors receive an enormous amount of technical support and assistance from many sources. For all their contributions, the authors want to sincerely thank:

- Drs. William Wulf and Vinton Cerf, whose Internet expertise provided a great wealth of information on many topics.

- Joel Skelton, for invaluable net surfing—er, research—that turned up a great deal of raw data for this effort.

- Sheila Rosenthal, who helped locate much of the reference material supporting the book.

- Jonathan Kamens, Scott Yanoff, Gene Spafford, David Lawrence, and Stephanie DaSilva, for their selfless efforts in creating and maintaining some of the most useful information on the Internet, and for allowing us to share it with our readers.

- Sarah Glinka and Rocco Varuolo of Advanced Network & Services (ANS), for connection to ANSRemote/IP and technical assistance in its use.

- Kimberly Brown of Performance Systems, International (PSI), for connection to PSILink.

- Michael Tague and the rest of the Computer Witchcraft crew, for connections to WinNET Mail, and permission to include the software for it on the companion disk.

- Annette Valle, Donna Laughlin, and Bob Williams of NetManage, for providing their Chameleon networking software.

- Beam & Whiteside Software, Limited, for its BWTCP software package for DOS and Windows.

- Christina Apap-Bologna of Distinct Corporation, for providing an evaluation copy of Distinct TCP/IP for Windows.

- Steve Berger, for an excellent technical review of the manuscripts, and the ideas that helped make this a better book.

- Microsoft Corporation, for providing Word for Windows 2.0 to the authors.

- The entire Que organization, for grace under pressure.

- The Internet community founders and members, for providing a wealth of information and the means for its exchange.

- Ed Guy of Guy Software, for providing his Racontex program to index the lists supplied on the accompanying disk.

- Jill Ellsworth, university professor and Internet expert, for her contribution of Appendix B.

The authors also want to extend their individual gratitudes:

William A. Tolhurst: My wife, Pamela, for providing emotional buoyancy and allowing me to have this baby as she carried our first child. My family, for love, guidance, support, and inspiration. The TTM crew 1976-1985, wherever you are, for everything.

Keith A. Blanton: My wife, Rycca, and daughter, Kathlene, for love, understanding, and support.

Mary Ann Pike: My husband, Tod, who provided me with moral and technical support throughout this project.

Trademarks

Contents at a Glance

Table of Contents

3 The Structure of the Internet   61

4 Finding and Using Internet Resources   103

6 The Future of the Internet   241

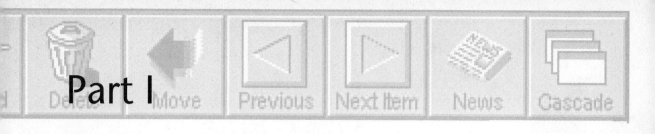

Part I

Introducing the Internet

coming Mail

NSFNET Packet Traffic

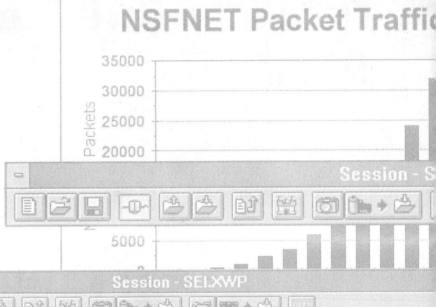

Session - SEI.XWP

PINE 3.07   MAIN MENU   Folder.inbox   1 Message

```
  ?    HELP       - Get help using Pine

  C    COMPOSE    - Compose and send a message

  I    MAIL INDEX - Read mail in current folder
```

Call

Mail in progress...

* ------ Mail Composition Editor ------ *

TO: ftpmail@decwrl.dec.com

CC:

ject: file request via ftpmail server

Edit   Done   Cancel

```
  Note: In Pine 3.0 we are encouraging folks to use the MAIL INDEX t
        mail instead of VIEW MAIL, so it is no longer on the main me
        in the mail index, it is available as usual as the "Y" comma
```

```
  Help          Quit          Folders       Other
  Compose       Mail Index    Addresses
```

## Chapter 1

The Internet: Infrastructure for the Information Age

The 1990s are witness to sweeping changes in the way we live, work, and interact. Communications and information have become the basis for much of the world's evolving post-industrial society. For businesses, changing global political and economic climates are at the same time creating more opportunities and more challenges. On a personal level, people are having to cope with more and more information in their jobs and as part of their daily lives. Computers, fax machines, cellular telephones, pagers, and other information "appliances" are becoming commonplace not only in the office, but also in the home. More and more, the distinction between home and office is blurring. Plans are under way for the largest information distributor, television, to offer two-way communications and hundreds of channels.

In this society, getting the information you need in a timely fashion is of immense importance, and presents immense problems to both the sender and recipient alike. If you are an information source, how do you make your data available to others who need it? As the recipient, how can you extract the information you truly need from the blizzard of data you are exposed to on a daily basis?

In companies worldwide, decentralizing and downsizing are the new business credos. Executives and managers are having to rethink the very concept of a business and its structure. The term *virtual company* has been coined to describe a new group of corporate entities that have few permanent employees and little equipment, instead relying heavily on acquiring contracted resources on an as-needed basis only. A major challenge presented to the modern business world is how to coordinate the efforts of employees or contractors who may be thousands of miles apart, but who nevertheless must work together productively on a day-to-day basis.

With legislation such as the *High Performance Computing Act*, which in part lays the foundation for an "information superhighway," the federal government is now taking an active role in forming the future of information distribution in America. Even the name implies a public works infrastructure that supports information traffic. Other national governments have followed or will follow suit. Not to be outdone, many electronics companies are partnering and even merging, with the single objective of developing their own portions of the highway.

So what do these fundamental shifts in the social order have to do with the Internet? They are the underlying reasons that an important but unassuming research project for investigating wide area computer networking has evolved into a system for transferring trillions of bytes of data among millions of people via thousands of computing machines in dozens of countries. The Internet is truly an infrastructure for the Information Age.

Who Should Buy This Book?

If you've gotten this far, and you didn't pick this book up by mistake, you must be seriously considering the purchase of a text about the Internet. Purchasers of such books generally fall into one of three experience classes:

- *The uninitiated.* As it has received a lot of word-of-mouth and press attention recently (to the point of hype, in some cases), you likely have heard or read about this entity called the Internet (often just the *net* to those already using it). The gist of many of these news pieces is that the Internet helps solve all sorts of communications problems for individuals, small businesses, and large corporations alike. This is one reason that the number of Internet participants has more than doubled every year since 1988, with no end in sight to this trend. To paraphrase an old cliche, your attitude is probably, *I've heard a lot about Internet, and now I'd like to try some.*

- *The Internet novice* (a *newbie* in net jargon). In this case, you're a new member of the Internet community (a *user*) and may feel a bit overwhelmed by the features and capabilities that the net provides. You need to know more about ftp, telnet, archie, Gopher, and the rest of the myriad of tools and techniques for transferring, translating, gathering, and distributing information.

- *The experienced user.* You know your way around the net pretty well but want more information on how best to use the tools, your options for increasing the sophistication of your connection, and even pointers on setting up a computer or network within the Internet itself (thereby adding a *host* to the net). You also need a handy reference for looking up things such as what the ftp`!` command does, or the length of the subnet portion of a class B IP address.

The special edition format of this book allows in-depth coverage of material of interest for all three groups. In addition, topics of interest for all experience levels are included, such as the history of the net and legal implications of its usage.

As an added bonus, the IBM PC format disk included in the back of the book provides PSILink software to get you connected to the Internet. Also included are several indexed files of Internet resources so that you can find what you need on the net as quickly as possible. A prime goal of this book is to provide you with everything you need to obtain an Internet connection and be immediately productive with it.

About *Using the Internet*

A number of good texts about the Internet are available; many of them were used as reference material for this one. This book is unique, however, because it's oriented toward business, professional, and individual users and also would-be users. Its primary goal is to assist those seeking to learn more about the Internet's usefulness as a tool to support them rather than as a technology for them to master (or to master them, for that matter). This book is not a "bits and bytes" guide, but a practical, useful reference for boosting your productivity and supporting your quest for information.

No prior knowledge of the Internet is assumed, except that you may have heard the word *Internet* before. It's assumed that you are comfortable using a personal computer, but no detailed knowledge of the machine itself is necessary. You don't have to know anything about networking. You don't even have to be a current user of the Internet; much of the information given here is specifically oriented toward helping you acquire the right kind of Internet features for your needs.

This book was motivated by the authors' search for just such a book to support them in their own quests for Internet how-to information. They also found that a lot of their business colleagues and friends were asking the same questions. Another way that *Using the Internet* differs from many other books is that the authors, although possessing a variety of technical backgrounds, can't in fairness be considered experts on computer networks, nor key members of the Internet community. Rather, they are all "plain ol'" users who have focused their writing toward addressing the same issues you will encounter as a user. Their expertise was acquired by having to do the same things you want to do.

Top 10 Things To Know about the Internet

Despite the bright light of media attention cast on the Internet recently, most non-users still know very little about the Internet's real features and uses. Unfortunately, the best sources for dispelling the myths—Internet users themselves—seem to get tongue-tied in awe of its vast potential. They tend to struggle for a succinct description that is meaningful to a non-user. Although it isn't worthy of David Letterman, the following 10-point list captures the essence of what the Internet is and is not:

1. The Internet *is* a medium for effectively communicating with others.

2. The Internet *is* a research support and information retrieval mechanism.

3. The Internet *is* flexible in cost and features.

4. The Internet *is* at once a local and an international entity, allowing interaction among users separated by an office wall or by an ocean.

5. The Internet *isn't* a specific piece of software or hardware.

6. The Internet *isn't* a single network, but a group of networks logically (but not physically) arranged in hierarchy.

7. The Internet *isn't* owned by any government, corporation, or university.

8. The Internet *isn't* the same everywhere (homogeneous), but vastly different (heterogeneous).

Introducing the Internet

9. The Internet *isn't* restricted to research only, non-commercial, or other appropriate uses, although some networks within it are.

10. The Internet *isn't* solely or even mostly inhabited by computer professionals, engineers, nerds, or techies. It is used daily by people from all backgrounds, interests, and personalities.

Chances are at least one of the preceding points refutes something you've heard about the Internet.

The Internet Summarized

In each of the chapters that follow, a specific area of the network is examined and explained. But before getting into details, it's best to provide you with a broad overview that should quickly answer most of the fundamental questions you may have about the net.

What Is the Internet?

The Internet is a collection of thousands of computer networks, tens of thousands of computers, and more than 10 million users who share a compatible means for interacting with one another to exchange digital data.

What Can I Do with Internet Access?

This is a lot like asking, *What can I do with electricity?* The short answer is, *Almost anything.* A tad more specifically, the Internet can be viewed as an information utility, whose benefits can be subdivided into eight major categories:

- You can exchange information quickly and conveniently.

- You can access experienced and expert individuals in thousands of fields.

■ You can receive regular updates on topics of interest.

■ You can gain wide-area access to your data.

■ You can build teams and enhance teamwork across geographic distance.

■ You can gain access to archived information.

■ You can translate and transfer data between machines.

■ You can have fun and be entertained.

Exchanging Information Quickly and Conveniently

Users of the Internet can interact with one another across town or across continents. The concept is somewhat like the *bulletin board systems* (BBSs) that many PC users are already familiar with. Unlike a BBS, however, the users don't have to dial in to the same machine. Through the Internet you can send information to users on different machines, running different operating systems, located in separate geographic areas.

By far the most popular application of this vast network is the exchange of *electronic mail* (e-mail). That is, users can send written (actually, typed) messages to one another. Why do this rather than simply call and leave a phone message? For example, you can completely compose your message before it's sent, thereby making sure everything you want to cover is in the message. Also, unlike with most phone answering machines, you can send messages of arbitrary length. You can also include other information within a message, such as executable programs or spreadsheet data.

Caution

Don't let the fact that you can send long messages tempt you to turn every memo into a treatise. While most people can talk on the phone and do other things at the same time, most cannot read and do other tasks in parallel. Try to avoid needlessly monopolizing the time of your message recipient.

For another, the cost of a phone call depends on its proximity, while sending an e-mail message can be sent to any other user without charge based on the destination. In this capacity the Internet serves as a international toll-free messaging service. Although it may not seem so important across town, the savings from a few transcontinental messages quickly add up. It's not uncommon for companies conducting business overseas to save thousands of dollars per month on long-distance phone charges after they become connected to the network. The power and usefulness of e-mail alone is enough for many people to make the decision to get an Internet connection. E-mail isn't the only type of information you can transfer via Internet, however. Data files can be exchanged as well, allowing users to move everything from satellite images to digital audio clips from one user to another. The most commonly used method for transferring files is called, oddly enough, the *file transfer protocol* (ftp). Chapter 8, "Using ftp and telnet," shows you how to use ftp, with plenty of examples that you can try directly on the net as exercises.

If you need to have a more interactive dialog with another user, ways to chat with one another on-line are available . Further, the capability is also evolving for transfer of voice and images in a real-time manner. These multimedia features now require a greater information transfer rate than is supported by all but the most sophisticated connections, but advances in data compression technology and network bandwidth will make them more readily available in the near future.

Accessing Experienced and Expert Individuals
How often have you wanted to ask for assistance from someone who has actually tried or is trying to accomplish the same task you are? Or wanted to get impressions of a product or service from real users, rather than rely on marketing literature or questionable benchmark results that may not reflect real-world

usage? The Internet is an invaluable resource for collecting just such information.

Although many computer professionals exist within the Internet community, they are certainly not the only ones. Active participants in the Internet include doctors, artists, musicians, attorneys, businessmen, homemakers, students, office workers, factory workers, clergy, government officials, scientists, and many others. They're from almost every walk of life and most countries on the planet. All are easily accessible and able to interact with you to exchange information, opinion, or simple pleasant conversation.

A certain gathering place exists on the net to allow users with specific interests to congregate and share tips, viewpoints, and other data on their topic of mutual interest. This place is called the USENET, which consists of literally thousands of smaller cells, called *news groups*. Would you like some insight on how well a computer system performs? The itinerary for the next space shuttle flight? Why your favorite character is leaving the hit soap opera *The Old and the Stagnant*? It's all available via USENET. You can join or resign from news groups easily and as often as you like, so you can modify the character of the news group data you receive (your news *feed*) as your needs or interests change.

Receiving Regular Updates on Interesting Topics

Many interest groups also exist that periodically publish newsletter-type documents. By joining one of these groups, or *mailing lists* in the Internet vernacular, you receive information automatically as it's placed on the net. Essentially, you can create your own personalized news source dedicated to the topics you're interested in, rather than have to search more general sources for relevant information. Subscribing to a mailing list is as easy as sending an e-mail message saying, "Sign me up!"

Gaining Wide-Area Access to Data

Travel is now an integral part of business life, not just for executives and salespeople, but for many employees. To be as productive in a remote location as you are at your home office, you need access to the same information; you have to make sure you anticipate everything you might need and bring it all with you. With the appropriate Internet connection, you don't have to take it with you when you go: you can get to it after you're there. Many service providers use Public Data Networks (PDNs) that provide toll-free dialup connections in hundreds of cities. Others use 800 numbers for easy nationwide access.

Note

Most business travelers know the frustration of getting to a customer site and then finding out an hour before a presentation that some figures have changed at the last minute. With the proper type of Internet connection, you can have access to the data you need to make your updates "on the fly."

Building Teams and Enhancing Teamwork across Geographic Distance

The economic forces at work today have lead to downsizing and restructuring businesses throughout the world. The emphasis is on smaller, more efficient organizations. This doesn't mean that the tasks to be completed have gotten any smaller, however. This implies that companies and their employees must distribute the load and work cooperatively to get tasks done that they cannot complete by themselves.

As a small example, the authors of this book used the Internet extensively to coordinate efforts, seek and exchange information, and review manuscripts. Some have never met face to face and may never meet in person. In addition, two of the authors in Atlanta work for a company that provides the complete

R & D resources of a firm in San Francisco. Face-to-face visits occur only a few times a year, usually for product demonstrations or strategy meetings. The Internet plays an essential role in the day-to-day coordination and project management between the companies.

Accessing Archived Information

Imagine being able to receive, almost instantly, back issues of your favorite magazines or newspapers, in a format that your computer can manipulate and perform searches on. How about receiving source code that shows you how to perform dynamic palette manipulation under Windows? Archives for many of the USENET news groups and mailing lists are readily available, and thousands of computers on the Internet make copies of public domain and shareware programs available to you. The programs from a single major host can fill several CD-ROMs.

In fact, the biggest problem you're likely to encounter is trying to find the specific files you're looking for. Fortunately, search utilities with funny names like archie, Gopher, and WWW have been constructed especially for helping you find your needle in this haystack. Chapter 13, "Aids to Navigating the Internet," describes many of these tools and how to use them.

Translating and Transferring Data between Machines

One often overlooked benefit that the network provides is a means for exchanging data between dissimilar machines. Because the Internet consists of many different types of computing platforms, the problem of transferring the data is solved by necessity. You also don't have to worry about finding a common media among the machines, such as floppy disk, tape, or CD-ROM. Utility programs also exist to convert from one data format to another.

Enjoying Recreation and Entertainment

The Internet is far from a cold, business-only environment. Although most users enjoy simply browsing through information on various topics (alternatively called *net surfing* or *net prospecting*), a wealth of games is available through the Internet. Some are played *on-line* (simultaneously in competition with other Internet users); others are meant for downloading and playing directly on your computer. Also, hundreds of news groups and mailing lists are dedicated to recreational topics like TV shows, motorcycling, sailing, and so on. If you somehow can't find a group for your particular interest, you can even start your own, as long as you're willing to take the responsibility of setting it up and maintaining it.

The value of these features, of course, depends a lot on who you are and what specific tasks you are trying to accomplish. Not all these features are provided by every type of Internet service, and some may limit your full use of them. By obtaining a connection that matches your requirements and interests, you can avoid paying for features you don't use.

How Can I Get Internet Access?

You need to arrange access through an organization that has established the necessary physical connections and equipment to offer an Internet connection. These organizations are referred to as *service providers*. Service is available from a wide variety of sources, including commercial ventures, non-profit groups, and universities. Depending on your needs and provider, your connection may be free, cost a nominal fee, or be thousands of dollars per month. Chapter 10, "Determining the Level of Internet Service You Need," defines four major levels of service and explains their differences in detail to help you figure out the level of service you truly need and can afford. Chapters 16 through 19 provide contact lists for each of the service levels. You can then call and shop around for the best deal available in your area.

What Equipment Will I Need?

The equipment you need depends on the level of service you choose. A personal computer (IBM PC, Macintosh, or other) is sufficient for individual-level services. Unlike other recently popularized areas of computing such as multimedia, the hardware requirements are quite reasonable. Your platform can be as simple as an original 8088 with a CGA monitor, or a Mac Classic, and still be able to take full advantage of your Internet connection. Obviously, more powerful machines that can run Windows, or System 7 for a Macintosh, may provide a more up-to-date user interface and other features, but the baseline capabilities of the net won't be enhanced.

A standard modem used for other telecommunications purposes, such as BBS or on-line service connections (such as CompuServe), is all that's needed for a wide variety of service options. Similarly, a standard, voice-grade telephone line is perfectly acceptable for connecting to your service provider's host computer. The most advanced levels of service require special hardware, and perhaps special telecommunications lines, however.

You also need software to control and direct the hardware and implement the communications protocols required to interact with your service provider. Again, applications used for other telecommunications tasks, such as a terminal emulation package, are often all that is necessary. In some cases, your service provider may require you to use its own software package, and the most advanced services require specific capabilities. Chapter 12, "Hardware and Software," discusses the hardware and software necessary for your particular service level and describes some of the commercial and shareware products available.

How Much Will It Cost?

Your costs for an Internet connection come from three sources: service provider charges, line connection charges, and set-up costs.

Set-Up Costs

Assuming that you already have some sort of personal computer, your main hardware cost is for a modem. A 2400 bit per second (bps) modem can be easily found and purchased for under $75. You also need communications software. For the most basic services, you can use terminal emulation software, whose prices range from $50 to $100 or so. For the more sophisticated service that can support the needs of a small business, you can expect to pay about $500 to $2,000 for hardware, plus another $500 or so for software.

The software cost of an Internet connection is being alleviated somewhat via a move by operating system developers to include Internet-capable software within the OS itself. For some time, UNIX operating systems have been Internet capable, and Microsoft Windows NT also includes the software support necessary to communicate with the network. Many of these same features are also expected in the next release of Windows.

Monthly Costs

Service provider charges obviously depend on the level of service you obtain and the price structure of your provider. As mentioned, under some conditions you can even get a free connection. If you use a fee-based provider, you can expect to pay from $10 to $30 per month for basic service suitable for an individual, and $20 to $50 for full-featured individual access. For service sufficient to support a small business, you should expect to pay from $100 to $500 per month. More expensive connections certainly exist, but they are designed generally for use by larger organizations that likely have dedicated staff for arranging and managing the connection.

You'll also want to figure in the charges from your phone company for connection time charges, if applicable. A popular trend among service providers is to offer an 800-number-based service, sometimes for a flat fee. This may or may not be cheaper than paying for connect time, but it does give you an option.

The Internet Operating Environment

As you read earlier, the Internet is not a single product or service. It's not governed or operated by a single national or corporate entity. It has many faces, many uses, many features, and many options. This is the kind of diversity needed to support research, but it can hamper new users. It also makes it a bit more difficult to describe the net because your interface to it may be vastly different than that of others.

The computers operating within the Internet can be everything from notebook PCs to supercomputers, running any number of different operating systems and application programs. Until recently, this diverse operating environment scared off a lot of would-be users, particularly in the personal computing world. Now a number of programs, existing on the DOS, Windows, and Macintosh platforms, make it much less painful to use; you see some examples of them in Chapter 12, "Hardware and Software."

Guidelines for Conduct on the Net

Before you dive into and onto the network, you should be aware of the rules of the road for using the Internet. These guidelines for behavior collectively make up network etiquette, or *netiquette,* for short. As always, most of these guidelines can be boiled down to common sense and general courtesy, but a few things bear pointing out because they may not be obvious to newbies.

Internet Access Is a Privilege, Not a Right
This is the first item to keep in mind. Neither the Constitution nor the Bill of Rights mention the inalienable right of Internet access. Consider yourself a guest of your service provider and the other hosts that you visit during your Internet travels.

These people have extended the courtesy to access their hosts strictly because they are good sports and fervently believe in the value of open access to information. In short, they're doing it solely for your benefit, with no benefit for themselves in return. Sometimes this open-door policy gets abused, either by accident or on purpose. Host administrators occasionally get burned so badly by ignorant, indifferent, or malicious users that they have to remove the public access to their systems. Then everyone loses. The most well-known example of abuse of this friendly environment was the Internet *worm*, which is discussed in Chapter 5, "Legal Considerations of Internet Usage."

> **Note**
>
> It must be stressed that the Internet worm affected only systems with a true presence on the Internet itself, and even then only certain kinds of machines. As a user, the chances of your PC being attacked by such a virus are essentially nil. Note that viruses can still be imbedded in programs that you obtain from the Internet. These viruses were already present when the file was placed on the net, however, and were not "caught" through the Internet itself.

Be Efficient in Your Information Distribution

You should be keenly aware of the distribution your messages can receive. E-mail is not usually a cause for much concern because only your designated recipients receive it. You therefore have a good idea of its distribution. This isn't necessarily the case for USENET news groups, however. Consider the following example. If you post a 1K file (about a 15-line text message) to a news group with ten thousand participants (less than .1 percent of net users), your message consumes at least 10M of the net's bandwidth. Because your message is relayed through other machines before reaching its final destinations, that number can easily climb to 40M or 50M. With this in mind, try to limit your distribution where possible to minimize wasting network bandwidth.

Be Polite in Your E-mail and USENET Postings

The Internet user community is by and large an informal group. But don't let the fact that you are a thousand miles from another user tempt you to be any less polite than you normally would be. In fact, just like when using the telephone, you should be bit more courteous and formal with your initial contacts. After you've been introduced to one another, you can relax the tone of your messages to normal conversation levels. Usually, your e-mail exchanges are with people you know personally or professionally, and therefore your manners are usually good, if not always at their best.

Note

As with any community, peer pressure plays an important role in governing the activities of the Internet. If you become annoying with your messages, you may find that no one seems to respond any more. Keep it up, and your fellow users will start sending messages again—to your service provider, asking that your access be terminated.

As a much more public forum, posting a message to a USENET news group is a lot like standing up and giving your message as a speech. Courtesy and diplomacy are extremely important assets in this context. One of the uglier sights on the network is a nasty message whose purpose is to attack another user on a personal level. This is called a *flame* in Internet lingo, because of its incendiary nature. If posted in a reasonably active news group, flames can quickly get out of control. Here, hundreds or thousands of people see it, and the urge to respond in kind is great. The result can be a deluge of ever more personal attacks, until everyone seems to forget the original point of the argument and resorts to demonstrations of their proficiency at name-calling. At one time, sending flames and having *flame fests* break out was mildly amusing, but with millions of users, such an outbreak can quickly generate a massive exchange that ends up rendering a news group virtually useless.

Some argue that flames are occasionally necessary to stop ignorant or indifferent violation of the proper use and intention of the network. They claim that flames help make up for the fact that no e-mail police, so to speak, exist to reprimand such violators. The reality is that despite what may seem a reasonable cause, very few folks will see your flame as constructive criticism, especially if administered in a public area like a news group.

This doesn't mean you shouldn't feel free to disagree with errors, or fail to offer alternative opinions. Just don't try dealing with an obnoxious user by being obnoxious yourself. If you really think another user is being truly abusive, make better use of your anger by complaining to his service provider. If enough complaints are received, the perpetrator can lose his connection. Remember too that your comments aren't anonymous, so your vicious flame of someone won't win you much sympathy if you commit a "flame-able" *faux pas* sometime in the future. The solution is easy: Just say no to flames.

Be Efficient in Your Information Transfers

One of the main attractions of the Internet is the ability to send and receive information from all over the world. The ease of moving data to and from distant locations requires a certain amount of self-discipline, however. So don't transfer that 10M file from a computer in Australia if you live in Atlanta and can get it from a machine at Georgia Tech. Even if it's via tax dollars, you can bet someone, somewhere, is somehow paying for the charges of getting that data between the continents. The bandwidth between continents is especially at a premium, so take some time to search out alternative sources that are closer to home.

Be Aware of the Humor-Impaired Nature of E-Mail

Another area where people get into inadvertent trouble is in having humor, especially sarcasm, mistaken for a serious comment. Because your e-mail message can't convey that smile on your face or the twinkle in your eye, it's sometimes very hard to discern whether you are serious or not. For example, what would you think of the attitude of a user whose message included the following line:

```
How dare you criticize me!
```

Was this person serious, or just joking? How can you tell? If you're like most people, your first reaction was probably, *What a jerk!* Then you might have thought about the possibility that he was jesting, but the damage to your initial impression of him is done. You don't have to make your messages devoid of humor—just watch for things that might be misinterpreted.

One mechanism that has been developed to gauge the seriousness of the author is the use of little textual icons called *smileys* or emoticons, which tell the reader not to take the aforementioned seriously. Because e-mail messages typically are limited to ASCII text characters, you have to be a bit inventive in visualizing smileys. In this case, it means turning your head sideways and looking at the result. For example, one fairly standard smiley is :-). If you turn your head sideways, you can see that :-) resembles a smiling person's face. So, now try that line in the last message again:

```
How dare you criticize me! :-) :-) :-)
```

Now it's pretty clear the author of the message was just joking. Certain abbreviations are also used to convey the context of the user's message, such as IMHO, which means *In My Humble Opinion*, or ROTFL, meaning *Rolling On The Floor, Laughing*.

Lastly, keep in mind that your audience, particularly in the case of news groups, may have vastly differing views and beliefs on things like politics, religion, and so on. Although some groups specifically address these issues for purposes of open debate, avoid commenting, particularly in an off-color manner, about such things in other news groups or your e-mail.

Understand Possible Legal Implications

The world is becoming an increasingly litigious place, and unfortunately the Internet can't be considered immune. Just remember that every message you send can be saved—meaning every time you speak (type), it's as though the recipient has a tape recorder rolling. Further, public electronic forums are not exempt from laws regarding slander, fraud, or theft. Another area to watch is in the transfer of information to certain countries that may be subject to trade or other restrictions. Chapter 5, "Legal Considerations of Internet Usage," is an excellent introduction to the legal aspects of Internet usage, written by an attorney experienced in computer-related law. You would do well to read that chapter before you accidentally end up in trouble, rather than after you're already in it.

Growth of the Internet

As mentioned at the beginning of this chapter, the growth of the Internet over the last few years has been phenomenal. The number of users is hard to determine with accuracy, but it's believed that more than 10 million people access the Internet daily, and perhaps as many as 25 million have some means of access.

You can gauge the growth of the net more easily by looking at the number of computers using it. As you can see from the numbers shown in figure 1.1, the increase in the number of machines has been staggering.

Consider also the amount of data traffic logged on NSFNET, which is just one major (albeit large) network within the Internet, as shown in figure 1.2.

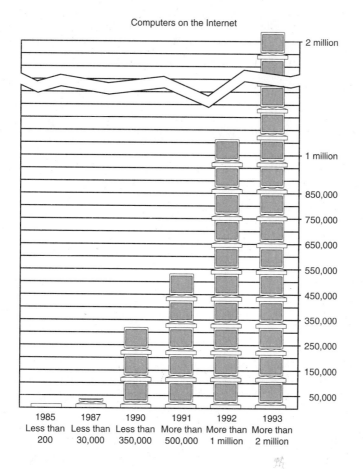

Computers on the Internet

1985	1987	1990	1991	1992	1993
Less than 200	Less than 30,000	Less than 350,000	More than 500,000	More than 1 million	More than 2 million

Fig. 1.1

The number of computers used on the Internet, by year.

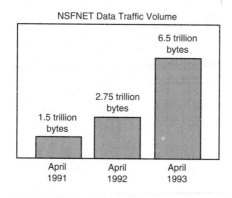

NSFNET Data Traffic Volume

1.5 trillion bytes — April 1991

2.75 trillion bytes — April 1992

6.5 trillion bytes — April 1993

Fig. 1.2

NSFNET data traffic volume.

Another very telling fact is that somewhere in the first half of 1993, commercially oriented traffic exceeded 50 percent of all Inter-net traffic for the first time. By some estimates, the current growth rate of the net is now more than 15 percent per month.

The Disk Included with This Book

An MS-DOS format, 1.44M diskette is included with this book. You will find it on the inside of the back cover. This diskette contains a program to help you connect to the net and information that will make your use of the net more productive. For more information on the contents of the disk, see Appendix A, "Using the Companion Disk."

What Should I Read Next?

Now that you're familiar with the basics of the Internet, where should you go from here? The answer depends again on your experience level. If you don't yet have a connection and have no prior experience with the Internet, you should read the first parts of Chapters 2 through 10. The information in these chapters catch you up on the history of the network, how it works, the kinds of features it provides, and what kind of services you can get to fit your needs and budget. You can then use the service provider contact information in Chapters 14 through 17 to shop around for a service provider. Be sure to check the special promotional offers in the back of this book. They can save you a considerable amount of money. After you get connected, you can look in more detail at the chapters in Parts II, III, and IV that describe how to use the facilities of the net.

Novice users will want to read at least Chapters 3 and 4 of Part I, and the chapters within Parts II, III, and IV relevant to the type of service they have. Experienced users should know enough to select their topics of interest from Parts II through V (Chapters 7 through 19). They should serve you well both as a reference and as refresher material.

Many of the Internet hosts use the UNIX operating system. If you are not at least somewhat familiar with UNIX, you should read the UNIX Quick Reference in Appendix B. This is especially true for those who choose a service that provides direct access to UNIX via a so-called *shell account*. See Chapter 10, "Determining the Level of Internet Service You Need," for the details of this type of service.

Now you're ready to begin using the Internet!

Introducing the Internet

Chapter 2

The History of the Internet

You may think that something as far-reaching and influential as the Internet must have been carefully planned, designed, and rigorously tested, with dozens of the world's most knowledge-able computer scientists working together to produce the world's most advanced computer network. But although lofty goals were set from the start, the development of the Internet was more of a need-driven response to the requirements of the nation's research computing communities than it was an orga-nized research effort. Not to say that it wasn't a rousing success, however.

The research that resulted in the Internet is the foundation for most computer networks in existence today, from internal cor-porate networks to commercial electronic bulletin boards. Things that the computer world takes for granted—such as elec-tronic mail, gateways (devices that allow access to machines on a different network), remote file access, and distributed process-ing—also derived from the original experimentation that led to the Internet.

The history of the Internet is the history of computer network-ing in general. The Internet and its predecessor, the ARPANET, have been the proving ground for almost all networking ideas in use today. This chapter traces the growth of the Internet from the first four sites that were connected to form the ARPANET to the multinational expanse of today's Internet.

Early Experiments in Networking

From the beginning, computers have been linked together in one form or another. From carrying boxes of punch cards from one system to another, through serial and parallel communications, scientists have realized that one way to make better use of computers is to have them exchange data.

In the early 1960s, computer scientists across the country began to explore new methods of connecting systems and their users over a shared network that would provide direct connections between any two machines. In the mid to late '60s, the U.S. government began to realize the tremendous impact that computers had—and would be having—on education and on military research and development. At the time, small, isolated networks of computers existed, generally serving the communities of a university or a military site. The government decided to fund an experimental network that would allow information to be exchanged between remote computers. This network, funded by the U.S. Advanced Research Projects Agency, was christened the ARPANET.

The ARPANET Is Born

On January 2, 1969, teams of software and hardware engineers funded by ARPA began to research new computer networking technologies. Bolt, Beranek and Newman, Inc. (BBN) of Cambridge, Massachusetts, was awarded the contract to build the initial components of the ARPANET. BBN, a commercial research and development firm with strengths in computer communications, acoustics analysis, and software development, developed and built the first Interface Message Processors (IMPs) for the fledgling network. These first four IMPs were delivered in September 1969 to the first four ARPANET sites: the Stanford Research Institute (SRI), the University of California at Santa Barbara, the University of California at Los Angeles, and the University of Utah. On September 2, 1969, these four IMPs were turned on and began exchanging information between these sites. The ARPANET was born.

The ARPANET was initially an experiment to see what type of network designs would work, how robust they would be, and how much information they could transfer. One of the main development efforts was to design a network that wouldn't be impaired seriously if physical sections of the network were lost. Another research goal was to develop a network built so that new nodes could be added or removed with minimal impact on service. The network also needed to be able to connect computers of many manufacturers and enable them to communicate easily with one another.

In a report to ARPA (which had become DARPA by then), *A History of the ARPANET: The First Decade*, BBN tells about the first public demonstration of the ARPANET, in October 1972 at the first International Conference on Computers and Communications in Washington, D.C. More than 1,000 attendees witnessed approximately 40 terminals accessing large computers at different locations on the ARPANET. The flawless demonstrations so impressed the attendees that they returned to their research centers with a vision of the promise of greater things to come.

The attendees had no idea that many frantic hours of debugging and testing preceded the conference. The quality of the demonstrations led the attendees to believe that the technology had been successfully operating for some time; in reality, however, some types of computers and terminals had been connected to the network only recently and hadn't been extensively tested before the demonstrations.

This situation probably reminds you of some of the demonstrations you have done or seen. (Or that used car or house that you bought, which had been tuned up or spruced up just before being put on sale.)

In a special issue of *ConneXions* magazine devoted to the 20th anniversary of the ARPANET, Robert Kahn, one of the original ARPANET researchers, tells how the research equipment was more advanced than the commercial telecommunications equipment. The ARPANET researchers had monitoring equipment that enabled them to see what data was being transmitted on the network, and detect when information was being lost. They could tell by the error rates on certain segments when the phone lines used for those segments were having problems. At that time, the phone company didn't have the technology to do the same type of remote problem analysis.

One of the major developments to come out of the ARPANET research was the development of a new type of network protocol. *Network protocol* is a formal set of rules that computers connected on the network use to talk to one another. All the computers, no matter who manufactured them, had to use the new protocol to be able to talk on the network. This new networking protocol involved a new technology called *packet switching*.

Packet-Switching Technology

Packet switching is one way many different network segments can share a common transmission media. Rather than send a large block of data over a dedicated line directly to the destination computer, a packet-switching network breaks the data into small chunks; each chunk is sent along a common transmission line in a "packet" that also contains source and destination information. This information allows many packets to flow through the same network, yet all reach their appropriate destination.

Dedicated network components called *packet-switching nodes* route these packets from source to destination, using the information contained in the packet itself. After all the packets from a particular transmission of data reach their destination, the source and destination information is removed, and the packets are reassembled into the original data. In this way, packets from any number of computers can share the communications network.

> **Note**
>
> The original protocol used by the ARPANET was Network Control Program (NCP), which the now widely used TCP/IP (Transmission Control Protocol/Internet Protocol) later supplanted.

To make sure that the packets went correctly from their source to their destination, much of the basic ARPANET research involved the development of routing algorithms. When a packet is sent, it is passed from one machine to another until it reaches its destination. This method is called *routing*. Many difficult problems can occur during routing. If your machines don't have enough information about the destination of the data or about where the packets have come from, you can end up with information that keeps going around the network and never reaches its destination. Also, if parts of your network become physically unavailable, you must be able to send your data by different paths to your destination—if the destination is still on the network.

TCP/IP Becomes the Standard

During the 1970s, researchers using the new ARPANET technology began experimenting with new communication protocols to provide reliable and simple network communications. This new communications protocol suite became the Transmission Control Protocol/Internet Protocol (TCP/IP), which replaced

NCP, the original Network Control Program. At the same time, the Xerox Palo Alto Research Center was exploring packet switching on coaxial cable, which ultimately led to the development of the EtherNet local area network. These two developments would change and expand the ARPANET into the current Internet.

At the same time, DARPA wanted to encourage the educational community to take advantage of the ARPANET. DARPA funded the company of Bolt, Beranek and Newman, as well as the University of California at Berkeley, to provide a low-cost implementation of TCP/IP. The result of this project was that the UNIX operating system, which was in use at most universities then, supported the TCP/IP suite. With this software base and the many computer science researchers already using the new network, groups in universities across the country began using the network to assist their research.

The Berkeley version of UNIX provided many of the network tools that Internet users are now familiar with: the File Transfer Protocol program (ftp), remote login and file copy operations (rsh and rcp), and a utility that soon would become the most popular of all—intercomputer electronic mail (e-mail). Berkeley also provided a simple-to-use software interface between user programs and the TCP/IP protocols, which enabled almost anyone to build a network program.

The Growth of the ARPANET

By 1975, the ARPANET was carrying much of the day-to-day Department of Defense network traffic, and control was transferred from DARPA to the Department of Defense, under the U.S. Defense Communications Agency. Under the DCA, the ARPANET technology became the basis of the Defense Data Network program (the DDN), which was intended to serve the computer communications needs of the DOD.

While computer researchers learned how to make a rapidly growing computer network run smoothly, they (and other users at their sites) discovered that they could use the ARPANET for other things. Electronic mail soon became a popular mechanism for exchanging information about the network and about current topics of the day. Computer mailing lists (or mail reflectors) started to allow users to broadcast their messages to a group of readers. Some central sites became repositories of information that allowed researchers at other sites to access the information using the File Transfer Protocol program (ftp). (See Chapter 8, "Using ftp and telnet," for more information.) Also at this time, the USENET news system was started. (See Chapter 9, "USENET," for more information.) Users began using the network for more than computer research.

Because the traffic was growing beyond the capability of the phone lines used to carry it, and because the military sites were becoming concerned about the amount of operational traffic on their experimental network, the ARPANET was split into two separate segments in 1983. The military sites and their network (which carried the DOD operational traffic) became known as MILNET; the civilian network, which continued to be used for network research and non-military operational traffic, was still known as the ARPANET. This split managed to reduce the traffic to reasonable levels—for a short time.

The Internet Is Born

During the early 1980s, all the networks were converted to the TCP/IP-based protocols, and the ARPANET became the *backbone*—the physical connection between the major sites—of the new Internet, which comprised all TCP/IP-based networks connected to the ARPANET. The ARPANET was still used by the DOD as a test bed for refinement of the TCP/IP suite, and many improvements were made. By 1983, the conversion to TCP/IP was complete, and the Office of the Secretary of Defense mandated that all computers connected to long-haul networks use TCP/IP.

At this point, the Internet was still small. By August 1981, 213 hosts were in the official ARPANET *host table* (a single file on every host computer connected to the ARPANET that contained the addresses of all other registered hosts). By February 1986, the Internet host table had grown to 2,308 hosts. The traffic among these hosts also was growing rapidly—the "legitimate" traffic of network research and, increasingly, the social traffic of the Internet community. (See "The Growth of the Internet" later in this chapter for some information on current expansion rates.)

NSF Supercomputers Spur Backbone Development

During the mid 1980s, the National Science Foundation (NSF) established six supercomputer centers around the country because researchers at various university and government organizations needed them to facilitate their research. In July 1986, the NSF funded a backbone network that directly connected the centers and allowed researchers access to the Internet so that they easily could share their findings and look for information. Initially, the NSF backbone was configured using 56 kbps (kilobits per second) lines. In July 1988, the backbone was upgraded to 1.5 Mbps (megabits per second) lines. This backbone network was dubbed NSFNET. Figure 2.1 shows a map of the NSFNET as of the fall of 1993.

The network initially was designed to connect the following supercomputer centers:

- John von Neumann National Supercomputer Center (JVNNSC), Princeton, New Jersey

- San Diego Supercomputer Center (SDSC), University of California

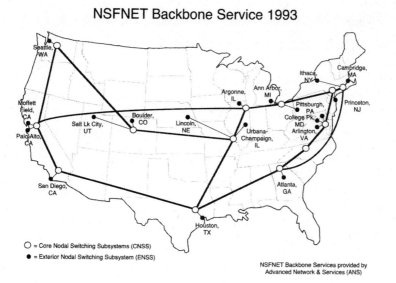

NSFNET Backbone Service 1993

○ = Core Nodal Switching Subsystems (CNSS)
● = Exterior Nodal Switching Subsystem (ENSS)

NSFNET Backbone Services provided by
Advanced Network & Services (ANS)

Fig. 2.1
The configuration of the 1993 NSFNET backbone communication lines.

■ National Center for Supercomputing Applications (NCSA), University of Illinois

■ Cornell National Supercomputer Facility (CNSF), Cornell University

■ Pittsburgh Supercomputer Center (PSC), operated jointly by Westinghouse Electric Corp., Carnegie Mellon University, and the University of Pittsburgh

■ The Scientific Computing Division of the National Center for Atmospheric Research (NCAR), Boulder, Colorado

Any researcher eligible for NSF support can use these supercomputer centers, which have computers from Cray Research, Control Data Corporation, IBM, and other manufacturers. The NSF decided on the Internet TCP/IP communication protocols, which allowed the supercomputer centers access to all the services available over the Internet: e-mail, ftp, remote use of resources, and file sharing. The NSF also provided seed money to fund many regional networks to allow connections to major institutions in a particular geographic area.

The NSFNET Backbone Comes under New Management

Because the NSFNET had become more general purpose, rather than provide direct support for the supercomputer centers, in 1987 the NSF solicited proposals for changing the funding and management of the network. Out of the six proposals received, the cooperative agreement with the NSF was awarded to Merit, the Michigan Educational Research Information Triad, a non-profit corporation managed by a consortium of eight Michigan universities. In cooperation with IBM and MCI Communications Corp., and with funding from the state of Michigan and a $14 million, 5-year award from the NSF, this cooperative effort between federal government, industry, and universities facilitated the rapid deployment of a high-speed, nationwide network backbone. Merit offered a technically superior communications network and a staff with network management experience at a low cost to NSF, made possible by the supporting funds from IBM and MCI.

Commercial Traffic on the Internet

Merit was chosen because the organization offered the best cost:benefit ratio of all the proposals. MCI provided the long-distance phone lines, IBM provided the routing equipment (including installation, maintenance, and operation), and Merit provided the network administration. In 1990, Merit, IBM, and MCI formed a non-profit corporation, Advanced Network & Services Inc. (ANS), to take over management and operation of NSFNET. In 1991, ANS created ANS CO+RE system, Inc., a for-profit corporation whose mission is to support research and education efforts and to provide network services for commercial clients.

This arrangement wasn't, at first glance, in accordance with the NSF acceptable use policy (AUP), which doesn't allow for any commercial traffic on the NSFNET. NSF decided, however, that

it was paying only for conveyance of NSFNET traffic, not buying equipment and facilities. As a result, the AUP applied only
to the traffic that flowed from NSF-funded organizations, while
allowing ANS to sell commercial access to the Internet through
the same facilities. The NSF put the following restrictions on the
connection of commercial sites, however:

- ANS must recover the average cost of any commercial use.

- Revenues recovered above costs will be placed in a pool.

- Money from the pool will be distributed to regional networks that agree to carry the commercial traffic with the
  purpose of improving the national and regional network
  infrastructure.

- The commercial traffic can't have a detrimental effect on
  NSF traffic service and support.

Because of the questionable practice of carrying commercial
traffic over the same backbone as NSFNET traffic (among other
things), Congress requested a review of the NSFNET program. A
report to Congress by the Office of Inspector General found that
neither NSF nor any original proposals for the management of
NSFNET anticipated or addressed the use of the NSFNET by
commercial traffic. Apparently, NSF didn't document or request
approval for the decision to allow commercial traffic over the
NSFNET facilities. The report concluded that the decision to
allow commercial traffic wasn't improper, because commercial
traffic doesn't degrade performance of NSFNET traffic; instead,
it provides funds to improve the network infrastructure. The
report, however, criticized the NSF for the lack of documentation and review, and admonished the organization to conform
to the appropriate procedures in the future.

Internet Information Services

One of the important parts of Merit's management of the Internet was the provision of information and technical support

services for the network. Merit created a centralized collection of documents related to Internet administration. Merit also monitored the performance of the Internet, producing monthly, quarterly, and annual reports with statistical analysis of the traffic. Another service provided by Merit was regional workshops to help campuses learn to connect to and use the Internet.

Merit's agreement with the NSF included the provision of the physical manifestation of the network and the information services for the network. When the agreement with Merit expired in 1992, the NSF decided to award separate agreements for the network information services (providing information about the network, and how to use it) and the traffic conveyance services (providing the physical connection and monitoring of the network).

The traffic conveyance agreement with Merit was extended to approximately the spring of 1994 to allow the NSF to solicit proposals for a new network provider. In March 1992, the NSF solicited proposals for one or more organizations to provide the information services for the NSFNET (which is also the backbone of the Internet, because it's the largest TCP/IP network in the country). The NSF required that the Network Information Services manager(s) provide the following services to the NSFNET community:

- Registration services, providing a central location where new Internet sites can obtain their network address and their domain name (the name and physical network address that can be used to access the site)

- A master directory that points to other directory services, possibly including the following:

  Lists of users by name, discipline, and organization

  Network sites and the characteristics of their connections

Organizations accessible by function

Resources available on the Internet (available computing facilities, libraries, databases, and so forth)

Databases of contributed material

Databases of Internet documents, such as FYIs (repositories of common Internet information), RFCs (documents used to propose standards and provide information about the Internet), and so on

Databases maintained for other groups, possibly for a fee

■ Network Reference Desk services (provided through phone, fax, e-mail, and U.S. mail) to answer general questions, distribute information related to general questions, direct inquiries to the appropriate information source, record and track inquiries and summarize the inquiries for NSF, and track problems and queries that can't be resolved immediately

■ Coordinated information sharing between component networks and the international networking community

■ Educational and training services, including the following:

Training courses for potential network users

Material dealing with network security

Help so that elementary, high school, and two- and four-year colleges can become more involved with the NSFNET

End-user training materials, information about resources available on the network, information about how to use the network, and a document describing NSFNET procedures and policies

The Current Network Information Providers

On April 1, 1993, the NSF awarded three 5-year cooperative agreements for the management of the Network Information Services. These providers intend to use innovative methods to respond and adapt to the projected explosive growth of the Internet over the next five years. The three cooperative agreements were awarded to the following companies:

- Network Solutions, which will provide the Internet registration services, including the assignment of IP addresses and registration of domain names.

- AT&T, which will maintain lists of ftp sites, various types of servers available on the Internet, lists of white- and yellow-page directories, library catalogs, and data archives. AT&T also will offer database design, management, and maintenance services to groups for material available to the Internet community.

- General Atomics, which will provide a Network Reference Desk, the Info Source (a database of network reference materials), training classes and documentation for running NIS groups, and coordinating services. The company also will provide an innovative hypermedia interface to the Info Source called NICLink, and will use a person in the role of info scout to search the Internet for new resources and innovative uses of the network that can be included in the Info Source.

Together, all these services are known as the InterNIC. In a press release announcing the NSFNET Network Information Services contract awardees, Steve Wolff, director of the NSF's Division of Networking and Communications Research and Infrastructure, said that the cooperation between these geographically dispersed organizations should exemplify the environment of distributed collaboration fostered by the Internet.

A Grander Vision

Without a direct need for resolution, a number of issues have been left unaddressed over the years, including standards development and commercial access to the Internet. Because of these issues, as well as the perception of a substantial national benefit from an advanced information infrastructure, Congress proposed the High Performance Computing Act to resolve these issues.

The High Performance Computing Act, signed into law by President George Bush in late 1991, provided in part for federal support of research into and implementation of a nationwide high-speed computing network known as the National Research and Education Network (NREN). This bill encourages network research comparable to the research effort that spawned the ARPANET in the late '60s and early '70s. The government recognizes that high-speed data transmission will be vital to the educational and economic health of the nation in the not-too-distant future, and that money spent in this area will bring great benefits in the future.

The NREN Takes Shape

The Federal Coordinating Council on Science, Engineering and Technology (FCCSET)—part of the White House Office of Science and Technology Policy—is directing the NREN project. This organization will provide a vision for network development that hasn't been present for a number of years. The NSF is coordinating the NREN project.

The government has directed that the NSFNET be used as the backbone for the NREN, providing the links between all the major government networks. The NREN consists of the NSFNET and portions of the networks operated by NASA (NSINET), the Department of Energy (ESNET), and the DOD (MILNET).

Because the NSFNET backbone will be the cornerstone of the NREN, NSF is responsible for managing the development of NREN facilities and sponsoring the continued improvement of the national computer networking environment.

New Goals for the NSFNET/NREN

The NSF is taking a different approach to the management of the NSFNET backbone with its current proposal solicitation. In this solicitation, the management of the network is divided into four separate areas:

- One or more Network Access Point (NAP) managers

- A routing arbiter organization

- A provider for Very High-Speed Backbone Network Services (vBNS)

- A set of regional networks that connect research/educational institutions

The NSF's goal is to remove itself from the direct funding of NSFNET. The NSF now is soliciting proposals for a new network manger that will advance the technology of the NSFNET to the next level. The NSF envisions the new configuration of the NSFNET as a series of NAPs where a number of networks can connect to a new high-speed backbone.

NSF also envisions an arrangement where networks would pay connection fees and an annual fee to use NAPs. Unlike the previous NSFNET proposal, this arrangement will provide for the conveyance of non-research/educational traffic. This arrangement would have the effect of removing some of the restrictions now in place on most Internet traffic. An AUP still will cover NSFNET traffic, but because the NAPs won't be subject to the AUP, they won't have any NSF-placed restrictions on traffic between two networks connected to a single NAP.

Although the NAPs will have no restrictions on commercial traffic carried on their own network, the NSF service provided by the NAP still must be maintained at acceptable levels to the NSF, which may mean that the NSF traffic receives priority over the commercial traffic. And, for a fee, commercial users would have access to the vBNS, which would give the commercial traffic access to high-speed communications services that they may need.

The NREN legislation provides that the NREN be a collaboration between government and industry, and shouldn't dampen the motivation for commercial development of similar networking technology and services. One of the main focuses of NREN is to encourage the continued development of new network technology, including standards that will make development coherent across vendors. Further areas to investigate are ways to make information available while guaranteeing copyright protection, and ways to charge for usage of the network and network facilities (such as databases and copyrighted materials). The intent is that companies that provide the hardware and services required for the NREN will be motivated to sell them commercially after they are developed for the NREN.

Internet-Related Organizations

A number of formal and informal groups have controlled the Internet over the years. Three groups that hope to direct the development of the Internet as the NSF reduces the government involvement in the Internet are the Internet Society, CIX, and FARNET.

The Internet Society

The Internet Society describes itself as an organization that "provides assistance and support to groups and organizations involved in the use operation and evolution of the Internet. It provides support for forums in which technical and operational questions can be discussed, and provides mechanisms through which interested parties can be informed and educated about the Internet, its function, use, operation, and the interests of its constituents."

The Internet Society intends to foster the creation of a world-wide networked community. It provides educational activities and information to the academic and scientific communities and the general public about the technology and use of the Internet. It also supports the evolution of the Internet and encourages involvement of the different user communities in the evolution.

Although it has no official say or control over the Internet, the Internet Society tries to bring together the communities that use the Internet, educate them about the Internet, and encourage them to become involved in the evolution of the Internet.

The Internet Society was organized by the Corporation for National Research Initiatives, EDUCOM (an organization whose members consist of educational institutions in the United States), RARE (a consortium of European research networks), and the Internet Architecture Board.

The Commercial Internet Exchange (CIX)

In 1991, three public networks—CERFnet, PSINet, and Alternet—formed the Commercial Internet Exchange (CIX) to provide commercial high-speed networking services. To be able to carry commercial network traffic, these organizations had to provide their own network interconnections rather than use the nationwide NSFNET because the NSF restricts the passage of commercial traffic over the NSFNET. Because CIX allows commercial traffic, companies can connect to distant offices electronically or get vendor updates over the wires instead of by delivery services.

FARNET

Some regional and special-interest networks interested in promoting research and education networking have joined to form an association called FARNET, the Federation of American Research Networks. The members of FARNET want to improve the accessibility of information on the Internet and assure the Internet's robustness and ease of operation. To these ends, the members have organized workshops and educational meetings, and used their combined size to negotiate better rates for products and services, among other things. FARNET also allows its members to have their voices heard in the development of NREN and international network standards.

Other Networks Accessible from the NSFNET

Although the NSFNET backbone is the major highway that allows access to all the networks that comprise the Internet, thousands of separate networks make up what is called the Internet. Some of these networks are large and most are in the United States, but a growing number are small networks, and many of them are overseas.

NSFNET has a number of network connections in other countries. Some countries have non-TCP/IP networks that can be reached through gateways.

Corporation for Research and Educational Networking (CREN)

Not all universities had access to the Internet. Several non-Internet networks developed to enable researchers at these universities to communicate with each other and with colleagues on the Internet. One of these networks was CSNET, the Computer and Science Network.

The CSNET was an NSF-funded network developed to provide Internet access—and, thus, contact with peers—for computer science researchers who otherwise couldn't connect to the Internet. Although the network was TCP/IP based, the only service initially provided to CSNET members was electronic mail. As time went on, some parts of the network began to support other common Internet services, such as file transfer and remote login.

Educational institutions that couldn't connect to the Internet or CSNET could provide a means of collaboration for their researchers through BITNET (Because It's Time Network). To be a member of the BITNET community, you needed only to lease a phone line connection to another BITNET site and agree to allow a new node to run a leased line to your site in return. BITNET provided facilities for electronic mail, file transfer, and interactive discussions between users. Because BITNET wasn't a TCP/IP-based network, however, exchanging information with organizations that were on the Internet wasn't easy.

Because their missions were similar, CSNET and BITNET decided to merge and form the Corporation for Research and Educational Networking (CREN), to provide computing services to small universities and sites not on the Internet. The merger also enabled the two networks to move toward the most recent network technology and to have more of a role in the development of the NREN.

Because the technologies of the two component networks are very different, CREN won't immediately be trying to merge the two networks. Instead, CREN initially will focus on providing a wide variety of network connection options and services. It will provide for the basic BITNET leased-line connection to provide file transfer, remote command capability, interactive messages, and electronic mail.

CREN also will provide for a central dial-up mail forwarding system that sends messages to other major mail networks.

Another service that will be provided is dial-up IP service, a SLIP-based dial-in service that will provide full TCP/IP access to the Internet. Some leased-line IP access also will allow connection to the Internet, and a new protocol will allow original BITNET sites to send information in IP format to the Internet.

> **Note**
>
> SLIP is an IP protocol that can be used over the phone lines. See Chapter 10, "Determining the Level of Internet Service You Need," and Chapter 16, "SLIP and PPP Service," for more information about SLIP.

With these network connections, the following services will be provided:

- Interactive messages

- File transfer

- Electronic mail

- LISTSERV (a means for setting up automated mail distribution lists)

- Basic IP services such as telnet, ftp, and Internet e-mail

- CSNET information service (providing mail response for Internet information and a hot line that provides technical, operational, administrative, and information services for CSNET service members)

The ultimate goal is to strengthen the presence of CSNET in the Internet world, and to make the BITNET services more compatible with the existing Internet services.

> **Note**
>
> CREN also is affiliated through BITNET with networks in approximately 35 countries, with Europe and Canada having the largest membership.

Introducing the Internet

International Networks

You can access a number of networks from other countries, most of them sponsored by governments, from the Internet:

- NORDUnet, the network that connects the individual networks in the Nordic research community (Denmark, Finland, Iceland, Norway, and Sweden). NORDUnet gives Nordic researchers access to each other and to other major networks (the Internet and EARN, among others).

- CA*NET, the Canadian equivalent of NSFNET. This network connects the Canadian regional networks and supports Canadian data communications related to research, academic, and technology transfer activities.

- NETNORTH, the Canadian equivalent of BITNET. This network provides e-mail, file-transfer, and interactive message capabilities between BITNET, EARN, and NETNORTH members. Like BITNET, NETNORTH can be reached from the Internet through gateways.

- EARN, the European equivalent of BITNET. This network provides e-mail, file-transfer, and interactive message capabilities between BITNET, EARN, and NETNORTH members. Like BITNET, EARN can be reached from the Internet through gateways.

Government Networks

The ARPANET was officially dismantled in 1990 because it had outlived its usefulness; the NSFNET now provides the main backbone connectivity. Because the military still needed an operational and an experimental network, however, the Department of Defense created the DDN (Defense Data Network), a secure operational network, and the DRI (Defense Research Internet) to carry on in the tradition of the ARPANET in research into high-speed reliable distributed communications. The new technologies developed by these networks are expected eventually to become available commercially, as military research by-products often do.

A number of other government agencies that have research programs—such as the National Institute of Health, the Department of Energy, and NASA—also have their own networks.

The Social Development of the Internet

Few people envisioned that the ARPANET would be used the way it was or that it would grow into what it is today. The initial designers of the ARPANET imagined that its main use would be for information exchange and remote processing. But one of the most widely used Internet applications—which wasn't foreseen—is electronic mail (discussed in more detail in the next section). This ease of communication with other Internet members has enabled the Internet to grow into a community whose members interact in complex relationships.

Before computer networks became so widespread, researchers depended on printed materials (such as journals, technical reports, and letters), conferences, and face-to-face meetings to exchange information about their research. Researchers were very isolated, with infrequent contact with any but their close colleagues. Researchers in different parts of the country could be pursuing the same goal, with no way of knowing that their efforts were being duplicated nor sharing the information that may enable them to collaborate or compare results.

One of the main goals of the ARPANET was to enable researchers to exchange information in a much more timely and convenient manner. Through the file-exchange facilities, one researcher could transfer reports and data easily to another researcher within a matter of hours, if not minutes. Programs developed at one site could be shared with others who were doing similar work. The resources of a powerful computer could be made available to labs that were too small to afford to buy such a machine for themselves.

All these goals have become a reality on the Internet. But the Internet has become something much more than a tool to allow researchers to share information and resources.

Electronic Mail

One of the most important uses of the ARPANET turned out to be electronic mail, which enables physically distant users to communicate in a very short period of time. Electronic mail, also called *e-mail*, can be received much faster than mail sent through the U.S. Postal Service. And although a phone call may put you in touch faster, e-mail enables you to send and receive large amounts of information in a form that you can store, print, or use as input to programs. E-mail also enables you to leave a message, even if the recipient can't read it immediately.

An outgrowth of the e-mail facility is the mailing list. A *mailing list* is a type of conference that enables list members to contribute articles discussing topics pertaining to the purpose of the list. Everyone participating in a mailing list receives via e-mail a copy of every article submitted to that list.

> **Note**
>
> See Chapter 7, "Using E-Mail," for details about using e-mail and mailing lists on the Internet.

Sometime after mailing lists became a popular means of communication, the USENET netnews system began operating (see Chapter 9, "USENET," for more information). USENET provides a type of conference forum capability, something like the forums on CompuServe. Unlike mailing lists, USENET articles aren't sent directly to a user's mailbox, but to a common disk area on a user's machine. Currently, thousands of public forums on the Internet (between USENET and the BITSERV mailing lists) provide discussion groups pertaining to everything from computer system administration to religion. Many different groups have technical topics, social topics, and recreational topics.

These different groups have created an amazing capability to communicate almost instantaneously with users on the other side of the world. Without the restrictions that physically close relationships place on people, friendships—and animosities— spring up with amazing quickness on the Internet. Users with similar interests can go to the network to find help and report successes. You also can collaborate on a project without ever meeting your colleagues. (This book, for example, was written by authors in two different states who communicated by phone, e-mail, and file transfer, without ever meeting physically.)

Explosive Growth

Back in the early days of the ARPANET—even as late as 1981— the Internet community was so small that users literally knew almost everyone on the network. Most sites were government or university research centers. If a researcher received a request for information from a colleague at another site, he or she generally would know that person—or at least know of that person—and would be able to spend a few hours or more of his/her time answering the request.

With the growth of the Internet, this type of personal response has become more difficult. The growth can be compared with a small town suddenly acquiring a large industry and expanding to 25 times its original size. Residents in the small town all used to know each other and were on speaking terms with most of their neighbors. Their children went to the same schools and grew up together. In the big city, residents keep their houses shut and come out only to drive to work or for other necessities.

Individuals don't have time to know their neighbors, except perhaps for one or two they have something in common with.

The Internet has become like this, in a way. So many users are on the Internet now that knowing even the people in your own organization (if it is large) is difficult, let alone others on the network. Perhaps users know a few dozen others who participate in a discussion news group, or other researchers that they have met at conferences or whose papers they have read in journals.

Even though the smallness has been lost, the Internet still provides a community, of sorts. Right now, access to the Internet is still relatively restricted. Compared to the more than 250 million people in the United States, the million or so that have Internet access is still a small number.

Malicious Use

Most use the Internet for its intended purpose: to exchange information or use remote computer resources unavailable to them locally. Usually this exchange is done in a friendly and honest manner. But some users abuse the Internet. Several incidents have come to the public's attention over the last few years, as the next two sections explain.

Espionage

In his book, *The Cuckoo's Egg*, Clifford Stoll tells about his experience with computer infiltration as a graduate student in astronomy at the University of California, Berkeley. While trying to find the reason for less than a dollar's worth of unaccounted for computer time, he discovered an international spy who was breaking into computers around the country with the apparent intent of finding government information. Stoll's book is a fascinating look at how the computers were accessed, the trails that the computer thief unknowingly left, and the way he was caught.

The Internet Worm

Another well-publicized Internet incident was that of the Internet Worm. A *worm* is a program that moves from one computer to another, sometimes damaging the systems it passes through. (Compare this to a virus, which enters a system as part of another program and usually damages the system it infects.) On November 3, 1988, Robert Morris, then a graduate student at Cornell, wrote a computer program that allegedly was simply an experiment to test a problem with the network mail transport mechanism. Reportedly, it unintentionally got out onto the Internet and became what is now known as the Internet Worm.

Although the worm didn't actively destroy any data on the systems it encountered, it did flood the network and tie up computer time by trying to make as many connections as it could to any machine it found on the network. Machines became so bogged down with the connections from the Internet that they became unusable.

To stop the attacks, many Internet segments disconnected themselves to keep from being reinfected after they cleaned up their systems. To keep new infestations from spreading, all subnetworks had to remain disconnected from the Internet until every subnetwork had cleaned itself of the worm. It was several days before all parts of the Internet were back on-line.

Ironically, Morris is the son of the then chief scientist of the National Security Agency's Computer Security Council. He was charged under the provisions of the Computer Fraud and Abuse Act of 1986, which makes impeding authorized use of federal-interest computers a felony. (Because the worm didn't destroy any physical property, he couldn't be charged with any standard crime.) He was found guilty but was sentenced only to three years' probation, 400 hours of community service, and a $10,000 fine.

Interestingly, this event lead to the development of new laws that declared intentional misuse of computer resources a crime.

The Internet Helps Democracy

Although the Internet enables users to exchange information of common interest, it can play a much bigger part in the world of communications. It can, for example, allow instantaneous reporting of events that are happening around the world. Regularly, members of the Internet community are among the first to find out about major earthquakes, the death of a notable person, or major accidents or storms.

When Slovenia declared its independence from Yugoslavia in June 1991, students and faculty at universities there sent their colleagues in the United States e-mail with reports on the bombing and the atrocities that were taking place.

When an attempted coup occurred in the then Soviet Union in 1991, the perpetrators took control of the print and broadcast media but couldn't get control over—or forgot about—the computer networks. Around the world, messages were sent from the government under attack detailing the true state of affairs, and the support that was sent back to it helped sustain its fight against the usurpers.

The Internet in Desert Storm

An article in the May 1992 issue of *ConneXions* magazine tells of how the Internet played an important part of another military operation—the 1991-92 Gulf War. The military requested and was immediately issued addresses to create 20 class B subnetworks (which would allow up to 65,536 addresses per subnetwork). The military decided to connect back to the Internet in the United States through satellite links. Until the satellite equipment could be brought over to Saudi Arabia, however, the military used a dedicated voice line to Fort Bragg, North Carolina, with a 9600-baud modem for the first 6 weeks of what turned out to be an eight-month network installation.

During Operation Desert Storm, the military used the Internet connection to send unclassified logistics data to different command centers in the Persian Gulf arena and on the continental United States. Military personnel also used the network to send messages home to their families.

The Internet Community

One interesting thing about communicating over the network is that it removes many preconceived notions that you form about people when you meet them in person. When you communicate with individuals over the network, you don't know (unless they tell you) their age, race, height, weight, or sometime even their gender. You don't know whether they're disabled, the president of a company, or a janitor. You can judge them only by their words.

For this reason, carefully choosing the words you use in your Internet communications is very important. The Internet, for the most part, is a friendly, open community. Because the chance of any real retribution is small, however, some users make vicious attacks on others. These users quickly lose credibility in the community, though, and may find themselves in trouble if they need to deal with someone they insulted or someone who was unimpressed by their abuse. The existence of people who abuse the open environment of the Internet is one of the few drawbacks of the Internet community, but one that has grown as the number of users on the Internet has grown.

The Internet community has features that physical communities have, but on a much larger scale. Two users from different parts of the country may strike up a friendship that eventually leads to a romantic relationship, or even marriage. On-line real-time conferences using services such as the Internet Relay Chat allow many users to converse in real-time about subjects they have in common. Internet users have all types of personalities: shy, aggressive, friendly, and even abusive. The Internet community truly represents society in general.

The Growth of the Internet

The growth of the Internet has been absolutely phenomenal, particularly over the last five years. During that time, many commercial TCP/IP providers have begun connecting to the network, and the number of research and educational institutions has expanded as well.

The traffic over the NSFNET backbone is monitored by the backbone manager, Merit, and the statistics are available on-line at Merit's anonymous ftp site (`nic.merit.edu`).

The following sections talk about the growth of the number of hosts and the amount of traffic on the Internet, and show graphically some of the information available from Merit. Although the figures refer only to NSFNET, this is the major TCP/IP backbone of the Internet and should be representative of the Internet growth in general.

Traffic Growth

The number of data packets that flowed through the NSFNET went from 85 million in January 1988 to 29.7 billion packets in May 1993 (see fig. 2.2). The byte traffic increased from 1.26 trillion bytes of data in March 1991 to around 6 trillion bytes of data in May 1993 (see fig. 2.3).

In addition to the general increase in traffic, looking at the type of traffic flowing through the network (and how this has changed) is also interesting. Approximately 45 to 50 percent of the current network traffic involves file exchange (ftp activity), up from 20 percent five years ago. Approximately 20 percent involves mail and USENET traffic, although this type of traffic has dropped considerably from a high of almost 30 percent. The interactive traffic (telnet, login, and finger) dropped from around 20 percent to about 6 percent of the traffic. Name service (Domain Name Lookup) has dropped from a high of around 15 percent to about 3 percent of the traffic. Other TCP services (such as Internet Relay Chat, talk, and X Windows) have grown from about 11 percent to almost 25 percent of the total traffic. Non-TCP services average about 2 percent of network traffic.

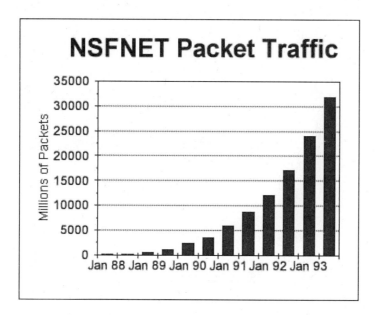

Fig. 2.2
The increase in NSFNET packet traffic from January 1988 to May 1993.

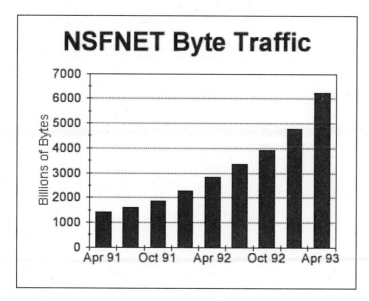

Fig 2.3
The increase in NSFNET byte traffic from March 1991 to May 1993.

Introducing the Internet

Host Growth

As of July 1993, 13,170 NSFNET-affiliated networks existed in 59 countries around the world, from Argentina to Croatia to Singapore to the Virgin Islands. The NIC Network registration has increased tremendously in the last 10 years. It has gone from assigning only 6 class B addresses in 1982 to assigning 12,678 class C addresses in 1992, and more than 4,000 class C addresses in the first two months of 1993 alone (see fig. 2.4).

Fig. 2.4

The increase in the number of networks on the Internet, from December 1982 through December 1992.

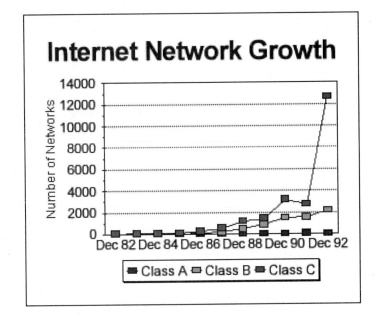

The number of hosts on the Internet has grown from 213 in August 1981 to 1,313,000 hosts in January 1993 (see fig. 2.5). The edu domain, for educational and research organizations, has the most hosts with 410,940. The commercial domain now has almost as many hosts with 347,486.

The program that searches the Internet to collect the host and domain information also collects information about the most common host names on the Internet. At last report, the most popular host name is venus, with seven of the planets showing up in the top 20 names. calvin and hobbes also show up, as do a number of more practical names such as pc1 and mac1. You may think your machine name is unique, but it's not too likely!

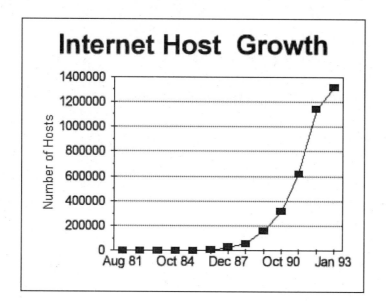

Fig. 2.5
The increase in the number of hosts on the Internet between August 1981 and January 1993.

Summary

The experiment that no one was sure what to do with has evolved into an indispensable part of many people's personal and professional lives. The Internet has evolved from a small network connecting four research sites in the United States to a huge international web of networks that reaches almost every country in the world.

Network technology has been evolving constantly since the first days of the ARPANET. The Internet community has evolved, too, from a few educational and research sites where everyone knew everyone else, to a huge community of several million users worldwide.

The Internet gives researchers access to resources that they would otherwise never have, such as powerful supercomputers. Electronic mail provides a means of exchanging information with colleagues who are geographically distant.

For a long time the Internet was restricted to research and educational sites. The recent and rapidly expanding addition of commercial sites has spurred the development of commercial services available on the Internet—at this point, a small number, but sure to increase as the community grows.

Chapter 3

The Structure of the Internet

Perhaps the hardest thing for a new user of the Internet to grasp is its incredibly non-uniform nature. Even its name, *the Internet*, sounds as though only one, massive network is connecting computing machines across streets or continents with equal ease and access. The fact that the software implementing the network struggles to make any differences between machines and connections invisible to you compounds this illusion.

A Dynamic Organization of Computers

In reality, the Internet is a tangled web of different machines in different networks with different users. Rather than settle down over time, the rate of growth and change in the Internet continues to increase. One way to describe the amorphous physical structure of the Internet is as a "cloud" of computers (see fig. 3.1), with the corresponding image of continuous melding and shifting over time.

So how can the structure of such a dynamic organization be captured and explained? By taking a step back and analyzing what sort of structural information you would require to use the resources of the Internet effectively. For instance, do you really need to know where a certain computer is physically located, the network protocols in use, or the details of the file format for its operating system? Do you even want to know? Almost universally, the answers to these questions are *no*. You do need to be able to locate, identify, and exchange resources such as programs, data files, or computational capability. Fortunately, looking at the Internet from a functional rather than physical level reveals a much more organized—if not truly rigid—structure.

Fig. 3.1

The Internet "cloud." Different computers and their users loosely joined to form a single, worldwide body.

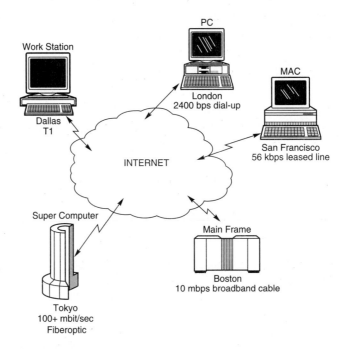

The participants in the Internet are a wide variety of machines, organizations, and individuals, all able to communicate and share information. The fundamental computing entities within this structure are called *hosts*, or *nodes*. Hosts may be massive, parallel processing supercomputers, data-processing mainframes, laboratory minicomputers, CAD system workstations, desktop PCs, or even laptops. These hosts are tied together through network connections that support data-transfer rates of from hundreds of bytes to hundreds of megabytes per second.

The hosts that comprise the Internet are collectively responsible for sending information to its intended destination, capturing and sorting incoming information, dispatching it to the proper recipient, forwarding data between hosts, and converting data formats and protocols (see fig. 3.2). To navigate within this structure successfully and confidently, you need to understand some of the basics of how a host operates to accomplish these tasks, and the services it provides you to make exchanging information a straightforward process.

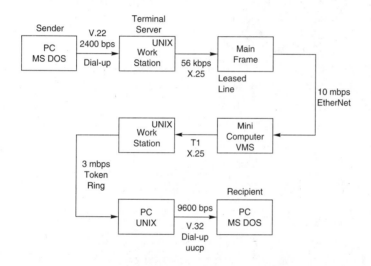

Fig. 3.2
An example of how several hosts cooperate to transfer a message across different networks until it reaches its final destination.

Obtaining an in-depth understanding of the configuration and operation of the Internet is a complex, challenging feat. Fortunately, you can safely ignore many details unless you are involved in network management or the oversight of a host. As a user, your interface to the Internet normally focuses on two structural areas: the name structure and the data storage structure.

The Name Structure

When you want to send a letter or make a phone call to someone, you need to know more than just that person's proper name. So it is when you send information through Internet. And just like a paper mailing address, an electronic address of an individual, computer, or organization on the Internet has several components. In Internet terminology, a name represents any entity on the Internet, such as a user account, an executing software process, or a machine having one or many such accounts or processes.

To include as much information as possible in a succinct, consistent fashion, you create names by using a convention called the Domain Name System (DNS). The DNS defines a template for the structure of names. Names are constructed going left to right, and from the more narrow to the more broad in scope. A name consists of several elements or labels, each separated by a delimiter (a @ or . character). The general format for a name is as follows:

```
<account>@[subdomain].[subdomain].[...].<domain>
```

As you can see, several fields appear within a DNS name. An address that complies with this format contains a special ASCII string, called a *label*, that defines these fields. The significance of each field is detailed in the sections that follow.

> **Note**
>
> In the DNS syntax, *italic text* indicates that you shouldn't type the text literally, but that you should replace it with the appropriate information. Square brackets denote optional items. Don't type the brackets as part of a DNS name.

Labels

Labels must be no more than 63 characters long; start with a
letter; end with a letter or digit; and contain only letters, digits,
or the hyphen. Examples of legitimate labels follow:

```
blondie
DAGWOOD
r2d2
C3p0
six-pack
LONG123456789112345678921234567893123456789412345678
```

The following are examples of illegal labels:

```
endedwithhyphen-
2notstartedwithletter
spaces not allowed
no#othercharacters
```

Obviously, you could define some pretty hard-to-remember
labels. As a practical matter, though, RFC 1032 "The Domain
administrators guide" suggests that labels be kept to 12 characters or less, to enhance human readability and memorization.

Domain Field

The domain for a name appears as its right-most label.
Domains, one of the few well-specified and regulated areas,
represent the top-most logical subdivisions of the Internet.
Within the United States, each host on the Internet is assigned
to one of the following domains based on its usage:

Domain	Description
gov	Non-military government affiliated
edu	Universities and other educational institutions
arpa	ARPANET members (largely obsolete now)
com	Commercial and industrial organizations

(continues)

Domain	Description
mil	Military
org	Other organizations, such as user groups
net	Network operations and service centers

Note

Many users initially confuse domains or subdomains with networks. This confusion is understandable because a subdomain consisting of only one network is often coincidentally true, especially for smaller organizations. But whereas a *network* is a grouping based on physical connectivity and the use of a similar communications protocol suite, a *domain* is a logical grouping that can contain multiple networks, entirely or partially. Thus, a host's domain hierarchy isn't necessarily dictated by its physical network (see fig. 3.3).

Fig. 3.3
Domains can encompass entire networks, or only certain computers within a network.

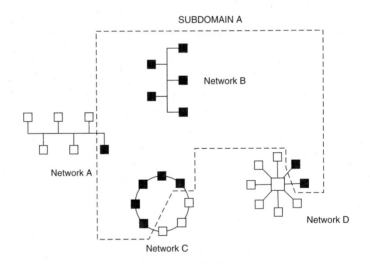

Outside the United States, each nation has a domain assigned to it that corresponds to its two-letter country code, as listed in table 3.1. These country codes are based on a document from the International Standards Organization (ISO), number 3166, which defines two-letter, three-letter, and numeric designations for each nation.

Note

This list is updated occasionally as international events deem necessary. The list was particularly active before this printing due to the breakup of the former Soviet Union and the split of Czechoslovakia and Yugoslavia into new republics. The following table lists the international domains.

Table 3.1 International Domains

Country	Code
Afghanistan	AF
Albania	AL
Algeria	DZ
American Samoa	AS
Andorra	AD
Angola	AO
Anguilla	AI
Antarctica	AQ
Antigua and Barbuda	AG
Argentina	AR
Armenia	AM
Aruba	AW
Australia	AU

(continues)

Table 3.1 Continued	
Country	**Code**
Austria	AT
Azerbaijan	AZ
Bahamas	BS
Bahrain	BH
Bangladesh	BD
Barbados	BB
Belarus	BY
Belgium	BE
Belize	BZ
Benin	BJ
Bermuda	BM
Bhutan	BT
Bolivia	BO
Bosnia Hercegovina	BA
Botswana	BW
Bouvet Island	BV
Brazil	BR
British Indian Ocean Territory	IO
Brunei Darussalam	BN
Bulgaria	BG
Burkina Faso (formerly Upper Volta)	BF
Burundi	BI
Byelorussian SSR	BY
Cambodia	KH
Cameroon	CM

Country	Code
Canada	CA
Cape Verde	CV
Cayman Islands	KY
Central African Republic	CF
Chad	TD
Chile	CL
China	CN
Christmas Island	CX
Cocos (Keeling) Islands	CC
Colombia	CO
Comoros	KM
Congo	CG
Cook Island	CK
Costa Rica	CR
Cote d'Ivoire (Ivory Coast)	CI
Croatia (local name: Hrvatska)	HR
Cuba	CU
Cyprus	CY
Czech Republic	CZ
Denmark	DK
Djibouti	DJ
Dominica	DM
Dominican Republic	DO
East Timor	TP
Ecuador	EC
Egypt	EG

(continues)

Table 3.1 Continued

Country	Code
El Salvador	SV
Equatorial Guinea	GQ
Estonia	EE
Ethiopia	ET
Falkland Islands (Malvinas)	FK
Faroe Islands	FO
Fiji	FJ
Finland	FI
France	FR
French Guiana	GF
French Polynesia	PF
French Southern Territories	TF
Gabon	GA
Gambia	GM
Georgia (a former Soviet Republic)	GE
Germany	DE
Ghana	GH
Gibraltar	GI
Greece	GR
Greenland	GL
Grenada	GD
Guadeloupe	GP
Guam	GU
Guatemala	GT
Guinea	GN

Country	Code
Guinea-Bissau	GW
Guyana	GY
Haiti	HT
Heard and McDonald Islands	HM
Honduras	HN
Hong Kong	HK
Hungary	HU
Iceland	IS
India	IN
Indonesia	ID
Iran, Islamic Republic of	IR
Iraq	IQ
Ireland	IE
Israel	IL
Italy	IT
Jamaica	JM
Japan	JP
Jordan	JO
Kazakhstan	KZ
Kenya	KE
Kiribati	KI
Korea, Democratic People's Republic of (North)	KP
Korea, Republic of (South)	KR
Kuwait	KW
Kyrgyzstan	KG
Lao People's Democratic Republic	LA

(continues)

Introducing the Internet

Table 3.1 Continued

Country	Code
Latvia	LV
Lebanon	LB
Lesotho	LS
Liberia	LR
Libyan Arab Jamahiriya (Libya)	LY
Liechtenstein	LI
Lithuania	LT
Luxembourg	LU
Macau (Macao)	MO
Madagascar	MG
Malawi	MW
Malaysia	MY
Maldives	MV
Mali	ML
Malta	MT
Marshall Islands	MH
Martinique	MQ
Mauritania	MR
Mauritius	MU
Mexico	MX
Micronesia	FM
Moldova, Republic of	MD
Monaco	MC
Mongolia	MN

Country	Code
Montserrat	MS
Morocco	MA
Mozambique	MZ
Myanmar	MM
Namibia	NA
Nauru	NR
Nepal	NP
Netherlands	NL
Netherlands Antilles (Dutch West Indies)	AN
Neutral Zone	NT
New Caledonia	NC
New Zealand	NZ
Nicaragua	NI
Niger	NE
Nigeria	NG
Niue	NU
Norfolk Island	NF
Northern Mariana Islands	MP
Norway	NO
Oman	OM
Pakistan	PK
Palau	PW
Panama	PA
Papua New Guinea	PG
Paraguay	PY

(continues)

Table 3.1 Continued	
Country	**Code**
Peru	PE
Philippines	PH
Pitcairn Island	PN
Poland	PL
Portugal	PT
Puerto Rico	PR
Qatar	QA
Reunion Island	RE
Romania	RO
Russian Federation	RU
Rwanda	RW
St. Helena	SH
St. Kitts and Nevis	KN
St. Lucia	LC
St. Pierre and Miquelon	PM
St. Vincent and the Grenadines	VC
Samoa	WS
San Marino	SM
Sao Tome and Principe	ST
Saudi Arabia	SA
Senegal	SN
Seychelles	SC
Sierra Leone	SL
Singapore	SG

Country	Code
Slovakia (Slovak Republic)	SK
Slovenia	SI
Solomon Islands	SB
Somalia	SO
South Africa	ZA
Spain	ES
Sri Lanka	LK
Sudan	SD
Suriname	SR
Svalbard and Jan Mayen Islands	SJ
Swaziland	SZ
Sweden	SE
Switzerland	CH
Syrian Arab Republic (Syria)	SY
Taiwan, Province of China	TW
Tajikistan	TJ
Tanzania, United Republic of	TZ
Thailand	TH
Togo	TG
Tokelau	TK
Tonga	TO
Trinidad and Tobago	TT
Tunisia	TN
Turkey	TR
Turkmenistan	TM

(continues)

Table 3.1 Continued	
Country	**Code**
Turks and Caicos Islands	TC
Tuvalu	TV
Uganda	UG
Ukrainian Soviet Socialist Republic (Ukraine)	UA
United Arab Emirates	AE
United Kingdom	GB
United States	US
Uruguay	UY
USSR (formerly)	SU
Uzbekistan	UZ
Vanuatu	VU
Vatican City State (Holy See)	VA
Venezuela	VE
Vietnam	VN
Virgin Islands (British)	VG
Virgin Islands (U.S.)	VI
Wallis and Fortuna Islands	WF
Western Sahara	EH
Yemen, Republic of	YE
Yugoslavia (formerly)	YU
Zaire	ZR
Zambia	ZM
Zimbabwe	ZW

Subdomain Field

Being able to refer to a logical gathering of user names as one entity, such as the employees within a department or students within a class, is convenient. The DNS enables you to group names into subdomains for just such purposes. Usually a company, department, or other organization (such as a user group) will have several subdomains, such as that given in figure 3.4.

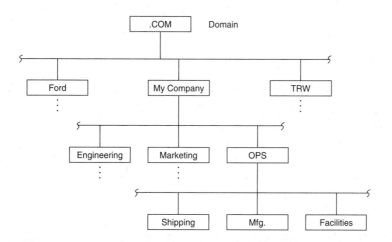

Fig. 3.4
An example subdomain structure for an organization with several departments, and groups within each department. Each successively lower level of this hierarchy adds another subdomain field to the names of the users in that subdomain.

Developing groups of groups also may be handy, so subdomains can beget subdomains in a practically endless fashion, such as in the legitimate uses shown in figure 3.5.

Fig. 3.5
Examples of subdomains for groups within a company.

Each name has a limit to how long it can be. Due to the way the DNS encodes the name, that length depends on the number of labels in it. RFC 1035 specifies that a name can be no more than 255 bytes. Each label is coded as a length octet, followed by the characters of the label. The terminating octet of all names is the null (0) octet. Therefore, the total number of characters available for a name, excluding the delimiters, is

254 – (number of labels in name)

In reality, you typically run out of groupings before encountering this limit.

> **Note**
>
> RFC 1035, titled "Domain names—implementation and specification," does not actually refer to a quantity called a *byte*, but instead to an *octet*, which is an equivalent eight-bit entity.

> **Note**
>
> It's troublesome for someone sending information to remember the address of a recipient that has lots of subdomains. One way around the problem of long names is for the host administrator to request that an *alias* be defined and registered for his host. An alias allows a user to replace the real name with a shorthand representation. The concept of an alias is discussed in more detail later in this chapter.

If you are sending a message to a user in your subdomain, you may find that specifying the entire name for that user is annoyingly tedious. But a machine powerful enough to be a part of the Internet is smart enough to assign a logical default to the parts of a name that aren't specified. If you don't specify a subdomain, the DNS assumes that you are referring to another user within your subdomain. So, in the earlier example, if Otto

wanted to send an e-mail message to his buddy Joe in the same
department, he would need to specify only

```
joe
```

as the recipient. Similarly, if Otto sent e-mail to Rick in marketing, he could use

```
rick@mkting
```

and `mycompany.com` would be assumed as the rest of the name.

The hierarchical structure of the DNS enables your host to make
such logical choices. To find a match for the name of the recipient of your message, your host works its way up the subdomain
hierarchy until it finds the one that the sender and recipient
share. It then moves down the hierarchy until it reaches the
recipient. Although this seems trivial when sender and recipient
names are located on one host, things quickly get more complicated when your local host has to begin traversing the Internet
looking for the recipient. (This process is explained in more
detail a little later in this chapter.)

User or Account Field

The left-most label defines the user or account, and is separated
from the remaining labels by an "at" symbol (@). The user label
generally is chosen to reflect the real identity of the owner. So if
Otto D. Smeadford has an account on a host, he would likely
have a name with a user label something like

```
osmeadford
ods
ottos
smeadfordod
```

Although it isn't mandatory, having your user label reflect your
real identity is a good idea, because it facilitates the use of tools
that another user can invoke to find your Internet name if he
knows something about you. One such tool, NETFIND, is discussed in Chapter 13, "Aids to Navigating the Internet."

Certain special functions also have user names. Many companies and organizations, for example, have a user name to which you can send mail to request that information be mailed back to you. If you wanted to get an overview of the Internet e-mail services provided by the Institute of Electrical and Electronics Engineers (IEEE) or the Association of Computing Machinery (ACM) to those organizations' memberships, you would e-mail your request to

```
info.email.services@ieee.org
```

or

```
Account-info@ACM.org
```

respectively. In these instances, the user label refers to an automated process, which extracts the sender's name from the header of your e-mail message and mails the requested information back to your name. The contents of such messages are irrelevant and can be left blank. All that is of value is your name, which is included automatically in the message header.

You may have noticed something a little unexpected in one of the above names—specifically, the account label in `info.email.services@ieee.org`. The reason this is a legitimate name is that in its processing, the DNS effectively makes no distinction between an "@" and a ".". The "@" is used as the delimiter after the account label to make it easier for us mere humans to remember names.

IP Address

As you can see, the DNS provides a logical means for developing names and grouping them in meaningful ways. Hidden from view by the DNS, though, is a more primitive means of identification called the Internet Protocol (IP) address. Users rarely access this address, which is the underlying identifier used by the protocols that govern Internet information exchange. Your host converts DNS names to IP addresses before starting the routing process that gets your message to your intended recipient (see table 3.2 for some example IP addresses). The intervening machines and network software also use IP addresses as your message is passed along.

Table 3.2 Example IP Addresses and Their DNS Names

IP Address	DNS Name
16.1.0.2	gatekeeper.dec.com
128.89.1.178	nnsc.nsf.net
128.252.135.4	wuarchive.wustl.edu
130.127.8.1	hubcap.clemson.edu
192.112.36.5	nic.ddn.mil

Note

Although addresses aren't case sensitive through the Internet, preserving the case of the name you communicate with is a good idea, for several reasons:

■ Many of your possible destinations for the information you send may not actually be on the Internet directly, but are accessed indirectly through other network services, such as CompuServe. Within these services, the specific software and protocols operating in that environment determine case sensitivity.

■ The RFCs that specify the naming conventions (1032-1035) require that case be maintained "just in case" a future implementation of the network software becomes case aware.

Similarities exist between an IP address for a host and a Social Security number for a human: a governing body assigns each to identify an entity uniquely, each is more machine-oriented than human-oriented, and each is rarely used as a means for reference during normal conversation. For IP addresses, the governing body is a member of the Internet Network Information Center (InterNIC) consortium; Network Solutions, Incorporated (NSI) of Herndon, Virginia, is the group within the consortium responsible for providing registration services. Technically, NSI assigns only a portion of the address (the network ID). The remaining portion (the host ID within that network) is assigned by those administering the network.

You don't often refer to your friends like "How's it going, 123-45-6789, dude?" do you? The creators of Internet realized that having to refer to hosts by their IP addresses would be just as cumbersome, and so the DNS developed as a much more suitable naming system for use by mere humans.

A host's IP address is a 32-bit value. Like a DNS name, the IP address also consists of fields, each separated by a period (.). For this reason, an IP address is sometimes referred to as a *dot address*. The number of octets in an IP address is fixed at four (8 bits per field), but the interpretation of the address varies based on the value of the first field. The address contains the host's network ID and host ID within the network. The value of the first field determines the length of each.

If the first octet has a value from 1 to 126, the IP address is class A format. In class A addresses, the network ID consists of the first octet, and the host ID uses the last three. This limits the number of nets to 126, but each net can have up to 16,777,214 hosts. Such addresses are limited to major service providers and participants.

Class B format addresses have a first octet range from 128 to 191 and use the first two octets for network IDs and the remaining two for host IDs. This gives 16,382 network ID values and 65,534 host IDs. Larger network organizations such as campus-wide systems for universities or larger businesses are assigned class B addresses.

Class C addresses have a first octet from 192 to 223, use the first three octets for the network ID, and use the last octet for the host ID. This class supports more than 2 million network IDs and only 254 host IDs for each net. This address class is typical for small networks or machines that aren't part of a local network.

Class D addresses have a first octet value of 224 to 239 and are used for *multicasting*, which is best described as broadcast by subscription. Multicasting allows a host to join or leave a multicast group dynamically. When a message is sent to a multicast address, all hosts in that group receive the message. This approach makes sending messages to groups of hosts easier and makes more efficient use of the available bandwidth.

Class E addresses, from 240 to 247, are reserved for future use.

Table 3.3 contains some real-world IP addresses for each class. In addition to the address classes, two special IP addresses are available. A message with its host ID set to all 1's indicates that the message is being broadcast to every host in the network. A host also may set the network ID to 0 if it wants to communicate on a network for which it doesn't know the actual net ID. In this instance, a net ID of 0 is interpreted to mean "this network I am on." The responses the host receives to these messages will include the actual network ID, so it can update this information and begin using it in its messages.

Table 3.3 Sample IP Addresses and Address Classes

IP Address	Net Owner	Address Class
12.0.0.0	AT&T	A
128.5.0.0	Ford	B
128.30.0.0	MIT	B
192.112.59.0	Kellogg	C

Aliases

In reality, the names of many hosts are quite long and have many subdomains. Again, the problem of having the name be tractable to humans rears its head. Fortunately, a shorthand way is available to refer to a name—*aliasing*. By defining an alias, your host administrator can "promote" a host that may be at a fifth-level subdomain to appear as though it were at the second level. In this way, the host name

```
myaccount@myhost.level4.level3.level2.com
```

can be referenced as

```
myaccount@myhostalias.com
```

which is a much easier name for your Internet partners to remember.

Although each host network connection can have only one IP address, by using aliases you can assign more than one name to the host address. One example of how you can use multiple names for a single host is to consider the situation where two companies are sharing the same network (perhaps one is a wholly owned subsidiary of the other). Both companies would like to appear as independent organizations. By using aliases, a user account such as

```
myaccount@smallfry.bigpotato.com
```

can be referenced as

```
myaccount@smallfry.com
```

and

```
myaccount@bigpotato.com
```

Note

An alias can't be the same as another DNS name. Thus, if a smallfry.com already exists, you will have to choose another alias.

Using an alias doesn't block any attempt to use your full DNS name. So in the preceding example, another member of your company who was aware of your full DNS name could use

```
myaccount@smallfry.bigpotato.com
```

without problems.

The Data Storage Structure

Now you can navigate through the naming structure of the Internet, but you also need to know how the data available on all those hosts is organized. You need a similar set of skills for navigating the data structures of the Internet.

File Structure

Fortunately, unlike the DNS, the data-storage organization on the Internet is more intuitive to most PC computer users. Although different operating systems implement the syntax of their file structures differently, almost all use some form of hierarchical tree-based structure of files and directories. An example file hierarchy is given in figure 3.6.

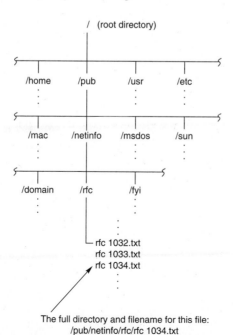

The full directory and filename for this file:
/pub/netinfo/rfc/rfc 1034.txt

Fig. 3.6

An example of a typical host file hierarchy. Each successive level of the hierarchy will add another field to the Location: field of an archie query for the files in that level.

You can use a tool called *archie* to locate files among the many ftp sites on the network. Chapter 13, "Aids to Navigating the Internet," provides the details about operating archie, but the following segment of output from an archie session shows some of the variation in syntax for directory and file names that you can find on the Internet. In this session, a search was performed for the file RFC1032.TXT, and two of the responses received were

```
Host maggie.telcom.arizona.edu    (128.196.128.233)
Last updated 06:26 16 Jul 1993
Location: /RFC.DIR;1/1000.DIR;1
FILE    -rwxrwx-w- 59 bytes 14:42  7 Apr 1988
RFC1032.TXT;1
```

and

```
Host nic.cerf.net    (192.102.249.3)
Last updated 05:56 17 Jul 1993
Location: /pub/infomagic_cd/doc/rfc
FILE    -r-xr-xr-x 28673 bytes 01:00 17 Feb 1992
rfc1032.txt
```

By examining the structure and syntax of the file specifications, an experienced user would assume that the first host, maggie.telcom.arizona.edu, most likely is running the VMS operating system, whereas nic.cerf.net is probably running UNIX. The syntax of the directory names given in the Location: field, as well as the file name syntax, give good clues. The overall impact from these differences is minor, though. You just as easily could ftp either file to your machine by specifying the file name in the proper form for the host of your choice.

One item that you may find a little confusing is *file links*. Some operating systems (such as UNIX) support the capability to add a file logically to a directory without actually having to copy the file's contents to the directory. Essentially, the linked file name acts as an alias, which points to the real file location. You can use a file link just as though it were any other file name, however, and the operating system will take care of getting or updating the information, wherever it really is.

Also, unlike PC operating systems, you don't have to be aware of which physical storage device you are accessing—that is, the files presented in a host's file hierarchy may reside on one hard disk or many, or perhaps other devices such as CD-ROMs. You don't have to be concerned with where the files are; the host's operating system worries about such things for you.

File Ownership and Access

One concept that PC users may not be familiar with is *file ownership*. Most PCs assume that they are being used primarily or exclusively by only one user. Their operating systems typically don't support identifying files as "owned" by a particular user, or limiting access to files based on who you are. This setup isn't so for larger machines—especially not for those connected to a network that allows access by users not associated in any way with the owning organization.

Most multiuser operating systems provide at least three levels of file access based on your relation to the file owner. If a file is assigned *read-only access*, you can view or copy the file. If you have *write* or *delete access*, you can erase, overwrite, or modify it. Finally, *execute access* allows you to run the file as an application.

Typically, the access level is specified for the types of user: the file owner, users belonging to the same previously defined group as the owner, and all other users. The example pictured in figure 3.7 shows how to interpret the access information provided from a directory listing. As the figure shows, access level is indicated as follows:

Level	Description
r	Read access
w	Write/delete access
x	Execute access

(continues)

Level	Description
d	Directory (in the directory flag)
–	Means no access available for that access type; in the directory flag, represents a file

Fig. 3.7
The access level
indicated in a
directory listing.

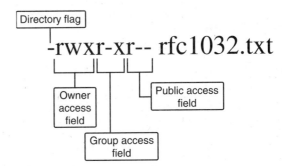

An Overview of DNS Operation

As mentioned in the introduction to this chapter, the process
that a host must go through to transfer information from a
sender to a recipient can be quite complex. Although you don't
have to have an understanding of DNS operation, such an understanding does help you appreciate what a host does for you
in locating the destination for your information. It's especially
informative to be familiar with the concepts of name servers,
name caches, resolvers, master files, and zones. These are the
entities that point your message in the right direction and help
get it there. A simple schematic diagram of DNS operation is
given in figure 3.8. Besides, certainly you're a little bit curious,
aren't you? Just a little?

Name Server

In the earliest implementations of the Internet, each host had a
file that contained all the information necessary to locate any
other host on the Internet. This approach made finding another

host and exchanging information simple for one host. Soon, however, the expanse and rate of change of the Internet meant that having such a complete picture of the Internet was impossible for every host. Before the current explosion of growth, such lists would become obsolete very quickly, and the network traffic required to keep these lists up-to-date was becoming overwhelming.

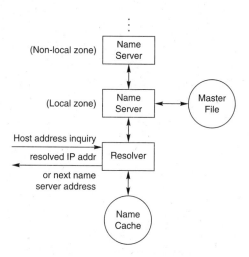

Fig. 3.8
A schematic of DNS operation. Your host's resolver makes use of name servers and name caches to obtain the IP address for your recipient.

To solve this problem, a more centralized approach was developed and implemented. In this approach, certain hosts are designated as *name* (or *domain*) *servers*. Name servers provide a means for getting the routing information and IP addresses for your destinations. Other hosts then need to know only the addresses of a name server or two to get the latest address information on a demand basis. Hosts that are listed with a name server are called *registered hosts* (the distinction between registered and unregistered hosts will be explained a little later in this section). Any registered host must have its name placed on at least two name servers, so in case of host or network failure, an alternate means for getting the host routing information is available.

Resolver

The *resolver* is the software that operates on a host trying to determine where the specified address is. When you specify a destination for the data you are sending, the resolver queries the name servers it knows of to find the IP address of the recipient's host. Now your host knows who to send the data to, but in a network topology as diverse as that of the Internet, you could take literally thousands of routes to get the data there. The problem is analogous to planning a trip from New York to Los Angeles: knowing the ZIP code of your destination doesn't tell you anything about which highways to take. Fortunately, the name server also provides the resolver with the routing information it needs to point the data in the right direction.

To speed things up, the resolver keeps around a *name cache*. A name cache is a high-tech way of referring to a file that keeps the addresses that were resolved in the recent past. You can safely assume, based on statistical studies of network traffic, that if you send data to someone once, you likely will do so again soon. The name cache takes advantage of this assumption by avoiding the overhead of the name server query for recently resolved names.

Master Files

On every name server exists a database of all the registered hosts. This database, called the *master file*, is updated three times a week (Monday, Wednesday, and Friday) from the InterNIC and distributed to the name servers through the Internet itself. The name server uses the master file to look up zone, IP, and routing information to return to the inquiring host.

Zones

If only registered hosts participated in the network, the operation of the DNS would require only that a host's resolver find and query its name server. Not all hosts are registered, however.

In fact, most aren't, and it's a good thing, too. You can imagine the headaches that would result from having to require that every host using the Internet be registered. Every time a computer within a company's network was added, removed, or transferred to a different network location, for example, the company would have to update its registration status.

To avoid this problem, the authority and responsibility for the domain name space is subdivided into zones, each with a registered host responsible for that portion of the name space. Within that portion of the name space, subdomains can be added or removed. For example, a registered host named `myzone.myprovider.com` would be responsible for the allocation and maintenance of the hosts and subdomains below it, such as `myhost.mysubdomain.myzone.myprovider.com`. One difference between a zone and a subdomain is that while unregistered hosts can also have subdomains, only the name space under a registered host can be designated a zone. As is true for subdomains, zones can exist within other zones.

Each name server is aware of other name servers responsible for the various zones, and if it receives a request for IP and routing information within a zone, it can contact that name server for information or direct its inquiring host to contact the appropriate zone name server. The former method is referred to as *recursive resolving*, because one name server may call another, which in turn may call another, and so on, until the name is resolved. The latter method is called *nonrecursive resolving*, because the inquiring host has to restart the resolving process with each new name server it's directed to.

Host Registration

As a user, you normally don't have to concern yourself with registering host names or aliases; your provider has taken care of that. If you are in the position of investigating what you need to do to register for your company or other organization, the following is provided to let you know what is involved.

You can obtain a domain questionnaire by using ftp to get the file `/templates/domain-template.txt` from host `ftp.rs.internic.net`. Fill out the questionnaire completely and return it through electronic mail to

    HOSTMASTER@rs.internic.net

If your application is in order, getting registered should take about two weeks. You can check the status of your registration by telneting to `rs.internic.net` and following the instructions given in the login header.

A registered host is not likely to be required by most purchasers of this book, so you should make certain that it is really necessary for the level of service you or your organization needs. When you are certain that you need to register a host, the best place to start the process is with your service provider. Service providers often can take care of registration for you and provide you with technical assistance on getting your network connection set up. You also will want to check out several of the texts listed in Appendix E. These texts have the more detailed information you need if you are going to be a budding network administrator.

Finding and Verifying a Registered Host

If you need to locate a host or verify its registration, you can use an on-line utility called *WHOIS* to accomplish this task. *WHOIS* gives network address data and contact information such as administrator names, phone numbers, and postal addresses. If your Internet service provider has given you access to *WHOIS*, you can use the command

    whois domain <domain name><return>

Alternatively, you can telnet to `rs.internic.net` and log in as `whois`. At the `Whois:` prompt, type the name you want information on.

The reply from *WHOIS* will supply the following information:

- The name and address of the organization "owning" the domain

- The name of the domain

- The domain's administrative, technical, and zone contacts

- The host names and network addresses of sites providing name service for the domain

You can use *WHOIS* to get contact information for your host or others on-line, rather than have to find a business card, note, or wait for an e-mail reply from someone.

The following are some sample *WHOIS* sessions:

```
Whois: unc.edu
University of North Carolina at Chapel Hill (UNC-DOM)
   Chapel Hill, NC 27514

Domain Name: UNC.EDU

Administrative Contact:
   Gogan, James P.   (JG452)   gogan@HERMES.OIT.UNC.EDU
   (919) 962-1621 (919) 962-0658 (FAX) (919) 962-5604
Technical Contact, Zone Contact:
   Averett, Shava Nerad   (SNA) shava@HERMES.OIT.UNC.EDU
   (919) 962-1603 (919) 962-0658 (FAX) (919) 962-5604

Record last updated on 27-May-93.

Domain servers in listed order:

NS.UNC.EDU                152.2.21.1
NS.BME.UNC.EDU            152.2.100.1
NCNOC.CONCERT.NET         192.101.21.1,128.109.193.1
```

```
Whois: nasa.gov
NASA Ames Research Center (NASA-DOM)
   Mail Stop 240-9
   Moffett Field, CA 94035

   Domain Name: NASA.GOV

   Administrative Contact, Technical Contact, Zone Contact:
      Medin, Milo  (MSM1)  MEDIN@NSIPO.NASA.GOV
      (415) 604-6440 (FTS) 464-6440

   Record last updated on 22-Feb-93.

   Domain servers in listed order:

   NS.NASA.GOV                 128.102.16.10, 192.52.195.10
   DFTSRV.GSFC.NASA.GOV        128.183.10.134
   JPL-MIL.JPL.NASA.GOV        128.149.1.101
   MX.NSI.NASA.GOV             128.102.18.31

Whois: internic.net
Network Solutions, Inc. (INTERNIC-DOM)
   505 Huntmar Park Drive
   Herndon, VA 22070

   Domain Name: INTERNIC.NET

   Administrative Contact:
      Zalubski, John  (JZ7)  johnz@INTERNIC.NET
      (703) 742-4757
   Technical Contact, Zone Contact:
      Kosters, Mark A.  (MAK21)  markk@INTERNIC.NET
      (703) 742-4795

   Record last updated on 23-Mar-93.

   Domain servers in listed order:

   RS.INTERNIC.NET             198.41.0.5
   IS.INTERNIC.NET             192.153.156.15
   NOC.CERF.NET                192.153.156.22

Whois: ibm.com
International Business Machines (IBM-DOM)

   Domain Name: IBM.COM

   Administrative Contact, Technical Contact, Zone Contact:
      Trio, Nicholas R.  (NRT1)  nrt@watson.ibm.com
      (914) 945-1850
```

```
Record last updated on 12-Dec-91.

Domain servers in listed order:

WATSON.IBM.COM              129.34.139.4
NS.AUSTIN.IBM.COM           192.35.232.34
```

```
Whois: acm.org
Association for Computing Machinery (ACM-DOM)
    1515 Broadway
    New York, NY  10036

Domain Name: ACM.ORG

Administrative Contact:
    Deblasi, Joe   (JD3017)  DEBLASI@ACM.ORG
    (212) 869-7440
Technical Contact, Zone Contact:
    Lemley, Bob  (BL162)  LEMLEY@ACM.ORG
    (817) 776-5695

Record last updated on 04-Jun-93.

Domain servers in listed order:

PASCAL.ACM.ORG              192.135.174.1
SESQUI.NET                 128.241.0.84
```

On-Line Domain Information

Several text files are available on-line that provide information
on Internet domains. The following on-line files, all available
by ftp from `ftp.rs.internic.net`, contain pertinent domain
information.

File	Description
/NETINFO/DOMAINS.TXT	A table of all top-level domains and the network addresses of the machines providing domain name service for them. This table is updated each time a new top-level domain is approved.

(continues)

File	Description
`/NETINFO/DOMAIN-INFO.TXT`	A concise list of all top-level and second-level domain names registered with the NIC. This list is updated monthly.
`/NETINFO/DOMAIN-CONTACTS.TXT`	A list of all the top-level and second-level domains, but also includes the administrative, technical, and zone contacts for each. This list is updated monthly.
`/TEMPLATES/DOMAIN-TEMPLATE.TXT`	The questionnaire to be completed before registering a top-level or second-level domain.

The Flow of Information from Host to Host

So far the process of moving information within a host or from one host to another has been taken for granted. You usually don't have to be concerned with the way in which data is moved through the Internet, but being familiar with the basic terminology and subsystems that are used helps.

Jumping across Network Boundaries

Because the Internet is a collection of smaller networks, any information that you send or receive probably has to cross several networks to get to its destination (see fig. 3.9). Some network boundaries result from physical limitations such as the length of cabling over which an electronic signal can reliably be driven and received.

A problem with reliability arises when you connect greater numbers of hosts together within a single network. In many instances, a single failure of the network disrupts all communications for the entire net. A *bridge* is a device that isolates one physical section of the Internet from another, so that a failure at one place disrupts communications for only that portion of the Internet on the same side of the bridge as the failure. Bridges usually require that both segments of the network use the same physical-level connection, such as EtherNet or token ring.

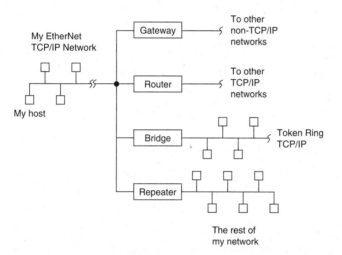

Fig. 3.9
As information traverses a network, it may encounter a variety of different hardware devices including repeaters, bridges, routers, and gateways.

If information is moving between two networks using the same protocol suite, such as TCP/IP, then a *router* acts as the means for tying them together. A router has knowledge of the protocol suite and addresses associated with both networks, and monitors each for messages that are bound for the other. The router receives and forwards these messages between the networks. A router also may be able to connect networks with different physical-level interconnection schemes.

If two networks have dissimilar protocols, then an interpreter called a *gateway* is required. Just like a human language interpreter, a gateway knows the protocol suites used by both networks it's serving to connect. A message bound for the other network is converted from its native protocol to that of the destination network. Typically, a gateway also performs the functions of a router.

Tip
You can use *repeaters* to extend the maximum effective extent of a network. You can think of a repeater as a simple amplifier that boosts the power of weak signals before sending them farther down the network.

Layers of Software

In this multilayer model of the software that implements TCP/IP (often called a TCP/IP stack, since one layer "stacks" on another), an example of an application would be ftp, telnet, archie, whois, or any of the other tools and utilities you use to exploit the capabilities of the Internet. An application may also be any other program that makes use of TCP/IP to transfer data, such as a local area network (LAN) software package.

Applications interact with the next lower layer, TCP, through a series of special commands called *service primitives* that the TCP layer makes available to the application. A few of these primitives are listed in table 3.4. As you can see, TCP provides a high-level means for the applications to communicate with each other. For example, a connection with another host is established via the OPEN primitive. A major goal of TCP is to obscure the details of the connection from the application so that the application doesn't have to account for network-specific items such as transfer rates and data formatting.

Table 3.4 Typical TCP Primitives

Service Primitive	Summary Description
OPEN	Establishes connection to remote host
SEND	Sends data to remote host
DELIVER	Makes data available from remote host
CLOSE	Shuts down connection
STATUS	Provides status of connection

The IP layer in turn converts the service primitives of TCP into the low-level functions provided by the subnetwork layer, and vice versa. The IP may segment the data from a TCP SEND primitive into a series of smaller messages. Lastly, the subnetwork layer is responsible for converting IP messages into a format suitable for the particular hardware and physical-level protocols being used to connect to the network. If your host is connected to a local network that uses a token-ring access control scheme, for example, the subnetwork interface will try to acquire a token so that it can send information. If, on the other hand, the connection is a dialup serial link, the subnetwork layer is responsible for tasks such as modem control (see fig. 3.10).

The goal of the TCP/IP stack approach is to limit and localize the changes that need to be made to accommodate different network configurations.

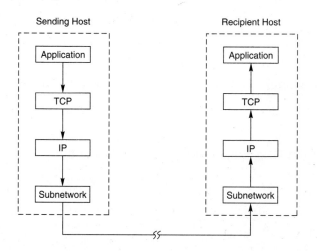

Fig. 3.10
Sample data flow between hosts through the TCP/IP stack. Information provided to an application such as ftp is processed through each layer of the stack until it's ultimately converted to a bitstream, which is transmitted to the recipient and reassembled.

Sharing the Interconnection Space

As many connections as are available throughout the Internet, efficient use of the available capacity (or *bandwidth*) of these connections is still a major issue. Even if you aren't paying the connection charges, you can rest assured that someone somewhere is. Try to keep these costs in mind when transferring information between hosts. Just because you can get a copy of an RFC from a host in Australia doesn't mean you should use it as your primary ftp site for RFCs if you live two blocks from a major university that can provide them.

Although it's an important Internet resource, usage of bandwidth still is not tightly regulated. Basically, if you don't make a true nuisance of yourself, no one will chase you down for an honest mistake or for an intercontinental transfer of a large quantity of data if done for a valid reason. Being wasteful is considered poor network etiquette, however, and you may receive a warning or even have your access terminated if you are a flagrant bandwidth hog. The goal of everyone using the Internet should be to use it efficiently.

The Host Administrator

Although most of your interaction with the Internet is electronic, a human element exists as well: your *host* (or system or network) *administrator* (HA). The HA is responsible for ensuring the reliable operation of your host within the proper usage guidelines established by the host owner and his service providers.

In your day-to-day use of the Internet, you shouldn't need any assistance from the HA. Please don't bother the HA with frivolous questions or as a way to get out of tracking down information on the Internet. One of the more embarrassing but frequent calls to an HA come from users who have forgotten their passwords.

You can expect to require some assistance from your HA a few times, however, as explained in the following sections.

Establishing or Reconfiguring Accounts
When the HA sets up your account, he/she assigns you to a host and a subdomain. Sometimes moving accounts from one host

to another is necessary to help balance the computational and storage loads.

Controlling Service Access

Due to the incredible amount of information available and traffic through the Internet, the HA likely will place some limits on your access, such as limits on connect time, the number of connections, total file space available, or lockouts on features such as USENET. If you need additional space or access to a currently unavailable resource, ask your HA if your account access can be adjusted.

Handling Trouble

You need to contact the HA if any of the following occur:

- Access problems

- Possible security breaches

- Violations of the proper use limitations (for example, profane messages)

- Bugs or other problematic behavior of network software

- You suspect you have encountered a malevolent program (such as a virus) that poses a threat to his system or the network at large

Just be very sure that you have really found a problem in operation and not just committed "pilot error." Before contacting the HA, check to see whether other users on your host are experiencing the same problems. See whether others on the same network but different hosts are affected. The more information on the scope of the problem you can provide, the more quickly the HA will be able to track down and fix the problem.

Summary

Uncounted man-hours of some of the brightest minds in computer science and engineering have been put to the task of designing the structure and operation of the Internet. This chapter has touched only the surface of their remarkable results, but gives you the practical knowledge you need to make sense of what often seems to the newcomer a bewildering maze of computers, networks, and files. In the next chapter, you will be taken on a guided tour of some of the useful resources that are available on the Internet as means of getting some hands-on experience exploring the structure of the Internet.

Chapter 4

Finding and Using Internet Resources

The Internet is certainly a valuable resource for obtaining information about virtually any field of inquiry. This chapter is dedicated to showing you how to find out more information about the Internet itself. The organizations that establish network policies are identified, and ways to obtain important documents pertaining to network operations are discussed. You easily can retrieve much of this documentation on-line through ftp (see Chapter 8, "Using ftp and telnet," for an example). Even if you don't have access to ftp, you still can obtain much useful information by using e-mail.

Many sites on the network allow—some even encourage—network users to access their files, databases, or specialized software packages. This chapter identifies several of the major network nodes that maintain substantial amounts of information of value to network users. Two computer programs that provide tutorials in basic Internet concepts and operations are discussed as well.

Although a diskette accompanies this book, the authors had to be extremely selective in choosing the material it contains (its contents are described in Appendix A). Much highly useful information and software couldn't be included because of storage limitations.

CD-ROMs designed specifically for the Internet user community also are available. These CD-ROMs contain an enormous amount of information that would be time-consuming for you to locate or tedious to download from the network yourself. As such, the CD-ROMs could be very cost-effective purchases if you want more detailed information about the Internet than is within the scope of this book.

Keep in mind that the Internet is very dynamic, and that descriptions of the major Internet sites, tutorial software, and CD-ROM offerings are subject to change over time. When using ftp to access files described in the text, always look for readme and index files to learn of new developments. Exploring directories containing files in which you are interested also is a good idea, because they may have something else of interest to you.

> **Note**
>
> Portions of the text of this chapter were taken directly from public-domain information available through anonymous ftp. The sources for these passages are attributed.

Organizations that Set Internet Standards and Policies

No one owns the Internet or receives a portion of the fee your Internet service provider charges you. Rather, the Internet is a loose affiliation of smaller networks that have agreed to use common standards for communicating with each other. The communications protocols are standardized, but not their implementations. As long as the technical standards are met and acceptable use policies are observed, a local system can connect with the network and communicate with other systems.

An organization was established, however, for overseeing the creation, distribution, and updating of standards regarding the

Internet. The Internet Society (ISOC) was formed in January 1992 as the umbrella organization given authority for all aspects of network administration. It is given "authority" by virtue of its members and other supporters; those members and supporters happen to include virtually the entire Internet user community in the United States.

ISOC also enjoys considerable support from European and other users outside the United States. Several major administrative bodies are part of ISOC, including the Internet Architecture Board (IAB), the Internet Engineering Task Force (IETF), and the Internet Research Task Force (IRTF).

The Internet Architecture Board (IAB) is concerned with overseeing development and evolution of network protocols. It has the authority to issue standards and allocate resources such as network addresses. The Internet Engineering Task Force (IETF) is charged with developing the specifications that eventually will become standards, if approved by the IAB. It conducts regular meetings to discuss technical and operational problems that have been encountered or that likely will be experienced in the near future. The Internet Research Task Force (IRTF) considers longer-term issues than does the IETF. The IRTF focuses more on information science and networking technology than on establishing policies and standards.

The Internet Society (ISOC)

With the explosive growth in new systems connecting to the Internet, an international administrative body that determines and publishes technical, procedural, and operational standards and policies is essential. The Internet Society fills this role and is responsible for guiding the future development of the network as well. Its charter is as follows:

The Society is a non-profit organization operated for academic, educational, charitable and scientific purposes, such as the following:

■ *To facilitate and support the technical evolution of the Internet as a research and education infrastructure and to stimulate involvement of the academic, scientific, and engineering communities, among others in the evolution of the Internet.*

■ *To educate the academic and scientific communities and the public concerning the technology, use, and application of the Internet.*

■ *To promote scientific and educational applications of Internet technology for the benefit of educational institutions at all grade levels, industry, and the public at large.*

■ *To provide a forum for exploration of new Internet applications and to foster collaboration among organizations in their operation and use of the Internet.*

Individuals and organizations can join the Internet Society, although only individuals can vote.

ISOC publishes the *Internet Society News*, a quarterly newsletter, and conducts an annual conference (called INET) open to all members and other parties interested in various aspects of the Internet. It also sponsors workshops and symposiums from time to time on topics of current interest to the Internet community.

Additional information about the Internet Society is available on-line through anonymous ftp to `nri.reston.va.us`. In directory `/isoc` you will find membership and other general information about ISOC as well as conference announcements. Under this directory are subdirectories containing the text of recent issues of the newsletter. For more information, you can contact the Internet Society as follows:

Internet Society
1895 Preston White Drive, Suite 100
Reston, VA 22091
Voice: (703) 648-9888
Fax: (703) 620-0913
E-mail: `isoc@isoc.org`

Internet Architecture Board (IAB)

The Internet Architecture Board (IAB) has authority to issue and update technical standards regarding Internet protocols. It doesn't have a role in day-to-day network operations. Originally founded in 1983 as the Internet Activities Board, its intent is to guide the evolution of the TCP/IP protocol suite and to provide research advice to the Internet community; it was placed under the Internet Society in June 1992. Its charter reads as follows:

The Internet Architecture Board (IAB) shall be constituted and shall operate as a technical advisory group of the Internet Society. Its responsibilities shall include:

- *Expert and experienced oversight of the architecture of the worldwide multiprotocol Internet.*

- *The editorial management and publication of the Request For Comments (RFC) document series, which constitutes the archival publication series for Internet Standards and related contributions by the Internet research and engineering community.*

- *The development, review, and approval of Internet Standards, according to a well-defined and documented set of "Procedures for Internet Standardization." Internet Standards shall be published in the form of specifications as part of the RFC series.*

- *The provision of advice and guidance to the Board of Trustees and Officers of the Internet Society concerning technical, architectural, procedural, and (where appropriate) policy matters pertaining to the Internet and its enabling technologies.*

- *Representation of the interests of the Internet Society in liaison relationships with other organizations.*

The IAB holds meetings in person on a quarterly basis. Additional meetings may be conducted at intervening times by telephone, e-mail, and computer-mediated conferences. The minutes of meetings of the Internet Architecture Board are available on-line through anonymous ftp. Connect with host venera.isi.edu and look under /pub/IAB for text files containing the minutes of the most recent meetings.

Internet Engineering Task Force (IETF)

The information in this section was taken directly from material provided by the Internet Engineering Task Force (IETF):

The Internet Engineering Task Force (IETF) is the protocol engineering, development, and standardization arm of the IAB. The IETF began in January 1986 as a forum for technical coordination by contractors for the then U.S. Defense Advanced Research Projects Agency (DARPA) working on the ARPANET, U.S. Defense Data Network (DDN), and the Internet core gateway system. Since then, the IETF has grown into a large open international community of network designers, operators, vendors, and researchers concerned with the evolution of the Internet protocol architecture and the smooth operation of the Internet.

The IETF mission includes:

- *Identifying and proposing solutions to pressing operational and technical problems in the Internet;*

- *Specifying the development (or usage) of protocols and the near-term architecture to solve such technical problems for the Internet;*

- *Facilitating technology transfer from the Internet Research Task Force (IRTF) to the wider Internet community, and*

- *Providing a forum for the exchange of relevant information within the Internet community among vendors, users, researchers, agency contractors, and network managers.*

Technical activity on any specific topic in the IETF is addressed within working groups. All working groups are organized roughly by function into 10 technical areas. Each is led by one or more area director, who has primary responsibility for that one area of IETF activity. Together with the Chair of the IETF, these technical directors (plus the Director for Standards Procedures) compose the Internet Engineering Steering Group (IESG).

The IETF holds week-long meetings three times a year. These meetings are composed of working group sessions, technical presentations, network status reports, working group reporting, and an open IESG meeting. A Proceedings of each IETF meeting is published, which includes reports from each area, each working group, and each technical presentation. The Proceedings include a summary of all current standardization activities.

Meeting reports, charters (which include the working group mailing lists), and general information on current IETF activities are available on-line by way of anonymous ftp from several Internet hosts. Connect to `ds.internic.net` or `nri.reston.va.us` and look in the `/ietf` directory for information regarding the IETF and in directory `/iesg` for minutes of Internet Engineering Steering Group meetings.

On-Line Internet Documentation

As is appropriate for a worldwide electronic communications system, Internet Standards, reports, and other documents are available on-line. They are stored on many of the major network nodes that allow anonymous ftp access, although some sites may carry only a partial set of documents. To make those documents easily accessible to the widest possible audience, they are all stored as ASCII files. PostScript versions of some documents are available as well.

The Request For Comments (RFC) series of documents contains all approved Internet Standards, as well as many other documents designed to explain various aspects of the Internet. As of this writing, nearly 2,000 RFCs have been issued. Although most of the RFCs are technical in nature, some contain more general information, such as suggestions for selecting computer names (RFC 1178), answers to common questions (RFC 1206 and RFC 1207), and Internet growth statistics (RFC 1296). Although anyone can submit a document for consideration as a future RFC, the Internet Architecture Board (IAB) is responsible for approving all RFCs before they are issued.

The For Your Information (FYI) and Standards (STD) series of documents are subsets of the RFC series. The FYI series is concerned with issues at a more general level than most RFCs. FYI documents are good places to look for short, to-the-point answers to common, high-level questions about using the Internet.

The STD series, however, is devoted to descriptions of key technical issues. The purpose of this subseries of the RFC documents is to clearly identify those RFCs that describe approved network standards. An RFC can be included in the STD series only if it has completed the full process of approval for Standards required by the IAB.

The descriptions of the RFC, FYI, STD, Internet Monthly Report, and Internet Drafts are taken from FYI 4, "Answers to Commonly asked 'New Internet User' Questions."

RFC: Request For Comments Series

The *Request For Comments documents (RFCs)* are working notes of the Internet research and development community. A document in this series may be on essentially any topic related to computer communication, and may be anything from a meeting report to the specification of a standard. You can submit Requests For Comments to the RFC Editor (`rfc-editor@isi.edu`).

Most RFCs describe network protocols or services, often giving detailed procedures and formats for their implementation. Other RFCs report on the results of policy studies or summarize the work of technical committees or workshops. All RFCs are considered public domain unless explicitly marked otherwise.

Although RFCs aren't refereed publications, they do receive technical review from the task forces, individual technical experts, or the RFC Editor, as appropriate. Now, most Standards are published as RFCs, but not all RFCs specify standards.

Anyone can submit a document for publication as an RFC by way of e-mail to the RFC Editor. You can consult RFC 1111, "Instructions to RFC Authors," for further information. RFCs are accessible on-line through anonymous ftp at a number of sites, including `nic.ddn.mil` (directory `/rfc`), `ftp.nisc.sri.com` (directory `/rfc`), and `nis.nsf.net` (directory `internet/documents/rfc`).

For a more complete list of RFC repositories, get the file `/in-notes/rfc-retrieval.txt` from host `isi.edu` (you can access this system through anonymous ftp). An index to the RFCs, arranged in descending order of RFC number, also will be in these directories. Two other indexes are available on some hosts: one arranged in alphabetical order by author, and one arranged in alphabetical order by title of the RFC.

After a document is assigned an RFC number and published, that RFC is never revised or reissued with the same number. Having the most recent version of a particular RFC is never in question. A protocol such as the File Transfer Protocol (ftp), however, may be improved and redocumented many times in several different RFCs. Verifying that you have the most recent RFC on a particular protocol is important. The "IAB Official Protocol Standards" memo (now RFC 1500) is the reference for determining the correct RFC corresponding to the current specification of each protocol.

FYI: For Your Information Series

For Your Information documents (FYIs) are a subset of the RFC series of on-line documents. FYI 1 states,

> The FYI series of notes is designed to provide Internet users with a central repository of information about any topics which relate to the Internet. FYI topics may range from historical memos to operational questions and are intended for a wide audience. Some FYIs will cater to beginners; others, meanwhile, will discuss more advanced topics.

In general, FYI documents tend to be oriented more toward general information, whereas RFCs are usually—but not always—more technically oriented.

FYI documents are assigned an FYI number and an RFC number. RFC 1325 ("Answers to Commonly asked 'New Internet User' Questions"), for example, also is denoted FYI 4; RFC 1207 ("Answers to Commonly asked 'Experienced Internet User' Questions") is the same document as FYI 7.

As with RFCs, if an FYI is ever updated, it is issued again with a new RFC number; however, its FYI number remains unchanged. This can be a little confusing at first, but the aim is to help users identify which FYI corresponds to a specific topic. For example, the document that today is designated FYI 4 will always be FYI 4, even though it may be updated several times and receive different RFC numbers during that process. At this writing, FYI 4 is RFC 1325; previously, it corresponded to RFC 1206, and before that, it was RFC 1177. Thus, you need to remember only the FYI number to find the proper document.

You can obtain FYIs in the same way as RFCs and from the same repositories. In general, look for an `fyi` directory at the same directory path level as the `rfc` directory. Also look for an index file in the `fyi` directory, which contains a complete listing of all FYI documents that have been issued to date.

STD: Standards Series

The newest subseries of RFCs are the *STDs (Standards)*. RFC 1311, which introduces this subseries, states that the intent of the STDs is to identify clearly RFCs that document Internet standards. An STD number will be assigned only to specifications that have completed the full process of standardization in the Internet.

Existing Internet Standards have been assigned STD numbers, which you can find in RFC 1311 and in the IAB Official Protocol Standards RFC (which is now RFC 1500). Like FYIs, after a

Standard is assigned an STD number, that number won't change, even if the Standard is reworked, respecified, and later reissued with a new RFC number.

> **Note**
>
> Differentiating between a Standard and a document is important. Different RFC documents always have different RFC numbers; however, sometimes the complete specification for a Standard is contained in more than one RFC document. When this happens, each RFC document that is part of the specification for that Standard will carry the same STD number. The Domain Name System (DNS), for example, is specified by the combination of RFC 1034 and RFC 1035—therefore, both RFCs are labeled STD 13. Thus, you sometimes need to obtain several RFCs to have the complete Standard denoted by a single STD number.

Some hosts establish special directories that contain the STDs. Directory `internet/documents/std` on host `nis.nsf.net`, for example, contains the files `std13-rfc1034.txt` and `std13-rfc1035.txt`, which are the same as `rfc1034.txt` and `rfc1035.txt`, respectively. Thus, if you performed the ftp command `mget std13-*`, you would retrieve all the documents that comprise STD 13.

On the other hand, some hosts keep an index file for the STDs in the same directory that stores the RFCs. The file `std-index.txt` in the directory `/rfc` on host `ftp.nisc.sri.com`, for example, has a complete list of all STDs issued to date. The list of RFCs that comprise each STD is given in this file, and you must retrieve the specific RFC documents you need by using the RFC numbers.

IMR: Internet Monthly Reports

The *Internet Monthly Report (IMR)* communicates on-line to the Internet Research Group the accomplishments, milestones reached, or problems discovered by the participating organizations. Many organizations involved in the Internet provide monthly updates of their activities for inclusion in this report. The Internet Monthly Report is only for Internet information purposes.

You can receive the report on-line by joining the mailing list that distributes the report. To be added or deleted from the Internet Monthly Report list, send a request to `cooper@isi.edu`. Back issues of the report also are available via anonymous ftp from the `/internet/newsletters/internet.monthly.report` directory of the host `nis.nsf.net`. The file names are in the form `imryy-mm.txt`, where *yy* is the last two digits of the year and *mm* is the two digits for the month. The September 1993 report, for example, is in the file `imr93-09.txt`.

I-D: Internet Drafts

Internet Drafts (I-Ds) are the current working documents of the IETF. Internet Drafts are in a format very similar to that used for RFCs, with some key differences:

- Internet Drafts aren't RFCs or a numbered document series.

- The words `INTERNET-DRAFT` appear in place of `RFC` *xxxx* in the upper left corner.

- The document doesn't refer to itself as an RFC or as a draft RFC.

- An Internet Draft doesn't state or imply that it's a proposed standard. To do so conflicts with the role of the IAB, the RFC Editor, and the Internet Engineering Steering Group (IESG).

An Internet Drafts directory has been installed to make draft documents available for review and comment by the IETF members. These documents ultimately will be submitted to the IAB and the RFC Editor to be considered for publishing as RFCs. Several machines contain the Internet Drafts directories, as follows:

- NSFNET Network Service Center (NNSC): `nnsc.nsf.net`

- U.S. Defense Data Network Network Information Center (DDN NIC): `nic.ddn.mil`

- SRI, International Network Information Systems Center (SRI NISC): `ftp.nisc.sri.com`

To access on-line Internet Drafts, access one of these sites using anonymous ftp and go to directory `/internet-drafts`.

Major Internet Nodes You Can Access

Nearly 2,000 sites on the Internet allow their systems to be accessed through anonymous ftp. This section describes several of the more notable hosts that make available documents and software pertinent in using the Internet. Anyone can access these sites through anonymous ftp and retrieve, for example, the latest RFCs or an application form to join the Internet Society.

These sites are great places to begin experimenting with the Internet and, in particular, to learn about ftp. If you can use ftp, you can connect with one of these hosts, explore those directories open to the general public, and try retrieving some files. You will find no shortage of interesting files—in fact, you likely will be overwhelmed by the amount of information available at just these sites.

Note

Keep in mind the volatility of the network. The nature of the information these sites store is subject to change over time. Some of the file and directory names may change. You may even find that some day, one of these hosts no longer accepts anonymous ftp users, or that a host with one of these domain names is no longer attached to the Internet.

Introducing the Internet

Defense Data Network Network Information Center (DDN NIC)

Host Name: `nic.ddn.mil`

You can find the RFC and STD series of documents on this host under directories `/rfc` and `/std`, respectively. The directory `/protocols` also has the specifications of communications protocols authorized by the Department of Defense. Look in `/templates` for commonly used forms that you can fill out and send by e-mail to register, for example, a user in the WHOIS database or a domain in the Domain Name System (DNS).

SRI, International Network Information Systems Center (SRI NISC)

Host Name: `ftp.nisc.sri.com`

In addition to maintaining a repository for all RFCs (directory `/rfc`) and FYIs (`/fyi`), this host also holds a number of other files containing general network information. Look in directories `/netinfo` and `/introducing.the.internet` for documents designed to help the novice Internet user become familiar with network resources and protocols. This site also maintains up-to-date reports and other information from the IETF (in `/ietf`) and IESG (`/iesg`). Internet Drafts are available in the directory `/internet-drafts`.

Merit Network, Inc. Network Information Center (Merit NIC)

Host Name: `nic.merit.edu`

Merit's Network Information Center host computer contains a wide array of information about the Internet, NSFNET, and MichNet. Directory `/introducing.the.internet` holds a number of documents oriented toward new Internet users.

Much information about the Internet is available in the sub-directories of `/internet`. Look in `/internet/documents`, for example, for RFC, STD, FYI, IETF, IESG, and Internet draft files. Also, Merit's A Cruise of the Internet (described later in this chapter) is available through this host, under `/internet/resources`.

SURAnet Network Information Center (SURAnet NIC)
Host Name: `ftp.sura.net`

SURAnet maintains its Network Information Center on this host under directory `/pub/nic`. Many documents available in this ftp archive are geared toward the new user of the Internet.

SURAnet has provided several how-to guides for network navigation tools such as telnet, ftp, and e-mail. These how-to guides are available in the directory `/network.service.guides`. The chapters of Richard Smith's e-mail-based introductory class are available in the `/training` directory. Also of interest is the SURAnet "Guide to Selected Internet Resources," which documents new and unique Internet resources. This document is in the file `infoguide.`mm-yy`.txt`, where yy is the last two digits of the year and mm is the two digits for the month of the most current dated version.

InterNIC Directory and Database Services
Host Name: `ds.internic.net`

This is a key site when it comes to storing documents generated by the major Internet administrative bodies. The RFC (directory `/rfc`), FYI (`/fyi`), and STD (`/std`) documents are available, as well as Internet Society (`/isoc`), IETF (`/ietf`), and IESG (`/iesg`) reports. Look in directory `/resource-guide` for ASCII text and PostScript versions of the Internet Resource Guide, a valuable compilation of facilities such as supercomputers, databases, libraries, or specialized programs on the Internet that are available to large numbers of users.

Corporation for National Research Initiatives (CNRI)
Host Name: `nri.reston.va.us`

This site maintains up-to-date documents pertaining to the Internet Society (ISOC) and several of its major components. Under directory `/isoc`, you can find ISOC membership information, announcements of INET conferences, and on-line files with the latest issues of the *Internet Society News* newsletter (in directory `/isoc/isoc_news`). Directory `/ietf` holds general information about the IETF and subdirectories containing reports by its various working groups. Look in directory `/iesg` for minutes of the most recent IESG meetings.

Mac Internet Tour Guide Visitors Center
Host Name: `ftp.farces.com`

This site, run by Arts & Farces, contains information and software helpful to Macintosh users. Look in directory `/pub/visitors-center/software` for the latest versions of Macintosh utilities, such as Eudora, MacTCP, TurboGopher, and Fetch. The directory `/pub/visitors-center/mac-internet-tour-guide` has a description of and order information for the book *The Mac Internet Tour Guide: Cruising the Internet the Easy Way* (described in greater detail later in this chapter).

Computer-Based Tutorials for Using the Internet

Given the millions of persons connected to the Internet, no wonder several computer-based tutorials have been developed to guide new users in exploring network resources. You can obtain, at no cost, the two programs described in this section through anonymous ftp. If you have the hardware and software required, these programs are worth trying. The program descriptions are based on information provided by the developers to the authors and are subject to change.

Merit's Cruise of the Internet

Merit Network, Inc. has produced a tutorial, called A Cruise of the Internet, that runs on an IBM PC or compatible under Windows 3.1. Your computer must be capable of displaying 640x480 pixels with 256 simultaneous colors. You also must be running Windows in Enhanced mode. A version also is available for the Macintosh II, LC, and Quadra computers. The Mac version requires 8-bit color and a color monitor (12 inches minimum), and you must be operating under System 6.0.5 or 7.x.

The tutorial briefly describes common Internet facilities, such as ftp, telnet, Gopher, archie, and WAIS. It also mentions several areas of special interest, such as supercomputing and space exploration, for which considerable information is available through the network.

To obtain A Cruise of the Internet, use anonymous ftp to connect to `nic.merit.edu` using `guest` as your password. If you want the DOS/Windows version, change to the `/internet/resources/cruise.dos` directory. If you have PKUNZIP, get the file `meritcrz.zip` (note that this requires that you use the binary ftp file transfer mode). This compressed file contains all the files you need to run the Internet Cruise. If you don't have PKUNZIP, get `meritcrz.txt` (an ASCII file) and `meritcrz.exe` (a binary file). The `meritcrz.txt` file has brief instructions for running the Cruise; `meritcrz.exe`, meanwhile, is the actual executable file for the program.

If you want the Macintosh version, change directory to `/internet/resources/cruise.mac`. Retrieve the `merit.cruise2.mac.readme` and `merit.cruise2.mac.hqx` files. You will need to use BinHex or StuffItLite to convert the `.hqx` file to a Mac executable form. The file `merit.cruise2.mac.readme` has brief instructions on configuring your computer and running the Cruise.

Alternatively, you can obtain a diskette containing the Cruise through postal mail. Send your name and address, specify which version you want to receive (DOS/Windows or Macintosh), and include a check or money order for $10 (payable to the University of Michigan) or your VISA/MasterCard number (including the expiration date and your signature) to the following address:

Merit Network, Inc.
Information Services
2901 Hubbard, Pod G
Ann Arbor, MI 48105

The software will be sent to you on a 1.44M diskette. You can request additional information by sending e-mail to `cruise2feedback@merit.edu`.

NNSC's Internet Tour

For Macintosh users, the NSF Network Service Center (NNSC) has developed an Internet Tour in HyperCard 2 format for novice network users. It is intended to be a fun and easy way to learn about the Internet. The stack has basic information including history; sample e-mail, ftp, and telnet sessions; and a glossary. To run this stack, you need to have HyperCard 2 and System 6.0.5 or higher.

You can obtain the Internet Tour through anonymous ftp to `nnsc.nsf.net`. Go to the `internet-tour` directory and retrieve the files `Internet-Tour-README` and `Internet-Tour4.0.2.sit.hqx`. The readme file will give you information about the latest enhancements and changes to the software, as well as details on system requirements and configuration.

> **Note**
>
> The Internet Tour files have been compressed and saved as a StuffIt 1.5.1 archive, and converted to BinHex format. To use the files, you need to reverse this process by using the Macintosh application StuffIt 1.5.1 or StuffIt Classic.

You also can obtain Internet Tour by way of electronic mail. To do so, send a message to INFO-SERVER@nnsc.nsf.net. You don't need a subject field, but the text of your message must be in a special format (this is very important). You will receive the file split into messages small enough to pass through most gateways to the Internet. Use an editor to re-assemble the original file and transfer it to your Mac. The file Internet-Tour-README in directory internet-tour on host nnsc.nsf.net has a description of the required e-mail message format. If you can't access this file through ftp, try to retrieve it by using ftpmail (see Chapter 8, "Using ftp and telnet").

Several Books and Periodicals of Special Interest

Many books have been written about the Internet; they range from short summaries of basic functions such as e-mail and network news to in-depth descriptions of specific aspects of the TCP/IP protocol suite. The following sections describe several books and periodicals that the authors feel, for one reason or another, are especially valuable to Internet users. Most of them are commonly available—your local computer bookstore or technical library will probably carry several of them.

The Whole Internet User's Guide & Catalog

Ed Krol; *The Whole Internet User's Guide & Catalog*; O'Reilly & Associates, Inc.; 1992.

This excellent book is oriented toward the general Internet user. Descriptions and explanations are crystal clear, and the coverage of most subjects is appropriate for the intended audience. Detailed information is given about how to use Internet tools such as ftp, telnet, and archie. The book also includes a 47-page Resource Catalog with brief descriptions of interesting items (covering dozens of topics) available through the Internet.

Internet: Getting Started

April Marine, Susan Kirkpatrick, Vivian Neou, and Carol Ward; *Internet: Getting Started*; PTR Prentice Hall, Inc.; 1993.

Another general-interest entry, this book contains very brief descriptions covering a large variety of Internet-related topics. As the title implies, it pays special attention to telling readers how they can receive value from connecting to the network, and then discusses follow-up topics, such as types of network connectivity and how to find a service provider. It also contains a number of useful tables and lists such as the RFC, FYI, and STD indexes; lists of major Internet service providers throughout the world; and a table showing the level of network connectivity available in every country.

Connecting to the Internet

Susan Estrada; *Connecting to the Internet: An O'Reilly Buyer's Guide*; O'Reilly & Associates, Inc.; 1993.

As the title implies, this short text focuses on issues pertaining to getting connected to the Internet. A wide range of options is explored, and lists of public dialup and dedicated line service providers are included. The book also leads you through the steps in establishing a network connection, from deciding which services and what level of system performance you require to evaluating specific providers. Facilities available through the network are only briefly mentioned, however, in the context of choosing the package of network services you need.

The Internet Companion

Tracy LaQuey with Jeanne C. Ryer; *The Internet Companion: A Beginner's Guide to Global Networking*; Addison-Wesley Publishing Company; 1993.

Oriented toward new Internet users—or nonusers wanting to know what the Internet can offer them—this short book is written in a high-level, descriptive fashion. The basic resources available through the network are discussed briefly, and a short list of network service providers is given.

The book is filled with interesting personal accounts of the experiences of actual Internet users, from computer simulations of real-world events (the Iraqi invasion of Kuwait) to a contest between a group of reference librarians and a WAIS user to see who could determine more quickly whether the Kremlin has a swimming pool.

The Matrix

John S. Quarterman; *The Matrix: Computer Networks and Conferencing Systems Worldwide*; Digital Press; 1990.

This comprehensive book discusses the worldwide matrix of computer networks in a very clear and thorough manner. Details about networks in every part of the world are given, including the protocols they use, interconnections they now have, and their plans for expansion. Valuable sections of the book are dedicated to a description of communication layers and protocols, a survey of international standard-setting organizations, and an in-depth discussion of legal issues in computer networking.

TCP/IP Network Administration

Craig Hunt; *TCP/IP Network Administration*; O'Reilly & Associates, Inc.; 1992.

If you now have or are considering a TCP/IP Internet connection, this book will provide you with information on all aspects of configuring and managing your network connection. The basic principles of TCP/IP are discussed, as are such considerations as obtaining an IP address and domain name, troubleshooting TCP/IP, and maintaining network security. Dialup

IP—that is, SLIP and PPP—and dedicated connections also are described. This book is strongly oriented toward administrators of UNIX-based systems.

Using UUCP and Usenet

Grace Todino and Dale Dougherty; *Using UUCP and Usenet*; O'Reilly & Associates, Inc.; 1991.

This short book discusses the basic concepts of communicating through UUCP. The UUCP set of programs is described in detail, and many examples are provided that show how to perform common tasks. Differences between flavors of UNIX are identified. The fundamentals of using network news are discussed, and explanations of how to read and post news are given. A list of news groups is provided that contains their official names and a brief (single sentence) description of each one.

!%@:: A Directory of Electronic Mail Addressing and Networks

Donnalyn Frey and Rick Adams; *!%@:: A Directory of Electronic Mail Addressing and Networks*; O'Reilly & Associates, Inc.; 1993.

This book begins with an introduction to electronic mail message formats and addressing conventions. An exhaustive discussion of the major computer networks throughout the world then follows. A brief description is given of each network, with a list of the facilities it offers its users, the addressing format it uses, contact information, and a brief description of future network plans. Another third of the book contains a listing of the registered U.S. and international domain names.

The Mac Internet Tour Guide

Michael Fraase; *The Mac Internet Tour Guide: Cruising the Internet the Easy Way*; Ventana Press, Inc.; 1993.

As indicated by its title, this book is designed to help introduce the Macintosh community to the Internet. It contains discussions of electronic mail, ftp, Gopher, and other network facilities, as well as descriptions of commonly available Macintosh network-related software such as Eudora, MacTCP, Turbo-Gopher, and Fetch.

The most interesting aspect of this book is that it comes with a diskette containing the Macintosh utilities Fetch, StuffIt Expander, and Eudora. People who buy the book also are eligible for two free electronically distributed updates to the information in the book.

Internet World **Magazine**

Internet World; Daniel P. Dern, editor-in-chief; published by Meckler.

Internet World magazine, published bimonthly, contains articles on areas of interest to the general Internet community. New network resources and publications are reviewed, and feature articles may include interviews with prominent Internet figures and overviews of specific network service providers. Contact Meckler for subscription information and a sample issue at

> *Internet World*
> Meckler Corporation
> 11 Ferry Lane West
> Westport, CT 06880
> **Voice:** (800) 635-5537
> **Fax:** (800) 858-3144
> **E-mail:** meckler@jvnc.net or ddern@world.std.com

Internet Society News **Newsletter**

The Internet Society publishes the *Internet Society News*, a quarterly newsletter that covers items of general interest to Internet users and providers. The text of these newsletters is also available on-line through anonymous ftp (see the earlier section "The Internet Society (ISOC)"). For more information, contact the Internet Society at

> Internet Society
> 1895 Preston White Drive, Suite 100
> Reston, VA 22091
> **Voice:** (703) 648-9888
> **Fax:** (703) 620-0913
> **E-mail:** `isoc@isoc.org`

CD-ROMs Useful to Internet Users

The Internet is a somewhat loose combination of an extremely large number of computer systems spread throughout the world. Several major sites act as repositories of useful network information. They usually carry the same core set of information files, but each also stores some unique files not carried by all the rest. Many other sites also carry files of value to the general network user community that aren't widely distributed.

Searching the Internet at large for files of interest to you can be time-consuming. Even if you are very familiar with the locations of key information files, loading them on your local computer can use a great deal of network connect time and storage on your local computer disk.

CD-ROM is an ideal medium for mass distribution of network information. With a capacity of more than 650M, a CD-ROM can store as much data as 450 1.44M diskettes. Furthermore, a CD-ROM can be manufactured so that it can be read on PC, Macintosh, and UNIX platforms.

With such a large amount of storage available, you also can store files without compression, thus eliminating the inconvenience of decompressing files, storing them on your local hard disk, and deleting them when you are done. You also don't have to worry if you have the correct decompression software installed on your local computer. This is especially troublesome if you want to access a file on your PC that has been compressed using the UNIX compress utility, for example.

> **Note**
>
> The descriptions in the following sections were taken from information provided to the authors by the sellers. This information is subject to change. If you are interested in these products, request the latest information about them directly from the firms themselves.

Atlantis Internet CD-ROM

Atlanta Innovation, Inc. offers a CD-ROM with a wide range of tools and information for accessing the Internet. This CD-ROM, called Atlantis, is updated regularly and features all the most widely used Internet documents, including the complete series of Requests For Comments (RFCs), For Your Information (FYIs), Namedroppers Forum, and Standards (STDs) documents.

The Atlantis CD-ROM also contains the latest on-line information from key groups involved in the design, maintenance, and expansion of the Internet, such as the Internet Society (ISOC), Internet Architecture Board (IAB), Internet Engineering Task Force (IETF), and Internet Engineering Steering Group (IESG). Many other valuable lists of network providers and Internet services are included on the CD-ROM as well, thus saving you considerable time and effort in tracking down such information yourself.

The Atlantis CD-ROM contains a wealth of software acquired from the Internet in a single, easy-to-use package. Communications packages, demonstration software for graphical user interface (GUI) Internet interfaces, computer-based tutorials about the Internet, and many other utilities are provided to help you get the most from the Internet, whether you are a novice user or an experienced professional. Utilities and documents are provided for all the most common computing environments, including the DOS, Windows, Macintosh, and UNIX operating systems. The Atlantis CD-ROM is frequently updated to ensure that you have the most up-to-date software and most recent network-related documents.

The Atlantis CD-ROM sells for $39.95, plus a shipping and handling charge of $4.95. (For orders shipped outside the United States, shipping and handling charges are $9.95.) You will find an order card for the Atlantis CD-ROM in the back of this book. You also will find an ASCII file on the enclosed diskette by the name of CD-ORDER.TXT, which contains a printable order form for fax, e-mail, or postal mail orders. An annual subscription service is also available.

For more information about the Atlantis CD-ROM, contact Atlanta Innovation at the following address:

> Atlanta Innovation, Inc.
> P.O. Box 767849
> Roswell, GA 30076
> **Voice:** (800) 285-4680
> **Fax:** (404) 640-8769
> **E-mail:** cdrom-info@atlinv.com

SRI International Internet CD-ROM

The Network Information Center of SRI International sells The Internet CD-ROM, which offers comprehensive documentation on the fundamentals of TCP/IP networking. The price is $195 for delivery within the United States and $200 for shipments outside the United States.

This CD-ROM includes all the on-line Requests For Comments (RFCs); all on-line Internet Engineering Notes (IENs); For Your Information documents; the GOSIP specification; and other protocol, security, and informational files. Archives of technical mailing lists that discuss protocol implementation issues also are provided.

IFIND, an easy-to-use search program, is included on each disk. The search program works on UNIX and DOS systems and searches indexes made from all RFC, IEN, and FYI files, and all TCP-IP and Namedroppers mail messages. As a free bonus, the CD includes public domain source code related to TCP/IP networking for those who don't have direct access to Internet file-transfer capabilities.

For more information, contact SRI at

> SRI International, Room EJ291
> 333 Ravenswood Avenue
> Menlo Park, CA 94025
> **Voice:** (415) 859-3695 or (415) 859-6387
> **Fax:** (415) 859-6028
> **E-mail:** nisc@nisc.sri.com

InfoMagic Internet CD-ROMs

InfoMagic has produced several CD-ROM titles of interest to Internet users. The Standards CD-ROM ($40) is described as a comprehensive collection of U.S. and international communications standards and documentation. Included are the complete Internet Engineering Notes (IEN) and Request For Comments (RFC) series, Internet Engineering Task Force (IETF) and Internet Engineering Steering Group (IESG) meeting minutes, and the Network Resource Guide.

InfoMagic also offers the Internet Tools CD-ROM ($40), which the company calls a comprehensive collection of public domain networking tools and utilities. It contains a wide range of networking software, including SLIP and PPP implementations, SNMP packages, and KA9Q (TCP/IP for PCs). The USENET CD-ROM ($20) comes with assorted archives of the USENET news groups. It also includes the Frequently Asked Questions lists (FAQs) for many news groups.

You can find a brief description of these CD-ROMs and other offerings in file `/isoc/cdrom.members` on host `nri.reston.va.us` (you can connect using anonymous ftp). Discounts are available for members of the Internet Society. For more information, contact InfoMagic at

> **Voice:** (609) 683-5501
> **Fax:** (609) 683-5502
> **E-mail:** `info@infomagic.com`

Summary

As you can see from this chapter, you can obtain a great amount of information about the Internet on-line through the Internet itself. The major administrative bodies for the Internet maintain their protocol standards, meeting reports, and newsletters on Internet hosts. Many other organizations keep other documents and software available on-line to anonymous ftp users. You should explore a few of the Internet sites described in this chapter to see for yourself the tremendous volume of documents and software that are easily accessible through the network.

Chapter 5

Legal Considerations of Internet Usage

This chapter is an attempt to provide you with a road map of a vast and complicated legal minefield. The information in this chapter is "computer law in a nutshell," a veritable mini-treatise that briefly discusses several of the more significant legal problems you may encounter as an Internet user, host, or telecommunications provider.

Disclaimer

Because this chapter deals with legal questions, we (the authors, editors, publishers, and any other contributors to this book) have to provide some legal disclaimers (we do it for good reason—it's too easy to get sued these days, and too many hungry lawyers are looking for lawsuits to file). We have to "read you the fine print." We have to note that this chapter is NOT intended to constitute legal advice from the authors or contributors. You MUST seek your own counsel if you have a legal problem or want more detailed information about running your business. If you follow everything we say in this book and in this chapter, you STILL may be sued and you STILL may lose. Thus, we take NO RESPONSIBILITY WHATSOEVER for the accuracy of the information or the viability of any of the laws we discuss. Rather, consider this chapter as a guide for asking further questions—further questions of YOUR lawyer.

Keep in mind that every state and country has its own laws, and rarely do two lawyers agree on an interpretation of a particular law (which is one reason there are so many lawsuits). If you find that you have a problem or concern about a potential problem that may create a risk of legal liability to your business, seek legal help immediately. Try to get advice *before* you do anything big. Prevention is the best cure; you can avoid many legal problems by governing your behavior in an acceptable manner and by attempting to abide by the known laws.

Chapter Overview

Now that the disclaimers are over, here are a few of the conclusions addressed in this chapter:

Courts might well view the Internet as just another electronic communications medium. If they do, many of the laws that apply to electronic communications will probably apply. In any event, such laws are a good place to start in your research for legal guidelines.

If you have a specific need to find out about certain laws, plan to hire a lawyer, or want to educate yourself (beyond what you can learn from this chapter), then find a good law library and start searching out the law. A good starting place for learning more is a detailed treatise on computer law, such as *The Law of Computer Technology,* by Raymond Nimmer.[1]

As an Internet user, you have certain rights to freedom of speech. Like all rights, however, those rights have certain limitations. Your freedom of speech does not extend to the point at which you are infringing the rights of others, for example, by distributing obscene or criminal materials, or by violating the copyright laws.

If you have created original works of authorship that you allow others to access via the Internet, plan ahead as to how you will protect your property interest, both legally and practically. Know the copyright laws, and set up secure systems.

If you run an Internet-accessible host, you have the right to protection against unauthorized or criminal access to your system. Just as criminal laws prohibit breaking and entering and stealing, you have civil legal remedies, typically in the copyright laws, for damages if someone copies your copyrighted material without authorization.

If you download materials from various hosts or other sources, be aware that, because of the copyright laws, you cannot copy the materials in their entirety; you only can make fair use of such materials. You don't have the right to copy the copyrighted works of others, even if they make such materials available to you on the Internet, and even if you are clever enough to figure out how to get past the security web.

You have the right to protection against unreasonable searches and seizures. You are most likely to be the subject of such a search or seizure if you run an Internet-accessible bulletin board or host and your facilities are used (by yourself or by someone who obtains access to your system) for criminal or unlawful purposes. Access to your system via telephone lines for purposes of gathering law enforcement information is governed by the Electronic Communications Privacy Act (ECPA), and requires a warrant in most circumstances.

You can't expect to maintain complete privacy in materials you communicate via the Internet. However, the ECPA imposes legal restrictions upon interception of electronic communications, and unauthorized access is prohibited, indeed criminal, except under certain tightly controlled circumstances.

Under the ECPA, an operator of a wire or electronic communication service (for example, an e-mail server or a gateway of a telecommunications provider) can intercept, disclose, or use a communication in the normal course of employment while engaged in any activity which is a necessary incident to the rendition of the service. The extent to which such a service provider can intercept communications, however, is not clear in the law.

Treating your communications through the Internet backbone as though you were broadcasting over the airwaves is probably a good idea—some might pick it up, but what they do with it is subject to certain legal limitations. Although these privacy considerations may change in the future with encryption, no real privacy exists now.

Be aware of the usage policies of the various hosts and gateways you use. The policies may not have the force of law (yet), but they can be legally invoked to bar your further access.

Policy versus Law

Because many people seem to think that the various usage policies promulgated by various hosts are the "law of the Internet," the distinction between policy and law governing use of the Internet is a topic worth special consideration. Basically, the Internet is a new communications medium, and very little law has been specifically developed for governing its usage and responsibilities. In keeping yourself legal when using the Internet, you need to be clear as to what is "legal" and what may violate a "policy." Merely because you are behaving legally does not necessarily mean you are following policy! By the same token, merely following a given host's policy does not necessarily mean you are behaving legally. In most circumstances, you minimize your business risks by staying legal AND following policy.

Although some host sites on the Internet have established usage policies, these policies do not have the force of law. Also, a given site's policy can apply only to things under the control of that particular entity. However, violation of a host's policy can have legal implications. Most Internet facilities, hosts, and tele-communication providers have contracts that govern access and usage. Violation of a policy may trigger a legal right of the host to invoke a clause in its contracts with other entities, as ex-plained in the following paragraph.

What happens if a packet containing material that violates a host's policy is transferred through the host? If the policy viola-tion is detected (which in and of itself is a difficult problem), then the entity probably is within its rights to claim a breach of contract with a connected party utilizing its facilities, if that party's facilities were used to commit the breach. For example, if you are a Delphi or CompuServe user, and you use those ser-vices to violate a policy of a host to which you are connected, you could trigger a right of the host to terminate Delphi's or CompuServe's right to access that host.

You can rest assured that one ultimate legal consequence of Internet usage is termination of usage privileges if you are the cause of one entity (for example, a telecommunications service provider) breaching an important commercial contract with another entity (such as a host site that everybody wants to log in to).

Aside from policy-related questions, public-access questions also pertain to Internet usage. The Internet has a certain "public" character about it that brings in considerations outside of con-tract law. If you think about it, you can come up with many questions as to the extent to which a host can promulgate a policy that affects the passage of information through it. Who owns the Internet? Who has the right to control it? Who determines who gets on and who gets kicked off? Who decides what can be made available on the Internet, and what right do they have to determine what is available and who can access it?

Most of these questions do not have clear answers. Many, however, have legal implications because of the effect of various laws in various places that may influence the questions' answers. In many respects, the law of the Internet is a bit like the law of the old West—no one clearly has control of the whole thing, but here and there are marshals with "guns" that serve as a kind of police. As long as you behave according to the "norm," whatever that is, and as long as you do not attract undue attention by heavy traffic volume or by getting caught doing something clearly illegal, you most likely will be left alone. On the other hand, you need to be aware of the stated anti-commercial bias on the Internet.

The rest of this chapter explores some of the many legal matters that affect you as a business person in your usage of the Internet. We cannot cover fully the legalities of using the Internet, because the subject involves too many unanswered questions and too many gray areas. We try to hit on the high points, however, so you can start out aware of the main pitfalls of using the Internet and then steer clear of known trouble areas. If your business depends heavily on Internet access, however, it is important that you get a good lawyer *before* you get in trouble. As in health care, preventative medicine for your business is always better than the cure—a lawsuit!

Customary Acceptable Use Policies

At least one host site on the Internet has established an acceptable use policy. The National Science Foundation's network, known as "NSFNET," has the most widely accepted model for the "law of the Internet," to the extent such a thing exists. Its policy is known as the NSFNET Backbone Services Acceptable Use Policy.[2] Supposedly, you can get an up-to-date version of the policy via anonymous ftp from `nic.merit.edu`, in the file `nsfnet/acceptable.use.policies/nsfnet.txt`. Remember, however, that "policy" is not "law"; but for all intents and purposes you should treat it as law, because violation of the policy may trigger violation of contractual provisions.

Because this book is intended for business as well as individual users, you need to be keenly aware that the NSFNET policy specifically lists as one of two "unacceptable" uses, "use for for-profit activities, unless covered by the General Principle or as a specifically acceptable use." As a practical matter, what specifically constitutes "use for for-profit activities" is not crystal clear. Because virtually every telecommunications provider is "for profit," and virtually every government contractor is "for profit."

However, the NSFNET is not the Internet—it is merely a piece of the Internet. Some branches of the Internet are not anti-commercial. Further, the impetus to commercialize the Internet is growing, because its commercial benefits are so clear.

The National Research and Education Network (NREN) is expected to build on and eventually replace the Internet. The NREN will have a speed of 1.2 gigabits per second, as compared to the present maximum of 45 megabits per second for certain Internet links. The NREN was authorized by the High Performance Computing Act of 1991[3] (HPCA), which was promoted by then-Senator Al Gore of Tennessee. Congress plans to spend $2.9 billion over 5 years to bring it in. The HPCA specifies that the NREN is to be "designed and operated so as to ensure the continued application of laws that provide network and information resources security measures, including those that protect copyright and other intellectual property rights, and those that control access to data bases and protect national security."[4]

Present factors, including the current Clinton administration's known interest in NREN, suggest that NREN is likely to become the proverbial "information superhighway" open to a broad spectrum of commercial, government, and educational users and suppliers. These factors also suggest that the present anti-commercial bias in promulgated policies will gradually disappear.

To close out our discussion on policy, we remind you that you should take up any questions about what is or is not acceptable for transmission on the Internet with your service or telecommunications provider. Your agreement with your service provider will most likely determine what is acceptable.

Legal Areas Affecting the Internet

Even though the law is still developing, users of the Internet should be aware of a number of legal areas. Any or all of these legal areas potentially can influence your usage of the Internet. Again, be aware of them! Generally, it is unsound business practice to be the one who "sets legal precedent" by suing and getting sued, even if you get your name and picture in the papers. Let someone else enjoy this publicity. Lawyers and lawsuits are expensive, and there are better (and less costly) forms of advertising.

As an overview, the broad categories of law that have some impact on Internet usage include the following: intellectual property law, contract law, tort law (private actions for wrongdoing), international trade law, criminal law, electronic transaction law, regulatory law, and privacy law. This list is not necessarily exhaustive, but these are the areas most likely to impact your business usage. Clearly, a full development of all of these legal subjects would require books, if not treatises. In the following sections, we direct your attention to significant aspects of each of these areas so that you can be on the lookout for developing problems and consult a legal expert before the problem gets out of hand.

Legal Structure of the Internet

As described elsewhere in this book, the Internet is a collection of independent but interconnected hosts, telecommunication pathways connecting hosts, and gateways to hosts or to pathways. Each of these items is an "Internet entity," meaning that it is a part of the Internet and forms a piece of the whole. Generally, you can consider the Internet as having three different types of legal entities that interact with one another—users, hosts, and telecommunications facilities. These entities sometimes become intertwined. For example, university students are "users" but rarely "hosts." On the other hand, a "host" can be a "user" and can provide some gateway functions and other telecommunications functions. A gateway entity such as Tymnet or Sprintnet is generally a telecommunications provider, but it may also operate a host site as a gateway for users in certain cities.

Each entity has a different and independent legal existence and legal structure. In other words, a host computer system is controlled and operated by some organization or individual that is legally recognized as the owner. Generally, the laws governing ownership and control of the host are the laws of the place or "jurisdiction" where the host is physically located—typically a state or a country. However, the governing laws also can be those of the legal home of the host's owner—for example, a corporation in Delaware can operate a computer in New York, and the laws of either state (or both) may apply.

The same is generally true of a telecommunications provider, except that telecommunications may overlap different legal jurisdictions and be subject to the laws of each or all of those jurisdictions. For example, Tymnet extends across the Atlantic between Great Britain and the United States. Arguably, therefore, the laws of both countries apply to Tymnet's usage. Tymnet is subject also to the laws of Georgia and Florida if it transmits communications between the two states, as well as to federal laws that govern interstate commerce.

Any legal matter that involves the Internet necessarily involves the laws of at least one jurisdiction. Often, the laws of different jurisdictions apply. Figuring out which jurisdictions are involved so you can look up the law of the appropriate jurisdiction and apply it to your problem may prove to be difficult and confusing. Lawyers speak of the questions surrounding whose law applies to a given problem as "conflicts of laws" questions.

We can't solve conflicts of laws problems for you here. Just remember that you can't necessarily stop thinking about a problem simply because the law of one state says that a given action is OK—another state's law may be different!

Intellectual Property Law

The laws that you as an Internet user are most likely to encounter are the intellectual property laws. Proprietors of databases accessible via the Internet and those who distribute software products via the Internet have particular concerns about how they can protect their property interest. Common knowledge tells us that software is protected to some degree by the copyright laws, and to a lesser degree (depending on the marketplace you are in) by the patent laws. Having a good handle on the extent to which you legally can protect software assets accessible and distributed via Internet transactions is important. You also need to know the extent to which you can legally use software assets that you download.

If you are of a mind-set that the intellectual property laws are somehow inherently evil because they restrict the free flow of information and freedom in general, you may want to track down and participate in the activities of the Free Software Foundation, Inc., Cambridge, Massachusetts (also called the "FSF"). This organization is responsible for creating and distributing a UNIX-compatible software system called "GNU," which stands for "Gnu's Not UNIX." The notice associated with programs distributed by the FSF says, "Permission is granted to anyone to make or distribute verbatim copies of this document as received, in any medium, provided that the copyright notice and permission notice are preserved, and that the distributor grants the recipient permission for further redistribution as permitted by this notice."[5] The intent of the Free Software Foundation, whether or not this restrictive notice is effective, is to eliminate restrictions on copying, redistribution, understanding, and modification of computer programs.

Keep in mind that this discussion about "legal protection" considers matters very different from those of "practical protection." Legal protection means that one has a civil cause of action in court against a person who has violated some legal right. Practical protection, on the other hand, involves use of self-help methods such as copy-protection for software, "dongles" (that is, hardware devices that prevent a program from running under certain conditions), and similar matters relating to physical security of a computer system. Issues of physical security of computer systems typically do not involve a civil cause of action. If your computer system is secure and a thief breaks into it and steals something, it is just as if someone broke into a house—both the homeowner and the computer system owner have suffered a legal trespass. If the thief takes something of value from you, you may have a criminal remedy (if you can get the police or district attorney's office interested). You also may have a civil remedy in the courts; such remedy entails use of the court system in an effort to get the value of the stolen property returned, or to get compensation for the loss in terms of damages. The criminal laws do not afford any methods for recovery of damages, they only allow fines or putting the perpetrator in jail.

Copyright and patent laws are civil laws. Although some criminal provisions are associated with these laws, such criminal provisions are invoked infrequently. Keep the distinctions between civil and criminal laws in mind when you consider this part of the discussion about copyright and patent laws, as well as the other sections of this chapter that pertain to criminal laws.

Copyright Laws

As the name suggests, copyright laws protect against copying. The present copyright laws evolved from an 18th-century law called the Statute of Anne,[6] which was one of the first parliamentary statutes enacted in England. The statute's primary purpose was to preserve the guild/apprentice system for printers. Centuries passed before computer software was created, and then several decades went by before the copyright laws were applied to protect software. In the United States, the copyright laws did not clearly apply to computer programs until the copyright laws were amended in 1980.

Copyright law is only federal; no valid state copyright laws exist[7] (although they did at one time). The federal copyright laws give authors the right to preclude others from making unauthorized copies of original works of authorship. Copyright does not protect ideas—it only protects expressions of ideas. The distinction between ideas and expressions is not always clear, and much copyright litigation involves arguments over what is an unprotected idea as opposed to a protected expression. In the software realm, this "idea/expression dichotomy" (a legal term you hear from copyright lawyers) has led to litigation over user interfaces—the idea for a spreadsheet program is not now protectible, but one's particular implementation (and user interface) of a spreadsheet program is, at least to some degree.

Determining the difference between the protected and unprotected aspects of a program isn't always an obvious, intuitive process. For now, suffice it to say that if you sit down and reverse-engineer the user interface of any widely marketed and popular software, instead of sitting down cold without any other programs as a guide—look out. You may well find yourself the subject of a copyright infringement lawsuit if (a) your program is successful enough to attract the attention of the company that put out the popular product, and (b) that company has enough money to pay lawyers to sue you.

The dilemma you face is the same one everybody else in the industry faces—you want to enhance the prospects for your own product's success by "emulating" the user interface of successful predecessors, but you have no way of knowing which of the predecessor's features are protected and which are not. Creating your own programs and user interface is always legally safer but is riskier business-wise because there is a clear marketplace reluctance to adapt anything truly new.

Developing all the themes of copyright protection for software is beyond the scope of this discussion. We must, however, in the interest of completeness, hit the high points.

Elements of Copyright Law

The U.S. Copyright Act lists several basic elements for determining whether a particular work is subject to protection under the Act's provisions: the work must be (1) original, (2) a work of authorship, (3) fixed in a tangible medium of expression, and (4) one that does not extend to any idea, procedure, process, system, method of operation, concept, principle, or discovery.[8] The law gives the owner of the copyright (the owner is always the author, at least in the beginning, and subject to the "work for hire" provisions, discussed later) certain exclusive rights to control reproduction (that is, copying), dissemination, and adaptation of the work (that is, creation of "derivative works").[9]

The Copyright Notice, ©

Until recently, one had to put a copyright notice on one's work in order to flag the work as protected and invoke the copyright law. Prior to March 1989, the U.S. law required that the author of a work place a visible copyright notice (for example, ©1993 Bill Smith) before distributing the work in order to preserve copyright protection. The requirement for use of a copyright notice changed in 1989, when the United States became a signatory to a treaty known as the "Berne Convention." (Some countries have been a member of this treaty for years.)

Note that we said "preserve"—not "create"—copyright protection. Copyright in a work exists and attaches with creation of the work. No legal action is required for the copyright to come into existence. Rather, it just used to be that you had to put the copyright notice on the work so as to prevent the work from entering the public domain.

Under the provisions of the Copyright Act implemented in connection with entry into the Berne Convention, affixation of a copyright notice is no longer required in order to preserve the copyright. Nonetheless—and mark these words keenly—putting the copyright notice on anything that even remotely may be protected by copyright law is still a very good idea. There is no law against putting copyright notice on things that are not protected, and who knows? You may be starting something new.

Consider, for example, how creators of virtual reality software might display a copyright notice. How on earth can you put a copyright notice in a virtual reality space? Well, what about creating a "virtual billboard" with flashing neon lights? Such a billboard might read, "WELCOME to the COPYRIGHTED VIRTUAL WORLD OF (fill in the blank for your weird space). This virtual reality and all its aspects are © COPYRIGHT 1993 VIRTUAL DIMENSIONS, INC. ALL RIGHTS RESERVED." Or, how about a virtual pop-up "copyright policeman" that comes up to you, thrusts a copyright notice and license in front of you, and requires your "virtual signature" before he allows you to pass into the world? Such scenarios are not all that far-fetched.

Proper Copyright Notice

Getting serious again, a proper copyright notice can defeat a defense that an alleged infringer copied the material innocently. And more importantly, the notice creates a practical deterrent to copying because it gives a clear signal that the owner intends to protect the work. Believe it or not, most of the world is law-abiding and tries to do the right thing, so putting a copyright notice on your work helps the law-abiding person know where the line is. Besides, the small percentage of people who are going to rip you off don't pay any attention to copyright notices anyway (or to security barriers), so you don't have anything to lose by affixing a proper notice.

A proper copyright notice contains the symbol © ("c" in a circle) or the word "Copyright," followed by the year of first publication, followed by the name of the owner of the copyright.[10] You often see the follow-up language "All rights reserved," which is acceptable but not required.

Where do you place the notice? The law does make registration of a claim to copyright and deposit of certain material important in enforcing a copyright claim, and affixation of notice in the manner set forth in the copyright rules facilitates registration. Current regulations allow placement of the copyright notice in one or more of the following locations: (1) notice embedded in the copy (for example, in the source or object code), so that it is visible on perceptible printouts, either with or near the title, or at the end of the work; (2) notice displayed on a user's terminal or computer screen at signup or bootup; (3) notice continuously displayed on the terminal or screen; or (4) labels or printing directly on media or containers for the media.[11] Preferably, if you want to claim copyright, you put the copyright notice in some or even all of these areas.

Copywrong? Copyleft?

If you do *not* want to claim copyright, then you may well have to affix a notice to the effect that the work is not copyrighted and may be freely copied. One thing the Berne Convention did to confuse things in the United States was to make it more difficult for authors to communicate that they don't want to treat something as copyrighted. However, this situation does not happen very often in a modern, free-market-based, technological society—most people want all the protection they can get.

If you want your works to be freely available to all, say so clearly; use a *non*-copyright notice such as "Not copyrighted— this work is not copyrighted by the author and may be freely copied and distributed without permission." You might want to obtain the materials from the Free Software Foundation (FSF), discussed earlier. The FSF scheme of non-copyright-protection, which some have dubbed "copyleft," has yet to be tested in the courts, but provides a framework for those who are of a like mind with the FSF.

Copyright Registration

Although registration of the claim to copyright is not a condition of obtaining or retaining a valid copyright, registration (like copyright notice) is a good idea if you really are serious about copyright protection. A prior registration is a "ticket to court"; that is, it is a jurisdictional requirement.[12] You must have your ticket before you can invoke the power of the court. After the Berne Convention, however, the registration requirement applies only to works that originated in the United States. For works published in other Berne Convention countries for which enforcement of the copyright is sought, registration is optional. In any case, registration is preferable because it definitely eases the way into court.

Registration serves as prima facie (that is, "on its face") proof of the validity of the copyright and of the accuracy of the matters stated in the registration certificate.[13] Facts stated in a registration are rebuttable in a lawsuit at trial, but having the presumption in your favor means that your opponent bears the burden of proof on the particular matter. Presumptions are always preferable in a legal matter because they guarantee that you automatically win if your opponent does not come up with sufficient evidence to rebut the presumption.

Getting a registration is relatively easy—fill out a form (Form TX for a computer program), pay a $20 filing fee, and submit the filled-out form and filing fee with appropriate deposit materials to the Register of Copyrights. You can generally do it yourself, without the assistance of a lawyer (assuming, of course, that you have figured out what you are doing and are prepared to take the risk of something going wrong).

What "deposit materials" are required? Under current Copyright Office regulations, deposit materials for computer programs in machine-readable copies from which the works cannot ordinarily be perceived without the aid of a machine comprise one copy of "identifying portions" of the program.[14] The purpose of such "identifying portions" is nominally to allow the Copyright Office to determine whether the work constitutes copyrightable authorship. In enforcement proceedings, the identifying materials are often used to piece together the whole program as evidence used at trial (because you do not normally deposit the entire program, if you can help it). For software, deposit materials consisting of "identifying portions" typically consist of the first 25 and last 25 pages of a source code printout of the work.

The Copyright Office accepts other types of printouts for deposit material, but you clearly should try to come up with some type of a source code printout. Deposit materials other than the "first and last twenty-five" may result in a registration under the so-called "rule of doubt," which means that you do not get the benefit of the legal presumptions we discussed earlier.

Copyrights and Trade Secrets

As some readers will know, many computer programs are treated as trade secrets. In particular, the source codes of most programs are treated as trade secrets, because skilled programmers can learn a lot about how a program operates by analyzing source code (well, very skilled programmers can learn from object code, but that undertaking is a lot more difficult).

The Copyright rules contain provisions for deposit of "trade secret" material as the identifying material of a program. These provisions allow the deposit of various other types of identifying material, such as the first and last 25 pages of source code with some portions blocked out, the first and last 10 pages of source code with no portions blocked out, the first and last 25 pages of *object* code plus any 10 pages of source code with no portions blocked out, or at least 50 percent of a program whose length is less than 25 pages total.[15] As mentioned earlier, however, using anything other than the "first twenty-five, last twenty-five pages of source code" rule as deposit materials generally results in a registration under the rule of doubt.

Copyrightability of Databases

One aspect of copyright law that is particularly significant for Internet users is the applicability of copyright to databases. Just because you can access a database through the Internet does not mean that you may freely download the whole thing. This limitation is true even if your modem and communications line is fast enough to do it without attracting attention, and even if you split up your on-line sessions and download only a piece of the database at a time. Databases, in short, are copyrightable subject matter.

Databases are typically viewed as "compilations" under copyright law. A "compilation" is a "work formed by the collection and assembling of preexisting materials or of data that are selected, coordinated, or arranged in such a way that the resulting work as a whole constitutes an original work of authorship."[16] Copyrightability of a database does not depend on any one entry in the database being copyrightable. Rather, copyrightability derives from the selection or arrangement of the database items.

Use of the information in a database typically is permitted by the database proprietor, particularly where the user pays a fee to access the database (for example, LEXIS, NEXIS, and DIALOG are three commercially available databases for which the database owner or gateway control system charges a fee to access). On the Internet, many data sources don't, or can't, charge a fee; the lack of a fee, however, does not mean that the database is not legally protected.

Any use of a database must be considered a "fair use" in order to avoid legal liability for copying the information from the database. Under the U.S. Copyright laws, "fair use" of a copyrighted work is not considered an infringement. Determining just what constitutes "fair use," however, is not easy. The copyright law has no specific definition of fair use; rather, there is a legal test for fair use that is intended to be flexible and reflect equitable considerations. The law states a non-exclusive list of factors to be considered in deciding whether a particular use of a copyrighted work is fair. The list includes such factors as (1) the purpose and character of the work (for example, is the work specifically intended for commercial purposes, to make money for the owner?), (2) the nature of the copyrighted work, (3) the amount or proportion of the original work that is used (copying the whole work is much more likely *not* to be fair use), and (4) the effect of the copying on the potential market for or value of the copyrighted work.[17]

As you may discern, these factors do not really tell you how to decide if your usage is a fair use or not. A number of recent court cases involving the copying of telephone directories have highlighted the difficulty of determining fair use.[18] Telephone directories are essentially databases published in paper media, whereas computer databases are "published" in electronic media. Although certain information in the databases (such as the YELLOW PAGE listings) might be public domain, the database proprietors have invested enormous sums selecting, coordinating, and arranging the data so that it is usable. Obviously, the database proprietors want to ensure that the data is used in a manner that serves to protect their huge investments. Consequently, people who copy the telephone directories to produce competing directories have had to fight in court over the question as to how much usage of the directory constitutes fair use and how much constitutes unlawful copying.

The recent U.S. Supreme Court case of *Feist Publications v. Rural Telephone Service* has cast serious doubt on the protectability of databases. Prior to this case, many courts recognized that effort in gathering information and putting it in a database should be protected. Such courts applied what was called the "sweat of the brow" test for copyrightability. The *Feist* case arguably removed the "sweat of the brow" doctrine from the law.

The current stated test for copyrightability (notwithstanding the clear statement in the copyright law that compilations[19] are protectable subject matter) is "originality"—however it is determined—and not the effort expended in creating the compilation. In order to be protected under recent decisions, a work must demonstrate some "minimal degree of creativity." What constitutes a "minimal degree of creativity" may be difficult to figure out; the use of headings and other arrangement organizers were held not to meet the test in later circuit court cases.

The implication of the *Feist* case for database suppliers is that fact-based databases, and much of the information in them as well as much of the format or arrangement of the information (for example, selection of which fields to put in which order, and so on), may not be protectable. More litigation concerning the protectability of databases is likely in the near future.

One thing is clear—the more of a work that you copy or use, the more likely yours will not be considered a fair use. Downloading an entire database, unless that database is clearly marked as unprotected (which is rare), in all likelihood will not be a fair use.

Derivative Works

Another copyright issue that you may face when obtaining and using information downloaded over the Internet is your right to modify that work. Suppose that you have found a really nifty host containing lots of C++ routines that you would like to use. Further suppose that there is no clear marking that any of the routines are copyrighted, or that anything on that host (except for obvious things such as the operating system and commercial software that you can access) is copyrighted. Can you use the routines "as is?" Can you modify the routines and use them?

We have already answered the first of these questions. Even without a copyright notice, the routines are copyrightable subject matter under post-Berne Convention law. If you want to use the routines in a commercial product, you'd better obtain permission from the author or other owner. Otherwise, you may find yourself subject to a lawsuit for copyright infringement.

The question of modifying the works raises slightly different problems, but many of the same considerations apply. In a nutshell, you need permission from the author to modify and then use the routines. The copyright law gives the owner of the copyright the exclusive right to prepare "derivative works."[20] A derivative work is a work that is based on one or more preexisting works.[21] For example, the screenplay for a movie based on a popular novel is a derivative work, as are the publication of a Spanish-language translation of the novel and the publication of an abridged paperback edition. Creation of a series of prints from an original oil painting is also a derivative work.

One curious thing about derivative works is that they can have plural authors, and more than one copyright can attach to the work. A derivative work qualifies as a separate, copyrightable work with respect to the new material and expression it contains. If the author of a copyrighted first work gives a second author permission to prepare a derivative work of a computer program by copying the first work and by adding to or modifying it, the resultant second work becomes a work of authorship copyrightable by the second author. Further, because the first work is copyrighted, the copyrights of both the first author and the second author attach to the work.

> **Note**
>
> You need permission of the first author before you can prepare a derivative work. Those in the Free Software Foundation might not like it, but you have no legal right to modify another's software, whether or not you have any commercial purpose in mind.

Technically speaking, you don't have the right to modify a copyrighted program even if you want only to modify it for your own private purpose. The law recognizes that the author's ability to benefit from the market for enhancements and updates may be diminished if users are free to make modifications in the author's original work.

Even so, the fair use provisions should excuse most modifications made entirely for personal non-commercial use. For example, if you add or delete certain program functions, or make changes to enhance the speed of performance or minimize storage requirements, you have made a derivative work. If you don't have permission from the copyright owner to make the modifications, you are a copyright infringer. Even though the likelihood of a legal problem is relatively small if you keep your modifications private, you are technically in violation of the law unless your usage is excused under one or more of the fair use exceptions.

Backups

Assuming that you are legally permitted to download copyrighted material (a program, graphics, data from a database, and so on), you have certain rights to use that material. No discussion of copyrights relating to the computer area would be complete without a consideration of the copyright implications of backups. The copyright laws grant the owner of a copy of a computer program rights to additional copies under certain conditions. The law presupposes you are an "owner" of a copy. The law's protection does not apply if you have obtained a copy unlawfully.

Section 117 of the Copyright Act[22] grants the owner of a copy of a computer program a limited right to make an additional archival copy and to adapt the program notwithstanding the exclusive rights of the author. You are entitled to prepare a copy of the program as an "essential step" in using the program on a computer—after all, when you load a program from disk into RAM, you have made another copy! You then have two copies in existence at the same time. Without Section 117, you would be an infringer for making the second copy, but it is impractical—no, IMPOSSIBLE—to run the program without loading at least some of it in RAM.

You can also make a copy for "archival purposes" (read, make a backup). Under the law, you technically cannot make multiple backups, although doing so is a widespread practice. Again, the likelihood of a legal problem with multiple backups is low, as long as the number of backups is small and the backup media are placed in safe storage and are not used. The practice adopted by some computer installations of rotating backups for each day of the week (with five different disk cartridges used on a rotating basis, with one or two cartridges used for weekly and monthly backups) is not strictly legal under current copyright laws. While the practice is acceptable (and recommended) for data backups, it is on the borderline between copyright infringement and fair use as respects to copyrighted application and operating system software.

Copies made pursuant to the provisions of Section 117 may be transferred without permission of the copyright owner as long as all rights in the copy are transferred to another person. In these circumstances, you are supposed to destroy the backup when you transfer your copy to another person. The common practice of selling used personal computers "loaded with lots of software" is unlawful unless the seller also parts with all the original diskettes, manuals, and so on and does not retain any part of the original works.

Works For Hire

The final subject for our copyright discussion is that of "works made for hire." This issue comes up often in discussions of ownership of programs that are created on a contract basis. If you are a contract programmer who is *not* an employee of the people for whom you work, then you need to know about the work-for-hire provisions of the copyright law. We can expect that as the Internet expands, and people use it to telecommute (in particular, by creating copyrightable works on their own computer systems, communicating via e-mail with those who hire them, and even distributing the resultant works via Internet file transfers), work-for-hire questions will come up.

In short, if you are an independent contractor, *not an employee*, and you create a copyrighted work for another, even if you are paid for the work, you are the owner of the work. An independent contractor owns the rights in his or her work. If you are an employee and you create a work within the scope of your employment, your employer owns the work as a "work made for hire."[23] In these circumstances, the employer is deemed the author, even though you as the programmer actually wrote the work.

If the indicia of an employment relationship are not present, then the relationship is probably that of an independent contractor. The common law concept of an independent contractor relationship is one in which the hiring party does not control the details of the work performance and has only the right to accept or reject the finished product. In contrast, an employee relationship is one in which the employer directs and controls the manner in which the work is performed.

The working relationship between an employer and employee is much closer than that between a hiring party and an independent contractor. If you are the proverbial programmer who writes code from the mountaintop, based only on the spec provided by the hiring party, you pay your own medical and worker's compensation insurance, you pay estimated taxes instead of having them withheld by another, and so on, then you probably are an independent contractor. Recent court cases have elaborated on the types of factors considered in determining whether a work is one made for hire.[24] You should consult the cases or your lawyer if you need more guidance.

As mentioned, the U.S. Copyright Act treats the employer as the author of works created by its employees within the scope of their employment. In addition, the law defines certain types of specially commissioned works as work for hire.[25] These specially commissioned works, such as contributions to a collective work, parts of a motion picture or audiovisual work, compilations, translations, supplementary works, instructional texts, tests, answer materials for tests, and atlases can be works for hire and owned (and authored) by the hiring party only if a written agreement specifically states that the works are expressly agreed to be works for hire.

Oddly, the list does *not* include computer programs *per se*, which are one of the most widely commissioned types of copyrightable subjects today. However, several of the items in the list may be parts of multimedia works—for example, contributions to a collective CD-ROM comprising a number of different scenarios, parts of a motion picture on the CD-ROM, and so on. People involved with multimedia projects thus should pay particular attention to the work-for-hire provisions.

Because computer programs are not automatically works for hire, they are owned by an independent contractor, absent an outright assignment to the hiring party. In case of any doubt, the independent contractor probably owns the program. Legal agreements involving computer programs and other works not on the list often include language to clarify that particular works are works made for hire and owned by the hiring party, and if for some reason such works are not considered works made for hire, the creating party/hired party assigns all of his or her right, title, and interest in and to the work to the hiring party in perpetuity. Legal agreements include such language to make it clear that the hiring party intends to be the owner and legal author (if not the actual author) of the work.

Thus, if you are a hiring party and want to own rights in the works you pay for, you'd better get an agreement that includes copyright assignment language. If you are an independent contractor and want to retain ownership of your works, you'd better make sure you are not assigning title to your works to the hiring party. Remember, just because someone paid for the work does not mean that he or she owns it! The copyright laws govern on this issue.

Patent Laws

Because a patent lawyer (who specializes in software patents) helped us write this chapter, we feel compelled to mention the patent laws before leaving the subject of intellectual property. The availability of patent protection for software-related technology is becoming surer and surer in the United States, and other developed countries are following suit slowly but surely. The United States has lead the way on this issue, as it has lead in the development of software technology in general.

Software Patents

Software patents are highly controversial. Indeed, an Internet discussion group is devoted solely to the subject of the wisdom and efficacy of software patents.[26] The arguments against software patents typically run like this:

> Software patents are bad because the Patent Office can't do a good job examining the patent applications, and many people are trying to patent things that were created long ago and are in the "prior art." It is not fair to allow people to get patents on programs or concepts for programs that others created before. Besides, patents (similar to copyrights and any other intellectual property law protection) slow down the dissemination of technological information and retard technological development. Only the big rich companies can afford software patents, and thus the patents are used to put the small companies out of business. Etc. Etc.

Lots of other reasons pro and con exist, many of which you probably know.[27]

The arguments in favor of software patents are essentially the arguments in favor of patents, period. People have long denounced patents for (purportedly) slowing down technological development and impeding the free flow of information. The arguments really are the same as they were 150 years ago, when the argument was made that the cotton gin shouldn't be patented because such important technology shouldn't be kept in the hands of a few entrepreneurs, but should be spread out so as to benefit all of society.

So, if you're going to be anti-software-patent, you logically have to be anti-patent as well.

The Patent Compromise

Well, patents themselves are a compromise of competing interests, designed to promote antithetical values in a free-market society. The very word "patent" means "open"—the information in patent is intended to be opened up to society so that all can benefit from the information and carry the technology further. Indeed, if a patent does not describe fully how one makes and uses an invention, then the patent is invalid.[28] However, the openness of a patent is subject to one very significant limitation—the 17-year grant of the right to exclude others from making, using, or selling the invention.[29]

Patents are an important tool for entrepreneurs as well as big businesses. Entrepreneurs obtain patents to increase value in a new concern so as to attract investment and keep the competition at bay long enough for the entrepreneur to develop market momentum. Both entrepreneurs and big companies use patents to build technological fences—staking out technological turf that has been acquired with investment of capital. If that investment cannot be protected, the entrepreneurs and the big businesses cannot keep unscrupulous copyists from reverse-engineering their products and selling products at much lower prices (because the copyists haven't the cost of capital sunk in research and development).

If products are sold at low prices, consumers may of course benefit for a short while because of the low prices, but technological development eventually is hampered if the capital invested in research and development cannot be protected. Few rational business people would choose to invest their capital in marketplaces that are risky and offer meager returns for products that require extensive (and expensive) research and development.

This short dissertation on the pros and cons of patents will probably not convince you one way or the other, but at least you now know what both sides are saying.

Critical Timing for Patent Applications

As a communications medium, the Internet can facilitate research and development by people in remote geographic areas. People needn't be physically present to collaborate on a research project, whether it involves software or hardware.

According to a recent article in the magazine *IEEE Spectrum*, engineers at Digital Equipment Corporation (DEC), in places including Massachusetts, Arizona, Colorado, Singapore, and Germany, collaborated via e-mail on the design of a new disk drive, without ever meeting and while using the telephone only rarely.[30]

If you are involved in a research venture using the Internet or other e-mail facilities, be aware that your efforts may be the subject of patent protection. Be aware, as well, of the cardinal principles of preserving patent protection:

(1) you must file a patent application in the U.S. before one year has passed from the date of first public use or offer for sale of a thing embodying an invention, or you cannot get a valid patent,[31] and

(2) if you are interested in obtaining foreign (non-U.S.) patents, you must file a patent application in some country (such as the U.S.) where convention filing priority can be claimed[32] *before* any public disclosure of the invention, such as at a trade show or through the presentation of a technical paper describing the technology; otherwise, your rights to seek a patent in many foreign (non-U.S.) countries are lost.

Note

If you are interested in obtaining foreign (non-U.S.) patents, the best rule to follow is: file a patent application *before any public disclosure*, (such as occurs when a product embodying a new technology is introduced at a trade show, when an article describing the technology is published, when the salesmen are told about the product, and so on), and you will, in all likelihood, preserve your patent rights everywhere—if you have any.

Other Issues Involving Patent Law and the Internet

Many, many questions of patent law could be discussed in connection with Internet usage. For example, the U.S. patent laws require an export license (see the discussion elsewhere in this chapter) before a non-U.S. patent application can be filed. What happens in the case of multinational, Internet e-mail collaboration on a new product (such as the DEC disk drive that involved engineers in the U.S., Germany, and Singapore)? Because non-U.S. nationals may be involved and already know of the technology, must an export license still be obtained? What if the owner of the technology wants to file in Germany first? How does one determine the locus of an invention for purposes of deciding whose patent laws apply?

These are all good questions. You may have other questions. Space does not permit development of this subject, so we provide no answers. If you need answers, seek out a patent lawyer (or, if you work for a company that already has an established patent program, seek out the company's patent lawyer).

Contractual Issues

A "contract" is a promise or set of promises, for breach of which the law gives a remedy, or the performance of which the law in some way recognizes a duty.[33] Obviously, business usage of the Internet is highly concerned with contract law.

Transactions between different entities, such as a buyer and a seller, or a host and a telecommunications provider, necessarily involve a contract. Dealings with customers generally involve contracts of one form or another. Sometimes, a contract in written or "express" form is involved. At other times, contracts are implied by law—typically involving the Uniform Commercial Code (UCC). And at yet other times oral understandings (which also are contracts if certain conditions are met) govern the business relationship.

Oral Contracts

In most instances an oral contract is valid. However, certain kinds of agreements by law must be evidenced by a writing signed by the parties sought to be bound. For example, in some states a contract that cannot be performed in a year must be in writing. Also, a promise for the sale of goods of $500 or more is not enforceable unless evidenced by a writing.[34]

Contracts for Internet Access

You likely will find that a contract is involved with access to the Internet. Because the Internet is not a legal entity, no such thing as an "Internet contract" exists. No single master controlling entity has the right to force you, or anyone else, to sign its contract to get on the Internet. Rather, you find that you have to abide by the contractual terms of some entity that is either an Internet host or an Internet gateway.

Generally, agreements exist between Internet hosts and various telecommunications services that connect to that host—for example, BellSouth Corporation, Tymnet, Sprintnet, and so on. Legal agreements between the hosts and the various service providers rarely are accessible to the general public. Terms of these contracts can affect users, but finding out ahead of time what these terms are is a difficult task. If you are going to rely heavily on Internet access for your business and are likely to be a volume user of telecommunications services or the services of a particular host, you should ask to see the agreements between that host and its telecommunications provider. Your request may be refused, but there is no harm in asking.

An Internet user is likely to have at least one contractual arrangement—that for access to the Internet itself. In a commercial setting, you probably will be required to have an agreement with a commercial host or gateway before you can access the Internet.

In a government setting, access is controlled by government policy. In a university setting, access may not be strictly governed by a contract. With university-owned computer systems, access is generally governed by the policy of the university. Arguably, the university and its students share a contractual relationship, the terms of which are at least partially set forth in the policy statement.

With some Internet service providers, you are asked to sign a written agreement before you get a user name and password. With other service providers, you may form an "electronic contract." In the Delphi system, for example, you can sign up for access during an on-line session. During the session, you are asked a number of questions and must give a credit card number before you are allowed on the system. If you answer the questions and supply the credit card number, you have met the conditions imposed by Delphi and (one can argue) you have entered a contract with Delphi—Delphi has promised to let you access the Internet by invoking certain commands, and you have promised to pay (with your credit card) for that privilege.

Electronic Contracts

A purely electronic contract has no provision for receiving a signature and involves no permanent "writing" in the sense of a written paper document. Yet, some would argue that a contract can be entered during an interactive on-line session. The legal efficacy of electronic interactive contracts has yet to be fully tested in the courts. Some of the difficulties associated with "shrink-wrap" license agreements often used with mass-marketed software apply here. An electronic on-line "contract" bears many similarities to a "contract of adhesion," which is unenforceable in some jurisdictions.[35] A contract of adhesion is a contract of specified form and not actually negotiated.

At least two factors make electronic agreements questionable. The first relates to the manner in which the transaction occurs. The terms of such contracts are seldom negotiated, but are always unilaterally imposed by the vendor. If you don't agree with the terms of the so-called "contract" or "license," why, you can package up the whole thing, send or take it back, and get a refund! These are the terms, take them or leave them—there is nothing to negotiate!

A second questionable aspect of electronic agreements relates to timing. In most circumstances you don't even see the terms until you have paid the money and opened the package. Repackaging the program and sending it back is inconvenient. And the vendor does not exercise the classic contractual control of withholding, which is that either you agree to the terms ahead of time, or you don't get the goods. In a mass-market context, it is unreasonable to expect that merchants will withhold goods from sale pending execution of a written agreement. The imposition of a so-called "contract" at the point of sale with someone other than the merchant is a bit ridiculous.

The same holds true for an on-line "contract." If you answer the questions in the on-line "contract," you are allowed access, but the vendor is not truly withholding the goods or services unless it gets a written contract signed by the customer.

Yet another source of potential limitations on unilaterally imposed contract or license terms are inferred from copyright and trade secret law. As discussed previously in this chapter, the copyright laws set forth clearly established rights of an "owner" of a copy, which insulate the owner from certain restraints. The U.S. Copyright Act provides to the owner of a copy limited rights of reproduction and modification of a program, as well as the right to make backups.[36]

It makes sense, both practical and legal, that a vendor may legally condition a transaction on acceptance of its terms. However, in the mass market software environment, license terms are often not disclosed until after the purchase is made. Although the purchase can arguably be reversed, it is inconvenient and impractical. It seems logical that a vendor would want to legally condition an electronic transaction with acceptance of terms in an electronic contract. As you should have noticed, however, in a real-time on-line environment, there are legal difficulties that the laws do not readily and conveniently handle.

Shrink-Wrap Contracts

Shrink-wrap contracts or licenses are often used by software vendors to impose "terms" on the sale of computer programs. Such agreements are characterized as "shrink-wrap" because of the manner in which they are a part of the package—a paper containing so-called terms of the agreement are bound up within the shrink-wrapping that often encloses the diskettes, CD-ROMs, and user manuals.

Shrink-wrap contracts or licenses, as well as on-line electronic contracts, raise potential issues associated with the general commercial law doctrine of "unconscionability" and the general reluctance of courts to enforce contracts of adhesion characterized by unequal bargaining power. Unconscionability is an issue primarily arising in consumer purchases, although efforts to apply the doctrine to small businesses have been intermittently successful.[37]

Interactive "Sign-Up/Follow-Up" Contracts

Some vendors (Delphi, for example) have tried the following solution to the problem of questionable legality of electronic contracts: (1) allow initial but limited access if satisfactory answers are given to certain on-line questions provided during an initial "sign-up" session, and (2) condition further access on satisfactory follow-up—receipt of a signed, written agreement. This solution can be called an "interactive sign-up/written follow-up" approach. While this approach may work for Delphi, CompuServe, and similar on-line services, the approach is impractical if you are going to sell goods (for the obvious reason that it's hard to get the goods back after they have been shipped). This solution also is impractical for Internet situations involving multiple hosts or multiple telecommunications services.

Caution

You should be careful if you are involved with an "interactive sign-up/written follow-up" deal, either as a user or a vendor. A written follow-up contract provided subsequent to the interactive assent to the terms may or may not be consistent with the interactive terms. If the terms of the follow-up contract are not consistent with those of the interactive sign-up, legal troubles—charges of fraud, bait-and-switch, and so on—can follow.

"Hidden" Charges

One specific problem that can occur with interactive sign-up/follow-up contracts relates to the notion of "hidden" charges. Have you ever been surprised, upon receiving your credit card bill, at how much on-line time you have accumulated? People do not like being charged unexpected fees for services, or fees in amounts that they are not expecting. Some on-line services impose separate communication charges through Tymnet or Sprintnet. These charges are the result of separate contractual arrangements between the on-line service provider and the telecommunications provider. Further charges often are imposed for access to certain "premium" databases. Some services, such as Delphi, impose still other charges for Internet access.

None of these additional charges are readily calculable upon initial subscription. You really have to be savvy and experienced to avoid nasty surprises when your credit card bill comes. You very easily can stumble into significant charges before you realize that at virtually every turn there is another opportunity for a charge and that you have contractually agreed to the charge!

Contracts Between Hosts and Communications Providers

Contracts also are necessarily in place between various hosts and between communications providers and hosts. Indeed, the Internet arose from an agreement between different host sites that wanted to communicate with one another; the data communications carrier and protocol for such communications were established by agreement, and the rest is history. Although the original agreement (which this author hasn't seen) may not have been a formal contract, you can believe that had big problems arisen that resulted in damage to one or the other of the host sites, lawyers would have found a breach of contract theory upon which to base a lawsuit.

As an Internet business user, you probably will never see the provisions of any of the agreements between host sites or the telecommunications providers. This fact makes it difficult to know whether any particular entity's policies have been violated. You have no way of knowing what these policies are without obtaining copies of and studying all relevant agreements—which is clearly and practicably impossible. Conceivably, therefore, you could be violating the policy of a particular host without knowing it.

The Contractual Distinction between "Goods" and "Services"

One particular contract characterization question that arises in Internet usage is the distinction between goods and services. Most states recognize a legal distinction between contracts for goods and contracts for services. This distinction determines the body of law that applies to the transaction. The Uniform Commercial Code (UCC), which has been enacted in most states, applies to goods; and, generally, common law and other statutes apply to services. The purchase of computer hardware constitutes the purchase of goods under the UCC. However, it is questionable whether the UCC applies to software contracts, since such contracts are not readily characterized as "goods."

If your business involves software distribution via the Internet or the sale of a service involving access to a proprietary database maintained by a particular host, the applicability of the UCC to your business may not be readily discernible. The UCC was drafted for transactions involving the conveyance and delivery of products. In contrast, common law and statutes dealing with personal service agreements are concerned primarily with labor issues. The main focus of service-oriented laws concerns matters such as control over work performance.

Typically, a service contract relating to data processing services will be upheld under the UCC.[38] Nonetheless, in most reported cases involving contract issues, that a software contract is a sale of goods under the UCC is usually stipulated between the parties or is not substantially contested.

Contract Issues Involving Electronic Data Interchange (EDI)

A term frequently used in the context of electronic commercial transactions is "EDI," which stands for *electronic data interchange*. EDI is another of those jargony acronyms of uncertain origin, and whose meaning varies depending on who you talk to. To some, EDI means any technology that enables one party to electronically transfer information and legally relevant "documents" to another party, often for the purpose of processing in the other entity's information systems.[39]

The term EDI also is used loosely to signify electronics funds transfer (EFT), service bureaus and processing, and issues relating to electronic contract formation. Payroll processors and computer service bureaus that process data for others come to mind as involved in "EDI."

The term EDI is probably appropriate in a business context where you, as a businessperson, are interested in setting up electronic transaction systems for the sale of goods or services. For example, as a merchant, you could distribute an electronic order "form" or particular protocol that you want your customers to use when ordering from you. The "form" could be distributed electronically to customers and distributors. You might agree that, so long as an order was provided on your form and received via e-mail or otherwise on the Internet, you would respond in a certain fashion. You could grant a particular discount, ship by a certain preferred method, or provide some other service.

If you expect to receive orders or "product" electronically, via Internet or otherwise, you conceivably have an EDI situation. You should then be concerned with the question of whether your EDI usage is legal and proper.

Responsibilities of Internet Communications Carriers

In a commercial transaction involving Internet usage, third-party telecommunications carriers and Internet hosts have needs and interests different from those of the people involved in the transaction. Many Internet hosts serve merely as message passers and have no involvement with a business deal. Telecommunications carriers are primarily interested in inducing EDI users to use their networks. You should make sure that any data carriers with whom you contract support the EDI protocol you want to use and do not impose complications on your scheme with their agreements.

Given the state of the law, the standard of care and duties that a carrier owes are unclear. If a data carrier is at fault by causing you to miss or botch up a major order, you may have a claim against the data carrier. Likewise, a host that causes you to miss or botch a job can also be subject to a claim. Fear of legal liability is one reason that certain Internet entities have anti-commercial policies. It is easier to argue in court that you are not legally responsible for botching up someone's data if that person's data was a violation of your usage policy.

Legal liability is imposed through traditional theories of breach of contractual duty, negligence, and intentional tort, and these theories should apply in Internet transactions. Other theories may be pursued through specific statutes such as dealing with unauthorized access to systems, unauthorized data tampering, or computer-related fraud. If you need help in pursuing a claim, again, seek a good lawyer. Before you do so, however, find a good book on EDI at your local law library.[40]

If you plan to conduct commercial transactions on the Internet, you should define the carrier's duties and liabilities completely in a "network agreement," which is a contract between the trading parties and the carrier. Such an agreement should set out duties the parties to the transaction owe the carrier, and the duties the carrier owes to the trading parties. At a minimum, the carrier's duties for transactions should include

(1) the accuracy of data transmissions;

(2) the timeliness of delivery of transaction records;

(3) delivery to the correct party or parties;

(4) the preservation of privacy and security from outside intruders;

(5) the preservation of privacy and security by the carrier, its employees and agents;

(6) reasonable access to any records involving the trading parties' transactions; and

(7) reasonable accuracy in accounting for any fees and charges imposed against the participants.

> **Note**
>
> Be aware that on the Internet, telecommunications carriers do not always have control over things such as timeliness of delivery of messages and preservation of privacy. If you use the Internet, you may want to consider encrypting your data if you want privacy (which leads to other legal considerations) or give up any expectations of privacy.

Warranties

Another legal issue related to contracts is that of warranties. A "warranty" is a promise that a proposition of fact is true. As a promise, a warranty can become part of a contract.

Warranties can be "express" or "implied." An *express* warranty is one in which a party affirmatively represents or expresses, typically in a writing, that a fact is true. For example, a printed statement on a software package such as "This software works on a Macintosh computer" can create a legal obligation for a refund if a Windows diskette is in the package. An *implied* warranty is one that is imposed by the operation of law, even though no real promise was ever made.

Express Warranties

Users of the Internet should be aware that express warranties are among the most significant factors in lawsuits under the Uniform Commercial Code. Under the UCC, an express warranty is any affirmation, promise, description, or sample that "becomes part of the basis of the bargain" between the parties.[41] It must be affirmatively created by action or statement. Any representation that creates an express warranty is by definition an element of the agreement and enforceable.

A good example of an express warranty is found in many software manuals. Many software vendors include language to the effect that, "We warrant the diskettes on which the software is recorded to be free from defects in materials and faulty workmanship under normal use for a period of 90 days after the date of original purchase." Note that this is not a warranty of the program, it is merely a warranty of the diskette. If you have ever been disappointed with a program governed by one of these express warranties that doesn't work as you thought it would, you probably found out the hard way that you can't get your money back. Your remedy, usually, is mere replacement of the diskette if the program does not run properly. You don't usually get your money back—unless the vendor is one of the few with a money-back guarantee!

Court cases involving express warranties frequently entail the interpretation of contract terms that seek to eliminate or reduce the effect of the express warranties' representations. Express warranties can be negated by a written agreement, and thus, in a sense, disclaimed.

Implied Warranties

In addition to express warranties, the terms of a transaction may be defined by implied warranties imposed by law or through the actions of the parties. Two implied warranties commonly are involved in cases under the UCC: one is the warranty of merchantability, and the other is the warranty of fitness for a particular purpose.

The implied warranty of merchantability is presumed present in any transaction where the seller is a merchant engaged in selling goods of a particular type. The warranty is that the delivered products would pass without objection in the trade and are fit for the ordinary purpose for which such goods are used.[42] For example, a software program delivered on a diskette made of inferior plastic and whose magnetic coating flakes off after only one or two insertions in a disk drive would probably not satisfy the implied warranty of merchantability.

The second implied warranty is the warranty that the delivered goods are fit for a particular purpose.[43] This warranty exists only if the seller has reason to know of the buyer's intended application of the product, and if the buyer is relying on the seller's skill or judgment to furnish suitable goods. A good example of the implied warranty of fitness for a particular purpose applies to a computer itself—if all the computer can do without crashing is run a simple screen-saver program, then it is not fit to be a general-purpose computer. A computer purchaser can claim that a computer seller impliedly warrants its computers to run useful programs. (Such implied warranties may be a useful tool if you have purchased an "IBM-compatible" computer that is not really compatible with any useful software.)

Both of these implied warranties can be disclaimed by vendors, but they must be disclaimed in a particular manner, namely, with appropriate and conspicuous language in the contract. If you don't have a written contract involved in an Internet transaction, then you may be providing these warranties without knowing it. You may want to consider including in your EDI format an appropriate warranty disclaimer. You must follow the provisions of the law[44] in order to effectively disclaim warranties. Again, seek an expert's advice if you believe you have problems in this area.

Magnuson-Moss Act

Another warranty concern that you might encounter on the Internet is that of the Magnuson-Moss Act.[45] The primary thrust of this law is the disclosure of terms. The Magnuson-Moss Act states that any warrantor of a consumer product sold to a consumer with a written warranty "must fully and conspicuously disclose ... the terms of such warranty" to the extent required by the regulations of the Federal Trade Commission (FTC). This law is one of the main reasons that you see warranty provisions included with packaging for consumer products that you buy. A thorough discussion of these standards is beyond the scope of this book, but it is likely that Internet transactions would be governed by this law if there are any consumer goods involved. If you are going to conduct any consumer-oriented business on the Internet, be aware that you will probably have to deal with Magnuson-Moss warranty issues.

License Agreements

License agreements are nothing more than contracts. They typically involve the legal "owner" of the software (that is, the owner of the intellectual property rights) and the "owner" of a copy of the software. Many purchasers of software fail to execute a license agreement or otherwise acknowledge agreement to it. Many mass-market software transactions are structured in a manner designed to infer acceptance of a license based on use of the program. Commonly, this structure involves a license form that purports to condition the purchaser's right to use the program on acceptance of the license, or it may involve forms that indicate that the act of opening a software package constitutes acceptance of the license provisions.

The "license agreement" mechanism also is used in providing access to Internet gateways and is expected to be used for indicating assent to certain contract terms via the Internet. In these cases, prior to completing an Internet transaction a purchaser would be asked whether he or she assented to particular license terms that would be displayed on-screen. Of course, the language will be drafted by lawyers, will probably be in a very small font, and will be difficult to read. Nonetheless, the transaction won't be completed unless you type "yes," or "I accept these terms," or something like that.

Shrink-Wrap and On-Line License Agreements

As we discussed earlier in this chapter, so-called "shrink-wrap licenses" with unilateral terms are often used in connection with mass-market software. On the Internet, electronic agreements or licenses with unilateral terms might be called an "interactive on-line" agreement or license. The effect of these conditioned agreements or licenses has not yet been fully resolved by the courts. Shrink-wrap licenses are so widespread in usage, and software marketers are so accustomed to them, however, that you can expect to see them in connection with Internet transactions; at present, no better (or widely accepted) way exists to simulate the arms-length bargaining that is typically required under current law to form a valid enforceable contract.

Again, use of any type of so-called "agreement" that does not afford the opportunity for negotiation raises questions of unconscionability and adhesion contracts, because you as the purchaser have no choice but to accept the terms if you want to consummate the transaction.

Tax Laws

As we have seen, Internet transactions can involve the sale of goods (for example, by running an Internet-accessible "mail-order" catalog) or the rendering of services (for example, by operating an Internet-accessible service bureau). The characterization of a particular transaction as involving "goods" or "services" may affect the body of law that applies in determining the rights of the parties in the contract—for example, whether the UCC applies to the transaction or not. The classification of the subject matter also is necessary when applying state tax laws to the transaction. In many states, sales or use taxes are a major source of tax revenues for the state. States impose sales or use taxes on property sold within a state or used in a state following acquisition in another jurisdiction.[46] You basically cannot buy anything from a merchant without paying a sales tax.

Tangible versus Intangible Items

In most states, sales and use taxes are limited to transactions involving tangible items—that is, things having a tangible existence. For example, a computer is a tangible thing, as is a software package, a modem, and RAM. On the other hand, a promissory note and a copyright are intangible things—you cannot grab hold of the promise to pay or the copyright (although you can hold the note itself or the copyright registration certificate). The issue of tangible versus intangible property commonly comes up in conjunction with intellectual property rights and financial securities such as stocks and bonds.

Sales and Use Tax on Internet Transactions

In your Internet business, you may need to determine whether aspects of your transactions fall within sales or use tax provisions. This determination may not always be easy to make, especially when sales and use tax laws generally aren't set up to handle computer-related businesses. Clearly, if you are conducting a business that involves taking orders for tangible goods over the Internet and delivering those orders to people in other states via a carrier such as UPS, Federal Express, and so on, you are likely to have sales or use tax requirements and must collect taxes. On the other hand, if your business primarily relates to providing a service such as access to a proprietary database or consulting services, or if your business serves as an intermediary between other parties, you may not have tax liability. At the risk of sounding like the proverbial broken record, see the experts! In this case, see a tax expert.

The relevant state laws on taxation are changing rapidly and are expanding, because states are beginning to realize that software is a potentially valuable source of tax revenue. The various state laws differ widely in effect and are published in various sources, many of which you can find in your local law library.

Tort Law

A "tort" is not a kind of a cake or pastry or an immoral English girl (you're thinking of a "tart"). A tort is a private or civil wrong or injury. The law provides remedies for injuries suffered as a result of such wrongs. When you hear of negligence cases, product liability cases, or fraud cases, you are generally hearing about torts. Sometimes, these wrongs carry criminal penalties; but tort law is what you use to obtain compensation from the wrongdoer.

In the computer context, tort law applies in cases where there has been a fraudulent misrepresentation, negligence, or product liability. Most of the cases involving fraudulent representation come up in contract law. However, tort law principles establish basic minimum standards, obligations, and duties that cannot be modified or avoided entirely by contract.

Tort liability involves at least three different paradigms or contexts, as follows:

(1) that between two parties in a direct contractual relationship;

(2) that pertaining to remote parties such as manufacturers and consumers; and

(3) that involving reliance by a user on information supplied by a vendor.

While space does not permit a full development of the subject of tort law, in the following sections we try to briefly describe each area that you may encounter as a user of the Internet.

Fraud

The first context of tort liability raises questions of fraud, although allegations of negligence and malpractice also may be raised. Note that the context presumes a contract relationship. Thus, allegations of fraud in a contract are often another legal issue in a contract suit, in addition to simple breach of the contract. For example, one party can raise fraud as a defense to a lawsuit for enforcement of the contract by the other party.

Tort law imposes penalties on active deception and grossly harmful behavior, regardless of what that behavior is called—fraud, misrepresentation, deceptive trade practices, and so on. As a result, you must follow standards of behavior, or you must pay the price. The standards are those generally acceptable to society, as codified in statutes or as determined by courts. Less directly, tort law may impose minimum obligations on the parties, despite contractual specifications to the contrary. Tort laws, in other words, establish limitations on your freedom to contract. You cannot legally contract to break or avoid the law.

In the realm of Internet usage, tort problems can occur in cases of outright fraud, where a user has deliberately placed wrongful or misleading information on the Internet. One who fraudulently makes a misrepresentation of fact, opinion, or law for the purpose of inducing another to act or refrain from action in reliance on it, is subject to liability to the other in deceit for pecuniary loss caused to him by his justifiable reliance on the misrepresentation.[47] Thus, a fraud is generally considered to be a type of wrong that requires proof of knowing misrepresentation of material fact, made with the intent to deceive, where the misrepresentation is in fact relied on by the deceived party to his or her detriment.[48] For example, it is probably a fraud if an Internet user, wanting to buy goods with someone else's credit card (intent to deceive), sends you an e-mail message claiming to be your bank officer (a knowing misrepresentation of material fact), gets you to reply with your VISA card number (reliance by the deceived party), and then uses your VISA number to buy mail-order goods shipped to another address (to the detriment of the VISA card owner who gets the bill).

Fraud law frequently serves to police contractual relationships by establishing minimum standards of fair dealing and honesty in a contract. However, fraud law is not limited to contractual situations, as our example of the credit card fraud illustrates.

The most commonly occurring cases of alleged fraud in a contractual context are those in which a vendor's description of the capabilities of its system or software is faulty from the outset. If the other party relies on the vendor's description of the product's capabilities, then there is a basis for an action of fraud.[49] True fraud is rare, but it occurs. Unless evidence shows that the fraud-perpetrator knew he or she was making the misrepresentation, fraud is difficult to prove. In most cases, the alleged perpetrator has some excuse, such as that the information was not really all that false, or that he or she was misunderstood.

Misrepresentation

Misrepresentation cases are related somewhat to fraud. Misrepresentation can occur from an outright false statement. In one court case,[50] a vendor sold a computer system that performed at unacceptably slow speeds and was sued by the customer. The basis for the legal action was that prior to the sale, the vendor had demonstrated to the customer a model that was specially designed for faster performance. The use of this sales model to induce the purchase demonstrated vendor knowledge of the sold model's flaws. In short, you'd better sell them what you show them!

An incomplete disclosure of information can amount to misrepresentation, but it is somewhat more difficult to make out as a case of fraud. Nonetheless, a failure to disclose material negative information can give rise to liability. Inaccurate representations about the suitability of a system for a buyer's application may result in liability under fraud theories. Estimates concerning benefits derived from a product such as increased information flow, time savings, or cost savings, also can give rise to a fraud claim.

There is no substitute for honesty in commercial transactions. Although we are not here to preach commercial morals, the seeming isolation of the Internet can lull you into complacency and carelessness if you don't watch out. Making exaggerated claims about your products or capabilities is all too easy when there is no one standing in front of you, looking you in the eye—but this attitude is dangerous. Any message passed on the Internet theoretically can be intercepted, archived, and come back to haunt you as evidence of a fraud or misrepresentation. Make sure that you speak the truth. If you are not certain about some aspect of your products or capabilities, provide disclaimers that your stated assessments of those aspects are "estimates" or "not verified," or that you "believe" your assessments to be true. Beliefs are harder to attack as fraud than are statements that can be taken as facts.

False Advertising

False advertising also bears some relationship to fraud as a legal theory for tort liability. False advertising cases (that is, *private* false advertising cases, not Federal Trade Commission false advertising cases) are brought under a broad area of the law known as "unfair competition." This area of the law is very trademark-like, in that its legal principles are very similar to those of the federal trademark laws. Although false advertising isn't strictly a common-law tort (it has its origins under federal commercial statutes[51]), false advertising may be thought of as a federal tort, because it involves a federal remedy for a civil wrong. Many states have counterpart laws to the federal law, often called "deceptive trade practices" laws.[52]

The federal unfair competition statute has been broadly interpreted by courts to cover a wide variety of unfair competition claims. Principal categories of cases that have arisen under these laws are as follows:

- common-law trademark infringement (that is, when there is no federal trademark registration)

- trade name infringement (involving names under which businesses are conducted)

- trade dress infringement (involving non-functional designs, such as the layout of a restaurant or the design of a product's package)

- false advertising

- character rights (involving the likeness of famous personalities, living and dead)

- passing off, palming off, and reverse palming off (involving substitution of goods)

Unfair competition cases are fact-intensive and concentrate on how bad was the defendant's behavior. Thus, the determination of whether certain behavior is legally actionable is very subjective, and the "black hat" factor plays a large role.

Because the Internet may be considered a form of media, as in the misrepresentation law, be careful that you are truthful in your Internet advertising. Whether you are advertising on the Internet through methods such as unsolicited e-mail and bulletin boards, or whether you advertise in other media, if you cannot verify the truthfulness of your assertions (especially if you compare your product against those of another), seek competent advice.

Negligence

Negligence is another form of tort. You often hear about negligence in medical malpractice cases and automobile product liability cases. The negligent design or manufacture of products, or the negligent provision of services, may cause liability under negligence and related legal theories. Obviously, you as a manufacturer, distributor, or programmer may be liable to people with whom you have a direct contractual relationship if your products cause physical harm. However, design and manufacture may create liability to third parties under products liability law, as discussed in the later section "Product Liability."

Generally, *negligence* is conduct that falls below the standard established by law for the protection of others against unreasonable risk of harm[53] (but does not include reckless conduct). In order to win a negligence case, you must prove that there is some legal standard against which the conduct should be measured, and that the risk of harm is unreasonable. The determination that a legal standard of conduct exists (for example, one is supposed to stay awake while driving a car) leads to a conclusion that one has a duty to abide by the standard (one has a *duty* to stay awake while driving!).

Unlike fraud, negligence theories are not bound by a focus on misstatements of fact. Indeed, you don't have to say anything to be found negligent—sometimes saying nothing when something should have been said amounts to negligence! Negligence derives from a failure to exercise care in the execution of an enforceable legal duty. Legal duties arise in a number of ways, including from contractual relationships defined in a contract. Legal duties also arise simply from a duty to society. For example, you are not supposed to operate an automobile in a manner so as to cause injury to other people. If you have a wreck and it's your fault (say, because you were looking out the window instead of at the traffic light), you probably will be found negligent!

It is sometimes difficult to distinguish between negligence and contract claims. The courts traditionally distinguish between misfeasance and nonfeasance of contract obligations. *Misfeasance* occurs when you perform your legal duty badly. *Nonfeasance* occurs when you don't do your job at all. In other words, performance of any contractual obligation carries an implied legal duty to exercise reasonable care. Fouling it up not only can breach the contract, but also can give rise to a negligence claim.

It is impossible to predict how negligence theories will be applied in the Internet realm. One particular example related to medical computing was alluded to by Cliff Stoll in his book, *The Cuckoo's Egg.*[54] Suppose that you operate an Internet-accessible computer system for a hospital, and you don't have extensive security on access. Suppose further that your database contains sensitive medical records, such as prescription information, surgery instructions, or a computer-controlled cancer radiation therapy device. Next, suppose a hacker logs into your system quite easily (because you didn't make it difficult) and while futzing around modifies some of those sensitive medical records. Now, suppose that a patient is given the wrong prescription, has the wrong organ operated on, or receives a fatal dose of radiation because those computer records were modified. Were you negligent for failing to erect a proper security barrier that would have prevented unauthorized entry to those sensitive medical records?

If this happens to you, you can bet your bottom dollar that some clever plaintiff's lawyer is going to be asking a lot of embarrassing questions about your computer system's security features! We all know that security makes computer systems more difficult to use (that's the point), even by those who are supposed to use them. But failure to exercise due care in preventing injury to people is what negligence law is all about.

If your Internet usage relates to sensitive areas such as medicine, credit ratings, nuclear power, or hazardous waste, you obviously will have to give some thought as to the extent of your obligations and possible legal duties to prevent injury. Make certain that your systems are secure to the extent commensurate with that duty. Find out what your legal duties are. Perhaps you already have a good idea that your business is litigation-prone, so you should be extra careful. If you are not sure, the best way is to seek a lawyer's advice as to what areas are currently hot for negligence cases, unless you want to spend the rest of your life in a law library looking up the law!

Product Liability

Tort liability under contractual, fraud, and negligence theories generally applies only where you have had some direct contact with or know the injured party (or at least you have "met" them in an accident!). Under other tort law theories, however, duties of care are owed to unknown third parties. The term "product liability" is the general label commonly applied to various legal theories through which a manufacturer or distributor of a thing may be liable to third parties with whom it has no direct contractual relationship. Product liability cases are increasingly common, because many cases are brought by "contingent fee" lawyers who get a cut of the proceeds if they win or settle the case favorably to the injured plaintiff.

The legal theories supporting third-party product liability include negligence, contract warranties, and concepts of "strict" liability. A primary controversy in product liability law pertains to strict liability. The following is a good definition of "strict" product liability:

(1) One who sells any product in a defective condition unreasonably dangerous to the user or consumer or to his property is subject to liability for physical harm thereby caused to the ultimate user or consumer, or to his property if

    (a) the seller is engaged in the business of selling such a product, and

    (b) it is expected to and does reach the user or consumer without substantial change in the condition in which it is sold.

(2) The rule stated in subsection (1) applies although

    (a) the seller has exercised all possible care in the preparation and sale of his product, and

    (b) the user or consumer has not bought the product from or entered into any contractual relation with the seller.[55]

We are not aware of any substantial litigation in the computer industry on strict liability. Current industry patterns show that product liability claims typically involve physical damage. The product liability cases relating to computer systems tend to involve computer-assisted machinery, robotics, aircraft guidance, medical diagnostics, or information systems used in activities that involve a foreseeable risk of physical injury to users and others.

If your business does not involve things that can cause physical harm to people if things go wrong, you probably have reduced chances of facing a product liability claim.

> **Note**
>
> As mentioned earlier, in his book Cliff Stoll expressed concern of
> physical harm caused by a hacker who might wrongfully disrupt
> medical files or images being utilized to diagnose or treat disease.
> If you have a computer system that is Internet-accessible, and your
> system contains information that, if erroneous for whatever reason,
> may cause physical harm, then you need to be aware of the potential
> for product liability claims. This liability would apply to you as the
> user or owner of the system, as well as to the manufacturer of the
> system.

We could go on and on about torts, because they are some of
the most widely visible aspects of the law. We leave the subject
now, however, because there are so many other things of a legal
nature you need to be aware of in regard to using the Internet.

International Trade Considerations

Because the Internet is clearly an international network, as an
Internet user you may face issues of transborder data flow and
export regulation. This prediction is especially valid if you plan
to conduct any type of foreign business transactions—aside
from simple e-mail messages about the current state of the
grape crop in Burgundy. Access to foreign markets can be critical to the economic health of a particular company or to an
entire segment of the technology industry. Foreign competition
can be the single most significant threat to a domestic concern.
Laws governing international competition are the laws you
are most likely to encounter in your international Internet
communications.

Two uniquely international issues are involved in computer
technology—military security and trade policy. In the United
States and elsewhere, computer technology is a vital tool of the

military. A set of laws has been designed to prevent the transportation of computer technology out of this country, especially to nations that are currently or potentially unfriendly to U.S. interests. In the mind-set of government officials, the potential transport of computer technology to unfriendly nations justifies governmental intervention in export transactions.

The trade policy issue involves foreign nations' policies that are inconsistent with U.S. law and domestic agendas for promotion of commercial growth. All countries have their own domestic and foreign policies that tend to favor their own citizens. Third-world countries are notorious for appearing to have some favorable trade policy designed to encourage the introduction of computer (and other) technology into their country. Usually, businesses in developed countries are interested in selling goods, technological or otherwise. On the other hand, lesser-developed countries usually are more interested in getting their hands on the technology necessary for setting up their own industries and providing jobs and cheaper goods for their own citizens. Some experienced politicians and international businessmen have discovered that trade policies in some countries that appear on the surface to encourage importation of technological goods often are nothing but a ruse to steal the technology.

These dominant themes—military security and trade policy— affect which international laws apply in your situation. As regards military security, the export laws are dominant. As regards trade policy, export and import laws apply. Thus, both issues affect product exportation and can affect product importation, as well.

Product Importation

If imported products are a threat to your business and you have intellectual property rights in your products, you have three basic ways to protect yourself: (1) enforce your intellectual property rights in the country of origin of the products; (2) enforce your rights at the point of importation into this country; or, (3) enforce your rights against sellers of the product in this country.

Enforcement of intellectual property rights against infringers in their own countries is costly and problematic; only a few who attempt such enforcement succeed. Certain U.S. laws are designed to enforce U.S. rights at the border by use of import restrictions based on imported products' infringement or contribution to infringement of U.S. rights. One such law, the Tariff Act of 1930, states:

> Unfair methods of competition and unfair acts in the importation of articles … or in their sale … the effect or tendency of which is to destroy or substantially injure an industry, officially and economically operated in the United States, or to prevent the establishment of such an industry, or to restrain or monopolize trade … are declared unlawful.[56]

Legal action under this law is called "Section 337 action" and is used to bar the importation of goods that meet certain requirements. The law does not establish a private civil right of action, but creates criteria for regulation of imports by the International Trade Commission (ITC). Enforcement of Section 337 begins with an ITC investigation that can be initiated by a complaint filed by an interested party.[57] Section 337 actions move very rapidly (relative to court cases involving patent or copyright infringement) and can be effective if you get the right help at the front end.

In 1984, Apple Computer sought general exclusion of Taiwanese computers that infringed its microcomputer copyrights and patents.[58] Apple established that the ROM chips in a number of imported microcomputers infringed the copyrights to portions of Apple's proprietary operating system. In most cases, the imports in question were exact duplications of Apple programs with only slight modifications designed to display the importer's, rather than Apple's, brand name. An exclusion order was issued against all computers incorporating programs substantially similar to Apple's copyrighted works.

> **Note**
>
> Predicting exactly what types of Internet businesses can make best use of Section 337 is a difficult task. If you are in the software business, and foreign pirated copies of your programs are being brought into this country, you may look into Section 337 as another way to stop the importation of the pirated software.

But what about electronic importation? This issue is more difficult, because getting the customs agents to "block" all the wires coming into this country would be difficult. Software piracy on the Internet has been reported.[59] The Software Publishers Association (SPA) reported in the spring of 1993 that software theft had occurred on the "warez" channel. Copies of the popular Norton Utilities, Paradox, AutoCAD, and MS-DOS programs were being downloaded by Internet users from a host site. Apparently the host site has displayed little fear of prosecution, ostensibly because it is not in the U.S. Also apparent is that the host sites from which the pirated software can be downloaded are not physically located in countries that have strong antipiracy laws. Because the Internet has no central police, cracking down on the perpetrator is a difficult task.

The theory has been promoted that the illegal importation may best be attacked by targeting specific sections of the Internet that are providing the gateway into the U.S. network for investigation and legal action. Section 337 is one legal tool that could be used. Plain old copyright law enforcement against recipients is another weapon available to the SPA and proprietors of the software. Increased investigatory and law enforcement activity might be expected in the future if Internet software theft persists.

Introducing the Internet

Export Laws

In addition to import considerations, use of the Internet also involves export considerations. These considerations typically revolve around military security. As mentioned earlier in this section, the domestic importation laws are designed primarily to protect domestic interests from competition that is deemed unfair or contrary to U.S. industrial and legal policy. However, U.S. companies also compete in foreign markets. Companies in the U.S. want to export technology and its related products, because technology is one of the principal areas in which the United States excels.

Based on national security and foreign policy interests, the United States has maintained export regulations since the 1940s. As presently structured, such regulation exists under two primary statutes, one of which is the Arms Control and Disarmament Act, also called the Export Control Act.[60] This law deals primarily with the control of export of products and technology related to arms and munitions.

More significant for most exporters is the Export Administration Act of 1979 (the EAA).[61] The EAA has expired under its own terms, but export administration in fact now occurs under the emergency powers available to the president. The export controls consist mainly of a complex licensing system that is keyed to classification lists administered primarily through the Office of Export Administration (OEA) of the Department of Commerce. The system also involves the Department of Defense (DOD).

The OEA maintains two lists that affect or may affect Internet usage. These lists are set forth in the Code of Federal Regulations (CFR).[62] The first of these lists is the Commodity Control List (CCL), which encompasses hardware components of computer exports, as well as other types of goods. Separate CCLs exist for major categories, including electronic components, computers, telecommunications and cryptography products, and many other things. Each major category of goods is divided into five subgroups of products that are affected: A—equipment, assemblies, and components; B—production equipment; C—materials; D—software; and E—technology. The regulations also provide definitions of the things affected, such as definitions of "technology" and "technical data."[63]

To legally export any goods included in a Commodity Control List, the seller must obtain an export license for export to any country to which controls are applicable. The government also maintains lists of countries to which certain types of exports are prohibited. In general, items on this list require a "validated license," which essentially is a license for the particular export only. This license requires application to the OEA.

Virtually all computer hardware exports require that the seller possess an export license. Obtaining the license usually leads to delays that are disruptive of computer technology commerce. Nonetheless, this export licensing is the law as of writing this book, and it may be expected to survive in some form or another for the foreseeable future.

If you plan to transmit over the Internet virtually any data whatsoever overseas, you may be affected by the export laws. You probably need a license to avoid trouble if the data pertains to any item listed on a CCL. Getting the license is not difficult after you have been through it once or twice, but the first time can be an ordeal if you do not know what to do or how to do it. Again, some lawyers specialize in this area. Ask them to show you how to obtain the license.

International Proprietary Rights Issues

Another international trade issue arises in the context of proprietary rights protection. For copyrights and patents, international treaties or "conventions" establish a degree of protection against international discrimination in protecting the rights of authors and inventors of one country from actions taken in another country. The primary patent law treaties are the Patent Cooperation Treaty (PCT) and the Paris Convention.[64] In the copyright realm, such protection is provided by the Berne Convention and the Universal Copyright Convention.[65]

The Paris Convention is administered by the World Intellectual Property Organization (WIPO). WIPO is a United Nations organization of experts on intellectual property law that makes rules governing implementation of the conventions it oversees. The Paris Convention expressly recognizes that patents granted in one country are independent of those granted in another (the underlying premise of territoriality in patent law). However, the Convention further provides that nationals of any member country must be granted access to the same patent protections that are available to nationals of the other member countries, provided that local formalities are complied with. A limited international filing date priority is provided under the Paris Convention. This filing date priority allows a patent filing in one participating country to have a right of priority in all others for 12 months.

Unless you are concerned with patents, these conventions may not be of interest to you. However, if you have a patent portfolio and anticipate significant foreign markets, consult with your patent attorney about foreign patents.

As mentioned earlier in this section, international copyright protections are governed by two distinct treaty systems. The first is the Berne Convention, in which the United States is now a party, and the second is the Universal Copyright Convention (UCC). The UCC, not to be confused with the Uniform Commercial Code, requires contracting countries to offer the same copyright protection for works of foreign citizens of other contracting countries as those provided for works of their own citizens.

While these international agreements establish some international consistency, national laws vary widely. Be aware that if copyright questions arise in an international context, you need to consider the territoriality of the question. If you sell mass-market software, you are no doubt aware that thieves can send a copy of the program over the Internet to one of those pirate hosts in a foreign country. You may be prudent to take extra steps to register your copyright or seek copyright advice in particular countries so that you can take steps to enforce your rights in certain foreign countries (such as gateway countries).

Transborder Data Flow

Another international trade issue is that of "transborder data flows." In addition to considering the import and export issues, Internet users should be aware that other countries have their own import and export laws that can affect Internet usage. A significant concern at any country's border is the reconciliation of competing interests—the international mobility of information assets, versus the government's desire to control internal assets and processes related to its economic and social systems. These concerns manifest themselves in various laws, aside from, strictly speaking, import and export laws.

Privacy laws are another international trade concern of users of the Internet, because each country has its own privacy laws. You probably are not surprised that every country doesn't take the same position on issues regarding privacy protection of electronically stored or transmitted data. Oddly, many countries have more stringent privacy protection than the United States. With the exception of data collection regulations, where U.S. consumerism has created restrictions second to none, privacy protection in the United States is relatively weak. In the U.S., privacy laws typically are organized around individual action in administrative or judicial forums to enforce individual rights. Such provisions are not common in many foreign countries.

Some western countries have established more elaborate administrative and licensing systems for personal data creation in use in computer systems.[66] Some European countries have data collection and usage guidelines that relate to privacy protection.[67] For the present, be aware that the European countries appear to be taking an active lead in the development of laws in the area of privacy protection, primarily due to the impetus of the European Community.

Computer Crime

A popular perception is that computer crime is a major social concern. Just how widespread computer crime has become is not clear. By their very nature, computer crimes often are difficult to detect and difficult to prove. One particular aspect of computer crime that comes up in connection with Internet usage is the question of unauthorized access to and use of computer systems owned by another. Although all accessible hosts on the Internet are, to some degree, like open doors that enable you to go in and look around, you generally have no right to go "behind the counter." Logging onto someone's host as a guest is very similar to walking into a store—you can look around and inspect the merchandise and buy it, if it's for sale. However, as in a store, you cannot legally poke into the cash register and take money (or steal cycles, because in computers, time is money), or go in the back room and pilfer the goods.

The Internet Worm and the Federal Computer Crime Act

No doubt the most celebrated case involving criminal law and the Internet was the case of Robert Morris. Morris, ironically enough, was the son of the computer security guru Bob Morris Sr., then chief scientist at the National Computer Security Center of the National Security Agency (NSA). In 1988, the junior Morris introduced a virus program (which some characterized as a "worm") that affected UNIX computers on the Internet.[68] The worm, transmitted by the Internet, rapidly multiplied out of control and caused many computer systems (estimated in the thousands) to shut down or become temporarily unusable. It took several days to figure out the program and disable it.

Morris was prosecuted under a major federal law called the Computer Fraud and Abuse Act[69] (also called the Computer Crime Act). This law deals with several forms of computer abuse involving computers operated by the United States government or computer systems that cross state lines. Among the prohibited activities are:

> accessing a computer that falls within specified security categories with intent or reason to know that the information is to be used to the injury of the United States or to the advantage of a foreign nation;

> accessing a computer to obtain information in a financial record of a financial institution, or a card issuer, or contained in a file of a consumer credit reporting agency on a consumer, as such terms are defined in the Fair Credit Reporting Act;

> accessing a computer system without authority or beyond authorized access in a system that is operated exclusively for the government or, where the access affects government use of the system;

> accessing a federal interest computer with intent to defraud or to obtain anything of value other than the mere use of the computer;

> intentionally and without authorization accessing a federal interest computer to alter, damage, or destroy information, or to prevent authorized use of the information or the computer; and

accessing information regarding passwords or similar access information that affects interstate or foreign commerce.[70]

Most of the prohibited acts of "accessing" are prefaced by terms such as "knowingly," "intentionally," "with intent to defraud," "without authorization or exceeding authorized access," or similar language. Thus, mere use of the computer by authorized users is permitted (as it should be), but exceeding one's boundaries can get one in trouble. It is important that system operators make their access policies clear up front, so that if problems from unauthorized access occur, proving that perpetrators exceeded their authorization will not be difficult.

Morris defended himself on the ground that he did not have the required intent to cause damage or deny others access to their computers. His conviction was upheld on appeal,[71] and he was sentenced to three years' probation, 400 hours of community services, and a fine of $10,000.[72]

Forms of Computer Abuse

Because the federal Computer Crime Act deals primarily with federal-interest computers, it does not provide a comprehensive, national, criminal-law framework for computer abuse. Nonetheless, the law does deal with many significant aspects of computer crime. You can discern three distinct forms of computer abuse by analyzing the provisions of the law. The first of these forms is computer abuse involving national security interests. It is a criminal offense to access a computer without authorization or to use the computer beyond authorization to obtain information falling within specified security categories, with the intent that the information so obtained be used to the injury of the United States or to the advantage of a foreign government. This provision, basically, is a computer espionage law.

A second type of computer abuse covered by the Computer Crime Act involves the use, modification, destruction, or disclosure of information in a computer system accessed without authority or used beyond the purposes of the authorized access. The provision against this form of abuse probably applies only to computers operated for or on behalf of the government of the United States. Thus, this aspect of the law has a distinctly federal-government-owned-computer flavor to it.

The third form of computer abuse covered by the Computer Crime Act may be the broadest. Certain aspects of the law provide a basis for enforcing individual financial privacy against unauthorized access in a computer environment. Under the law, it is a criminal offense to access a computer without authorization and obtain information contained in a financial record of a financial institution. Violation of these laws is a felony punishable by up to 10 years in prison and a $10,000 fine.

Wiretapping and the Electronic Communications Privacy Act

Several of the provisions of the Computer Crime Act clearly show that Congress was concerned with privacy issues when it passed the law. The "Privacy Issues" section, later in this chapter, gives further consideration to this area of the law. Here, however, we need to make mention of the other principal federal statute that applies to computer crime. In 1986, Congress passed the Electronic Communications Privacy Act, also called the ECPA.[73] This law was an amendment to preexisting federal wiretapping regulations. The ECPA extended the wiretapping laws to data communications and by prohibiting various nonaural interceptions of private communications. Basically, the law created a new federal crime of unauthorized access to stored communications. The crime consists of the following types of activities:

> intentionally accessing without authorization a facility through which an electronic communication service is provided;

intentionally exceeding an authorization to access that facility.

Summarized, the meaning of this law is that someone who logs in to a computer system under someone else's name and password without the individual's consent, or who figures out a way to hack in through a back door without authorization, commits a federal crime. Likewise, one who intercepts another's e-mail messages without authorization (for example, a valid search warrant) also commits a federal crime.

The ECPA, because it was born from federal wiretapping laws, was primarily intended to force government agencies to obtain warrants for wiretaps in connection with criminal investigations. The law also was intended to close a gap in the wiretap laws that were ambiguous as to their application to data communications. The ECPA's principal focus is on data in transit, rather than on information that has already reached its destination and is merely being stored. However, in the Internet e-mail context, messages that are being routed from one system to the next, with interim storage in a way station, may be subject to the law.

Arguably, if the sender or the recipient of an e-mail message consents to the wiretap, the wiretap is not a violation of this law. On the other hand, the viewing of others' e-mail messages passing through your system may be subject to the law. No law requires that e-mail facilities be provided on anybody's system anywhere. Arguably, however, the ECPA requires that if you undertake to pass private messages, you abide by these regulations, because reading the e-mail of others technically violates the law.

Considering these laws, it is probably a good idea to post a notice to e-mail users that their mail is not private and that the system operator and others may read and inspect the content of any unencrypted messages. Because the ECPA has so many aspects aside from its criminal penalties, we discuss this law in greater detail later in the "Privacy Issues" section.

Computer Fraud and Embezzlement

Aside from viruses and the breaking and entering paradigm, various types of acts attain a criminal aspect when implemented through a computer. For example, an embezzlement scheme might be more lucrative by virtue of high-speed data transmissions—one can transfer a lot more money a lot more quickly by a wire transfer than by carrying cash. Cash is easy to spot and more difficult to launder, and banks are required to report cash transaction of more than $10,000. Wire transfers are fairly tightly controlled, but in some senses, credit card account numbers are like cash. "Postings" and other communications of stolen credit card numbers have been reported.[74]

As we mentioned earlier, computer crimes are difficult to detect and prove. Of course, problems of detection and proof are exacerbated by electronic media; the evidence itself is somewhat transient unless it is made tangible by printouts or by storage on a tangible medium. Because electronic storage is by nature changeable, the probative value of electronically stored evidence is questionable. Reportedly, the case of the California BBS sysop (system operator) who posted stolen credit card numbers was dropped because the prosecutor anticipated difficulty proving that the sysop knew that stolen credit card numbers were posted on his system.[75]

State Computer Crime Laws

The federal laws relating to computer crime typically require some type of federal or interstate involvement. Most crimes involving Internet usage will more likely than not have an interstate flavor. Even though the Morris case was one of the first involving criminal law and the Internet, it probably will not be the last, because Internet communications generally have some interstate and international aspects.

Individual states have an interest in controlling computer crime within their jurisdictions. Most states have their own computer crime legislation. Each state's law is slightly different. The federal government does not have a specific "computer crime" statute that can be generally applied, but it has long recognized various types of computer-related activities as being criminal. As long ago as 1976 (a veritable eternity in computer time), the federal government classified four basic categories of activities as types of computer crime:

(1) introduction of false data into a system,

(2) unauthorized use of computer facilities,

(3) altering or destroying data, and

(4) taking money or services through a computer.[76]

These activities also are generally the same types of activities that are on the books of various states as state computer crimes. The federal government did not implement a specific computer-crime-related law until the Computer Crime Act. The various types of activities classified as "computer crime" in many states include other types of behavior. Georgia's computer crime law, in its entirety, is as follows:

> 16-9-93. **Computer crimes defined; exclusivity of article; civil remedies; criminal penalties.**

> (a) *Computer Theft.* Any person who uses a computer or computer network with knowledge that such use is without authority and with the intention of:

> > (1) Taking or appropriating any property of another, whether or not with the intention of depriving the owner of possession;

> > (2) Obtaining property by any deceitful means or artful practice; or

(3) Converting property to such person's use in violation of an agreement or other known legal obligation to make a specified application or disposition of such property

shall be guilty of the crime of computer theft.

(b) *Computer Trespass*. Any person who uses a computer or computer network with knowledge that such use is without authority and with the intention of:

(1) Deleting or in any way removing, either temporarily or permanently, any computer program or data from a computer or computer network;

(2) Obstructing, interrupting, or in any way interfering with the use of a computer program or data; or

(3) Altering, damaging, or in any way causing the malfunction of a computer, computer network, or computer program, regardless of how long the alteration, damage, or malfunction persists

shall be guilty of the crime of computer trespass.

(c) *Computer Invasion of Privacy*. Any person who uses a computer or computer network with the intention of examining any employment, medical, salary, credit, or any other financial or personal data relating to any other person with knowledge that such examination is without authority shall be guilty of the crime of computer invasion of privacy.

(d) *Computer Forgery*. Any person who creates, alters, or deletes any data contained in any computer or computer network, who, if such person had created, altered, or deleted a tangible document or instrument would have committed forgery under Article 1 of this chapter shall be guilty of the crime of computer forgery. The absence of a tangible writing directly created or altered by the offender shall not be a defense to the crime of computer forgery if a creation, alteration, or deletion of data was involved in lieu of a tangible document or instrument.

(e) *Computer Password Disclosure.* Any person who discloses a number, code, password, or other means of access to a computer or computer network knowing that such disclosure is without authority and which results in damages (including the fair market value of any services used and victim expenditure) to the owner of the computer or computer network in excess of $500.00 shall be guilty of the crime of computer password disclosure.

(f) *Article not Exclusive.* The provisions of this article shall not be construed to preclude the applicability of any other law which presently applies or may in the future apply to any transaction or course of conduct which violates this article.

(g) *Civil Relief; Damages.* (1) Any person whose property or person is injured by reason of a violation of any provision of this article may sue therefore and recover for any damages sustained and the costs of suit. Without limiting the generality of the term, "damages" shall include loss of profits and victim expenditure.

   (2) At the request of any party to an action brought pursuant to this Code section, the court shall by reasonable means conduct all legal proceedings in such a way as to protect the secrecy and security of any computer, computer network, data, or computer program involved in order to prevent possible recurrence of the same or a similar act by another person and to protect any trade secrets of any party.

   (3) The provisions of this article shall not be construed to limit any person's right to pursue any additional civil remedy otherwise allowed by law.

(4) A civil action under this Code section must be brought within four years after the violation is discovered or by exercise of reasonable diligence should have been discovered. For purposes of this article, a continuing violation of any one subsection of this Code section by any person constitutes a single violation by such person.

(h) *Criminal Penalties.* (1) Any person convicted of the crime of computer theft, computer trespass, computer invasion of privacy, or computer forgery shall be fined not more than $50,000.00 or imprisoned not more than 15 years, or both.

(2) Any person convicted of computer password disclosure shall be fined not more than $5,000.00 or incarcerated for a period not to exceed one year, or both.[77]

You may note that the Georgia law includes provisions relating to criminal modification of data. These laws probably would relate to data vandalism, where someone modifies or corrupts the data of others. Introduction of a virus can involve these laws, because a virus often causes the modification or corruption of key security files or other critical system functions. One obvious threat is that an unauthorized user may intentionally or negligently destroy or alter data in the system, causing harm to someone. More than 15 states have direct criminal sanctions for unauthorized alteration, modification, or destruction of computer data, including computer programs.

Other state laws are similar. For example, New York's laws prohibit the following types of acts:

unauthorized use of a computer service;

computer trespass (which goes beyond mere unauthorized access or use, and involves intent to commit a felony or gain access to confidential information);

computer tampering (which involves altering data or programs, and probably introducing a virus);

unlawful duplication of computer-related material (which may be unconstitutional by virtue of the operation of the preemption provisions of the Copyright Act[78]); and

knowing possession of programs or data that were unlawfully copied.[79]

Other State Criminal Laws

Various state laws that are already on the books and pertain to various types of crimes are applicable whether or not a computer system is used. Thus, certain types of criminal activities are "criminal" whether or not they involve the use of a computer. Nonetheless, the term "computer crime" often is invoked when a computer is used in conjunction with such crimes. In such cases, traditional theft crimes, computer fraud, information theft, trade secret theft, criminal access to a computer, and criminal modification of data all are lumped together with computer crime, although the elements of each of these crimes vary widely from state to state.

In regard to traditional theft crimes, financial fraud involving computers can be prosecuted under state laws by applying traditional theft-related criminal statutes. Traditional theft crimes include larceny, embezzlement, false pretenses, forgery, and similar crimes. General financial fraud cases do not require any new thinking about the application of criminal law on fraud and theft.

Because each state has different laws, you need to check out what the laws are in your state. Be on the lookout particularly for statutes that pertain specifically to computers.

Theft of Trade Secrets and Information

Another criminal activity is that referred to as "information theft." This category of activity is sometimes considered together with "trade secret" laws. Information theft may be considered to have occurred in a situation involving access to and the copying or taking of information in the form of data, computer programs, formulas, and the like. Such concepts may apply even if the material taken is not copyrightable subject matter (which has its own civil and criminal penalties). Note that this activity may be distinguished from that involving money, real estate, or other tangible property that formerly was controlled by a victim. Cash and personal property are tangible, identifiable items. A criminal who accesses a database and obtains secret information takes intangible property.

Some states have modified their laws to redefine "property" taken under theft statutes to include computer data and software. Again, users should consult the laws in their own jurisdiction.

Further, a significant body of state law prohibits theft or misappropriation of trade secrets. Trade secret laws are often used to provide legal civil law protection for information that may have commercial value, such as the masks for an integrated circuit, the source code of a computer program, a list of customers, and so on. Usually, the owner of valuable commercial information attempts to keep it secret by requiring that all persons who have access to the information bind themselves via contract (for example, a nondisclosure agreement) to keep the information secret and not to use it to their own personal financial advantage. The taking of trade secrets also can have criminal implication, aside from the civil implications of being sued in civil court for misappropriation of a trade secret.

Many state trade secret laws include definitions of "trade secret" and specify acts involving the improper taking of trade secrets that amount to civil or criminal wrongs. The Georgia law is instructive and exemplary in this regard:

> As used in this article, the term:
>
> (1) "Improper means" includes theft, bribery, misrepresentation, breach or inducement of a breach of a confidential

relationship or other duty to maintain secrecy or limit use, or espionage through electronic or other means. Reverse engineering of a trade secret not acquired by misappropriation or independent development shall not be considered improper means.

(2) "Misappropriation" means:

    (A) Acquisition of a trade secret of another by a person who knows or has reason to know that the trade secret was acquired by improper means; or

    (B) Disclosure or use of a trade secret of another without express or implied consent by a person who:

        (i)   Used improper means to acquire knowledge of a trade secret;

        (ii) At the time of disclosure or use, knew or had reason to know that knowledge of the trade secret was:

            (I)   Derived from or through a person who had utilized improper means to acquire it;

            (II) Acquired under circumstances giving rise to a duty to maintain its secrecy or limit its use; or

            (III) Derived from or through a person who owed a duty to the person seeking relief to maintain its secrecy or limit its use; or

        (iii) Before a material change of position, knew or had reason to know that it was a trade secret and that knowledge of it had been acquired by accident or mistake.

    ...

(4) "Trade secret" means information including, but not limited to, technical or nontechnical data, a formula, a pattern, a compilation, a program, a device, a method,

a technique, a drawing, a process, financial data, financial plans, product plans, or a list of actual or potential customers or suppliers which:

(A)   Derives economic value, actual or potential, from not being generally known to, and not being readily ascertainable by proper means by other persons who can obtain economic value from its disclosure or use; and

(B)   Is the subject of efforts that are reasonable under the circumstances to maintain its secrecy.[80]

Information contained on a computer system can be a trade secret. Merely because information is on an Internet-accessible computer does not necessarily mean that the information cannot be a trade secret. Such information's status as a trade secret, however, will depend on the "efforts that are reasonable under the circumstances to maintain its secrecy"—for example, factors such as the security barriers erected to prevent unauthorized access, encryption of secret files, whether there is a user agreement specifying that certain information in certain files is a trade secret and should be kept secret, the use of notices to warn that certain areas are restricted, and so on. Aspects of computer programs also can be trade secrets, but note in the Georgia law that reverse-engineering of a trade secret not acquired by misappropriation or independent development is not considered "improper means."

Other states' trade secret laws are similar to Georgia's in many respects. Some civil laws relate to trade secrets, as do some criminal laws. All such laws typically define the subject of the taking as material that possesses relative novelty and secrecy, and material that possesses a commercial benefit by not being generally known to others. In California, theft of a "trade secret" is generally defined as the taking of any "scientific or technical information, design, process, procedure, formula, computer program or information stored in the computer …

which is secret and is not generally available to the public and [which] gives one who uses it an advantage over competitors who do not know of or use the trade secret."[81] Criminal theft of a trade secret can occur regardless of whether a nondisclosure agreement exists between the proprietor and the thief, although the existence of a contractual arrangement can give rise to civil liability as well as criminal liability.

In concluding our discussion of trade secrets, we point out that system operators should be careful to identify aspects of their Internet-accessible systems that may contain trade secrets and take steps to prevent unauthorized access. Such steps may include password protection, partitioning the storage resources to prevent external access to trade secret materials, posting authorization access notices (see the next section), and obtaining secrecy agreements with key personnel who may have legitimate access to the materials.

The Use of Notices To Prove Unauthorized Access

As we discussed earlier, many computer crime laws are premised on someone exceeding their authorization, or accessing a system without any authorization whatsoever. In the Robert Morris case, Mr. Morris defended (unsuccessfully, we might add) on the ground that he was authorized to be on all those systems he shut down. Clearly, it is trickier to pin the blame for a computer trespass on someone who has lawful access to your system. The Georgia law listed earlier uses the language "without authority," which arguably (but not expressly) covers the situation where one either exceeds one's authority or operates with no authorization at all. Proof that someone accessed your system "without authority" would help your case when the criminal is tried in court.

Under New York's laws, unauthorized use of a computer service by an otherwise authorized user can be proven more easily if users are provided with notice not to go beyond a certain point.

If you run a BBS or data files accessible on the Internet, you may want to consider displaying a notice similar to this:

> IMPORTANT NOTICE—Only users pre-authorized by the system operator are permitted to access, download, or upload files in this area. If somehow you have obtained access to this notice and this area of the system without express authorization by the system operator, please log off immediately or return to an area in which you are authorized. You are hereby notified that persons accessing the files, programs, or other information in this section without authorization will be subject to prosecution to the full extent of the law.[82]

The Prodigy user agreement includes the following language, which (one could argue) at least puts users on notice of authorization to access:

> Unauthorized access to the Service, to restricted portions of the Service, or to the telecommunications or computer facilities used to deliver the Service, is a breach of this Agreement and a violation of law.[83]

The legal effect of such an "authorization notice" has not yet been fully tested in the courts. However, such a notice may prove instrumental in proving lack of authorization, and you are probably well advised as a system operator to include such a notice.

Other Federal Criminal Laws May Apply

The interstate aspects of Internet usage complicate the determination as to which state's law may apply if a criminal act is perpetrated in one state that has one set of laws, and the crime carries over into another state that has another set of laws. Given the interstate and international aspects of the Internet, one may expect that federal criminal provisions will come into play in such cases as those just described. The federal government usually doesn't get involved in property crimes, however, and leaves such matters to state and local governments.

Traditionally, the federal government has taken a secondary role in defining and enforcing property crimes, except when those crimes infringe on federal institutions or interests. The Computer Crime Act is a classic example of the U.S. government's reluctance to encroach upon states' rights in this regard. One federal statute that could be used for computer-related offenses prohibits theft, embezzlement, or conversion of United States property.[84] Of course, this statute would apply only where the United States has some property interest in the subject of the theft.

Other, not strictly computer-related, federal criminal statutes could be applied to a computer crime, as could various state laws, especially when a crime has distinctly interstate or international attributes. Current laws prohibit mail fraud, and they apply to any use of the mails to execute or attempt a scheme to defraud.[85] Additionally, current "wire fraud" laws expressly apply to any use of wires, radio, or television communication to accomplish fraudulent purposes across state lines.[86] Both statutes may apply to computer crimes that involve interstate communications, especially the wire fraud laws, because they expressly refer to the use of wires.

Federal laws prohibit the engagement in electronic surveillance under color of law (except as authorized by statute).[87] The laws appear to apply to any interceptions of information (aural or nonaural), interception from stages of data communications, and disclosure or use of information obtained under color of law by electronic surveillance.

Interstate transportation of stolen goods is a federal crime.[88] The statute, although it expressly applies to the transportation of tangible goods, might be applied in cases where intangible data such as stolen trade secrets are transported across state lines.

Another statute relates to criminal activities under the Electronic Funds Transfer Act (EFTA).[89] This statute defines electronic funds transfer as any "transfer of funds ... which is initiated through an electronic terminal, telephonic instrument, or computer ... [to] authorize a financial institution to debit or credit an account." To the extent a computer-based activity results in wrongful charging of an account via a stolen credit card number, the EFTA criminal provisions may be applicable.

In closing out our discussion on computer crime, we need to remind you that you should familiarize yourself with the computer crime laws in the states in which you plan to conduct activities, to get an idea as to the types of activities you need to be on the lookout for. If you discover that a hacker or other person is engaging in unauthorized access, tampering, is in possession of unlawful materials, and so on, you have a firmer grasp of the situation if you already know which state laws apply. Prosecutors in state courts probably will be less computer literate than you are, and you will find it easier to attract their interest in a case if you already know the laws that apply and have a start on gathering information that might serve as evidence. Keep a paper trail of the events that lead to your discovery of the problem. Read Cliff Stoll's book, mentioned earlier in this chapter, for a good overview of the type of data that needs to be kept, preferably in paper form for ultimate introduction as documentary evidence in a court proceeding.

Finally, if you suspect an interstate or international connection to the problem, you may very well have to approach federal authorities with your information. You will want to try to invoke one or more of the federal laws pertaining to computer crime. As with a state computer crime, you will need to keep careful records, preferably in a permanent form such as a paper printout that is less susceptible to electronic alteration.

Privacy Issues

In the United States especially, individual privacy is a significant societal value. Where else in the world can one expect, in general, to be let alone? Certainly not in the (present or former) Soviet Union, or some other socialist states. The desire to be let alone, especially in areas of religious freedom, led to the formation of this country.

Most people will agree that individual privacy is protected by constitutional provisions. Many people fail to remember, however, that privacy in any organized society is not absolute, and that privacy protection represents a tradeoff between the interests of the society in law and order and the interest of the individual to be let alone. Even in civilized society, balancing these interests against each other involves debate and political struggle.

Much of that debate revolves around the extent to which the law should protect individual privacy and balance the need for privacy against societal concerns. The United States probably is unique in drawing the line as close as it does to individuals than to the society. In 1928, Justice Brandeis described the right to privacy as "the right to be let alone—the most comprehensive of rights and the right most valued by civilized men."[90] Privacy may also be defined as the claim of individuals, groups, or institutions to determine for themselves when, how, and to what extent information about them is communicated to others. This aspect of privacy law primarily comes into play in connection with the gathering and selling financial information, a typical credit bureau activity.

As you consider your privacy concerns as an Internet user, you are wise to keep in mind that, because we live in a society, privacy is not an absolute principle. This advice is even more significant when one realizes that the Internet itself is not merely a communication between an individual and a computer, but involves the shared access of a number of different individuals to various resources, sometimes simultaneously. Thus, users themselves must establish a balance between individual interests in privacy and the interests of society, or find greater government involvement in its use.

Aspects of Privacy

Privacy issues manifest themselves in two principal aspects. The first of these aspects has to do with the right to privacy in telecommunications. Does anyone have a right to inspect or monitor your communications with others? This right comes to mind when considering whether the information transmitted pertains to a private business transaction, or whether the information may be judged obscene or seditious. The issue is particularly significant in respect to e-mail (more discussion on this topic occurs later in the chapter).

A second and significant aspect of the privacy question pertains to the collection of information about individuals and the access or lack of access to that information. Many people perceive the accumulation and use of data about individuals to be a major threat. Obviously, accumulating data about individuals makes little sense unless the information is to be used for some particular purpose. While none of us particularly care for the notion of the Internal Revenue Service collecting information about us, society has an interest in insuring that taxes are paid (although many may disagree with this statement).

The realm of data collection encompasses four principal aspects of individual and societal rights of privacy. First is the right of the government to collect data about its citizens. Second is the right of members of society to request and receive the data collected by the government. Third is the right of private entities—typically, businesses such as credit bureaus—to collect data about people. Finally comes the right of individuals to see that privately collected data is accurate (we can't do much to stop private data collection that is lawfully performed).

Space does not permit a full exploration of these complex issues. However, the United States has on the books several major laws that govern these four principal aspects of privacy in data collection. In the following sections we highlight several of these major laws and leave you with the usual admonishment to seek counsel if you have a particular problem in a particular area.

Privacy in Telecommunications

Internet usage involves telecommunications of various natures—between host and host, user and host, user and user via e-mail, and so on. These telecommunications are similar in many respects to simple telephone conversations. Indeed, digitized telephone conversations are often intermixed with data communications by the communications transport companies, and many Internet users obtain access to the network via telephone line dialup line. It would be normal to expect that many of the same laws should apply to both Internet communications and "regular" communications.

When a stand-alone computer system operates in a private manner and does not invite or facilitate intrusions, you naturally may expect it to be afforded the same protection given to any other private property. However, when a system is connected to an internetwork such as the Internet, where the whole idea is communications, different rules of protection must apply. In today's society, anyone is silly to expect that if they open the door and leave it wide open, nobody will come in. But that is just what some people try to achieve—they open the door because they want to come and go as they please, and they are not inviting you in just because they leave their door open. Most of us know that this behavior is somewhat unrealistic in a crowded, urban environment—and that perfectly describes the Internet environment.

Although the "front door" analogy is not strictly applicable, it does illustrate the principle, and it highlights the current movement toward encryption and security in computer communications. Such security measures are designed to allow users to come and go with (hopefully) minimal inconvenience, but to keep unwanted intruders out. Efforts presently are underway to develop and deploy Internet Privacy Enhanced Mail (PEM).[91] If secure e-mail systems such as PEM can be implemented successfully, it will become increasingly difficult for others (including legitimate government investigators with search warrants) to come in the "door." We can expect much more activity on this front in the coming years.

As we have discussed earlier, most states define unauthorized access to a computer system as a criminal offense. Criminal laws are not, strictly speaking, privacy laws; nonetheless, they often are used to enforce the right of a person to be let alone. Breaking and entering is a crime, whether you are talking about someone's house or about someone's computer system whose "door" is a telecommunications pathway. With the computer crime laws and a few separate privacy laws, society has established at least the beginnings of a zone of expected privacy and security for computer systems.

Breaking and entering a computer system (for example, obtaining unauthorized access) is, rather clearly, criminal behavior. This criminality would apply whether the burglar is seeking commercial information, trying to plant a virus, or attempting to monitor the communications (e-mail) on a mail server. After a communication leaves the originating computer system and enters the Internet, it is a different story. The communication has left the expected zone of privacy around the originating computer; the communication is "out in the street." As all urban dwellers know, when you're in the street, you might get mugged.

Fortunately, an electronic mugging is just a unlawful as an actual physical mugging. The operator of the telecommunications provider (Tymnet, AT&T, MCI, Telenet, the local phone company, and the local cable company, to name a few) has its own zone of expected privacy and security. The mugger who intercepts the Internet packet from AT&T is just as much a criminal as the mugger who has unauthorized access to the telecommunications line. Wiretapping is a federal crime.

But what about the situation where the interceptor is authorized to be there—for example, the sysop of a bulletin board or e-mail server, the operator of a commercial service like Prodigy or CompuServe, or a law enforcement officer engaged in a criminal investigation? In some situations, authorized people have legal access to communications on their system, and they may lawfully intercept communications between various entities.

The Constitutional Basis for the Right of Privacy

The basic constitutional provision relating to intercepted communications, at least in the case of government interceptions, comes from the Fourth Amendment. This amendment relates to the right to be protected against unreasonable searches and seizures. Generally, a governmental authority must have a warrant before it can search. Note, however, that the Fourth Amendment is intended to protect against unwanted *governmental* intrusion, and does not pertain to private action. Of course, no private person has the right to search and seize the property of another (except in certain contractual contexts), but this prohibition says nothing about the mere monitoring of telecommunications—arguably, monitoring does not amount to either a search or a seizure.

Generally, then, courts do not find a reasonable expectation of privacy from the mere use of a communication system. Indeed, there have been cases in which users of cordless and cellular telephones were found not to have a justifiable expectation of privacy for their conversations.[92] These cases are premised on the simple fact that the airwaves are public, and if you use the airwaves, you should expect that others may listen. Those who are installing wireless radio or optical data networks should be aware that it is possible for eavesdroppers to pick up the signals.

In regard to governmental monitoring or listening, two principal federal statutes apply. Both have their origins in the field of wiretapping and surveillance. One of these statutes is the Communications Act of 1934, which prohibits any action to intercept an interstate or foreign communication (by wire or radio) and divulge the communication.[93] The statute has been applied to unauthorized access to an electronic database system.[94]

The Electronic Communications Privacy Act

A second federal statute, which we mentioned earlier in connection with computer crime, is the Electronic Communications Privacy Act of 1986 (ECPA).[95] The ECPA amended existing wiretapping laws and made the laws more clearly applicable to electronic data communications, as contrasted with traditional telephone-type wiretapping. The ECPA is not limited strictly to governmental interception. It also applies to private interception.

Before the wiretapping laws were amended in 1986 by the ECPA, how the law applied to pure data communications was somewhat uncertain. The 1986 amendments made it clear that the wiretapping laws apply to any form of electronic communications. The ECPA generally prohibits any unauthorized interception or disclosure of wire, oral, or electronic communications. Thus, the ECPA's focus is on data "in transit," as opposed to data that has already reached a destination, either a final destination or an interim destination such as an e-mail server. Again, the key word is "unauthorized," so consent to interception makes a different story. As we discuss later, whether the law prohibits reading e-mail on an interim server is not clear.

The civil and criminal liability penalties for unauthorized interception are limited to cases where some effort has been made to restrict access to the system. No criminal or civil liability exists for intercepting an electronic communication made through an electronic communication system that is configured so that such electronic communication is "readily accessible" to the general public.[96] For example, a transmission may be readily accessible if it has not been scrambled or encrypted.[97] This treatment parallels trade secret law and is analogous to the open-door situation—if you put a lock on your door (encryption), you intend that the room (the communication) is private; but if you leave the door open, one may come in and browse with impunity (criminal and civil liability).

The ECPA sets forth criminal and civil penalties for unauthorized interception. In the case of interception of a private satellite video or radio transmission that isn't encrypted or scrambled, damages are limited to $500 or $1,000, depending on whether the violation is a first violation and whether the interception is for tortious or commercial gain. These provisions clearly are intended for the cable and satellite TV "private pirate" situation. In other cases, damages are the greater of either the actual damages to the plaintiff and the wrongdoer's profits, or statutory damages of a maximum of $10,000.[98]

The above penalties relate to private actions against unauthorized interception. In the case of governmental interception, the ECPA places significant procedural hurdles in the way of government agencies who conduct criminal investigations. While such hurdles are consistent with the American notion of privacy under the U.S. Constitution, they do make it harder for the government to enforce the law. Basically, any government agency must obtain a warrant before intercepting a communication, be it aural (telephone) or nonaural (data communications), and to obtain a warrant, must be able to show probable cause supported by oath or affirmation, specifying the place to be searched and the things or persons to be seized. This is straight Fourth Amendment stuff, except that the ECPA may be even more restrictive.

Can They Read My E-Mail?

Before turning to the question of how these laws affect e-mail, note again that any privacy right hinges to some degree on consent. Any communication necessarily implies at least two parties—a sender and a recipient. Consent by either party to monitoring or wiretapping can negate the protections afforded by law. Those who run bulletin boards, mail servers, or other communications-related services that use the Internet may want to explore the possibility and desirability of a contractual consent to the interception or monitoring of messages that pass through their system. For example, in its User Agreement, Prodigy prohibits certain types of potentially offensive materials, but claims that it will not read your e-mail:

> The Service lets you share information with other Members. You agree not to use the Service to send, or submit for public posting, any abusive, obscene, profane, sexually explicit, threatening, or illegal material, or material containing blatant expressions of bigotry, racism or hate. Prodigy reserves the right (but is not obligated) to review and edit any material submitted for display or placed on the Service, excluding private electronic messages. Prodigy may refuse to display or may remove from the Service any material that Prodigy believes violates this Agreement or any policies or guidelines posted by Prodigy on the Service, or is harmful to other Members, to Merchants or information providers, or to the Service or the business interests of Prodigy....

> Prodigy will comply in all respects with the Electronic Communications Privacy Act of 1986, as amended, relating to private electronic messages on the Service. "Private electronic messages" are only those messages sent to a Member for receipt through the Service's Message Center feature. Prodigy will not inspect the contents of private electronic messages, or disclose their contents to anyone

other than the writer or an intended recipient, without the consent of either the writer or an intended recipient, except as permitted or required by law.[99]

Although Prodigy did not require consent to inspection of e-mail as a condition of using the service, no apparent legal reason prohibits such a requirement. Even so, no clear evidence indicates that an e-mail server can readily circumvent the requirements of the ECPA merely by requiring consent to interception of messages as a condition of usage.

The law appears to offer no clear or consistent protection against government interception of transmissions if there is a contractual consent to interception. More and more commercial e-mail providers may be expected to utilize such consents in their user contracts, following the example of Prodigy (unless, of course, the users revolt). Commercial gateways to the Inter-net are in a better position than some to impose such a requirement as protection against the usage of their systems for criminal purposes. However, some governmental and educational institutions may not as readily impose contractual conditions upon usage.

Interim E-Mail Servers

Based on the ECPA, as an Internet e-mail user you have a reasonable expectation of privacy—at least some privacy. Any e-mail messages you send are not subject to being inspected by the government without a warrant—at least the messages are not subject to such inspection while "in transit." But what about the situation where the e-mail is stored in an interim server; and what about the e-mail service provider itself? Can these entities access and read your e-mail? Probably, yes.

There may be no constitutional protection of e-mail messages in an interim server. The Constitution may or may not offer such protection, but the issue has yet to be considered in the courts.

In most e-mail systems, messages are passed over public network facilities and often stored in a third-party computer for later access. The delayed access nature of computer systems makes the situation very different from traditional telephone or mail systems, because the service provider (the network) is the custodian of the message for at least a limited time.

In this regard, the ECPA has the following provision that appears to relate to telecommunications providers, interim e-mail servers, gateways, and the like:

> It shall not be unlawful under this chapter for an operator of a switchboard, or an officer, employee, or agent of a provider of wire or electronic communication service, whose facilities are used in the transmission of a wire communication, to intercept, disclose, or use that communication in the normal course of his employment while engaged in any activity which is a necessary incident to the rendition of his service or to the protection of the rights or property of the provider of that service, except that a provider of wire communication service to the public shall not utilize service observing or random monitoring except for mechanical or service quality control checks.[100]

This provision is the very first of a long list of exceptions to the general prohibition against unauthorized interception and disclosure of electronic communications. The provision seems to suggest that it's OK for an operator of an interim server, gateway, or other e-mail facility to intercept communications. The permissibility of the interception is premised on the meaning of "normal course of his employment while engaged in any activity which is a necessary incident to the rendition of his service." As long as the interception occurs somewhat casually—such as while running routine deletion of e-mail messages over 180 days old, when moving files around while conducting system maintenance, or while troubleshooting a problem—then reading the e-mail of others is permitted and not criminal. Thus, users of e-mail cannot have expectations of complete privacy.

Contrast this against another provision of the ECPA:

(a) **Offense.**—Except as provided in subsection (c) of this section whoever

    (1) intentionally accesses without authorization a facility through which an electronic communication service is provided; or

    (2) intentionally exceeds an authorization to access that facility;

and thereby obtains, alters, or prevents authorized access to a wire or electronic communication while it is in electronic storage in such system shall be punished as provided in subsection (b) of this section.

   ...

(c) **Exceptions.**—Subsection (a) of this section does not apply with respect to conduct authorized—

    (1) by the person or entity providing a wire or electronic communications service;

    (2) by a user of that service with respect to a communication of or intended for that user; or

    (3) in section 2703, 2704 or 2518 of this title. [The latter sections relating to government wiretaps].[101]

This portion of the ECPA again is premised on the notion of "authorization," and suggests that system operators, telecommunications providers, and others who have legitimate responsibilities in connection with an "electronic communication service" are permitted to access the contents of the service. But what they can do with such access is another matter.

Another section of the ECPA relates to disclosure of the contents of electronic communications. This section appears to prohibit disclosure of the contents of e-mail messages (or other communication), even if the person accessing the e-mail was authorized to do so:

(a) **Prohibitions.**—Except as provided in subsection (b)—

   (1) a person or entity providing an electronic communication service to the public shall not knowingly divulge to any person or entity the contents of a communication while in electronic storage by that service; and

   (2) a person or entity providing remote computing service to the public shall not knowingly divulge to any person or entity the contents of any communication which is carried or maintained on that service—

       (A) on behalf of, and received by means of electronic transmission from (or created by means of computer processing of communications received by means of electronic transmission from), a subscriber or customer of such service; and

       (B) solely for the purpose of providing storage or computer processing services to such subscriber or customer, if the provider is not authorized to access the contents of any such communications for purposes of providing any services other than storage or computer processing.

(b) **Exceptions.**—A person or entity may divulge the contents of a communications—

   (1) to an addressee or intended recipient of such communication or an agent of such addressee or intended recipient;

(2) as otherwise authorized in section 2617, 2511(2)(a), or 2703 of this title;

(3) with the lawful consent of the originator or an addressee or intended recipient of such communication, or the subscriber in the case of remote computing service;

(4) to a person employed or authorized or whose facilities are used to forward such communication to its destination;

(5) as may be necessarily incident to the rendition of the service or to the protection of the rights or property of the provider of that service; or

(6) to a law enforcement agency, if such contents—

  (A) were inadvertently obtained by the service provider; and

  (B) appear to pertain to the commission of a crime.[102]

Absent specific statutory protection beyond the ECPA, which has its limitations, there is no clearly defined absolute privacy interest in e-mail, especially after it reaches an interim destination. Further, the ECPA clearly indicates that e-mail can be intercepted and read if one of the parties to the communication has consented to the interception,[103] or if the e-mail service provider is looking at the mail in furtherance of the service provider's normal administrative duties.

Some legal commentators believe that, because information on a BBS is essentially on public display, electronic mail and bulletin board systems are subject to routine inspection of their message content by law enforcement agencies without a search warrant.[104] The bottom line is that while you may have some privacy, it is not absolute, and that the laws are complex, wordy, and in constant change.

One final note about the ECPA—180 days is a magic number if you are an e-mail server. If an e-mail message has been in storage less than 180 days, a search warrant is required by a government agency to obtain the message.[105] After 180 days, however, you can be forced to produce any stored or archived messages with only a subpoena. A subpoena is much easier for a government agency to generate than a search warrant—a judge is required to sign a warrant, while a subpoena can be issued by a clerk of court. This fact provides an incentive to delete messages before they become 180 days old.

Because much of the privacy law affecting Internet usage may well come from ECPA, a summary of some of the ECPA's more significant provisions may be helpful to you. The following summary of ECPA provisions affecting system operators comes from the book *SYSLAW—The Sysop's Legal Manual*:[106]

> You have a right to be protected against users who invade your system via tricks or false pretenses and destroy or tamper with messages or data.
>
> Law enforcement authorities must obtain a search warrant to obtain information on your system under 180 days old.
>
> You should have no liability to a user for wrongful disclosure as long as you are acting in response to a warrant, subpoena, or court order.
>
> You must not disclose information on your system that you have promised your users (via their service contracts or otherwise) will be private.
>
> You must provide user records, user lists, time records, etc. maintained on your system (as opposed to user messages such as e-mail) in response to a subpoena.
>
> The government can require you to keep a backup copy of user information, but you have to give notice to the individual whose files the government is seeking. This provision is presumably designed to ensure the survival of certain data.

The government can obtain a gag order prohibiting you from disclosing pending legal proceedings to anyone (presumably including the press and your users). This is to keep you from jeopardizing an ongoing investigation or a trial.

As you may have perceived, the ECPA is perhaps the most dominant law affecting privacy rights on the Internet. If you are or plan to be a sysop on the Internet, you are well advised to get a copy of the entire ECPA (we have reproduced only portions of it here), or read a good overview of its requirements, such as the book *SYSLAW*.

If you conduct business transactions on the Internet, you should be aware that some or all of your messages may be intercepted and that protecting your communications, in practicality, may be difficult. You may want to join the increasing number of computer users who encrypt their communications, but be prepared for more political maneuvering over encryption before the rules in this area are clear.

Privacy in Data Collection and Dissemination

We will close our privacy considerations on the subject of *content* of information, as opposed to *communication* of the information. As mentioned earlier in our discussion on privacy, existing laws affect how you gather information, and what you can (and must) do with the information you have gathered. The subject breaks down into two primary categories—information gathered by governments, and information gathered by private entities such as credit bureaus.

Government Data Collection

Federal, state, and local governments collect a great deal of information about their constituents through census data. In general, responding to these queries is only annoying due to the time it takes to gather the data or fill out the form. But what if you are asked a question that you feel is impertinent or too personal in nature? Do you have to respond? The short answer to this question is "no," but a qualified "no."

If you are a participant in some government-funded program and are receiving government benefits of some type, then the government *can* ask you sensitive questions. They also can put the information on a database. This practice is called "data collection," and it is a normal part of modern day governance—if you receive a government benefit, then the government has the right to know what its money is being spent for. Unfortunately, you give up some of your privacy when you participate in a government program of virtually any type. (And taxes are a government program from which many will complain they receive *no* benefits, just hassles!)

As we mentioned earlier, the constitutional right to privacy is fairly well defined, although you won't find the word "privacy" mentioned in the U.S. Constitution. The privacy right was judicially recognized by the United States Supreme Court in a landmark case involving birth control counseling.[107] The privacy right defined in that case and in related Supreme Court decisions, however, is different from *informational* privacy interests. The privacy right coming from this case can be traced to the coalescence of various amendments to the constitution. However, the Supreme Court has never held that U.S. citizens have an absolute right to informational privacy, as opposed to personal privacy. Personal privacy was the major focus in most of the cases involving privacy interests.

A significant Supreme Court decision pertaining to informational privacy as it relates to government data collection is *Whalen v. Roe*.[108] In that case, the State of New York proposed a central computer databank containing the names and addresses of all persons who obtained particular drugs pursuant to a doctor's prescription. The objective was to develop monitoring of drug abuse that resulted from the abuser obtaining multiple prescriptions of controlled drugs. The Supreme Court held that there were no constitutional barriers to the proposed system.

Under present court decisions such as *Whalen v. Roe*, the government can continue to collect all kinds of data, even sensitive data such as abortion information. Only if the data collection itself adversely affects a protected constitutional interest will the courts prohibit the collection, and the protected privacy interest alone is probably not enough.

The Privacy Act of 1974

The Privacy Act of 1974[109] is the major federal legislation concerning individual privacy as respects data collection. Portions of this law restrict data collection and retention by federal agencies to information that is relevant to the activities of the agencies. Further, a law called the Paperwork Reduction Act of 1980[110] provides that the federal Office of Management and Budget (OMB) may refuse to allow data collection if the OMB concludes that another agency has already collected the information, or if it does not believe that the agency proposing to collect information will in fact be able to use it.

The Privacy Act expressly encourages data collection directly from individuals where possible. The Privacy Act also provides that subject to certain exceptions, an individual may inspect the data collected. If there are inaccuracies, an individual may file a statement disagreeing with the record.

Sharing Information with Other Agencies

Fortunately, after an agency has gathered information about you and put that data in its database, it is subject to some restrictions on sharing the information with other agencies. The Computer Matching and Privacy Protection Act of 1988[111] provides a framework for what is called "data matching" between federal agencies. "Data matching," as defined in the law, involves computerized comparison of two or more automated systems of records, typically to verify eligibility for government benefits or compliance with regulations. For example, in some cases, matching between Social Security and veterans' records has occurred, with the result of reductions in benefits.[112] The 1988 law imposes procedural safeguards and reporting requirements on government agencies that utilize matching programs. If you are involved with government computer system, you need to know about this law.

Clearly, the government can collect data about you, and it can share it among different agencies. You have no true means of preventing data collection, so what can you do? You can try to make sure the information is correct! Great harm can result to you if the data is wrong.

Getting the Information Yourself

The Privacy Act sets forth procedures for accessing information collected about you as an individual (if you can figure out who is gathering the information) and ensuring that the information collected is correct. The problem is that you must first have some reason to believe that there was an error in the collected data or at least some other basis for reviewing an agency file. Also, because government bureaucracy necessarily is involved, and government agencies are not known to be particularly cooperative in this area, be prepared for a time-consuming, expensive, and painful process.

Disclosure of Information Gathered by the Government

Although many don't like the fact that the government has the right to accumulate data, little question remains that the right exists. Given that a complex society cannot function without data collection, perhaps our concern is best focused on the accuracy of the data.

With the myriad of databases now accessible via the Internet, and the many more that are expected to be added with the "information superhighway," we reasonably can expect that some may contain significant personal information. Usually, information that is impersonal, such as Food and Drug Administration research reports, Department of Agriculture research information, or NASA Extragalactic Database,[113] doesn't cause many people problems. It's when the government starts collecting information related to taxes and health (for example, searching databases of the Internal Revenue Service for delinquent taxpayers or searching databases of the Communicable Disease Center for people that are HIV-positive) that most of us get the willies.

Because the whole purpose of government data collection is to gather information that helps the government function, obviously they can use that information themselves for that purpose. The government's right, or even obligation, to disclose the information to outside third parties poses a thornier question. The government is a vast repository of data, and many—especially curious Internet users—would like to obtain government-collected data for commercial or other purposes. Why gather data if the government has already done it for you?

In some circumstances, the government can freely disclose information to whomever wants it. For example, the Supreme Court has held that the government can disseminate a list of active shoplifters derived from arrest records, without infringing the privacy interest.[114] The public interest in open information in this case dominated over any privacy right. Apparently, if your name is on such a list by mistake, you have the right under the Privacy Act to get it corrected.

Although, cases occur here and there that involve the government's voluntary dissemination of data, these cases are few in number. After all, few people truly expect the government to do anything, such as publish data, without being forced to. Cases involving federal and state laws mandating disclosure of information are far more common, because people can sue under specific statutes to seek information they want.

The Freedom of Information Act

The Freedom of Information Act (FOIA)[115] is the principal legal vehicle used to force the government to divulge information it has gathered. FOIA is subject, of course, to certain exemptions relating to national security, material specifically exempted by statute, trade secrets, law enforcement, and so on. Generally speaking, FOIA provides that upon a request for records that reasonably describes the records and is made in accordance with published rules of an agency, the agency shall make the records promptly available. The law contemplates that the person requesting the data will pay the reasonable fees for the cost of the disclosure. It also provides for judicial intervention to enforce the obligation to disclose.

However, FOIA is not clearly set up to facilitate electronic requests and replies by government agencies. Requesters are not guaranteed access to information on materials other than paper.[116] In short, if you have a reasonable idea as to what information a government agency may have collected (electronic or otherwise), you can ask for it, as long as you go by the agency's rules. But expect to have to pay for it, and don't expect that an electronic answer will be readily forthcoming.

Conceivably, rules could be established for an electronic FOIA request, with an electronic FOIA reply, both via the Internet. At this stage, we haven't heard that any government agency will respond to formal FOIA requests via e-mail. However, government agencies that have computers connected to the Internet may expect that they will receive such inquiries and may have to establish formal electronic FOIA procedures. No doubt, many e-mail requests for data from government agencies have already been made and data has been provided, perhaps via ftp, but we do not know whether any agencies have established Internet FOIA rules.

Data Processing as Part of FOIA Requests

Obviously, the data maintained on government computers is indexed, stored, and processed in a manner that suits the agency's purposes. If a FOIA request is received, how much effort must the government agency expend to put the data in a form usable by a FOIA requester? Some balance must be maintained between the public's right to obtain the information, and the right of the agency to fulfill its public mandate without dropping everything to run out 100+ boxes of data printouts.

No generally accepted rule governs how far an agency must go to satisfy a FOIA request. One case has said that the agency must make a reasonable effort geared to the achievement of the required disclosure.[117] The agency in that case was required to make a diligent effort calculated to uncover a requested document, but did not have to restructure its entire system to satisfy the request. The competence of a search for the record had to be determined in relation to the circumstances of the case.

The obligation to search probably does not extend to undertaking statistical analyses on behalf of the FOIA requester. The agency does not have to become a data processing service to the public[118]—presumably, you can get the records and process the data yourself.

Commercial Data Collection and Disclosure

As we mentioned at the beginning of our privacy discussion, private entities such as credit bureaus have the right to collect data about people. Other entities, such as cable TV companies, educational institutions, banks, and so on, also gather data about people. System operators for such entities need to know that if their systems are available on the Internet, specific laws concern the collection and disclosure of data in their areas. In this section, we list a few of the more significant federal laws, and warn that others probably exist.

As most people know, credit bureaus sell their data for a fee. A well-developed body of law pertains to how such entities collect the data and how a consumer can correct the data. As regards credit, for example, the Equal Credit Opportunity Act imposes restrictions on collection of data regarding race, sex, religion, and marital status, except for limited uses by creditors and employers.[119] The Fair Credit Reporting Act[120] regulates credit reporting agencies and information concerning an individual's credit history.

Educational Files

If you have student records on a network-accessible system, note that the Family Educational and Privacy Rights Act[121] imposes restrictions on disclosure of educational files. If you are a college student, you may be interested to know this law imposes restrictions on the disclosure of your educational files. Sysops at universities should be especially careful that their grade files are secure. This act is keyed to federal funding of educational institutions, and it prohibits an institution from disclosing the content of a student's file except to school officials with a need to know, research organizations, governmental education officials, and people with enforceable subpoenas.

The Cable Communications Policy Act of 1984

The Cable Communications Policy Act of 1984[122] places restrictions on the collection, use, and dissemination of information by the operator of a cable system about its subscribers. The law requires a cable operator to provide a subscriber with annual notification about the nature of any personally identifiable information that it collects about the individual, the intended use for the information, and the nature and frequency of any disclosure of the personally identifiable information that may occur.

The Electronic Funds Transfer Act

The Electronic Funds Transfer Act[123] encompasses all point-of-sale electronic transfer systems, as well as transfers involving automated teller machines. If you plan to conduct any type of funds transfers on the network that are not within the list of the exclusions set forth in the law, you may fall under the governance of this law. Again, seek expert advice. The law is intended to focus on electronics transfer systems with a direct impact on consumers. Because the law is primarily drafted to govern the operation of financial institutions in the manner in which they conduct their consumer accounts, it includes a number of express exclusions, such as:

(1) transfer initiated by checks;

(2) non-transfer systems, like check guarantees and authorization services;

(3) wire transfers through systems that are primarily business systems;

(4) transfers for the purchase of securities or commodities that are regulated by other agencies;

(5) transfers initiated by telephone, but not part of a pre-arranged plan of recurring transfer; and

(6) transfers among a consumer's account or between a consumer and the institution holding the account.

Privacy Issues in Other Countries

This section has discussed U.S. privacy laws. Many countries (especially in the European Community) have more stringent limitations than the United States on collection of data in the private sector.[124] If your operations are international, be reminded that each country has its own laws about data collection, disclosure, and privacy. Do any privacy obligations affect data pertaining to foreign citizens collected and stored in the

United States but Internet (and, therefore, internationally) accessible? On this question, the laws are murky at best.

Legal Action for Invasion of Privacy

To conclude our discussion of privacy, you should be aware that a body of common law cases have established tort actions for invasion of privacy. These causes of action have typically been subdivided into categories of: (1) appropriation of an individual's name or likeness, which is also called the right of publicity; (2) intrusion into an individual's private affairs; (3) public disclosure of embarrassing, private facts; and (4) publicly placing an individual in a false light.[125] The nature and extent of such tort actions vary from state to state. If you violate a privacy right by making information about a person available on the Internet, you may be subject to a private law suit by the offended person.

These subjects are complex, and if you have databases on Internet that contain any information that may be considered "personal" in nature, be aware that you must watch out for a veritable mine field of laws. We have mentioned a few of the more significant federal laws that affect privacy, but be aware that relevant state laws and other federal laws exist. You simply must be familiar with these laws before you make any personal or private data available on the Internet.

Summary

As we warned at the beginning of this chapter, we can provide only a brief survey of the myriad of laws that might affect your usage of the Internet. As distasteful as it may seem, you may have to hire a lawyer to help you sort all these out, because it seems that every way you turn, a different law applies. We wish we could simply say, "Just behave yourself and you'll be okay," but the answer isn't that easy. In societies as complex as those of the United States, Europe, and Japan, it is simply not possible for a mortal human being with a finite brain capacity to keep track of all the laws and regulations that might govern one's actions.

If you want to use the Internet's facilities to help you navigate your way through the maze of laws and regulations, we suggest that you get a copy of "The Legal List, Law-Related Resources on the Internet and Elsewhere," by Erik J. Heels, 39 Main St., Eliot, ME 03903. This document lists various legal information sources available on the Internet, including detailed instructions on addresses, telnet, ftp, Gopher, WAIS, and other resources. "The Legal List" includes a listing of LISTSERV groups for many of the topics discussed here, including privacy, copyright, software patents, computer law, and so on.

"The Legal List" is available via anonymous ftp from `ftp.midnight.com` (137.103.210.2) (Midnight Networks Inc.) as `pub/LegalList/legallist.txt`. You should connect to `ftp.midnight.com` by anonymous ftp ONLY. Please do not telnet to `ftp.midnight.com`. If you do not know how to ftp the file, ask someone for help. If you have problems with ftp-ing to `ftp.midnight.com`, you can send an e-mail message to `admin@midnight.com` or `justice!legal-list@nic.unh.edu`.

All things considered, common sense plays a large part in avoiding legal problems on the Internet (as in the rest of your life). If you are an honest, small-time business user, you probably don't have too much to worry about. But if your business depends on continued access to the Internet and the continued ability to conduct transactions, then you would be well advised to obtain the services of a good computer-literate lawyer if you find you are getting in over your head. Be careful out there "on the net."

I

Footnotes and References

1. Nimmer, Raymond T., *The Law of Computer Technology* (2d Ed. 1992) (hereinafter, "Nimmer"). This is a detailed "computer law" treatise that may be a much more detailed reference than many will need, but it is a good overview of the law relating to computer technology and of many aspects of telecommunications law.

2. See Appendix C, Krol, *The Whole Internet User's Guide And Catalog* (1992).

3. 15 U.S.C. §§ 5501-5528 (1991). For more information on the NREN, see Walter, Priscilla and Sussman, Eric, "Protecting Commercially Developed Information on the NREN," 10 *The Computer Lawyer* 1 (April 1993).

4. 15 U.S.C. 5512(c)(5).

5. See Tichane, David, "Copyright: Restrictive Notices on Quasi-Public Domain Software," *The Licensing Journal* (April 1993), p. 18.

6. 8 Anne, c. 19 (circa 1710) (English laws).

7. The preemption provisions of 17 U.S.C. § 301 did away with common law copyright.

8. 17 U.S.C. § 102.

9. 17 U.S.C. § 106.

10. 17 U.S.C. § 401.

11. 37 C.F.R. § 201.20(g).

12. 17 U.S.C. § 411(a).

13. 17 U.S.C. § 410(c).

14. 37 C.F.R. § 202.20(c)(vii).

15. 37 C.F.R. § 202.20(c)(vii)(A)(2).

16. 17 U.S.C. § 101.

17. 17 U.S.C. § 107.

18. *Feist Publications, Inc. v. Rural Telephone Service Co.*, 111 S.Ct. 1282 (1991); *BellSouth Advertising and Publishing Co. v. Donnelley Information Publishing, Inc.*, 999 F.2d 1436 (11th Cir. 1993) (en banc).

19. 17 U.S.C § 101. ("A 'compilation' is a work formed by the collection and assembling of preexisting materials or of data that are selected, coordinated, or arranged in such a way that the resulting work as a whole constitutes an original work of authorship.")

20. 17 U.S.C. § 106(2).

21. 17 U.S.C. § 101.

22. 17 U.S.C. § 117.

23. 17 U.S.C. § 201(b).

24. *Community for Creative Non-Violence v. Reid*, 490 U.S. 730, 109 S.Ct. 2166 (1989).

25. 17 U.S.C. § 101. (Definition of "work made for hire.")

26. If you want to participate in the debate on software patents, you might try to e-mail the Free Software Foundation at gnu@prep.ai.mit.edu.

27. For a discussion of some of these pros and cons, see John R. Harris, "Software Patents: An Overview," Intellectual Property in the Computer Age, A Special Supplement of the *Fulton County* (Georgia) *Daily Report*, December 7, 1992.

28. 35 U.S.C. § 112.

29. 35 U.S.C. § 271.

30. Perry, Tekla. "E-mail at work," *IEEE Spectrum* (October 1992), p. 24.

31. 35 U.S.C. § 102(b).

32. 35 U.S.C. § 119.

33. Restatement (Second) of Contracts § 1.

34. Uniform Commercial Code (UCC) § 2-201(1).

35. See *Vault Corp. v. Quaid Software Ltd.*, 655 F.Supp. 750 (E.D. La. 1987), aff'd 847 F.2d 255 (5th Cir. 1988). (Shrink-wrap license form not enforceable since it constituted a contract of adhesion.)

36. 17 U.S.C. § 117.

37. See White & Summers, *Uniform Commercial Code 170* (2d Ed. 1980).

38. See, for example, *Computer Servicenters, Inc. v. Beacon Mfg. Co.*, 328 F. Supp. 653, 655, aff'd, 443 F.2d 906 (4th Cir. 1971).

39. See Nimmer, § 14.22, p. 14-45.

40. A good survey of EDI law is a book titled *Electronic Contracting Law - EDI in Business Transactions*, by Al J. Kutten, Bernard D. Reams, Jr., and Alan E. Strehle (Clark Boardman Callaghan, 1993).

41. UCC § 2-313.

42. UCC § 2-314.

43. UCC § 2-315.

44. UCC § 2-316. A warranty disclaimer must be conspicuous, in writing, and specifically mention "merchantability."

45. 15 U.S.C. § 2301 et seq.

46. See State Tax Guide 6011-6016, § 60-000 (CCH); Hollman, "Sales Taxation of Software," 1 *The Computer Lawyer* 31 (March 1984).

47. Restatement (Second) of Torts § 525.

48. Prosser, The Law of Torts, § 105.

49. See *APLications* [sic]*, Inc. v. Hewlett-Packard Co.*, 501 F. Supp. 129 (S.D.N.Y.), aff'd, 672 F.2d 1076 (2nd Cir. 1982).

50. *Glovatorium v. NCR Corp.*, 684 F.2d 658 (9th Cir. 1982).

51. See Lanham Act § 43(a), 15 U.S.C. § 1125.

52. See, for example, O.C.G.A. § 10-1-370 et seq. for the Georgia law of deceptive trade practices.

53. Restatement (Second) of Torts § 282.

54. Cliff Stoll, *The Cuckoo's Egg*, Pocket Books/Simon & Schuster Inc. (1990). Page 213 relates to the Bevatron particle accelerator used for radiation therapy.

55. Restatement of Torts (2d) § 402A.

56. Tariff Act of 1930, 19 U.S.C. § 1337.

57. See *Bally/Midway Mfg. Co. v. U.S. ITC*, 714 F.2d 1117 (Fed. Cir. 1983).

58. See "In re Certain Personal Computers and Components Thereof," No. 337-TA-140 (ITC 1984).

59. See Willett, Shawn, "SPA investigates reports of rampant piracy on the Internet," *INFOWORLD*, March 22, 1993, page 12.

60. 22 U.S.C. §§ 2551 et seq. (1982).

61. 50 U.S.C.App. § 2401 et seq. (1980).

62. 15 C.F.R. § 799.1. (Computers are listed in ECCN1565A; disks in 1572A(D).)

63. 15 C.F.R. § 799.1, Supp. No. 2, Supp. No. 3.

64. See 1883 Convention of the Union of Paris, as revised June 2, 1911, 38 U.S.T. 1645, amended November 6, 1925, 47 U.S.T. 1789, amended October 31, 1958, TIAS No. 4931, amended July 14, 1967, TIAS No. 6923, 7727.

65. Berne Convention, Paris text, July 24, 1971; Universal Copyright Convention (July 1971).

66. Burkert, "Institutions of Data Protection: An Attempt at a Functional Explanation of European National Data Protection Laws," 3 *Computer/Law J.* 167 (1982).

67. See Organization for Economic Cooperation and Development, "Guidelines on the Protection of Privacy and Transborder Flows of Personal Data" (1981).

68. A good discussion of the events leading to the discovery and neutralization of the virus is contained in the Epilogue of Cliff Stoll's *The Cuckoo's Egg*.

69. 18 U.S.C. § 1030. This law, enacted in 1984, primarily pertains to computer systems having some "federal interest" involved.

70. See Nimmer, § 12.18.

71. *United States v. Morris*, 928 F.2d 504 (2d Cir. 1991).

72. See Johnson, Dell, "The Future of Electronic Educational Networks: Some Ethical Issues," U.S. Dept. of Education, Office of Educational Research and Improvement, Document No. ED 332 689 (May 1991).

73. 18 U.S.C. §§ 2510 et seq.

74. See Wallace & Morrison, *SYSLAW—The Sysop's Legal Manual*, LLM Press, New York, New York (1988), for the story of Tom Tcimpidis, a California BBS operator who was prosecuted for posting stolen credit card numbers on his BBS.

75. Ibid., p. 32.

76. See "Computer Related Crimes in Federal Programs," Government Accounting Office (GAO) (1976).

77. O.C.G.A. § 16-9-93 (Ga. L. 1991, p. 1045, § 1).

78. 17 U.S.C. § 301.

79. See Wallace & Morrison, *SYSLAW*, p. 66.

80. O.C.G.A. § 10-1-761.

81. Cal. Penal Code § 499(c)(9) (1983).

82. See *SYSLAW*, supra note 74, p. 67 for an exemplary notice. Consult with counsel before you adopt any particular legal notice language.

83. PRODIGY User Agreement, Prodigy Services Co., Sept. 1993.

84. 18 U.S.C. § 641.

85. 18 U.S.C. § 1341.

86. 18 U.S.C. § 1343.

87. 50 U.S.C. § 1809.

88. 18 U.S.C. § 2314.

89. 15 U.S.C. § 1693 et seq.

90. *Olmstead v. United States*, 277 U.S. 438, 478 (1928) (Brandeis, J., dissenting).

91. Kent, Stephen, "Internet Privacy Enhanced Mail," *Communications of the ACM*, August 1993, p. 48.

92. See *Tyler v. Berodt*, 877 F.2d 705 (8th Cir. 1989); *Edwards v. State Farm Ins. Co.*, 833 F.2d 535 (5th Cir. 1987). However, New York apparently has an anti-eavesdropping statute; see *People v. Fata*, 159 AD2d 180, 559 NYS2d 348 (App. Div. 1990).

93. 47 U.S.C. § 605 (as amended in 1988).

94. *Telerate Systems, Inc. v. Caro*, 689 F.Supp. 221 (S.D.N.Y. 1988). (In its user agreement, an investment information database supplier only allowed access to its database via its own software.)

95. 18 U.S.C. §§ 2510 et seq.

96. 18 U.S.C. § 2511(g)(i).

97. 18 U.S.C. § 2510(16)(A).

98. 18 U.S.C. § 2520.

99. PRODIGY User Agreement, Prodigy Services Company (Sept. 1993).

100. 18 U.S.C. § 2511(2)(a)(i).

101. 18 U.S.C. § 2701.

102. 18 U.S.C. § 2702.

103. 18 U.S.C. § 2511(2)(c) - (d).

104. Cf. Haynes, "The Envelope Please: Problems and Proposals for Electronic Mail Surveillance," 14 Hastings Const. L. Q. 421 (1987).

105. 18 U.S.C. § 2703.

106. *SYSLAW*, supra note 74.

107. *Griswald v. Connecticut*, 381 U.S. 479 (1965).

108. 429 U.S. 811 (1977).

109. 5 U.S.C § 552a.

110. 44 U.S.C. § 3501 et seq.

111. 5 U.S.C. § 552a(o). (Amendment to Privacy Act of 1974.)

112. *Jaffess v. Secretary, Dept. of HEW*, 393 F.Supp. 626 (S.D.N.Y. 1975).

113. These are only a few of the government databases that can be accessed via the Internet. Many Internet reference texts such as Krol, supra note 2, have access details and addresses.

114. *Paul v. Davis*, 424 U.S. 693 (1976).

115. 5 U.S.C. § 552.

116. See Grodsky, Jamie, "The Freedom of Information Act in the Electronic Age: The Statute is Not User Friendly," 31 *Jurimetrics J.* 17 (Fall 1990). See also *Dismukes v. Dept. of Interior*, 603 F.Supp. 760 (D.D.C. 1984) (agency not required to give computer tape to requester).

117. *Miller v. Dept. of State*, 779 F.2d 1378 (8th Cir. 1985) (amateur historian seeking information on the 1967 attack on the U.S.S. Liberty by Israeli defense forces).

Introducing the Internet

118. See *In re Guerrier v. Hernandez-Cuebas*, 165 AD2d 218 (N.Y. App. Div. 1991) (no obligation to make special computation of number of murder convicts on work release where agency did not have a program that enabled such analysis). See also Nimmer, § 16.11.

119. 15 U.S.C. §§ 1691 et seq.

120. 15 U.S.C. §§ 1681 et. seq.

121. 20 U.S.C. § 1232g.

122. 47 U.S.C. §§ 521, 551.

123. 15 U.S.C. § 1693.

124. See Millard, "Data Protection and Privacy Considerations in Transnational Distribution: A European Perspective," 6 *Comp.L.Ass'n Bulletin* 17 (1991). See generally, Nimmer, § 11.14.

125. See Restatement (Second) of Torts § 652A.

Chapter 6

The Future
of the Internet

What can we look forward to in the future of the Internet? For the business world, being able to connect electronically with suppliers and customers will have a big effect on the way business is done. Being connected to the global network also can affect internal corporate communications. Connecting government to the Internet will change the way we interact with our representatives. The Internet will present many opportunities for elementary and high school students. And researchers in many fields—not just the computer scientists who have used it until now—will find the Internet to be a powerful tool. All these areas—and more—will benefit from the power of high-speed electronic communications.

Already today, tens of millions of people can communicate electronically through e-mail. As more people become connected to the Internet, more services will become available; more social interaction will occur. The Internet could help turn this world into a truly global society by letting everyone work and play with people from all over the earth. This chapter will show how networking—and the Internet, in particular—will affect our daily lives.

Note

As discussed in Chapter 2, "The History of the Internet," the U.S. government is supporting the creation of a national data superhighway, designated the National Research and Education Network (NREN). The NSFNET, the National Science Foundation's network, is the backbone of the NREN and of the Internet in the United States.

In addition to providing a network for research and educational organizations, having all businesses and individuals connected to the data superhighway is also the goal of the government. However, it isn't clear whether this service will be Internet based or based on a service offered by commercial communications providers (such as the phone company or cable TV operators). So, although this chapter discusses the future applications of the Internet, these applications can be applied to whatever data superhighway is eventually implemented.

The Internet's Effect on Corporations

Until recently, only research and academic organizations could connect to the Internet. Initially, commercial organizations were allowed to connect to the Internet only if they had research divisions or if their services were needed by research or educational institutions on the Internet.

Now that commercial organizations are allowed to connect to the Internet for any purpose (as discussed in Chapter 2), the number of commercial sites has grown tremendously. Some organizations are using the Internet to connect geographically distant offices, and some are using the Internet to communicate with their customers and suppliers. Being connected to the Internet also can have an effect on the internal operations of many businesses, especially if the business didn't previously use an electronic communications network.

Note

Researchers Lee Sproull and Sara Kiesler have written a book called *Connections: New Ways of Working in the Networked Organization,* which explores the effect of electronic communications in an organization. Their book was used as a reference for some of the material in the following sections.

The Networked Office

A connection to the Internet is often the first experience that a company has with electronic communications. An Internet connection not only connects the employees to others external to the company, it also connects them internally to each other. This creation of an electronic community may change the way employees interact—often for the better.

When a company is completely networked, members of the corporate community begin to communicate electronically. Many companies are beginning to distribute company newsletters and company-wide memos electronically. Using electronic distribution over the Internet can simplify distribution between remote divisions of a company. Such a distribution technique saves paper and reduces the desktop clutter that occurs when employees take their mail out of their boxes and throw it on their desks.

On-Line Corporate Information

Although today's company newsletter may look jazzier on paper than on-line, because of the proliferation of low-cost color desktop workstations and reasonably priced graphics scanners, soon full-color documents, complete with photos and graphics, will be distributed on-line. And as the technology advances, video and audio can be added to the "document." Companies also could personalize on-line copies of the newsletter by division, with the company-wide section distributed over the Internet and division-specific information added before distribution.

One area now under research on the Internet is the broadcast of live video and audio over the network. Imagine attending the company president's weekly staff address while seated at your computer halfway across the country. You also would be able to ask questions and have the president respond to you—all in real time.

The Effect of E-Mail on Corporate Communications

E-mail already is replacing the interoffice memo and has become a standard way of distributing meeting minutes. Because e-mail isn't as intrusive as a phone call, it can present the information being exchanged in a convenient format for the recipient. Electronic communication also provides a record of a process (product development, for example) and reasons behind decisions.

The capability to broadcast electronic mail over the Internet allows instant communication to all employees, even at remote sites. For example, managers can send a request for urgent information to employees at remote company sites, possibly on another continent, with the likelihood of receiving the requested information in a relatively short period of time. (All employees may not be reading their mail, but those who aren't can get word from those who are.) Last-minute opportunities for training or other things can be offered through this quick means of communication.

Research has found that the pervasiveness of networking in the office encourages communication that may otherwise not occur. Junior employees who may feel uncomfortable speaking in person or on the phone with their department head or company president have less hesitation about sending an e-mail message to these people. And e-mail messages from junior staff look just like those from more "important" employees, and as such may give workers more opportunity to have their ideas heard. Also, many executives read their own electronic mail; physical correspondence and phone calls, on the other hand, often go through secretaries.

Electronic Meetings

Researchers have found that the ability of aggressive individuals to dominate the discussion is limited when meetings are conducted electronically (using real-time discussion programs like Internet Relay Chat) or when electronic communications are used to supplement meetings. Also, all participants tend to get a fair hearing. As a matter of fact, meeting participants have more of a tendency to listen to the ideas of junior workers. In face-to-face discussions, junior or shy participants' ideas often are discounted, even though they may be the best solutions to the problem.

This capability to communicate quickly and with less inhibition allows problems to be addressed and resolved more quickly— and with a larger pool of talent to draw from—because sites from around the country can communicate easily. It enables people to play more of a role than they may in a traditional corporate environment because they can be more aware of what's going on and become more easily involved. This sharing of responsibilities should mean that organizations can run more efficiently and with less middle management.

Problems can result, however, if electronic communications are used inappropriately. In electronic discussion, participants don't really know how others feel about the things that have been discussed. Research has found that electronic discussions tend to take longer than face-to-face discussions to get all the participants' clarifying information. And decisions made electronically when participants didn't have enough time to fully express themselves can lead to more extreme decisions made with lack of information. In some cases, the lack of face-to-face interaction leads to socially inappropriate messages being sent.

A Distributed Development Team

Some large computer companies already have sped up their product designs by assembling geographically dispersed design teams. In this way, they can have individuals whose talents most fit the project needs, no matter where they are located. They also use geographically distributed sales and marketing teams. Teams communicate through e-mail and phone. Data is available for transfer to any project site over the Internet.

The advantages to this type of project development are that the company can use resources (people) it already has. The expenses of a temporary assignment aren't necessary. And an employee can choose a place of permanent residence without worrying about having to transfer to take a better project assignment.

Perhaps corporations eventually won't have a large number of permanent, on-site employees. They instead may be able to call on the services of consultants who will work over the network, out of their homes or a local office, for the specific period of the project. Consultants can work for several clients at once, remotely attending meetings and submitting reports and delivering products. In addition to providing benefits for employer and employee, *telecommuting*—that is, working at home—can help the environment by preventing some congestion and pollution caused by employees driving to their workplace.

Communicating on the Road

Employees whose jobs require their being out of the office can use portable computers to contact their co-workers and access up-to-the-minute information about pricing, policies, or needed technical information over the Internet. This is a great boon to the company, because it doesn't require that a live person answer the phone to supply the remote employee with the needed information (so the employee can give a quicker response to the customer). Also, it allows the remote employee to converse more with management, making him or her feel more a part of the overall organization.

The Negative Social Effects of Being Networked

So far, some of the positive effects that come from connecting an organization to the Internet have been discussed. Some unexpected negative social effects also can result, however. Telecommuting hasn't turned into the corporate boon it was predicted to be. Sometimes the ease of accessing remote information negatively affects people who were considered experts. And the presumption that information can be found very quickly using the Internet can cause people to become sloppy when allocating time needed for project activities.

Telecommuting

One of the big predictions that appeared when computer networks became more prevalent was that large numbers of workers would telecommute. The thinking behind telecommuting was that it would enable companies to save facility expenses while enabling workers to have many benefits, such as living far from the office in a location that they desired, decreased cost of child care, more flexibility for work schedules, more time to spend with their families, and so forth.

Telecommuting hasn't become all that popular, however, for a number of reasons. Employers don't like the loss of control over employees when they aren't on site. Parents may find that working on company property gives them a break from their small children.

Workers at home also lose the ability to network socially with others in the company. This informal networking often leads to opportunities for advancement or project responsibility. Because telecommuting employees have less personal interaction with management, they feel less a part of the company. Perhaps if the technology improves to the point of having almost face-to-face interaction with other employees on a regular basis while at home, telecommuting may become more practical. (When the Internet research on live video and audio broadcasting that is now in progress becomes practical, interaction with remote co-workers should improve dramatically.)

Changing Social Structures

Shifting the power of different people in an organization some-times has unexpected social effects. With network technology, people can bypass *gatekeepers* (people who hold the key to information access) and get information directly. This should be an advantage because now anyone can access the information, but it may have undesirable effects on the gatekeeper. For example, say you have an organization where customer inquiries are handled by long-time employees who are intimately familiar with all the company's products. If you then install a computerized system that allows anyone to access product information from all over the company by accessing databases at different divisions, the long-time employees who used to do this work will feel devalued because their importance to the company is lost.

Expecting Instantaneous Communication

Research has found that one problem brought about by the capability to communicate instantly is an expectancy of instant response. Because the technology exists to allow rapid retrieval of information, people come to expect that they will be able to get information they need almost immediately. When people expect this type of quick response, they begin to plan for it in their projects without allowing time for unexpected delays. When a request for information takes some time to generate a response, and a project becomes delayed because no slack was designed in, frustration and anger result.

The Interaction of Network Organizations

The possibility exists for positive and negative effects when organizations interact over the Internet. How will widespread networking affect organization interaction? Consider the following:

- Organizations may interact more automatically. For example, a person could send in an electronic order for supplies, have the packing list generated automatically, and have an invoice and shipping order sent back to the customer's computer.

- Psychological dependence on computer-induced relationships may occur. Through e-mail and electronic conferences, buyers may get to know their suppliers so well that they are reluctant to switch to another supplier.

- Suppliers may offer electronic extras to attract clients (perhaps when you connect to your supplier, you automatically get sports highlights or movie reviews).

- Rather than return overstocked products to a central inventory site, companies can check to see whether certain regional distributors are understocked in a particular product and then ship that product directly to those distributors.

The Resistance of Business To Join the Internet

Although many businesses have connected to the Internet to compete, other businesses have resisted. Concerns exist about the security of data and the possibility of malicious intrusion, as do concerns about unauthorized access to information and user impersonation. Questions exist about whether statements made through e-mail are legally binding. These businesses also are concerned about legal ownership and distribution. But even companies who don't want to commit themselves just yet are reserving addresses on the Internet in fear that it will reach capacity and leave them shut out.

The Effects of the Internet on the Marketplace

Not only will the Internet affect the way commercial organizations interact with their employees, it also will affect how they interact with their customers and with other businesses.

Customers can connect to their suppliers to check for the availability of stock and place their orders. Businesses can provide marketing information and technical support over the network. The Internet can even be a vehicle for market research, providing more accurate and less costly methods for accessing customer needs and satisfaction with products.

On-Line Selection and Ordering of Products

The Internet offers many opportunities for improving the process of selecting and ordering products. Businesses may give customers access to on-line multimedia catalogs so that they can see pictures of the products they are ordering, and perhaps even view a simulation of how the product is used. Similarly, consumers may be able to view products on-line, select their merchandise, and approve payment, all without human interaction. Paper money may become obsolete, with wages being directly transferred to a bank and bills being paid automatically or with approval from the consumer.

On-Line Problem Reporting

A number of companies already are using the Internet so that their customers can submit product problem reports on-line. This approach can speed up problem-debugging time, because the customers can supply a complete written description of the problem that a customer service representative will read as soon as one is available. This way, the customers save time because they don't have to try back if the customer service line is busy or wait on hold for a service representative to become available. This approach also helps the service representative, who can work on one problem without being interrupted with a phone call about another problem.

Also, if further communications between the customer and a customer service representative are necessary to solve a problem, the requests for information and the necessary data can be exchanged by e-mail at the convenience of the involved parties, rather than end up in a prolonged game of telephone tag. If necessary, customers' problem files can be ftp-ed or e-mailed to the vendor.

Eventually, many companies may do customer support in this manner, perhaps even running remotely on the customer's site to do the debugging. This way, the companies can investigate problems that may arise due to a customer's particular configuration, which may not be easily reproduced at the vendor's site. Software suppliers also may be able to distribute product upgrades, or even new products over the network after proper security and authorization methods are developed.

On-Line Marketing Research

Companies also can use the Internet to collect marketing information by observing how customers are using their products, and what they like and don't like about the products. Many Internet mailing lists and USENET news groups, for example, are devoted to a particular product or product type. By reading these forums, companies can see what product features are liked, what features aren't used, and what features are needed. This approach can reduce the need for focus groups and other expensive marketing tools.

Note

News groups and mailing lists are types of discussion forums. Mailing lists are discussed in Chapter 7, "Using E-Mail"; news groups are discussed in Chapter 9, "USENET."

On-Line Availability of Printed Materials

Another area that should rapidly expand as the Internet grows is that of the publishing industry. Books, catalogs, newspapers, and magazines all can be offered on-line.

Some of the problems in this field, however, are charging for the use/purchase of materials and protecting copyrights. Because of the way people now access Internet information repositories, no provision is established for charging for information, and no method is set up to make sure that people give credit for information they pick up from a site. On-line material is much easier to copy and distribute without permission from or any indication of the author. But both problems are under investigation now so that this area can develop.

The Internet's Effect on Research and Education

The function of the Internet and its predecessor, the ARPANET, has always been to provide a way for researchers to have better access to each other and to tools that facilitate their research. But the Internet can provide much more for educational institutions at the college, elementary, and high-school levels. The Internet offers the capability to conduct remote classes, provides access to a tremendous variety of information, allows access to remote libraries, and creates an environment where students can have innovative cooperative learning experiences.

College-Level Research and Education

Researchers used to be fairly isolated. Perhaps they had a few colleagues who worked with them, but, generally, they couldn't keep in close contact with other major researchers in their fields. Also, some researchers had access to superior laboratory facilities, whereas others didn't. Doing certain types of research was impossible to do at some universities because those campuses couldn't afford to buy the appropriate equipment. And government grants wouldn't cover the cost if the government thought enough money already had gone toward equipment in that research area.

These problems restricted the research in different fields to sites that had the facilities for that research. And because the number of positions at any one site are limited, the number of people doing research in any particular area is likewise limited.

But the Internet removes all these barriers and limitations. The Internet allows timely discussions with peers about proposed theories and the results of experiments to take place. Researchers have access to tools and information that they otherwise wouldn't. Future technical advances in the Internet will allow for real-time remote graphic simulations and other advanced research methods.

Internet Communication with Peers

Already researchers can exchange ideas almost instantaneously through e-mail. Researchers can send ideas to peers for feedback before they spend large amounts of time investigating a new theory. They also can share methods easily between each other. Researchers at physically distant sites can collaborate closely on work by using e-mail to coordinate their investigations and using file transfer to share data and reports.

Note

Now, researchers with Internet connections can use resources available at only a few select sites (like supercomputers or specialized scientific instruments such as powerful telescopes). Not having to buy the same equipment for multiple sites saves money and allows the equipment to be fully utilized because many people can access it.

The Internet and Remote Simulations

Within the next few years, researchers not only will be able to exchange data, but also will be able to observe live experiments. As the Internet *bandwidth* (the amount of information it can carry) improves, live video and real-time computer simulations can be observed from any site on the Internet. Researchers at one site could view a live simulation of almost any type of scientific investigation—the modeling of complex organic compounds, complicated microcircuits, or the effects of cholesterol-reducing drugs on clogged arteries.

The Internet and College Students

The opportunity exists for the Internet to revolutionize education. Approximately one-third of all colleges in the United States now have Internet access. When multimedia transmission becomes commonplace, you may be able to attend one university physically while you take classes remotely at universities around the country. Your research may involve using supercomputers or instruments (such as an electron microscope) at a university thousands of miles away. And with corporations becoming members of the Internet community, researchers can explore more closely how they can apply their findings to product development, or investigate the cause and effects of various stimuli on corporate culture.

The Internet in Social and Humanitarian Research

You may expect that a nationwide network would be of greatest use to scientists and engineers. You also may think that a nationwide computer network would have much less of an effect on research in the humanities and the arts, because they would have little need for access to unusual tools or blazingly fast supercomputers. But the Internet does give them access to a vast wealth of knowledge, much of which they may not know about or have difficulty accessing without the Internet.

William Wulf, a computer science professor at the University of Virginia and former assistant director of the National Science Foundation, gives some examples of the advantages of being networked. He says that all classical Greek literature is now online, and researchers in this area are all avid computer users because they are excited about having such easy access to such of wealth of source material. Also, Dr. Wulf says that many art historians, English professors, and archaeologists have become Internet users because of the access it gives them to rare book collections, paintings, and artifacts.

One related application that already is expanding is the accessibility of library databases on-line. Many public and university libraries have their catalogs of available books on-line; many of these are available over the Internet, enabling researchers to find books that they didn't know existed and getting access to them through interlibrary loans.

Chapter 18, "Host Resource Guide," has a section titled "Libraries" that tells about some of the on-line libraries available. One of these sites, `ariel.umn.edu`, has a file that lists the Internet addresses of all libraries connected to the Internet. Accessing on-line libraries is done by using the telnet command (discussed in Chapter 8, "Using ftp and telnet") to connect to the library. Usually, when you connect to the library, the library's interface software will give you instructions for how to do on-line searches.

You usually can search by author, title, subject, or other parameters. In addition to searching the contents of the library's holdings, you often can search through databases of periodical abstracts. After you find something that you need at a library, you probably must go to your public or school library to request an interlibrary loan for the item. Librarians also can make requests over the Internet for photocopies of material (journal articles, for example) that you can't borrow from the remote library.

Note

Some libraries also have Gopher sites that contain reference information, in addition to the telnet address to their on-line catalog. *Gopher* is an information retrieval system discussed in Chapter 13, "Aids to Navigating the Internet."

The Internet makes collections of rare books or books on particular topics accessible to a wider audience. Although rare books may not be available for interlibrary loan, the researcher at least can travel to see the materials, whereas he or she may not have even known of their existence otherwise. Eventually, the entire contents of libraries' holdings may be on-line, not just the catalogs. This way, researchers will have access to the remote materials themselves. They actually will be able to view the book on-line and print the pages they are interested in (you must consider copyright protection when something like this is implemented). Some sites have some classical literary works, such as Dante's *Divine Comedy*, on-line in their entirety but, currently, the number of works on-line is very limited.

In addition to the information access, Dr. Wulf gives an example of how the use of the computing power can help all researchers, not just scientists, use interesting approaches to analyzing the information that they have. For example, a researcher was investigating the development of railroads in the Southwest. By using a program that plotted population densities against different variables, he showed that a relationship existed between the depletion of bat guano (bat droppings) in the Caribbean and the extension of railroads into the Southwest. As bat guano, a natural fertilizer, became less available, the cotton farmers in the South moved West to more fertile areas, and the railroads followed them to bring supplies and take their product to processing plants. Discerning such a relationship would be difficult without the capability to process enormous amounts of information.

The Internet in Primary and Secondary Education

Another area where the Internet will be having a big impact is primary and secondary education. Children will have access to an incredible wealth of reference material over the Internet. Students also can have greater access to their teachers, sending them e-mail to ask questions about assignments or to clarify class discussion outside of class time.

In secondary education, network connections will give students at small schools the opportunity to take classes that may not have been practical otherwise. If only a few students at a school want to take a foreign language course, for example, the course could be offered remotely to a number of different schools. The Internet also can give school districts access to educational programs developed by federal and non-profit organizations.

Using networked computers may change the way teaching is done. Students can get assignments, take tests, and submit homework and papers from home or other sites connected to the Internet. Eventually, classrooms may not be necessary at all; students could receive their lectures live using the latest interactive multimedia capabilities of the Internet (currently under research), allowing them to ask questions and have discussions right from their desks at home. Of course, a big part of any educational system as it stands now is the socialization of students, and what effect decentralization would have on students' social skills would have to be studied in great detail.

Note

A May 18, 1992, *Wall Street Journal* article titled "Classrooms Without Walls" discusses some of the problems that can occur if teachers aren't thoroughly introduced to technology and its ramifications before using it in the classroom. Many children are more comfortable using a computer than their teachers are. Also, some teachers see the use of remote classes as a loss of control in their classrooms. They also feel threatened because they are no longer the only source of information for their students. But even if students discover things on the Internet that their teachers can't explain immediately, seeing what the teacher does to find answers to their questions is a great learning experience.

Novel Learning Experiences

Connections to the Internet can even lead to novel learning experiences. American students participating in a program sponsored by the French government can exchange e-mail messages with students in France. Students from both countries get a chance to practice conversation in another language. They also can learn a great deal about each other's cultures through their conversations—what they do for recreation, what they eat, what they read, even what types of music they listen to.

Another example, mentioned in the previously cited *Wall Street Journal* article, is Kids Network, a program developed by *National Geographic* in conjunction with TERC (an educational research and development firm in Massachusetts). Kids Network allows teams of students from around the world to collect data for an experiment, compare it to the data of their global teammates, and get help interpreting the data from a scientist on the network.

Another program developed by TERC is the Global Laboratory. This program enables students and teachers to be involved in ecological experiments that scientists around the world are conducting. Children not only can help scientists gather data, but they also can design their own experiments and get other children around the world to help them collect data, while scientists help them analyze their data.

The Effects of the Internet on Our Political System

The ability to talk to our political representatives and access government information over the Internet has the possibility of greatly affecting our political system. At the national and local levels, having the voting public on-line can affect the way politicians campaign and the way government interacts with the people. Recently, the White House and some Congressional representatives have been connected to the Internet, giving the public a new way of voicing their opinions. A California city gives us a glimpse of how an on-line local government might work.

The 1992 National Election

An October 1992 *IEEE Spectrum* article titled "Electronic Mail: Forces for social change" reports that the 1992 presidential election was the first in which computer networks played some role in the candidates' interaction with the voters. In the 1992 primary election, Jerry Brown had accounts on CompuServe and other public networks to take questions from voters on his political stands. He also spent two hours live on one of CompuServe's forums, fielding questions from voters. George Bush and Bill Clinton presented their viewpoints and answered questions on Prodigy during their campaigns. Jim Warren, a computer rights activist who is on the board of Autodesk Inc., made an effort to get a number of the candidates to participate in a debate carried on USENET.

The Federal Government On-Line

In the summer of 1993, the White House went on-line with the establishment of an Internet address for the president and the vice president. Congress also established trial Internet addresses for some of its members, with the intention of eventually getting all representatives (House and Senate) on-line. An attempt also was made to have a live Congressional hearing broadcast over the Internet, in conjunction with an electronic town hall to get feedback from the on-line public.

Talk to the White House on the Net

In 1993—in large part because of Vice President Al Gore's support of technology—voters could access the White House from the Internet. When the system was started in June 1993, it acknowledged electronic mail sent to the Vice President or President Clinton (vice.president@whitehouse.gov and `president@whitehouse.gov`). The content of each message was noted, but individual responses weren't provided. It was hoped that by the end of 1993, individual responses to many messages also will be possible.

Talk to Your Representative on the Net

In addition to the president and vice president going on-line, a few members of Congress have agreed to participate in a pilot program called the Constituent Electronic Mail System. Because access to computer mail is becoming much more common, this program is an attempt to make congressional servants even more available to their constituents.

The initial participants are Reps. Ja y Dickey (AR-7), Sam Gejdenson (CT-2), Newt Gingrich (GA-6), George Miller (CA-7), Charlie Rose (NC-7), Fortney "Pete" Stark (CA-13), and Melvin Watt (NC-12). The designations following the representatives' names are the state and congressional district that they represent.

In the initial phases of the program, the representatives will respond to the electronic mail through the U.S. Postal Service to ensure confidentiality. Constituents first will need to send a post card to their representative to express interest in participating in the program and to provide their name, postal address, and Internet address.

As the pilot program progresses, information will be collected and the system will be modified and improved as needed. When the system proves to be stable, more representatives will be added. For more information, send a request for information to `congress@hr.house.gov`.

Witness Live Congressional Debates on the Net

Along with having congressional representatives accessible to their constituents over the Internet, a consortium of industry and government organizations attempted to have a July 1993 congressional hearing broadcast live over the Internet. The hearing of the House Subcommittee on Telecommunications and Finance was to have been titled *The Role of Government in Cyberspace*, and demonstrations of different Internet services were to have been given to the committee members and any who attended the public hearing. A "town hall" address also was to have been created so that regular Internet users could testify to the importance of a national information infrastructure.

Unfortunately, this initial attempt at an Internet congressional session didn't occur. A number of commercial suppliers had donated equipment and services to make the town hall possible. One supplier raised questions about whether supplying equipment would violate a congressional ethics law prohibiting in-kind donations over a certain value to Congress. A few months will be spent trying to resolve these questions and establish that the on-line hearings are in the public interest. The organizers are hoping that having an on-line hearing still will be possible.

Local Governments On-Line

The attempts at bringing Congress on-line are just the beginning of introducing the information age to government. Although the federal government probably will come on-line faster because many of its agencies already are connected to the Internet, eventually many local governments also may come on-line, thus giving residents of their communities quick access to their local representatives and to information pertaining to local issues.

As an example, the *IEEE Spectrum* article cited earlier talks about how the city of Santa Monica, California, installed a computer system accessible to any resident. The system enables users to send e-mail to their council members, access databases containing information about council activities, tap into the public library catalog, and access conferences discussing city-related topics such as rent control. Residents have used this system to influence the council's spending allocations and decisions on zoning. If, as the government hopes, everyone eventually is connected to the Internet (or whatever data superhighway is implemented), setting up this type of system for all local governments would be a relatively simple task.

Government of the Future

The attempts at bringing Congress on-line are just the beginning of introducing the information age to government. The availability of good quality long-distance communications and the accessibility of government records to the general public eventually could change the structure of our government.

Imagine what may happen in the future. As new technology improves the capability for electronic conferences, the need to have a geographically centralized government may decrease. Representatives could spend more time in their home districts by attending meetings and visiting electronically.

As more government information becomes accessible on-line, the general public will become more knowledgeable about what is going on in the government. Citizens then will be able to express their opinions directly to their representatives. Perhaps eventually, the general public will have a larger, direct role in government affairs, with the representatives restricted to situations where negotiation or problem solving is necessary.

Who Will Shape the Internet of the Future?

Who should fund the development of a national network is a source of disagreement. The government believes that because of the projected importance of the data network with respect to the development of the economy and commercial sector, development must be done quickly. In an interview published in

The New York Times in January 1993, Vice President Al Gore expressed his concern that the private sector isn't moving fast enough to create the type of network needed. Also, many public services—such as libraries, hospitals, and schools—are concerned that if the data highway is purely a commercial venture, they won't be able to afford to be connected to it. Some computer and telecommunication companies, however, feel that the government is stepping in and competing with private industry. Other commercial organizations hope that they can develop the network in partnership with the government.

The government is now sponsoring the development of NREN, a nationwide network for educational and research organizations. This network will be based on the Internet, whose backbone is currently the National Science Foundation's NSFNET. In addition to government-sponsored research, the not-for-profit Corporation for Research Initiatives (CNRI) seeks to involve government and the private sector in improving the nation's information infrastructure. Another not-for-profit organization, the Internet Society, encourages everyone to participate in the Internet, and administers some of the groups that direct the Internet.

Government's Role in the Development of a National Network

What is the government's intent with the NREN? The government doesn't want to be in the business of supplying network services. What the government is trying to do, as it has done with other research in the past, is prime the pump—enable the technology to develop to a point where it becomes commercially viable. The government believes that because this technology is so important to the future of our country, it is worth supporting in the initial stages, because commercial organizations probably would be unwilling to fund initial development of such a network. Because a national network is such a large, expensive undertaking, a commercial developer would have little incentive to build it, especially without supporting services already in place. And no one is going to develop the supporting services without the existence of a stable, usable network.

The NSF's Plans

Since establishing its network in the late 1980s (see Chapter 2, "The History of the Internet," for details), the National Science Foundation (NSF) has directly paid for the costs of the traffic that is sent over its network (NSFNET) by research institutions. Now that the NSFNET is the backbone of the NREN, the goal of the NSF in the second stage of the NREN is to reduce direct funding of the NSFNET over the next five years. Although the NSF now pays the network service provider directly for conveyance of NSFNET traffic, the current plan calls for the reduction of the direct funding over the next five years and instead to fund the NSF researchers who will then pay for the NSFNET services that they use.

When the NSFNET was initially developed, it wasn't clear that the organization that won the first solicitation for the installation of the NSFNET would benefit from the project. But with the growth of the Internet and the structuring of the next version of the NSFNET to allow some commercial traffic, the providers selected for the latest solicitation likely will be in a position to gain financially from the arrangement, not just from the contract, but from commercial traffic that will be carried over the same hardware put in place for the NSFNET. The commercial traffic that is carried by these providers should help spur the development of more network services for non-research organizations, providing the early pieces of the nation's information infrastructure.

Effects of a National Network on the Economy

The development of a national communication network can be compared to the building of the national highway infrastructure in the 1950s. The U.S. government funded the national highway system because no commercial incentive—for

example, no services to get to—existed to build the highways.
But after the highways were in place, they had a tremendous
effect on the economy, interstate commerce, and the social
structure of the country.

For example, people could live much further from the city because they could get to work faster. As a result, suburban "bed-
room communities" cropped up, thus expanding the housing
industry, one of the largest segments of our economy today.

The highway system also encouraged the manufacture and use
of cars. The automobile industry, along with supporting services
such as the petroleum industry, gasoline stations, automobile
repair shops, and so on, is another large segment of the
economy.

Similarly, the development of a national "data superhighway"
should lead to commercial development in many areas. Some
network-related services that will be necessary are billing services and services that provide for secure data transmission. But
the things that will drive the economy are the services that will
be provided to the people connected to the network. Things like
customized on-line newspapers, presenting news stories selected
from major news services based on predefined reader interests,
may be the first "gas station" of the data superhighway.

The Corporation for National Research Initiatives

One organization driving the development of a national computer network is the non-profit Corporation for National Research Initiatives (CNRI). CNRI was founded in 1986 by Robert
Kahn, who until the year before had been a director at the federal Defense Advanced Research Projects Agency (DARPA).

Kahn thought that although DARPA had successfully involved
a large number of the nation's universities and research centers
in the development and use of a national computer network,
no relationship was developing with private industry. Believing
this relationship with private businesses was critical to the

future of the nation's economy and technological advancement, Kahn wanted to start an organization that would help combine government, academic, and private efforts to develop a national network.

Currently, the government is providing some funding for CNRI, but a greater amount is actually coming from private industry. Academic research centers also are participating in the projects that CNRI is sponsoring.

Driving the Development of the Gigabit Network

One project that CNRI is now overseeing is the development of *gigabit transmission speed networks*, networks that will be capable of carrying information at the speed of a billion bits per second. Fast networks will allow real-time broadcast of video and audio data, remote access to real-time graphical animation of computer models, and three-dimensional medical imaging, among other things.

Not only is developing transmitters and receivers that can operate at this speed necessary, developing routers or switches that will pass the data onto the next node in the network at high speeds also is necessary. A promising technology toward this end is asynchronous transfer mode (ATM) switching, a type of hardware switching that will provide a temporary circuit that allows a large amount of information to be transmitted directly between two sites. (This is opposed to packet switching, where each packet of data may take a different route to a destination, and packets from many sources flow over the same network circuits.) Carnegie Mellon University in Pittsburgh recently announced the development of a low-cost, high-speed, high-performance ATM switch.

CNRI has now established 5-gigabit test beds, which all involve geographically dispersed academic, government, and private industry groups working as teams. The test beds are working on developing the hardware and software necessary to implement the gigabit networks. They also are working on the development of applications that will showcase the capability of high-speed data transmission. Some of the applications under development are for video conferences, atmospheric storm modeling, multimedia digital libraries, geophysical modeling, chemical reaction modeling, and imaging for medical radiation therapy.

Developing On-Line Knowledge Repositories

Another area that CNRI feels is top priority to the advancement of the information age is on-line access to huge knowledge databases, including, for example, library holding, all published works, and research reports. If all the information that existed in this country were accessible on-line, everyone would benefit—researchers, high school students, and corporations, to name a few. People could find information that they didn't know existed, or could get faster access to information they knew of to help speed up their work. But the problem is that even if all the information was on-line, it would be an overwhelming task to sift through it for the things that were pertinent to you.

Researching Knowbots

CNRI hopes to remove this problem through its research into *knowbots* (the term comes from *knowledge robots*). These robots aren't mechanical men with computers for brains, as most people envision robots. CNRI's knowbots are computer programs that, given a type of information to look for, go off and search through the on-line world for items pertinent to that topic.

The April 1991 issue of *Discover* magazine quotes Vinton Cerf, vice president of CNRI, as saying that knowbots are analogous to mechanical robots because they "serve humans as their surrogates in the world of electronic data, just as mechanical robots serve as surrogates in the physical world."

The *Discover* article goes on to investigate the pros and cons of knowbots. These knowbots have been likened to viruses—programs that go off on their own, visiting any machines they can find on the network. But viruses are usually viewed as being malicious and destructive; knowbots would be "good" viruses, only asking for information.

Even if they aren't intended as malicious, care must be taken in the design of knowbots. Some things that need to be taken under consideration in the development of knowbots are as follows:

- Asking/granting permission for a knowbot to access a certain information repository

- Charging fees for the use of the information it finds

- Packaging the information so that it isn't unwieldy to transport

- Developing a way to specify the information the knowbot is looking for in a concise yet complete manner

Also, if knowbots do have virus-like behavior, that behavior must be kept under control to keep the knowbot from becoming a drain on system performance, and keep it out of places where it shouldn't be. And if charges are being made for the information the knowbot is accessing, some type of mechanism will have to be built into the knowbot to limit its searches to stay within its owner's budget.

The Internet Society

Another organization involved in shaping the future of the Internet is the recently formed Internet Society (ISOC). The Internet Society was organized by CNRI, EDUCOM (an organization of that helps colleges and universities integrate computer networking into their institutions), RARE (a consortium of European research networks), and the Internet Architecture Board.

The Internet Society encourages the formation of a global communications network and attempts to facilitate the operations of the Internet. ISOC provides forums for the discussion of Internet-related topics, and provides educational materials and informational training. The organization also serves as the secretariat for the Internet Architecture Board and its Internet Engineering Task Force (IETF), organizing and coordinating the work of hundreds of volunteers for these organizations worldwide.

> **Note**
>
> The Internet Architecture Board, previously the Internet Activities Board, is a committee of volunteers who help coordinate the design, engineering, and development of the Internet. The IETF is a task force of the IAB whose members are volunteers interested in exploring technical developments that will enhance the evolution of the Internet.

ISOC sponsors the INET conference, which brings Internet users and potential users together to discuss topics such as regional network status, network policy, applications, and technical developments.

Vinton Cerf, a founding member of the Internet Society, explains that among other things, the organization's goals are to take responsibility for standards-making work and to encourage the use of network technology for humanitarian purposes. Volunteers In Technical Assistance, for example, is an organization that uses the Internet to coordinate disaster relief and other humanitarian activities.

The Internet Society also encourages the use of the Internet in international applications. The World Bank uses the Internet to coordinate investment transactions. The United Nations is on the Internet, as is the French Embassy, which uses the Internet to stay in touch with French scientists.

One area that the ISOC is interested in is getting technologically poor nations on-line. In an article in the December 1992 issue of the *Communications of the ACM*, Larry Press discusses some of the issues related to getting the Internet into these "less industrialized nations" (as he calls them). Even rudimentary connections to the Internet can have great benefits for these countries. But the software allowing these connections is cryptic to use and difficult to install, requiring knowledgeable, well-trained users. To train a small number of people to start these networks isn't difficult, but to provide systems that average citizens of these nations can use is more difficult. Larry Press has established an ftp site to archive papers on global networking at `dhvx20.csudh.edu` in the `global_net` directory (see Chapter 8, "Using ftp and telnet," for information about retrieving information from ftp sites). He also moderates a news group that discusses global networking.

Who Will Protect Internet Members' Privacy?

One area that needs to be addressed in the networked society of the future is that of privacy. Computer networks offer the opportunity for monitored surveillance and unwanted intrusion.

Until the last few years, the Internet community was relatively small and composed of people that wouldn't be inclined to harm another member's property intentionally or spy on other members. Growth of the Internet community itself wouldn't necessarily lead to privacy problems, if the new members were the traditional research and academic individuals. But the composition of the community is changing, because now almost anyone can get an Internet account through one of the commercial providers. Unfortunately, individuals who don't respect the privacy of anyone can get an Internet account and are becoming a concern. Ways of protecting people without diminishing the usefulness of the network must be found.

Obviously, companies who connect to the Internet want to keep their proprietary information from being accessed by people who don't have any business with it. Also, copyrighted material must be protected from inappropriate use. Having medical records on-line would be very valuable for patients being treated in an emergency or by out-of-town physicians, but access to medical records is a very sensitive issue. Also of concern is the on-line availability of large amounts of sensitive data, even if this data is accessible only to members of the organization that collected it. For example, in the summer of 1993, it was announced that IRS employees had been snooping through on-line income-tax returns.

The Internet, as it stands now, isn't "run" by anyone. No one sets rules, and no one can impose penalties on those who use the network destructively. Who, therefore, if anyone, should police the Internet? Traditional law enforcement agencies have no experience with computer crime, although the federal government is trying to address this area. Currently, several groups have formed to address the issues of computer users' rights and responsibilities.

The Role of Traditional Law Enforcement

Crimes involving computers may be beyond the comprehension of many traditional law enforcement organizations, on the federal level as well as the local level. Law agencies often don't know how to judge the seriousness of crimes committed by computer or crimes that involve the incapacitation of computers. (See Chapter 2, "The History of the Internet," for some examples of the malicious use of computers.) In several cases over the last few years, the FBI has confiscated hardware and software in unfounded or misunderstood accusations against small software developers and electronic publishers.

The FBI would like to have wiretap access to all public and private data networks. The Clinton administration initially supported this request, and President Clinton was going to sign legislation requiring all computer equipment to use a form of data encryption that the FBI would be able to decode. However, concerns of the computer industry and members of the computer-using public about requiring this type of access to private information have caused the administration to rethink its position.

This requirement could be very expensive to the computer and telecommunications industries, because they would have to redesign equipment and retrofit existing equipment. Corporations that want to use private encryption methods to send sensitive data over the Internet are worried that using a known encryption method would lead to unauthorized access to their private data.

In support of its request that the industry re-engineer its networks, the FBI argues that wiretaps are vital to national security. The proposed legislation would provide for two neutral organizations to hold the encryption keys and would require the FBI to obtain search warrants to get the keys. But industry opponents still think that this system would put an undue burden on the computer manufacturers and end users.

Computer Professionals for Social Responsibility

Tip
You can get more information about CPSR by sending e-mail to cpsr@cpsr.org.

Several organizations are concerned about the issues of computer privacy and law enforcement. One of them is the Computer Professionals for Social Responsibility (CPSR). CPSR was originally formed in 1983 because of concerns about the reliability of software developed for military applications. Over the years, CPSR has become concerned about many social issues that involve the use of computers.

Concerns of Privacy

Privacy of on-line records is one area of most concern to CPSR. With the ease of data exchange, companies with marketing lists easily can sell a person's private information to anyone who is willing to pay for it. Although sometimes this information involves only the person's name, address, and phone number, sometimes the information includes such things as approximate household income, types of frequently made purchases, and other facts of a more personal nature. And many people object to any information—especially their phone number—being distributed without their knowledge.

Although the U.S. courts have ruled that a person loses rights to information that that person gives to someone else (1976, *U.S. v. Miller*), CPSR believes that perhaps individuals could claim rights to their information under the copyright law. Lotus Development Corporation, for example, tried to market a product called MarketPlace, which was a CD-ROM-based system containing marketing information about millions of American consumers. When consumers found out about this product, tens of thousands of them contacted Lotus to have their names removed from the product. (Lotus eventually withdrew the product.) CPSR suggests that a situation like this may be okay if the consumers were compensated for the use of their data.

Concerns of Catastrophic Technical Failure

In addition to concerns of privacy, CPSR is concerned about the ethical design and use of computer applications. One potential problem area is that of large software systems being widely used for applications that may involve putting a human life in danger. Software designers must be very careful that a system such as this is thoroughly tested before it is installed, and that system errors are handled in a safe manner. Potential disasters may occur if a widespread problem would appear in hundreds or even thousands of locations using an application such as this at the same time.

Concerns of Workers and Technology

CPSR also is concerned about the issue of technology replacing workers. The organization is encouraging employers to use technology to enhance workers' skills, not to replace workers.

CPSR also is concerned that federal research and development funding not decrease as military funding (one area that traditionally drives R&D) decreases. Another concern is reducing environmental pollution caused during the production of technological devices. The organization encourages all computer professionals to take social responsibility for their professional activities when at all possible.

Electronic Frontier Foundation

Tip
For more information about the EFF, send e-mail to info@eff.org.

Another organization concerned about the social problems created by the computer industry is the Electronic Frontier Foundation (EFF). EFF was founded in 1990 by Mitchell Kapor, founder of Lotus Development Corporation, and John Perry Barlow, rock lyricist and computer enthusiast, in response to perceived infringements of computer users' rights by law enforcement organizations. EFF's main concern is protecting the rights of computer users in a world that isn't sure how to apply traditional legal rights to complicated new technologies. The organization also wants to help shape public policy in the emerging area of computer-based communications.

Emerging Technologies

Research is going on in many areas to improve the usability of the Internet. Two of these areas are a capability to broadcast information simultaneously to multiple hosts on the Internet and the capability to have mobile Internet nodes.

The MBONE is the experimental high-speed, high-bandwith Internet backbone, where researchers are experimenting with the broadcast of live video. Other researchers are investigating the technology necessary to provide Internet links that ships or other mobile computing units could use. One application that currently doesn't require any technical innovations, but is an innovation in services, is Internet Talk Radio, an audio program that you can access over the Internet.

Faster Communications

The *bandwidth* of the network refers to volume of information that it can carry. Higher bandwidths can carry more information in the same period of time. Although relatively low bandwidths can carry quite a bit of text and even voice transmission, live video and computer-generated animation require a large bandwidth to carry enough information to have them reconstituted correctly in real time. Researchers are currently investigating these areas.

The MBONE

Currently, an experimental network is set up to test audio and video broadcasts over the Internet. Although this network, called the Multicast Backbone (MBONE), uses the physical Internet to carry its traffic, it needs special router hardware and destination machines that understand the format of the data packets to send and receive the data. As the hardware and software becomes efficient and robust, many commercial vendors are expected to build into their products the capability to use the MBONE (or its commercial version).

One of the major ways of testing the MBONE is by broadcasting live video from the IETF meetings. The 1993 summer meeting of the Internet's IETF was held in Amsterdam, the Netherlands. Video and audio coverage of all the sessions was broadcast over the MBONE. Users with the proper software could receive the conference right at their workstations, anywhere in the world.

Although the video quality of the initial broadcasts wasn't great, as the technology improves, users will be able to get live video coverage over the Internet. Eventually, the technology should allow interactive video conferences. Imagine attending a conference without ever leaving your office. The presenter could receive a live video image of each participant when that person had a question or comment. People who can't afford the cost of traveling to a conference could use this low-cost alternative. Of course, remote conferences may not present the opportunity for peer interaction that exists in a face-to-face meeting, but this limitation also may be overcome—someday.

Internet Talk Radio

Tip
For information about how to retrieve and play the files, and for other information about Internet Talk Radio, send e-mail to info@radio.com.

In an attempt to provide a useful quasi-commercial application on the Internet, Internet Multicasting Service (a non-profit corporation) has started offering Internet Talk Radio, a professionally produced audio file distributed over the Internet. The "show," done in the format of National Public Radio, is intended to provide news about the Internet. The "show" isn't a live broadcast; instead, it is a file that you can retrieve over the Internet using ftp. It can be played on any workstation that can produce audio output, including PCs and Macintoshes.

The main feature of Internet Talk Radio is "Geek of the Week," an interview with a prominent Internet personality. Book reviews, restaurant reviews from different sections of the Internet community, analysis of current technical proposals, and, eventually, coverage of industry events (conferences, trade shows, and so forth) also are available. Internet Talk Radio even carries two NPR shows—*TechNation: Americans and Technology* and *SOUNDPRINT*. Each daily program runs between 30 and 90 minutes.

Although the program is now modeled after a radio broadcast (because of the limited number of facilities that can support more advanced features), the producers expect that as multimedia becomes standardized and widely used, video and real-time interaction eventually will be integrated into the broadcast. The producers also hope to get the show to be a self-sufficient Internet news service.

Mobile Internet Hosts

Another area now under research is mobile computing. Researchers are experimenting with maintaining Internet connections networks within vehicles such as ships or space-craft. Individual mobile hosts for anything from a laptop to a robotic unit are another research area.

Unfortunately, the current cellular phone system isn't suited for data communication because the data is *analog* (a continuous wave, like a radio wave), as opposed to *digital* (in its most simple terms, a series of ones and zeros), which is needed for high-speed communications. Also, the number of simultaneous calls allowed in a cell is limited, which would make cellular technology unsuitable because a large number of Internet connections likely would occur in a small geographical area. A complex satellite network is proposed to provide the needed connectivity for mobile networking technology.

Future Uses of the Internet

This section discusses a few areas where the Internet could provide tremendous improvement for researchers and scientists. These areas include the National Research Council's idea for a collaboratory to develop research projects (for which the Internet would provide the communications links). Although most simulations of this type are currently research-based, eventually these types of simulations could be used for commercial or public-service applications.

Collaboratories

The 1993 National Research Council report *National Collaboratories: Applying Information Technology for Scientific Research* discusses a major application for a nationwide computer network. It proposes that research be performed by groups of researchers in *collaboratories*, a term coined by William Wulf when he was the assistant director of the National Science Foundation's Directorate for Computer and Information Science and Engineering. The report gives a number of examples of possible areas that would benefit from collaboratories.

A collaboratory—a combination of the terms *collaboration* and *laboratory*—is used to indicate a research environment where geographically distant researchers can share instruments, data, and computing resources to work closely on projects.

Oceanography is a young science of growing importance in areas such as the predictions of global weather patterns. Traditionally, data is difficult to gather. Researchers who have devoted a great deal of time to gathering a data set haven't had much incentive to share their data with other researchers in the discipline. A collaboratory in this area of research could serve to bring colleagues in more frequent contact with each other, to share the effort of data collection, and to allow the data to be shared among projects. Efforts now are under way to create an Internet link for sea-going research vessels so that they can interact with land-based researchers as they gather data and can transmit the data quickly back to researchers' machines.

Molecular biology is an area in which a number of collaborative efforts already are under way. Researchers trying to unlock the mysteries of human DNA use computers to store DNA patterns, compare them to find similarities, and analyze their findings. A group of molecular biologists who are studying a particular nematode worm is developing a model collaboratory. The approximately 500 researchers around the world use a common set of tools to search data transparently from all their research sites. Researchers can retrieve database items for study and can submit new items to be available to all the other participants.

In any collaboratory, the Internet could provide a wealth of resources in addition to the data collection and storage capabilities. Distant researchers could work together, building models and observing their results remotely. Models could guide the planning of the field researchers' work, and interfaces could be built to help the field researchers understand the models' results. Eventually, research efforts will be published on-line, providing immediate access to the most recent discoveries in a field. The tools that do these things should provide transparent access to the researcher, freeing him or her from knowing where to find all the information needed.

Weather Forecasting

It would be very valuable if weather forecasters could predict sudden severe storms that produce flash floods and tornadoes. Supercomputers available on the Internet could provide this capability.

An article in the July 25, 1993, *Pittsburgh Post-Gazette* talks about a weather simulation program running at the Pittsburgh Supercomputer Center. A Cray C90 at the Pittsburgh Super-computer Center accurately predicted a fierce storm that occurred a few hours later in Oklahoma. Data of the current weather conditions provided the information to allow the atmospheric modeling program to predict the storm. Such models could allow time to warn people in an area where a flash flood will occur, or to allow snow-removal crews to be alerted only when a storm is certain, thus saving lives and money.

Summary

The Internet continues to expand at an incredible rate that will bring the Internet into every facet of our lives, from reading a personalized copy of the newspaper with breakfast; to personalized course selections for primary, secondary, and college students; to telecommuting; to the weather forecast we get on our evening news.

As the Internet expands, research is needed not only in the areas of the hardware and software required to implement it, but also in the effects it will have on society. The Internet can make us a truly global society, making information available to lesser-developed countries and remote areas of the United States, and giving everyone an opportunity to develop to their full potential. Although issues need to be addressed to ensure that privacy and other rights aren't breached, the Internet can serve to be a powerful and positive driving force for improvement in society.

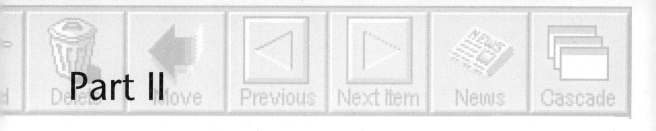

Part II

Features and Services

? HELP   - Get help using Pine

C COMPOSE   - Compose and send a message

I MAIL INDEX - Read mail in current folder

Mail in progress...

"------ Mail Composition Editor ------ "

ftpmail@decwrl.dec.com

Edit   Done   Cancel

file request via ftpmail server

Note. In Pine 3.0 we are encouraging folks to use the MAIL INDEX to
      mail instead of VIEW MAIL, so it is no longer on the main menu
      in the mail index, it is available as usual as the "V" command

Help   Quit   Folders   Other
Compose   Mail Index Addresses

Delete   Move   Previous   Next Item   News   Cascade

coming Mail

NSFNET Packet Traffi

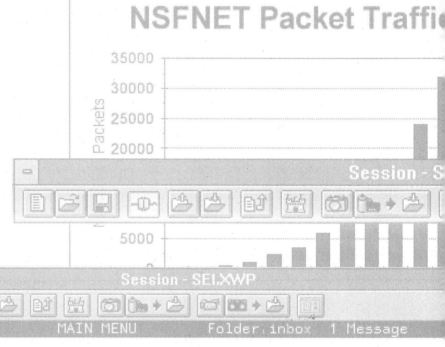

35000
30000
25000
20000

Packets

Session - S

5000

Session - SEI.XWP

PINE 3.07   MAIN MENU   Folder:inbox   1 Message

```
?    HELP        - Get help using Pine

C    COMPOSE     - Compose and send a message

I    MAIL INDEX  - Read mail in current folder
```

Call

Mail in progress...

* ------ Mail Composition Editor ------ *

TO: ftpmail@decwrl.dec.com   Edit   Done   Cancel

CC:

ject: file request via ftpmail server

```
Note. In Pine 3.0 we are encouraging folks to use the MAIL INDEX t
      mail instead of VIEW MAIL, so it is no longer on the main me
      in the mail index, it is available as usual as the "Y" comma
```

Help   Quit   Folders   Other
Compose   Mail Index   Addresses

Chapter 7

Using E-Mail

Electronic mail is one of the major uses of the Internet, and certainly one of the easiest to take advantage of. Just as you can drop a letter in a postal box, you can electronically write, address, and send an e-mail message to someone. This chapter will give you the information you need to use this powerful tool.

What Is E-Mail?

E-mail (short for *electronic mail*) is a method of sending a message from a user on a computer to a recipient user on a destination host. This message is made up of a set of *header lines*, which tell the computer system how to deliver the message, and the *message body*, which can contain any text (such as an office memo or personal letter).

Historically, electronic mail has been one of the main uses of the Internet, and was one of its first applications. Early in the development of the Internet, computer users needed to send messages to other users; electronic mail applications were developed to make this communication possible. Electronic mail applications are now part of almost all computer systems on the Internet.

In general, two distinct sets of programs are used to handle e-mail. The first is called the *user agent*, which is the program that the user interacts with to compose outgoing mail, read incoming mail, and perform all the housekeeping chores necessary to deal with mail messages (such as deleting old mail or reorganizing the mail messages in a logical format).

The second set of programs, which users can't see operating, are the *mail delivery* programs. These programs are responsible for taking a mail message from the user agent program and delivering the mail message to the remote host. Mail delivery programs generally run as part of the underlying operating system on the originating and destination hosts; they are not run by users directly.

The format of electronic mail messages is specified in the Internet RFC (Request For Comments) number 822, available by way of anonymous ftp to `ds.internic.net` in directory `/rfc`. This RFC defines all the required headers and any optional parameters that you can use in mail messages. Read this RFC if you want to understand why certain information is required in your message.

Note

You don't need to read the RFCs that define what a mail message looks like (unless you are interested in knowing more about the mail standards), but you do need to make sure that your mail software follows these standards. Ask your software supplier to make sure.

If you want to interchange mail with other hosts on the Internet, the mail user program on your machine must generate mail messages that follow the RFC 822 standard. Most machines connected to the Internet also use mail transport programs that communicate by using the *Simple Mail Transport Protocol (SMTP)*, which is specified in RFC 821. This RFC defines the commands and options used by mailers that speak the SMTP protocol; you should read this RFC if you want to understand how the mail transport programs on the Internet operate.

This isn't to say that other mail transport mechanisms and mail formats aren't in use, but SMTP is the most widely used mail message transport protocol, and RFC 822 is the only common mail message interchange format accepted on the Internet.

The Format of an E-Mail Message

As mentioned earlier, an electronic mail message is composed of the mail headers and the message body. In general, the mail programs generate most of the mail headers automatically, but the user must specify some of the important information.

You can understand how the mail header information is used by thinking of an example out of a familiar situation: an office memo confirming receipt of a delivery.

```
To: David Smith, Shipping Department
CC: William Price, Purchasing Department
From: Roberta Page, Production
Date: April 1, 1993
Subject: Delivery of the widget shipment

Dave:
   I assume that we have received the widget shipment in
its entirety. If we have not, please inform me at once.

        Thanks,

        Roberta
```

The headers of a mail message appear at the top of the message and are separated from the message body by a blank line. Each header line starts with a keyword followed by a colon; for example, a valid header line is one starting with `From:`. Each header line can extend across several lines; wherever space can be allowed in a header line, you can use a carriage return followed by at least one space. The exact syntax of the header lines is fully defined in RFC 822, but summaries of the commonly used header lines follow.

Destination Header Lines

The headers of the mail message hold several different (and important) types of information. First of all, the address specification lines (or *destination lines*) give information that the mail programs use to deliver the message to the intended recipients. These header lines begin with any of the following key words: `To:`, `Resent-To:`, `CC:`, `Resent-CC:`, `BCC:`, or `Resent-BCC:`. The function of these lines is clear; they tell the system who is supposed to receive the message.

In the earlier office memo example, we see that two people are supposed to receive the memo: one specified by a `To:` address (David Smith) and one in a `CC:` address (William Price). The sample e-mail message would have header lines starting with `To:` and `CC:` and have the e-mail addresses of these two recipients.

All the destination lines specify an address (of the form *user@host*), with the `To:` address being the primary recipient(s) of the message. Addresses on any `CC:` line are the secondary recipients of the message (the primary recipients see these addresses), and addresses on any `BCC:` receive *blind carbon copies* (the primary recipients don't see that these people are receiving carbon copies) of the message.

The destination lines that begin with `Resent-` are treated the same as the equivalent lines without the `Resent-` part, but indicate that the mail message is being forwarded from another user who was the original recipient of the message.

For example, one of the recipients of the memo may want to forward the memo to one of his managers. With a paper memo, you could add a new recipient and just send a copy along; with an e-mail message, you would add a `Resent-To:` header with a new recipient address.

Originator Header Lines

The *originator headers* are those beginning with the key words
`From:`, `Sender:`, `Reply-To:`, `Resent-From:`, `Resent-Sender:`, and
`Resent-Reply-To:`. In the sample office memo earlier, there is
only one originator (Roberta Page); if the memo was from a
group of people, there could be many originators.

These header lines give information about the user who sent, or
originated, the mail message. In general, the mail programs that
users run generate these lines automatically, but the accuracy of
the header information isn't guaranteed. It is quite possible for
the sender to insert any information into these lines, so users
shouldn't treat these originator lines as proof of who actually
sent the message. (More information about *mail forging* is given
later in this chapter.)

The `From:` line gives the primary (or only) author of the message. The mail programs should set this field to be the address
of the person or program who caused the message to be sent.
If this line isn't present, the `Sender:` line must be present.

The `Sender:` line also gives the primary person (or program) who
sent the message. What makes the `Sender:` line different from
the `From:` line is that `Sender:` is used when the sender of the
message isn't the author of the message, or to indicate which
author from among a group of authors actually sent the message. A mail message may be listed as from a particular user, for
example, but may have been generated by an automatic program. In this case, the `From:`line designates the user, but the
`Sender:` line designates the program that actually generated
the message.

Again looking at the office memo, suppose that Roberta Page
wrote the memo but had her secretary (Jim Short) actually send
it out. In this case, the `From:` header line would have Roberta
Page's address, but a `Sender:` line would give Jim Short's address.

II

Features and Services

The `Reply-To:` header line gives the mail address to which replies to this message should be addressed. Often, if the message is from a program or mailing list, the `Reply-To:` line indicates a person or list maintainer who should receive any replies. This way, users can reply to automatically generated messages without having to know the person associated with them.

As with the destination lines, the originator header lines that begin with `Resent-` indicate that the message was re-sent from a second user, who was the original recipient of the message. In the memo example, if William Price re-sent the message to one of his co-workers (for example, Carol Cage), a `Resent-To: Carol Cage` line and a `Resent-From: William Price` line would appear (using their e-mail addresses instead of their names, of course).

Other Mandatory Headers

Other header lines give information about the enclosed mail message. The `Date:` and `Resent-Date:` give the date and time that the message was sent (or re-sent). The date field is in the form of the current date followed by the time (in the local time zone or Greenwich Mean Time). The day of the week may be included before the date.

The `Return-Path:` line, automatically added by the final mail transport program, gives a definitive route back to the originating address. Often, you can use this line if the address given in the `From:` header isn't valid. This is as though the postal carrier stamped your home address on the outside of the envelope when he picked it up from your mail box; even if you didn't sign your letter on the inside, the recipient can still see who sent the message.

Other header lines are generated automatically by the mail delivery programs and record information about the mail delivery process. The `Received` header lines record the different machines that the mail message passed through during the delivery process. It is as though each post office that handled a letter would put a stamp on the outside, indicating where it had been.

Different parts of the Received headers give information about which host, mail program, and protocols were used in handling the mail message. This information can be extremely useful in debugging possible mail problems, but in most cases, you can ignore it.

Optional Mail Headers

According to RFC 822, mail programs may add other header lines for their own use, but the mail delivery programs don't require these headers. Some examples of these headers are as follows:

- Message-ID: and Resent-Message-ID:, which define a unique text string identifying the current message

- In-Reply-To: and References:, which refer to a message that this message is in reply to

- Keywords:, Subject:, and Comments:, which enable the user to insert text to identify the contents of the message body

- Encrypted:, which defines the program used to encrypt the message body and may optionally give an indication of the key used to encrypt the message

The user or the mail programs also may insert other headers, which the mail transport system will ignore. The user should be careful in using non-standard headers, however, because the mail transport programs may not understand them and may lose or misdirect your mail.

Addressing E-Mail Messages

The most difficult idea for new users of electronic mail to understand is mail addresses. A *mail address* is the way to specify the recipient of a mail message; every person who can receive mail messages on the Internet has a unique mail address.

Using mail addresses isn't difficult, but the process of finding out the mail address of a person can be difficult.

User and Host Names

A mail address consists of two separate parts: the *host address* and the *user name*. These parts, separated by the at sign (@), make up a full mail address, such as `postmaster@no-machine.com`. In this example, the host address is `no-machine.com` and the user name is `postmaster`.

In most cases, the host address part of the mail address for a user is the name of the machine they use to connect to the Internet. As explained in Chapter 3, "The Structure of the Internet," the host address is a *fully qualified domain name*, which uniquely specifies the host on the Internet. The network administrator at the host's site assigns this host name.

The user name part of the electronic mail address is really an arbitrary string set by the systems administrator of the user's site. In most cases, it corresponds to the login name of the user, but some sites set up mail addresses that consists of the first and last name of the user.

> **Note**
>
> The user name field doesn't have to be associated with a real user. A site administrator can set up a *mail alias* that allows mail to a particular address to be delivered to a program (to retrieve files, for example) or to a mailing list. Both types of mail aliases are discussed later in this chapter.

Note that this type of mail address is the simplest form, although it is the one you usually encounter when communicating with users who are directly connected to the Internet. At times, though, you see more complicated address forms, especially when the user you are contacting is on some other network connected to but not a part of the Internet.

For example, mail for a user on another network (such as BIT-NET or UUCP networks) must go through a *gateway* machine that understands how to communicate between the Internet and the foreign network. Many times, to get mail to one of these users, you must manually tell the mail programs to contact this gateway machine.

Look at an example of this mail routing. Many machines not directly connected to the Internet use a protocol called *UUCP* (UNIX to UNIX Copy) to send mail and other information. If the administrator of one of these machines configured the machine to receive mail from the Internet, the host address for the machine usually ends in .uucp (for example, mail addresses for the machines look like user@machine.uucp).

The problem for Internet users is that the .uucp domain really doesn't exist for them—it simply indicates that mail should be sent through the gateway machine, which understands how to route the mail to the right place. So to send mail to a user in the .uucp domain, you usually must route the mail manually through the appropriate gateway machine. For example, if you receive mail from a user on a machine that is connected using UUCP, for example, the return address will be something like uunet!host1!user. This means that the mail goes through the machine uunet, then the machine host1, and then is delivered to the user (called simply user in this example). The gateway machine in this example is the leftmost machine in the address. In this case, the gateway machine is uunet, which on the Internet is called uunet.uu.net.

Features and Services

II

> **Note**
>
> Unfortunately, there is no central machine that you can use to route all mail to people on UUCP machines. The machine uunet.uu.net is one of the central hubs that connect the UUCP machines to the Internet, however, so it is a fairly common gateway.

So, in this case, you can address the mail by using an address of host1!user@uunet.uu.net (by removing the first part of the address and sending it manually through the uunet gateway), or even user%host1.uucp@uunet.uu.net (which is just a different way of writing the same address). While this process is somewhat complicated, your mail software often will generate the correct return address for you when you reply to a message.

Often, a user experienced on a network that needs special routing tells you explicitly how to reach him. You also can find information about how to route between the Internet and other networks by reading the Updated_Inter-Network_Mail_Guide file posted periodically to the news group comp.mail.misc, and also available by way of anonymous ftp to rtfm.mit.edu in the directory /pub/usenet/comp.mail.misc. (You can retrieve this also through ftpmail if you don't have direct ftp capabilities or access to USENET. ftpmail is discussed later in this chapter and also in Chapter 8, "Using ftp and telnet.")

How To Find the E-Mail Address for a User

When you deal with electronic mail, one of the most common questions you hear is, *How do I find out the address for a user?* Often, this question isn't easy to answer due to the diverse nature of the Internet and the number of users connected to it. Just think how complicated trying to find out someone's postal address would be if no directories were available to list the information centrally! This is exactly the problem with finding electronic mail addresses: now very few central databases of mail addresses are on the Internet, and those that do exist list only a fraction of the people who can receive mail.

Even though very few central databases of electronic mail addresses exist, you can still use many resources to locate an address. The more information you have about the person you are looking for, however, the better the chance you have of locating that person on the Internet.

Some of the resources you can use to locate a user's address on the Internet are as follows:

- Direct contact with the person in question

- The Internet WHOIS databases

- The USENET address server

- College and university address servers

> **Note**
>
> Don't distribute people's electronic mail addresses without their permission. Although you often can locate a person's address by looking in a public database, you shouldn't distribute that person's address widely (to a large mailing list, for example) without asking that person first. The user in question may not know that his or her address is publicly available, or that user simply may not want his or her electronic mail box flooded with unwanted mail. (As electronic junk mail becomes more prevalent, distribution of an e-mail address becomes an open invitation for a flood of electronic junk mail.)

Direct Contact

Because of the lack of databases of e-mail addresses, quite often the easiest way to discover the mail address for a particular user is to ask that person directly. If you have some other contact with a user (for example, a business card or postal address), you often can simply call or write the user in question and ask if he or she has a valid electronic mail address. In fact, many companies with Internet connections now print their e-mail addresses right on their business cards.

Alternatively, if you have seen a netnews post from a user and you want to send electronic mail to that user, you can often examine the headers of the netnews post to determine the return address for the user. This information usually is given in the `From:` or `Reply-To:` header lines in the post, or the user may include an e-mail address in his *signature*—text included automatically at the end of his post. See Chapter 9, "USENET," for more information about news posts.

The WHOIS Databases

Originally, the WHOIS databases were set up to register the host and network administrators at the various sites on the Internet. These databases have been expanded to include other people as well, including people who are not administrators. Two different sites now run major WHOIS databases: `nic.ddn.mil` and `whois.internic.net`.

> **Note**
>
> The databases are referred to as the WHOIS databases because many of the original systems on the Internet had a command called `whois` that would connect to this database and automatically look up the information you wanted. This command is still part of many systems on the Internet.

These two databases contain similar information, but for different parts of the Internet. The database at the site `nic.ddn.mil` contains information only on machines that are part of the Department of Defense military network, while the database at the site `whois.internic.net` contains information on the rest of the Internet.

For each of these databases, you can find information such as the names and addresses (electronic and postal) for the administrators who run a particular domain, or part of the Internet. You can find information about individual sites on the Internet, sometimes including which machines at that site are connected to the Internet and who uses them.

To use the WHOIS databases, you can telnet to the WHOIS server machine and run the command whois after you are connected. The whois command allows you to ask for information about a user, host machine, or network. You can use the command whois host ds.internic.net, for example, and receive information about the address of the machine, the administrator of the machine, and some of the users of the machine that are registered with the WHOIS service.

The search keywords that the WHOIS server supports are domain, network, host, gateway, organization, or group. whois searches that don't specify a keyword are assumed to be searching for a user name.

If you can't telnet directly to the WHOIS server, you also can use the database by sending electronic mail to the address whois@whois.internic.net (or service@nic.ddn.mil for military addresses). If you send a message with help in the message body, you will receive more information about the mail server.

You also can access the WHOIS database by using a *Gopher* client to connect to the two machines. For more information about Gopher, see Chapter 13, "Aids to Navigating the Internet." Some computer systems (most UNIX systems, for example) also have a local whois command that connects automatically to the central WHOIS database and does a query for you. Check with your local site administrator to see if such a command is available on your system.

The WHOIS database is a valuable resource for finding out information about sites on the Internet. Because all networks must be registered with the network registration services and must provide the name of a person to contact for the network, you have a very good chance of finding out a contact name for a particular network. On the other hand, many users or hosts aren't in the WHOIS database, so you aren't as likely to find information about individual users there.

Other sites on the Internet run local WHOIS servers to provide information about their local users. Unfortunately, finding out exactly which sites do so is difficult, unless you ask administrators there. One list of sites that run WHOIS servers is available by way of anonymous ftp to the site `sipb.mit.edu` in the file `/pub/whois/whois-servers.list`. See Chapter 8, "Using ftp and telnet," for more information about how to use anonymous ftp.

USENET Addresses Server

If the person you are looking for posts articles on netnews, finding out an address for that person is possible by using the USENET addresses server. This database server, run on the machine `rtfm.mit.edu`, scans all USENET posts and stores the addresses it finds in a central database.

To ask the server for an address, send an electronic mail message to the address `mail-server@rtfm.mit.edu` with a message of the form `send usenet-addresses/`*string* in the message body. You should replace *string* with a list of words to search for. For example, if you were looking for the address of the user `mjohnson`, you could send the request `send usenet-addresses/mjohnson`.

The server will send a mail message back to you with all the addresses that match any words you specify. You should include in the search string items that will help identify the user in question, such as the user's first and last name, and possibly the site that person may post from.

Because the database search matches any of the words you gave, you may get quite a few addresses in response. The server will return only a maximum of 40 addresses, however, so if you get 40 addresses back and the address you want isn't among them, you should eliminate some of the words to reduce the number of matches.

The USENET addresses database is also available through WAIS, on the machines `rtfm.mit.edu` and `cedar.cic.net`. On both machines, the database is called `usenet-addresses` and can be reached on port 210. For more information on the WAIS program, see Chapter 13, "Aids to Navigating the Internet." For more information about USENET and netnews posts, see Chapter 9, "USENET."

Looking Up Addresses at Colleges and Universities

If the person you are looking for is a student or employee of a college or university, you may be able to find out information about the electronic mail addresses by looking in the *College Email Addresses* postings in the news group `soc.college`.

This set of articles gives the electronic mail address policies for many universities and colleges across the country, and can often give enough information so that you can look up a particular user at that site.

You can retrieve these articles by looking in the `soc.college` netnews group (see Chapter 9, "USENET," for more information about reading news groups), or by anonymous ftp to `rtfm.mit.edu` in the directory `/pub/usenet/soc.college`. The articles are the ones starting with the name *FAQ:College-Email-Addresses*.

Other Tools and Techniques for Finding Addresses

You can use many other tools and techniques to look up electronic mail addresses, and more of these tools and techniques are being introduced every day.

Many companies run central servers to provide mail addresses for their employees, and even some countries have mail address servers (called *white pages* or *X.500 servers*). These servers are set up quite like a telephone directory, and the information in them is divided into small pieces called *organizations*.

An organization is like a single phone book, while the X.500 server is like a whole library of phone books.

One way to locate and use these servers is to use Gopher and WAIS clients. Many of these servers are advertised through these services, and you can browse around different sites without having to know which sites actually offer the services. If you know the name of the site where the person is (the college or university, or the company they work for), you can use a Gopher or WAIS client to look for a server at that site and get information about users there.

Gopher and WAIS are very valuable tools that can help you find an incredible amount of information about the Internet as a whole, and users on the Internet in particular. See Chapter 13, "Aids to Navigating the Internet," for more information about using these services.

Other services available for finding information about mail addresses, such as *netfind* and the *Knowbot Information Service*, are described in the `finding-addresses` Frequently Asked Questions post. You can find this post in the netnews group `comp.mail.misc`, and you can retrieve the file by way of anonymous ftp to `rtfm.mit.edu` in directory `/pub/usenet/comp.mail.misc`.

If you know the site where a user is but can't find out any information about the user name to use, you can ask the postmaster at that site for help. Every site on the Internet is required to have a mail address called `postmaster`, which is set up to be a person who can answer questions about the site. So you can send mail to the address postmaster at the site in question, and at least be reasonably sure that you will get an answer.

When you contact the postmaster at a site, you need to remember a few things. First of all, be specific about the user you are looking for, and be polite! The user who is designated as postmaster is quite often a systems administrator, and almost always very busy. Answering mail probably isn't something that is high on his priority list, so you should be patient. You probably will get a response within a few days. That said, almost every post-master on Internet sites takes the job seriously and will make every effort to find the information for you.

As a last resort, you can post a message to the news group `soc.net-people` and ask for the electronic mail address for the person. Because this is like advertising in the *New York Times*, asking if anyone has an address for your old college roommate, you should try this only when all other attempts—including calling the person in question—have failed. You should be as specific as possible when identifying the person, and you probably shouldn't get your hopes up too high. If all the aforementioned techniques have been tried and failed, the readers of `soc.net-people` probably won't have much better luck. For information about posting to news groups, see Chapter 9, "USENET."

Determining the Host Address

Most of the techniques given so far assume that you know at least a little about the site where a user is. If you don't know even this information, you probably won't be able to find the electronic mail address for the person. However, if you know something about the person (such as where they work or go to school), you often can deduce the site name for that person.

First, you need to determine the domain part of the address. As described in Chapter 3, "The Structure of the Internet," host names are made up of words separated by periods. For example, the name `charon.mit.edu` is a valid host name. The parts of the name go from the least specific at the right side (the `edu` part, called the *domain*) to the most specific at the left (`charon` in the preceding host name).

You can deduce the domain of the person's site if you know what type of institution he or she is at. For example, if the person is at a university, that person probably will have an `edu` domain. If the person works at a company, the domain probably will be `com`. Similarly, if the person lives in a foreign country, the domain will be the one associated with that country (for example, `fr` is the domain for France).

After you determine the domain, you need to find the site name. This name is often related in some way to the institution the person is affiliated with. For example, if the user is at Stanford University, the site name is `stanford.edu`. In other cases, acronyms are used. For example, the site name for Carnegie Mellon University in Pittsburgh is `cmu.edu`. These two examples show the most common ways that domains are named.

The WHOIS databases described so far are a very good way to look up these domain names. If you connect to the appropriate server, you can find all sites that match a search string. For example, you can use a command such as `whois carnegie` and search through the results until you find the entry for Carnegie Mellon University. This entry reveals that their domain name is `cmu.edu`. Another example is to use the command `whois international business` to find out that the site name for International Business Machines is (not surprisingly) `ibm.com`.

Getting Access to Electronic Mail

Now that you have read a little about the format of electronic mail messages and discovered how to find out how to address those messages, it is time to discuss how to get access to electronic mail.

When you try to get access to e-mail, the first consideration is what level of service you want to have. Although setting up and configuring electronic mail servers and applications isn't especially difficult, it may require some understanding of

networking and operating systems. Fortunately, several ways of
getting access to electronic mail don't require any administration on your part at all.

Public Access Sites

If you don't have a specific need to have electronic mail running directly on your local machine, the easiest way to get
access to it is to use one of many *public access sites* available on
the Internet. These public access sites are machines connected
to the Internet that provide accounts on a commercial basis.
Almost all these systems provide electronic mail; many also
provide access to netnews and other Internet services, such as
Gopher and ftp. The fees charged by these sites vary widely;
some don't have a usage fee, others charge a small fee to cover
their costs. Some are commercial providers that have levels of
service running from inexpensive to quite expensive.

The advantage of using a public access site is that you don't
need to worry about setting up and maintaining an electronic
mail system; someone already has done it for you. All you need
to do is log in to the machine (usually by way of telnet from
your local machine) and use the local mailer to send your mail.

The disadvantages of using such as public access site is that you
have no say (usually) about the configuration of the mail system. You must use the software the site administrators provide,
and you must observe whatever policies they maintain concerning the content of electronic mail (such as prohibitions
on commercial use). Also, because you often are using terminal
emulation software, the software you run to send mail usually
isn't graphical in nature. Given the number and variety of public access sites, however, these usually aren't problems—you can
often find a site that suits your needs.

II

Features and Services

> **Note**
>
> Explaining exactly the use you will make of the public access machine account when you apply for it is always best. Although censorship is almost unheard of on the Internet, some public-access machines do have restrictions on commercial use (such as receiving orders for merchandise) or material offensive to minors. You are much better off talking about your needs in advance rather than have the administrators of the machine "discover" your possible abuse of their policies later on.

After you decide to use a public-access site, several resources are available to help find one. To locate a public-access site, consult the lists provided on the disk included with this book in the file PDIAL.TXT. The PDIAL document is updated as the maintainer gets information about new public-access sites. It is kept at an ftp site (identified within the file) on the Internet and posted regularly to certain news groups, which also are identified in the file.

After you have the names of sites that may be able to provide the news access you need, you should contact the administrators at that site (given as the contact for information in the listings) to determine the features of the mail system on that machine. You need to ask about the following:

- *What mail programs are available to compose and send mail?* Most of these programs will be terminal oriented (that is, they don't have a graphical user interface), and several do have help features built in. Common mail interfaces are Elm, Pine, and MH, although many others exist. Some examples of the different mail interfaces used on public-access sites are discussed later in this chapter.

- *How much disk space is allocated to store user mail?* If you expect to receive large amounts of mail (you want to subscribe to several mailing lists, for example), you want to make sure that the system has sufficient disk space available to store it, and that you won't go over whatever amount is allocated to you. Some of the more active mailing lists can send you several megabytes of mail per week!

■ *What are the system policies regarding the content of electronic mail messages?* Also, can the systems administrators examine users' mail at will, or are there policies against it? You want to make sure that both you and they are comfortable with what you will be doing, and how they run the system.

Off-Line Mail Readers

An *off-line mail reading system* is another way to get access to electronic mail without having to administer the actual mail delivery programs on your local machine. Off-line mail systems use a local communications program to connect to a remote system or service. In general, you read your existing mail and compose new mail messages when you aren't connected to the remote machine; you connect periodically to send any new mail and to receive any mail that is waiting on the mail server machine.

This type of setup is more efficient than connecting to a remote machine and performing your mail tasks on-line. Because reading and composing mail are time-consuming tasks, you can save the connect time on the remote system (which often costs money!) by doing those tasks on your local machine.

Many different organizations offer off-line mail (and netnews) services. Most of these organizations now have Windows-compatible programs that provide a simple-to-use interface to the remote system, as well as easy-to-understand tools for managing your local mail (reading, filing, and sorting your mail messages, for example). Some of these organizations also feature other on-line services, such as an interactive "chat" service or file downloading capabilities.

> **Note**
>
> An *interactive chat program* allows you to talk to several people at once. These other people can be on the same machine you are on, or they can be on a machine anywhere else on the Internet.

Examples of these off-line mail services include Computer Witchcraft, Inc., which offers a system called WinNET Mail (which also offers netnews capability—see the chapter on netnews for more information about this part of their service), and General Videotex Corporation, which offers a service called BIX. BIX, accessible through a program called BIXnav, offers on-line chat programs and other services. Some examples of these programs are given later in this chapter.

If your system is running DOS only (that is, not Microsoft Windows), an off-line mail service from PSI (Performance Systems, Inc.) can be used to send and receive mail. This system, available in a DOS and a Windows version, has options to read and send mail, as well as read USENET news and retrieve files.

Setting up a Local Mail System

Setting up a mail system on your local machine isn't an easy task. Some experience with computer networking and the operating systems that are running on your systems will be required to make the mail programs run correctly. You also may have to buy some additional computer systems to act as mail gateway machines. Also, someone at your site must be designated as the postmaster and should monitor the mail system to make sure that it continues to work as expected.

To decide what mail software is appropriate to your site, you will first have to review what existing software your mail programs will have to work with. If, for example, you have existing mail software, and you simply want to be able to communicate with mailers on the rest of the Internet, you will have to run significantly different software than you would if you don't have any existing software.

The simplest type of mail system to set up is a stand-alone mail system. In this case, you have a single machine that communicates with the rest of the Internet. This type of system is simple, because you have only to set up and maintain a single computer system and mail programs.

To communicate with the majority of machines on the Internet, the mail system you run must be able to speak the Simple Mail Transport Protocol to communicate with the remote mail system. If you also want to receive your incoming mail on your local machine, it should also run an SMTP server that can accept mail from other Internet machines.

One option for sending and receiving mail on your local machine is PC-Eudora. This software is available by way of anonymous ftp to `ftp.qualcomm.com`. It uses the SMTP protocol to send mail to a remote server machine (usually, your Internet service provider will have a machine you can route mail through), but uses a different protocol called the *Post Office Protocol Version 3* (POP3) to receive mail. This configuration requires that you have a second machine to receive your mail and run the POP3 server.

Note

The Post Office Protocol is a way to have your electronic mail sent to a central machine and to allow you to pick up the messages on your personal machine whenever you want. A program on your local machine connects to the central mail machine and copies in any mail you have waiting.

Another option for a single machine to send and receive electronic mail is a commercial product called SelectMail from Sun Microsystems Inc. This product—available in Microsoft

Windows and MS-DOS versions—supports SMTP for sending mail and requires a POP server for receiving mail. Many other mail programs run on stand-alone machines; check with your computer system or software vendor to see what they have available.

Integrating with Existing Networks

If you already have some networking systems running at your site, your choices of electronic mail systems are very different and will depend on what you already are running.

If, for example, you already are running an internal network of computers with a product such as Microsoft Mail or Lotus Notes, you probably will want to buy a product that allows these systems to send mail through the SMTP protocol to the rest of the Internet. These products are available from the vendor from whom you bought your existing mail products. Third-party products that interface these systems to normal Internet mail systems also may be available.

If you are running a Novell network on your local system but don't have a mail system already, several inexpensive products can give you e-mail access. One mail system that uses the Novell MHS system to send mail locally is called Pegasus Mail. This system is available by way of anonymous ftp to `ftp.uu.net` in the file `/systems/ibmpc/msdos/simtel20/novell/pmail235.zip`.

Although Pegasus Mail can be used to send mail between systems on your local Novell network, you will need a gateway system to send mail to other Internet sites using SMTP. One such gateway product is called XGate, which is a shareware product available by way of anonymous ftp at the site `wuarchive.wustl.edu` in the file `/systems/novell/lan/xgate140.zip`. XGate must run on a separate dedicated personal computer system on your Novell network.

XGate is a MHS to SMTP gateway, but it also requires an
SMTP agent to handle the actual transmission of the mail.
Two such products are available, XSMTP and Charon.
XSMTP is a shareware product available from ftp Software
(but usually is included in the shareware version of XGate),
and Charon is a freely available software product of Clarkson
University. Charon is available by way of anonymous ftp to
`sun.soe.clarkson.edu` in the file `/pub/cutcp/charon.zip`.

Configuring XGate with XSMTP or Charon is beyond the scope
of this chapter, but documentation is included with the packages. Because these are shareware products, you can obtain
them and experiment with them before paying the registration
fee. The main cost of these packages is the expense of operating
a separate gateway machine for the XGate software. XSMTP
runs on the same machine as XGate, but Charon also requires
a separate computer system to run on.

Examples of Different Mail Systems

This section shows examples of several different mail systems
that you can use, on your own system or on a remote service
provider. The first examples are of character-oriented interfaces,
Pine and MH, which you can use if you are using a public access
site as your mail server. Later examples are from different off-
line mail readers that run on your PC.

Examples of the Pine Mail System

The Pine mail system is a simple screen-oriented interface to
sending electronic mail. This system is often used on public-
access sites, because it is easy to use and includes on-screen help
for novice users. If your public-access site has the Pine mail system available, you will normally use the command `pine` to run
the program after you log in to the public-access system.

II

Features and Services

When you first run Pine, you will see the main menu screen, which gives you the commands that are available. The main menu screen is shown in figure 7.1.

Fig. 7.1
The Pine Mailer main screen, which shows the main commands available and how to get help.

The I command will give you a list of the new mail messages that you have received, and allows you to select the message you want to view. At this point, you can use the V command to view a message, as shown in figure 7.2.

Fig. 7.2
The Pine View Message screen.

Other Pine commands enable you to move a message into a different *folder*. For example, you may have a folder for all mail from your boss, or different folders for mail relating to different projects you are working on. This way, you can organize your mail for easy access. You can also, of course, delete mail messages when you no longer need them.

The Pine c command allows you to compose, or send, new mail messages. An example of the compose screen is given in figure 7.3.

Fig. 7.3
The Pine Compose Message screen.

Examples of the MH System

The MH mail system is another common mail system you may encounter on a public access system, especially if that system runs the UNIX operating system. MH is a *command line* oriented mail system—you issue MH commands at the operating system prompt.

MH, available for many different operating systems, can be obtained by way of anonymous ftp to the site ftp.uu.net in the directory /mail/mh. MH is made up of many commands that enable you to read, send, or manipulate your mail messages. MH also includes the idea of mail "folders," where you can keep mail messages that are related in some way.

Examples of commonly used MH commands are as follows:

Command	Description
inc	Reads your system mail file into your inbox, which is the default folder created the first time you ran an MH command. Messages in your inbox (or any other folder, really) are numbered, and MH keeps track of the current message for you.
show	Displays your current message.
next	Moves to the next message in your folder and displays it.
prev	Moves to the previous message in your folder and displays it.
scan	Displays the headers of the messages in your folder. You can specify a range, or list, of the messages you want to look at.
comp	Allows you to compose a message to send to someone.
rmm	Removes the current message (or the one you specify).
repl	Replies to the current message.
refile	Lets you move a mail message into another folder.

Quite a few other MH commands manipulate messages or folders. MH is a very flexible mail system, and it works even when you don't have a graphical environment available.

Examples of the WinNET Mail System

WinNET Mail is an off-line mail system that allows you to read and compose mail messages while not connected to the service provider; you can then call the provider to actually deliver your mail (and receive new mail messages if any exist). WinNET

Mail, a Microsoft Windows application, is a product of Computer Witchcraft, Inc. The WinNET Mail system consists of the main user interface program, the communications module that contacts the server system to transfer your incoming and outgoing mail, and several support programs. (WinNET Mail is included on the disk accompanying this book.)

When you start up WinNET Mail, you will see your main mail folder, which lists all the messages you now have received. This screen has icons that you can use to move among the mail messages, compose new mail, reply to or forward a mail message, or move a mail message to another folder. This mail screen is shown in figure 7.4.

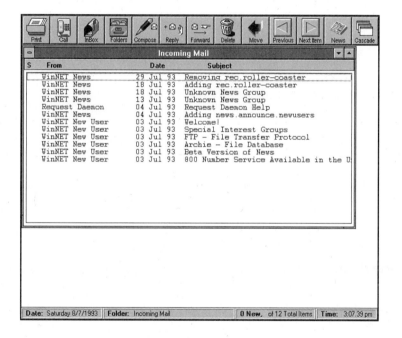

Fig. 7.4
The WinNET Mail main screen.

You can read a mail message by double-clicking the line for that message. A second window comes up, displaying the message you selected. You can have many different windows with different mail messages displayed, as shown in figure 7.5.

Fig. 7.5

Reading mail in
WinNET Mail.

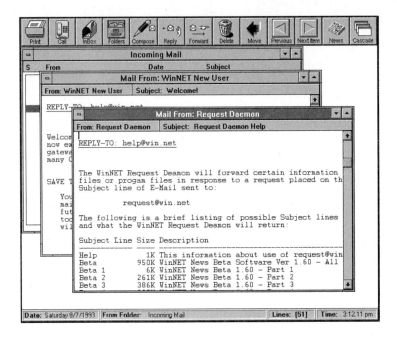

To send a new mail message, click the Compose icon, which
brings up the Mail Composition Editor to edit your outgoing
mail message. After you edit your mail message to your satisfaction, you can send the mail message by clicking the Done button. This queues your mail message on your local disk, where it
waits until you connect to the server machine. Figure 7.6 shows
the Mail Composition Editor window.

Using Electronic Mail

When you have access to electronic mail, you have access to
most of the resources of the Internet. Of course, the primary use
of e-mail is to send messages to other individual users on the
Internet. You can do many other things with electronic mail,
however, as described in the following sections.

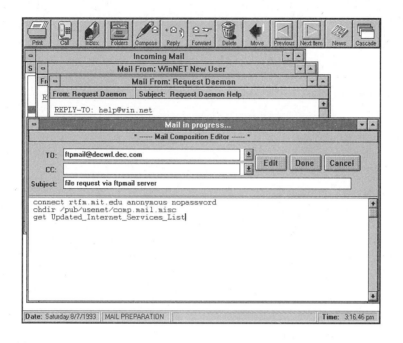

Fig. 7.6

The WinNET Mail Mail Composition Editor window.

Mailing Lists

Early in the development of the Internet, a problem was encountered with electronic mail: people with a common interest wanted to distribute mail messages to a group of people. One way to send these mail messages was to send around the addresses of everyone in the group. Each person would then address his or her mail message to everyone on the list of people. The problems with this idea soon became obvious: everyone had to have the same list of names, and adding or removing people from the list was hard to do. Everyone on the list also had to be able to get mail to everyone else on the list.

From these early attempts at group communications, the current concept of a *mailing list* evolved. Rather than each person in a group have the address of everyone in the group, one person at a central site keeps track of who is on the list. The mail administrator at this central machine then sets up a mailing address for the list. Mail sent to this address is redistributed (usually by way of some intermediate software) to everyone on the list. Usually, a second address is set up to deal with requests to the list administrator, which enables people to communicate with the person maintaining the list without explicitly knowing who that person is.

The advantages of the central mailing list are obvious. With only one copy of the addresses, who is on the list is never in question. Because a central person maintains the mailing list, no confusion exists about who is supposed to keep track of additions or deletions to the list. Also, only the central site needs to be able to contact every address on the list; the other sites need to be able to contact only the central site.

The centrally maintained mailing list has a few disadvantages, however. If the central site is unavailable (because of a hardware failure or a network problem, for example), the entire mailing list is unavailable. Also, if the maintainer of the list goes on vacation or is simply busy, it may be hard to be added to or removed from the list.

Most mailing lists are set up to send out automatically all messages submitted to the list. These lists usually are called *mail reflectors*, as everything sent in is reflected out to the entire list. This type of list works well for low-volume lists or those where little controversy exists. Other types of lists exist to deal with unusual situations.

Moderated Mailing Lists

One of these types is the *moderated* list. With this list, submissions to the list are mailed to the list maintainer, or *moderator*. This person reviews the message, and if it meets his or her criteria for acceptance, it is then sent out to the rest of the list. Usually, the list moderator weeds out messages that are off-topic for the list or those that contain objectionable material. This type of list works well for topics that may be controversial, or where a particular user often disrupts the list with objectionable material.

Although the moderator has absolute control over the messages that flow through the list, in almost every case, his job simply is to keep the topics discussed on the list relevant to the charter of the list. The moderator of the list almost always publishes the criteria he uses for selecting the articles, but these are in fact approved by the people who subscribe to the list.

There have been cases where the moderator of a mailing list has refused to allow certain topics or posts from legitimate users to pass to the list; such censorship is relatively rare, however. Ultimately, the only recourse the readers of the list have to deal with an objectionable moderator is to start another mailing list.

Mailing List Digests

In cases where a very high volume of messages exists, the list may be set up to condense the messages. In this case, submissions to the list are accumulated and then sent out in one large message, called a *digest*. This reduces the load on the central site, because one large message is easier to process than a great deal of little messages. Usually with the mailing lists, the digests are sent out at regular intervals (daily or hourly, for example).

Finding Mailing Lists

Mailing lists exist on almost every topic imaginable. Any time a group of people have a common interest, a mailing list usually is set up so that these people can communicate. Because of the dynamic nature of the Internet, these mailing lists have a tendency to begin and grow quickly, and then decline and disappear as the need or interest declines. Some mailing lists last a few months to deal with a particular problem or interest; others have lasted for many years.

You can find a list of publicly available mailing lists posted periodically in the news group `news.announce.newusers`. The list (in five separate files) is also available by way of anonymous ftp to `rtfm.mit.edu` in directory `/pub/usenet/news.announce.newusers` in files starting with the name `Publicly_Accessible_Mailing_Lists`.

This file is updated frequently by the list maintainer, Stephanie da Silva (who you can reach through e-mail at the address `arielle@taronga.com`), but the information may be out of date. You should contact the individual list maintainers to see whether the list still exists and what the topics covered by the list are. These files are also on the disk included with this book and are listed in Chapter 20, "USENET News Groups Descriptions."

Mailing List Etiquette

To join a mailing list, or to talk to the maintainer of the list, you should always send mail to the "request" address listed for the mailing list. In most cases, the address for submitting requests to the list maintainer is the same as the address for submissions to the list, but with `-request` added on the end.

> **Note**
>
> Please don't send your requests to the entire list; this will greatly annoy the people who subscribe to the list and probably won't get you the information you want.

For example, if the mailing list address for submissions is `network-talk@some.machine.com`, the address for the list maintainer is usually `network-talk-request@some.machine.com`.

After you are on the list, remember that every message you send to the list will be re-sent to everyone on the list. If you are simply agreeing with another list message, you probably should respond just to the person who originated the message. Also, if you send in a request for information to the list, a usual practice is to send in a summary of the responses to your question after a reasonable period of time.

If the list is moderated, the moderator may reject one of your submissions, for any of several reasons. Someone else recently may have asked your question (in which case the moderator often supplies you with an answer), or your question may be one that causes long and prolonged arguments in the list (in which case the moderator probably will explain the trouble it causes). In any case, you often can reword your request or ask the moderator how to get the information you need. Don't simply argue with the moderator about why the message was rejected; the moderator's job is to keep the list on topic and the people on the list happy.

Sending Non-Text Data

Most of the time, your mail messages contain only printable characters (called *ASCII data*). In some cases, however, you will want to send binary data in a mail message. This binary data may be an executable program file, sound or graphic file, or any of a number of binary formats. Because the mail transport programs in use today were designed to handle printable (ASCII) data only, you must take some special measures to make sure that your binary data gets through correctly.

The first step you must take to transmit binary data in a mail message is to translate the binary into ASCII. This step usually is done with a command such as uuencode, which encodes the binary data as a series of printable ASCII characters. Most UNIX systems have the uuencode program available on it as a standard system program. Versions of uuencode are available for other systems; you should use archie to find a version for your system. (See Chapter 13, "Aids to Navigating the Internet," for more information on archie and other tools for finding programs.)

After you use uuencode to translate your binary file into ASCII data, you can include it in your mail message. You should note, however, that if the encoded file is longer than about 1,000 lines, you should split the data into several parts by using a text editor or some other tool. These parts can be enclosed in separate mail messages.

When you send encoded binary data, always include information in the messages that tell the remote user what the data was originally. You also should include information on what method was used to encode the data, and information about which part of a multipart message this one is (for example, you can say that this message is part two of five total parts). This information allows the remote user to take the message, assemble the different parts if the file was split up, and then decode the file (using the uudecode program) into its original binary form. If everything worked correctly, the destination user will have an exact copy of the original binary file.

Multimedia Electronic Mail

As outlined earlier in the section on sending non-text data, the process of sending binary data through the normal mail channels is a somewhat complicated one. Many possible locations exist where a slight error will cause the file extracted on the remote side to be wrong, often in a subtle way. Multimedia electronic mail is designed to simplify the process of sending binary data and extracting the data on the receiving side.

A multimedia electronic mail system automatically encodes binary data to send along with a mail message and automatically decodes and processes binary data in incoming mail messages. For example, you can send a binary file containing a voice message along with a normal mail message. The receiving mail program automatically plays this sound file when the mail is received. Because the process is automatic (and handled by the mail programs themselves), the user doesn't have to be concerned with the details of the process. Of course, if the computer system the user is on can't deal with the binary data (it doesn't have a speaker for playing the sound file, for example), the user is simply notified that the binary data exists.

Multimedia is a relatively new idea, and the details of the exact format of the messages are still in the process of being worked out. As this book is being written, the standards for multimedia electronic mail are being finalized, and mail systems that implement these standards are being written. A few mail systems that implement multimedia e-mail are already available: the "metamail" package from AT&T Bell Laboratories is one. You can retrieve the "metamail" package by way of anonymous ftp to the site `ftp.uu.net` in the directory `/networking/mail/metamail`. It is also available from many other sites around the Internet.

Retrieving Files Using Electronic Mail

Although the primary means of retrieving files on the Internet is by use of the ftp file transfer program, sometimes this isn't the best way to get access to files. Many sites on the Internet don't have the direct Internet connection that ftp requires, or their Internet connection may be over a slow line, making the ftp transfer too slow to be practical.

In any case, many more sites have access to electronic mail than can use the ftp program directly. The logical question, then, is whether you can retrieve files using electronic mail. The answer is *yes*—several ways exist for retrieving files using only e-mail.

The way that the ftp-by-mail servers (commonly called *ftpmail servers*) work is that a mail message containing a file retrieval command is sent to the server mail address. On some ftpmail servers, the command must be in the `Subject:` header; on others, the command must be in the message body.

Features and Services

> **Note**
>
> Almost every ftpmail server supports a help command. You should always try this command first to determine what commands the ftpmail server expects. Most of the time, if you give the server a command it doesn't recognize, it will send you back a mail message telling you how to get help.

As an example, you can look at one ftpmail server provided at the site `decwrl.dec.com`. You can use this server by sending mail to the address `ftpmail@decwrl.dec.com`. Sending a message with the word `help` in the message body returns the commands that the server understands. This server is unusual in that it supports a `connect` command that allows you to connect to any ftp server on the Internet and retrieve files. Most ftpmail servers let you retrieve files only on the machine they are run on.

In this case, if you wanted to retrieve the file `/pub/test.message` on the machine `some.machine.com`, you can use the following commands to the decwrl ftpmail server to get it:

```
connect some.machine.com anonymous anypassword
chdir /pub
get test.message
```

The first line tells the server to connect to the machine that has the file, using the user name `anonymous` and the password `anypassword`. The server is then told to change to the directory `/pub` and then to get the file `test.message`. This file will be mailed to you.

This ftpmail server has many other options, and other servers have other commands.

> **Note**
>
> The ftpmail server at `decwrl.dec.com` is provided as a service to the Internet community, and it shouldn't be abused. Try to limit your use of the server to hours late at night, and don't retrieve many files through it, because it will overload the machine quickly.

Other Services by Electronic Mail

Many other services are available on the Internet by way of electronic mail, and more are being added every day. You can access a list of these services (as well as other

Internet services) through anonymous ftp to `rtfm.mit.edu` in file
`/pub/usenet/alt.internet.services/Updated_Internet_Services_List`.
This list also is posted to the news group `alt.internet.services`
at least monthly.

Here is a sampling of services offered on the Internet by way of
electronic mail:

■ *An archie lookup service* is available via e-mail to addresses
`archie@archie.rutgers.edu` and `archie@archie.sura.net`. If
you send a message with `help` in the body, the server will
give you a list of commands available. See the chapter on
archie for more information about the archie service.

■ *An IP address resolver service* is available by mailing to the
address `resolve@cs.widener.edu`. You can look up the address for a machine or network by sending the phrase
`site` `hostname` in the message body; replace `hostname` with
the name of the machine or network you want to look up.

■ *A WHOIS service* is available by mailing to the address
`service@rs.internic.net`. You should send a message
with the subject `help` to get the list of commands
available. Also, if you send a message with the subject
`send` `RFC-XXXX.TXT` (where you replace the *XXXX* with
the RFC number you want), the server will send the
appropriate RFC file to you.

As you can see, many services can be reached with only electronic mail—if you read the appropriate news groups and read
the lists (and experiment a little!), you can find a wealth of information on the Internet.

II

Features and Services

Common Problems with Electronic Mail

As with any other Internet function, electronic mail has its own set of problems and pitfalls. This section deals with some of the most common ones, and gives tips on how to get around the problems.

Most mail systems do an amazingly good job of delivering mail to the various sites on the Internet. When mail is sent out, the user-level mail programs place your outgoing mail message into some kind of queue for the mail delivery program to act on. Generally, the mail delivery program is run at intervals (once an hour is common; sometimes more frequently, depending on the configuration). When the mail delivery program runs, it tries to connect to the remote computer and deliver the mail message.

If the attempt to deliver the mail fails, one of two things can happen. If the mail delivery program encounters what it believes is a temporary error condition (the remote machine appears to be down, for example), the outgoing mail message will be placed back in the queue for another attempt later on. The number of times the mail delivery program will try to send the message varies, but quite often the message will be held for a day before the message is returned in a mail message to the user with an indication of the error encountered.

If the mail delivery program encounters what it believes is a fatal error condition (the user address wasn't valid or the remote machine couldn't be located), the program immediately returns a mail message, indicating the failure to the sender with the error.

> **Note**
>
> The error message sent when a mail message fails is often called a *bounce message*, because the message bounced back to the sender rather than get to its destination. You may often hear the lament, "My mail bounced again!"

In either case, the result is that the mail message is returned to the sender. The error message (which is actually a mail message sent to the original sender of the message) lists the reason the message failed, and almost always includes the entire original message so that you can figure out the message that failed. Because error messages are generated automatically by the mail transport programs, the reasons why a message failed are often hard to understand.

Mail errors can occur for many different reasons, many of which are out of the control of the person sending the original message. The following sections talk about some common problems and how to resolve them.

Mail Addressing Problems

Mail addressing problems are the most common problems that users of electronic mail run into. These problems usually are indicated by error messages such as User unknown or Host unknown from the mail transport programs. Often, the Host unknown error messages are sent by your local mail transport program, indicating that it couldn't find the remote host. The mail transport program on the remote machine usually returns User unknown errors; that mail transport program is the only one that knows whether the user name is valid.

II

Features and Services

Because mail addresses are often non-intuitive and hard to type, the first thing you should check is the spelling of the user name or host name (depending on the error received). For example, check to make sure that you didn't confuse the number 0 with the letter O or the number 1 with the letter l. Mail addresses are case insensitive, so it doesn't matter if letters are in upper- or lowercase.

If this is the first time you have sent mail to this address, you should go through the process listed earlier in this section for finding out a person's electronic mail address to verify that the address you have is correct. If the host name you have is incorrect, you can check the WHOIS database to determine a valid host name, for example. If the host name you have is correct, but the user name is invalid, you can often send mail to the postmaster address at the host to ask for a valid user name.

If, however, you sent mail to this address before without difficulty, and this time it failed, several possible problems exist. First of all, the condition that caused the failure may be temporary. The remote network or host may have been unavailable due to a hardware failure, or a configuration problem may have caused the user name to be temporarily invalid.

Other problems may have happened to cause an address that previously worked to stop working. If the user name is returned as invalid, the user possibly is no longer at that host. A student user may have graduated (or left the school), which caused that person's account to stop working. Similarly, an employee of a company may have left, or the host the user was on may have been removed from service or been renamed to something else. Quite often, only by sending mail to the postmaster for the site in question can you find out this type of information.

Mail Configuration Problems

Sometimes you will receive an error message that indicates a mail configuration problem. These errors are usually some of the more cryptic ones, such as `No permission to write` or `No such file or directory`. In these cases, you must first determine whether the error came from your local mail delivery program, or the one on the remote machine. You can determine this information by examining the mail error message itself. The sender of the message is usually the mail program (sometimes called *mail daemon*) from the system that found the error.

In general, these conditions can be corrected only by the mail administrator on the machine in question, so you should notify the postmaster at the site where the error has been found. When reporting a mail problem to the postmaster, you always should include the error message you received, with as much detail as you can. You don't need to include any of the text of the original message you sent, however; in most cases, the postmaster needs to see only the headers of the messages.

> **Note**
>
> If the mail configuration is incorrect enough to cause mail to be returned, the mail to the postmaster possibly may be returned also. In this case, you can try to find a telephone number for the administrator of the machine (by using the WHOIS database, for example) and contact the administrator that way (if the problem is urgent). Or you can wait and hope the administrator notices the problem and fixes it.

Unwanted Mail Messages

As electronic mail becomes more prevalent, receiving unwanted mail messages becomes more common. Unwanted e-mail can be anything from a "business opportunity" from someone you don't know (electronic junk mail) to harassing or threatening mail. Dealing with this problem is often difficult because of the lack of control on the Internet.

II

Features and Services

Most of the unwanted electronic mail is of the junk mail variety. This type of message, while annoying, is generally the easiest to ignore. The main problem with electronic junk mail is that if you are paying for your Internet access, you are probably paying for each junk mail message you receive. Some ways of dealing with these messages are as follows:

- Delete the mail message.

- Send a mail message back to the sender, asking him not to do it again.

- Send a mail message to the sender's postmaster, asking him to get the person to stop.

- Send a mail message to the administrator of the system that provides the sender with Internet access, asking them to cut off the person's account.

Naturally, you should start at the top of the list and work down, depending on how many messages you get from the person.

If you receive harassing or threatening electronic mail from a person, you should treat it seriously—as seriously as a threat in a postal letter. The first thing to do is to bring it to the attention of your local postmaster or systems administrator. This person should be able to examine the message and determine whether it's a hoax or forgery.

If your local administrator or postmaster thinks the problem is serious, you should involve your local police in the matter. One main problem with this approach is that in many cases, the local police don't have experience in dealing with electronic mail, so you may have to educate them in this matter.

Mail Security Issues

Although receiving and sending electronic mail messages usually doesn't cause security problems, users and administrators must be aware of several issues when dealing with electronic mail.

First of all, the programs that deliver mail to users are generally run as a system-level program, one that has access to write or modify almost any system file. The system administrator should make sure that the mail delivery programs don't have any bugs or loopholes that may enable a remote user to overwrite important system files. In fact, one of the ways that the famous Internet Worm (detailed in Chapter 2, "History of the Internet") got into systems was by exploiting a debugging feature of a common mail delivery program.

A remote user also can cause system problems, perhaps inadvertently, by sending enough mail to a user to fill up the disk the mail is stored on. Or a misconfigured mail program can cause a mail "loop," where a single message is routed through a series of machines forever, with the message getting a little larger each time. This can cause a severe load on the machines and networks the message is looping on.

Forging of Mail Messages

Forging mail messages is another security issue that users need to be aware of. When they receive a electronic mail message, most users believe that the message is from who it says it is from. But this may not necessarily be the case. Because the mail delivery programs generally have no way to verify the contents of the mail message headers or message body, those programs simply pass along the information to the recipient.

In fact, the sender of a mail message can put anything he or she wants into the message headers and body. A knowledgeable user can cause a mail message to appear to be from whomever he or she wants, and only a close examination of the mail headers can point to a possible forgery. One of the main ways to detect a mail forgery is to examine the `Received By:` header lines to see which hosts the message has passed through. If these lines do not match the host name indicated by the originator header lines, the message may be a forgery.

Although the exact mechanism of forging mail messages is beyond the scope of this book—and is to be discouraged in any case—users should be skeptical of the contents of electronic mail. For example, if you receive a mail message claiming to be from your systems administrator telling you to change your password to something suggested in the message, contact your administrator to verify that the message is valid.

Caution

The preceding example isn't just an example; computer system intruders regularly use this trick to break into systems.

In fact, if you receive any suspicious mail, you should talk to your administrator; the potential damage caused by someone breaking into the system is well worth a few minutes looking over a suspicious mail message. As you gain more familiarity with electronic mail, you will soon be able to tell what mail is normal and what is not.

Mail Message Authentication and Privacy

Another issue related to mail message forging is mail message authentication. Several mechanisms have been proposed to deal with the problem of mail forging by allowing the user to determine the real originator of the mail message. These mechanisms generally use some kind of digital signature to encrypt the message; the receiver can get the sender's decryption key and therefore determine that the presumed sender was the actual sender of the message.

Considerable work is going on in the Internet community to develop standards for allowing electronic mail to be secure. The primary one, called *Privacy Enhanced Mail* (PEM), is described in Internet RFCs 1421 through 1424. Mail programs that fully implement PEM aren't generally available, but one implementation of a subset of PEM is called RIPEM.

RIPEM is publicly available, but it depends on the public key encryption mechanism written by RSA Data Security Inc. You can get the RIPEM code and information about RSA by way of anonymous ftp to `rsa.com` in the directory `/rsaref`; read the README file there for more information about the RSA algorithms.

The other side of the encryption problem is that of mail privacy. Although electronic mail is generally private, in many cases a mail message has been read by unintended parties, intentionally or unintentionally. Common causes of this problem include the following:

- The sender misaddressed the message. The message was sent to another user (or, even worse, is posted to a public bulletin board system).

- An error occurred in the mail delivery program, causing the message to be sent to someone else, probably the postmaster at the source or destination machine.

- A system administrator was trying to find the cause of a mail delivery problem and read the user's mail files.

- A person who can read mail files was being nosy and read the user's mail files.

In any case, the best way to go is to assume that mail messages can be read by anyone at any time. You shouldn't say anything in an electronic mail message that would cause you embarrassment, legal problems, or worse.

In fact, if you talk to any experienced postmaster or systems administrator, you always can find an example of a personal message being misaddressed and winding up on a public USENET group or electronic bulletin board. Also, sending a private message to a public mailing list is very easy (remember to check the destination address when replying to a mail message from a mailing list). It is very embarrassing when someone's job performance review is posted on the company electronic bulletin board!

The use of PEM-based mail products, however, can provide some relief from this problem by encrypting the mail message so that only the intended reader can actually read the message.

Summary

Electronic mail is one of the great conveniences of the Internet. The capability to send a message instantly to anyone on the global Internet is one of the main reasons for getting access to the Internet. After you decide the level of mail service you require and what programs you need to get the service set up, you can begin to take advantage of this remarkable service.

With a little experience in finding people's electronic addresses and how to send mail to the various networks connected to the Internet, communicating electronically becomes easy. And the mailing lists and services available via e-mail provide a wealth of information.

Chapter 8

Using ftp and telnet

In Chapter 7, "Using E-Mail," you saw how to send and receive electronic mail. Although e-mail is a powerful communications tool, it isn't truly interactive. Two-way communications using electronic mail consists of sending someone an e-mail message, waiting for it to reach its destination, waiting for your addressee to become aware of your mail message and read it, and, finally, waiting to receive a reply. This process is like playing "telephone tag"—communicating with people only through their telephone answering machines instead of directly speaking with them on the phone.

Internet itself has the capability for interactive communications. Many service providers allow you to connect with remote computers in such a way that you can interactively examine directory contents, change directories, upload or download files, or even run programs on remote computers. Furthermore, you can do these things almost as easily on the remote computer as you can on your local computer. Not all service providers offer this interactive Internet access, however. Ask whether your provider supports *ftp* (File Transfer Protocol) or *telnet*, the main topics of this chapter. If not, you still can access files non-interactively through *ftpmail*, which also is described in this chapter.

The theme of this chapter is how to access resources of remote computers interactively through the Internet. Some of the procedures show how to transfer text and binary files using ftp and how to log in to a remote computer using telnet. The programs ftp and telnet ask you for the user name and password of your account on the remote computer. However, many computers have guest accounts for ftp users called *anonymous* accounts, which are available to the general public.

> **Note**
>
> No single standard set of commands exists for ftp or telnet. The command set and issues such as case-sensitivity can vary from system to system. In this chapter, a common UNIX implementation is described. It is the implementation you are most likely to encounter, although there is even some variance in ftp and telnet across UNIX systems. UNIX is case-sensitive, so you must enter commands and file names with this in mind.

Using ftp To Access Files of Remote Network Computers

Many computers on the Internet support *ftp* (File Transfer Protocol) access, a simple way for you to interactively examine their file directories and exchange files with them. You need the following to use ftp:

- An account with an Internet service provider that allows you to use ftp to connect with remote computers.

> **Note**
>
> Your provider doesn't need to allow other network computers to access its files using ftp.

- The name of the system on the network that has the files you want to obtain, or on which you want to place files. In other words, because you want to use ftp to access files on a remote computer, you need to know the name of the system containing the files in which you are interested. For remote systems containing many files, you also should try to know beforehand in which directories the files you want reside.

- A valid user name and password to use on the remote computer. Many remote computers that you encounter, however, allow *anonymous ftp*, where you use the user name anonymous (see the following section on anonymous ftp).

Tip

This book has several real-life examples that include specific file and host names. To obtain a list of file names (and their hosts) for a specific topic, use a navigational aid such as archie (see Chapter 13).

The ftp program is designed specifically to simplify file access between network computers. You may move from directory to directory on a remote computer, examine the contents of its individual directories, transfer files from the remote computer to your computer, and put files from your local computer onto the remote computer.

> **Note**
>
> You can't use ftp to perform non-file-oriented operations on a remote computer. For example, ftp has commands to rename and delete files on the remote computer, but you can't run programs on the remote machine.

Be aware that no single standard way exists to implement ftp. The ftp program you run on one computer may appear (and behave) differently than the one you run on a different computer. UNIX implementations of ftp are very similar, however, although differences do exist. You may find that the version of ftp offered by your provider varies significantly from that described in this chapter. Before using ftp for the first time on an unfamiliar system, you first should examine the command structure of that particular version of ftp. Furthermore, you may encounter remote computers that don't process ftp commands in a manner compatible with your local computer's ftp program. Incompatibilities rarely are experienced these days and shouldn't be a problem when connecting with major sites offering anonymous ftp access.

Now, tremendous growth is occurring in the amount and types of information available through ftp, with much of it accessible through anonymous ftp. Many government agencies, educational institutions, and other organizations make databases and other information available to ftp users.

For example, the Association for Computing Machinery (ACM), the society for computer professionals, has established an anonymous ftp server that rapidly and easily can provide information of use to its members. The ACM has the advance program and registration forms for its SIGGRAPH (special interest group for computer graphics) conference available through anonymous ftp to `siggraph.org`.

Of course, ftp is extremely useful for transmitting data rapidly between sites that are working jointly on projects. Using ftp eliminates many of the usual considerations, including the following, in transferring files between computers:

- You don't need to worry about requiring both computers to be able to use the same types of floppy disks or tapes to transfer files. An astronomical observatory in Chile, for example, could transmit new digital images to an astronomer in Georgia in minutes using ftp. The two facilities could be using different types of computer systems, and many megabytes of image data could exist, yet the ftp servers on the two systems would handle all these issues without human intervention.

- You can transmit large files as is; you don't have to break up a file into several smaller files because the larger file won't fit on a single floppy disk.

Your Internet service provider may not make ftp access available to you. In this case, you may use a facility called *ftpmail* to get files from remote computers. File retrieval through ftpmail can be quite tedious, and your file access has several significant limitations. However, ftpmail does provide you with an automated method to retrieve files and requires only that you be able to send and receive electronic mail over the Internet. The ftpmail facility is discussed in more detail later in this chapter.

Anonymous ftp

When you try to connect to a remote computer using ftp, you are asked for a user name and password. Many facilities have information that they want to allow people without accounts on their computers to be able to access. These common types of connections, called *anonymous ftp*, mean simply that you enter anonymous as the user name. The system gives you instructions regarding what to enter as the password. Often, you are asked to enter your Internet e-mail address for the password.

Allowing essentially anyone in the world to access one's computer involves some amount of risk. Therefore, when you establish an anonymous ftp connection with a system, you likely will have significantly restricted access, compared with someone using a personal account on that computer. You should expect to be able to see only files and directories that the systems administrator considers appropriate for unlimited distribution (again, this literally means to anyone anywhere in the world). Also, you may not be able to place any of your files on the remote computer. This restriction is to keep anonymous users from consuming the system's disk storage and to prevent the system from being used for unauthorized purposes.

> **Note**
>
> Anonymous ftp is a great way to explore remote computers on the Internet. Thousands of sites, spanning a tremendous diversity of topics, accept anonymous ftp users. Try connecting to some of the major sites described in Chapter 4, "Finding and Using Internet Resources," as a starting point for your own personal exploration of Internet resources available through anonymous ftp.

A Sample ftp Session

The following example illustrates how easy using ftp is to get files from remote computers. In it, ftp connects to the Network Information Center (NIC) and retrieves several Internet Request For Comments (RFC) documents. A quick search is made for a master index to the RFCs (which is found and retrieved). Then, files containing RFC 1206 (titled *Answers to Commonly asked "New Internet User" Questions*) and RFC 1207 (titled *Answers to Commonly asked "Experienced Internet User" Questions*) are accessed.

> **Note**
>
> The following example is an actual ftp session and preserves all text appearing on-screen during the session. For clarity, text the user types is in a special **boldface** typeface; the remote or local computer generates all other text. The example represents many ftp sessions where the goal is to examine directories on a remote computer and transfer some of its files to your local computer. The specific actions of the commands used in the example are explained and a more detailed explanation of individual ftp commands follows in a later section.

First, the ftp program is invoked and directed to connect the local computer with the NIC, whose Internet node name is `nic.ddn.mil`. Because you don't have an individual account on this system, the anonymous account is used.

```
atlinv.com> ftp nic.ddn.mil
Connected to nic.ddn.mil.
220-*****Welcome to the Network Information Center*****
     *****Login with username "anonymous" and password "guest"
     *****You may change directories to the following:
        ddn-news          - DDN Management Bulletins
        domain            - Root Domain Zone Files
        iesg              - IETF Steering Group
        ietf              - Internet Engineering Task Force
        internet-drafts   - Internet Drafts
        netinfo           - NIC Information Files
        netprog           - Guest Software (ex. whois.c)
        protocols         - TCP-IP & OSI Documents
        rfc               - RFC Repository
        scc               - DDN Security Bulletins
        std               - Internet Protocol Standards
220 And more!
Name (nic.ddn.mil:kb): anonymous
331 Guest login ok, send "guest" as password.
Password:
230 Guest login ok, access restrictions apply.
```

Note that **guest** was entered as the password (as the remote computer had requested), although the password didn't appear on-screen.

The welcome message indicated that RFC documents are stored in the rfc directory on this system. Therefore, the cd command in the following listing is used to set the default directory to rfc. Having an index to all the many RFCs would be handy. Such a file, if it exists in the rfc directory, likely will have a name like index or Index. Therefore, the dir command is used to make a listing of all files matching the pattern *ndex*. (The two * wild-card characters used in this fashion mean that any file name with the contiguous characters *ndex* is a match.)

Note

Entering the dir command without an argument produces a listing of the contents of the entire directory. Because (for this directory) this listing likely will occupy more than a thousand lines on-screen, a more restrictive directory listing was specified.

II

Features and Services

```
ftp> cd rfc
250 CWD command successful.
ftp> dir *ndex*
200 PORT command successful.
150 Opening ASCII mode data connection for /bin/ls.
-r--r--r--  1 postel   1     6254 May 27 15:14 fyi-index.txt
-rw-r--r--  1 postel   1   181249 Jun 10 19:31 rfc-index.txt
226 Transfer complete.
remote: *ndex*
138 bytes received in 0.87 seconds (0.16 Kbytes/s)
```

This strategy for finding an index to the on-line RFCs was successful, having found the file rfc-index.txt. This file is retrieved simply by using the get command, shown in the following listing. Because this is a text file, the file transfer type doesn't need to be changed because, by default, it's set to ascii (see the ascii and binary commands later in this chapter for further discussion of this issue).

```
ftp> get rfc-index.txt
200 PORT command successful.
150 Opening ASCII mode data connection for rfc-index.txt (181249 bytes).
226 Transfer complete.
local: rfc-index.txt remote: rfc-index.txt
185823 bytes received in 5e+02 seconds (0.36 Kbytes/s)
```

Now you can obtain both of the desired RFCs by using the mget command, which prompts the user before retrieving each file to verify that it should be transferred. The user responds with y at each prompt, as shown in the following listing, thereby causing the transfer to occur. Note that if the prompt command had been executed previously, this prompting would have been disabled.

```
ftp> mget rfc1206.txt rfc1207.txt
mget rfc1206.txt? y
200 PORT command successful.
150 Opening ASCII mode data connection for rfc1206.txt (70685 bytes).
226 Transfer complete.
local: rfc1206.txt remote: rfc1206.txt
72479 bytes received in 1.5e+02 seconds (0.48 Kbytes/s)
mget rfc1207.txt? y
200 PORT command successful.
150 Opening ASCII mode data connection for rfc1207.txt (32543 bytes).
226 Transfer complete.
local: rfc1207.txt remote: rfc1207.txt
33385 bytes received in 72 seconds (0.45 Kbytes/s)
```

Finally, the ftp session is terminated and control is returned to the local computer (shown as follows). Three new files now should be in the default directory on the local computer.

```
ftp> bye
221 Goodbye.
atlinv.com>
```

Summary of ftp Commands

This section partitions the ftp commands into groups of commands related by the functions they perform. No single standard exists for defining the ftp commands—they may vary from system to system. The commands described in the following sections are the ones you likely will find in UNIX implementations of ftp. Fortunately, ftp on other systems usually closely resembles the UNIX implementations, especially regarding the most commonly used commands.

Strictly speaking, the ftp program you run is actually a user interface to a low-level set of commands called the *File Transfer Protocol Service Commands*. This lower-level command set is standardized (see RFC 959), but few ftp user interfaces exploit the full capability of entire command set.

In the following descriptions, the full command syntax is given. Anything you enter literally (such as the command name) is represented in a special typeface—for example, get. Command arguments that you must supply are *italicized*. Optional arguments are enclosed in [brackets]. For example, the syntax

```
get remote_file_name [local_file_name]
```

indicates that you type the word get, followed by the name of the file you want to retrieve from the remote system, followed (optionally) by the name you want this file to have on your local computer.

> **Note**
>
> Do not actually type the brackets when entering your ftp command line.

Starting an ftp Session

Syntax: ftp [-div] [remote_host]

Entering ftp followed by the name of a remote computer causes ftp to try to establish a connection with that computer. If no computer name is given, ftp starts its command interpreter and responds with a prompt such as ftp>.

> **Note**
>
> You can establish a connection later in the session through use of the open command.

The optional flags may differ for different implementations of ftp, but common ones are as follows:

-d   Turn on debug mode (see ftp **debug** command)

-i   Turn off interactive prompting for multiple file transfers (see ftp **prompt** command)

-v   Turn on verbose mode (see ftp **verbose** command)

You can terminate ftp by executing the bye or quit commands.

Getting Help on ftp Commands

Commands: `help, ?`

Syntax: `help [command]`

                    `? [command]`

The `help` and `?` commands perform identical functions. If `help` or `?` is entered without a valid ftp command, a brief listing of all the available ftp commands, such as the following, is printed on-screen:

```
ftp> help
Commands may be abbreviated.  Commands are:
!            cr           ls           prompt       runique
$            delete       macdef       proxy        send
account      debug        mdelete      sendport     status
append       dir          mdir         put          struct
ascii        disconnect   mget         pwd          sunique
bell         form         mkdir        quit         tenex
binary       get          mls          quote        trace
bye          glob         mode         recv         type
case         hash         mput         remotehelp   user
cd           help         nmap         rename       verbose
cdup         image        ntrans       reset        ?
close        lcd          open         rmdir
```

If a valid ftp command follows `help` or `?`, a brief (usually one line) description of that command is given.

Establishing and Terminating an ftp Connection

Commands: `open`

                    `close`

                    `disconnect`

                    `bye`

                    `quit`

These commands establish and terminate ftp sessions with remote computers. You can connect with a sequence of sites by using the `open` and `close` commands. When you are finished with all your ftp accesses, you can use the `bye` command to exit ftp.

II

Features and Services

Establishing an ftp Connection to a Remote Computer
Syntax: `open remote_host`

The `open` command attempts to establish a connection with the indicated remote computer. If you want to connect with only a single site while running ftp, you don't need to use the `open` command. Instead, you can specify the site name on the command line invoking ftp. To end the connection, use the `close` or `bye` command.

Ending an ftp Connection to a Remote Computer
Syntax: `close`
                     `disconnect`

The `close` and `disconnect` commands are identical; they terminate the connection with the remote host. Because they don't terminate ftp, you can establish another connection by using the `open` command.

Terminating the ftp Program
Syntax: `bye`
                     `quit`

The `bye` and `quit` commands are synonymous. They close the current connection, if one is open, and then terminate the ftp program.

Changing Directories and Examining Their Contents
Commands: `cd`
                     `cdup`
                     `pwd`
                     `dir`
                     `ls`

These commands enable you to move about the directory structure on the remote computer and list the files contained within a directory. You can change the default directory on the local computer through the `lcd` command, which is discussed in more detail later in the section "Executing Commands on the Local Computer in an ftp Session."

Changing the Directory on the Remote Computer
Syntax: cd *new_directory*

`cd` changes the default directory on the remote computer to *new_directory*.

Moving to the Parent Directory on the Remote Computer
Syntax: cdup

The `cdup` command changes the default directory on the remote computer to the parent of the current directory. If the remote computer is UNIX-based, for example, `cdup` is equivalent to the `cd ..` command.

Showing the Current Directory's Name on the Remote Computer
Syntax: pwd

The `pwd` command shows the name of the current default directory on the remote computer.

Showing a Full Directory Listing on the Remote Computer
Syntax: dir [*directory*] [*local_file*]

The `dir` command produces a full listing of the contents of the indicated directory on the remote computer. The optional *directory* argument may contain wild cards in the syntax supported by the remote computer. If *directory* isn't specified, a listing of the current working directory on the remote computer is given.

If you specify a *local_file*, the listing is placed in a file of that name on the local host. Otherwise, the directory listing is printed to your screen.

Using dir produces a "full" directory listing, meaning that information such as owner, date, size, and protections are given for each file. The remote computer determines the actual set of listed information. For example, the command dir *ndex* may produce the following listing:

```
-r--r--r-- 1 postel   1    6254 May 27 15:14 fyi-index.txt
-rw-r--r-- 1 postel   1  181249 Jun 10 19:31 rfc-index.txt
```

Showing a Brief Directory Listing on the Remote Computer

Syntax: ls [*directory*] [*local_file*]

The ls command is identical to dir, except that ls produces a "brief" listing of the directory contents—only the file names are given. For example, the command ls *ndex* may generate the following output:

```
fyi-index.txt
rfc-index.txt
```

Getting Files from a Remote Computer

Commands: get
                        mget
                        recv

You can retrieve individual files by using the get command and multiple files with the mget command. Make sure that the file transfer type you are using matches the types of the files you are actually transferring. The default type is ASCII but can be changed through the ascii (for printable files) and binary (for graphics, executable, ZIP, and other non-printable files) commands. You can abort a file transfer by typing the terminal interrupt key (usually Ctrl+C).

Often you encounter files that are stored in a compressed form. Remember that you have to use a binary transfer to retrieve them. You usually can tell these files by their file extension. A file with the extension Z was most likely compressed with the UNIX compress utility. To restore the original file, use the UNIX uncompress program. Files ending in .zip were compressed using the utility PKZIP and can be decompressed with PKUNZIP. This compression scheme is the most widely used for PCs. For Macintosh users, the most common compression programs are BinHex 4.0 (extension hqx) and StuffIt (extension sit). Information services like CompuServe often carry decompression programs for these file formats.

> **Note**
>
> The recv command is identical to the get command but may be considered obsolete. Its use is not encouraged.

Retrieving a Single File from the Remote Computer

Syntax:

```
get remote_file_name [local_file_name]
recv remote_file_name [local_file_name]
```

The get and recv commands are identical; they retrieve the single file named *remote_file_name* from the remote computer and copy it to your local machine. If you don't specify a *local_file_name*, the copied file is given the same name on your local computer as it had on the remote computer (or at least as closely as possible, if *remote_file_name* isn't a valid file name on your computer). If you specify - in the *local_file_name* field, the file is printed on-screen.

Retrieving Multiple Files from the Remote Computer
Syntax: mget *remote_file_names*

The mget command retrieves multiple files from the remote computer and copies them to your local machine. The argument *remote_file_names* may be a list of file names and may use wild-card characters. Use the syntax of the remote computer for specifying wild cards and file name lists. If you don't want to be prompted before each file is retrieved, issue a prompt command before you issue the mget command.

Putting Files on a Remote Computer
Commands: put
                       mput
                       send

Individual files are written to a remote computer using the put command. The mput command transfers multiple files from your local computer to the remote computer. You must set the file transfer type properly for the type of files you want to transfer. ASCII is the default type but may be changed by the ascii or binary commands. You can abort a file transfer by typing the terminal interrupt key (usually Ctrl+C).

> **Note**
>
> The send command is identical to the put command but may be considered obsolete. Its use is not encouraged.

Writing a Single File to the Remote Computer
Syntax: put *local_file_name [remote_file_name]*
                          send *local_file_name [remote_file_name]*

The put and send commands are synonyms. They write the single file *local_file_name* on your computer to the remote computer. If *remote_file_name* is specified, the transferred file is given this name on the remote computer. If `remote_file_name` isn't specified, the transferred file keeps the same name as on your local machine (or at least as close to the original name as possible, if `local_file_name` isn't a valid file name on the remote computer).

Writing Multiple Files to the Remote Computer

Syntax: mput `local_file_names`

The `mput` command writes multiple files from the local computer to the remote computer. The argument `local_file_names` may contain wild cards and file lists in the syntax of the local computer. If you don't want to be prompted before each file is transferred, use the `prompt` command.

Selecting the File Transfer Mode

Commands: ascii
                        binary

The file transfer mode *must* match the type of file being transferred. If it doesn't, the transferred files almost certainly will be totally useless. When ftp is started, by default it begins in ASCII mode.

> **Note**
>
> Examples of ASCII and binary files are given in their respective sections.

Setting File Transfer Mode to ASCII

Syntax: ascii

This command indicates that subsequent file transfers will be comprised solely of printable ASCII characters. Examples of such files are text files, programming language source files, and PostScript files. Using the binary command changes the file transfer mode from ASCII to binary.

Setting File Transfer Mode to Binary
Syntax: binary

By specifying the binary command, you indicate that subsequent file transfers will involve only files that should be transmitted exactly as is (that is, without carriage control conversion) between the remote and host computers. Examples of such files are most word processor files (such as WordPerfect and Microsoft Word), executable programs, compressed files (such as PKZIP or UNIX compress), and most backup files (such as UNIX tar).

The ascii command changes the file transfer mode from binary to ASCII.

Deleting Files on a Remote Computer
Commands: delete
mdelete

You can delete an individual file on the remote computer by using the delete command. To remove multiple files, use mdelete.

> **Note**
>
> You must have delete privilege on the remote computer for files you want to delete.

Deleting a Single File on the Remote Computer
Syntax: delete *remote_file_name*

The delete command deletes the *remote_file_name* on the remote computer. For this command to succeed, you must have
sufficient privilege to delete this file on the remote computer.

Deleting Multiple Files on the Remote Computer
Syntax: mdelete *remote_file_names*

Use the mdelete command to delete the indicated files on the
remote computer. The *remote_file_names* argument may contain
wild cards in the syntax of the remote computer. This command won't succeed unless you have sufficient privilege to
delete these files on the remote computer.

Getting Status Information
Commands: status
                         bell
                         hash
                         prompt
                         verbose

These five commands can help you monitor the progress of
your file transfers or your ftp session in general. Your ftp implementation probably has more modes than those mentioned
here, so look at your documentation for additional information.

Getting Overall Status Information
Syntax: status

The status command prints information concerning the current
state of the ftp session to your screen. In particular, the values
of binary-valued mode flags that the user can set are displayed.

An example output from the status command follows:

```
ftp> status
Connected to nic.ddn.mil.
No proxy connection.
Mode: stream; Type: ascii; Form: non-print; Structure: file
Verbose: on; Bell: off; Prompting: on; Globbing: on
Store unique: off; Receive unique: off
Case: off; CR stripping: on
Ntrans: off
Nmap: off
Hash mark printing: off; Use of PORT cmds: on
```

Ringing the Bell after Completion of Each File Transfer
Syntax: bell

The bell command toggles a mode flag that indicates whether
the bell (beep) should be sounded at the completion of each file
transfer command.

Printing # after Each Data Block Is Transferred
Syntax: hash

The hash command toggles a mode flag specifying whether the
character should be printed on-screen after each data block is
transferred. By using this command, you can verify that your
transfer is proceeding and, if you can determine the data block
size through your documentation or experimentation, calculate
what percentage of your transfer has completed.

Toggle Prompting for Multiple File Transfers
Syntax: prompt

By default, the mget and mput commands (discussed earlier) ask
you to confirm each file to be transferred. The prompt command
toggles the mode flag controlling this. Using the prompt command before an mget, for example, instructs mget not to ask you
before it retrieves each file. Executing prompt again means that
mget would now prompt you before transferring each file.

Toggling Verbose Mode
Syntax: verbose

In verbose mode, all responses from the ftp server are
displayed, as well as the data transfer statistics for file transfers.
The verbose command toggles the use of this mode.

Executing Commands on the Local Computer in an ftp Session
Commands: lcd
                       !

Often, you will want to execute commands on your local computer without ending your ftp session. You may want to change
directories, get a directory listing, or examine the contents of
a file on the local computer. The lcd command changes your
local working directory; the ! command executes a system
command on your local machine.

Changing the Directory on the Local Computer
Syntax: lcd [*new_directory*]

lcd changes the default directory on the local computer to
new_directory. If you don't specify *new_directory*, the user's
home directory is used.

Executing a Command on the Local Host
Syntax: ! [*command*]

The specified command is executed on your local computer. If
no command is given, an interactive shell is started on the local
host. To get back to ftp, exit the shell as you normally would for
a local host shell.

II

Features and Services

Non-Interactive ftp through E-Mail

Unfortunately, many users who can send and receive electronic mail through the Internet don't have access to ftp. If you fall under this category, you can use a facility called *ftpmail* to receive files from remote computers through e-mail. Although using ftpmail involves numerous restrictions and limitations, it is a simple, automated way to obtain files.

> **Note**
>
> The first thing to do if you want to try ftpmail is to get the help document describing how to use it. You can have this document mailed electronically to you by sending an e-mail message to `ftpmail@decwrl.dec.com` with the single word `help` in the body of the message. You should receive a brief description of the ftpmail command set and notes regarding the proper usage and limitations of ftpmail.

To use ftpmail, send to `ftpmail@decwrl.dec.com` an e-mail message in which each line in the body of the message contains an ftpmail command (described in later sections). The subject of your message appears in the subject field of the replies you receive from the ftpmail server. When the server receives your request, you then receive an immediate reply verifying receipt of your ftpmail request, indicating any errors in processing your request, and indicating the number of ftpmail requests ahead of yours. When your request is actually processed, you receive an e-mail message containing a log of the ftp session the ftpmail server conducted to fulfill your request. Thus, for every ftpmail e-mail message you send, you receive two status e-mail messages, plus the e-mail messages containing the files you are trying to get.

Capabilities and Limitations of ftpmail

The ftpmail facility isn't ftp. Its command set is different and much less capable than that of ftp. You can't send files to other users using ftpmail—you can only receive them. You also can't change directories more than once. Furthermore, you can't get more than 10 files from a single ftpmail request.

ftpmail also can be quite slow. The documentation states that you should receive the results of your ftpmail session in approximately one day; however, it could take considerably longer. Also, if an error occurs in processing your request, you have to resubmit it, thus incurring an additional cycle of delay.

The limitations of Internet electronic mail also greatly hamper ftpmail. Internet e-mail was designed to carry relatively short packets of ASCII data. Thus, ftpmail will easily retrieve small printable ASCII files. You must convert binary—that is, non-ASCII—data into some kind of ASCII representation before mailing it. ftpmail offers two ways to do so: uuencode format and btoa format. Programs that encode and decode files using these formats are commonly available for UNIX-based computers and for PC and Macintosh computers. (CompuServe should have programs that perform these operations.)

A more annoying aspect of Internet e-mail is the limitation in message length. Commonly, messages are limited to no more than 64,000 characters. You must split files longer than the maximum length of an e-mail message into multiple files and transmit them separately. You can specify the maximum characters to be transmitted in a single e-mail message (by using the chunksize command), but the maximum message size which ftpmail can use is 100,000 characters. Many RFCs, for example, are larger than 100,000 characters; ftpmail would have to send them through multiple e-mail messages. Binary files often exceed this limit.

ftpmail does support two types of data compression: compress and compact. The compress compression type uses Lempel-Ziv encoding; `compact`, on the other hand, uses adaptive Huffman coding. Decoding programs called `uncompress` and `uncompact` are commonly available on UNIX-based computers and also can be found for PC and Macintosh systems. These compression techniques are especially useful in reducing the number of mail messages into which a large binary file must be broken.

> **Note**
>
> If you compress or compact a file, you must transmit it as a binary file, even if the original file is ASCII.

A Sample ftpmail Request

The following example illustrates how to retrieve a single file using ftpmail. Like the example ftp session detailed earlier in this chapter, this ftpmail request causes the document RFC 1206 to be mailed to you. Because the file containing this document is larger than 64,000 characters, it is divided into two sections, which are sent in two separate e-mail messages.

Your request is mailed to ftpmail@decwrl.dec.com. You can use anything you want in the subject field of the message, but it should remind you of the particular file retrievals you are performing in this ftpmail request. In this example, an appropriate subject would be *Get RFC1206 from the NIC*. The body of the message is as follows:

```
connect nic.ddn.mil
chdir rfc
get rfc1206.txt
quit
```

After you send this message, you receive confirmation from the ftpmail server that your request has been placed on the queue. When processing is complete, you receive three additional mail messages: a log of the ftp session ftpmail conducted to fulfill your request and two messages containing portions of the file `rfc1206.txt`. You must combine these two pieces to re-create the complete document but, because the original is an ASCII file, you easily can concatenate the two parts using a text editor.

Summary of ftpmail Commands

ftpmail commands are simpler to use than their corresponding ftp commands, and fewer of them exist. The commands are described briefly in table 8.1, but you should refer to the ftpmail help message for further information.

Table 8.1 ftpmail Commands

Command Syntax	Description
reply *your_address*	The string *your_address* is used as the e-mail address to which all responses will be sent. If the request doesn't contain a reply command, the responses are sent to your address as indicated in your requesting e-mail message.
connect [*hostname* [*username* [*password* [*account*]]]]	This command specifies the name of the host and the user information to use when connecting with that host. A command in the form connect *hostname* will try to establish an anonymous ftp connection on the system *hostname*.
ascii	Use this command when retrieved files are printable ASCII.
binary	Use this command when retrieved files aren't printable ASCII. Examples of binary files are compressed files, executable files, and graphics files.
chdir *new_directory*	The argument *new_directory* is selected as the default file directory. You can have at most one chdir command in a single ftpmail request.
compress	Use this command to perform Lempel-Ziv encoding before transmitting the file. You have to decode the files you receive.

(continues)

II

Features and Services

Table 8.1 Continued	
Command Syntax	**Description**
compact	Use this command to perform adaptive Huffman encoding before transmitting the file. You have to decode the files you receive.
uuencode	Mail binary files using the uuencode format. You have to unformat the files you receive.
btoa	Mail binary files using the btoa format. You have to unformat the files you receive.
chunksize *max_size*	Use this command to break files into portions no larger than *max_size* characters. The default for *max_size* is 64,000, and it can't be larger than 100,000.
ls *[directory]* or dir *[directory]*	Either command lists the contents of the indicated *directory*. If *directory* isn't specified, the command lists the contents of the current default directory.
get *file_name*	This command retrieves and mails the indicated file. You can issue no more than 10 get commands within a single ftpmail request.
quit	Use quit to end the ftpmail session. Any further lines in your requesting e-mail message are discarded.

Typical Problems Encountered Using ftp

This section describes problems frequently encountered when trying to use ftp. Even if you aren't experiencing any difficulties now, you probably should scan this section to become familiar with common pitfalls. Almost all new ftp users ask themselves at least one of these questions while gaining experience with ftp. Although you can figure out the recommended solutions to each of the following situations from the information given in this chapter, having a short list of the most frequently asked questions is often convenient.

Problem: I don't have a password on the remote computer I want to access.

Recommendation: Try using anonymous ftp (see the earlier "Anonymous ftp" section). If the remote computer maintains information of general use to Internet users, it may accept anonymous users. If not, you have to obtain an account through the systems manager of the system you want to access.

Problem: I transferred a program/image file/ZIP file from a remote computer but it won't execute/can't display correctly/ won't UNZIP properly.

Recommendation: You must specify a binary transfer for all non-ASCII files. Examples of binary files include executable programs, object code, graphics files, and compressed files (created, for example, by PKZIP or UNIX compress). Non-ASCII files that are transmitted without previously using the `binary` ftp command do not transfer correctly.

Problem: I want to get several files, but doing a `get` command for each one is very tedious.

Recommendation: The ftp command `mget` retrieves multiple files. Furthermore, it accepts wild-card characters in the file name specification. Even if you want to transfer only a single file, `mget` is often more convenient than `get` if the file name is long.

Problem: The remote computer has many files and directories—I'm not sure where the files I want are located.

Recommendation: After you connect with the remote system, look for index, help, and readme files in the directories you examine. Note that the file names are likely to be case-

II

Features and Services

sensitive and not restricted to some arbitrary length. Issuing the command `dir *ndex*`, for example, lists the files `index`, `Index`, and `Index-public-files`, but doesn't list the file `INDEX`.

Problem: I want to transfer files using ftp, but my Internet provider doesn't allow me to have interactive Internet access.

Recommendation: You can use ftpmail to retrieve files in a noninteractive manner. The commands of ftpmail are different than those of ftp, and ftpmail has significant limitations compared with ftp. Otherwise, many remote computers have servers that can send you specific files through e-mail. RFCs and FYIs, for example, can be retrieved through the RFC-Info service, and you can request the instructions for ftpmail by sending an e-mail message to `ftpmail@decwrl.dec.com` with the single word `help` in the body of the message.

Problem: I want to look at the contents of a file without having to transfer it to my local computer.

Recommendation: Often, you aren't sure whether a file contains the information you desire. Other times, you need only a very specific piece of information from a file and don't need to transfer it to your local computer. The command

```
get remote_file_name -
```

prints the file contents on your computer screen. Unfortunately, it prints the entire file. On UNIX systems you can use the command

```
get remote_file_name - "| more"
```

which pipes the output through the `more` filter, or

```
get remote_file_name - "| grep string"
```

which sends lines of the file having only the character string `string`.

> **Note**
>
> For more information on grep, see Appendix C, "UNIX Quick Reference."

Problem: I am retrieving a large file; how can I tell that the transfer is proceeding?

Recommendation: Use the hash command before beginning your file transfer. This command causes the # character to be printed on your screen after each data block transfer.

The documentation for your system's implementation of ftp may state the size in bytes of a single data block. If so, you can calculate the number of bytes transferred at a particular time from the number of # characters appearing on-screen.

Logging in to Remote Network Computers Using telnet

The *telnet* facility allows you to execute commands on a remote host as though you were logged in locally. Like ftp, you need to know the name of the computer you want to access and have a valid user name and password for that computer.

Unlike ftp, telnet has no common analog to anonymous ftp. Although many remote sites allow guest logins, no convention exists on the user name and password a guest may use. Furthermore, guest logins aren't nearly as common as anonymous ftp accounts. This makes sense because a remote site is more likely to want you to be able to access certain files than for you to be able to execute software on it.

In essence, a telnet session allows you the same capabilities on the host computer you would have if you were logged in locally under the same account. A common situation, however, is for telnet users to run a special operating environment shell that restricts their actions. This shell is especially common for guest accounts under telnet.

Tip

This particular NASA system is designed to provide easy access to educators, journalists, and other persons seeking information about space exploration.

The NASA Marshall Space Flight Center, for example, allows telnet access to the host spacelink.msfc.nasa.gov for persons interested in space technology. If you don't now have an account on this system, enter newuser as the user name and password. The system then allows you to set up an account for yourself by choosing a user name and password for future logins.

Although your telnet session is actually running software directly on this host, you will be running a program that prevents you from accessing the general capabilities of that computer. Specifically, you will be running a menu-driven system whose main menu is as follows:

```
NASA Spacelink Main Menu
1.    Log Off NASA Spacelink
2.    NASA Spacelink Overview
3.    Current NASA News
4.    Aeronautics
5.    Space Exploration: Before the Shuttle
6.    Space Exploration: The Shuttle and Beyond
7.    NASA and its Centers
8.    NASA Educational Services
9.    Instructional Materials
10.   Space Program Spinoffs/Technology Transfer
Enter an option number, 'G' for GO TO, ? for HELP, or
   press RETURN to redisplay menu...
```

As you can see, this operating environment prevents you from exploring the file system of the remote computer and running any unauthorized programs. In this case, you enter the number corresponding to the category in which you are interested. Any other responses are invalid.

Another common use of telnet is for users to be able to log in to their computers from remote locations. In this case, users enter their own user names and passwords and, therefore, have the same user privileges they would have when logged in without using telnet. Usually, the only losses in capability are slower access and having to use a terminal-type environment rather than a window-type environment (if that was available on the host). Thus, users away from the office can read their own e-mail, edit files, or run programs off their own computer. Public computers with telnet access are becoming more common at professional conferences so that attendees can keep in touch with their organizations.

Summary of telnet Commands

Like ftp, no single standard is available for defining the telnet command set; the commands may vary from system to system. This section describes commands commonly found in UNIX implementations of telnet. Quite likely you will need to use only a handful of the total telnet commands.

Command	Description
open	Establishes a telnet connection with a remote host
close	Terminates a telnet connection
quit	Closes the current (if any) telnet connection and terminates telnet
z	Suspends telnet so that commands can be executed on the local computer
?	Obtains help on using telnet commands

Furthermore, because you can specify the host name as a command-line argument when invoking telnet, and because the quit command closes the current connection, you don't need to use the open and close commands unless you want to contact several hosts without terminating telnet.

II

Features and Services

Note

To learn about telnet's specific command set and capabilities, refer to the documentation for your particular implementation of telnet.

Most versions of telnet support two modes of operation: character and line. Character mode—the preferred mode of operation—sends each character to the remote computer as it is typed. Character mode is usually the default mode. In line mode, all characters are echoed and edited locally, and a line is transmitted only when it is completed. The main difference to a telnet user is that typed lines are edited locally (using the local computer's line editing capabilities) in line mode and are edited under control of the remote computer in character mode.

Normally during a telnet session, your local computer acts as though it were a terminal connected to the remote computer. You temporarily can escape from interaction with the remote computer by entering the telnet escape character, which normally is the ^] (Ctrl+right bracket) character. The telnet escape character may vary from system to system; you can tell telnet that you want to use a specific escape character with the set escape command. When the escape character is entered, telnet enters its command mode, and you see a prompt such as telnet> on-screen. In this mode, lines you type are interpreted as telnet commands. To leave telnet command mode, enter a carriage return at the telnet prompt (that is, a blank line).

Note

The telnet escape character shouldn't be confused with the ASCII escape character (ESC).

In the following descriptions, the full command syntax is given. Anything entered literally (such as a command name) is represented in computer-like type—for example, mode. Command arguments that you must supply are *italicized*. Optional arguments are inside [brackets]. For example, the syntax

```
open remote_host
```

indicates that you type the word open, followed by the name of the remote computer with which you want to establish a connection. The syntax

```
? [command]
```

specifies that you can enter ? by itself, or ? followed by the name of a telnet command.

Starting a telnet Session
Syntax: `telnet [remote_host]`

Entering telnet on the command line of your local computer begins a telnet session. If the name of a remote host follows the word telnet, Internet tries to establish a connection to that computer. Otherwise, telnet begins in its command mode with no connection established.

> **Note**
>
> Some implementations of telnet have additional command-line options defined.

Establishing a Connection with a Remote Computer
Syntax: `open remote_host`

The open command attempts to establish a connection with the specified remote computer. Executing an open command isn't necessary if telnet had been invoked with the name of a remote host and the connection was successful.

Ending a telnet Session
Syntax: `close`

The `close` command terminates the connection with the remote computer and returns to telnet command mode. You now can make another connection to a remote computer by using the `open` command.

Exiting telnet
Syntax: `quit`

The `quit` command closes any open connection and terminates telnet. If you now are connected, you will be disconnected from the remote computer, and your local computer will regain process control.

Suspending telnet
Syntax: `z`

The `z` command temporarily suspends telnet so that you can enter commands on your local computer.

> **Note**
>
> This command isn't available on all implementations of telnet—not even all UNIX implementations. Consult the documentation for your particular version of telnet to determine whether the z command is available and, if so, how to unsuspend telnet after a z command.

Obtaining Help on Using telnet Commands
Syntax: `? [command]`

Use `?` to obtain a brief description (usually one line per command) of the telnet command set available to you. Enter `?` followed by the name of a telnet command to get a brief description of that command and any options it may have.

Selecting Character or Line Mode

Syntax: mode *type*

Most implementations of telnet can transmit to the remote computer in character-by-character or line-by-line mode. If *type* is specified as line, characters are transmitted only when the line they are on is complete. If *type* is character, each character is sent to the remote host as it is typed.

Showing the Current Status of a telnet Session

Syntax: status

The status command shows the current state of telnet—including whether line mode or character mode is now in use—and may show the current escape character.

Sending One or More Special Character Sequences to the Remote Host

Syntax: send *argument1* [*argument2* [...]]

You can use the send command to send special telnet command sequences to the remote computer. Use send ? to obtain information about the specific command sequences supported.

Showing the Settings of One or More telnet Variables

Syntax: display [*argument1 argument2* ...]

telnet uses a number of variables to store internal states and other information. Most likely, the only one of interest to you is the escape variable, which specifies the character that causes telnet to enter command mode.

Entering display with no arguments lists the current values of all telnet variables. Entering display followed by a valid telnet variable shows the value of that particular variable. You can change variables through the set, unset, and toggle commands.

II

Features and Services

Setting the Value of a telnet Variable
Syntax: `set telnet_variable value`

Tip
You can examine the current settings of variables by using the `display` command.

You can use the `set` command to change the value of a telnet variable. The command `set ?` gives a brief description of the telnet variables that you can change through the `set` command. The only one likely to be of interest to you is the `escape` variable, which specifies the character that causes telnet to enter command mode. For a binary-valued variable, the value `off` disables the action associated with the variable.

Unsetting the Value of a telnet Variable
Syntax: `unset telnet_variable`

You can use the `unset` command to set binary-valued telnet variables to false and turn their associated functions off. You can use the `display` command to show the current values of telnet variables.

The `unset` command isn't available on all telnet implementations. Use `unset ?` to obtain a brief description of the telnet variables that you can change with the `unset` command.

Toggling the Value of a telnet Variable
Syntax: `toggle telnet_flag`

The `toggle` command toggles binary-valued flags that control how telnet responds to events. Use `toggle ?` to get a brief listing of the flags that you can alter through the `toggle` command. You can use the `display` command to show the current values of these flags.

Summary

The ftp and telnet facilities are the most important interactive Internet utilities. With ftp, you can transfer ASCII and binary files of unlimited size across the network. Many hundreds of hosts accept anonymous ftp users, which means that you can have easy access to several million files. You can log in to remote computers using telnet and use them just as though you were logged in locally. You also can connect to sites offering publicly available navigational aids such as archie, Gopher, and WAIS through telnet.

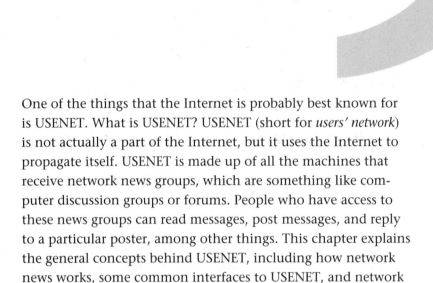

Chapter 9

USENET

One of the things that the Internet is probably best known for is USENET. What is USENET? USENET (short for *users' network*) is not actually a part of the Internet, but it uses the Internet to propagate itself. USENET is made up of all the machines that receive network news groups, which are something like computer discussion groups or forums. People who have access to these news groups can read messages, post messages, and reply to a particular poster, among other things. This chapter explains the general concepts behind USENET, including how network news works, some common interfaces to USENET, and network news history.

What Is the Network News?

The network news (commonly referred to as *netnews*) is a mechanism for broadcasting messages, called *articles*, from your local host to a large number of hosts across the world. The transport mechanism used is called *store and forward*, which means that each host that receives a netnews article stores it locally and then forwards, or *feeds*, it to other hosts that are part of the USENET network. Because a single host may feed the article to any number of other hosts, who then may feed it to additional hosts, this mechanism ensures that each article can reach a very large number of hosts (and readers) in a very short period of time.

On each individual host, the netnews system is split into two distinct systems. The first system is for receiving articles, storing them, and forwarding them to other sites. You probably don't need to worry about this system unless you directly receive a news feed at your site. The second system allows local users to read articles and post new articles (this system commonly is called a *news reader*). These two systems are distinct and are treated separately in this chapter.

The Structure of Netnews

This section talks about the different news groups, how they are organized, and how to determine what topics are discussed in each group. Before you can make effective use of the information available in news groups, you should understand how to locate the appropriate group and how to contribute to that group.

News Group Organization

Each article posted to netnews is placed into one or more *news groups*. Each group is a place in netnews where conversations about a particular topic occur. News groups have names made up of several components, separated by periods. For example, a valid news group name would be `comp.sys.ibm.pc.games`. The name's different components tell you something about the topic of discussion in the group, with the left-most name component being the most general (`comp` stands for computer-related topics), and the right-most name component being the most specific (`games` indicates that only games are discussed in the group). Taken as a whole, the group `comp.sys.ibm.pc.games` discusses games running on IBM personal computers.

The most general of the name components are the so-called "top-level" names, or *hierarchies*. These hierarchies are well established, and new top-level hierarchies are created very rarely.

The most commonly used hierarchies include the following:

Hierarchy	Designates
comp	Computer-related topics
rec	Recreational topics
sci	Topics related to sciences
soc	Topics related to social issues
news	Topics related to the operation and administration of a netnews system
talk	Conversational topics, often controversial
misc	Miscellaneous topics not covered elsewhere

In addition to these standard top-level hierarchies, quite a few other news group hierarchies exist. Many of these other hierarchies relate either to a specific topic or a local geographic area. For example, here are a few of these alternative hierarchies:

Hierarchy	Designates
alt	An alternative hierarchy with relaxed rules for new group creation
vmsnet	A hierarchy devoted to systems running the VMS operating system from Digital Equipment Corporation
bionet	A hierarchy devoted to biological sciences
k12	A hierarchy devoted to education in grades kindergarten through 12

You can use the information presented so far to locate the news groups that hold the information you are interested in. In addition, your local news system may have a copy of a news groups file, which has a one-line description of each news group. You

II

Features and Services

should ask your local news administrator to see whether a copy is available. If you cannot locate one, you can get a copy using anonymous ftp to the machine `ftp.uu.net` and retrieving the file `/archive/uunet-info/news groups`. This file lists almost all the groups carried by USENET sites around the world; your local site probably does not carry all these groups. See Chapter 8, "Using ftp and telnet," for more information about how to use anonymous ftp.

Contributing to a News Group

Although a newcomer to netnews may know the definite set of topics discussed by each news group, the newcomer may have difficulty understanding a group's background and how the people who read that news group are expected to behave. You can picture netnews with its many news groups as a building with a large number of rooms, each of which is identified only by a name on the door. In some of these rooms, you find a small number of people politely discussing a topic of mutual interest while others quietly listen. In other rooms, you find a large crowd with everyone shouting out their opinions and paying no attention to anyone else in the room. Both of these types of news groups, and many other types in between, can be found in netnews.

Although this topic is discussed in further detail in the later section dealing with the culture of netnews, for now you should realize that you need to learn about the history of each individual news group before joining in the discussion (called *posting to the group*). Some topics may be discussed frequently (or just recently), and the group participants may not want to talk about them again. Other topics may be the cause of protracted arguments (called *flame wars*) and probably won't make you popular with group regulars.

> **Note**
>
> You should read the introductory information contained in the group `news.announce.newusers` before posting to any group on netnews. It contains valuable information about how USENET works and how to post effectively. Information about the history of USENET, posting etiquette, and writing style are also available in this group. See the sections "Subscribing to News Groups" and "Reading News Articles" for information on how to read `news.announce.newusers`.

News Distributions

In addition to news group names, netnews also involves the idea of *news article distribution*. A distribution is a keyword (such as "us" or "local") that can be placed in a news article. The article distribution controls which machines can receive an article posted to a news group. Distributions generally are associated with a geographic area and are used to ensure that an article is received only by machines in that geographic area. The news administrator for each site determines which distributions that site will accept from other USENET sites.

Why would you want to limit the distribution of an article? Many articles are not of interest to people across the entire USENET. For example, not many people reading news in California are interested in buying a car you have for sale in New Jersey. Similarly, if you are posting an announcement for a meeting of a local organization, people outside your immediate community probably won't be interested. And, bear in mind, posting a message worldwide can cost the network hundreds, even thousands, of dollars.

You limit the distribution of your news article by including a `Distribution:` line in the headers of the message. Often, this distribution header is generated automatically by your news posting mechanism (using a default value provided by your news administrator); you can edit this value if it is not appropriate. If the distribution header is not included automatically, you may be able to include it manually by editing the headers of your post. The format of this header line is the word `Distribution:`, followed by a space (after the colon), and then a value that identifies the distribution you want for your article. See the section "Posting an Original Article" for more information about how to post.

Commonly used distribution values follow:

Value	Identifies This Distribution
local	By convention, the article won't leave your local news machine; often used for groups that are private to your organization.
pa	The posting will be propagated to all machines in the state of Pennsylvania; all states in the United States have their own distribution code (that is the same as the state's postal code), and other countries often have distribution codes for the state or province level.
us	This article will be propagated to all machines in the United States; other countries have their own distribution code, and it is generally the same as their postal country code.
na	The article will be propagated to all machines in North America.

By default, if no distribution header is included in the article, the article propagates to all machines receiving the groups the article is posted to—including machines worldwide.

Many other distributions exist for local cities and regions. You should consult the periodic postings in the group `news.announce.newusers` for the valid news distributions in your area. The section "Reading News Articles" gives more information about how to read a particular group.

The Process of Reading and Posting News

This section discusses the basic steps necessary for reading and posting news articles. In addition, you learn formatting and content guidelines to be used when composing articles. Examples of some specific netnews interfaces are given later in the section "Examples of News Readers."

Subscribing to News Groups

To read news, you first need to decide to which groups you want to subscribe. Most news readers provide you with a way to view all the available news groups. Some, like the WinNET Mail system, mail you a list of the available news groups. Other systems, such as PSILink, automatically download the list to your system when you first connect and keep a local list on your machine that is updated automatically each time you call in to your account. See the section "Examples of News Readers" for more information about specific news readers.

You can determine from the news group's name or the news group's file (discussed in the section "News Group Organization") whether it may be of interest to you. You then subscribe to the groups you are interested in joining. Your news reader software explains in detail how you subscribe to a news group. In most cases, subscribing involves marking the news groups so that the news reader knows to save and/or show you articles from this group automatically, whenever you read news. After you subscribe to a news group, you see any new messages that have been posted to that group. You can unsubscribe from a group if you find that it doesn't interest you.

Reading News Articles

After subscribing to a news group, you are ready to begin reading articles. Your news reader may display each article one at a time sequentially, or it may display a list of the subjects and

II

Features and Services

authors and allow you to pick which articles you want to see displayed. Some news readers are *threaded*, which means that they display sequential listings of articles grouped by topic, rather than a sequential listing of all articles in the news group.

When you display an article, you see information at the top of the article about what news group(s) it was posted to, who posted it, and what subject the article discusses. Other information also may be listed at the top of the article, such as the organization the sender works for, keywords related to the main topic of articles (some news readers allow you to search for keywords), a short summary of the article, and possibly a few other things that you may not care about. In most news readers, after you display an article, you aren't shown that article again (only new messages are shown). The article continues to exist in the group for a while, but you may have difficulty going back to it.

Posting a Follow-Up Article

After reading an article, you may decide that you want to add something to the discussion, or comment about the author's viewpoint. If you think that your comments may be of general interest to everyone who reads the news group, most news readers allow you to post a follow-up article. When you give the follow-up command, your news reader creates a blank message with a header that contains the name of the news group, your return address, and a subject line that is the same as that of the original article, but with Re: attached to the front of it. See the discussions of individual news readers in the "Examples of News Readers" section for examples of follow-up commands.

Some news readers automatically include in the follow-up article the text of the original article, and some give you the option of including it or not. If you are going to include the original text, you should remove any of the text that is not relevant to the point you want to make. This editing makes the follow-up article easier to read and saves network resources.

Replying to an Article with E-Mail

If your comments are intended only for the author of the article, most news readers enable you to compose a mail message directly to the author. When you use the command in your news reader to reply to the message, the news reader uses the information in the article to generate a mail message to the author of the article. Some news readers also enable you to include text from the article automatically in the e-mail message. The news reader then displays an editor that enables you to edit the mail message. After you have finished editing the message, the mail message is sent to the author of the news article, using your computer system's electronic mail system. See Chapter 7, "Using E-Mail," for more information about electronic mail.

Posting an Original Article

If you want to post an article on a completely new subject, use your news reader's Post command. This command asks you to identify what news groups you want to post to and the subject of your article, and then puts you into an editor to allow you to compose your article. After you finish editing, you simply exit the editor and use your news reader's Send command. Most news readers have a provision for aborting a message if you decide not to send it. The store-and-forward systems, like WinNET Mail or PSILink, place your news post into a queue on your local system, where it waits for you to connect to your account on the central computer system. Some of these systems allow you to edit and delete messages that are in the queue if you've not connected to the system yet. When you are connected, the messages you have composed are no longer on your system and cannot be edited or deleted.

Guidelines for Composing Your Article

When you compose a news article, you should keep a number of things in mind. Try to make your subject relatively brief, but descriptive. For example, "Information needed" is too short, but

"Information needed about the best way to test for out-of-bounds errors" is too long. A better subject would be something like "Question about error testing." Also, you need to follow a number of formatting guidelines when composing your article, to make it easier to read. Here are a few guidelines:

- Use text characters only. Control characters do odd things to different types of displays.

- Keep your line length under 80 characters (the maximum line length of some displays).

- Break up your text into medium-size paragraphs with blank lines between them. This format is much easier to read than long, solid blocks of text.

- Use mixed case, because text in all uppercase is hard to read and is generally used for emphasis in your message. A message in all uppercase is considered "shouting" and should be avoided.

In addition to the above guidelines for how you format the text of your article, you should follow some guidelines concerning the content of your article. Most of these guidelines involve common courtesy towards USENET readers and authors:

- Commercial advertising is not permitted on netnews groups (but advertising personal items of interest to other members of the group usually is permitted). Some forms of advertising do occur on netnews groups, but a blatant advertisement posted to inappropriate groups is frowned on and won't gather much support for the advertiser. A separate hierarchy (called `biz`) was created specifically to allow companies to form groups for their products. Also, the group `comp.newprod` contains postings for new-product announcements.

- Try to keep the length of individual articles to 1,000 lines or less. Longer articles can break some older news transport mechanisms.

- Postings of binary files (files that contain control characters in addition to text) should be encoded using a program such as uuencode, because current news transport mechanisms don't pass binary data correctly. (Many news readers make provisions to use uuencode automatically when you send a binary file.) In addition, post binary files only to those groups that accept them.

- Posting an e-mail message without the sender's permission is greatly frowned on and may in fact violate copyright restrictions. If you have any question about the legality of posting the mail message, you should contact the author first.

- When you quote someone else's article, indicate the quoted material with some character in the left-hand column—most news readers use the greater-than sign (>) as the standard indicator of quoted material.

- Posting large amounts of information (usually binary files) is frowned on. Because netnews is transmitted by a store-and-forward mechanism, every article you post costs people around the world some amount of money for its reception and transmission. In the case of sites that still use UUCP links to transmit and receive news, the telephone charges for netnews transmission can be considerable (especially overseas, where phone charges are much higher than in the United States). Statistics that indicate which people and sites have posted the largest number of articles each month, and which news groups are most popular, are posted to the group `news.groups`.

- If you are posting information that some people may not want to read (like the plot of a new movie, or something that might be offensive to some people) use the rot13 format command to encrypt the text. Most news readers have commands to encrypt text into rot13 format and to decode encrypted text so that it can be read.

Your Signature

When you post an article or a follow-up to an article, your news reader software may not generate a proper return e-mail address in the From: line of your article. Even if you have a valid return address in your headers, and your article is requesting or giving information about your local area, people who are reading your article may not recognize your site name or know where that local area is. So it's a good idea to include a signature at the bottom of your message that contains a valid return e-mail address and, at least, the geographical area that you are posting from, if not a complete identification of the organization with which you are affiliated.

Many people put a favorite quote or a picture made out of text characters in their signature. Most news reader systems, however, suggest that you limit your signature to a maximum length of four lines, to avoid wasting network resources on unnecessary information. With most news readers, after you set up your signature, the news reader automatically appends that signature to each article that you post. On UNIX, for example, you can have a .signature file in your home directory that is appended automatically to your news posts.

The Culture of USENET

As with any large group of people (estimates indicate that well over a million people are USENET users), USENET has a unique culture that you should become familiar with before beginning to read (and certainly post to!) news groups. Just as you would not join a conversation before understanding what is being talked about, you should not post to a news group before you understand the culture of USENET. As a USENET user, you can make better use of the information available and encounter fewer problems if you have a good idea of how USENET works.

First, USENET is made up of all the machines that receive network news groups. These machines, and the users on those machines who read and post articles, make up a very diverse community. Netnews reaches the United States, Canada, and most of the rest of the world. As a result of this international span, every article you post on USENET may be read by someone in virtually any part of the world. You can't assume, therefore, that everyone who reads your article speaks English as a native language or shares your cultural background.

USENET also reaches many different kinds of sites. Because the Internet initially was a research and educational network (and still is, to a great extent), many sites receiving netnews are educational institutions. Since the Internet has become more diverse, however, the number of commercial, governmental, and private sites receiving netnews has increased.

Even though USENET reaches thousands of sites and many thousands of readers, no central authority controls USENET. No central group or organization dictates which groups are carried by a site. In fact, there is no way that a particular person or site can impose rules or restrictions on how other sites run USENET. This lack of central authority always confuses new netnews readers, who have a hard time adapting to the idea that USENET has no central authority to run things or complain to; the local site administrator is the only authority, and he or she can control only that site.

So, if no central authority controls USENET, how does it continue to run and grow? Even though USENET has no hard and fast laws and no authority to enforce laws (if they did exist),

USENET is run by cooperation between sites, and a set of customs and conventions that have grown up during the years that USENET has existed. In addition, the opinions of certain people are respected by a large number of site administrators. These respected individuals have gained authority by expressing reasonable opinions over a number of years; quite often, they have contributed considerable time to USENET, either writing and maintaining the netnews software or administering netnews sites.

USENET, therefore, represents a diverse, multicultural community. It is significantly different than any other group, both in its diversity and its size. Rather than be guided by laws or some governing body, it is run according to the customs, conventions, and opinions of respected members of the community. Given this loose organization, it is amazing that USENET has managed to grow, and indeed flourish. The continued existence of USENET is a tribute to the cooperation of the people using it.

The Culture of a Particular News Group

As USENET in general has a culture associated with it, so each individual group has its own particular culture. As discussed earlier, a group can be polite and friendly, easily welcoming new users, and patiently explaining what has gone on in the past. Other groups can be decidedly unfriendly, with opinions flying rapidly and no regard for newcomers.

In general, groups in the "serious" hierarchies such as comp, news, and sci are more likely to place emphasis on discussing facts rather than opinions. Groups in these hierarchies often are less likely to tolerate the expression of opinions that lack supporting facts, and they generally are more tolerant of newcomers who are willing to listen to "reason."

On the other hand, groups in the soc and rec hierarchies are more oriented toward opinions on topics and are thus more likely to be argumentative. People in these groups are likely to listen to the opinions of a newcomer. But if you join one of these groups and express your opinions, be prepared to receive other people's opinions in return—opinions that may not be the same as yours!

Finally, groups in the talk and misc hierarchies definitely tend toward inflammatory topics, such as politics and abortion. Discussions in many of these groups often generate much more heat than light (discussions often referred to as having a low "signal-to-noise ratio"), and you are wise to tread lightly when entering these groups for the first time. Expressing a strong opinion in one of these groups will certainly elicit a strong response, and you should be prepared for negative reactions to your posts. Although you will not (and in fact cannot) be forbidden to post to a group, you may find other readers of a group ignoring your posts (if they hold differing opinions), or responding negatively (or abusively) to your posts, either in follow-up posts or by electronic mail directly to you.

And, although anyone can post to most of the news groups, some news groups are "moderated." In a moderated news group, before articles can be posted, they must be approved by a person who is the moderator of the group. All articles are sent to the moderator, who decides whether the content of each article is appropriate to the topic and tone of the group. If the article meets the moderator's approval, the moderator then posts the article to the news group. Moderated news groups tend to have few problems with abusive and/or inappropriate postings. Most news readers automatically send to the moderator all articles posted to a moderated group. Your news-reading software usually informs you if a group is moderated, and the news groups file (discussed earlier in the section "News Group Organization") also indicates whether a group is moderated.

II

Features and Services

Getting To Know a News Group

So, how do you know the culture of a news group when you first begin reading the articles in it? The answer is that you don't. And you shouldn't make any assumptions about the group before understanding its culture.

The best way to understand the culture of a group, and netnews in general, is to read it for a while. Before you post an article to a group, it's a good idea to read the group for at least a month before attempting a post; read it longer if you don't have any pressing questions.

Read the Frequently Asked Questions Lists

Some groups maintain a list of frequently asked questions (called a *FAQ*), which the groups post periodically (generally once a month). Always read a group's FAQ before posting any questions to the group. Quite often, your question has been asked before (possibly many times), and asking it again won't generate any new information.

All the FAQ postings for netnews groups are available for anonymous ftp to the site `rtfm.mit.edu`. These postings really are a wealth of information about numerous topics, and are well worth reading. The FAQs also are posted to the groups `news.answers`, `comp.answers`, `soc.answers`, and so on.

After you have read a news group for a while, you begin to get a feeling for its culture. You learn to recognize the group's common topics (and those that cause the most problems!), the regular posters to the group (including the most and least respected), and how new users are treated. At this point, you have the background information necessary to "live" in the group.

Problems with News Group Discussions

The most important thing to remember when posting to a news group is that no matter how hard you try, you can't please everyone reading your articles. The number of people reading netnews is just too large, and the USENET community too diverse, for you to expect everyone involved to share your opinions. Even if you post a simple request for information in a polite news group, you are likely to receive mail from people either asking for you to forward the same information to them (called "me too" messages) or complaining that your message was inappropriate for the group you picked. On the other hand, you will almost always receive an answer to your question, and the chances are good that the answer will be correct. The USENET community contains experts on almost every field.

One serious problem with holding discussions in a news group is that you may experience long propagation delays between the time you post your article and the time it gets to the many user sites. If you're directly connected to the Internet, your post will be available on many other directly connected sites within a few hours. Because some sites still use UUCP to transfer their news, and many overseas sites get their news in batches only a few times a day, several days may pass before all netnews sites receive your article.

Similarly, replies to your article may take several days to reach your site. What may happen, then, is that the news group contains your original article, replies to your article, replies to the replies, and so on. These articles appear in the news group in a more or less random order and may take many days to die out (depending on how much discussion your article generates), as people in distant parts of USENET finally get your article and respond to it. You may find that in a discussion with many replies, the topic is still being discussed long after most of the people in the news group are tired of the subject!

Netiquette

Netiquette is a term that refers to common netnews etiquette. Enforcing any particular code of behavior on posters to a news group is almost impossible (see the section "Dealing with Problem Users" for more information). However, most people voluntarily follow the many rules of common courtesy that exist in the USENET community. And, when you post an article, remember that you don't know who may be reading your post, including your boss, your spouse, or a future employer! The section "Guidelines for Composing Your Articles" discusses the content and form of your article this section addresses the tone of your article and how people may react to it.

When you are composing an article, make sure to word your post carefully so that it accurately communicates your thoughts. With the lack of immediate feedback from your reader, and the absence of your voice inflection, tone, and physical indicators (facial expressions, hand gestures, and so on), the intent of your message easily can be misunderstood. Also, your message may be read by someone who is not a native speaker of your language, or who doesn't understand your culture. Your message may be reaching hundreds of thousands—or even millions—of readers, many of whom are in places with which you've never dreamed of holding communication. And when communicating on USENET, you cannot quickly correct a misunderstanding by your reader.

Don't post *flames*, articles that are personal attacks on another poster or tirades about a topic. Although flaming is accepted (and even encouraged) in some groups, members of most groups lose respect for someone who does it frequently. Before you take offense at an article, have an e-mail discussion with the author to clarify that individual's position; you may have misunderstood what the author was trying to say. When you get angry after reading an article, don't respond immediately. If you're still angry after you investigate to uncover any misunderstanding on your part, think carefully about how you best can respond.

When you read an article, read all the replies to that article before you post your reply. Someone else may have already replied with the same point that you were going to make. It just wastes time and computer resources for you to post the same response. Due to delays in receiving replies, of course, multiple replies do get posted; you may post your reply and later receive one that makes the same point.

Finally, try to avoid lengthy conversations over netnews with a particular individual. You and another reader may share opinions on an issue or have widely opposing ones. After a few messages about the topic go back and forth, however, you should move the conversation to personal electronic mail.

Expressing Emotions without Visual Cues

One of the main problems in communicating with people over netnews is that you aren't talking with them face to face. Your netnews communications lack the many visual cues that you use to express feelings and emotions, and, as a result, their meanings can be misinterpreted.

You can draw on a number of commonly used conventions to try to put some of the more physical aspects of communication into articles. Shouting is indicated with all uppercase letters (for example, `THAT IS NOT TRUE!`). You can emphasize a phrase by enclosing it with asterisks (for example, `*do this step first*`).

Another way to indicate emotions in your messages is to use commonly understood symbols (often called *emoticons*, or *smileys* after their main use). For example, to indicate that you are making a joke, you can use `:-)`. (Hint: Look at the symbol sideways!) Here are a few of the most common emoticons:

Emoticon	Description
:-)	Smiley (happy) face
:-(	Sad face

(continues)

Features and Services

Emoticon	Description
;-)	Winking
:-0	Surprise (or shouting)
8-)	Wide-eyed smile
:->	Sarcastic smile
:-{)	Smiley with mustache

These examples are only a few of the many emoticons you can use to express feeling. You can, of course, simply write that you are joking in your post, which prevents any misunderstanding!

Always remember, however, that the best way to avoid misunderstandings is to express yourself as clearly and concisely as possible in your messages. Your readers will know nothing about you other than what they learn from reading your postings. Rather than assume that the reader of your post will know when you are joking or being sarcastic, you should tell them explicitly. Humor can be indicated by spelling out the intended physical clue in angle brackets (for example, <grin>).

Using Abbreviations in Your Articles

In addition to the emoticons, you will find that news articles often contain abbreviations for commonly used phrases. Some of the more common abbreviations are IMHO, which means *In My Humble* (or *Honest*) *Opinion*; BTW, for *By The Way*; FYI, which means *For Your Information*; OTOH, which stands for *On The Other Hand*; and FWIW, which means *For What It's Worth*. You can also abbreviate <grin> with <g>. You probably will come across other abbreviations as you read news articles; the meanings of most of them are obvious from their context in the message. Abbreviations are a way to save space and network resources by reducing the number of characters in an article.

Dealing with Problem Users

Eventually, you will have a problem with another user on USENET. Someone may send you abusive mail concerning a post you made, or a person may disrupt a news group with repeated, unwelcomed posts. Occasionally, someone posts a message that appears to be from another person (called *forging* a post). Even more rarely, problems such as death threats or other forms of harassment are reported.

The first thing to try as a means of dealing with problem users is to ignore them. If a person is posting articles that annoy you, just don't respond to those posts. Many news readers support a feature called a *kill file*. This feature automatically removes (kills) articles specified by criteria you set. The kill file feature enables you to kill all posts from a particular user, posts that regard a particular subject, or that meet any other criteria. Check the documentation on your news reading software to see Whether it supports such a mechanism. Using the kill feature of your software is often very effective in reducing the amount of annoyance generated by netnews.

If the problem user is going further than simply posting annoying articles (such as sending harassing e-mail), you can try to contact the administrators at the user's site. See Chapter 7, "Using E-Mail," on how to contact the administrator at a user's site.

How Do You Get Access to USENET?

Two common methods exist for individual PC users to gain access to USENET. The first of these methods is through a store-and-forward system, which enables you to read and compose news articles on your PC and connect to an Internet provider only when you want to receive or send your news and e-mail. Alternatively, you can connect on-line through a terminal interface to an account on an Internet provider's host. In either case,

II

Features and Services

you don't have to worry about setting up a mechanism on your PC to manage news groups. The Internet provider does all the news group management and sends you (or gives you access to) the news articles that are of interest to you. Most Internet providers give you information about how to use the particular news reader that they supply.

In some cases, users may want to receive an actual local news feed. Information on using and receiving a local news feed appears later in this chapter, in the "How To Receive Netnews" section.

Examples of News Readers

This section discusses examples of a number of different news readers that you may encounter from your Internet provider. This section outlines common news reader features and provides examples of some of their commands.

Common News Reader Features

Some news readers give you the option of ignoring certain threads (articles with the same subject), ignoring posts from certain people, marking articles as unread (so that you see the header of these articles the next time you read the group), marking an entire thread as read, or marking an entire group as read. This last option is valuable if you return from vacation, for example, and find a large number of articles in a news group, and you don't have time to read them all. You can use the "catch up" feature to discard the unread articles. You can then start reading new articles as they appear.

Expiring Articles

Because of the huge volume of messages that arrive daily for all the thousands of news groups, most news group managers "expire" articles after a certain period of time. After an article is expired, you can't call it up again on USENET, so you may want to save articles that are of particular interest to you to a permanent file on your local disk. Even if you are getting the news articles downloaded to your local disk by the provider, you probably need to save interesting articles to a separate file, because the provider's news group reader needs to delete articles occasionally to keep your disk from filling up.

The rn News Reader

The rn news reader commonly is available on UNIX hosts. You may need to use this news reader if you are connected through a terminal interface directly to your Internet provider's UNIX host. To use rn, you can give the command rn followed by the name(s) of the news group(s) you want to read. Or, if you have used rn's subscription feature, you can just give the rn command by itself, because rn keeps a file in your account of all the groups you have subscribed to.

> **Note**
>
> The trn news reader has the same commands as the rn news reader, but it groups articles into threads. The rn reader displays articles in the order they are received on your news system.

After you give the rn command, you see a list of the news groups you specified with information about how many new messages are in each group. The rn news reader then cycles through this list of news groups and asks, for each group, whether you want to read the new articles. As a rule, you answer by pressing y to read the group immediately, or n to go on to the next group in the cycle. Alternatively, you can press p to return to the previous group, or q to quit reading news.

The rn news reader enables you to read new articles sequentially, in the order they appear in the news group. It displays as much of the current article as fits on your screen, and it displays a command line at the bottom of the screen. You can perform a number of different functions in rn by entering single-character

commands. Table 9.1 lists the most common commands.
The h command gives help at every prompt.

Table 9.1 rn News Reader Commands	
Command	**Action**
<space>	Display the next page of the current article
n	Go to the next unread article
N	Go to the next article, read or unread
P	Go to the previous unread article
p	Go to the previous article, read or unread
b	Back up one page
M	Mark this article as unread
k	Mark as read all articles with the current subject (kill a subject)
r	Reply to the author through e-mail
R	Reply to the author through e-mail, quoting the article
f	Post a follow-up article to the news group
F	Post a follow-up article quoting the article
s*file*	Save the current article to *file*
w*file*	Save the current article minus headers to *file*

The rn news reader is complex and powerful (if not very user-
friendly). For more information on using rn, refer to the UNIX
manual page (type man rn at your UNIX prompt). And be aware
that rn doesn't enable you to post new articles (only follow-
ups). If you use this news reader and want to post a new article,
you can use the postnews command, which prompts you to indicate your article's subject and the name of the news group to

which you want to post the article. The command then puts you in an editor where you can compose your article. When you exit the editor, you have the option of sending or aborting the article.

The tin News Reader

The tin news reader is screen oriented and much more user-friendly than rn. The tin news reader enables you to subscribe to groups and post new articles directly. Further, tin is a *threaded* news reader, which means that it organizes articles both in sequence and by topic; thus, you don't have to go through a sequential listing of all articles in the news group if you are interested only in those articles pertaining to a specific topic.

When you start tin (by using the `tin` command), it displays all the news groups to which you have subscribed (like rn, it keeps track of your news groups in a file). You see an on-screen list of those news groups and the number of new articles in each group to which you have subscribed. You can use the up- and down-arrow keys to move to the group that you want to read; then press Enter to read that group, or u to unsubscribe from that group. Other commands allow you to search for a group by name, move a group to a different place in the group list (so you can put your most frequently read groups first), or subscribe to a group that is not already in your list of read groups.

Table 9.2 lists some tin news reader commands and their actions.

Table 9.2 tin News Reader Commands

Command	Action
<Enter>	Read the current article
N	Move to the next article
n	Move to the next threaded group of articles

(continues)

| **Table 9.2 Continued** | |
Command	Action
P	Move to the previous article
p	Move to the previous threaded group of articles
K	Kill and mark as read the entire current thread
w	Post an article to the current group of articles
q	Return to the news group selection screen
Q	Quit tin

The tin news reader has many more commands for selecting, viewing, or deleting articles. On-screen help is available at all times, and the h command gives you a description of all available commands. You also can view the UNIX manual page for the tin program by using the man tin command at the UNIX prompt.

The WinNET Mail News Reader

The WinNET Mail news reader (available from Computer Witchcraft, Inc.) is an example of an "off-line" news reading service that enables you to receive news (and mail) destined for your site. WinNET Mail is a Microsoft Windows program that connects through a modem on your computer to the WinNET Mail central computer. Using that connection, WinNET Mail downloads the news and mail for your site onto your local disk. After transferring all the files, the program disconnects, enabling you to read your news and mail without running up expensive phone bills. Because the program uses the Windows interface, reading and posting news on WinNET Mail is very easy.

Chapter 7, "Using E-Mail," discusses the procedures for reading and sending mail with WinNET Mail, but the mail and news parts of the program are very similar. The WinNET Mail

program starts up in mail reading mode. If you click the News
icon on the startup screen (on the button bar), the Usenet News
Group Folders window shown in figure 9.1 appears.

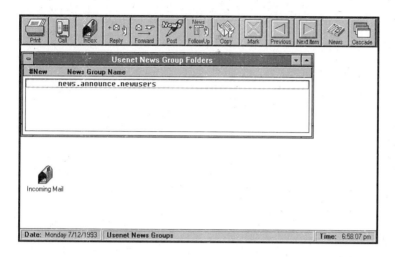

Fig. 9.1
The WinNET
Mail News Group
Folders window.

After you are in the Usenet News Group Folders window,
you can see the news that has arrived in a news group by
double-clicking the name of the news group in the News
Group Name column. For example, you double-click the
news.announce.newusers line to read the articles in that group.
This opens a new window with the list of articles that you have
received in that group, as shown in figure 9.2.

This screen shows that four articles have arrived in the news
group news.announce.newusers. To read a news article, double-
click the line that contains that article's name. So, for example,
if you want to read the last article in the group (from Ron
Dippold), double-click that line. The article then appears in a
new window, as shown in figure 9.3.

You can click the Next Item icon in the button bar at the top of
the WinNET Mail screen to move to the next article; click the
Previous icon to move to the previous article. Other icons enable you to print, move an article to another folder, or post and

delete news articles. You subscribe to a new news group by using the Subscription item on the News menu. This item displays a dialog box that asks you for the group to subscribe to. When you register your WinNET Mail account, you receive instructions (through electronic mail) for using the system that include lists of available news groups. More information about the program is also available through the on-line Windows help.

Fig. 9.2
The articles available in a news group.

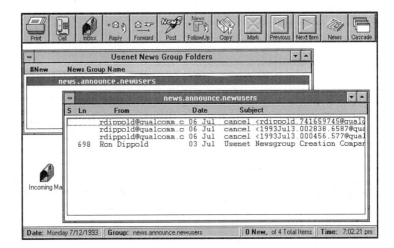

Fig. 9.3
The news article window.

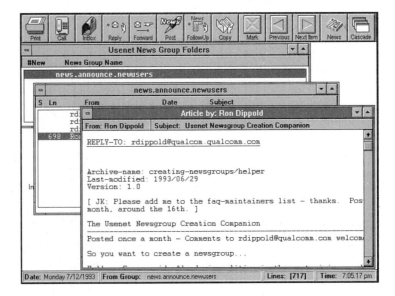

The PSILink News Reader

The PSILink software (available from Performance Systems International, Inc.) is another example of an off-line news reader. The software connects to the PSI news server to retrieve the articles available in the groups you have subscribed to. The PSILink software is available in DOS and Windows versions (both versions operate in much the same way). When you enter the PSILink DOS version, you see the main screen, as shown in figure 9.4.

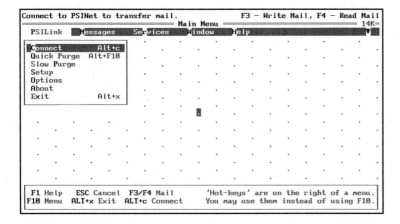

Fig. 9.4
The PSILink main screen.

You can activate menus and issue commands to the PSILink software by choosing menus and menu items either with the mouse or by pressing Alt plus the highlighted letters for the items. For example, you activate the Messages menu by clicking it or by pressing Alt+M.

To subscribe to news groups, for example, you choose Messages followed by Subscribe To News. This choice brings up a list of all available groups. This very large list, a portion of which is shown in figure 9.5, is transmitted to your system the first time you connect to the PSI server. You can scroll through this list and choose the groups in which you are interested. Pressing the space bar subscribes (or unsubscribes) to the current news group, and you can search for a particular group by using the s command.

Fig. 9.5

The PSILink news subscription screen.

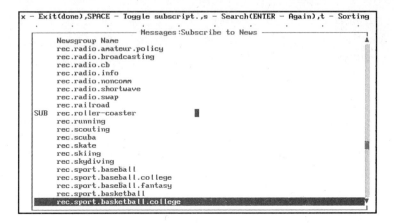

Reading news in PSILink is exactly the same as reading mail. You use the Read Mail/News menu item under the Messages menu to bring up the list of available mail and news folders. Press Enter to read the news or mail available in the selected folder; the Next and Prev menu items move around the available folders and messages.

You post news with the Write News option in the Messages menu. Choosing Write News brings up the New Messages screen, shown in figure 9.6. This screen prompts you to enter the name of the news group to which you want to post the article and to indicate the subject of the message. You then can edit the article and post it to the group. The File menu allows you to send or cancel the article, and the Header menu allows you to change one of the header lines. The Edit menu allows you to cut and paste and perform other edits on your message.

More information about the PSILink software is available in the program's on-line documentation and the printed manuals.

A Brief History of Netnews

Although computer bulletin boards, where users can post a message for many people to read, have been popular almost from the beginning of the computer age, the idea of sending messages from a local bulletin board to a similar board on another machine wasn't explored until the early 1980s. Electronic mailing lists enabled a user to send a single message to a number of other users, but this practice wasted resources because every user that wanted to read the article had to receive a private copy of the article. Thus, if you had 20 people on a system who were also on a mailing list, the system received 20 copies of each message sent to the list. It is more efficient, however, if a single copy of the message is placed where each of the 20 users can read it, which is what a bulletin board system does.

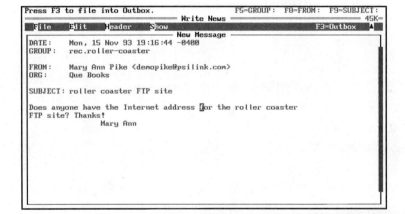

Fig. 9.6
The PSILink New Messages screen.

News Transport Systems

In early 1980, computer programmers at Duke University and the University of North Carolina set up a rudimentary system to forward messages between their two systems. Using a UNIX Version 7 utility called UUCP (UNIX to UNIX Copy), the system transmitted, through modems and phone lines, articles posted to a local news group to the other machine.

This news transport system was presented at the 1980 summer Usenix (a professional organization of UNIX users) conference, where it generated a small amount of interest in the UNIX community. With a few improvements, the system was released to the public domain and was called "A news" (as the first version of the netnews system). Although it was slow, the message transport system worked. The system's authors expected it to handle only about 10 messages per day to a few news groups.

Soon, a few more computers were linked into this UUCP network, and the flow of articles increased. The early success of the A release of the news article transport system soon pointed up its failings, and a complete rewrite of the software was begun at the University of California at Berkeley. This release, known as "B news," was made available in 1982. B news was designed to handle a large number of news groups and articles, and it remained the standard for many years. The final version of B news was released in late 1986, and the system has been stable since then.

The UUCP system soon became too slow to handle the amount of articles it was called on to handle, and the phone calls were often expensive. With advancements in the development of the Internet, many people realized that it should be used to transmit news articles. In 1986, a program to implement NNTP (Network News Transport Protocol) was written, and that program became the standard for the transmission of netnews articles across the Internet. NNTP is defined by the Internet RFC 977. (RFC stands for Request For Comment, an Internet standard.)

With the advent of NNTP, the already fast growth of netnews exploded. The B news release, although relatively robust and well used, became too slow to handle the flow of news. In 1987, Henry Spencer of the University of Toronto released the "C news" version of the netnews transport mechanism. This release featured increased speed, reliability, and configurability, and quickly became the standard in use on the Internet.

As of this writing, several other systems also are used to transmit netnews articles, such as Waffle and Fido BBS (a network of PC systems that communicate through telephone lines) and INN (Internet News), which is similar in use to C news. These systems, although not as widely used as C news, perform the same function of transmitting news articles between machines.

In a later section, this chapter discusses the operation of some of the available PC-based news transport systems.

News Reader Systems

Although the news transport mechanism has changed to reflect the increase in volume of news, relatively few transport systems have been in use. On the other hand, the number of news reader systems has been greater, to reflect different user needs and tastes. Some news readers are easy to learn and use, although others have very complex interfaces but allow users to sort through large numbers of articles quickly.

While an in-depth description of the many news readers currently available is beyond the scope of this book, the features of many of the readers are similar. Because this book is oriented toward users with PC systems, this chapter discusses some of the news readers available for that platform.

With the original B news release came a very simple news reader, called *vnews*. The sections "The rn News Reader" and "The tin News Reader" earlier in this chapter discuss two other popular news readers in detail. Another popular news reader is trn (a threaded version of rn). These programs all can be compiled and run on many different platforms, are available at no cost on the Internet, and are actively supported by their authors.

All of these news readers allow users to read and post articles, and many allow users to follow "threads" of conversations (articles that are related to the same topic). Other features in popular news readers are discussed in the section "Examples of News Readers."

News Group Creation

One of the most frequently asked questions about netnews is: How are new news groups created? This topic is one of the most central to the administration of netnews; in fact, quite a lot of the history of netnews is tied to the process of creating news groups.

How Groups Used To Be Created

When the bulk of the netnews traffic was being carried by the
UUCP method of transmission, most people who carried netnews had to pay telephone charges to receive and transmit
news. When the amount of traffic was small, these charges
weren't excessive; but as netnews became popular, these telephone charges were a burden on sites.

Some central sites (such as Duke, the University of Toronto, and
others) imported the news hierarchies into a certain area and then
distributed them to local sites. Many of these central sites could
absorb the telephone charges because the benefits of receiving the
news transmissions at their site was worth the cost. However,
because these sites (called the *backbone*) essentially were providing
a service to the rest of the net free of charge, they held a certain
authority over the process of creating news groups. In fact, if these
backbone sites refused to carry a certain group, it was impossible
to get that group to a large number of users.

So although the UUCP transport mechanism was still carrying
the majority of news, the group of administrators at these backbone sites (sometimes called the *backbone cabal*) were the final
authority on news group creation. Users and administrators
would propose a news group publicly, and the administrators of
the backbone sites would raise any objections that they had to
the group. If no one objected to the proposed news group, the
group was created on the backbone sites, and everyone on the
netnews network (called USENET) began receiving the group.

Although the backbone cabal was an effective way to control the
creation and deletion of news groups (and in fact created the current main hierarchies in the so-called *great renaming* of the mid-
1980s), many people in the netnews community wanted a more
liberal approach to the creation of news groups.

One way of dealing with the strict rules for news group creation in
the main news hierarchies was the creation of the alt hierarchy.

Initially proposed by Brian Reid at the Digital Equipment Corporation, the `alt` hierarchy has very liberal rules for the creation of new groups; literally anyone with the capability to post an article to the news system can create a new group under the `alt` hierarchy. You should note, however, that although the `alt` hierarchy has some groups that are carried by a majority of netnews sites, most `alt` groups are carried by few news sites worldwide.

In the end, it wasn't the objections of users or some political process that caused the end of the backbone cabal. It was, instead, the growth of the use of the NNTP transport mechanism that reduced, and finally ended, the influence of the backbone administrators. Sites that used the NNTP transport could receive their news from literally any other site on the Internet (instead of the local UUCP backbone site). If the local site refused to carry a particular news group, the chances were that, somewhere on the Internet, you could find a site that would feed the desired group to you.

How Groups Are Created Now

The current news group creation mechanism came into being to replace the influence of the backbone administrators. The current mechanism for creating news groups is described fully in periodic postings to the news group `news.announce.newusers`, but the process (in brief) is as follows:

1. The group's name and a brief description of the topics it is expected to cover are posted to the `news.announce.newgroups` group (as well as to any news groups with topics related to the new group). This proposal is called a "call for discussion" (often abbreviated CFD) and is expected to generate discussion about the validity and usefulness of the new group.

2. Following a two-week discussion period, if no serious objections to the name and charter of the new group are raised, a "call for votes" (often abbreviated CFV) is posted to the same news groups as above. In this call for votes,

the electronic mail address for the "vote taker" (who is supposed to be an independent, nonpartisan person) is given. The vote taker collects the names of people voting for and against the news group proposal. During the voting process, the vote taker periodically posts the names of the people who have voted on the proposal (but not how they voted) so that people can verify that their vote has been received. The vote taker is explicitly forbidden from publishing the current number of votes for or against the group proposal.

3. After the two-week vote process is completed, the vote taker announces the results of the vote. To pass, the news group proposal must receive at least 100 votes in favor of the group; the proposal must receive at least 100 more Yes votes than No votes; and the Yes votes must be at least two-thirds of the total votes. If all these criteria are met, the group is approved and, after a one-week waiting period, is created.

The important thing to remember about the process of creating a news group is that the group must be accepted by a legitimate vote. Even when a majority of the votes is for the new group proposal, if the news administrators on the various machines receiving netnews feel that the group is not legitimate, they will not carry the group on their machine. For all the democratic appearances of the above process, the local news administrator is free to do what he/she wants with his/her site's machine. One of the facts of life in netnews is that you generally cannot control someone else.

Why You Shouldn't Create a News Group
One final note on creating a news group. One of the most common mistakes made by new readers of netnews is to try to create a news group before understanding the process and culture of netnews. A new user often begins reading netnews,

discovers that a group covering his or her favorite topic is not available, and immediately proposes the creation of such a group. This kind of proposal is almost certain to fail because the group proposed probably does not have sufficient interest to gather the required number of Yes votes.

New readers of netnews should read the material in the groups news.announce.newusers and follow the discussion in groups such as news.groups (which often discusses the creation, deletion, and renaming of news groups) for at least six months before trying to propose a new group. If you cannot wait that long, you should at least get someone who has read netnews for an extended period of time to make the actual new group proposal. If you don't do this, your new group proposal will probably not be well received, and ultimately the group will probably not be created.

How To Receive Netnews

If you want to receive netnews on your personal machine, or a central machine at your organization, you need to learn how to manage netnews. The first thing that you must decide before getting access to netnews is what level of service you want to receive. Because the reception of netnews on a local machine can require significant resources (depending on the number and type of news groups you want to receive), you may decide on one of several options that don't require you to dedicate local resources to netnews in order to read the news.

The resources required to have netnews on a local system vary with the number of groups received locally, but in general, you need a machine with enough disk space and CPU power to handle a large amount of traffic. At this writing, a full feed of the main hierarchies (including the alt hierarchy) averages almost 80M of data per day. So, if you want to keep a week's worth of news articles on your system, you need more than 500M of local disk storage, plus a few megabytes for storage of the news binaries and sources.

II

Features and Services

Similarly, you need a CPU that can handle this amount of traffic moving into your system. A personal computer with an 80386 or 80486 processor is necessary to handle the load of a fairly large number of groups.

As you can see, getting a local feed of more than a few groups is not something to be undertaken lightly. Fortunately, other ways of getting access to netnews exist that don't require significant local resources.

Public-Access News Sites

If your site is one at which only a few people want to have access to netnews, and you don't need to have control over the length of time a particular news article is available on a system (how long until an article *expires*), you may want to get access to netnews on one of many public access machines around the country.

For a monthly fee, you can get an account on a public access machine. These systems, called *public-access sites*, are connected to the Internet and may provide services such as electronic mail, netnews feeds, ftp, or other Internet services to their customers. Often, these sites are set up to allow people who do not have direct Internet access to dial in via a modem and connect to their site. If you already have an Internet connection, you don't need to use a modem, but instead you can simply telnet to the remote machine and log in.

These public-access sites are available around the country, and you should pick the one which gives you the best service for your money. If your primary need is simply netnews access, you should pick a site that receives the groups you're interested in and keeps the groups on-disk for an amount of time acceptable to you. Generally, you should require the site to keep the groups you require on-disk for at least four days so you can skip reading the news over an extended weekend without missing any articles.

Another item you should consider when picking a public-access site is the site's reputation. Because any posts you make to a news group display the public-access site from which they originate, you should try to find a site that has a professional reputation—one that won't cause people to discount your posts. Try to find a site that allows you to customize your outgoing posts so that the organization name and return mail address listed in the article headers reflect your actual organization and Internet mail address (rather than the public access site). This arrangement enables you to receive replies to your post at your regular mail address, if you choose.

To locate a public-access site, consult the lists provided on the disk included with this book in the file PDIAL.TXT. The PDIAL document is updated as the maintainer gets information about new public-access sites. The file is kept at an ftp site (identified within the file) on the Internet and is posted regularly to certain news groups that also are identified in the file. After you have the names of sites that may be able to provide the news access you need, you can contact the administrators (given as the contact for information in the listings) at those sites to determine their news policies and features.

Remotely Reading News with NNTP

You may have a few problems reading news at a public-access computer. For example, if you want to keep a news article around for future reference, you probably need to transfer it to your local site by using the ftp program (discussed in Chapter 8, "Using ftp and telnet"). Further, you may not like the news readers available on the remote site, and you generally have to pay a per-hour fee for the time you spend reading news (which can be a significant amount, given the amount of news available!).

If you have only a few people at your site who want to read news, and you don't want to use a public-access site to read news, another option available to you is to set up a local news

II

Features and Services

reader that accesses the news stored on a remote machine. These news readers use the NNTP protocol (the same one used to transfer news between sites that feed each other) to retrieve individual articles that you want to read. The rn and tin news readers can be set up to use the NNTP protocol to read articles; most other popular news readers have this capability also.

The advantage of using an NNTP-based news reader is that you have control over the news reading interface you use—you can pick the news reader that suits your tastes. In addition, because the news reader is running on your local machine, any articles you save for future reference are stored locally. You don't need to devote large amounts of computer resources to receive a local news feed.

One disadvantage of using the NNTP-based readers is that you transfer the articles you want in real time. Network congestion, the load on the remote machine, and other factors can slow the transfer of articles to your news reader and can result in slower responses than reading the news off of a local disk.

Getting access to a system that supports NNTP-based reading is similar to finding a public-access site. Your choices are somewhat broader, however, because you require only an NNTP connection and don't require a login account on the remote machine. Many of the same public-access sites that allow news reading also allow NNTP access to their news. Also, commercial news providers such as UUNET and PSI provide NNTP-based news access. To locate such a site, consult the public-access site list (PDIAL.TXT) included on the disk provided with this book.

Also, local universities and even some commercial sites allow NNTP-based readers; check around in your local area for such sites.

Getting a Limited Number of Groups via Electronic Mail

Quite often, the people at your site don't require a full netnews feed to receive the groups whose articles they want to read. If the total number of requested groups is small, and few articles are posted in those groups, receiving the news groups via electronic mail is often easier than the normal netnews transport mechanisms.

To receive the news articles via electronic mail, your site should need to receive less than 5M of information per day (or a few hundred articles). If your site receives more than this amount of information, you may find it more efficient to use the normal news transport mechanisms that are designed to handle a large flow of articles. Also, news reader programs are somewhat more efficient at presenting news articles in a logical, readable format than most electronic mail reading programs.

That said, you can set up an electronic mail-based news feed by contacting the same type of sites as listed above. Because an electronic mail-based feed is not a "normal" type of news feed, however, you may have better luck contacting some of the commercial news providers, such as UUNET, because they are accustomed to setting up these types of feeds. Any of the public-access sites, however, may be willing to set up an e-mail feed; you can contact the administrators at these sites for availability and prices of such a feed.

In addition to getting someone to feed you news via electronic mail, you need a mechanism that enables you to post messages to news groups via electronic mail. The site that provides you with a feed may set up such an e-mail-based posting mechanism (usually done with mail aliases), but if the site is unwilling to set it up, several sites are on the Internet that provide mail-to-news gateways.

II

Features and Services

One of these mail-to-news gateways is at the machine decwrl.dec.com; you can post to a group such as news.admin.misc by sending a message to news.admin.misc.usenet@decwrl.dec.com (in effect, you use the netnews group name with .usenet appended to it as the user name for the mail). Other gateways exist at the machines pws.bull.com and news.cs.indiana.edu (using addresses such as news.admin.misc), and at the machine cs.utexas.edu (using addresses such as news-admin-misc). The news group news.admin.misc is also a good place to ask for advice in setting up your news feed or locating someone to feed you news.

Because these sites may restrict gateway access to users at their site, or the gateway may be turned off at any time, you should always check with the administrators at the individual sites before using their gateway. You generally can contact the news administrator at a netnews site by sending electronic mail to the address usenet or netnews at the site. Don't post large amounts of news through these gateways, however, as these large postings place a burden on the remote site; if people abuse these gateways, they will be turned off.

Getting a Full or Partial News Feed via NNTP

Only a few reasons support a decision to receive your news feed locally; these reasons outweigh the costs of necessary hardware and administrative time. Some of these reasons follow:

- You want to control how long groups are kept on-line.

- You want to control fully which groups you have access to.

- You want to create groups that are local to your site only (perhaps containing proprietary information).

- You want to be able to provide news feeds to other sites.

If you have made the decision to receive more than a few news groups locally, you probably are going to be using one of the

NNTP-based transport mechanisms. These mechanisms are the only ones in widespread use carrying news over the Internet and are designed to carry a large volume of news efficiently. Given this, make your choice of news transport systems based on the operating system you want to run on your news machine.

UNIX-Based News Transport Mechanisms

Most of the news transport systems in wide use on the Internet are written based on the UNIX operating system. Although setting up and running a UNIX system may seem intimidating to people who are accustomed to the DOS world, several inexpensive (even free) versions of UNIX are available for the PC platform. The initial trouble in setting up the single UNIX machine often pays for itself many times over by allowing the use of an efficient, well-tested news transport system.

Of course, after you have the single news transport machine set up, the rest of your local system can read the news from the UNIX machine, either by having the news area on a Novell network disk (or by some other network disk scheme such as PC-NFS), or by using an NNTP-based reader, as described earlier in the section "Remotely Reading News with NNTP."

The popular C news transport mechanism compiles and runs on systems running SCO UNIX as well as many other variants of UNIX for the PC platform. The C news release is currently available from its archive site `cs.toronto.edu` via anonymous ftp. After you retrieve and extract the release files, the on-line instructions lead you through the building process. Help for setting up a C news system is available from the system's authors and several netnews groups.

The recently released INN (InterNet News) transport system also can compile and run under SCO UNIX. INN is available at the site `ftp.uu.net` and also has full on-line instructions for building and setting up the feed.

After you build your news transport mechanism and test it with local posts, you have to find someone to feed you news via NNTP. As already described, local universities, public-access sites, and commercial netnews providers are all possible NNTP-based news feed sources. You also can post a message to news.admin.misc asking for a local feed, using one of the mail-to-news gateways described earlier.

When setting up an NNTP-based feed, you need to tell the remote site your machine name and Internet address, plus the news groups or hierarchies that you want to receive. The remote site then configures their NNTP feed program to contact your site at regular intervals and transfer the news to your machine. Similarly, you need to set up your outgoing transmission program to feed any posts your users have made locally to your feed site so that your posts can be transmitted to the rest of the world.

During the initial few days of receiving a news feed, you should monitor the news system closely to make sure that it is working correctly. You also should monitor the programs that remove old news from your system (called *expiration programs*) to make sure that your disk doesn't fill up.

DOS-Based News Transport Mechanisms

A couple of options are available to you if you must run your news transport mechanism under DOS. Basically, these systems are bulletin board systems that have functions to receive, send, and read news and mail.

One system in fairly wide use for receiving news is Waffle, a shareware product available on the Internet through anonymous ftp to the site halcyon.com in the file /pub/waffle/waffle/waf165.zip. Waffle is a bulletin board system that offers news reception and reading, as well as electronic mail, conferencing, and other features commonly found on bulletin boards. If you don't need the full functionality of a bulletin board system, you can use only the parts of Waffle that you need.

The details of setting up a Waffle system are beyond the scope of this book, but the ZIP file contains complete instructions on installing, configuring, and operating the Waffle functions. Additional assistance is available via electronic mail to the author Tom Dell (`dell@vox.darkside.com`) and in the netnews group `comp.bbs.waffle`. The "frequently asked questions" file posted monthly to `comp.bbs.waffle` gives a good overview of the Waffle system and is also available via anonymous ftp to `rtfm.mit.edu` in the file `/pub/usenet/comp.bbs.waffle/W_F_A_Q_(F)`.

Further, many additional packages have been written to work with Waffle to provide more functionality (such as different editors, news or mail readers, or gateways to other BBS systems). These packages also are available on the Internet via anonymous ftp to `halycon.com` in the directory `/pub/waffle`.

Waffle was designed to receive and transmit news and mail through a telephone link using the UUCP protocol; but by getting the optional file `waf165nn.zip` (for the current version), you can receive news via the NNTP protocol. This package is limited in regard to which network adapter cards and network software it supports, so make sure that your hardware and software are supported before trying to set up an NNTP-based Waffle news site.

Other PC-based bulletin board systems that also receive and send netnews (as well as mail) exist, but these are all based on modems and UUCP transfers of data. Systems such as Fido, Wildcat, and other BBS systems are available through the Internet.

Summary

USENET is a relatively simple system for sending messages to thousands of others who are interested in the message's topic. Most of the members of the USENET community are friendly and helpful, but some others are adversarial and downright malicious. But the latter group of people are in the minority, and USENET tends to reflect the composition of the societies who have access to it.

II

Features and Services

USENET can be an amazing resource. It allows you (relatively) quick access to thousands of people who have the same interests as you do. You can post a request for information and, within a few days, receive replies from all over the world. Something that may have taken you weeks or even months to discover can be found within hours or days by tapping that vast resource of experts who make up the USENET community. We're all experts on something, whether it's astronomy, gardening, or child raising. Everyone can contribute to the success of the USENET community.

Chapter 10

Determining the Level of Internet Service You Need

The previous chapters have shown you many services available through the Internet. Many firms offer some type of Internet access; the options they offer span the spectrum of possible service levels. Some offer only an electronic mail gateway, whereas others provide true interactive Internet access through a T3 (44.746 Mbps) link. As a result, Internet services have a broad price range. You already may have a computer account that enables you to send and receive electronic mail, access network news, and run ftp and telnet, for example, without incurring any charges. But at the other extreme, you may need to provide Internet access to a large number of users divided into several groups. Such an arrangement may cost tens of thousands of dollars a year in Internet access fees alone. And high-volume network usage implies a commitment of substantial computer, facility, and personnel resources, just to manage your organization's network access.

This chapter will help you determine the level of service you need from your Internet service provider. It prepares you for several of the subsequent chapters in this book by exploring the issues involved in choosing levels of service and by giving

II

Features and Services

numerous examples of the service requirements of various types of users.

After you make certain key decisions, you will be ready for the chapters in Part IV, "Service Providers," which give detailed information about major Internet service providers. You also will be prepared for Chapter 12, "Hardware and Software," which discusses methods of configuring computer systems to access the Internet. Chapter 11, "Connections Beyond the Internet," also provides an in-depth examination of Internet access through popular information services such as Compu-Serve and MCI Mail.

Deciding Which Internet Services You Need

As the earlier chapters of this book show, the Internet is rich in resources, and the growth of its capabilities is explosive. You must decide, however, which services are essential to your networking needs. If all you really need is an electronic mail address and you plan to check your mail only once or twice a day, you don't need to pay for a more expensive service that also enables you to run ftp.

You probably will have to compromise when choosing a service provider. Ideally, you may like to maintain a 24-hour-a-day connection, but perhaps you can't justify the fee of several hundred dollars per month for such service. You may find, however, that you obtain satisfactory results for $20 to $30 a month from a dialup service that you check once an hour to check for new electronic mail messages.

> **Note**
>
> Changing network service providers is relatively easy. Because providers realize this fact, they compete vigorously for your business. Expect to see more services at the same, or even lower, prices.

Electronic Mail

Electronic mail is the most fundamental service offered; essentially all providers include it in their service packages. You need to answer two questions before deciding on your e-mail service:

- How quickly do you need to be notified of new incoming e-mail?

- Do you need multiple, independent e-mail addresses?

If you maintain a continuous connection to the network, you are notified immediately of incoming mail. Otherwise, you must access the network to check for new mail. Periodically checking for new events is called *polling*. You may find that polling your provider enables you to respond satisfactorily to new mail. Just make sure that you can poll as often as you like! You may find that connecting to your provider during certain times of the day is difficult, or that the connection fees are expensive for this method of access.

Many network providers give you one e-mail address and set up a single mail folder per account. If multiple users access the account, they share the e-mail address, and all their mail is placed in the same folder. Thus, they can read and reply to each other's mail. This state of affairs can be confusing, even with a small number of users sharing an account. And an individual user may want to have several independent e-mail addresses as well, to distinguish between mail messages (separating personal mail from business mail, for example). Users also may want to set up separate addresses for different projects or activities.

Of course, remaining on-line while composing or reading mail messages isn't actually necessary. You can do this work at your leisure on your local computer, thus reducing connect-time fees (if you are charged in this manner). Furthermore, simple operations such as downloading your e-mail can be automated to reduce further the actual time you are connected to your provider. Many common communications packages (such as

PROCOMM PLUS) allow you to write *scripts*—programs to control your communications sessions—to do this and other straightforward, commonly used procedures. Service providers like the idea that you do not tie up a communications line while examining and responding to your e-mail. CompuServe, for example, offers its CompuServe Information Manager, which can retrieve your mail and then immediately disconnect you from the network.

Network News

Most providers offer USENET and other news feeds to their users. If you want to have access to network news, you need to consider two main issues:

■ Your provider needs to carry the news groups in which you want to participate. Your provider may not receive each one of the several thousand news groups available, because they cumulatively generate around 90M of news every day. Investigate the news feeds carried by potential providers; if a provider of interest doesn't carry a news group you want to follow, ask whether it can be added to the daily feed.

■ Estimate the resource cost for accessing your news groups. Remember that you can spend a great deal of time just reading the news, and use a significant amount of disk space or connection time in accessing it. Loading a large amount of news each day to your computer over a 2,400 bps connection, for example, could be quite expensive.

Although you may be tempted to participate in many news groups, only a few of them will be of use to you on a regular basis. Most providers that carry network news make changing the news groups you receive easy. Thus, you can try out a news group for a while and then drop it when it's no longer of interest to you.

Interactive Access to Remote Computers

If you want to use ftp and telnet, you need interactive access to the Internet. The main issue for you to consider before choosing this level of service (offered by many providers) is the cost of connect time. Because you are connected to the network during your entire interactive session, you can incur large expenses if you are charged for connect time. Try to plan your accesses off-line as much as possible and disconnect from the network whenever you pause for more than a few minutes (to examine downloaded files on your local computer, for example).

If you plan to transfer frequently large amounts of data using ftp, make sure that the data rate of your network connection is cost effective. A 14.4 Kbps connection, for example, can transfer data six times faster than a 2,400 bps connection. Compression schemes such as V.42*bis* also can increase the effective transfer rate by as much as a factor of four.

Network Navigation Aids

Navigation aids such as archie, Gopher, and WAIS are invaluable when you need to locate network resources. You can use all these tools—and others as well—by way of publicly accessible telnet accounts. If you can connect to remote computers using telnet, you can use these common navigation aids.

Many service providers install one or more of these programs on their local systems; these locally installed tools are sometimes more responsive. Your provider also may offer a version of your favorite tool with a more advanced user interface.

Real-Time Textual Chatting

Real-time interactive character-based communications is commonly available to Internet users with interactive access. Many providers offer facilities such as *talk* and *Internet Relay Chat (IRC)*. If you plan to use these features often, you need to consider two major issues:

II

Features and Services

- As with ftp and telnet, you must remain connected to the network for the duration of each chatting session. Compare the cost of chatting through the Internet to other means of communicating, such as telephone calls or e-mail. Unlike ftp usage, chatting is a very low data rate activity; faster connections don't improve performance significantly.

- As with electronic mail, you must be connected to the network to be aware that someone wants to chat with you. And you can't effectively poll your service provider (as you can with e-mail) to monitor requests to chat. Statistically speaking, the person trying to reach you almost certainly will give up before you respond. That means you must have a continuous network connection if you want people to be able to initiate requests to chat with you at any time of day.

Teleconferencing over the Internet

You can transfer audio and video data in real time through the network, but these processes require an extremely high-speed connection. Note that the complete path between all the teleconferencing sites must support an adequate data transfer rate. Generally speaking, such support is now too expensive for individuals and small organizations to justify.

Although most network teleconferencing capabilities are experimental at this time, interest in them is growing, especially in the business community. Transfers of real-time audio through the network are likely to become more common in the near future. But to become a viable alternative, real-time audio teleconferencing has to be cost-competitive with conference telephone calls and fax communications.

Allowing Network Users To Access Your Computer

You may want to allow outside users to establish ftp and/or telnet connections to your local system. You may want members of your organization who are traveling, for example, to be able to access your local computer from another location that is connected to the Internet. You also may want to make a resource such as a database or specialized software package available to outsiders through the network.

If you want to allow users to access your computer from the Internet, you must set up a server on your local system and connect it to the network as an Internet host. In such a case, you probably want a continuous connection and need a fast communications link to support the anticipated volume of network traffic. For security reasons, if you plan to allow unregistered network users to access your system (through anonymous ftp, for example), you should set up a dedicated system for this purpose. If possible, this system normally shouldn't be connected to other computers in your facility.

You Already May Have Internet Access and Not Know It

Many people can obtain Internet access easily, without any cost to themselves, through their schools or workplaces. Professional societies, especially in fields involving computers, are beginning to offer some Internet-related services to their members. Local users' groups in your area also may offer some type of Internet connection for a small fee, or for free. Of course, you must observe some restrictions on your Internet usage when using accounts obtained through such organizations.

You may find that accessing the network through such an account provides you with all the Internet services you need. And even if connections such as these don't handle your full Internet requirements, you can use them to learn more about the network and to experiment with the services provided. Your initial Internet connection will help you acquire information about other service providers and currently available hardware and software for accessing the network.

Educational Institutions

If you are a student at a large university, chances are good that you already have a computer account through which you can send and receive electronic mail and run ftp and telnet. You may have no idea that this account exists. Many colleges and universities automatically set up accounts for all new students, regardless of their majors. Such accounts also may be established for part-time and non-degree-seeking students. Many colleges provide each student with an individual account on their central computer system to facilitate course registration, allow access to the library's on-line databases, and handle electronic mail within the university community.

Contact the manager of your educational institution's central computer facility for information concerning the availability of computer accounts, the level of Internet access they provide, and their acceptable use policies. Also ask faculty members (your academic advisor, for example) and the administrator of your department's computer facility (if one exists). If you obtain an account through an educational institution, remember that its acceptable use policy almost certainly prohibits for-profit use and extensive use for private or personal business. These prohibitions are imposed by the NSFNET backbone, through which most educational institutions receive their Internet access.

Employers

Commercial activity on the Internet has been increasing steadily and now comprises more than half the traffic on the network. The critical mass of network participants has been reached; justifying the costs of Internet access now is easy for many businesses. If you use a computer that's connected to other computers at work, ask the systems administrator if the local network can access the Internet. If it can, you may find that you can send and receive electronic mail but can't run interactive applications such as ftp or telnet. If you want more extensive network privileges, ask your company's computer systems administrator if you can have a special account that allows you interactive Internet access.

Although you may think a business would encourage its employees to use the rich resources on the Internet—after all, large universities do—commercial institutions can be very restrictive concerning network access for a number of reasons. If you use your employer's Internet connection, keep in mind the considerations discussed in the following paragraphs. Otherwise, you may find your network privileges revoked and your job in peril. The bottom line is to act like a respectful guest when using your employer's Internet connection for non-job-related purposes.

Businesses are very sensitive to security issues. The process of connecting their computers to a world-wide network with millions of users in dozens of countries carries some risks. Employees easily can send sensitive information to persons outside the company—intentionally or by accident or negligence. Employers also worry about reduced productivity caused by employees using the Internet connection for personal uses during their work time. Non-work-related Internet activity (receiving large USENET news feeds, for example) also can place a significant load on the employer's computing facility, decreasing network performance for genuine work-related access. Always remember that your employer may be monitoring your networking activities; never assume any privacy when sending or receiving messages or files by way of an employer's computer.

Professional Societies

Some professional societies are experimenting with offering their members Internet-related services. The most common of these is an e-mail forwarding service. The Institute of Electrical and Electronic Engineers (IEEE), for example, the principal electrical engineering professional society in the United States, offers its members a permanent e-mail address of the form *xxx.yyy*@ieee.org, where *xxx.yyy* uniquely identifies the member within the domain `ieee.org`. The IEEE allows you to keep this address as long as you are a member of its organization.

The IEEE, however, doesn't store your e-mail messages—you must provide the electronic mail handler at `ieee.org` with an e-mail forwarding address. All mail sent to your permanent e-mail address *xxx.yyy@ieee.org* is forwarded to another e-mail address, which you are free to change from time to time. The advantage of such a scheme is that you have a permanent e-mail address that remains the same, even if you change employers, choose a different Internet service provider, or move to a different part of the country (or even the world).

Your professional society may provide additional Internet services in addition to forwarding your e-mail. For instance, the Association for Computing Machinery (ACM), the principal society for computer professionals in the United States, offers two types of accounts: a mail forwarding account and a full service account. The full service account provides electronic mail, network news, and Internet tools such as ftp, telnet, archie, and Gopher.

Keep in mind that these services are new for most societies and are therefore subject to rapid change. You also should review the acceptable use policy for Internet access through your professional society's connection. You may find significant restrictions (for example, no for-profit activities allowed) that severely limit its usefulness to you. Such policies often are due to the professional society receiving its network connection through NSFNET. But you may feel that a permanent e-mail address is valuable to you, especially when it's provided at an extremely low charge (or even at no cost at all).

Local Users' Groups

Some associations established in your community may allow you to access the Internet through their members' connections. The services offered are usually electronic mail and network

news through a UUCP connection. Such groups, if they exist in
your local area, are usually composed of volunteers dedicated to
promoting Internet awareness and experimentation.

The Atlanta Regional Network Organization (ARNO), for example, offers this kind of service to the greater metropolitan
Atlanta area. ARNO describes itself in the following terms (taken
from information provided by ARNO):

- A volunteer group of interconnected local hub systems
  that provide non-Internet sites with UUCP network connectivity to the Internet and other sites

- A means to provide UUCP connectivity to the rapidly
  growing small-system community (including Waffle and
  UUPC users)

- A central contact point where requests for UUCP connection may be sent (so that new systems don't have to search
  for a site that will provide them with a UUCP connection)

- A means to provide netnews feeds for those sites wanting
  this service

- A way to provide domain registration to the `atl.ga.us` domain for all who want it (and get rid of those long "bang"
  path e-mail addresses)

ARNO is *neither* of the following things:

- An attempt to compete with any commercial enterprise
  that provides UNIX access

- A UNIX support group or UNIX education group (those
  facilities are available elsewhere)

You can obtain this information as well as additional information about ARNO by sending an e-mail message to
`arno-post@mathcs.emory.edu` or `arno-post@gatech.edu`.

You may have to do some hunting to determine whether a similar group can provide you with network access. Ask the computer facilities managers at local colleges and universities (and other experienced network users in your area) about such organizations.

Often no fee or a token charge is assessed for connections obtained in this manner. Be forewarned, however, that their service reliability can vary from good to unacceptable, and reaching someone may be difficult if you experience problems or have questions. Of course, faulting this type of provider is difficult if your connection is provided at no cost to you.

Types of Internet Service Providers

Now that you are aware of the services you can obtain through the Internet, you are prepared to investigate the ways Internet services are typically packaged. You aren't likely to find exactly what you want for the price you are willing to pay. But you almost certainly can find a provider in your price range that offers the set of essential services you need. Keep in mind that changing from one service provider to a more suitable one is generally easy. Your Internet service easily can evolve with your networking needs.

The headings of the following sections correspond directly to the chapters in Part IV, "Service Providers," which list providers and give important information about each one. The information provided was current as of the date this book went to press; as you probably realize, however, the Internet is very dynamic and the information in these lists is subject to change. Directly contact providers that you are interested in for their current service offerings and rate structures.

BBS, UUCP, and Other Polled Services

Providers such as these don't offer interactive Internet access. Electronic mail and (in some cases) network news are the only Internet services available. These providers may offer other non-Internet-related services, however. The cost depends on the total package of services available and the profit orientation of the system owner. Prices for these providers typically range from no charge to around $30 per month.

Such a provider generally operates in one of two ways. In the first method, the host system is set up so that you log in using a modem and a terminal (or a computer running a terminal emulation package, such as PROCOMM PLUS from Datastorm Technologies or Microsoft Windows Terminal). After logging in, you enter commands to accomplish your tasks (such as instructing the system to show you new mail received since your last connection). After you finish a session, you disconnect from the host. All your transactions occur when you are connected to the host.

In the second method of operation, your local computer runs software such as Waffle (developed by Darkside International), which acts as a network server. It buffers all outgoing traffic, such as electronic mail messages originating from your computer. When your computer connects with the host computer, it sends all outgoing traffic to the host and receives any incoming traffic in a batch. The connection is terminated immediately after all traffic is exchanged. Your computer then stores any traffic it received from the host for you to review at a later time. Check with your system administrator to see what software you need to connect with a specific provider and how much it will cost (you may not be charged).

On-Line Services and Terminal Servers

These service providers offer the quickest and easiest way for you to establish an Internet connection. Essentially, you are given an account with a single electronic mail address on their computer system. Services such as CompuServe and Delphi enable you to sign up by telephone (by voice or modem). You don't even need a computer to access the network through these providers—you need only a terminal with a modem.

> **Note**
>
> You must pay long-distance charges unless your dialup provider has a local phone number in your area or a toll-free 800 number.

If you use your computer to access these services, the only software you need is a terminal emulation package. Low-cost graphical user interface (GUI) software is now available from some providers, and additional providers are expected to offer GUI front-ends to their systems in the near future.

This class of service provider can be subdivided further into two basic types. The only Internet access offered by the first type, exemplified by CompuServe and MCI Mail, is electronic mail. Of course, such providers typically offer many more non-Internet-related services that you may find valuable. The cost of service can depend to a great extent on the total package of services provided. You also may find that your charge for connect time depends on the speed of your modem. For purposes of comparison, CompuServe's standard service costs $8.95 per month, which includes $9 worth of free electronic mail (at the time of this writing). Sending or reading an Internet message normally costs 15 cents for the first 7,500 characters and 5 cents for each additional 2,500 characters. With this pricing structure, you can send or receive up to 60 Internet mail messages containing no more than 7,500 characters (approximately up to three pages in length) every month for $8.95.

The second type—Delphi, CRL, or Netcom, for example—provides interactive access to the Internet and allows subscribers to run ftp, telnet, navigational aids, and other facilities. Again, these providers offer additional services, such as databases and software archives, that may interest you. They usually charge a fixed monthly fee or else accrue charges on a connect-time basis. Charges to typical users are usually in the range of $10 to $20 per month.

> **Note**
>
> Even though you basically are logging in to one of your service provider's computers, you may be presented with a specialized user interface rather than enter the native operating environment. Such interfaces sometimes are provided as a service to you, to make performing network operations easier. They also are provided to enhance system security by preventing you from using the full set of commands and resources available through the operating system.

The *Public Dialup Internet Access List (PDIAL)*, compiled by Peter Kaminski, lists providers offering inexpensive public access to the Internet through an ordinary phone line using your regular modem and computer. PDIAL lists only providers directly connected to the Internet. This document is included on the disk accompanying this book.

SLIP and PPP Service

When you use an on-line service to access the Internet, you basically are given an account on a computer that's connected to the network. You log in to your provider's system by way of an ordinary telephone line to perform your Internet transactions. *Serial Line Internet Protocol (SLIP)* and *Point-to-Point Protocol (PPP)*, on the other hand, enable you to connect your computer directly to the Internet using an ordinary telephone line. Your computer, in turn, can be connected to other computers on your local network, thus permitting all these computers to have direct Internet access. This class of service is often called *dialup IP*.

With SLIP and PPP connections, you can use the full range of Internet services. The relatively slow speed of your communications link and the number and duration of your network connections impose the only restrictions.

You don't want to use a dialup IP connection with anything slower than a 9,600 bps modem. The slow communications link limits the number of computers you can use through a single dialup IP connection. If most of your local computers perform light, infrequent Internet accesses, they generate little network traffic. SLIP and PPP are generally considered suitable for connecting a single computer or a very small local network to the Internet.

> **Note**
>
> You don't need to maintain a continuous connection to the Internet. You can disconnect from the network whenever you want. Because you likely won't be charged for connect time when using SLIP or PPP, the main reason you may choose to operate in this fashion is to avoid dedicating a phone line to your Internet access. You also may want to access your connection from multiple locations, such as your home and office.

These connections are considerably more expensive than the connections offered by the providers discussed previously. You can expect to pay $150 to $300 per month for your Internet connection alone. Also, you must obtain dialup IP software to run on your local computer (at an approximate cost of $300 to $600). Also consider that, although not required, you may want to dedicate a phone line—and even a complete computer system—to the task of handling your Internet communications.

Dedicated Connections

If dialup IP is inadequate for your direct Internet connection needs, you can obtain a connection through a high-speed dedicated communications link. But if you do so, be prepared to spend a substantial amount of money and to make a major commitment to maintaining your connection. Available speeds range from 56 Kbps through nearly 45 Mbps. Expect to pay roughly $1,000 to $1,500 per month for a 56 Kbps connection and approximately $3,000 to $4,000 per month for a T1 connection (1.544 Mbps).

Your connection fees usually include the network router, customer support, and field service on all equipment provided. Furthermore, most service providers help you set up your site and register your network with the DDN Network Information Center.

With a dedicated connection, you can connect essentially as many computers to the network as you like. You have a 24-hour-a-day presence on Internet and can use any services the network provides. The main limitation in this case, again, is the speed of your communications link.

> **Note**
>
> Obviously, only organizations with a substantial amount of Internet traffic can justify the expense of this type of network connection. Typically, large organizations with a large base of network users utilize dedicated connections.

Determining the Network Performance You Need

Now that you have some ideas concerning which package of network capabilities you want, you must consider the level of performance you need from your connection. An organization that wants to connect many individual users obviously places a greater burden on the connection than a single user making short, infrequent accesses.

A multiuser organization may be able to justify a more costly connection, because the extra expense is distributed among more users. Network performance is usually equated with response time, which obviously is affected by the maximum data transfer rate your connection supports and by the amount of network traffic you expect. You also need to consider how well your connection can handle the number of your users having access to the network.

Who Will Use Your Internet Connection?

In general, Internet connections take one of two forms. Your connection can be a domain or a user account on a host in someone else's domain. In the first case, you can set up multiple user accounts (and subdomains, if you like) off your domain. Individual users can have their own private e-mail addresses and mail folders. You can monitor network usage by individual users. You can even establish subdomains to correspond to groups of users within your organization. Also, you may find that setting up certain e-mail addresses that automatically reply to incoming mail with informational messages is useful.

In the second case, you appear to the Internet as an individual user on someone else's host. Essentially, you have a single account on a computer that has an Internet connection. All mail sent to your account is placed in the same incoming mail folder. If several persons use the account, each user can read and reply to any incoming electronic mail messages. This may cause difficulties, even if only a few people share the account. With a single user account, you can't break down network usage by individual. Further, you may find that only one person is allowed to use the account at a time.

> **Note**
>
> You should monitor each user's on-line time to determine the amount and type of use he or she is giving the network. On-line time can be addictive and—if used for personal endeavors—expensive to your company.

What Data Transfer Rate Will Work for You?

Before choosing your network connection, you need to determine how many persons will be allowed Internet access, how many of them likely will use the network at the same time, and how much network traffic will be generated on average. You need to estimate the peak usage. You also should have an idea of how much delay in response time is acceptable. The particular services you choose partly determine these issues.

At present, network data rates can be grouped into two main categories: those supported by ordinary telephone lines, and those available through dedicated, high-speed connections. Low-cost modems capable of transferring 14,400 bps over ordinary telephone lines are readily available. Compression schemes such as V.42*bis* can increase the effective transfer rate by as much as a factor of four. Faster modems, although relatively expensive, are already available; even faster ones are being developed. You may find, however, that some network service providers support only dialup speeds up to 9,600 bps (or even 2,400 bps) and don't support data compression.

Dedicated connections, on the other hand, can offer rates from 56 Kbps to 44.746 Mbps (for T3 links). Unless you have a high-speed dedicated communications link, you can't use the high-end interactive network services such as teleconferencing. Most users can't justify the cost of such a link just to send real-time audio and video through the network. The two most likely reasons why you would need high data-transfer rates are as follows:

- You are servicing a large number of simultaneous interactive users

- You are receiving and transmitting massive amounts of data in items such as news feeds and large ftp transfers

If you can restrict these activities to times of days when few users are accessing the network, you may do fine with an ordinary telephone line connection. Note that you can transfer a megabyte of data in less than 12 minutes with a 14,400 bps rate.

How Often and How Long Will You Connect to the Network?

You need to consider three main issues concerning the number and length of your network connections:

- *Connect-time fees.* If your service provider charges you for connect time, maintaining a connection for more than a few hours per day, on average, is relatively expensive. If you need extended network connection time, you can cut costs by finding a provider that charges a flat monthly rate.

- *User access conflicts.* If you share your account with other users and your service provider doesn't allow multiple simultaneous logins using the same account, the persons sharing the account may have to wait long periods of time before they can connect. If access conflict is frequently a problem, you may want to set up an additional account or two.

- *Continuous connection.* You obviously can't be aware that you have new mail or that someone wants to chat with you over the Internet unless you are connected. A continuous connection enables you to receive instant notification of incoming mail. The less frequently you connect, the less responsive you are to correspondence conducted through the network.

Many people find that they need to connect to the network only infrequently. You may determine, for example, that your network needs are limited to electronic mail and an occasional ftp transfer or Gopher access. Checking for new mail several times a day may be okay in your situation. In this case, you don't need to be connected to the network constantly; a provider that charges on a connect-time basis may be a good choice. If you want to be notified immediately when incoming mail is received, on the other hand, your local host must maintain a continuous Internet connection.

What Systems Administration Burdens Can You Handle?

You can access the Internet interactively without even having a computer at your location. You can use such on-line services as Delphi with just a computer terminal, a modem, and your home telephone line. At the other extreme, you can set up a dedicated computer for network activity with a dedicated communications link to an Internet provider.

The larger the facility, the larger the burdens of systems administration will be. Dedicated resources must be managed and maintained; security and reliability issues must be addressed. Sometimes a service interruption can be a serious condition (depending on your network usage). If so, you may need to maintain multiple systems with active, independent network connections to ensure continuous service.

The cost of a dedicated facility and staff for managing network access can surpass the access fees charged by your provider and the expense of your communications link combined. Estimating the costs—including money and hassle—of connecting to the network is important. To determine the amount of system supervision necessary in your case, consider the impact of two conditions on the organization:

- A temporary loss of network connection

- A security violation involving your network connection

The network connection could be interrupted due to equipment failure, pauses for routine maintenance and system upgrades, or a problem with your service provider. A security breach could arise from the actions of someone at your facility or from unauthorized access of your local system by someone on the network.

After you consider all these issues, you will have to determine the number of persons needed to manage your network connection and the expertise required of them. Remember to include staff for non-business hours, weekends, and holidays if you need coverage during these periods. Also, you may need more than one connection to the Internet to provide redundancy.

Evaluating a Specific Provider

Although evaluating the packages of services an individual provider offers is relatively easy, assessing issues such as system reliability, customer service, effective system speed, and ease of access is much more difficult. The explosive growth in Internet usage has placed many providers in the position of being overwhelmed, in effect, by their own success. User activity quickly can outgrow the providers' system capacity, resulting in poor performance.

Unfortunately, an access provider (especially a BBS or dialup service) with a user base too large for its computer or personnel resources—at least, with respect to providing Internet access—is common. This condition occurs for two primary reasons:

■ Internet users usually need to access the network several times a day. Depending on your needs, you may want to poll your provider to check for new e-mail messages as rarely as once a day or as often as once every 15 minutes. Your provider may not have enough inbound phone lines to allow its users this frequency of access.

■ Your provider's access to the network may be inadequate. Remember that your provider must, in turn, have a service provider that connects it to the network. Your service provider's network connection may use a data rate that can't support network traffic properly. In fact, the bottleneck you experience when using the network may not be directly due to your provider—another system in the connection between you and the network may be causing the problem.

If you are a commercial Internet user, you likely have low tolerance for poor system performance. You probably conduct critical communications with clients, vendors, and colleagues by sending e-mail through the Internet. If so, you depend on your service provider to be continually available to you. Business users of dialup services, for example, expect to connect to the network nearly every time on the first attempt. After logging in, they expect their transactions to be processed with essentially no system delays. They want data to be transferred at rates approaching the maximum rates supported by their modems. If they have questions about setting up their equipment for accessing the network, or about the use of network services, they expect help to be readily available.

At a minimum level, these expectations mean that an adequate number of knowledgeable customer service representatives must be available by phone during normal business hours. Also, questions or requests for assistance made outside business hours should receive prompt responses. Generally speaking, a commercial user should avoid obtaining network access through an organization that doesn't consider providing such a service to be an important revenue-generating activity. In other words, a free or cheap connection is no bargain if it is undependable.

Use the following three methods to evaluate a network service provider:

1. Find out whether the provider also offers non-Internet-related services. If so, try to determine whether providing Internet access is considered a primary function or whether it's just a bonus offering added to the provider's mainstream business.

   Also, try to ascertain whether you fit one of the user profiles for the system. You can expect better service from an organization dedicated to providing Internet access to users like you. Someone who wants an Internet connection for commercial purposes, for example, may be disappointed by the service provided through a BBS used mainly for playing computer games.

2. Talk to other users about their experiences with a particular provider. You might even use an on-line forum where other users discuss problems and make suggestions for system improvements. Again, look for comments from users with needs similar to yours.

3. Some providers offer free trial periods during which you can explore their services. Such offers can take the form of a certain amount of free connect time or a usage credit for a specific monetary amount.

   If available, a trial period is clearly the best way to determine whether the provider can meet your needs. Make sure that you understand the complete terms of the trial period before beginning, and that you can cancel the service without further obligation at any time.

Summary

For most potential Internet users, the main decision is whether you require interactive access to the network. If not, you may find the access you need through a service such as CompuServe, WinNET Mail, or a UUCP connection. These service types can be very cost-effective ways to use electronic mail, and many such providers also offer USENET news feeds.

If this type of service doesn't satisfy your needs, shell accounts and low-cost SLIP/PPP connections are available that provide interactive access to the Internet. From such an account you will be able to use ftp, telnet, and navigational aids such as Gopher, in addition to accessing e-mail and network news.

Organizations that need to connect a large number of users may need to establish a dedicated network connection. This undertaking is fairly expensive; such a connection also implies a significant administrative burden.

Fortunately, changing Internet service providers is fairly easy. Many firms offer some type of Internet access. If your organization outgrows its connection, you should have no difficulty finding a provider that can provide the service you require.

II

Features and Services

Chapter 11

Connections Beyond the Internet

As discussed in Chapter 3, the Internet isn't a single unified entity, but a patchwork of thousands of interconnected smaller networks. Many of these networks were developed to support the on-line services, corporate communications networks, and research consortia that proliferated in the 1980s. Although the Internet existed at that time, it still was used primarily as a tool for network research and for communications between universities, research institutes, and government-affiliated organizations. Restrictions governing much of the network infrastructure prevented effective commercial use.

Most on-line services targeted owners of early PCs as their main market. Because modem transfer rates ran between 300 and 1,200 bps and PC disk space was limited, the idea of Internet connectivity for PCs seemed unrealistic at best. Of course, computer technology has progressed at a tremendous pace since those early days. Modems operating at 14.4 kbps are commonplace, and high-performance PCs now rival low-end workstations in computational power and disk capacity.

In recent years, high-powered computing platforms placed in network environments have become commonplace (even for smaller schools and businesses). During that time, many individual users came to appreciate the advantages of e-mail and file transfer through the local network, and many gained their first access to the Internet through their local system. As more users came to appreciate the advantages of an Internet connection, they also began to expect that any communications service they used would provide such global connectivity.

Today, every major on-line service provides a gateway to the Internet for e-mail exchanges. Some even support file transfer and other services for their customers.

Unfortunately, communicating with a member of one of these other networks isn't as simple as you may think. Although the physical and protocol-level connections may exist for moving data from one network to another, many application details are unique to each network. One of the most frustrating things about moving your e-mail to or from these other networks is that they aren't required to conform to the Domain Name System (DNS) naming schemes explained in Chapter 3, "The Structure of the Internet."

The Internetwork Cross-Reference

This chapter provides an internetwork addressing cross-reference—in other words, it provides a means for translating the addresses of one network type to an Internet name, and vice versa. It doesn't cross-reference every network's address to every other network; to do so would probably take several volumes. Instead, only the most popular networks and messaging services are listed here.

Getting the Cross-Reference from the Internet

This cross-reference is based in part on *The Inter-Network Mail Guide*, which is compiled and posted periodically by Scott Yanoff (`yanoff@csd4.csd.uwm.edu`). You can get the list by way of anonymous ftp (described in Chapter 8, "Using ftp and telnet") from `csd4.csd.uwm.edu`, or you can use the finger utility on Mr. Yanoff's account name to get information about other ways of acquiring it.

If you need a more detailed and well-presented list in print, O'Reilly and Associates, Inc. publishes a book by Donnalyn Frey and Rick Adams titled *!%@:: A Directory of Electronic Mail Addressing and Networks*. The 1993 edition of this text gives feature and address information for more than 180 research, educational, and commercial networks. It also provides a comprehensive list of U.S. and international subdomains and their owning organizations. The subdomain list can be very useful for finding the network subdomain associated with a known company or organization.

Using This Chapter's Network Cross-Reference

The cross-reference is organized in alphabetical order by network name. Each entry in the list briefly describes the capabilities of the network and explains how to send e-mail to and from these networks. Conversion to and from the Internet DNS is given if needed, along with any limitations or restrictions you should know about.

In this chapter, the address formats that you use with each network service appear in computer-like typeface, such as `user@attmail.com`. Placeholders—that is, phrases you need to replace with the actual name—are *italicized*.

America Online

America Online is a commercial on-line service based in the United States that provides e-mail, forums, and file archives. Dialup access is available through Public Data Networks (PDNs) such as Sprintnet, so most users can log in with a local call. America Online uses proprietary software available for PC and Macintosh platforms.

It now provides only mail gateway service to the Internet.

Sending an e-mail message to an Internet name from America Online is simple. Merely address your message to the DNS name of the recipient—*recip@subdomain.domain*, for example—when you compose it.

To send e-mail to America Online users, you must convert their account names to DNS-compliant names by removing spaces and entering all characters in lowercase. Then add the America Online domain—aol.com—to each name. To send a message to the America Online account of John Q, for example, address the message to johnq@aol.com.

> **Note**
>
> When you send mail to an America Online account, the content of your mail is limited in two ways:
>
> ■ Messages are truncated to a maximum length of 32K characters
>
> ■ Non-printable characters are translated into spaces.

AppleLink

Apple Computer employees and organizations, dealers, developers, and users use the AppleLink information service. AppleLink is managed and operated on contract with General Electric Information Services (providers of GEnie). It provides e-mail, file archives, and on-line technical support for Apple and participating third-party products.

AppleLink supports an e-mail gateway to the Internet. To send e-mail to an Internet DNS name from AppleLink, add the string @internet# to the name. The address for an e-mail message to *dnsuser@sub.domain*, for example, would be as follows:

```
dnsuser@sub.domain@internet#
```

> **Note**
>
> The address of an outbound message from AppleLink must be less than 35 characters. The AppleLink/Internet e-mail gateway supports transfers of up to 4M long, thus allowing mail transfer of uuencoded binary files.

To send mail from Internet to an AppleLink user, simply add the address of the gateway to the user's name. To send mail to `alinkuser`, for example, address your message to `alinkuser@applelink.apple.com`.

AT&TMail

AT&TMail was developed initially to fulfill the business communications needs of AT&T. Since its inception, however, it has integrated other customers and services, including the former Western Union EasyLink service. AT&TMail provides e-mail, file transfer, BBS, and fax services.

To send e-mail to an Internet name such as `dnsuser@sub.domain`, address your message to `internet!sub.domain!dnsuser`.

To convert an AT&TMail user account name to a DNS name, simply connect the gateway name to the user name with an `@`. To send e-mail to `attmailuser`, for example, address the message to `attmailuser@attmail.com`.

EasyLink accounts are referenced by 8-digit numbers that start with `62`—`62123456`, for example. To send mail to an EasyLink account, use `eln.attmail.com` to represent the gateway.

BITNET

BITNET is a global network of commercial organizations, research institutes, and universities. E-mail and file transfer services are available between BITNET and the Internet. BITNET user names are formatted as follows:

    USER@NODE

II

Features and Services

Tip
To obtain a list
of organizations
within the BITNET,
subscribe to
listserv@bitnic.
educom.edu or ftp to
bitnic.educom.edu.

Several gateways between Internet and BITNET are available. Two of the better known are cunyvm.cuny.edu and mitvma.mit.edu.

The means for sending e-mail from BITNET to the Internet vary depending on the mail program running at the BITNET host. First, try addressing mail to the DNS name itself—dnsuser@sub.domain, for example. If that doesn't work, try addressing mail to dnsuser%sub.domain@gateway, replacing gateway with an actual BITNET gateway name such as cunyvm.cuny.edu.

To send e-mail from the Internet to BITUSER@BITSITE, address your mail to bituser%bitsite.bitnet@gateway, replacing gateway with the correct BITNET gateway name.

BIX

BYTE magazine created BIX—the Byte Information eXchange—to provide an on-line service oriented to its technically adept readership. BIX maintains an Internet gateway and has recently begun to offer access to Internet features such as ftp and telnet.

To send e-mail from BIX to Internet name dnsuser@sub.domain, address your message to INTERNET:dnsuser@sub.domain.

To send e-mail to a BIX user such as bixuser, address your message to bixuser@bix.com.

Calvacom (France)

Calvacom is a commercial messaging service provided within France.

To send e-mail from Calvacom to an Internet DNS name such as dnsuser@sub.domain, address your message to EM/dnsuser@sub.domain.

To send e-mail to a Calvacom user such as caluser, address your message to caluser@calvacom.fr.

> **Note**
>
> Message lengths are limited to 100,000 characters.

CompuServe

CompuServe is the largest and best-known on-line service provider in the United States. Dialup access of 1,200, 2,400, and 9,600 bps is available by way of a local call in most U.S. cities. Many forums available cover various discussion topics; a number of vendors such as Microsoft, Borland, and Lotus also offer technical support information.

A CompuServe account name consists of two numeric fields separated by a comma, such as `71234,1234`.

CompuServe provides global public access to e-mail, forum, file transfer, and on-line chat services. Now, only an e-mail gateway is provided to the Internet, although connecting to CompuServe via telnet is possible. This method of connecting doesn't circumvent the fees charged with normal access, however.

To send e-mail to the Internet DNS name dnsuser@sub.domain from CompuServe, address your message to

```
INTERNET: dnsuser@sub.domain
```

CompuServe supports individual and organizational accounts. How you address your Internet e-mail depends on the account type of the CompuServe recipient. To send e-mail to an individual account, simply replace the comma in the address by a period and add the gateway name. To send e-mail to CompuServe user `71234,5677`, for example, address your message to `71234.5677@CompuServe.com`.

For a CompuServe organizational account of the form *organization:department:csuser*, address your e-mail to *csuser@department.organization*.CompuServe.com.

II

Features and Services

> **Note**
>
> The *department* field may not be present for some organizational accounts.

Connect

Connect is a professional information network, providing e-mail and file archive services. Connect maintains an e-mail gateway to the Internet.

To send e-mail from Connect to the Internet DNS name *dnsuser@sub.domain*, address your message to DASN and enter `"dnsuser@sub.domain"`@DASN as the first line of your message.

To send e-mail to a Connect user such as CONUSER, address your message to CONUSER@connectinc.com.

DFN (Germany)

DFN is the *Deutsches ForschungsNetz* (German Science Network), a large, X.400-based network connecting universities and research institutions. Some of its sites are also EARN/BITNET sites.

To send e-mail from DFN to an Internet DNS name such as *dnsuser@sub.domain*, try addressing your message to the DNS name directly. Another option you can try is BITNET style addressing, using *dnsuser%sub.domain@gateway* (replacing *gateway* with the address of a BITNET gateway).

How you address a DFN user depends on whether the user's host is connected by way of X.400 or EARN. To send e-mail to an X.400-based user such as *dfnxuser*, address your message to *dfnxuser@sub.domain*.dbp.de. For an EARN-based user such as *earnuser.earnsite*, send your message to *earnuser@earnsite*.bitnet.

> **Note**
>
> An address conversion program is available by telnet to
> `sirius.dfn.de`. Log in as `adressen` with no password. Address
> conversion is also available through e-mail by sending a message
> whose body contains the addresses to be converted (one per line) to
>
>   `C=DE; ADMD=DBP; PRMD=dfn; S=adrserv`
>
> from DFN or
>
>   `adrserv@dfn.dbp.de`
>
> from the Internet.

EARN

EARN is the European Academic and Research Network. EARN
connects universities and research institutes throughout Europe, the Middle East, and Africa. EARN uses BITNET style
addressing—*EARNUSER@EARNSITE*.

> **Note**
>
> Network traffic within EARN is subject to an acceptable use policy
> forbidding commercial use.

The means for sending e-mail from EARN to the Internet vary,
depending on the mail program running at the EARN host.
First, try addressing your mail to the DNS name itself—
dnsuser@sub.domain, for example. If that doesn't work, address
mail to *dnsuser%sub.domain@gateway*, replacing *gateway* with a
BITNET gateway name such as `cunyvm.cuny.edu`.

To send e-mail from the Internet to EARN user *EARNUSER@EARNSITE*,
address your mail to *earnuser%earn.bitnet@gateway*, replacing *gateway*
with a BITNET gateway name.

II

Features and Services

EASYnet

EASYnet is a network service operated by Digital Equipment Corporation (DEC). EASYnet now connects more than 100,000 computers worldwide, using a variety of connection protocols including DECnet and TCP/IP.

EASYnet provides e-mail, file transfer, USENET news, remote logins, and conferencing services.

The form of address to use when sending e-mail to the Internet from EASYnet depends on the operating system and software running on your host:

- Within the VMS operating system using DECnet mail, address your message to `nm%DECWRL::`*`"user@domain"`*.

- From within Ultrix, address your message to *`user%domain`*`@decwrl.dec.com`.

- From within All-In-1, use *`user@domain`* `@Internet`.

> **Note**
>
> Notice the space between *domain* and the second @ symbol in the All-In-1 address form.

Sending e-mail to an EASYnet user also depends on the address form of the recipient. To send mail to *`EASYHOST::EASYUSER`*, for example, use the DNS name *`easyuser@easyhost`*`.enet.dec.com`. To send mail to an All-In-1 address such as `John Public@AI1SITE`, address your message to `John.Public@AI1SITE.MTS.DEC.COM`.

Envoy (Canada)

Envoy is an X.400-based commercial messaging service provided by Telecom Canada. Envoy provides an e-mail gateway to the Internet.

To send e-mail from Envoy to Internet name *dnsuser@sub.domain*, address your message to

```
[RFC822="user(a)sub.domain"]INTERNET/TELEMAIL/US
```

> **Note**
>
> You may need to convert some characters of your address. For @, use (a), as shown in the preceding example. Also convert ! characters to (b) and blanks to (u).

To send e-mail to an Envoy user, send your message by way of UUCPnet to `uunet.uu.net!att!attmail!mhs!envoy!`*envoyuser*.

EUnet

EUnet is a consortium of 25 national service providers of European network connectivity. One top-level domain is provided for each nation:

Domain	Country
at	Austria
be	Belgium
bg	Bulgaria
ch	Switzerland
cz	Czech Republic
de	Germany
dk	Denmark
eg	Egypt
es	Spain
fi	Finland
fr	France

(continues)

Domain	Country
gb	Great Britain
gr	Greece
hu	Hungary
ie	Ireland
is	Iceland
it	Italy
lu	Luxembourg
nl	Netherlands
no	Norway
pt	Portugal
si	Slovenia
sk	Slovakia
su	Former Soviet Union
tn	Tunisia

EUnet uses Internet-style addresses.

FIDOnet

FIDOnet is a public network of bulletin board systems (BBSs). FIDOnet hosts consist of widely differing operating systems and platforms, including UNIX, DOS, Windows, Macintosh, Amiga, Atari, and others.

FIDOnet provides e-mail, file transfer, forum, and USENET services. Because the particular capabilities of each site depend on the BBS administrator (called a *system operator*, or *sysop*), not all services are available at all sites.

FIDOnet addressing is based on a hierarchical organization of zones, networks, and nodes. The zone, network, and node fields are all numeric values. The general address form looks like the following:

```
firstname lastname@zone:net/node
```

A sample address, then, may be `john public@1:10/100`.

FIDOnet also hosts a number of *virtual* networks such as K12net, a network for educators dealing with topics of educational interest.

To send e-mail from FIDOnet to an Internet DNS name such as *dnsuser@sub.domain*, address your message to

```
dnsuser@sub.domain ON 1:1/31
```

To construct an Internet DNS name for a FIDOnet user, use the following template:

```
first.last@f<node>.n<net>.z<zone>.fidonet.org
```

To send e-mail to FIDOnet user `john public@1:2/3`, for example, address your message to `john.public@f3.n2.z1.fidonet.org`.

GEnie

GEnie is an on-line service provided by General Electric Information Services. GEnie provides e-mail, forums, file archives, and fax services to its customers. GEnie maintains an Internet e-mail gateway.

To send e-mail to an Internet name such as *dnsuser@sub.domain*, address your message to *dnsuser@sub.domain@INET#*.

To send e-mail to a GEnie user, such as *geuser*, address your message to *geuser@genie.geis.com*.

Tip

To obtain information on FIDOnet sites and network organization, send mail to `Hostmaster@f1.n1.z31.fidonet.org`.

II

Features and Services

GeoNet Mailbox Services, GmbH

GeoNet is a commercial messaging service. GeoNet addresses have the form *user@host*, where *host* is geo1 (for Europe), geo2 (United Kingdom), or geo4 (US).

To send e-mail to Internet name *dnsuser@sub.domain*, address your message to DASN and enter *dnsuser@sub.domain!subject* as the subject line of the message.

To send e-mail to a GeoNet user such as *geouser@geohost*, address your message to *geouser@geohost*.geomail.org.

Gold-400 (United Kingdom)

Gold-400 is an X.400-based commercial messaging service operated by British Telecom.

To send e-mail to an Internet DNS name such as *dnsuser@sub.domain*, address your message to

/DD.RFC-822=*dnsuser*(a)*sub.domain*/O=uknet/PRMD=uk.ac/ADMD=gold 400/C=GB/

> **Note**
>
> You may need to convert some characters of your address. For @, use (a), as shown in the preceding address. Also convert ! characters to (b), % characters to (p), and " characters to (q).

To send e-mail to a Gold-400 user such as John Q. Public at JohnsOrg, address your message to

    john.q.public@JohnsOrg.prmd.gold-400.gb

gsfcmail

Gfscmail is the in-house e-mail system for NASA's Goddard Space Flight Center.

To send e-mail to Internet name *dnsuser@sub.domain*, address
your mail to

```
(SITE:SMTPMAIL,ID:<dnsuser(a)sub.domain>)
```

or to

```
(C:USA,A:TELEMAIL,P:SMTPMAIL,ID:<dnsuser(a)sub.domain>)
```

Alternatively, you can send your message to POSTMAN and enter

```
To: dnsuser@sub.domain
```

as the first line of the message.

To send e-mail to a gsfcmail user such as *gsfcuser*, address your
mail to *gsfcuser*@gsfcmail.nasa.gov.

IBM VNET

VNET is a network of mainframe computers using the Network
Job Entry (NJE) protocols. VNET maintains an Internet e-mail
gateway.

To send e-mail to Internet name *dnsuser@sub.domain*, address
your message to the DNS name directly.

To send e-mail to a VNET user such as *vnetuser*, address your
message to *vnetuser*@*vmnode.ibm_subdomain*.ibm.com.

> **Note**
>
> VNET provides an e-mail WHOIS name/address service. To look up
> *vnetname*'s address, for example, send a message including the line
> WHOIS *vnetname* to nic@vnet.ibm.com.

Keylink (Australia)

Keylink is an X.400-based commercial messaging service
provided by Telecom Australia.

Tip

For help concerning
interactions with
gsfcmail, phone (800)
858-9947.

II

Features and Services

To send e-mail to John Q. Public with an Internet DNS name such as `jpublic@`*`sub.domain`*, address your message to

`(C:au, A:telememo, P:oz.au, "RFC-822":"John Public<jpublic(a)`*`domain`*`>")`

> **Note**
>
> You may need to convert some characters of your address. For @, use `(a)`, as shown in the preceding address. Also convert ! characters to `(b)`, % characters to `(p)`, and " characters to `(q)`.

To send e-mail to Keylink user `John Public` of `JohnsOrg`, address your message to `John.Public@JohnsOrg.telememo.au`.

MCI Mail

MCI Mail is a commercial messaging service that provides an e-mail gateway to the Internet.

MCI Mail addresses consist of a user name and ID. The user name is sufficient for addressing, provided that it is unique. If it isn't unique, you must use the ID also. An example of an MCI Mail address is `John Public (123-4567)`.

MCI Mail offers e-mail and telex to its customers. No file transfer or other network services are provided.

To send e-mail to John Q. Public with an Internet DNS name such as *`dnsuser@sub.domain`*, address your message by entering the following information at the mail composer prompts:

```
To: John Public (EMS)
EMS: INTERNET
Mbx: dnsuser@sub.domain
```

To send e-mail to an MCI Mail user such as *`mci_user`* with ID `123-4567`, address your message to *`mci_user`*`@mcimail.com` if *`mci_user`* is unique; use *`mci_user`*`/1234567@mcimail.com` otherwise. (Note the conversion of a space in the name to an underscore.)

NASA Mail

NASA Mail is an enterprise wide messaging system for the National Aeronautics and Space Administration.

To send e-mail to Internet name `dnsuser@sub.domain`, address your message to (`site:smtpmail,id:<user(a)domain>`).

To send e-mail to a NASA Mail user such as `nasauser`, address your message to `nasauser@nasamail.nasa.gov`.

> **Note**
>
> You can get help with NASA Mail by phoning (205) 544-1771 or (800) 858-9947.

Prodigy

Prodigy, one of the newest on-line services, was the result of a cooperative effort by Sears and IBM. From its introduction, Prodigy has been targeted at a more casual computer user audience than most other on-line services.

Prodigy uses proprietary software that provides a graphical user interface (GUI) for its users. This software is available for PC and Macintosh platforms.

To send e-mail to a Prodigy user from the Internet, address your message to `userid@prodigy.com`, replacing `userid` with the user ID that Prodigy assigned to the recipient.

Prodigy users also can send e-mail to other Internet addresses, but they must have a software package called Mail Manager (which is available only for IBM-compatible PC users). To send e-mail to an Internet address, simply use the appropriate DNS name.

II

Features and Services

Relcom

Relcom provides network connectivity to the former Soviet Union. Relcom provides top-level domains for the following nations:

Domain Name	Country
by	Byelorussia
ee	Estonia
ge	Georgia
lt	Lithuania
lv	Latvia
su	Former Soviet Union
ua	Ukraine

Relcom uses Internet-style addressing.

SprintMail

SprintMail is an X.400-based messaging service. Dialup access to SprintMail is available through Public Data Networks (PDNs) such as Sprintnet, so most users can log in with a local call.

SprintMail provides e-mail, BBS, file transfer, telex, and fax services to its customers. It maintains an Internet e-mail gateway.

To send e-mail to Internet name *dnsuser@sub.domain*, address your message to

`(C:USA,A:TELEMAIL,P:INTERNET,"RFC-822":<dnsuser(a)sub.domain>) DEL`

Note that the @ in the name has been converted to (a).

To send e-mail to a SprintMail user such as `John Public` at `JohnsOrg`, address your message to `john_public@JohnsOrg.Sprint.com`.

> **Note**
>
> You can get help with SprintMail within the United States by calling (800) 336-0437 and pressing 2 on a Touch-Tone phone.

UUCPnet

UUCP (UNIX-to-UNIX Copy program) is a means for transferring data between machines, usually over a serial line or modem connection. UUNET is an organization that provides networked UUCP connections. UUCPnet uses *bang path* addressing, which reverses the order of DNS address fields and uses ! (referred to in UNIXdom as a *bang* symbol) rather than . as the field separator.

UUNET provides a gateway between UUCPnet and Internet.

To send e-mail to an Internet DNS name such as `dnsuser@sub.domain`, address your message to `uunet!domain!sub!dnsuser`. To send e-mail to a UUCPnet user such as `uunet!domain!sub!uucpuser`, address your message to `uucpuser%sub.domain@UUCP`.

Summary

As you can see from this chapter, most of the larger networks around the world have some type of connectivity with the Internet. Electronic mail can, in general, be sent between these networks and Internet hosts, and some networks also support file transfers as well.

In the future, you can expect many of these networks to adopt Internet-style e-mail addresses. As the number of Internet hosts continues to increase rapidly, many will also provide to their users a way to access the Internet interactively. In fact, some networks probably will switch to the TCP/IP protocol suite to ensure compatibility with other networks and allow for future growth.

II

Features and Services

Part III

Tools and Technology

Session - SEI.XWP

PINE 3.07   MAIN MENU   Folder.inbox   1 Message

    ?   HELP   - Get help using Pine

    C   COMPOSE   - Compose and send a message

    I   MAIL INDEX   - Read mail in current folder

Mail in progress...

* ----- Mail Composition Editor ----- *

O: ftpmail@decwrl.dec.com   Edit   Done   Cancel

C:

ct: file request via ftpmail server

    Note. In Pine 3.0 we are encouraging folks to use the MAIL INDEX to
          mail instead of VIEW MAIL, so it is no longer on the main menu
          in the mail index, it is available as usual as the "V" command

    Help   Quit   Folders   Other
    Compose   Mail Index Addresses

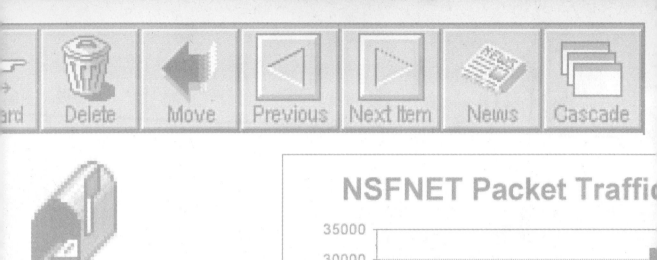

| ard | Delete | Move | Previous | Next Item | News | Cascade |

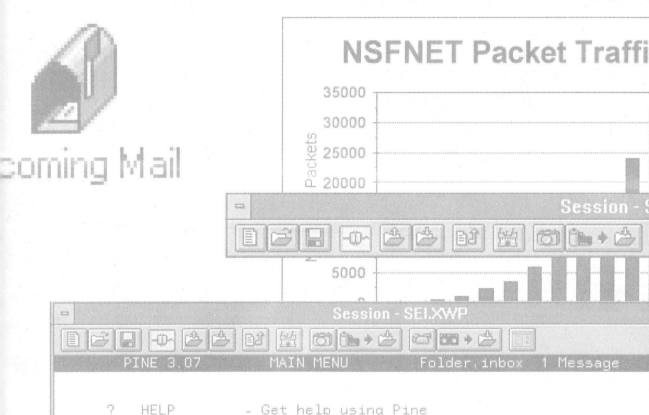

NSFNET Packet Traffic

35000
30000
Packets
25000
20000

5000

Session - S

Session - SEI.XWP

PINE 3.07   MAIN MENU   Folder:inbox 1 Message

?   HELP   - Get help using Pine

C   COMPOSE   - Compose and send a message

I   MAIL INDEX - Read mail in current folder

Call

Mail in progress...
* ----- Mail Composition Editor ----- *

TO: ftpmail@decwrl.dec.com   Edit   Done   Cancel
CC:
oject: file request via ftpmail server

Note: In Pine 3.0 we are encouraging folks to use the MAIL INDEX t
      mail instead of VIEW MAIL, so it is no longer on the main me
      in the mail index, it is available as usual as the "Y" comma

? Help   Quit   F Folders   Other
C Compose   I Mail Index A Addresses

Chapter 12

Hardware and Software

Now that you are familiar with some of the features an Internet connection provides and have used Chapter 10, "Determining the Level of Internet Service You Need," to select the class of connection you need, you probably can use some information to help set up your local system and make best use of your connection. This chapter looks at some of the hardware and software options you have that can support your Internet connection.

This chapter is also the one that is rather specific to one type of computer: IBM PCs and compatible. Macintosh owners may want to examine *The Mac Internet Tour Guide: Cruising the Internet the Easy Way*, for information specific to their computing platform. Novice UNIX pilots will likely find the information they need in Appendix C, "UNIX Quick Reference."

One of the most common complaints leveled against the Internet is that its interface is cumbersome. As you found out in Chapter 10, no single type of Internet connection exists, so this blanket criticism is immediately on shaky ground. Also, a number of software packages have been developed to make your interface to the Internet painless, and in some cases, even pleasant. Some of these packages rival programs such as CompuServe's WinCIM for providing an intuitive, useful interface to the Internet. In the section on software, you'll get a look at several offerings, including commercial, shareware, and service provider proprietary packages.

Hardware

Adding Internet connectivity to your PC is one of the few popular additions that doesn't require a powerhouse machine. Unlike multimedia, graphics, or GUI operating environments like Windows and OS/2, a 286 system with 640K of memory and a decent modem can use the Internet quite effectively. Of course, a machine with greater power will have better overall performance and a wider range of software options, but the basic capabilities for e-mail, USENET news, ftp, telnet, and so forth aren't at all limited to power users with the latest hot-shot computing platforms. Machines that can run Windows or other GUI environments do benefit from software packages that make your interface to the Internet a more friendly and intuitive one, however.

Storage Requirements

One feature that may put a strain on a minimally configured machine is USENET. USENET traffic is growing tremendously. As of August 1993, a full feed generated about 50M of data per day, or 1.5 gigabytes per month.

Although ordinarily you wouldn't subscribe to anything close to a full feed, without frequent purging of old files, a 30M hard disk can quickly be filled to capacity. Again, the easiest way to control this is to make sure that you're using USENET efficiently. Avoid the temptation to subscribe to more groups than you can read. And don't forget that archive sites exist for most news groups, relieving you of having to save messages locally.

Modem

For most individuals and small businesses, the medium by which you connect to your service provider is an ordinary phone line. To make use of your Internet connection, you need some way of converting the digital data signals your PC understands into a form suitable for sending and receiving over that phone line. A *modem*—the term is short for *modulator-demodulator*—performs that conversion.

Because of the popularity of BBS and on-line services such as CompuServe, modems have become commonplace on millions of PCs. Although the following sections can't substitute for a course in telecommunications or a modem user's guide, they provide a brief description of the principles of modem operation and some practical advice on choosing and configuring your modem.

Basic Modem Operation

For a number of reasons, digital signals aren't suitable for transmission over a common phone line. One of the major stumbling blocks is that phone lines were designed to provide only enough bandwidth to exchange intelligible speech from one person to another. A certain amount of signal degradation and distortion was considered acceptable as long as one person could still understand what the other was saying. Obviously, the same level of degradation couldn't possibly be tolerated during the transfer of data.

To get around these limitations, a modem converts bit values into an equivalent analog representation, manipulating three parameters of an analog signal: amplitude, frequency, and phase. The goal for the designers of modem communications techniques is to create as many unique combinations of these parameters as possible, while simultaneously keeping each combination as far from the others as possible. This separation reduces the chance of one symbol being confused with another. Figure 12.1 shows the basic operation of a modem.

Fig. 12.1

In basic modem operation, the sending computer provides (to the modem) digital data, which is converted into analog signals sent through telephone lines and reconverted into digital information by the receiving computer's modem.

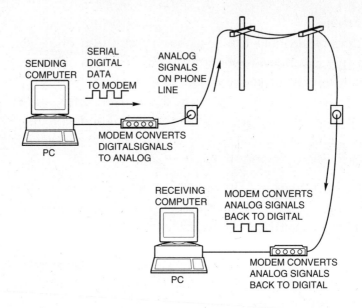

Basic Modem Operations

Thus, when two modems communicate, they convert the representation for digital data values into an analog form suitable for transmission through the phone system. They then reconvert these signals back to digital form on receipt.

Flow Control

A modem connection can link two very different types of computers, such as a PC and a supercomputer, as long as they share a common modem protocol. But given the disparity of machines, that one system could transfer data faster than the other seems likely. A difference in data transfer rates also could happen when connecting similar computers, if one of the computers has additional tasks that must be performed periodically, thus taking its attention away from the communications link momentarily. What happens if the sending or receiving equipment can't keep up with its partner? A technique called *flow control* is used to regulate the transfer of data between a computer and its modem to avoid losing information. Two types of flow control are used: hardware and software.

When *software flow control* (XON/XOFF) is used, a special character is reserved to be placed in the data stream to indicate "start sending data (XON)" or "stop sending data (XOFF)." Because sending this command will take some real—albeit small—amount of time to transfer between the computer and its modem, the XOFF command must be sent before the point at which the receiver can no longer store information. Sending XOFF ahead of time is necessary to allow for the delay between when XOFF is sent, and when the transmitting unit quits sending additional data.

Another way to signal the status of the connection is with separate status lines between the computer and modem. This approach is often called *hardware flow control*, because the generation and detection of the flow-control signals is performed by hardware components within the PC and modem. Hardware flow control is more efficient than software flow control and is especially preferred for higher speed modems. A similar flow-control issue exists between modems but is normally handled by the protocols within which they communicate, and hence is invisible to the user.

> **Note**
>
> Because UUCP and SLIP connections use their own flow-control protocols, you shouldn't enable XON/XOFF flow control when using these connections.

Modem Configuration and Wiring

If you buy a modem that plugs directly into your PC as an add-in card, you must assign one of the PC's serial ports to the modem. To do so, choose the interrupt request line (IRQ) and I/O base address that corresponds to the port to which you're assigning the modem. The assignment usually is accomplished by jumpers on the modem or a software configuration program that came with it. The IRQ and base address for the serial ports available within the PC are as follows:

Port	IRQ	I/O Base Address
COM1	4	0x3F8
COM2	3	0x2F8
COM3	4	0x3E8
COM4	3	0x2E8

You need to make sure that another piece of hardware doesn't already use the IRQ and I/O address you select. A common mistake is to configure your modem for operation as COM2 when the PC already has a COM2 serial port. You must check your system documentation and disable the PC's COM2 port before using your modem in this case.

Many users also run into trouble when trying to use COM3 and COM4 under DOS and Windows. The reasons vary, such as lack of software support for these ports or insufficient hardware support in your PC clone. Therefore, the safest thing to do is to configure your modem for COM1 or COM2 operation, if possible.

> **Note**
>
> Only IBM Micro Channel Architecture (MCA) computers seem capable of sharing interrupts reliably.

An alternative is to use a modem that plugs directly into one of the serial ports already provided by your PC. An external modem is more portable and can be used on machines other than a PC. Often, external modems also are fitted with an LED or LCD display that indicates the status of your connection; such a display can prove to be a valuable aid when you are trying to get modem configuration details sorted out. For these extra conveniences, external modems typically cost $20 to $40 more than their internal counterparts. You also lose one of your existing serial ports to support the modem.

The use of an external modem also requires a cable to connect it to the PC's serial port. You can easily buy pre-assembled serial cables, but just in case you need to build or troubleshoot a serial cable, table 12.1 gives the signal assignments for DB-9 and DB-25 serial ports for the PC.

Table 12.1 Serial Port Signal Pin Assignments

Signal Name	Pin Number	
	DB-9	DB-25
Carrier Detect (CD)	1	8
Transmit Data (TD)	2	2
Receive Data (RD)	3	3
Data Terminal Ready (DTR)	4	20
Signal Ground (SG)	5	7
Data Set Ready (DSR)	6	6
Request To Send (RTS)	7	4
Clear To Send (CTS)	8	5
Ring Indicator (RI)	9	22

Transfer Rates

The single biggest factor that separates modems by price and performance is the transfer rate they can support, expressed as *bits per second* (bps). The least expensive modems offer data transfer using the v.22 specification, which yields a rate of 2,400 bps. Modems that support v.32 can transfer data at 9,600 bps. At the current upper-end for readily available modems is the v.32bis standard, which accommodates 14,400 bps transfers.

> **Note**
>
> A new specification, dubbed *v.fast*, also is nearing release at the time this book goes to press. It should provide transfer rates of at least 28,800 bps. Some v.32bis modems offered today are based on programmable processors and claim to be software upgradable to the v.fast standard.

To figure out the number of bytes per second that correspond to a given transfer rate, you may be tempted simply to divide the bps rate by 8. (After all, 8 bits are in a byte.) The nature of serial transmission requires some overhead, however, usually one bit preceding and one bit following the data. So dividing by 10 is more accurate. The following table gives byte transfer rates for various modem connection classes:

Bits per Second	Bytes per		
	Second	Minute	Hour
2,400 (v.22)	240	14,400	864,000
9,600 (v.32)	960	57,600	3,456,000
14,400 (v.32bis)	1,440	86,400	5,184,000

Data Compression

Another way to boost the effective data transfer rate between you and your provider is to use a compression algorithm on the data before it is sent, and then decompress it when it's received. A common hardware compression scheme built into some modems is v.42bis. With v.42bis compression, a v.22 modem connection can reach equivalent effective transfer rates to that of a v.32 modem without compression. On text files, a compression factor of 4:1 is possible, meaning that the compressed data is one-fourth the volume of the input stream; for executable files, on the other hand, the result is closer to 2:1.

Another compression scheme is the Microcom Networking Protocol, Class Five, or just MNP-5. MNP-5 has a maximum compression factor of 2:1.

In some circumstances, however, such compression shouldn't be used. Compressing an already compressed file can have the unexpected result of actually making the file larger. For something like a UUCP connection, whose files are already compressed before transfer, you usually get the best overall performance by setting up your modem with all compression schemes turned off.

Modem control

Virtually every modem manufactured for PCs uses a standard set of commands to control its functionality. This set of commands was first developed by Hayes Microcomputer for that company's modems. Over time, this command set has become the *de facto* standard for modem control. The commands consist of ASCII character strings. Table 12.2 lists some of the more common commands.

Table 12.2 Common Hayes-Compatible Commands

Command	Description
AT	Attention (precedes all other commands listed in this table)
A	Set modem to auto-answer
D	Dial the number that follows

E(0,1)	Command echo control:
	    0 = no echo
	    1 = echo

H	Hang up phone line

(continues)

III

Tools and Technology

Table 12.2 Continued	
Command	**Description**
M(0,1,2)	Speaker control: 0 = off 1 = on until connected 2 = always on
Q(0,1)	Result code control: 0 = return codes 1 = don't return codes
T	Use Touch-Tone dialing tones
V(0,1)	Result code type: 0 = return numeric codes 1 = return words
Z	Reset modem
,	Pause
+++	Escape sequence

To direct your modem to dial the number 555-1212 with Touch-Tone dialing tones, for example, your communications software would send the following command, terminated with a carriage return:

    ATDT5551212

Notice that the AT command string begins a command string, and that multiple commands (D and T in this instance) can be used in the same string. Most modems have dozens of commands, making the task of configuring your modem potentially challenging and frustrating. Fortunately, many software packages include a number of predefined configurations for the more popular modem types. The best course of action is to get your modem working in a simple configuration such as 2,400 bps and no flow control. Then add additional capabilities such as compression, flow control, and higher transfer rates.

Software

Whereas the hardware requirements for an Internet connection are rather general purpose, the software you use for interfacing to the Internet can vary widely based on your operating environment and type of service. The purpose of the following sections is to introduce you to the types of software available, and to give you guidelines for matching appropriate software to the type of service you have. Because numerous software vendors are available for each class of product, not every package is mentioned.

The examples in the following sections aren't meant to serve as product endorsements, but merely to show you the kinds of features you can expect for a given class. Where practical, shareware as well as commercial offerings are examined. Many of these shareware packages are available from the Internet itself, and in these cases ftp sites are given where you can obtain them.

> **Note**
>
> Remember that shareware is NOT free. Please support shareware developers by registering and paying for the programs you find useful.

Lastly, although contact information has been provided for the commercial packages, your best bet is to consult with your local software retailer for current pricing and feature comparisons.

III

Tools and Technology

Terminal Emulation

The most common type of communications software provides a capability known as *terminal emulation*—that is, its main purpose is to make your interface to the remote machine appear like a computer terminal. This paradigm is borrowed from the days of mainframe systems, when groups of terminals were connected to a single, large computer. These terminals weren't truly computers in their own right, but units with a keyboard for data entry and a CRT for displaying results. Terminal emulation software makes your computer function like a terminal, but also lets you perform functions such as file exchanges.

Terminal emulation software can support shell-account-type Internet connections such as those from NETCOM, CRL, and Delphi. Because it also can be used for BBS and other dialup services, you can use it to fulfill your other serial communications needs. Another advantage is that the software is fairly mature, so refined and robust products are available for a comfortable price.

Useful Features

A terminal emulation package can be a very complex piece of software, with hundreds of major and minor features. Five major items of interest can reasonably summarize the capability of a terminal emulator:

- *Serial port interface.* The maximum data transfer rate the package can support is quite important, especially if you're using a high-speed modem with compression. A v.32bis modem with v.42bis compression would benefit from a connection speed of at least 57.6Kbps, and many packages today support rates as high as 115Kbps.

- *Scripting capability.* Scripting enables you to develop a "program," much like a DOS batch file, that can direct the action of the software automatically. Because some login procedures can be cumbersome, the capability to develop scripts is very useful and saves you from having to remember things like typing **@d** to get a 2,400 bps connection.

■ *Dialing directory*. Some programs store only the last phone number dialed, which is perfectly all right as long as you have only one number to call. But most users need to be able to save several different phone numbers and system configurations. A dialing directory provides the capability to save configuration details for each remote system.

■ *File transfer protocols*. A file transfer protocol provides the procedures for your computer to exchange files. XMODEM, YMODEM, ZMODEM, and Kermit are the most widely used protocols.

■ *Terminal types*. Although many different types of terminals used to be in use, today ANSI (or BBS), VT-102, and VT-220 are about the only ones necessary to connect to most systems.

PROCOMM PLUS for DOS and Windows

PROCOMM PLUS, from Datastorm Technologies, is a commercial package that originally was distributed as shareware. It retails for around $100. PROCOMM PLUS supports a wide variety of terminal types and file transfer protocols, including XMODEM, YMODEM, ZMODEM, and Kermit. Dialing directories and an extensive script file capability also are provided. Figure 12.2 shows PROCOMM PLUS connected to the Delphi on-line service.

For information about PROCOMM PLUS, contact

Datastorm Technologies, Inc.
P.O. Box 1471
Columbia, MO 65205
Voice: (314) 443-3282
Fax: (314) 875-0595

III

Tools and Technology

Fig. 12.2
PROCOMM PLUS
connected to the
Delphi on-line
service, which
provides Internet
services such as
e-mail, ftp, and
telnet to its users.

Crosstalk for DOS and Windows

Another full-featured terminal emulation package available for
DOS and Windows is Crosstalk, from Digital Communications
Associates (DCA). Crosstalk also costs around $100 and provides
essentially the same features as PROCOMM PLUS. Crosstalk
seems to be a favorite among users who require IBM 3270
terminal emulation for working with mainframe machines.

For information about Crosstalk, contact

> Digital Communications Associates, Inc.
> 1000 Alderman Drive
> Alpharetta, GA
> **Voice:** (404) 442-4000
> **Fax:** (404) 442-4364

Terminal for Windows

Windows users don't have to spend a hundred dollars or so for
a full-featured terminal emulation package. A package called
Terminal—one of the mini-applications, or *applets*, provided

with Windows—may be enough. Although it's not the most powerful or flexible package, it's still quite usable, especially for terminal server access. Figure 12.3 shows Terminal being used to connect to the Delphi on-line service.

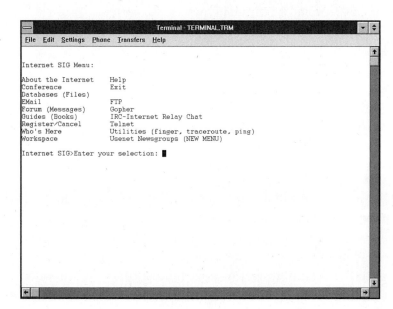

Fig. 12.3
The Terminal applet, included with Microsoft Windows at no charge, connected to Delphi.

Terminal has a number of limitations, however. It can't support a modem-to-computer connection transfer rate of more than 19.2Kbps. Only XMODEM and Kermit file transfer protocols are supported. Only TTY, VT-100 (ANSI), and VT-52 terminal types are supported. A dialing directory or script file capability also isn't available. It does have a nice feature that lets you view a local text file, however, which is quite useful if you can't quite remember the correct name of the file.

QuickLink for DOS

Simple terminal emulation packages often are bundled with new modems. One of the most common is QuickLink. Like Terminal for Windows, QuickLink bears consideration if for no other reason than that you get it for free.

III

Tools and Technology

QuickLink is quite a bit more capable than the Terminal applet, supporting all the major file transfer protocols and high-speed modem transfer. The most recent versions also include fax capability—provided your modem supports it. A dialing directory is available, and most terminal types are supported.

For information about QuickLink, contact

> Smith Micro Software, Inc.
> P.O. Box 7137
> Huntington Beach, CA 92615
> **Voice:** (714) 362-5810

Telix for DOS

The freeware and shareware markets are awash with communications programs. To name and briefly describe the features of all of them easily would fill a book this size. Of the available packages, only a few could be considered standards. Procomm certainly was until it was converted into a "payware" product. Another is Telix, which is still distributed as shareware and enjoys quite a following. It is widely available through traditional shareware channels such as diskette and CD-ROM collections, bulletin boards, and the Internet. One Internet host that archives Telix is `wuarchive.wustl.edu`, in the directory `/systems/ibmpc/msdos/telix`. At the time this book went to press, the latest version of Telix was housed in four files, `tlx321_1.zip` through `tlx321_4.zip`. You can retrieve these files via anonymous ftp.

Telix supports XMODEM, YMODEM, ZMODEM, Kermit, CompuServe B+, and other file-transfer protocols. A dialing directory and script language are included. A .PIF file also is included that enables Telix to operate successfully under Windows, thus allowing you to place Telix in the background while file transfers are in progress.

The registration fee for Telix is $39, and includes a registered copy of Telix on disk mailed to you. A printed manual is available for $12. A Windows version of Telix (also shareware) is expected to be released early this year.

For information about Telix, contact

deltaComm Development
P.O. Box 1185
Cary, NC 27512
Voice: (919) 460-4556
Fax: (919) 460-4531
BBS: (919) 481-9399

WinQVT for Windows

Several shareware terminal emulators are available for Microsoft Windows as well. One such package is WinQVT, available via of ftp from cica.indiana.edu in directory /pub/pc/win31/util. Figure 12.4 shows WinQVT in action. At the time this book went to press, the most recent version of WinQVT was contained in the file wnqvt480.zip. The registration fee for WinQVT is $50.

Fig. 12.4
WinQVT terminal emulation package for Windows, connected to Delphi.

For information on WinQVT, contact

> QPC Software
> P.O. Box 226
> Penfield, NY 14526
> **E-mail:** `76676.1420@compuserve.com`

UUCP-Based Software

UUCP software implements the UNIX to UNIX Copy protocol on PC systems. These packages usually can support multiple users, but don't provide interactive ftp or telnet capability.

Because of the number of configuration items, UUCP systems can be difficult to set up. Be sure to seek assistance from your service provider or technical support personnel when choosing your software. Your best bet is to choose a package they are familiar with and can help you properly configure. Sometimes your provider will preconfigure your software with your account information, making it easier for you to begin using your connection.

Tip
Two USENET news groups also are available for Waffle users: `alt.bbs.waffle` and `comp.bbs.waffle`.

Waffle

Waffle is a shareware package that runs under DOS. It provides e-mail, USENET news groups, and file transfer. Waffle also has a built-in bulletin board system (BBS) that allows callers access to UUCP features. Waffle is available via ftp from `ftp.halcyon.com` in the directory `/pub/waffle/waffle`. At the time this book went to press, the latest version of Waffle was contained in three files: `wafl165.zip`, `wutl10.zip`, and `waf165nn.zip`. The registration fee is $30.

For information on Waffle, contact

> Thomas E. Dell
> P.O. Box 4436
> Mountain View, CA 94040
> **E-mail:** `dell@vox.darkside.com`

UUPC

UUPC is another shareware package that runs under DOS and supports a UUCP Internet connection. UUPC provides e-mail and file transfer capability but currently doesn't support USENET news groups. UUPC is available via ftp from `ftp.clarkson.edu` in directory `/pub/uupc`. A number of files collectively contain UUPC, all of which start with `uupc`. The registration fee is $20 to $40.

For information on UUPC, contact

Kendra Electronic Wonderworks
P.O. Box 132
Arlington, MA 02174-0002

Tip
UUPC also has a USENET news group: `alt.bbs.uupcb`.

On-line Service Proprietary Software

As mentioned in Chapter 11, CompuServe and America Online have an e-mail gateway to the Internet. Both also provide easy-to-use interfaces under Windows.

CompuServe's WinCIM

The Windows CompuServe Information Manager (WinCIM) provides one of the best-designed interfaces to an information service. The refined interface uses the latest features, such as a button bar with icons that implement common functions. In addition to the user interface, WinCIM also has facilities that can reduce your connect time charges. WinCIM, for example, enables you to compose messages off-line, and then connect to CompuServe only on an as-needed basis to send and receive messages.

Note

A DOS-based version of CIM is also available.

III

Tools and Technology

WinCIM is available commercially, but is often distributed with promotional material for joining CompuServe. The version the authors use was provided through the Microsoft Developer's Network, as you can see in the title bar in figure 12.5.

Fig. 12.5
By using the standard mail creation facility in WinCIM, you can receive Internet e-mail by way of Compu-Serve.

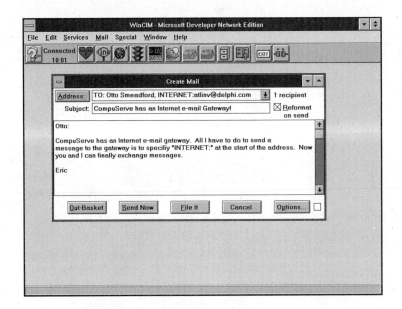

For information on WinCIM, contact

CompuServe
P.O. Box 20212
Columbus, OH 43220-9922
Voice: (800) 848-8990

America Online

America Online also has developed extensive Windows, DOS, and Mac front-ends for its on-line service. Currently, this interface is also being distributed with promotional materials for joining America Online. Figure 12.6 shows an example of how to use America Online's interface to send an Internet e-mail message.

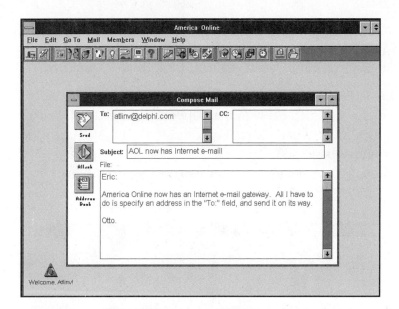

Fig. 12.6
Internet e-mail, by way of America Online. The AOL interface allows you to access the Internet e-mail gateway simply by specifying the appropriate address during mail composition.

For information on America Online, contact

> America Online
> 8619 Westwood Center Drive
> Vienna, VA 22182-2285
> **Voice:** (800) 827-6364

Service Provider Proprietary Software

A few service providers have developed their own software packages for the Internet. Their main reason for this is to give you a more human, intuitive, graphical interface to work with and to minimize system setup issues and potential software compatibility problems. This software is usually available free of charge from the provider directly, or by way of a BBS or ftp. These packages have the added advantage of being built specifically for their corresponding Internet services.

PSILink DOS/Windows

Performance Systems International (PSI) provides a UUCP-based service that includes proprietary software to put a

III

Tools and Technology

friendlier face on the Internet. PSILink provides 1,200, 2,400, 9,600 bps, and 14.4Kbps connections via local call to many U.S. cities, and the software is available for DOS and Windows.

The DOS software for PSILink gives the user a character-based window and menu system that supports e-mail, USENET news groups, and ftpmail file-transfer capabilities. PSI also provides Windows-based software for its PSILink service. Figures 12.7 through 12.11 demonstrate the look and feel of PSILink's user interface.

Fig. 12.7
The PSILink for Windows main window. Double-click the mailbox icon in the lower left corner to open the mail window. You also can create icons for your outgoing mail and USENET news groups.

Mailbox icon ——

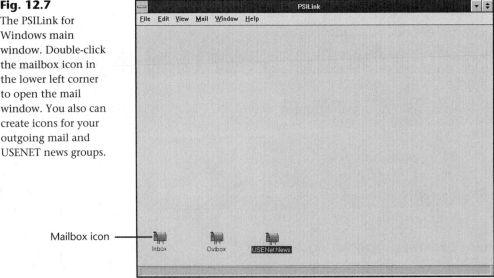

For information on PSILink, contact

Performance Systems International
510 Huntmar Park Drive
Herndon, VA 22070
Voice: (703) 904-4100
Fax: (703) 904-4200
E-mail: info@psi.com

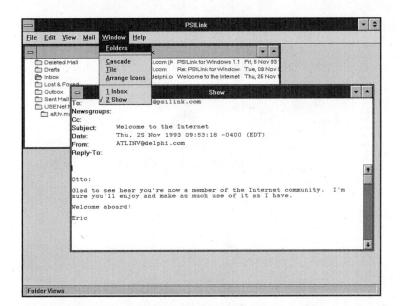

Fig. 12.8
The PSILink for
Windows mail
window, listing all
your currently active
messages. An envelope
icon denotes whether
you have read
(opened) a message.

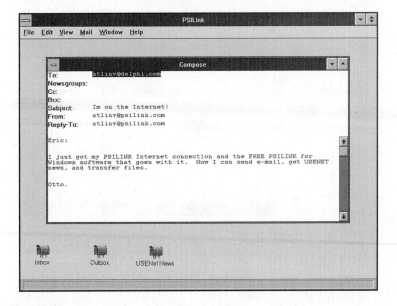

Fig. 12.9
The PSILink for
Windows Mail
composition window.
Separate fields are
provided for the
sender, receiver, and
"carbon copy" recip-
ients. Placing a
USENET news group
name in the appropri-
ate field posts the
message to that
group.

WinNET Mail

Computer Witchcraft has developed a UUCP-based service/
software package called WinNET Mail. WinNET Mail provides
e-mail, USENET news group, and file-transfer capabilities.

The software is freely distributed on the Internet, CompuServe, and on bulletin boards, or will be sent to new subscribers on diskette if they cannot acquire it through on-line means.

Fig. 12.10
The PSILink for Windows USENET news group subscription window. The list on the left provides the groups to choose from; the right-hand list contains groups subscribed to.

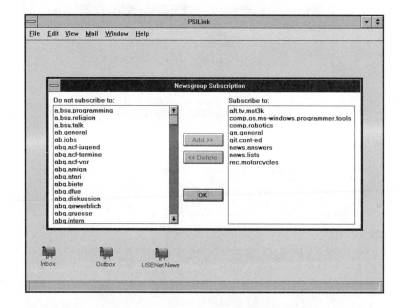

Fig. 12.11
The PSILink for Windows connection monitor, which enables you to track the operation of your connection with the PSILink host.

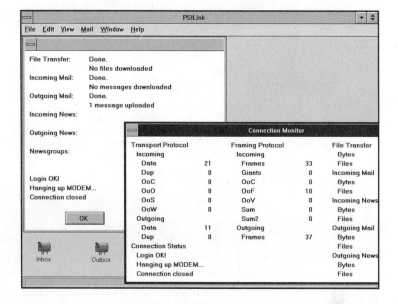

WinNET Mail also is included on the diskette accompanying this book. Figures 12.12 through 12.18 demonstrate the look and feel of WinNET Mail's user interface, but for a complete examination of WinNET Mail, including installation from the disk, see Appendix A.

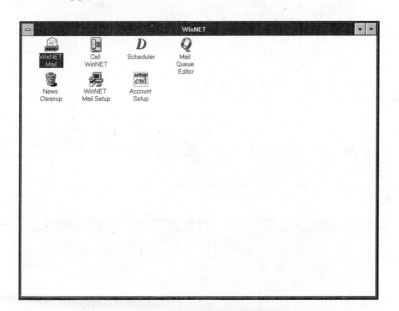

Fig. 12.12
The WinNET Mail group. Separate icons represent the programs provided, including account setup, communications with the host, and deletion of old messages.

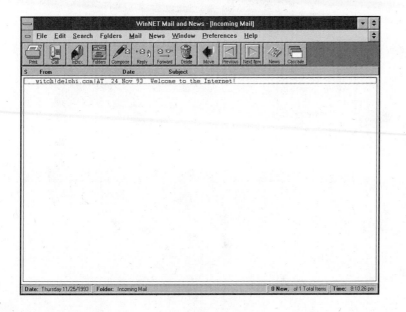

Fig. 12.13
The WinNET Mail main screen. The toolbar under the menus enables you to perform common tasks such as sending mail and reading USENET news with a single mouse click.

III

Tools and Technology

Fig. 12.14
Reading an e-mail
message in WinNET
Mail.

Fig. 12.15
Composing an e-mail
message in WinNET
Mail.

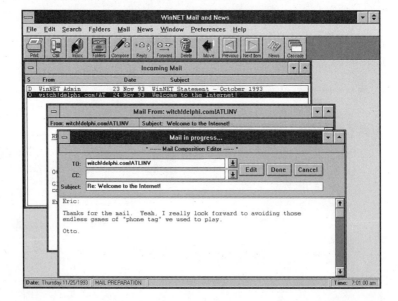

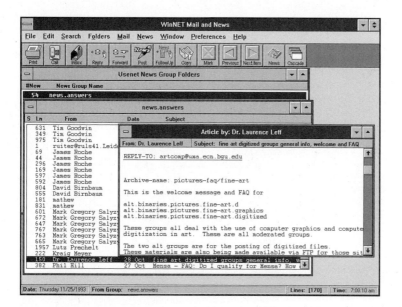

Fig. 12.16
Reading USENET news in WinNET Mail. WinNET Mail uses the Windows multiple document interface (MDI), which enables you to open several messages at once.

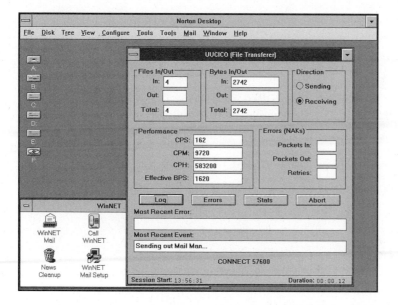

Fig. 12.17
You can communicate to the WinNET Mail host in the background while you run other programs.

III

Tools and Technology

Fig. 12.18
If new mail is
received, WinNET
Mail creates an icon
on your desktop to
alert you of its arrival.

New Mail icon ——

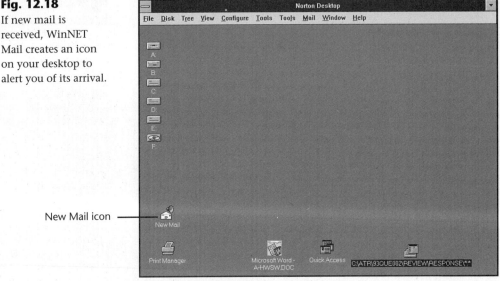

One additional benefit that Computer Witchcraft provides is an 800 number to connect to its service. Although the phone company won't charge you for use of an 800 number, Computer Witchcraft does charge you for it as part of your connection time charges. The primary benefit of the 800 number is that it makes the service available nationwide. The rates are usually better than for long-distance direct dialing, however.

For information on WinNET Mail, contact

> Computer Witchcraft, Inc.
> P.O. Box 4189
> Louisville, KY 40204
> **Voice:** (502) 589-6800
> **Fax:** (502) 589-7300
> **E-mail:** help@win.net

SLIP/PPP

As you read in Chapter 11, the Serial Line Internet Protocol (SLIP) and Point-to-Point Protocol (PPP) allow your system to become a full Internet host. Special software is needed to provide ftp, telnet, mail, and other services associated with a SLIP connection.

The popular commercial packages that provide SLIP capability are actually much more than a connection to the Internet. They are full-featured networking software packages that can provide TCP/IP networking within your local network as well as to your remote host.

Unfortunately, this added capability can make initial setup of the software an arduous task, especially for the network novice. As with UUCP software, you should speak with your service provider's technical support staff to find out which software packages they are familiar with setting up. Doing so could save you hours of frustration.

NetManage's Chameleon

NetManage has developed a network software package called Chameleon that implements TCP/IP within Windows, including support for SLIP connections. Chameleon provides a full suite of utilities, including e-mail, ftp, telnet, news, finger, ping, and others. NetManage also has started distributing a "sampler" package, which provides a scaled-down version of Chameleon that's pre-configured for SLIP connection to several of the major service providers (including ANS, PSI, and NETCOM). This package provides e-mail, ftp, telnet, and ping utilities. Figures 12.19 through 12.24 demonstrate the look and feel of Chameleon's user interface. The retail price for Chameleon is $399.

For information on Chameleon, contact

> NetManage, Inc.
> 20823 Stevens Creek Blvd.
> Cupertino, CA 95014
> **Voice:** (408) 973-7171
> **Fax:** (408) 257-6405
> **E-mail:** support@netmanage.com

III

Tools and Technology

Fig. 12.19

The Chameleon group. Icons are provided for many of the common Internet functions and utilities, such as e-mail, ftp, and telnet.

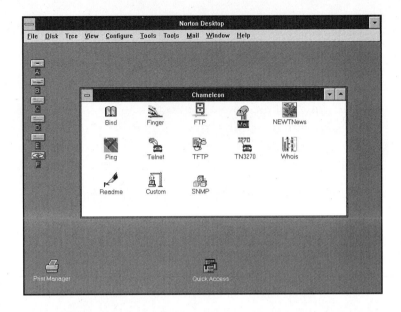

Fig. 12.20

The custom interface configuration window that is invoked by double-clicking the Custom icon in the Chameleon group. This defines and initiates the SLIP connection to your host.

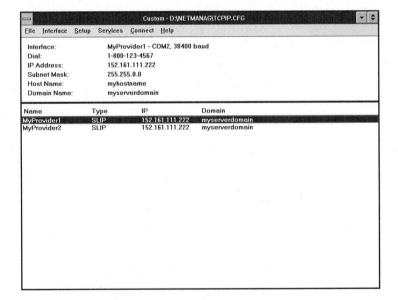

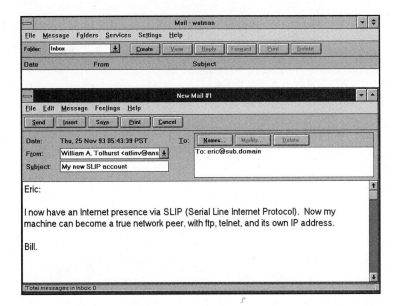

Fig. 12.21
Composing an e-mail message using Chameleon's mail utility.

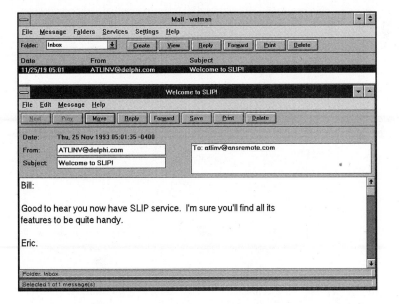

Fig. 12.22
Reading an e-mail message within Chameleon. By using buttons, you easily can save or reply to the message.

Fig. 12.23
The ftp utility in
Chameleon. Note that
you can transfer files
easily to or from the
host and view text
files before transfer-
ring them.

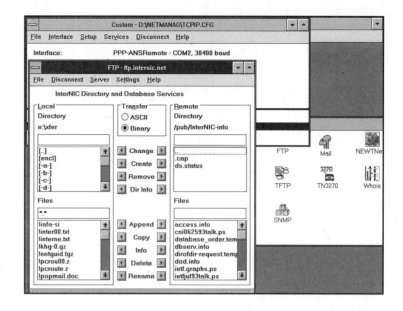

Fig. 12.24
telnet operation in
Chameleon.

Distinct TCP/IP

Distinct Corporation also offers a TCP/IP networking package
suitable for use as a front end for your SLIP connection. One
nice feature it includes is a demand dialing system, which

establishes your SLIP connection automatically when you invoke any utilities that require it (such as ftp, telnet, and so on). Distinct TCP/IP is available for Windows and DOS. The retail price is $395. Figures 12.25 through 12.27 demonstrate Distinct's look and feel.

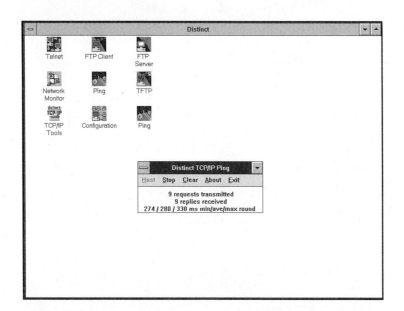

Fig. 12.25
Distinct's main group, overlaid with an operating ping utility. Note that software is provided for you to configure your machine as an ftp server.

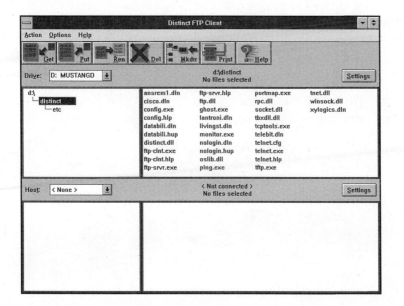

Fig. 12.26
The ftp client interface in Distinct TCP/IP for Windows. A toolbar and split window display make accessing the files you need easy.

III

Tools and Technology

Fig. 12.27
The network
monitoring utility
within Distinct
provides you with a
performance analysis
and troubleshooting
tool.

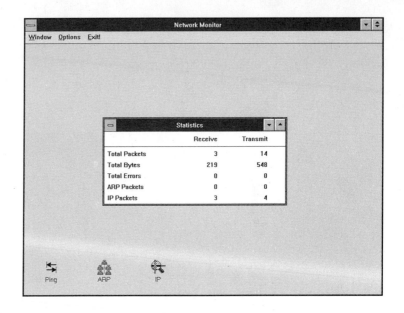

For information on Distinct TCP/IP, contact

> Distinct Corporation
> P.O. Box 3410
> Saratoga, CA 95070-1410
> **Voice:** (408) 741-0781
> **Fax:** (408) 741-0795

Beam & Whiteside's BWTCP

Beam & Whiteside's BWTCP provides DOS and Windows TCP/IP network support in a single package. BWTCP supports e-mail, ftp, telnet, ping, finger, and many other useful utilities.

For information on BWTCP, contact

> Beam & Whiteside Software Ltd.
> P.O. Box 8130
> Dundas, Ontario
> Canada L9H 5E7
> **Voice:** (416) 764-0822
> **Fax:** (416) 765-0815
> **E-mail:** support@ns.bws.com

PC-Eudora

PC-Eudora is a Windows freeware product based on a package titled Eudora, which originally was developed for the Macintosh. It doesn't include a means for establishing a SLIP connection (such as a phone dialer) nor the software required for implementing the TCP/IP protocol within Windows, WINSOCK.DLL. PC-Eudora is available via ftp from `ftp.qualcomm.com` in the directory `/pceudora/windows`. Figure 12.28 illustrates PC-Eudora's user interface.

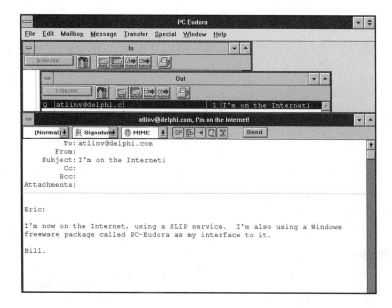

Fig. 12.28
PC-Eudora also uses MDI to allow the user to open several windows at once within the application—in this case, incoming mail, outgoing mail, and message composition.

For information on PC-Eudora, contact

> Qualcomm, Incorporated
> 10555 Sorrento Valley Road
> San Diego, CA 92121
> **E-mail:** pc-eudora-info@qualcomm.com

III

Tools and Technology

Note

Qualcomm is an RF (Radio Frequency) products manufacturer, and is not in the business of developing Internet software. Please respect this fact by deferring contact with the company except by e-mail.

QVTNet for Windows

QVTNet is a shareware TCP/IP networking product that can support SLIP connections. QVTNet provides e-mail, ftp, and telnet capabilities. QVTNet doesn't currently support the Windows sockets interface, WINSOCK.DLL. Instead, packet drivers must be loaded as terminate-and-stay-resident (TSR) drivers before starting Windows. The software is available via anonymous ftp from `cica.indiana.edu` in directory `/pub/win31/util`.

For information on QVTNET, contact

QPC Software
P.O. Box 226
Penfield, NY 14526

Utilities

In addition to the communications software, having a few utility programs available is also convenient. Because many different types of computers support and use the Internet, it's not surprising that the files can exist in one of several formats. You need a set of tools that allows you to convert between the popular file formats found on the Internet and a DOS/Windows compatible format.

The utilities mentioned in this section are available from most Internet hosts that archive PC software. All are available from `wuarchive.wustl.edu` via anonymous ftp, from the directories and file names given in the following sections. Table 12.3 lists the major file compression and encoding techniques used on files that circulate on the Internet.

Note

Keep in mind that `wuarchive.wustl.edu` is an extremely popular host. You may want to check around the archives of your other frequently visited hosts first.

Table 12.3 File Extensions and Their Associated Utilities	
File Extension	**Compression/Archival Type**
HQX	BinHex
SIT	Stuffit
tar	tar (Tape ARchiver)
Z	compress
ZIP	PKZIP

BinHex

BinHex is a binary file encoding method used primarily by the Apple Macintosh platform. A BinHex file is coded in a manner that uses only ASCII characters. In this way, it is an alternative method to using uuencode on a binary file before transferring it through e-mail. By convention, files that have been processed by binhex bear the HQX extension.

Several programs are available from Internet hosts to perform BinHex decompression. One such program is `xbin.exe`, which is archived as `xbin23.zip` in directory `/systems/ibmpc/msdos/mac`.

> **Note**
>
> `xbin.exe` can perform only the decoding operation on a BinHex file.

The compress Utility

`compress` is a UNIX file compression utility. By convention, files that have been processed by `compress` bear the Z extension. An MS-DOS version of compress can perform compression of DOS files into .Z files and decompression of .Z files. One DOS implementation of compress, `com430d.zip`, is located in directory `/systems/ibmpc/msdos/compress`, as are other implementations.

III

Tools and Technology

> **Note**
>
> Remember that the UNIX operating system uses case-sensitive file names; as a result, *file.Z* isn't the same as *file.z*.

PKZIP

PKZIP is the *de facto* compression standard and archival software used in the DOS and Windows computing environments. By convention, files that have been processed by PKZIP bear the ZIP extension. PKZIP is available from many on-line sources, including most Internet hosts that carry PC-compatible software.

To unzip a file, use the following command-line syntax:

```
PKUNZIP filename
```

If you just want a list of the files within the .ZIP file, simply add the -v option:

```
PKUNZIP -v filename
```

For information on other options, simply invoke PKUNZIP without any parameters or file names.

The tar Utility

Tip

tar and compress often are used together to create a compressed archive file, with either a .tar.Z or .taz extension.

tar is a Tape ARchiver utility developed for UNIX systems. As its name implies, tar originally was designed to archive data for backup onto magnetic tape. By convention, files that have been archived using tar bear the .tar extension. Files that have been archived and then compressed bear the tar.Z extension. A number of DOS-based tar programs are available in `tar4dos.zip` in directory `/systems/ibmpc/msdos/filutl`.

uuencode and uudecode

As you read in Chapter 7, "Using E-Mail," you can send binary files through e-mail, provided that you have properly encoded the files. If a file is longer than 64K bytes, it also must be separated into segments less than 64K. The uuencode utility provides a means for compressing files, converting those files into an ASCII representation, and subdividing the file into 64K or smaller segments. The uudecode process, intuitively, reverses these operations to reconstruct the original file on the recipient's machine.

One of several MS-DOS implementations of the uuencode algorithm is contained in `uuexe521.zip`, which is located in the `/systems/ibmpc/msdos/decode` directory. This file contains `uuencode.exe` and `uudecode.exe`. These programs perform the necessary file translations, including subdividing a long file into 64K segments and reassembling a segmented file.

Stuffit

Stuffit is an Apple Macintosh archival and compression utility. By convention, files that have been archived using Stuffit bear the SIT extension.

One of the better implementations of a Stuffit de-archiving program for DOS machines is contained within `unsiti.exe`, a self-extracting archival program that when run creates `unstuff.exe` and its support files on your disk. `unsiti.exe` is archived in the directory `/systems/ibmpc/msdos/mac`.

> **Note**
>
> `unstuff.exe` can perform only the decoding operation on a Stuffit file.

III

Tools and Technology

Other Compression Formats

You may encounter on various hosts a number of older or less popular file compression formats for the PC; the .ARJ, .ARC, .LZH, and .ZOO formats are among the most likely. For programs that can help you decompress these formats, check the contents of directories `/systems/ibmpc/msdos/util`, `/systems/ibmpc/msdos/filutl`, `/systems/ibmpc/msdos/archivrs`, and `/systems/ibmpc/msdos/zoo`.

Summary

Now that you've had the opportunity to review some of the software available to support your Internet connection, as well as the options for service in Chapter 10, "Determining the Level of Internet Service You Need," you should know enough to meet the challenge of configuring your Internet connection. The next chapter details how to use a number of the software tools that exist on the Internet to help you tackle another challenge: finding what you want among all the information that is out there.

Chapter 13

Aids to Navigating the Internet

The Internet is vast—it literally spans the globe. Finding useful resources easily available to you can be difficult because of the sheer number of hosts allowing some form of public access. Furthermore, there is certainly no universal body ensuring uniformity in file and directory naming schemes, or forcing sites to maintain thorough and up-to-date indexes to their public archives and databases. Even the file names of the RFCs, one of the most fundamental series of on-line documents, can vary from site to site. RFC 1206, for example, may be stored in file `rfc1206.txt` on one system and in file `1206.txt` on another.

Fortunately, several facilities designed to help ease navigation of the Internet are readily available to the general Internet community. This chapter describes the three most commonly used Internet navigators: *archie*, *WAIS*, and *Gopher*.

The first Internet navigator, archie, maintains a database of all the publicly accessible files on many sites that accept anonymous ftp users. You can use archie to search for files that have certain substrings in their names. archie also has a smaller keyword database on some files, which allows for searches to be performed on specific topics.

WAIS (Wide Area Information Server) facilitates searches of indexed databases. By using WAIS, you can request files that contain one or more keywords. WAIS also gives a score to each document it finds in performing your search. This score is an estimate WAIS makes of how pertinent it thinks a document is for the indicated search request.

Gopher integrates many functions provided by ftp, archie, WAIS, and telnet. It is extremely easy to use and greatly reduces the effort of examining directories and files on remote computers and viewing or downloading them to your own computer.

Other navigators are also available, and new ones are appearing relatively frequently. The three described in this chapter require only a minimal interactive Internet connection. A shell account accessed through an ordinary telephone line will work just fine. These navigational aids are also widespread and relatively mature, at least by Internet standards.

Using archie

The *archie* system maintains a database with the names of all publicly accessible files on hundreds of Internet sites accessible through anonymous ftp. The database is updated monthly and can be queried by any of the numerous archie servers located throughout the world. archie is very easy to use; you can make searches interactively or through electronic mail.

Suppose that someone gives you, or tells you about, a file originally obtained through the Internet by using anonymous ftp. You know the file name but, unfortunately, not the name of the site from which it was retrieved. You want to see whether an updated version of the file is available and explore the directories on the remote host for similar files of interest to you. In this case, chances are good that archie can help you find the particular host that interests you.

Of course, you always can try to search for files you want by guessing parts of their file names. You may assume, for example, that a graphics file containing an image of the planet Mars would have the string mars in its file name. You also can use archie to search for files using keywords through the whatis command. Unfortunately, only a small percentage of files in the archie database have keywords associated with them.

Using archie through telnet

If you can use telnet, you can access archie by connecting with one of the sites listed in table 13.1. All archie sites contain exactly the same database, and all receive database updates at the same time. Choose the closest host to you (in the geographic sense) to try to minimize unnecessary network traffic. Although you never know the precise network route between you and the archie site, assuming, for example, that someone in the eastern United States should use one of the U.S. servers rather than the Australian server is reasonable.

Table 13.1 telnet Connection Sites

Service Area	Host Name	Address
ANS server, N.Y.	archie.ans.net	147.225.1.10
AT&T server, N.Y.	archie.internic.net	198.49.45.10
Rutgers University server	archie.rutgers.edu	128.6.18.15
SURAnet server Md.	archie.sura.net	128.167.254.195
SURAnet alt. Md.	archie.sura.net(1526)	128.167.254.195
University of Nebraska, Lincoln server	archie.unl.edu	129.93.1.14
Australian server	archie.au	139.130.4.6

(continues)

III

Tools and Technology

Table 13.1 Continued		
Service Area	**Host Name**	**Address**
Austrian servers	`archie.edvz.uni-linz.ac.at`	40.78.3.8
	`archie.univie.ac.at`	131.130.1.23
Canadian server	`archie.uqam.ca`	132.208.250.10
Finnish server	`archie.funet.fi`	128.214.6.102
German server	`archie.th-darmstadt.de`	130.83.22.60
Israeli server	`archie.ac.il`	132.65.20.254
Italian server	`archie.unipi.it`	131.114.21.10
Japanese servers	`archie.kuis.kyoto-u.ac.jp`	130.54.20.1
	`archie.wide.ad.jp`	133.4.3.6
Korean servers	`archie.kr`	128.134.1.1
	`archie.sogang.ac.kr`	163.239.1.11
New Zealand server	`archie.nz`	130.195.9.4
Spanish server	`archie.rediris.es`	130.206.1.2
Swedish server	`archie.luth.se`	130.240.18.4
Swiss server	`archie.switch.ch`	130.59.1.40
Taiwanese server	`archie.ncu.edu.tw`	140.115.19.24
United Kingdom server	`archie.doc.ic.ac.uk`	146.169.11.3

To begin a session with archie, telnet to one of the archie sites and login as `archie`. No password is necessary. A prompt appears, and you now can enter archie commands. To end the archie session, enter `quit`.

A Sample archie Session

The following example is taken from an actual archie session. Some of the text generated by the remote computer was removed to enhance readability. An ellipsis (...) indicates long passages of omitted text. For clarity, text the user types is in **bold** typeface; all other text is generated by the remote or local computer.

This example is representative of many archie sessions where the goal is to search remote hosts for file names containing specific substrings. The session is analyzed step by step, and the specific actions of the commands are explained. A more detailed explanation of individual archie commands follows in a later section.

First, select one of the archie sites listed in table 13.1 and establish a telnet connection to it. Login as `archie` (no password is requested), as follows:

```
atlinv.com> telnet archie.sura.net
Trying 128.167.254.195 ...
Connected to yog-sothoth.sura.net.
Escape character is '^]'.

SunOS UNIX (yog-sothoth.sura.net)
login: archie
Last login: Wed Oct 27 21:35:39 from vega.selu.edu
SunOS Release 4.1.3 (NYARLATHOTEP) #3: Thu Apr 22 15:26:21 EDT 1993
              Welcome to the ARCHIE server at SURAnet
Please report any problems to archie-admin@sura.net
        .
        .
        .
archie>
```

Now you can search the file database by entering archie commands. Assume that you want to see what files, if any, are available through anonymous ftp that pertain to scuba diving. You guess that searching for file names containing the string `scuba` would be a good place to start.

archie can perform several types of file-name searches. You specify the type of search you want by setting the *search* variable. First, you should display the current value of this variable, because its default value may differ from system to system. To display values of variables, use the `show` command and modify them through the `set` command.

III

Tools and Technology

```
archie> show search
# 'search' (type string) has the value 'regex'.
archie> set search sub
```

The value of *search* was originally set to regex, which means
that search strings will be treated as UNIX regular expressions.
The value was changed to sub, indicating that all files names
containing the specified substring will be considered matches.
sub also specifies that case-insensitive comparisons are to be
used.

The prog command actually starts the search. As the search is
performed, archie reports its progress by indicating the number
of matches found and the percentage of the database searched
so far. The line containing this information is overwritten each
time the progress report is updated. Thus, in this example,
after searching the entire database, 64 matches were found.
The matching file names are then displayed.

```
archie> prog scuba
# matches / % database searched:    64 /100%
Host ames.arc.nasa.gov    (128.102.18.3)
Last updated 03:26  4 Oct 1993

     Location: /pub
        DIRECTORY rwxr-xr-x    5120  Aug 23 05:37     SCUBA
     Location: /pub/SCUBA
        FILE        rw-r--r--   1388  Sep 21  1992     scuba_joke.txt
        FILE        rw-r--r--  26037  Aug  3  1992     scubamag.txt

Host cs.dal.ca    (129.173.4.5)
Last updated 03:46 24 Oct 1993

     Location: /comp.archives
        DIRECTORY rwxrwxr-x     512  May 28  1992     rec.scuba
        .
        .
        .
```

As you can see, both directories and individual files match the
string scuba. archie has now told you everything it knows about
files containing scuba in their names; it's up to you to examine
or retrieve the files you want by using ftp.

Sometimes determining a file's contents from its name is fairly easy. The file `scuba_joke.txt`, for example, contains a joke with a scuba theme, and `scubamag.txt` has brief descriptions of scuba magazines. You can't really tell much about the `scuba` directory on `ames.arc.nasa.gov` from the preceding report generated by archie. If you connect to this host via anonymous ftp, however, you will see that this directory is an archive for reports on scuba equipment and dive sites.

Types of File-Name Searches

As noted in the preceding sample session, the value of the `search` variable establishes the criterion used to determine whether a file name matches the string you specified in your `prog` command. archie supports four types of file-name matching, as listed in table 13.2.

Table 13.2 archie Search Types	
Type	**Description**
exact	The string must match a file name exactly.
sub	If the search string appears as a substring in a file name, it's considered a match. The case isn't considered in this type of match. The search string scuba, for example, matches file names `scuba_joke.txt`, `Best_Scuba.zip`, and `SCUBA_4.gif`. This search type is the most frequently used.
subcase	This search type is the same as sub, except the matching is case-sensitive. Thus, the search string scuba matches the file name `scuba_joke.txt` but doesn't match `Best_Scuba.zip` or `SCUBA_4.gif`.
regex	In this case, the search string is treated as a UNIX regular expression. The use of regular expressions allows you to specify complex rules for file name matching, although it isn't for the faint-hearted. Detailing how to specify regular expressions is beyond the scope of this book, but information is available in the UNIX manual pages for archie and ed (the basic UNIX line editor).

III

Tools and Technology

To find out the current value of the *search* variable, enter the archie show command as follows:

```
archie> show search
```

You can change the *search* variable by using the archie set command:

```
archie> set search search_type
```

where *search_type* is one of the four types listed in table 13.2.

Searches Based on Keywords

In the example in the "A Sample archie Session" section, a guess was made for likely file names containing information about scuba diving. Although the guess was fruitful in this particular example, no guarantee exists, of course, that archie will report file names of genuine interest. For example, the search

```
archie> prog diving
```

finds a few of the scuba diving files, but most of the files found by archie pertain to skydiving.

archie has a means to search for files based on keywords. A separate keyword database called the Software Description Database (SDD) is available. To perform a keyword search, use the whatis archie command. Suppose that you want to find utilities for processing TIFF graphics files available through the network. The command

```
archie> whatis tiff

tif2ps        convert TIFF to PostScript
tif2rast      Source Code for TIFF->SunRaster
tif2rast-p2   Source Code for TIFF->SunRaster
tiff2rast     Convert TIFF files to Sun raster files
tifftopgm     Convert a TIFF file into a portable graymap
xtiff         TIFF previewer (X11)
```

returns a list of files that have the keyword TIFF associated with them. In contrast, the command `prog tiff` returns approximately a thousand items.

Unfortunately, only a small fraction of files in the archie database have keyword entries. The search **whatis scuba**, for example, finds no files. Also, the database used by the whatis command may not be as accurate as the database used by the prog command. This situation can happen when someone makes an entry in the SDD, but later deletes the file without updating the database. Because the database used by prog is regenerated monthly, the database is updated relatively quickly. The SDD, however, probably will be corrected only when someone reports the problem to McGill University at archie-admin@archie.mcgill.edu.

Summary of archie Commands

This section partitions the archie commands into groups of commands related by the functions they perform. In the descriptions in the following sections, the full command syntax is given. Anything you enter literally (such as the command name) is represented in computer-like typeface, such as set. Command arguments that you must supply are *italicized*. Optional arguments are inside [brackets]. For example, the syntax

```
set variable [value]
```

indicates that you type in the word set, followed by the name of the *variable* you want to modify, followed (optionally) by the *value* to which you want this variable set.

Note

Do not actually type the brackets when you enter an optional argument on your archie command line.

III

Tools and Technology

Getting Help on archie Commands

Command: `help`

Syntax: `help [`*`command`*`]`

If `help` is entered without a valid archie command, a brief listing of all the available archie commands, such as the following, appears on-screen:

```
archie> help

Help gives you information about various topics, including
all the commands that are available and how to use them.
Telling archie about your terminal type and size (via the
"term" variable) and to use the pager (via the "pager"
variable) is not necessary to use help, but provides a
somewhat nicer interface.

 Currently, the available help topics are:

      about   - a blurb about archie
      bugs    - known bugs and undesirable features
      email   - how to contact the archie email interface
      help    - this message
      list    - list the sites in the archie database
      mail    - mail output to a user
      prog    - search the database for a file
      quit    - exit archie
      set     - set a variable
Press return for more:
      show    - display the value of a variable
      site    - list the files at an archive site
      unset   - unset a variable
      whatis  - search for keyword in the software description
                database

 For information on one of these topics type:

   help <topic>

 A '?' at the help prompt will list the available sub-topics.


Help topics available:
         about   bugs    bye      email
         list    mail    nopager pager
         prog    regex   set      show
         site    term    unset    whatis

Help topic?
```

If a valid archie command follows `help`, a brief description of that command is given. For instance, the following example shows the informational message available for the `show` command:

```
archie> help show

'show' is used to display the value of a particular
variable, or all variables. Its usage is:

show <variable-name>

to display the value of a particular variable, or

show

to display the value of all variables.

Example:

show maxhits
```

Searching the archie Databases
Commands: `prog`

                          `whatis`

These commands cause a search to take place. The `prog` command searches the file name database; `whatis` performs a keyword search.

Search for Matching File Names
Syntax: `prog` *search_string*

The `prog` command finds all file names in the archie database that match the string *search_string*. You can specify the matching criterion you want by setting the *search* variable (see the earlier section "Types of File Name Searches" or the later section "Set the Value of an archie Variable" for additional information).

Search for Files Using Keywords
Syntax: whatis *search_string*

archie searches the Software Description Database (SDD) for files with keywords containing the substring *search_string*. The search is case-insensitive. Although only a small percentage of files in the archie database have keywords associated with them, this type of search still can be very useful, especially for commonly desired information.

Displaying and Changing archie Variables
Commands: show

                set

                unset

archie maintains a number of variables used to specify the matching criterion and control reporting of the matching file names. Three types of variables are available: *Boolean, numeric,* and *string.* You can display the value of any type of variable with the show command. You can change numeric and string variables by using the set command. Change Boolean variables to TRUE with the set command, and to FALSE with the unset command. For example, the commands

```
archie> set pager
archie> unset status
```

cause the *pager* variable to be TRUE and the *status* variable to be FALSE.

Summary of archie Variables
Table 13.3 describes the more important archie variables. The default values assigned to them when you begin an archie session can vary from system to system. To find out the current values of all archie variables, use the show command.

Table 13.3 An Overview of archie Variables

Variable	Description
pager	This Boolean variable specifies that all screen output should be formatted through the UNIX `less` filter. You can examine the UNIX man page for `less` to obtain additional information, but basically, output will appear a screen at a time. To go to the next screen, press the space bar (don't follow this with a carriage return). To display the next line, press the carriage return key. Entering **q** (again, without pressing the carriage return) will delete all remaining screen output and return you to the archie command mode.
status	archie can display a line reporting its progress as it performs a database search. This line tells you the number of matches found so far and the percentage of the database that already has been searched. Setting the *status* Boolean variable causes this line to appear when a search is in progress. Unsetting it means that no progress information displays as the search is being conducted. You probably should set this variable so that you will know how far along archie is toward completing searches you request.
maxhits	This numeric variable specifies the maximum number of matches archie should report. A search is terminated after *maxhits* matches have been found.
search	This string variable establishes the criterion used to determine whether a search string matches a file name. Four legal values for *search* are available: exact, sub, subcase, and `regex`. The earlier section "Types of File Name Searches" explains these values in detail.
sortby	The output from the `prog` command can be sorted before it appears on-screen. This string variable indicates the sorting order you want to use. Use the `help set sortby` command for a complete description of types of sorting available.
term	If you are displaying your output with the *pager* variable set, you need to check that archie knows certain information about your terminal (or terminal emulator, for most of us). The *term* string variable stores this information for use by the *pager*, if selected. The syntax of the set `term` command is `set term terminal_type [num_rows [num_columns]]`

(continues)

III

Tools and Technology

Table 13.3 Continued	
Variable	**Description**
	The integers *num_rows* and *num_columns* specify how many rows and columns, respectively, your screen displays. The string *terminal_type* indicates the type of terminal emulation you are using and can be any of the typical terminal type abbreviations used by UNIX.
mailto	This string variable specifies the e-mail address to be used for archie `mail` commands that don't explicitly specify an e-mail address.

Show the Value of an archie Variable
Syntax: show [*variable*]

The show command displays the current value of the indicated variable. If no variable is specified, the values of all variables are shown.

Set the Value of an archie Variable
Syntax: set *variable* [*value*]

The set command changes the value of the indicated variable. You must enter a value if *variable* is of numeric or string type. If this variable is Boolean, the set command will cause it to be TRUE.

Set a Boolean Variable to FALSE
Syntax: unset *variable*

Using the unset command causes the indicated Boolean variable to be set to FALSE.

Obtain a List of the Sites Included in the archie Database

Command: `list`

Syntax: `list [search_string]`

If no search string is given, this command returns a list of all
the sites represented in the current archie database. The site
name and the last date that updated information from this
site was included in the database are displayed. If you include
`search_string` in the command line, the string is interpreted as
a UNIX regular expression, and only site names matching this
pattern will be listed.

List the Contents of a Specific ftp Site

Commands: `site`

Syntax: `site [host_name]`

The `site` command returns a listing of all files and directories
on the indicated host that anonymous ftp users can see.

Mail the Output of the Last Search

Command: `mail`

Syntax: `mail [e-mail_address]`

This command causes the output of the last search to be sent
to the indicated destination via e-mail. If no address is specified
on the command line, the value of the `mailto` variable is used as
the address. (Table 13.3 describes the `mailto` variable.)

Using archie Through Electronic Mail

You also can access archie through e-mail. The command set
isn't as rich as that allowed for interactive access, however, and
variables aren't supported. Furthermore, `prog` can perform only
`regex`-type searches—although this search type is the most
general type archie supports.

Sometimes, you may want to perform archie searches through e-mail even if you can use telnet. For example, the archie servers nearest to you may be too busy to permit you to login. You can then submit your archie request through e-mail. Alternatively, you may not want to stay on-line (possibly accumulating connect-time charges) while archie processes your request, so you submit it via e-mail.

If you decide to use archie through e-mail, the first thing you should do is obtain the latest instructions for this mode of operation. To do this, send a message to your favorite archie server (the address is archie@server_name) with the single word **help** in the Subject: field or the body of the message. This message will give you details about the commands the archie e-mail interface will process.

> **Note**
>
> If your message contains a help command anywhere in it, everything else in your message will be ignored.

When accessing archie via e-mail, each line of your e-mail message will contain an archie command. Note that the Subject: line is interpreted as your first archie command line; you can leave it blank or enter a valid command.

> **Note**
>
> An invalid archie command in your message causes the archie e-mail interface help message to be sent to you.

Using an archie Client

You also can conduct file-name searches by using a client/server form of archie. If the archie client is installed on your local computer, you can perform `prog`-type searches by entering command lines of the form

```
atlinv.com> archie [-flags] search_string
```

The *flags* can specify such things as which matching criterion to use in the search and the name of the archie server that you want to actually perform the search.

Using a client can be the easiest way to run archie. Because you enter command lines on your local computer, you can develop scripts, macros, and even graphical user interfaces to automate much of the search specification. archie sites prefer that you access archie from a client because it reduces the number of simultaneous interactive logins they must accept.

For more information, see whether an archie client is installed on your local host. If so, examine its documentation and try using it instead of connecting to an archie site with telnet.

Using Gopher To Access Internet Resources

The Internet *Gopher* is one of the most popular utilities available on the Internet, and for good reason. Unlike many other facilities such as archie and ftp, even the most primitive version of Gopher is menu-based. In other words, you can use the arrow keys on your keyboard to specify your input, rather than always type command lines. Gopher can even retrieve files for you to view or download directly to your computer.

Versions with graphical user interfaces are available for some computers and generally follow the same user interface style as other software on the client machine. Thus, an X Windows Gopher client would use the mouse to specify choices from a dialog box, and a Macintosh client would use hypertext stacks.

III

Tools and Technology

The simplest, most widely available type of Gopher client uses a menu system based on a terminal emulator and lets you select your choices through the arrow keys and single keystrokes. This version is used in the Gopher examples and descriptions in this chapter.

All information Gopher displays is partitioned into screen-sized pieces. You easily can examine the contents of a file by looking at one screen at a time. Single-keystroke commands cause Gopher to advance to the next screen, go back to the previous screen, search for a text string you specify, or go back to the previous menu.

That your local host will have a Gopher client installed on it is very probable. If so, all you need to do is execute the Gopher program to begin a Gopher session. If your local host doesn't have a Gopher client, try using one of these publicly accessible Gopher clients: ux1.cso.uiuc.edu or consultant.micro.umn.edu. Enter the user name **gopher**; no password will be requested. Gopher will begin automatically when accessed in this manner.

A Sample Session with Gopher

The goals of this sample session are the same as that of the sample ftp session in Chapter 8, "Using ftp and telnet." In the sample session, Gopher connects to an anonymous ftp site (in this case, InterNIC) and retrieves several Internet Request For Comments (RFC) documents. First, a quick search is made for a master index to the RFCs, which is found and retrieved. Then, files containing RFC 1206 ("Answers to Commonly asked 'New Internet User' Questions") and RFC 1207 ("Answers to Commonly asked 'Experienced Internet User' Questions") are accessed.

From the sample session, you should be able to tell how much easier you can examine and retrieve these files with Gopher than with ftp. The menus do a good job of leading you in the right direction and greatly reduce the tedium of exploring remote sites.

This session is analyzed step by step, and the specific actions of the keyboard entries are explained. As you may expect, learning the basics of a menu-based or graphical user interface-based system is easier if you try it rather than read about it. Try Gopher for yourself and discover how much more quickly and effectively you can explore the Internet and use many of its resources. The exact look of the menus produced by your own Gopher client may vary from the ones in this section but should be fairly similar in nature.

To use Gopher, simply start the local gopher program:

```
atlinv.com> gopher
```

This causes Gopher to display its main menu:

```
              Internet Gopher Information Client 2.0 p18

              Root gopher server: gopher2.tc.umn.edu


  -->   1.  Information About Gopher/
        2.  Computer Information/
        3.  Discussion Groups/
        4.  Fun & Games/
        5.  Internet file server (ftp) sites/
        6.  Libraries/
        7.  News/
        8.  Other Gopher and Information Servers/
        9.  Phone Books/
        10. Search Gopher Titles at the University of Minnesota <?>
        11. Search lots of places at the University of Minnesota <?>
        12. University of Minnesota Campus Information/



Press ? for Help, q to Quit, u to go up a menu          Page: 1/1
```

The final line on-screen tells the user that pressing q will terminate Gopher, ? will display a help message, and u will return to the parent menu of the current one (because Gopher is now at the top-level menu, the u command has no effect at this particular time). These commands are available in every Gopher menu.

III

Tools and Technology

> **Note**
>
> These are single-keystroke commands; you don't enter a carriage return after pressing one of these keys.

The help message displayed by the ? command gives a brief description of many additional Gopher commands. You can use these additional commands, for example, to step through a displayed file page by page, download a file, and search for the occurrence of a text string.

To select the fifth menu entry, Internet file server (ftp) sites, press the down-arrow key four times (so that the symbol --> points at this entry) and then press Enter. The next menu then allows you to select, among other things, the specific ftp site with which you want to connect. Because InterNIC is an extremely popular host for anonymous ftp users, it even has its own entry in the menu. Move the arrow to item 2, InterNIC: Internet Network Information Center, and then press Enter to select this choice:

```
              Internet Gopher Information Client 2.0 p18

                    Internet file server (ftp) sit

      1.   About FTP Searches.
 -->  2.   InterNIC: Internet Network Information Center/
      3.   Popular FTP Sites via Gopher/
      4.   Query a specific ftp host <?>
      5.   Search FTP sites (Archie)/
      6.   UnStuffIt.hqx <HQX>
```

To search through the file archives on InterNIC, select entry 4, InterNIC Directory and Database Services, as shown in the following menu. This category contains Internet documentation and much other useful information.

```
            Internet Gopher Information Client 2.0 p18

          InterNIC: Internet Network Information Center

     1.  Information about the InterNIC/
     2.  InterNIC Information Services (General Atomics)/
     3.  InterNIC Registration Services (NSI)/
  -->  4.  InterNIC Directory and Database Services (AT&T)/

  Press ? for Help, q to Quit, u to go up a menu      Page: 1/1
```

The next menu even indicates which entry should be chosen for RFCs. Select entry 6, `Internet Documentation (RFC's, FYI's, etc.)`.

```
            Internet Gopher Information Client 2.0 p18

         InterNIC Directory and Database Services (AT&T)

     1.  About InterNIC Directory and Database Services/
     2.  InterNIC Directory of Directories/
     3.  InterNIC Directory Services ("White Pages")/
     4.  InterNIC Database Services (Public Databases)/
     5.  Additional Internet Resource Information/
  -->  6.  Internet Documentation (RFC's, FYI's, etc.)/
     7.  National Science Foundation Information/
```

As you can see in the following listing, separate entries are included for FYI and STD documentation. Internet Society (ISOC), Internet Engineering Task Force (IETF), and Internet Engineering Steering

Group (IESG) documents also are present. Select the RFC entry from this menu.

```
            Internet Gopher Information Client 2.0
     p18

            Internet Documentation (RFC's, FYI's,
     etc.)

     1.  Current IETF Conference Documents (Houston -
         November 1993)/
     2.  FYI's (For Your Information RFC's)/
     3.  IETF Internet Drafts/
     4.  IETF Meeting Minutes and Information/
     5.  IETF Steering Committee (IESG) Documents/
     6.  Internet Society (ISOC) Documents/
  -->  7.  RFC's (Request For Comments)/
     8.  STD's (Standard RFC's)/
```

III

Tools and Technology

At this point, the menu structure has been traversed far enough so that you are presented with a list of files that you can examine and download. Because one of the goals of this example is to retrieve the RFC index, the arrow is moved to the file `rfc-index.txt`, as shown in the following listing. At this point, you can download the file by pressing D (as explained in the help message produced by the ? command). Instead, you may want to examine the file briefly to verify that it is indeed the one you want. Press Enter to view the file.

> **Note**
>
> The screen management provided by Gopher makes examining large directories much more comfortable than through ftp. Unlike the ftp `get` *filename* - command, Gopher allows you to look at your file one page at a time, search for a particular text string, or even examine the file in reverse order.

```
            Internet Gopher Information Client 2.0 p18

                    RFC's (Request For Comments)

        1.   Keyword Search of the Internet RFC Documents <?>
        2.   rfc-by-author.txt.
        3.   rfc-estrin-requirements2.dvi.
        4.   rfc-estrin-requirements2.ps.
   -->  5.   rfc-index.txt.
        6.   rfc-instructions.nroff.
        7.   rfc-instructions.txt.
        8.   rfc-retrieval.txt.
        9.   rfc10.txt.
        10.  rfc1000.txt.
        11.  rfc1001.txt.
        12.  rfc1002.txt.
        13.  rfc1003.txt.
        14.  rfc1004.txt.
        15.  rfc1005.txt.
        16.  rfc1006.txt.
        17.  rfc1007.txt.
        18.  rfc1008.txt.

    Press ? for Help, q to Quit, u to go up a menu     Page: 1/52
```

The screen now displays the contents of file `rfc-index.txt` (shown in the following listing). This file is relatively large, but note that you didn't have to transfer it to your local system before viewing it, or deal with trying to perform flow control on the output of an ftp get command sent to the screen.

```
rfc-index.txt (248k)
0%
+----------------------------------------------------------------+
                          RFC INDEX
                          ---------

This file contains citations for all RFCs in reverse numeric
order.  RFC citations appear in this format:

####      Author 1, ... Author 5., "Title of RFC",  Issue date.
          (Pages=##) (Format=.txt or .ps)  (FYI ##) (STD ##) (RTR ##)
              (Obsoletes RFC####) (Updates RFC####)

Key to citations:

#### is the RFC number; ## p. is the total number of pages.

The format and byte information follows the page information in
parenthesis.  The format, either ASCII text (TXT) or PostScript (PS)
or both, is noted, followed by an equals sign and the number of bytes
for that version (Post- Script is a registered trademark of Adobe
Systems
+----------------------------------------------------------------+
[PageDown: <SPACE>] [Help: ?] [Exit: u]
```

Pressing D at this point will cause the file to be retrieved. Gopher supports several communications protocols, and you are prompted to choose one, as shown in the next listing.

The file is transferred directly to your local computer, which is very convenient if you are using a shell account. If, for example, you dialed up a service provider such as CRL and retrieved this file using ftp, you first would have to transfer the file from the remote site to your Internet service provider's computer. If it's a very large file, you may have problems with disk quotas your provider has in effect. After the file is on your provider's

III

Tools and Technology

computer, you still need to transfer it to your own computer. Often, you may be stuck with a relatively inefficient transfer protocol such as Kermit, because that may be the only protocol you and your service provider support. With Gopher, however, the transfer to your computer takes place in a single step, and you have several communications protocol options.

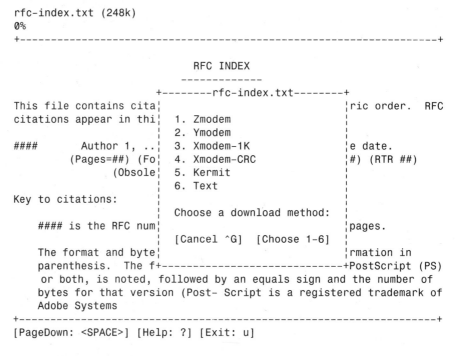

```
rfc-index.txt (248k)
0%
+-------------------------------------------------------------------+

                              RFC INDEX
                              ---------
                        +--------rfc-index.txt--------+
This file contains cita¦                             ¦ric order.  RFC
citations appear in thi¦  1. Zmodem                  ¦
                       ¦  2. Ymodem                  ¦
####        Author 1, ..¦  3. Xmodem-1K              ¦e date.
          (Pages=##) (Fo¦  4. Xmodem-CRC             ¦#) (RTR ##)
                (Obsole¦  5. Kermit                  ¦
                       ¦  6. Text                    ¦
Key to citations:      ¦                             ¦
                       ¦  Choose a download method:  ¦
    #### is the RFC num¦                             ¦pages.
                       ¦  [Cancel ^G]  [Choose 1-6]  ¦
    The format and byte¦                             ¦rmation in
    parenthesis.  The f+-----------------------------+PostScript (PS)
    or both, is noted, followed by an equals sign and the number of
    bytes for that version (Post- Script is a registered trademark of
    Adobe Systems
+-------------------------------------------------------------------+
[PageDown: <SPACE>] [Help: ?] [Exit: u]
```

The RFC index has been successfully loaded. Now you can search for the two specific RFCs (1206 and 1207) in which you are interested. Pressing u while viewing the RFC index file returns you to the RFC directory listing. Pressing / (again, look at the commands discussed in the help message displayed by the ? command) indicates you want to search for the occurrence of a specific text string. Enter **rfc1206** as the search string and press Enter.

```
                 Internet Gopher Information Client 2.0 p18

                        RFC's (Request For Comments)

           1.  Keyword Search of the Internet RFC Documents <?>
           2.  rfc-by-author.txt.
           3.  rfc-estrin-requirements2.dvi.
           4.  rfc-estrin-requirements2.ps.
      -->  5.  rfc-index.txt.
           6.  rfc-instructions.nroff.
      +------------RFC's (Request For Comments)---------------+
      |                                                       |
      | Search directory titles for:                          |
      |                                                       |
      |   rfc1206                                             |
      |                                                       |
      |               [Cancel: ^G] [Erase: ^U] [Accept: Enter]|
      +-------------------------------------------------------+
          15.  rfc1005.txt.
          16.  rfc1006.txt.
          17.  rfc1007.txt.
          18.  rfc1008.txt.

      Press ? for Help, q to Quit, u to go up a menu    Page: 1/52
```

As expected, the two desired files are indeed available in this directory, as shown in the following listing. By pressing D, you can download the file rfc1206.txt. Similarly, you can retrieve rfc1207.txt by moving the arrow down one line and pressing D. If you need no further assistance from Gopher, pressing q will terminate your Gopher session.

III

Tools and Technology

```
                          Internet Gopher Information Client 2.0 p18

                             RFC's (Request For Comments)

             217. rfc1196.txt.
             218. rfc1197.txt.
             219. rfc1198.txt.
             220. rfc1199.txt.
             221. rfc1200.txt.
             222. rfc1201.txt.
             223. rfc1202.txt.
             224. rfc1203.txt.
             225. rfc1204.txt.
             226. rfc1205.txt.
      -->    227. rfc1206.txt.
             228. rfc1207.txt.
             229. rfc1208.txt.
             230. rfc1209.txt.
             231. rfc1210.txt.
             232. rfc1211.txt.
             233. rfc1212.txt.
             234. rfc1213.txt.

     Press ? for Help, q to Quit, u to go up a menu    Receiving file../
```

Performing archie Searches with Gopher

This section shows how you can access archie through Gopher. The same search for files containing the substring scuba is performed as in the earlier archie section.

Using archie through Gopher has two principal advantages:

- The menu or GUI interface reduces the monotony of entering archie commands.

- After archie locates files of interest, you can view or download them with a single keystroke.

Thus, Gopher has—in a sense—unified archie, ftp, and other facilities as well.

As before, start the Gopher program (this example uses the publicly accessible client ux1.cso.uiuc.edu). The main menu (on this particular server) has a listing for Internet File Server (ftp) Sites. Select this entry.

```
              Gopher Courtesy Account Client v1.12S

               Root gopher server: gopher.uiuc.edu

     1.  Welcome to the University of Illinois at Urbana-Champaign Gopher.
     2.  Campus Announcements (last updated 11/01/93)/
     3.  What's New?  (last update: 10/21/93)/
     4.  Information about Gopher/
     5.  Keyword Search of Gopher Menus <?>
     6.  Univ. of Illinois at Urbana-Champaign Campus Information/
     7.  Champaign-Urbana & Regional Information/
     8.  Computer Documentation, Software, and Information/
     9.  Libraries and Reference Information/
    10.  Newspapers, Newsletters, and Weather/
    11.  Other Gopher and Information Servers/
    12.  Phone Books (ph)/
-->13.  Internet File Server (ftp) Sites/
    14.  Federal Register Online (trial subscription)/
```

The next menu you see has an item titled Search of Most FTP
sites (archie). It seems fairly clear that this entry is the one
that you should choose to perform an archie search.

```
              Gopher Courtesy Account Client v1.12S

                Internet File Server (ftp) Sites

      1.  About this directory.
      2.  About Anonymous FTP.
-->   3.  Search of Most FTP sites (archie) <?>
      4.  Keyword Search of Entries in FTP Menus <?>
      5.  FTP.CSO: University of Illinois CCSO's Main FTP Server/
      6.  FTP.NCSA: University of Illinois NCSA's Main FTP Server/
      7.  UXC: University of Illinois/
      8.  Boombox at Minnesota, Home of the Gopher and POPmail/
      9.  Type in the ftp site name for direct access <?>
     10.  Wuarchive.wustl.edu 128.252.135.4   GNU, X.11R3, GIF,IEN, RFCs,/
     11.  Popular FTP Sites via Gopher/
     12.  FTP sites that start with 'a'/
     13.  b/
     14.  c/
     15.  d/
     16.  e/
     17.  f/
     18.  g/
```

When you specify that you want to undertake an archie search,
Gopher asks you for your search string. Enter the string **scuba**,
and then press Enter.

```
                    Gopher Courtesy Account Client v1.12S

                    Internet File Server (ftp) Sites


        1.  About this directory.
        2.  About Anonymous FTP.
 -->    3.  Search of Most FTP sites (archie) <?>
        4.  Keyword Search of Entries in FTP Menus <?>
+----------Search of Most FTP sites (archie)----------+
|                                                      |
| Words to search for  scuba                           |
|                                                      |
|                  [Cancel ^G] [Accept - Enter]        |
|                                                      |
+------------------------------------------------------+
        12. FTP sites that start with 'a'/
        13. b/
        14. c/
        15. d/
        16. e/
        17. f/
        18. g/
```

The same 64 files (shown in the following listing) are found as in the earlier example. You can use Gopher screen management to examine the output easily. Like always, you can page forward or backward through the listing and search for an occurrence of a particular text string. If you want to view one of these files, move the arrow to it and press Enter. Pressing D will download the selected file for you.

```
                    Gopher Courtesy Account Client v1.12S

                    Search of Most FTP sites (archie): scuba


 -->  1.  nctuccca.edu.tw@/USENET/FAQ/rec/scuba//
      2.  athene.uni-paderborn.de@/doc/FAQ/rec.scuba//
      3.  relay.cs.toronto.edu@/pub/usenet/news.answers/scuba-faq.Z <Bin>
      4.  1th.se@/pub/netnews/news.answers/scuba-faq.gz <Bin>
      5.  walton.maths.tcd.ie@/news/news.answers/scuba-faq.Z <Bin>
      6.  athene.uni-paderborn.de@/doc/FAQ/news.answers/scuba-faq.gz <Bin>
      7.  athene.uni-paderborn.de@/doc/FAQ/rec.answers/scuba-faq.gz <Bin>
      8.  athene.uni-paderborn.de@..tions_about_Scuba,_Monthly_Posting.gz <Bin>
      9.  procyon.cis.ksu.edu@/pub/mirrors/news.answers/scuba-faq.Z <Bin>
     10.  bloom-picayune.mit.edu@/pub/usenet-by-group/news.answers/scuba-faq.
     11.  bloom-picayune.mit.edu@/pub/usenet-by-group/rec.answers/scuba-faq.
```

```
12. bloom-picayune.mit.edu@/pub/usenet-by-group/rec.scuba//
13. bloom-picayune.mit.edu@..sked_Questions_about_Scuba,_Monthly_Posting.
14. bloom-picayune.mit.edu@..by-hierarchy/news/answers/scuba-faq <PC Bin>
15. bloom-picayune.mit.edu@..-by-hierarchy/rec/answers/scuba-faq <PC Bin>
16. bloom-picayune.mit.edu@/pub/usenet-by-hierarchy/rec/scuba//
17. bloom-picayune.mit.edu@..stions_about_Scuba,_Monthly_Posting <PC Bin>
18. nctuccca.edu.tw@/USENET/FAQ/news/answers/scuba-faq.gz <Bin>
```

Performing Keyword Database Searches Using WAIS

Basically, *WAIS* (Wide Area Information Server) is a tool to search databases that have been indexed with keywords. WAIS is a relatively new Internet service but is gaining popularity as a navigational aid.

You can access WAIS in three ways:

- You can use a WAIS client on your local host—the preferred method. Unfortunately, WAIS clients aren't nearly as common as Gopher clients.

- You can perform WAIS searches through Gopher.

- The least desirable alternative is to connect to one of the sites offering a character-oriented user interface to the general Internet community. Although certainly usable, this interface is rather awkward and somewhat difficult to use.

WAIS sorts the list of documents it returns to you after a search by using a somewhat peculiar scoring system. The document that it thinks best fits the search request receives a score of 1,000; the other documents receive lower scores. The trouble is that you must be careful when setting up your search, or some less useful—or perhaps even useless—documents may be given high scores. Remember the differences encountered in searching for scuba versus diving in the examples in the section on archie in this chapter. The bottom line is to vary your search request if WAIS can't find genuinely useful documents for you.

III

Tools and Technology

If your local host supports a WAIS client, it most certainly will have a graphical user interface for an environment such as X Windows. Refer to the documentation available through your host for specifics on how to use WAIS in this fashion. If you don't have access to such a client, try using WAIS from Gopher. If you really feel adventurous, you can try the character-based WAIS client, described later.

Using WAIS through Gopher

For many people, Gopher is the best way to use WAIS. Recall that the main menus from the two different servers used in the Gopher examples both had entries named Other Gopher and Information Servers. Selecting this entry causes the following menu to appear:

```
              Internet Gopher Information Client v1.11

                 Other Gopher and Information Servers

        1.   All the Gopher Servers in the World/
        2.   Search titles in Gopherspace using veronica/
        3.   Africa/
        4.   Asia/
        5.   Europe/
        6.   International Organizations/
        7.   Middle East/
        8.   North America/
        9.   Pacific/
        10.  South America/
        11.  Terminal Based Information/
  -->   12.  WAIS Based Information/
```

Select the WAIS Based Information entry to access WAIS. You will see a list of databases from which you may perform keyword searches. Of course, all the usual Gopher display control functions are available when using WAIS through Gopher. You can perform keyword searches on databases and display or download any files that are found.

Accessing WAIS from a Character-Based Client

You can use WAIS through a publicly accessible client. Accessing WAIS in this manner is fairly tedious, however, mostly because the UNIX ex line editor is used to display documents. As an example of the basic steps involved in using this WAIS client, a search will be made for information about anonymous ftp from the Internet Society (ISOC).

One publicly available client is on quake.think.com. telnet to this system and log in as **wais** (no password is requested).

```
telnet quake.think.com
Trying 192.31.181.1 ...
Connected to quake.think.com.
Escape character is '^]'.

SunOS UNIX (quake)
login: wais
Last login: Tue Nov  2 05:35:13 from perch.afit.af.mi
SunOS Release 4.1.1 (QUAKE) #3: Tue Jul 7 11:09:01 PDT
1992
Welcome to swais.
Please type user identifier (optional, i.e user@host): maxrd@atlinv.com
TERM = (vt100)
Starting swais (this may take a little while)...
```

When WAIS actually begins, you will see a screen like the following one. You may select the source you want to use for your searches by using the arrow keys on your keyboard. You probably should examine the list of available commands by pressing the ? key (don't follow this by pressing Enter).

```
SWAIS                           Source Selection
Sources: 499
   #              Server              Source              Cost
001: [            archie.au] aarnet-resource-guide        Free
002: [ndadsb.gsfc.nasa.gov] AAS_jobs                      Free
003: [ndadsb.gsfc.nasa.gov] AAS_meeting                   Free
004: [      munin.ub2.lu.se] academic_email_conf          Free
005: [wraith.cs.uow.edu.au] acronyms                      Free
006: [     archive.orst.edu] aeronautics                  Free
007: [ ftp.cs.colorado.edu] aftp-cs-colorado-edu          Free
008: [nostromo.oes.orst.ed] agricultural-market-news      Free
009: [     archive.orst.edu] alt.drugs                     Free
010: [      wais.oit.unc.edu] alt.gopher                   Free
011: [sun-wais.oit.unc.edu] alt.sys.sun                   Free
012: [      wais.oit.unc.edu] alt.wais                     Free
013: [alfred.ccs.carleton.] amiga-slip                    Free
014: [      munin.ub2.lu.se] amiga_fish_contents           Free
015: [         150.203.76.2] ANU-Aboriginal-EconPolicies $0.00/
                                                          minute
016: [    coombs.anu.edu.au] ANU-Aboriginal-Studies       $0.00/
                                                          minute
017: [         150.203.76.2] ANU-Ancient-DNA-L            $0.00/
                                                          minute
018: [         150.203.76.2] ANU-Ancient-DNA-Studies      $0.00/
                                                          minute
```

To search for a specific source, use the / command. After you
press this key, you are prompted for the search string you want
to use. In this example, because information about the Internet
Society is desired, the search string **isoc** will be entered.

```
SWAIS                           Source Selection
Sources: 499
   #              Server              Source              Cost
253: [    sunsite.unc.edu] internet-mail                  Free
254: [       wais.cnam.fr] internet-rfcs-europe           Free
255: [       nic.merit.edu] internet-standards-merit      Free
256: [    ds.internic.net] internet-standards             Free
257: [       pinus.slu.se] Internet-user-glossary         Free
258: [    munin.ub2.lu.se] internet_info                  Free
259: [    munin.ub2.lu.se] internet_services             Free
260: [    ds.internic.net] internic-directory             Free
261: [    is.internic.net] internic-infosource            Free
262: [    ds.internic.net] internic-internet-drafts       Free
263: [    rs.internic.net] internic-whois                 Free
264: [ucmp1.berkeley.edu] InvertPaleoDatabase             Free
265: [       wais.cic.net] irtf-rd                         Free
266: [    ds.internic.net] isoc                            Free
```

```
267: [ ftp.bio.indiana.edu]   IUBio-arcdocs              Free
268: [ ftp.bio.indiana.edu]   IUBio-fly-address          Free
269: [ ftp.bio.indiana.edu]   IUBio-fly-amero            Free
270: [ ftp.bio.indiana.edu]   IUBio-fly-clones           Free

   <space> selects, w for keywords, arrows move, <return> searches, q quits, or ?
```

Now the line with the ISOC database is in reverse video.
By pressing the w key, you can search this database for keywords. Entering the keywords **anonymous ftp** causes the following output to appear:

```
 SWAIS                             Search Results
 Items: 40
   #  Score  Source           Title                        Lines
 001: [1000] (isoc)  /ftp/isoc/isoc_news/issue1-1/n-1-1-rev1   5475
 002: [1000] (isoc)  /ftp/isoc/isoc_news/issue1-1/n-1-1        5385
 003: [ 492] (isoc)  /ftp/isoc/info/nren.for.all                580
 004: [ 475] (isoc)  /ftp/isoc/isoc_news/issue1-3/n-1-3-015.2    187
 005: [ 458] (isoc)  /ftp/isoc/isoc_news/issue1-4/n-1-4-040.3    129
 006: [ 441] (isoc)  /ftp/isoc/isoc_news/issue1-1/n-1-1-040.3     55
 007: [ 424] (isoc)  /ftp/isoc/internet.bibliography             843
 008: [ 424] (isoc)  /ftp/isoc/internet.bibliography             843
 009: [ 424] (isoc)  /ftp/isoc/isoc_news/issue1-1/n-1-1-040      263
 010: [ 424] (isoc)  /ftp/isoc/isoc_news/issue1-2/n-1-2-040.3     63
 011: [ 424] (isoc)  /ftp/isoc/isoc_news/issue1-2/n-1-2-040      134
 012: [ 424] (isoc)  /ftp/isoc/isoc_news/issue1-4/n-1-4-900      104
 013: [ 424] (isoc)  /ftp/isoc/info/tao                         1067
 014: [ 407] (isoc)  /ftp/isoc/nominations-committee-rpt         183
 015: [ 407] (isoc)  /ftp/isoc/nominations-committee-rpt         183
 016: [ 390] (isoc)  /ftp/isoc/isoc_news/issue1-1/n-1-1-020.0     74
 017: [ 390] (isoc)  /ftp/isoc/isoc_news/issue1-1/n-1-1-040       64
 018: [ 390] (isoc)  /ftp/isoc/isoc_news/issue1-3/n-1-3-040       98
```

Each line in this listing represents an individual document that
may be examined. You can use the arrow keys to choose a specific document (the current choice will be in reverse video).
After you position the cursor at the document you want, you
can view it by pressing Enter. Moving the cursor to /ftp/isoc/
internet.bibliography, for example, and pressing Enter causes
this file to appear (as shown in the following listing). See documentation on the ex editor for information on how to examine
different portions of the selected document.

III

Tools and Technology

```
Network Working Group
J. Quarterman
Request for Comments: 1432
MIDS
                                           March 1993

                  Recent Internet Books
```

Status of this Memo

    This memo provides information for the Internet community.
    It does not specify an Internet standard. Distribution of
    this memo is unlimited.

Abstract

    This article originally appeared in Volume 2 Number 12,
    (December 1992) of Matrix News, the monthly newsletter of
    Matrix Information
:

Summary

Using navigational aids can greatly improve your ability to find Internet resources. Facilities like Gopher make browsing publicly available archives much easier, because you can download files or examine their contents with single-keystroke commands.

The tools described in this section no doubt will be improved as time passes. Other navigators are also available, and some are gaining acceptance by a significant portion of the Internet community. Furthermore, new navigational aids under development may make searching for and retrieving information on the network even easier.

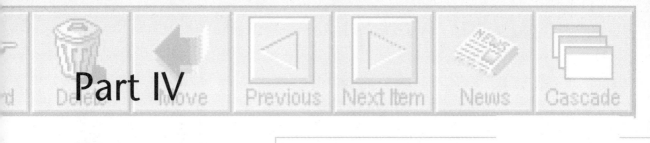

Part IV

Service Providers

PINE 3.07   MAIN MENU   Folder inbox   1 Message

?   HELP   - Get help using Pine

C   COMPOSE   - Compose and send a message

I   MAIL INDEX   - Read mail in current folder

Mail in progress...

----- Mail Composition Editor -----

TO: ftpmail@decwrl.dec.com   Edit   Done   Cancel
CC:
ct: file request via ftpmail server

Note: In Pine 3.0 we are encouraging folks to use the MAIL INDEX to
      mail instead of VIEW MAIL, so it is no longer on the main menu
      in the mail index, it is available as usual as the "Y" command

Help   Quit   Folders   Other

Delete | Move | Previous | Next Item | News | Cascade

coming Mail

NSFNET Packet Traffic

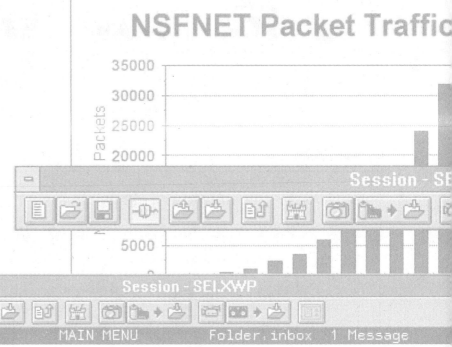

Session - SE

Session - SEI.XWP

PINE 3.07   MAIN MENU   Folder.inbox   1 Message

?   HELP   - Get help using Pine

C   COMPOSE   - Compose and send a message

I   MAIL INDEX   - Read mail in current folder

Call

Mail in progress...

* ----- Mail Composition Editor ----- *

TO: | ftpmail@decwrl.dec.com | | Edit | Done | Cancel |

CC: | |

ject: | file request via ftpmail server |

Note: In Pine 3.0 we are encouraging folks to use the MAIL INDEX to
      mail instead of VIEW MAIL, so it is no longer on the main mer
      in the mail index, it is available as usual as the "Y" commar

 Help   Quit   Folders   Other
Compose   Mail Index   Addresses

Chapter 14

BBS, UUCP, and Other Polled Services

This chapter is the first of four chapters that list contact information for Internet service providers. Each chapter corresponds to a level of service defined in Chapter 10, "Service Levels": bulletin board (BBS) and UUCP services, on-line and terminal services, SLIP/PP, and dedicated connections.

This chapter lists BBS, UUCP, and other non-interactive Internet access providers, organized by state and country. Each listing contains the provider name and phone number. Additional information—including e-mail addresses, system operator or contact name, and a brief list of services—is provided, if available.

BBS-based Internet access is now the fastest growing connectivity option. Its main benefits are that access is generally inexpensive to start up and maintain (sometimes even free), and is sufficient for daily mail checks, limited USENET group downloads, and mail-based ftp. The host BBS system also may put a friendlier face on your access to the Internet, such as a menu-driven or graphical interface.

Due to the growth of this type of service and the fact that many BBS systems rely on word-of-mouth awareness of their existence, this list is not complete. Particularly in major cities, you may have more options for BBS-based service than those given here. Use the list as a place to start, and once connected you likely will begin hearing of other service options to try in your area.

> **Note**
>
> Bulletin board systems tend to be more volatile than the other services, so you should verify the number before calling. Few things are more annoying than getting a hundred modem calls a night to your home voice line. A good practice is to verify that the phone number is answered by a modem by placing a voice call to the number before dialing with your modem.

Organizations Providing BBS, UUCP, and Other Polled Services

The following is a list of organizations providing BBS, UUCP, and other polled services with access to the Internet. This list provides a starting point for locating a provider of these services.

These organizations are listed by geographical area, as indicated by area code. In some cases, the organization may provide services in several diverse geographical locations. The information is organized as follows:

> **Geographical area**
>
> > **Organization name** (often the most common name or alias)
> > > Location
> > > `E-mail address`
> > > Contact name or system operator
> > > Phone number(s)
> > > Services

> **Note**
>
> A question mark appearing in a field means that that information is not available.

Phone numbers designated as voice are known to be voice only (not fax or data) and should never be called by modem. Some of these organizations provide dial-in services and will have data lines available, which you easily can verify with a voice call, as described earlier.

United States, Nationwide

Computer Witchcraft, Inc.

Louisville, KY

help@win.net

800-800-1482 (dialup)

502-589-6800 (voice)

502-589-7300 (fax)

UUCP, USENET, e-mail

Performance Systems, International

Herndon, VA

info@psi.com

703-904-4100 (voice)

703-904-4200 (fax)

UUCP, USENET, e-mail

Alternet

Falls Church, VA

alternet-info@uunet.uu.net

800-488-6384 (voice)

703-204-8000 (voice)

703-204-8001 (fax)

UUCP, SLIP/PPP, dedicated

Alabama

The MATRIX #1

?

matrix.sbs.com

Rocky Rollins

205-323-2016

USENET, Files

Alaska

Computer Dynamics Online Service

?

`compdyn.questor.org`

Al Mellis (`al_mellis`)

604-255-9937

USENET, Files

The Burrow

?

`burrow.cojones.com`

`!uunet!coldbox!burrow`

Bilbo

907-561-7209

USENET, UUCP

The Old Frog's Almanac #1

?

`oneb.almanac.bc.ca`

Ken McVay

604-245-3205

USENET news groups, All

Victoria Free-Net

Victoria, British Columbia, Canada

`freenet.victoria.bc.ca`

?

604-595-2300

Free net

indlink

Vancouver, British Columbia, Canada

?

?

604-576-1214

Internet or USENET

Arizona

coyote

Tucson
?
?
602-293-3276
Internet or USENET

telesys

Mesa
?
?
602-649-9099
Internet or USENET

xroads

Phoenix
?
?
602-941-2005
Internet or USENET

Arkansas

Courts of Chaos

?
chaos.lrk.ar.us
Dave Williams (dave.williams)
501-985-0059
USENET, Tech

The GrapeVine #1

?
grapevine.lrk.ar.us
Jim Wenzel (jim.wenzel)
501-753-8121
USENET, Files

California

Batchelor Pad

?

`batpad.lgb.us`
Mike Batchelor
310-494-1024
Internet News, All

E&S Systems UNIXLand BBS #1

?

`cg57.uucp:202/217`
Steve Froeschke (`steve`)
619-278-8267
IBM, UNIX, USENET

Hip-Hop BBS #1

?

`hip-hop.suvl.ca.us`
David L. Black
408-773-0768
Linux, UNIX, USENET, X Windows

KAIWAN Public Access Internet Systems #1

?

`kaiwan.com`
Luke Hwang
714-539-5726
Internet, USENET

Quake

?

`quake.sylmar.ca.us`
Jeff Skaletsky
818-367-2142
USENET, e-mail, IBM

SAC-UNIX

?

`sactoh0.sac.ca.us`

Eric J. Nihill
916-722-6519
USENET News, Internet Mail

SPACE BBS #1

?

spacebbs.com
Owen Hawkins (owen.hawkins)
415-323-4193
USENET, Files, GIFs

SnS BBS

?

jack.sns.com
J. Steven Harrison
510-623-8652
Internet, All

The Missing Link

?

?

Pete Bowden
805-925-1129
USENET, Mail

The QED BBS

?

qed.cts.com
Tim Capps
310-420-9327
USENET, Files

Woodowl

?

woodowl.UUCP
William
510-294-8591
USENET, Internet

California (continued)

abode

El Monte

?

?

818-287-5115

Internet or USENET

alchemy

Corona

?

?

714-278-0862

Internet or USENET

alphacm

Cypress

?

?

714-821-9671

Internet or USENET

atrium

Pasadena

?

?

818-793-9108

Internet or USENET

barbage

El Sobrante

?

?

510-223-9768

Internet or USENET

bdt

Oakland

?

?
510-530-9682
Internet or USENET

btr

Mountain View
?
?
415-967-9443
Internet or USENET

conexch

Santa Anna
?
?
714-842-5851
Internet or USENET

dhw68k

Anaheim
?
?
714-635-2863
Internet or USENET

gorn

Santa Cruz
?
?
408-458-2289
Internet or USENET

net01

El Osjon
?
?
619-569-4072
Internet or USENET

California (continued)

net12

Del Mar

?

?

619-259-7757

Internet or USENET

quack

Santa Clara

?

?

408-249-9630

Internet or USENET

sectoh0

Sacramento

?

?

916-649-0161

Internet or USENET

stanton

Irvine

?

?

714-894-2248

Internet or USENET

starnet

Los Altos

?

?

415-949-3133

Internet or USENET

stb

Santa Monica

?

?

310-397-3137
Internet or USENET

szebra
Sunnyvale
?
?
408-739-1520
Internet or USENET

uuwest
Sunnyvale
?
?
408-245-7726
Internet or USENET

wet
San Francisco
?
?
415-826-0397
Internet or USENET

zorch
San Jose
?
?
408-254-0246
Internet or USENET

Colorado

Denver Free-Net
Denver
`freenet.hsc.colorado.edu`
?
303-270-4865
Free net

Colorado (continued)

nyx

Denver
?
?
303-871-4824
Internet or USENET

Connecticut

admiral

Greenwich
?
?
203-661-1279
Internet or USENET

Florida

Medical Informations Health Network #1

?
`medinfo.jax.fl.us`
Peter Booras (`peter.booras`)
904-246-1481
USENET, Internet, Files

Starlight BBS

Overlord
?
?
305-948-0183
USENET, Files

amaranth

Pensacola
?
?

904-456-2003
Internet or USENET

jwt

Orlando
?
?
407-438-7138
Internet or USENET

vicstoy

Orlando
?
?
407-299-3661
Internet or USENET

Georgia

Ed Hopper's BBS

?
ehbbs.gwinnett.com
Ed Hopper (ed.hopper)
404-446-9462
USENET, All

The Data Dimension

?
datadim.com
Ricky Lacy
404-921-1186
Files, USENET, Internet

The King's Palace BBS

?
kingsp.gwinnett.com
Paul Gamber (paul.gamber)
404-781-8435
USENET, RIME, Files

Illinois

HCS Data Center

?

?

Victoria Kee

309-676-0409

USENET, Internet

The Heartland Free-Net

Peoria

`heartland.bradley.edu`

?

309-674-1100

Free net

chinet

Chicago

?

?

312-283-0559

Internet or USENET

gagme

Chicago

?

?

312-714-8568

Internet or USENET

pallas

Springfield

?

?

217-789-7888

Internet or USENET

IV

Service Providers

point

Chicago
?
?
312-338-0632
Internet or USENET

vpnet

Villa Park
?
?
708-833-8126
Internet or USENET

wa9aek

Lisle
?
?
708-983-5147
Internet or USENET

Indiana

Digital Underground

?
`digund.com`
`digund.uucp:2320/150`
Chris Nalley
812-941-9427
USENET, All

aquila

Evansville
?
?
812-421-8523
Internet or USENET

Indiana (continued)

gator

South Bend

?

?

219-289-0280

Internet or USENET

sir-alan

Bloomington

?

?

812-333-0450

Internet or USENET

Kentucky

disk

Louisville

?

?

502-957-4200

Internet or USENET

unatix

Lexington

?

?

606-263-5106

Internet or USENET

Louisiana

Southern On-line Services

?

sosinc.com

Russell Jackson (russell.jackson)

504-356-0790

Internet, Windows, OS/2, DOS, Files

...#1

`1ablues.UUCP`
Jon Meier and Patrick Delahanty
207-777-3465
IBM, Apple, Mac, USENET Mail

Northern Lights

?

`nlbbs.uucp`
Jack Kilday
207-761-4782
Internet, USENET, Files

Maryland

Grey Hawk #1

?

`ghawk.com`
Walter Ames
410-720-5083
Files, OLGs, Internet, USENET

The NetWork BBS

?

`netbbs.com`
Howie Michalski
410-247-3793
USENET, Windows

The Wright Place

?

`%twplace@wb3ffv.ampr.org ron.wright`
Ron Wright
410-882-4481
Files, USENET, Internet

Maryland (continued)

digex

Greenbelt

?

?

301-220-0462

Internet or USENET

highlite

Laurel

?

?

301-953-7233

Internet or USENET

wb3ffv

Baltimore

?

?

410-625-0817

Internet or USENET

Massachusetts

Channel 1 #1

?

channel1.com

Brian Miller and Tess Heder

617-354-8873

Internet, USENET, All

SCHUNIX #1

?

schunix.uucp

schu

Robert Schultz

508-853-0340

UNIX, IBM, USENET

csys

> Quincy
>
> ?
>
> ?
>
> 617-471-9675
>
> Internet or USENET

genesis

> North Reading
>
> ?
>
> ?
>
> 508-664-0149
>
> Internet or USENET

UNIXland

> Natick
>
> ?
>
> ?
>
> 508-655-3848
>
> Internet or USENET

Michigan

HAL 9000

> ?
>
> hal9k.ann-arbor.mi.us
>
> Victor Volkman (sysop)
>
> 313-663-4173
>
> ASP, Shareware, Internet

The Michigan BBS

> ?
>
> sycom.mi.org
>
> Ronald Kushner
>
> 313-939-6666
>
> Adt, CB, GIF, JPEG, USENET

Michigan (continued)

anubis

Jackson

?

?

517-789-5175

Internet or USENET

lopez

Marquette

?

?

906-228-4399

Internet or USENET

lunapark

East Lansing

?

?

517-487-3356

Internet or USENET

m-net

Ann Arbor

?

?

313-996-4644

Internet or USENET

nucleus

Clarkston

?

?

313-623-6309

Internet or USENET

ybbs

Jeniston

?

?
616-457-1964
Internet or USENET

Minnesota

net51

Minneapolis
?
?
612-473-2295
Internet or USENET

Mississippi

Oasis BBS

?
oamsbbs.com
Geoff Lewis (geoff.lewis)
601-853-2688
Files, Msgs, USENET, Internet

Montana

Big Sky Telegraph

Dillon
192.231.192.1
?
406-683-7680
Free net

New Hampshire

mv

Litchfield
?
?
603-429-1735
Internet or USENET

New Jersey

Dan's Domain

?

?

Dan Speers

201-366-5018

Internet, USENET, Files

Synergy Online Communications #1-#30

?

syncomm.com

Jim Boxmeyer (jim.boxmeyer)

201-331-1797

Files, Internet, USENET, adt, Chat

tronsbox

Belleville

?

?

201-759-8450

Internet or USENET

New Mexico

Land of Enchantment BBS #1

?

loebbs.com

Frank Lerner (sysop)

505-857-0836

Files, Msgs, Internet, USENET

New York

Buffalo Free-Net

Buffalo

freenet.buffalo.edu

?

716-645-6128

Free net

Hardgoods-East

?
hardgood.com
John Fix (john.fix)
914-961-8749
USENET, Doors, Files

anana

Ithaca
?
?
607-273-3233
Internet or USENET

sixhub

upstate
?
?
518-346-8033
Internet or USENET

Invention Factory #1

New York City
factory.com
Michael Sussell
212-274-8110
USENET, Files

dorsaidm

New York City
?
?
212-431-1944
Internet or USENET

magpie

New York City
?
?
212-420-0527
Internet or USENET

New York (continued)

marob

New York City

?

?

212-675-7059

Internet or USENET

North Carolina

rock

Research Triangle Park

?

?

919-248-1177

Internet or USENET

wolves

Durham

?

?

919-499-7111

Internet or USENET

Ohio

Cincinnati Computer Connection #1

?

`cccbbs.uucp`

Bob Emerson

513-752-1055

USENET, adt

Cleveland Freenet

Cleveland

`cleveland.freenet.edu`

Case Western Reserve University

216-368-3888
All, USENET News, Msgs

Lorain County Free-Net
Elyria
`freenet.lorain.oberlin.edu`
?
216-366-9721
Free net

Railnet
?
`railnet.nshore.org`
Rick DeMattia
216-786-0476
Railroad, USENET

The Youngstown Free-Net Youngstown
Youngstown
`yfn.ysu.edu`
216-742-3072
Free net

Tristate Online
Cincinnati
`cbos.uc.edu`
?
513-579-1990
Free net

cinnet
Cincinnati
?
?
513-779-8209
Internet or USENET

Ohio (continued)

ncoast

Cleveland

?

?

216-582-2460

Internet or USENET

Oregon

bucket

Portland

?

?

503-254-0458

Internet or USENET

m2xenix

Portland

?

?

503-297-3211

Internet or USENET

techbook

Portland

?

?

503-644-8135

Internet or USENET

Pennsylvania

Satalink Information Systems

?

`satalink.com:273/203`

Ron Brandt

215-364-3324
USENET, Files

Telerama Public Access Internet
?

telerama.pgh.pa.us
Kristin McQuillin (info)
412-481-5302
Internet, USENET, Files

The Circuit Board
?

%cktbd@ka2qhd.de.com
Jim Decatur (jimd)
717-676-9339
IBM, Pocono Mt., Internet, USENET

cellar
Horsham
?
?
215-654-9184
Internet or USENET

compnect
Harrisburg
?
?
717-657-4997
Internet or USENET

cpumagic
Bellefonte
?
?
814-353-0566
Internet or USENET

Pennsylvania (continued)

eklektik

Pittsburgh

?

?

412-431-8649

Internet or USENET

jabber

Doylestown

?

?

215-348-9727

Internet or USENET

Rhode Island

Terminal Madness #1

?

madness.network23.com

Chris Mathis (chris.mathis)

401-848-9069

USENET, Files

anomaly

Esmond

?

?

401-455-0347

Internet or USENET

South Dakota

oft386

Rapid City

?

?

605-348-2738

Internet or USENET

Tennessee

Amiga Central! BBS

?

amicent.raider.net

Guru Meditation (root)

615-383-9479

Amiga, USENET, Internet

East Tennessee Adult Connection

?

etacbbs.knox.tn.us

Charlie Vance (sysop)

615-690-4716

Adt, Msgs, Internet

aider

Murfreesboro

?

?

615-896-8716

Internet or USENET

edsys

Kingsport

?

?

615-288-3957

Internet or USENET

Texas

Black Box #1

?

?

?

713-480-2685

USENET News, Games

Texas (continued)
Connect America
?

1:382/10

William Degnan

512-459-3351

FIDOnet, USENET, DOS, Windows, OS/2

Data Warp Premium BBS
?

dwarp.sccsi.com

Mike Meyer (mike.meyer)

713-355-6107

Files, USENET

Future Quest Info Services
?

fquest.fidonet.org:19/23

Kevin Basey and Jason Hoogervorst (root)

512-451-0891

Commodore, Internet, USENET, Adt

German Connection
?

?

Dieter Belletz

512-532-4756

IBM, USENET

The Brewer's Witch BBS
?

?

713-272-7350

USENET News, All

The Cutting Edge
Houston

cutting.hou.tx.us

David Bonds (`david.bonds`)
713-466-1525
USENET, All

The Pet Project

?

?

Richard Hasting
512-251-6273
USENET, All

Unka Phaed's UUCP Thingy

?

`unkaphaed.uucp`
Phaedrus
713-481-3763
USENET News, Music, Radio

bigtex

Austin

?

?

512-346-2339
Internet or USENET

neis

Dallas

?

?

214-254-3404
Internet or USENET

nuchat

Houston

?

?

713-668-7176
Internet or USENET

Texas (continued)

sdf

?

`sdf.lonestar.org`

smj & sp & jack & larry

214-436-3281

UNIX, Internet

sugar

Houston

?

?

713-684-5900

Internet or USENET

taronga

Houston

?

?

713-568-0480

Internet or USENET

Utah

bitsko

Salt Lake City

?

?

801-566-6263

Internet or USENET

Virginia

tnc

Fairfax

?

?

703-803-0391

Internet or USENET

wyvern

Norfolk

?

?

804-627-7841

Internet or USENET

Washington

Eskimo North #1

?

eskimo.com

Nanook (nanook)

206-367-3937

Internet, Msgs, 206 BBS List

Halcyon

?

halcyon.com

Ralph Sims

206-382-6245

USENET, UNIX Programming

The 23:00 News

?

halcyon.wa.com

206-292-9048

Internet Mail, news

Northwest Nexus Inc.

?

info@nwnexus.wa.com

?

206-455-3505 (voice)

UUCP, SLIP, PPP, feeds, DNS

Washington (continued)

polari
Seattle
?
?
206-328-4944
Internet or USENET

visual
Spokane
?
?
509-536-4062
Internet or USENET

Washington, D.C.

Foggy Bottom
Washington, D.C.
?
R. Allbritton
202-337-2369
Mac, Internet, USENET

PerManNet
Washington, D.C.
?
M. Prodo
202-296-7778
Internet, Science

West Virginia

Lost Horizons
?
?
Arc Angel
614-487-2599
Apple, IBM, Mac, USENET

luemoon

Reynoldsburg

?

?

614-868-9980

Internet or USENET

Wisconsin

BlackWolf's Den

?

blackwlf.gwinnett.com

blackwlf.atl.ga.us

BlackWolf

414-642-9933

GIFs, USENET, MS-DOS, Windows

adnix

Madison

?

?

608-273-2657

Internet or USENET

edsi

Appleton

?

?

414-734-2499

Internet or USENET

mixcom

Milwaukee

?

?

414-241-5469

Internet or USENET

Australia

Cloud Nine

> ?
>
> cloud.apana.org.au
>
> 3:635/552
>
> Hamish Moffatt (hamish)
>
> 61-3-803-6954
>
> Text, Msgs, USENET

kralizec

> Sydney
>
> ?
>
> ?
>
> 61-2-837-1183
>
> Internet or USENET

Canada (Alberta, British Columbia, and Saskatchewan)

Edmonton Remote Systems #1

> Edmonton
>
> ersys.edmonton.ab.ca
>
> Dave McCrady
>
> 403-454-6093
>
> USENET News, Files

Magic BBS #1

> ?
>
> debug.cuc.ab.ca
>
> Rob and Nikki Franke
>
> 403-569-2882
>
> USENET, Legal Info

Purgatory

> ?
>
> purg.uucp
>
> ?
>
> 403-462-6976
>
> USENET, All

T-8000 Information System

?

t8000.cuc.ab.ca:134/160

Brian Simpson

403-246-4487

IBM, Internet, USENET, UltraSound

Canada (Ontario)

Baudeville BBS #1

?

bville.gts.org:250/304

Ian Evans (ian.evans)

416-283-6059

USENET, Msgs

NETRIX, Inc

?

netrix.on.ca

southport.com

southport.on.ca:250/148

416-512-8558

Networking, Data Communications, Internet

National Capital Free-Net

Ottawa

freenet.carleton.ca

?

613-780-3733

Free net

R-node Public Access UNIX/USENET

?

r-node.gts.org

Marc Fournier

416-249-5366

Internet, USENET News

Canada (Ontario) (continued)

ZOOiD BBS

?

zooid.guild.org
David Mason
416-322-7876
USENET

atour

Ottawa
?
?
613-237-0792
Internet or USENET

icor

Orlean
?
?
613-837-3029
Internet or USENET

telly

Brampton
?
?
416-452-0926
Internet or USENET

tmsoft

Toronto
?
?
416-461-2608
Internet or USENET

IV

Service Providers

Canada (Quebec)

ichlibix

Blainville

?

?

514-435-8896

Internet or USENET

Finland

Field of Inverse Chaos

?

ichaos.nullnet.fi

Juha Laiho

358-0-506-1836

USENET, UNIX, PC

France

gna

Paris

?

?

33-1-40-35-23-49

Internet or USENET

Germany

Infosystems Hamburg

?

?

Mike Loth

49-40-494867

USENET and Internet Mail, UNIX

Germany (continued)

gold

Baldhath

?

?

49-8106-34593

Internet or USENET

isys-hh

Hamburg

?

?

49-40-494867

Internet or USENET

scuzzy

Berlin

?

?

49-30-691-95-20

Internet or USENET

Ireland

Galway On-Line #1

Galway

`online.lol.ie`

Barry Flanagan (`barry.flanagan`)

353-91-27454

Internet, USENET

Italy

xtc

Rimini

?

?

39-541-27858

Internet or USENET

Netherlands

Ster BBS

?

sterbbs.nl #1–#10

Frans Kleijweg (kleijweg)

31-1880-40035

Files, Chat, Adt, Internet, OLGs

New Zealand

Acme BBS #1

?

acme.gen.nz

Craig Harding (postmaster)

64-6-355-1104

USENET, Mail

Actrix Information Exchange #1-#2

?

actrix.gen.nz

Paul Gillingwater and John Vostermanns

64-4-389-5478

USENET, Internet, Files, Msgs

Andrew's Folly #1

?

folly.welly.gen.nz

3:771/150

Andrew McMillan

64-4-233-9126

OS/2, USENET, Internet, Msgs

City Net #1-#7

?

kosmos.wcc.govt.nz

Roger Brockie

64-4-801-3060

USENET, Internet

New Zealand (continued)
Deep Thought

> ?
>
> deepthnk.kiwi.gen.nz
> Nick Warburton
> 64-9-443-7636
> USENET, Mac, IBM, Windows

Equinox Networks #1-#4
> ?
>
> equinox.gen.nz
> Geoff McCaughan and Peter Moore
> 64-3-385-4406
> Files, USENET News

InfoBoard #1
> ?
>
> infoboard.nacjack.gen.nz
> 3:772/140
> Colin Swabey
> 64-9-833-8788
> IBM files, USENET

Pinnacle Club
> ?
>
> pinn.nackjack.gen.nz
> 3:772/115
> Bernadette Mooney
> 64-9-631-5382
> General, USENET, Internet

Sideways
> ?
>
> sideways.welly.gen.nz
> Patrick Cain
> 64-4-569-5695
> Waffle, IBM, adt files, USENET

IV

The Cave III #1-#2

?

cavebbs.welly.gen.nz

The Bear

64-4-564-3000

USENET, IBM, OS/2, Files

The Cave/2

?

cave2.welly.gen.nz

3:771/130

Charlie Lear

64-4-564-2317

OS/2 only, FIDOnet, USENET

The Dawghaus

?

dogbox.acme.gen.nz

Alan Brown (postmaster)

64-6-357-9245

All, USENET

Tornado

?

tornado.welly.gen.nz

Sai

64-4-233-1843

USENET, Files, Commodore, IBM

actrix

Wellington

?

?

64-4-389-5478

Internet or USENET

New Zealand (continued)

cavebbs

Wellington
?
?
64-4-564-2317
Internet or USENET

kcbbs

Auckland
?
?
64-9-817-3725
Internet or USENET

Norway

Thunderball Cave #1

?
`thcave.no`
Jon Orten (`jon.orten`)
47-22-299441
USENET, Internet, Files

Spain

ABAFORUM

?
`abaforum.es`
David Llamas (`david.llamas`)
34-3-5893888
Files, USENET, Internet

Switzerland

Active-Net BBS #1

?

?

Martin Altorfer (`martin.altorfer`)

41-55-261815

Files, Internet, USENET

ixgch

Kaiseraugst

?

?

41-61-8115492

Internet or USENET

United Kingdom

Almac BBS

?

almac.co.uk

Alastair McIntyre (`alastair.mcintyre`)

44-324-665371

USENET, Internet

Connect #1

?

ibmpcug.co.uk

Adrian Hall

44-81-861-5522

IBM, Internet

United Kingdom (continued)

INFOCOM Systems

?

infocom.co.uk

Dave Hunt and Philippe Goujard

44-734-340055

Files, USENET

UKnet

?

uknet.ac.uk

postmaster@uknet.ac.uk

44-227-475497

Dedicated, dialup, UUCP

dircon

London

?

?

44-81-377-2222

Internet or USENET

## Chapter 15

On-Line Services and Terminal Servers

As you read in Chapter 11, "Connections Beyond the Internet," e-mail access to the Internet is provided by many of the established on-line services. To date, only BIX and Delphi have given their subscribers full access to the net by way of ftp, telnet, Gopher, and other utilities.

Most of the providers listed in this chapter provide terminal service, which is also often called a *shell account*. These providers actually create a user account for you on their machine (usually UNIX based), which gives you broad access to the operating system and utility programs rather than limit your activities to those provided in the context of a BBS or on-line service. This provides an opportunity for you to access UNIX as well as Internet services.

Tip
If you are a UNIX novice and plan to use a terminal service, be sure to check out the UNIX quick reference provided in Appendix C.

Organizations Providing On-Line Services and Terminal Servers

Use the following list as a starting point for locating a provider of on-line services and terminal servers with access to the Internet. These organizations are listed by geographical area, as indicated by area code.

In some cases, the organization may provide services in several diverse geographical locations. Although they are listed by their home state, it's worth calling or sending e-mail to find out whether service has been extended to your area. Those known to provide service nationally through a Public Data Network have *(national)* placed next to their names.

The information is organized as follows:

> **Geographical area**
>> **Organization name** (often the most common name or alias)
>>
>>> Full or official name
>>> E-mail contact address for more information
>>> Phone number(s)
>>> Services provided

Phone numbers designated as voice are known to be voice only (not fax or data) and should never be called by modem. Some of these organizations provide dial-in services and will have data lines available, which you easily can verify with a voice call.

On-Line Services

National

bix

Byte Information eXchange
info@bix.com
Mail, ftp, telnet, Gopher

delphi

General Videotext Corporation
walthowe@delphi.com
800-365-4636 (sign-up only)
800-544-4005 (voice)
ftp, telnet, feeds, user groups, wire services, member conferencing

Terminal Servers

California

a2i *(national)*

a2i communications

info@rahul.net

408-293-9010

408-293-9020

Shell, ftp, telnet, feeds

class *(national, member libraries only)*

Cooperative Library Agency for Systems and Services

class@class.org

800-488-4559 (voice)

ftp, telnet, Gopher, WAIS, hytelnet

crl

CR Laboratories Dialup Internet Access

info@crl.com

415-389-UNIX

415-381-2800 (voice)

Shell, ftp, telnet, feeds, SLIP, WAIS, 800 service

cyber

The Cyberspace Station

help@cyber.net

619-634-1376

Shell, ftp, telnet, IRC

dial-n-cerf

DIAL n'CERF USA

help@cerf.net

619-455-3900 (voice)

800-876-2373 (voice)

Dedicated, shell, menu, IRC, ftp, hytelnet, Gopher, WAIS, WWW, terminal service, SLIP

California (continued)

holonet *(national)*

HoloNet

info@holonet.net

510-704-1058

510-704-0160 (voice)

ftp, telnet, IRC, games

netcom

Netcom Online Communication Services

info@netcom.com

408-554-UNIX (voice)

Shell, ftp, telnet, IRC, WAIS, Gopher, SLIP, PPP, ftp space, feeds, DNS

portal

The Portal System

cs@cup.portal.com

info@portal.com

408-973-8091

408-725-0561

408-973-9111 (voice)

Shell, ftp, telnet, IRC, UUCP, feeds, BBS

well *(national)*

The Whole Earth 'Lectronic Link

info@well.sf.ca.us

415-332-6106

415-332-4335 (voice)

Shell, ftp, telnet, BBS

Colorado

cns

Community News Service

klaus@csns.com

719-520-1700

719-579-9120 (voice)

IV

Service Providers

UNIX shell, e-mail, ftp, telnet, IRC, USENET,
ClariNet, Gopher, 800 service

csn

Colorado SuperNet, Inc.

info@csn.org

303-273-3471 (voice)

Shell/menu, UUCP, SLIP, 56K, ISDN, T1, ftp, telnet,
IRC, Gopher, WAIS, domains, anonymous ftp
space, e-mail-to-fax

oldcolo

Old Colorado City Communications

dave@oldcolo.com

thefox@oldcolo.com

719-632-4111

719-632-4848 (voice)

Shell, ftp, telnet, AKCS, home of the NAPLPS
conference

Illinois

ddsw1

ddsw1,MCSNet

info@ddsw1.mcs.com

312-248-0900

312-248-6295

Shell, ftp, telnet, feeds, e-mail, IRC, Gopher

Maryland

express

Express Access - Online Communications Service

info@digex.com

301-220-0462

410-766-1855

301-220-2020 (voice)

Shell, ftp, telnet, IRC

Massachusetts

The World *(national)*

Software Tool and Die

office@world.std.com

617-739-9753

617-739-0202 (voice)

Dedicated, shell, ftp, telnet, IRC

nearnet

NEARnet

nearnet-join@nic.near.net

617-873-8730 (voice)

Dedicated, SLIP, e-mail, feeds, DNS

Michigan

MSen

MSen

info@msen.com

313-998-4562 (voice)

Dedicated, shell, WAIS, Gopher, telnet, ftp, SLIP, PPP, IRC, WWW, Picospan BBS, ftp space

michnet

Merit Network, Inc. - MichNet project

info@merit.edu

313-764-9430 (voice)

telnet, SLIP, PPP, outbound Sprintnet, Autonet and Ann Arbor dialout

New Jersey

jvnc

The John von Neumann Computer Network

info@jvnc.net

800-35-TIGER (voice)

609-258-2400 (voice)

Dedicated, ftp, telnet, SLIP, feeds, shell

IV

New York

mindvox

MindVOX

info@phantom.com

212-988-5030

212-988-5987 (voice)

Conferencing system, ftp, telnet, IRC, Gopher, hytelnet, archives, BBS

panix

PANIX Public Access UNIX

alexis@panix.com

jsb@panix.com

212-787-3100

212-877-4854 (Alexis Rosen)

212-691-1526 (Jim Baumbach)

Shell, ftp, telnet, Gopher, WAIS, IRC, feeds

North Carolina

rock-concert

Rock CONCERT Net

info@concert.net

919-248-1999 (voice)

Shell, ftp, telnet, IRC, Gopher, WAIS, feeds, SLIP

Ohio

wariat

APK - Public Access UNI*Site

zbig@wariat.org

216-481-9436

216-481-9425

216-481-9428 (voice)

Shell, ftp, telnet, IRC, Gopher, feeds, BBS

Ohio (continued)

OARnet

OARnet

nic@oar.net

614-292-8100 (voice)

Dedicated, e-mail, ftp, WWW, telnet, newsfeed

Pennsylvania

PREPnet

PREPnet

prepnet@cmu.edu

412-268-7870 (voice)

Dedicated, SLIP, terminal service, telnet, ftp

telerama

Telerama BBS

info@telerama.pgh.pa.us

412-481-5302

412-481-3505 (voice)

Shell, ftp, telnet, feeds, menu, BBS

Rhode Island

Anomaly

Rhode Island's Gateway to the Internet

info@anomaly.sbs.risc.net

401-331-3706

401-455-0347

401-273-4669 (voice)

Shell, ftp, telnet, SLIP

ids

The IDS World Network

sysadmin@ids.net

401-884-9002

401-785-1067

401-884-7856 (voice)

ftp, telnet, SLIP, feeds, BBS

IV

Texas

metronet

Texas Metronet

`srl@metronet.com`

`73157.1323@compuserve.com`

`GEnie:S.LINEBARG`

214-705-2902

214-705-2917

214-401-2800 (voice)

Shell, ftp, telnet, feeds, SLIP

sugar

NeoSoft's Sugar Land UNIX

`info@NeoSoft.com`

713-684-5900

713-438-4964 (voice)

BBS, shell, ftp, telnet, IRC, feeds, UUCP

Virginia

grebyn

Grebyn Corporation

`info@grebyn.com`

703-281-7997

703-281-2194 (voice)

Shell, ftp, telnet

psi *(national)*

PSI's Global Dialup Service (GDS)

PSILink - Personal Internet Access

`all-info@psi.com`

`gds-info@psi.com`

703-620-6651 (voice)

Dedicated, telnet, rlogin, e-mail, newsfeed, ftp

Washington

Halcyon

Halcyon

info@halcyon.com

206-382-6245

206-955-1050 (voice)

Shell, telnet, ftp, BBS, IRC, Gopher, hytelnet

eskimo

Eskimo North

nanook@eskimo.com

206-367-3837

206-362-6731

206-367-7457 (voice)

Shell, ftp, telnet

nwnexus

Northwest Nexus Inc.

info@nwnexus.wa.com

206-455-3505 (voice)

UUCP, SLIP, PPP, feeds, DNS

Australia

connect.com.au

connect.com.au pty ltd

connect@connect.com.au

61-3-5282239 (voice)

SLIP, PPP, ISDN, UUCP, ftp, telnet, NTP, ftpmail

Quebec, Canada

CAM.ORG

Communication Accessibles Montreal

info@CAM.ORG

514-281-5601

514-738-3664

514-923-2103

514-466-0592

514-923-2102 (voice)

Shell, ftp, telnet, feeds, SLIP, PPP, fax gateway

United Kingdom

ibmpcug

UK PC User Group

info@ibmpcug.co.uk

44-081-863-6646

44-081-863-6646 (voice)

ftp, telnet, BBS, IRC, feeds

Demon Internet Service (UK)

internet@demon.co.uk

44-081-349-0063

Shell, SLIP, PPP

Chapter 16

SLIP and PPP Service

Although an individual account through a BBS or terminal server may be sufficient for a single user, it usually can't serve the needs of small businesses and other organizations well. As a stepping stone between individual accounts discussed in Chapter 15, "On-Line Services and Terminal Servers," and dedicated Internet presence discussed in Chapter 17, "Dedicated Connections," the Serial Line Internet Protocol (SLIP) and it successor, the Point-to-Point Protocol (PPP), provide a cost-effective means for obtaining the benefits of host presence on the Internet at minimal cost.

As you read in Chapter 10, "Determining the Level of Internet Service You Need," these benefits include faster connections and the capability to provide ftp and telnet access from the Internet to your machine, which itself becomes an Internet host with SLIP/PPP. You also can define subnetworks and provide accounts for a number of users. You may be able to request your own IP and subdomain addresses, and you may register an alias for your subdomain. Check with your service provider for availability and cost of these features.

SLIP/PPP is offered by way of dialup and dedicated lines, with transfer rates from 9,600 to 57.6k bits per second. This kind of connection requires special software and perhaps dedicated hardware, depending on the specific nature of the service. Chapter 12, "Hardware and Software," has examples of some of the available choices. Making your system a part of the Internet involves setting up user accounts, installing and configuring network software, and controlling anonymous ftp, thus increasing your system administration effort.

Organizations Providing SLIP and PPP Service

This section lists organizations providing SLIP and PPP access to the Internet. This list provides a starting point for locating a provider of Internet access. These organizations are listed by geographical area, as indicated by area code. In some cases, an organization may provide services in several diverse geographical locations.

The information is organized as follows:

> **Geographical area**
>> **Organization name** (often the most common name or alias)
>>> Full or official name
>>> `E-mail contact address for further information`
>>> Phone number(s)
>>> Services provided

Phone numbers designated as voice are known to be voice only (not fax or data) and should never be called by modem. Some of these organizations provide dial-in services and will have data lines available. This is easily verified with a voice call.

> **Note**
>
> A question mark appearing in a field means that information for that field is not available.

United States, Nationwide

Alternet

alternet-info@uunet.uu.net

800-488-6384 (voice)

703-204-8000 (voice)

703-204-8001 (fax)

UUCP, SLIP/PPP, dedicated

California

BARRNET

BARRNET

gd.why@forsythe.stanford.edu

415-723-3104

Dedicated, dialup, SLIP, PPP

a21

a21 communications

info@rahul.net

408-293-9010

408-293-9020

Shell, ftp, telnet, feeds

class

Cooperative Library Agency for Systems and Services

class@calss.org

800-488-4559 (voice)

ftp, telnet, Gopher, WAIS, hytelnet

crl

CR Laboratories Dialup Internet Access

info@crl.com

415-389-UNIX

415-381-2800 (voice)

Shell, ftp, telnet, feeds, SLIP, WAIS, 800 service

California (continued)

cyber

The Cyberspace Station

help@cyber.net

619-634-1376

Shell, ftp, telnet, IRC

dial-n-cerf

DIAL n'CERF

help@cerf.net

619-455-3900 (voice)

800-876-2373 (voice)

Dedicated, shell, menu, IRC, ftp, hytelnet, Gopher, WAIS, WWW, terminal service, SLIP

holonet

HoloNet

info@holonet.net

510-704-1058

510-704-0160 (voice)

ftp, telnet, IRC, games

netcom

Netcom Online Communication Services

info@netcom.com

408-554-UNIX (voice)

Shell, ftp, telnet, IRC, WAIS, Gopher, SLIP, PPP, ftp space, feeds, DNS

portal

The Portal System

info@portal.com

408-973-8091

408-725-0561

408-973-9111 (voice)

Shell, ftp, telnet, IRC, UUCP, feeds, BBS

well

The Whole Earth 'Lectronic Link

info@well.sf.ca.us

415-332-6106

415-332-4335 (voice)

Shell, ftp, telnet, BBS

Colorado

cns

Community News Service

klaus@csns.com

719-520-1700

719-579-9120 (voice)

UNIX shell, e-mail, ftp, telnet, IRC, USENET,
ClariNet, Gopher, 800 service

csn

Colorado SuperNet,Inc.

info@csn.org

303-273-3471 (voice)

Shell/menu, UUCP, SLIP, 56K, ISDN, T1, ftp, telnet,
IRC, Gopher, WAIS, domains, anonymous ftp,
space, e-mail-to-fax

oldcolo

Old Colorado City Communications

dave@oldcolo.com

thefox@oldcolo.com

719-632-4111

719-632-4848 (voice)

Shell, ftp, telnet, AKCS, home of the NAPLPS
conference

Illinois

ddsw1

ddsw1,MCSNet

info@ddsw1.mcs.com

312-248-0900

312-248-6295

Shell, ftp, telnet, feeds, e-mail, IRC, Gopher

Maryland

express

Express Access - Online Communications Service

info@digex.com

301-220-0462

410-766-1855

301-220-2020 (voice)

Shell, ftp, telnet, IRC

Massachusetts

The World

Software Tool and Die

office@world.std.com

617-739-9753

617-739-0202 (voice)

Dedicated, shell, ftp, telnet, IRC

nearnet

NEARnet

nearnet-join@nic.near.net

617-873-8730 (voice)

Dedicated, SLIP, e-mail, feeds, DNS

Michigan

MSen

MSen

info@msen.com

313-998-4562 (voice)

Dedicated, shell, WAIS, Gopher, telnet, ftp, SLIP, PPP, IRC, WWW, Picospan BBS, ftp space

michnet

Merit Network, Inc. - MichNet project

info@merit.edu

313-764-9430 (voice)

telnet, SLIP, PPP, outbound SprintNet, Autonet and
Ann Arbor dialout

New Jersey

jvnc

The John von Neumann Computer Network
`info@jvnc.net`
800-35-TIGER (voice)
609-258-2400 (voice)
Dedicated, ftp, telnet, SLIP, feeds, optional shell

New York

mindvox

MindVOX
`info@phantom.com`
212-988-5030
212-988-5987 (voice)
Conferencing system, ftp, telnet, IRC, Gopher,
hytelnet, archives, BBS

panix

PANIX Public Access UNIX
`alexis@panix.com`
`jsb@panix.com`
212-787-3100
212-877-4854 (Alexis Rosen)
212-691-1526 (Jim Baumbach)
Shell, ftp, telnet, Gopher, WAIS, IRC, feeds

North Carolina

rock-concert

Rock CONCERT Net
`info@concert.net`
919-248-1999 (voice)
Shell, ftp, telnet, IRC, Gopher, WAIS, feeds, SLIP

Ohio

wariat

APK - Public Access UNI*Site

zbig@wariat.org

216-481-9436

216-481-9425

216-481-9428 (voice)

Shell, ftp, telnet, IRC, Gopher, feeds, BBS

Ohio/West Virginia

OARnet

OARnet

nic@oar.net

614-292-8100 (voice)

Dedicated, e-mail, ftp, WWW, telnet, newsfeed

Pennsylvania

PREPnet

PREPnet

prepnet@cmu.edu

412-268-7870 (voice)

Dedicated, SLIP, terminal service, telnet, ftp

telerama

Telerama BBS

info@telerama.pgh.pa.us

412-481-5302

412-481-3505 (voice)

Shell, ftp, telnet, feeds, menu, BBS

Rhode Island

Anomaly

Rhode Island's Gateway to the Internet

info@anomaly.sbs.risc.net

401-331-3706

401-455-0347

401-273-4669 (voice)

Shell, ftp, telnet, SLIP

ids

The IDS World Network

sysadmin@ids.net

401-884-9002

401-785-1067

401-884-7856 (voice)

ftp, telnet, SLIP, feeds, BBS

Texas

THEnet

Texas Higher Education Network Information
Center

info@nic.the.net

512-471-2444

Dedicated, dialup, SLIP

metronet

Texas Metronet

srl@metronet.com

73157.1323@compuserve.com

GEnie:S.LINEBARG

214-705-2902

214-705-2917

214-401-2800 (voice)

Shell, ftp, telnet, feeds, SLIP

sugar

NeoSoft's Sugar Land UNIX

info@NeoSoft.com

713-684-5900

713-438-4964 (voice)

BBS, shell, ftp, telnet, IRC, feeds, UUCP

Virginia

VERnet

VERnet

jaj@virginia.edu

804-924-0616

Dedicated, dialup, SLIP, PPP

grebyn

Grebyn Corporation

info@grebyn.com

703-281-7997

703-281-2194 (voice)

Shell, ftp, telnet

psi-gds

PSI's Global Dialup Service (GDS)

PSILink - Personal Internet Access

all-info@psi.com

gds-info@psi.com

703-620-6651 (voice)

Dedicated, telnet, rlogin, e-mail, newsfeed, ftp

Washington

Halcyon

Halcyon

info@halcyon.com

206-382-6245

206-955-1050 (voice)

Shell, telnet, ftp, BBS, IRC, Gopher, hytelnet

eskimo

Eskimo North

nanook@eskimo.com

206-367-3837

206-362-6731

206-367-7457 (voice)

Shell, ftp, telnet

IV

nwnexus

Northwest Nexus Inc.

info@nwnexus.wa.com

206-455-3505 (voice)

UUCP, SLIP, PPP, feeds, DNS

West Virginia

WVnet

WVnet

cc011041@wvnvm.wvnet.edu

Harper Grimm

304-293-5192

Dedicated, SLIP, PPP

Wisconsin

WiscNet

WiscNet

dorl@macc.wisc.edu

608-262-8874

Dedicated, limited dialup, SLIP, PPP

Australia

AARNet

AARNet

aarnet@aarnet.edu.au

61-6-249-3385

Dedicated, SLIP, PPP

connect.com.au

connect.com.au pty ltd

connect@connect.com.au

61-3-528-2239 (voice)

SLIP, PPP, ISDN, UUCP, ftp, telnet, NTP, ftpmail

Quebec, Canada

CAM.ORG

Communication Accessibles Montreal

info@CAM.ORG

514-281-5601

514-738-3664

514-923-2103

514-466-0592

514-923-2102 (voice)

Shell, ftp, telnet, feeds, SLIP, PPP, fax gateway

United Kingdom

ibmpcug

UK PC User Group

info@ibmpcug.co.uk

44-081-863-6646

44-081-863-6646 (voice)

ftp, telnet, BBS, IRC, feeds

Chapter 17

Dedicated Connections

The most sophisticated Internet connection services available are provided through special connections that aren't limited to the signal transfer rates available by traditional phone lines and data telecommunications equipment. These connections transfer data at rates approaching that of many local area networks and rely on communications services provided by phone companies specifically to meet these demands. Your local telephone service provider or your long-distance carrier can help you assess your needs and acquire the telephone connection.

Dedicated service requires more human and financial resources than many of you are likely to have. You must have current knowledge of the required communications equipment and services, and you must coordinate the efforts of the Internet service provider, the telephone company, and your computer support personnel. The cost for a dedicated connection easily reaches $10,000 for system setup, and several thousand dollars a month for the service itself. A typical candidate for a dedicated connection would be a medium to large company or other organizations with a staff handling computing and communications needs.

Chapter 10, "Determining the Level of Internet Service You Need," describes basic dedicated connection service.

Organizations Providing Dedicated Connections

This section lists organizations providing dedicated access to the Internet. The list provides a starting point for locating a provider of dedicated access to the Internet.

These organizations are listed by geographical area, as indicated by area code. In some cases, the organization may provide services in several diverse geographical locations. The information is organized as follows:

Geographical area

Organization name (often the most common name or alias)

Full or official name
Postal address
E-mail contact address for more information
Phone number(s)

Phone numbers designated as voice are known to be voice only (not fax or data) and should never be called by modem. Some organizations provide dial-in services and will have data lines available. This is easily verified with a voice call.

> **Note**
>
> A question mark appearing in a field means that information for that field is not available.

United States, Nationwide

Alternet

?
Falls Church, VA
alternet-info@uunet.uu.net

800-488-6384 (voice)
703-204-8000 (voice)
703-204-8001 (fax)

California

BARRNET

BARRNET
Pine Hall Room 115
Stanford
gd.why@forsythe.stanford.edu
415-723-3104

Los Nettos

Information Sciences Institute
4676 Admiralty Way
Marina del Rey
los-nettos-request@isi.edu
310-822-1511

dial-n-cerf

DIAL n'CERF
?
help@cerf.net
619-455-3900 (voice)
800-876-2373 (voice)

Colorado

Westnet

601 S. Howes, 6th Floor South
Colorado State University
Fort Collins
pburns@yuma.acns.colostate.edu
303-491-7260

Colorado (continued)

csn

Colorado SuperNet,Inc.

?

info@csn.org

303-273-3471 (voice)

Hawaii

PACCOM

University of Hawaii, ICS

2565 The Mall

Honolulu 96822

torben@hawaii.edu

808-956-3499

Illinois

netIllinois

Bradley University

501 W. Bradley Ave.

Peoria

joel@bradley.edu

309-677-3100

Massachusetts

The World

Software Tool and Die

1330 Beacon Street

Brookline

office@world.std.com

617-739-9753

617-739-0202 (voice)

nearnet

NEARnet

?

nearnet-join@nic.near.net

617-873-8730 (voice)

Michigan

ANS

Advanced Networks and Services
2901 Hubbard Road
Ann Arbor 48105
`maloff@nis.ans.net`
313-663-7601

CICnet

ITI Building
2901 Hubbard Drive, Pod G
Ann Arbor 48105
`info@cic.net`
313-998-6103

MSen

MSen
?
`info@msen.com`
313-998-4562 (voice)

Minnesota

MRNet

Minnesota Regional Network
511 11th Ave. S., Box 212
Minneapolis
`info@mr.net`
612-342-2570

Nebraska

MIDnet

MIDnet
29 WESC
University of Nebraska
Lincoln
`dmf@westie.unl.edu`
402-472-5032

Nevada

NevadaNet
University of Nevada System
Computing Services
4505 Maryland Parkway
Las Vegas
?
702-739-3557

New Jersey

jvnc
The John von Neumann Computer Network
?
info@jvnc.net
800-35-TIGER (voice)
609-258-2400 (voice)

Ohio/West Virginia

OARnet
OARnet
?
nic@oar.net
614-292-8100 (voice)

Pennsylvania

PREPnet
PREPnet
?
prepnet@cmu.edu
412-268-7870 (voice)

Pittsburgh Supercomputing Center
4400 5th Ave.
Pittsburgh
hastings@psc.edu
412-268-4960

Texas

THEnet

Texas Higher Education
Network Information Center
Austin
info@nic.the.net
512-471-2444

Virginia

SprintLink

Sprint International
3221 Woodland Park Drive
Herndon 22071
mkiser@icml.icp.net
703-904-2156

VERnet

Academic Computing Center
Gilmer Hall UVA
Charlottesville
jaj@virginia.edu
804-924-0616

psi-gds

PSI's Global Dialup Service(GDS)
?
gds-info@psi.com
703-620-6651 (voice)

Washington

NorthWestNet

NorthWestNet
2435 233rd Place
Redmond
ehood@nwnet.net
206-562-3000

West Virginia

WVnet

WVnet

?

cc011041@wvnvm.wvnet.edu

304-293-5192

Wisconsin

WiscNet

WiscNet

1210 W. Dayton Street

Madison

dorl@macc.wisc.edu

608-262-8874

Australia

AARNet

AARNet Support

CPO Box 1142

Canberra ACT 2601

aarnet@aarnet.edu.au

61-6-249-3385

British Columbia, Canada

BCnet

BCnet Headquarters

419-6356 Agricultural Road

Vancouver, Canada

BCnet@ubc.ca

604-822-3932

United Kingdom

UKnet

UKnet Support

?

postmaster@uknet.ac.uk

44-227-475497

Part V

Resource Reference

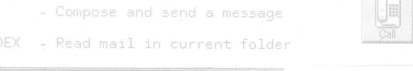

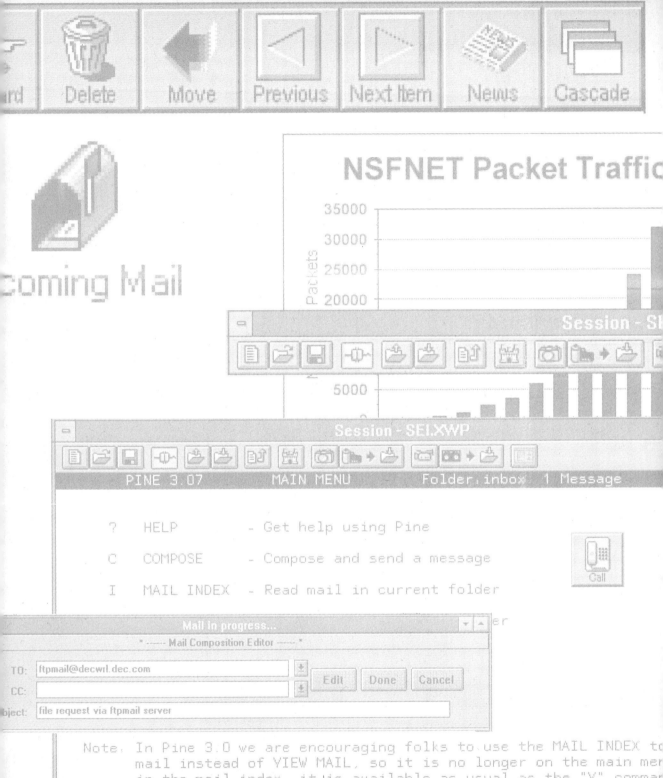

Delete **Move** **Previous** **Next Item** **News** **Cascade**

coming Mail

NSFNET Packet Traffic

35000
30000
25000
20000

Packets

Session - SI

Session - SEI.XWP

PINE 3.07   MAIN MENU   Folder.inbox   1 Message

5000

?   HELP   - Get help using Pine

C   COMPOSE   - Compose and send a message

I   MAIL INDEX - Read mail in current folder

Call

Mail in progress...

* ----- Mail Composition Editor ----- *

TO: ftpmail@decwrl.dec.com   Edit   Done   Cancel

CC:

bject: file request via ftpmail server

Note: In Pine 3.0 we are encouraging folks to use the MAIL INDEX to
      mail instead of VIEW MAIL, so it is no longer on the main men
      in the mail index, it's available as usual as the "Y" commar

? Help   Q Quit   F Folders   O Other
C Compose   I Mail Index A Addresses

Chapter 18
Host Resource Guide

New users of the Internet often have a difficult time locating the programs, documents, or other information they are interested in. This chapter intends to describe a few of the sites on the Internet that provide services such as anonymous ftp or Gopher. This chapter also describes some of the information available on the Internet that is related to special interests (professional, hobby, and so on). Although this list certainly is not exhaustive (new sites and documents appear on the Internet daily), the information provided here is a good starting point.

The sites presented in this chapter are organized by the type of service they provide (ftp, Gopher, and so on). Each listing gives the name of the site (and the Internet address, in case your system doesn't understand the name) and a list of the information available there. If a specific contact person at the site can answer questions about the material there, that name is also listed. If no specific contact name is given, you can send mail to that site's postmaster address for more information.

Following the list of sites are the special-interest categories. Some of the information is available via anonymous ftp and some via Gopher or some other information retrieval service; the individual sections outline the best way to find the information you are looking for.

Internet ftp Sites

In this section, individual sites on the Internet providing anonymous ftp services are listed, with details on what can be found there. You can locate specific information on the Internet by browsing large anonymous ftp sites (those that have large archives of information). This section lists some large sites that are a good starting place in your search for programs or information. For more information about how to use anonymous ftp, see Chapter 8, "Using ftp and telnet."

The file locations for directories and files are given from the top of the anonymous ftp area for each site. The directories are shown in a UNIX format (/directory), and subdirectories are indented under the upper-level directories. When you log in via anonymous ftp, you can use the cd command to move to the directory listed. From there you can use the ls or dir commands to get listings of the individual files in each area.

ftp.uu.net

Site name: ftp.uu.net (192.48.96.9)

Contact: archive@uunet.uu.net or tale@uunet.uu.net

Description: UUNet, an Internet services provider, is also one of the central distribution sites for all netnews traffic across the Internet. The ftp archive at ftp.uu.net is one of the largest and most complete on the Internet—almost everything can be found here! It has a very broad collection of programs and informational files; it's essential that you get the index files and search them for the information you want.

Location	Description
/index	Lists of what files are available
/systems	Software for various types of systems
/amiga	Software for Amiga computers

Location	Description
/next	Software for NeXT computers
/apple2	Software for Apple II computers
/gnu	Free Software Foundation software
/pyramid	Fixes for Pyramid system software
/sun	Software and documentation for Sun systems
/vms	Software for VMS systems
/iris	Software for SGI Iris systems
/mac	Info-mac mailing list archives, mainly
/msdos	Lots of software for MS-DOS machines
/unix	Software for UNIX systems (LINUX and so on)
/simtel20	Copy of the Simtel20 PC software archive
/mach	Software for systems running MACH
/apollo	Software for Apollo computers
/vendor	Information from many computer vendors
/info	Information about UUNET and the ftp area
/index	Index files for this ftp site
/news	Software for netnews transport and reading
/published	Information from publishers
/mail	Software for mail reading and transport
/pub	Miscellaneous software and information
/ai	AI (artificial intelligence) journals and information
/archiving	Compression and archiving software
/database	Information on different databases
/economics	Information on economics
/games	Game software for various computers

(continues)

Location	Description
/linguistics	Linguistic information
/physics	Software for physicists
/security	Security software packages (COPS and so on)
/shells	Shell software for UNIX systems
/text-processing	Editors and text processing systems
/window-sys	Window system software (X Windows and so on)
/inet	Information on the Internet
/aups	Acceptable use policies from sites
/ddn-news	DDN management bulletin archives
/doc	General network documentation
/ien	IEN documents
/iesg	Internet Engineering Steering Group documents
/ietf	Internet Engineering Task Force documents
/internet-drafts	IETF draft documents
/isoc	Internet Society documents
/maps	Maps of the Internet and subnets
/netinfo	General network information
/nren	NREN documents and information
/protocols	Information about different network protocols
/resource-guide	The Internet Resource Guide
/rfc	All Internet RFC documents
/networking	Different network software packages
/doc	Documents of general interest

Location	Description
/dictionaries	Various language dictionaries
/libraries	Lists of libraries on the Internet
/music	Musical scores for various instruments
/patents	Patent documents
/political	Political documents (U.S. Constitution, for example)
/security	Computer security related documents
/standards	Standards documents (IEEE, ISO, and so on)
/style	Written style documents
/supreme-court	U.S. Supreme Court decisions
/graphics	Graphics software and documentation
/languages	Computer language software

wuarchive.wustl.edu

Site name: wuarchive.wustl.edu (128.252.135.4)

Description: This site (at Washington University at St. Louis) is one of the biggest ftp sites on the Internet. It mirrors, or holds copies, of software archived at many different Internet sites. It holds very large collections of IBM PC and Apple Macintosh software, as well as software and documents covering almost every topic.

Location	Description
/decus	DEC User's Society tapes
/systems	Software for different computer systems
/aix	IBM AIX software (large collection)
/amiga	Amiga computer software
/apple2	Software for Apple II computers

(continues)

Location	Description
/atari	Software for Atari computers
/aux	Apple AUX software (large collection)
/cpm	Software for CPM machines
/gnu	All Free Software Foundation software
/hp	Software for Hewlett-Packard machines and calculators
/ibmpc	Huge amount of IBM PC software
/linux	Software for machines running LINUX
/mac	Huge amount of Macintosh software
/minix	Software for systems running Minix
/misc	Miscellaneous software for various systems
/next	Software for NeXT machines
/novell	Software specifically for Novell NetWare
/os9	Information and software for OS/9 systems
/penpoint	Software and information on PenPoint
/sinclair	Software for Sinclair systems
/sun	Software from Sun Exchange
/svr4–pc	UNIX System V.R4 for PC systems
/unix	Software for UNIX systems
/vax–vms	Software for people running VAX VMS
/xenix	Software for Xenix systems
/mirrors	Copies of information on different sites across the Internet
/info	Information about this site
/languages	Information about the Ada language
/packages	Different software packages
/TeX	The TeX document formatting system

Location	Description
/X11R5	The X11R5 windowing system
/benchmarks	Different computer benchmark software
/compression	Compression and archiving software
/dialslip	Serial Line IP dialup software
/dist	Software distribution software
/gopher	Gopher client and server software
/mail	Mail reading software
/news	Netnews software
/wuarchive–ftpd	The special ftp daemon written here
/www	The World Wide Web software system
/graphics	Different computer graphics packages
/usenet	Archives of some USENET groups
/doc	General documents
/EFF	Electronic Frontier Foundation information
/bible	The Bible in electronic form
/graphics–formats	Different graphics formats
/ietf	Internet Engineering Task Force documents
/nsfnet	NSFNET network-related documents
/nsfnet–stats	Network statistics collected by NSF
/rfc	Network Request For Comments (RFC) documents
/techreports	Reports from various universities
/edu	Software and information for educational sites
/multimedia	Multimedia data files
/audio	Internet Talk Radio files
/images	Pictures in different formats

V

Resource Reference

sunsite.unc.edu

Site name: `sunsite.unc.edu` (152.2.22.81)

Contact: `ftpkeeper@sunsite.unc.edu`

Description: Sunsite is run by the University of North Carolina as a major site for academic information. It contains collections of software and information for many academic areas, and also is a central site for information about computers manufactured by Sun Microsystems, Inc.

All directories listed below for this site are under the `/pub` directory. You should issue a `cd /pub` command after logging in.

Location	Description
`/Linux`	Software for sites running LINUX
`/X11`	Distribution and information about X11
`/academic`	Software for academic use, arranged by area of knowledge
`/agriculture`	
`/astronomy`	
`/athletics`	
`/biology`	
`/business`	
`/chemistry`	
`/computer-science`	
`/data_analysis`	
`/economics`	
`/education`	
`/engineering`	
`/environment`	
`/fine-arts`	

Location	Description
/geography	
/geology	
/history	
/languages	
/library	
/mathematics	
/medicine	
/physics	
/political-science	
/psychology	
/religious_studies	
/russian-studies	
/archives	Archives of mailing lists, USENET news groups, and publications
/docs	Written materials, Internet documents, computers, literature, politics
/gnu	All Free Software Foundation software
/languages	Compilers and interpreters of computer languages
/micro	Software for micro computers
/mac-stuff	Archives of Mac software
/mips-pc	Archives of MIPS PC software
/pc-stuff	Archives of IBM PC software
/multimedia	Software and information about computer-based video and sound
/packages	Large source distributions for UNIX
/TeX	The TeX document production system (sources)

(continues)

V

Resource Reference

Location	Description
/bbs	Bulletin board systems
/cygnus	Software from Cygnus Corporation
/gopher	Gopher client and server software
/infosystems	Different information retrieval systems
/Mosaic	Mosaic clients
/WWW	World Wide Web system
/Z39.50	Software implementation of Z39.50
/archie	archie clients for different machines
/ftp-archive	Software to run an ftp archive
/gopher	Gopher client and server software
/wais	WAIS client and server software
/mail	Different mail packages
/news	Different news software
/pctelnet	telnet protocol for PC systems
/terminal-emulators	Terminal emulation software
/sun-info	Information about Sun computer systems
/catalyst	Copies of Sun's Catalyst catalog
/development-tools	Tools for software development
/sun-dist	Sun distributed patches for its software
/sun-fixes	Security fixes from Sun
/sun-managers	Archives of Sun-Managers mailing list
/sunenergy	Archives of SunEnergy bulletins
/sunflash	Archives of SunFlash newsletters
/sunspots	Archives of SunSpots mailings
/white-papers	Copies of different Sun white papers
/talk-radio	Audio files from Internet Talk Radio

oak.oakland.edu

Site name: oak.oakland.edu (141.210.10.117)

Description: oak.oakland.edu is a major *mirror site*, which means that it holds copies of the software at other sites. Because Oak is very well connected to the Internet, this makes retrieving the software easier.

Location	Description
/pub	
/ada	Simtel20 Ada language archives
/misc	Simtel20 miscellaneous software (lots!)
/msdos	Very large archive of MS-DOS software
/pc–blue	PC-BLUE archive of PD and user-contributed PC software
/pub2	
/cpm	Software for CPM machines (lots!)
/cpmug	CPM User's Group software
/macintosh	Very large Macintosh software archive
/unix–c	Very large archive of UNIX software

rtfm.mit.edu

Site name: rtfm.mit.edu (18.70.0.224)

Description: This site is important in that it holds the archives of all the Frequently Asked Questions (FAQ) informational postings made to various netnews groups. If you have a question about a topic covered by a netnews group, you should check here to see whether it is covered by one of the FAQ postings.

V

Resource Reference

Location	Description
/pub	
/pcm	A PC emulator package
/popmail	The Post Office Protocol mail package
/usenet–by–group	FAQ postings organized by news group
/usenet–by–hierarchy	FAQ postings organized by news hierarchy
/usenet–addressed	Database and information on the USENET address server

ftp.cica.indiana.edu

Site name: ftp.cica.indiana.edu (129.79.26.102)

Description: This archive, a central site for Microsoft Windows applications, is run by the Center for Innovative Computer Applications at Indiana University. If you are looking for a Windows application, check here first.

Location	Description
/pub	
/laser	Information on Laser Sailboating
/next	Software and information on NeXT machines
/pc	IBM PC software
/borland	Software and information from Borland International
/misc	Miscellaneous PC software and information
/starter	Important first software (UNZIP, uudecode, and so on)
/win3	Microsoft Windows applications

Location	Description
/unix	Miscellaneous UNIX software
/wx	Weather files (GIF images and so on)

ds.internic.net

Site name: ds.internic.net (198.49.45.10)

Description: The InterNIC sites (ds, is, and rs) collectively form the InterNIC services. They provide different types of information, but ds is the most useful for new users. This site has collections of all Internet documents and information; it is a good site to look for answers to questions about the Internet.

Location	Description
/dirofdirs	Pointers to information at different sites, organized by category
/fyi	Internet FYI (informational) documents
/iesg	Internet Engineering Steering Group documents
/ietf	Internet Engineering Task Force documents
/internet-drafts	Drafts of common Internet documents
/internic.info	Information about the InterNIC
/isoc	Internet Society documents
/nsf	National Science Foundation documents
/policies-procedures	Network policies and procedures from sites
/pub	Other information
/conf.announce	Conference announcements
/current-ietf-docs	Documents under IETF review
/internet-doc	General Internet documents (zen, EARN)

(continues)

Location	Description
/netpolicies	NSFNET acceptable use policy
/the-scientist	On-line issues of *The Scientist*
/z39.50	Databases available using the Z39.50 protocol
/resource-guide	The Internet Resource Guide
/rfc	Internet Request For Comments (RFC) standards
/std	Internet Activities Board standards

ftp.eff.org
Site name: ftp.eff.org (192.88.144.4)

Description: This site is maintained by the Electronic Frontier Foundation, an organization interested in exploring the legal aspects of computers and networks.

Location	Description
/pub	
/EFF	Electronic Frontier Foundation information
/SJG	Notes on the Steve Jackson Games case, in which a bulletin board system was impounded because of alleged illegal material on the system (the EFF represented Games in the case)
/academic	Information from academic sites
/cpsr	Notes from the Boston chapter of Computer Professionals for Social Responsibility
/cud	Archives of the Computer Underground Digest
/internet-info	Copies of Internet documents
/journals	Various journals on-line

ftp.cso.uiuc.edu

Site name: ftp.cso.uiuc.edu (128.174.5.61)

Description: This is a large, general-purpose site run by the University of Illinois at Urbana-Champaign. It holds a good variety of programs and information, but an especially large collection of software for Amiga, IBM PC, and Macintosh computers.

Location	Description
/ACM	UIUC's student Association for Computing Machinery information
/pgsi	Power glove serial interface project documentation and software
/amiga	
/amoner	On-line *Amoner* magazine
/cucug	Champaign-Urbana Commodore User Group
/fish	Fred Fish collection—500 disks' worth!
/virus	Virus scanners for Amiga systems
/bbs	Information on local bulletin board systems
/doc	General computing related documentation
/pcnet	Lists of compression and network software
/mac	
/MUG	Champaign-Urbana Macintosh User Group collection of software
/eudora	E-mail package for Macintosh computers
/virus	Antivirus software for Macintosh
/mail	sendmail and smail packages
/math	PD math software and source code
/mrc	Index to materials available at the CSO resource center

(continues)

Resource Reference

V

Location	Description
`/pc`	
`/adf`	IBM Adapter Description Files and other PS/2-related items
`/exec-pc`	Index and sample files from Exec-PC BBS
`/local`	Collection of local files and software
`/pbs`	Disks from Public Brand Software
`/pcmag`	*PC Magazine* files from Exec-PC or PC-Magnet
`/pcsig`	Files from the largest PC-SIG (Special Interest Group) CD-ROM
`/scripts`	Kermit and other login scripts
`/virus`	UIUC collection of antivirus files
`/tandy`	Tandy Model 100/102 laptop files
`/uiuc`	MOTIF and X11R4 for various systems
`/unix/virus`	UNIX information and patches, Internet worm information, Sun sendmail & ftpd

wiretap.spies.com

Site name: `wiretap.spies.com` (130.43.43.43)

Contact: `archive@wiretap.spies.com`

Description: This site collects interesting information that flows over the Internet. It has a large and eclectic collection of documents ranging from jokes to White House press releases. If you are looking for an official document, such as a government charter or report, this is definitely the place to look.

Location	Description
/Clinton	White House press releases
/Economic_Plan	Clinton's economic plan
/GAO_Reports	Government Accounting Office reports
/Gov	Government and civics archives from around the world
/Aussie	Australian law documents
/Canada	Canadian documents
/Copyright	Copyright laws
/Economic	Clinton's economic plan
/Forfeit	Civil Forfeiture of Assets laws
/GAO–Report	GAO miscellaneous reports
/GAO–Risk	GAO high-risk reports
/GAO–Tech	GAO technical reports
/GAO–Trans	GAO transition reports
/Maast	Maastricht Treaty of European Union
/NAFTA	North American Free Trade Agreement document
/NATO	NATO press releases
/NATO–HB	NATO handbook
/Other	Miscellaneous world documents
/Patent	Patent office reform panel final report
/Platform	Political platforms of the United States
/Treaties	Treaties and international covenants
/UCMJ	Uniform code of military justice
/UN	United Nations resolutions (selected)

(continues)

V

Resource Reference

Location	Description
/US–Docs	U.S. miscellaneous documents
/US–GOV	U.S. government today
/US–History	U.S. historical documents
/US–Speech	U.S. speeches and addresses
/US–State	Various U.S. state laws
/World	World constitutions
/Library	Wiretap on-line library of articles
/Articles	Various articles
/Classics	Classic literature
/Cyber	Cyberspace documents
/Document	Miscellaneous documents
/Fringe	Fringes of reason
/Humor	Funny material of all types
/Media	Mass media
/Misc	Miscellaneous unclassified documents
/Music	Music scores and lyrics
/Religion	Religious articles and documents
/Techdoc	Technical information of all sorts
/Untech	Non-technical information
/Zines	Magazines

Internet Gopher Sites

Because Gopher is based in a hierarchical structure, you can browse easily among many sites. This section lists a few of the major Gopher sites to get you started.

In addition to the sites listed in the following sections, which
provide access using a Gopher client program, here are the sites
that allow telnet access to Gopher. These sites let you access the
Gopher system without you having any client software on your
end, just the telnet program.

Host Name	Address	Login	Area
consultant.micro.umn.edu	134.84.132.4	**gopher**	U.S.
ux1.cso.uiuc.edu	128.174.5.59	**gopher**	U.S.
panda.uiowa.edu	128.255.40.201	**panda**	U.S.
gopher.msu.edu	35.8.2.61	**gopher**	U.S.
gopher.ebone.net	192.36.125.2	**gopher**	Europe
info.anu.edu.au	150.203.84.20	**info**	Australia
gopher.chalmers.se	129.16.221.40	**gopher**	Sweden
tolten.puc.cl	146.155.1.16	**gopher**	Chile
ecnet.ec	157.100.45.2	**gopher**	Ecuador
gan.ncc.go.jp	160.190.10.1	**gopher**	Japan

gopher.micro.umn.edu

Site name: gopher.micro.umn.edu (128.101.62.12)

Description: This is the Gopher home site, the site where the
Gopher software was developed. As such, it has the complete
list of all available Gopher sites around the world and also keeps
the most recent information about Gopher on-line.

Menu Items

Information about Gopher
   Gopher FAQ
   comp.infosystems.gopher archive
   New stuff in Gopher
   Computer Information
   Other Gopher and information servers (complete list)

V

Resource Reference

boombox.micro.umn.edu

Site name: boombox.micro.umn.edu (134.84.132.2)

Description: This site, also run by the University of Minnesota, holds the source code for most of the Gopher servers and clients. If you do not already have Gopher client code running, you can use anonymous ftp to this machine to retrieve the current versions.

wiretap.spies.com

Site name: wiretap.spies.com (130.43.43.43)

Description: Also described under the earlier anonymous ftp section, wiretap contains many interesting documents that have moved over the Internet. All the following headings have more categories under them—there are too many interesting files to list.

Menu Items

About the Internet Wiretap
Clinton press releases
Electronic books at Wiretap
GAO transition reports
Government documents (U.S. and world)
North American Free Trade Agreement
Usenet alt.etext Archives
Usenet ba.internet Archives
Various ETEXT resources on the Internet
Video game archive
Waffle BBS software
Wiretap on-line library
Worldwide Gopher and WAIS servers

gopher.internic.net

Site name: gopher.internic.net (198.49.45.10)

Description: The InterNIC site is the central Network Information Center for the Internet. The Gopher site allows you to find
easily information about the Internet and many of its resources.

Menu Items

Information about the InterNIC
InterNIC Information Services
    Welcome to the InfoSource
    Getting connected to the Internet
    InterNIC store
    About the InterNIC Information Services
    Getting started on the Internet
    Internet information for everybody
    Just for NICs
    NSFNET, NREN, national information infrastructure
      information
    Beyond InterNIC: Virtual treasures of the Internet
    Searching the InfoSource by keyword
InterNIC Registration Services
    InterNIC registration archives
    WHOIS searches for InterNIC registries
    WHOIS searches for non-MILNET individuals
InterNIC directory and database services
    InterNIC directory of directories
    InterNIC directory services ("White Pages")
    InterNIC database services (public databases)
    Additional Internet resource information
    Internet documentation (RFCs, FYIs, and so on)
    National Science Foundation information

gopher.nsf.gov

Site name: gopher.nsf.gov (128.150.195.40)

Description: This is the main Gopher server run by the National Science Foundation, and as such it is a central clearing
house for many scientific reports and documents. This server

V

Resource Reference

also provides pointers to many other government Gopher servers; if you are looking for information from a government office or department, look here.

Menu Items

NSF publications
BIO—Director for Biological Sciences
CISE—Director for Computer and Information Science and
    Technology
EHR—Director for Education and Human Resources
ENG—Director for Engineering
GEO—Director for Geosciences
MPS—Director for Math and Physical Sciences
NSB—National Science Board
OIG—Office of the Inspector General
Office of the Director
SBE—Director for Social, Behavioral, and Economic
    Sciences
SRS—Science Resources Studies Division
Other US Government Gopher Services
    Extension Service, USDA
    Federal Information Exchange (FEDIX)
    LANL Physics Information Service
    Library of Congress MARVEL
    NASA Goddard Space Flight Center
    NASA Mid-Continent Technology Transfer Center
    NASA Network Application and Information Center
    National Institute of Standards and Technology (NIST)
    National Institutes of Health (NIH)
    National Science Foundation (NSF)
    Protein Data Bank—Brookhaven National Lab
    US Environmental Protection Agency (EPA)
    USDA National Agricultural Library Plant Genome
    USDA-ARS GRIN National Genetic Resources Program

Special-Interest Topics

This section lists a few of the many special-interest topics that have information available on the Internet. In some cases, the information is available via anonymous ftp; in other cases, you can use telnet to log in to a host and get information on the topic. Each individual entry lists the method of access and all the information necessary to get access to your topic.

This section is by no means complete; it is simply intended to give a feel for the types of information available and how to get access to it.

Agriculture

Several different services offer agricultural information on the Internet. Some services are weather and crop related; others provide information related to health.

Access method: `telnet caticsuf.csufresno.edu` (129.8.100.15)

> **Log in:** `super`

Description: This service, the Advanced Technology Information Network, provides information about agriculture and biotechnology. It is located in California, so the information is somewhat biased towards that area; but it is useful for people in other areas also. Information offered includes daily agricultural market reports; weather, labor, and job reports; safety information; and schedules of events.

Access method: `telnet psupen.psu.edu` (128.118.36.5)

> **Log in:** `state_code`

Description: This service, PENpages, is provided by the Pennsylvania State University. It provides access to agricultural prices and commodity reports, as well as USDA and 4-H information. Also available is the International Food & Nutrition Database, as well as a rich assortment of weather information.

Access method: `gopher esusda.gov` (192.73.224.100)

Description: This Gopher server is run by the Extension Service of the USDA. It provides access to various educational and information services of the Cooperative Extension System, as well as links to other agricultural Gopher servers around the country. This Gopher also provides information such as White House press releases, the Clinton health plan, the federal budget, and more.

Access method: `ftp ftp.sura.net` (128.167.254.179)
`get file /pub/nic/agricultural.list`

Description: This document, titled "Not Just Cows—A Guide to Internet/Bitnet Resources in Agriculture and Related Sciences," contains pointers to many resources on both BITNET and the Internet for the agricultural sciences. This document is fairly large (about 2,700 lines), so you should peruse it on-line when you retrieve it.

Access methods:
`mail almanac@esusda.gov`

`mail almanac@ecn.purdue.edu`

`mail almanac@oes.orst.edu`

`mail almanac@ces.ncsu.edu`

`mail almanac@silo.ucdavis.edu`

`mail almanac@joe.uwex.edu`

`mail almanac@wisplan.uwex.edu`

Description: The almanac servers provide e-mail access to different agricultural information based on the server. You should send a mail message with **send guide** in the message body to one of the preceding addresses to receive a guide on how to use the server. A mail message with **send catalog** returns the list of available information.

Aviation

The following services offer aviation information on the Internet. These services provide a repository and weather and flight-planning information.

Access method: `gopher av.eecs.nwu.edu`

Description: This site is run by Northwestern University as a repository for aviation information. Some of the information is from the USENET `rec.aviation` group, but quite a bit is contributed from individual pilots on the Internet. Stories, pictures, and flight-planning information are available.

Access method: `telnet duat.gtefsd.com` (131.131.7.105)

       or   `telnet duats.gtefsd.com` (131.131.7.106)

Description: The DUAT service (Direct User Access Terminal) is provided by the FAA to give aviation weather and flight-planning information for pilots. The first address is for certified pilots, the second one is for uncertified ones.

> **Note**
>
> Although this service is provided under contract from the FAA, it is now being reviewed and may be terminated.

Books

Access method: `ftp mrcnext.cso.uiuc.edu` (128.174.201.12)
                    `cd /pub/etext`

Description: This site maintains an archive of the Project Gutenberg files. Project Gutenberg is aimed at producing 10,000 of the most widely read books in electronic form. Some of the books already available at this site are *Alice in Wonderland, The CIA World Fact Book, Roget's Thesaurus,* and *Moby Dick.*

V

Resource Reference

Calculators

Access method: `telnet hpcvbbs.cv.hp.com` (15.225.72.16)

Log in: `new`

Description: This is a bulletin board system for owners of Hewlett-Packard calculators. It features conferences with information and programs for HP calculators, plus real-time conversations with other HP users.

Computer Security

Access method: `ftp ftp.cert.org` (192.88.209.5)
`cd /pub`

Description: The Computer Emergency Response Team (CERT) is a federally funded organization that acts as a clearinghouse for computer security information. On their ftp site are archives of all their security bulletins, some computer security tools, computer virus information, and other computer security related items.

Databases

For access to databases, check out the following sites. You can tap into databases on libraries, compact discs, and education, among others.

Access method: `telnet echo.lu` (158.64.1.36)

Log in: `echo`

Description: This system, run by the European Commission Host Organization, provides databases on scientific and R & D projects, business, economy, languages, and others. Because the server is located in Europe, it is most useful to sites there, but anyone can find interesting material.

Access method: `telnet pac.carl.org` (192.54.81.128)

Description: CARL, run by the Colorado Alliance of Research Libraries, provides access to various library catalogs, indexes to current articles, and an information database. Access to many library databases is available.

Access method: `telnet columbia.ilc.com` (38.145.77.221)

  Log in: `cas`

Description: The ILC server provides a search and purchase database for bookstores, VHS video cassettes, music CDs, laser disks, and UNIX software. You must have a verified account to order merchandise, but browsing the database is open to anyone.

Access method: `telnet holonet.net` (157.151.0.1)

  Log in: `cdc`

Description: This system provides an on-line search and purchase database for compact disks of all types. If you have a credit card, you can order disks.

Education
Access method: `gopher nysernet.org` (192.77.173.2)

  or   `telnet nysernet.org`

  Log in: `empire`

Description: The Empire Schoolhouse is one of the options under the Nysernet Gopher server (under the K-12 special collection), but is accessed directly via telnet. This server has information about education from grades kindergarten through 12, including the Educational Resource Information Center and the Empire Internet Schoolhouse.

Games

The Internet isn't all seriousness. You still can have fun, as the following sites will show.

Access method: `telnet coot.lcs.mit.edu 5000`

or `telnet 18.52.0.70 5000`

Description: This is the Chess server; it allows you to play a game of chess, or watch others play. Type **help** for information about the available commands and how to play.

Access method: `telnet astro.temple.edu 12345` (129.32.1.100)

or `telnet argo.temple.edu 12345` (129.32.32.102)

Description: Both of these sites provide a *fortune cookie*—a random quote from a large database of quotes. You get a different quote each time you connect.

Access method: `telnet castor.tat.physik.uni-tuebingen.de` (134.2.72.153)

Log in: `games`

Description: This site (in Germany) provides access to several different on-line games, such as Tetris, NetHack, and Multiuser Dungeons.

> **Note**
>
> Because this site is in Europe, your response time (how fast the system appears) may be very slow, because the Internet connection between the United States and Europe is fairly slow.

Genealogy

If you are looking up your roots and need some help, the following sites may be just what you need. They provide information on genealogy, including database programs.

Access method: `ftp wood.cebaf.gov` (129.57.32.165)
              `cd genealogy`

Description: This site contains a large amount of information
on genealogy, including information on the PAF genealogy
program, genealogy database programs, and text files relating to
genealogy.

Access method: `ftp vm1.nodak.edu` (134.129.111.1)
              `cd roots-l`

Description: This site contains a large number of text files
relating to genealogy. Retrieve the file `FAQ.INDEX` for a beginning
on how to use the information in this directory.

Geography

If you want to access information about populations, ZIP codes,
and other geographical data from the United States and around
the world, try the following sites.

Access method: `telnet martini.eecs.umich.edu 3000`
              (141.212.99.9)

Description: This server holds U.S. Geological Survey and U.S.
Postal Service information about U.S. cities, counties, and states.
You can perform searches by ZIP code or city name, and the
server returns information such as population data, latitude,
longitude, ZIP code, and so on.

Access method: `telnet glis.cr.usgs.gov` (152.61.192.54)

       Log in: `guest`

Description: The Global Land Information System offers land
use maps of the United States, along with graphs and data.
Using a PC client or an X Windows client, you can display
maps and information on your local system.

V

Resource Reference

Government

You can access data provided by the Federal Information Exchange and the Food and Drug Administration, as described in the following sites.

Access method: `telnet fedix.fie.com` (192.111.228.33)

Description: The Federal Information Exchange offers information on federal opportunities, minority college and university capability information, and higher education opportunities for minorities and women.

Access method: `telnet fdabbs.fda.gov` (150.148.8.48)

   Log in: `bbs`

Description: This site, run by the Food and Drug Administration, contains information about drug enforcement reports, drug and device approvals, the center for devices and radiological health, current information about AIDS, the FDA consumer magazine index (with selected articles), and other information. You can search the FDA files for summaries of FDA information and also retrieve the text of testimony at FDA congressional hearings. Even veterinary medicine news is available!

Health

Access method: `gopher gopher.nih.gov`

Description: Run by the National Institutes of Health, this Gopher site has health and clinical information, grants and research information, molecular biology databases, and links to the National Institute of Allergy and Infectious Disease and National Institute of Mental Health Gopher sites. This Gopher also features information relating to cancer (CancerNet information) and AIDS. Access to the National Library of Medicine is also available.

History

Several different servers provide information of interest to historians. Information about the history of the United States, as well as the rest of the world, is represented.

Access method: `telnet ukanaix.cc.ukans.edu` (129.237.1.30)

>   **Log in:** `history`

Description: The University of Kansas HNSource is a central information server for historians. From the main menu, you can get information on ftp sites with historical information and databases, information about discussion lists, and bibliographic information.

Access method: `ftp byrd.mu.wvnet.edu` (129.71.32.152)
>   `cd /pub/history`

Description: This site offers documents on many different historic categories, including diplomatic, ethnic, maritime, and U.S. history.

Access method: `telnet clus1.ulcc.ac.uk` (192.12.72.60)

>   **Log in:** `ihr—uk`

>   **Password:** `ihr—uk`

Description: This site gives on-line resources for historians in the London area, as well as on-line resources for historians in the United Kingdom and the rest of the world. It uses a very well-organized hypertext system to allow you to locate resources and information easily.

Law

Several law schools offer extensive resources on the Internet for lawyers and others interested in the law. Some of these are discussed in the following sections.

Access method: `gopher fatty.law.cornell.edu` (132.236.108.5)

V

Resource Reference

Description: This site, run by the Cornell University law school, features information such as a directory of legal academia; discussion and LISTSERV archives; U.S. law (primary documents and commentary); foreign and international law (primary documents and commentary); and other legal resources (such as government agencies and Internet sources). This is a very complete and valuable site for all legal references.

Access method: `gopher gopher.law.csuohio.edu` (137.148.22.51)

Description: This site, run by the Cleveland State University law school, features information such as electronic forms of many legal sources, legal sources on the Internet, course schedules, and links to other Gopher sites.

Libraries

Libraries are very well represented on the Internet. They have historically been a major user of the Internet, and many university and public libraries are connected to the Internet. The sections below are only a fraction of the libraries available.

Access method: `telnet library.dartmouth.edu` (129.170.16.11)

Description: The Dartmouth library server offers the capability to search for text in several on-line literary works. Use the command `connect dante` to search through Dante's *Divine Comedy*. Use the command `select file bible` to search the Bible. The commands `select file s plays` and `select file s sonnets` allow you to search Shakespeare's plays and sonnets, respectively.

Access method: `telnet access.usask.ca` (128.233.3.1)

 Log in: `hytelnet`

or   `telnet info.ccit.arizona.edu` (129.196.76.201)

 Log in: `hytelnet`

or   `telnet laguna.epcc.edu` (192.94.29.3)

 Log in: `library`

Description: The hytelnet servers (additional ones are available in other countries) provide links to many libraries and other information services around the world. hytelnet is an easy-to-use, menu-driven way to explore many of the resources of the Internet. Services include library catalogs, other resources (such as archie, electronic books, and others), an Internet glossary, and help on the library catalogs. This is a very valuable resource for new Internet users.

Access method: `telnet liberty.uc.wlu.edu` (137.113.10.35)

> **Log in: `lawlib`**
>
> or   `gopher liberty.uc.wlu.edu`
>
> or   `ftp liberty.uc.wlu.edu`
>   `cd /pub/lawlib`

Description: Run by Washington and Lee University, this site is very well run and set up. It not only provides access to W & L's law library (with a very large amount of information on-line), but also has connections to a great number of other libraries and information sources on the Internet. The Gopher interface is easier to work with, but the telnet interface is usable also, if you do not have access to Gopher.

Access method: `ftp ariel.unm.edu` (129.24.8.1)
                   `get file /library/internet.library`

Description: This document lists all the libraries accessible from the Internet. It is very large (over 8,800 lines) and should be viewed on-line if possible—it's too big to print easily!

Access method: `telnet marvel.loc.gov` (140.147.254.3)

> **Log in: `marvel`**
>
> or   `gopher marvel.loc.gov`

Description: This site is run by the Library of Congress and, as such, has information about the library, the U.S. Congress, and the federal government, and also copyright and employee information. It also has the Global Electronic Library, with information on many subjects such as library science, philosophy and religion, the arts, social sciences, law, economics, and others.

V

Resource Reference

Mailing Lists

Access method: `ftp ftp.nisc.sri.com` (192.33.33.22)

`get file /netinfo/interest–groups`

Description: This file contains a complete listing of all available electronic mailing lists on the Internet. Updated quarterly, it has mailing lists from `A.Rice` (discussing Anne Rice books) to `YUNUS` (the Turkish TeX Users Group).

> **Note**
>
> This file is *enormous*—please don't print it if you can avoid it.

Mathematics

Access method: `gopher e–math.ams.com` (130.44.1.100)

or   `telnet e–math.ams.com`

Log in: `e–math`

Password: `e–math`

Description: This site is run by the American Mathematics Society to provide an electronic forum for AMS members and others interested in mathematics. Topics include mathematical publications, mathematical preprints, mathematical discussion lists and bulletin boards, general information of interest to mathematicians, and professional information for mathematicians.

Music

Musicians have access to several archives of information, including scores, guitar tablature, and lyrics of popular songs.

Access method: `ftp ftp.nevada.edu` (131.216.1.11)

`cd /pub/guitar`

Description: This directory contains tablature or chords written for guitar. People from all over the world submit songs that

they have transcribed into tablature form, but please make sure
that if you submit something, it is not copyrighted.

Access method: `ftp ftp.uwp.edu (131.210.1.4)`

     `cd /pub/music`

  or   `gopher ftp.uwp.edu`

Description: This server has archives of information about
music, including articles about music composition, archives of
music by artist name, classical music buying guide, folk music
files and pointers, lyrics archives, and more.

Networking

Access method: `ftp dhvx20.csudh.edu (155.135.1.1)`

     `cd global_net`

Description: This site maintains an archive of documents pertaining to the effort to bring network access to lesser-developed
nations and the poorer parts of developed nations.

Many other networking documents are available, as described
in the host-specific section earlier. The site `ds.internic.net` is a
primary source for all documents and information about the
Internet and networking in general.

Recipes

Several Internet mailing lists and USENET groups are devoted to
cooking and recipes. Over quite a few years, these recipes have
been collected into several archives on the Internet.

Access method: `ftp gatekeeper.dec.com (16.1.0.2)`

     `cd /pub/recipes`

Description: The archive at `gatekeeper.dec.com` has many different items of interest. The recipes area has hundreds of items
submitted by users over a period of several years. This archive is
organized by recipe title.

Access method: `ftp mthvax.cs.miami.edu (129.171.32.5)`

     `cd /pub/recipes`

V

Resource Reference

Description: This site holds the archives for the USENET group `rec.food.recipes`. Recipes here are organized by food type (that is fish, chicken, and so on). Programs for indexing and reading the `rec.food.recipes` archives are also available on this site (for the Macintosh and IBM PC computers); see the file `/pub/recipes/readme` for information.

Religion

Many different religious texts and informational files are available on Internet servers. These sites are a good place to find many of these texts.

Access method: `ftp wuarchive.wustl.edu` (128.252.135.4)
            `cd /doc/bible`

Description: A complete edition of the King James Bible, including cross references. There are versions for the IBM PC and Macintosh computers under this directory. You probably want to get the README file first to understand how to use the files.

Access method: `ftp quake.think.com` (192.31.181.1)
            `cd /pub/etext/koran`

Description: This directory contains an electronically scanned version of M.H. Shakir's translation of the Holy Qur'an, as published by Tahrike Tarsile Qur'an, Inc. There are files for each chapter, and you can retrieve each one individually.

Access method: `ftp nic.funet.fi` (128.214.6.100)
            `cd /pub/doc/bible/hebrew`

Description: This directory contains the Torah from the Tanach in Hebrew, the Prophets from the Tanach in Hebrew, and the Writings from the Tanach in Hebrew. Also included is a program to display Hebrew letters on an IBM PC monitor and a Hebrew quiz with biblical Hebrew language tutor. This site is in Europe, so you may want to limit your file transfers somewhat.

Roller Coasters

Access method: `ftp gboro.rowan.edu`
`cd /pub/Coasters`

The anonymous ftp site `gboro.rowan.edu` has roller-coaster-related information in `/pub/Coasters`. There are more than 100 GIF format pictures of roller coasters, and almost 100 reviews of amusement parks and/or roller coasters. There's also a coaster census, the `rec.roller-coaster` news group FAQ (Frequently Asked Questions) article, and several AVI (Video for Windows) full-motion animations of the Top Gun roller coaster at Paramount Great America amusement park in California.

Science (General)

Access method: `gopher gopher.hs.jhu.edu`

Description: This server is run by the History of Science Department at Johns Hopkins University. Available topics include "scientists on disk"—that is, a collection of important documents by scientists, the history of science (including departmental information such as memos and correspondence), classes about the history of science, and other information in the "grab bag" category. The collection includes papers by Darwin and Oppenheimer, and also information about the Royal Society of Science. This server is a valuable resource for people interested in the history of science and scientists.

Seismology

For various information on earthquakes—including dates, times, and magnitudes—the following sites may yield the data you need.

Access method: `telnet geophys.washington.edu`

Log in: `quake`

Password: `quake`

V

Resource Reference

Description: This server gives recent earthquake information, either reported by the USGS National Earthquake Information Center or by the University of Washington. Information includes the date, time, and magnitude of the earthquake, and the latitude, longitude, and description of the location.

Access method: `telnet bison.cc.buffalo.edu`

select `INDX` followed by `QKLN`

Description: This site offers the NCEER Quakeline Earthquake resource database. You can search for information on earthquakes, earthquake engineering, natural hazards mitigation, and related topics.

Space

Space flight in general, and information from NASA in particular, has been extremely popular on the Internet for quite a few years. Many NASA sites are directly on the Internet; the sites listed here are only a sampling of the ones available.

Access method: `telnet spacelink.msfc.nasa.gov`
(192.149.89.61)

Description: This site, run by NASA, provides the latest NASA news. It includes schedules of space shuttle launches and information about satellites and other topics. You are asked for information and assigned a login name and password that you can use for future login sessions.

Access method: `finger nasanews@space.mit.edu` (18.75.0.10)

Description: This site provides a daily news summary from NASA headquarters in Washington, D.C. It gives information on current and planned shuttle flights and other NASA projects.

Access method: `telnet stinfo.hq.eso.org` (134.171.8.4)

Log in: `stinfo`

Description: This site is run by the European Space Organization and provides status reports on the Hubble Space Telescope and European HST news.

Access method: `telnet lpi.jsc.nasa.gov` (192.101.147.11)

> **Log in:** `envnet`
>
> **Password:** `henniker`

Description: This site is run by the NASA Lunar and Planetary Institute (LPI). It contains information about the LPI, including the Lunar and Planetary Bibliography database, the image retrieval and processing system (IRPS), and the Mars exploration bulletin board system.

Access method: `telnet ned.ipac.caltech.edu` (134.4.10.118)

> **Log in:** `ned`

Description: This site offers access to the NASA Extragalactic Database. It provides search capabilities into the database of more than 200,000 astronomical objects and also information about astronomical publications.

Sports

Access method: `telnet culine.colorado.edu` (128.138.129.83)

Description: The `telnet` command lets you specify a port number to connect to, and this server takes advantage of that ability. There are actually four different sports servers at this machine, each of which works at a different telnet port. To get schedules for NBA teams, connect to port 859. Others are listed as follows:

Port	Sport
859	National Basketball Association
860	National Hockey League

(continues)

V

Resource Reference

Port	Sport
862	Major-league baseball
863	National Football League

Stock Market Reports

Access method: telnet a2i.rahul.net (192.160.13.1)

> **Log in:** guest
>
>> Select n and set your terminal characteristics (you are prompted for this information)

Description: This site is an Internet access provider and has many interesting items available. The stock market reports are under the current system information menu. Other information is also available about the Internet and the A2I site.

Television

Television—a major part of modern culture—is well represented on the Internet. Information about many current and past television shows is available; the following is a small sample.

Access method: ftp ftp.cs.widener.edu (147.31.254.132)
cd /pub/simpsons

Description: This directory contains information about the television show *The Simpsons*. Information includes plot summaries, an episode guide, air dates for each episode, and even information about the Simpsons pinball game. If you watch the show and want information about it, this is the place.

Access method: ftp ftp.uu.net (192.48.96.9)
cd /usenet/rec.arts.startrek

Description: This directory contains archives of information about the *Star Trek* television show. Information here includes parodies written by fans, information about the various *Star*

Trek spin-off shows, archive of articles posted to the USENET `rec.arts.startrek` group, and other information.

The directory `/usenet/rec.arts.tv` on `ftp.uu.net` contains information about hundreds of television shows. Everything from *The A-Team* through *The Young and the Restless* is represented here. Most of the files are compressed using the UNIX compress program, so you should have an uncompress program ready.

Weather

Everyone is interested in the weather, and you can find out current weather information at several sites on the Internet. Weather maps, forecasts, and historical data are among the data you can find.

Access method: `telnet exnet.iastate.edu (129.186.20.200)`

   Log in: `flood`

Description: This server, run by the Iowa State University Extension, contains articles on flooding and dealing with the results of floods. The server allows you to read or download the information.

Access method: `finger forecast@typhoon.atmos.colostate.edu`

Description: This server returns the seasonal forecast for the Atlantic ocean. It also reports how the current season compares with previous years.

Access method: `telnet downwind.sprl.umich.edu 3000`

   or   `telnet 141.212.196.177 3000`

Description: This server, running at port 3000 on the listed site, returns the current forecast for given cities. If you know the city code for the desired location, you can enter it at the prompt; otherwise, you should press Enter and use the menu system. Other information available are a national weather summary, ski conditions, and severe weather and hurricane advisories.

V

Resource Reference

Access method: `telnet wind.atmos.uah.edu 3000`

or `telnet 146.229.8.2 3000`

Description: This server is similar to the `downwind` site in the preceding description, but it does not have the initial prompt for your city code. In addition to the general information available above, it also allows access to the "wx" weather system, which can display weather maps and other information on your local computer if you are running the X Windows system.

Access method: `gopher wx.atmos.uiuc.edu` (128.174.80.10)

Description: This server is the University of Illinois Weather Machine. It gives Gopher access to weather information for many different regions, including many major cities in the United States. In addition, it allows access to image files from different satellites. These images are in GIF format and may be displayed on your local machine after you have retrieved them.

ZIP Codes
Access method: `ftp oes.orst.edu` (128.193.124.2)

```
cd /pub/almanac/misc
get zipcode
```

Description: This file gives a list of all postal ZIP codes for the United States (and territories) as of the current date of the file. The file is of the form `zipcode:city` (that is, `15001:Aliquippa`, `PA`), which allows for easy searching.

Summary

The information presented in this chapter is available through several different methods. Anonymous ftp is discussed in detail in Chapter 8, "Using ftp and telnet." Gopher is discussed in more detail in Chapter 13, "Aids to Navigating the Internet." E-mail and mailing lists are discussed in Chapter 7, "Using E-Mail."

Chapter 19

USENET News Groups Index

In Chapter 9, you read about USENET news groups and the wealth of information and assistance that is available through them. You can subscribe to literally thousands of groups, and as of this writing the receipt of all USENET news postings (also called a *full USENET feed*) requires the transfer and storage of more than 1.5 gigabytes per month. In addition to the USENET groups, you also can subscribe to thousands of mailing lists that periodically send you e-mail containing the latest information on your topic of interest.

This chapter and the next are designed to work together. This chapter contains an index of subjects for the two lists in the next chapter. The next chapter contains those two lists: the first is a list of USENET group names, accompanied by a short description of the group's focus, and the second identifies many of the available mailing lists, describes their focuses, and provides contact information.

Use this chapter's index to look up topics you are interested in. Then use the mailing list or news group name(s) mentioned in the index to look up the full description of the mailing list or news group in the next chapter.

Alternatively, use the disk that accompanies this book to find mailing lists and news groups of interest. The on-disk lists have been indexed electronically so that you quickly can search on keywords. See Appendix A, "Using the Companion Disk," for more information.

> **Note**
>
> The disk also includes a list of periodic postings made to each USENET group. Due to its size, this list exists only on the disk accompanying this book in the file named PERIODIC.TXT. See Appendix A for more information on how to use this list.

Be aware that over-subscribing yourself is a constant temptation. You need to read what you receive, and many groups can generate hundreds of messages per day. Also remember to watch the download time your news feed takes, particularly if your provider has prorated connection charges. Many people will also tell you that, like e-mail, USENET can become quite addictive. As a brewer's advertisement warns, "Know when to say when."

Category Index

Activism

act–up–request
@world.std.com
action–alert–request
@vector.intercon.com
ae852@yfn.ysu.edu
alt.activism
alt.activism.d
alt.activism.death-penalty
alt.censorship
alt.comp.acad-
freedom.news
alt.comp.acad-
freedom.talk
alt.dads-rights
alt.discrimination
alt.individualism
alt.missing-kids
alt.revolution.counter
alt.save.the.earth
alt.society.ati
alt.society.civil-liberties
alt.society.civil-liberty
alt.society.resistance
alt.whistleblowing
altinst–request
@cs.cmu.edu
Ar–news–request
@cygnus.com

ar–talk–request
@cygnus.com
ba–liberty–request
@shell.portal.com
bikecommute–request
@bike2work.eng.sun.com
bit.listserv.envbeh-l
bit.listserv.free-l
bit.org.peace-corps
ca–liberty–request
@shell.portal.com
clari.news.gov.corrupt
clari.news.group
clari.news.group.women
clari.news.issues.civil_rights
clari.tw.environment
eagles–request
@flash.usc.edu
el406010@brownvm.brown.edu
fairness–request
@mainstream.com
femail–request
@lucerne.eng.sun.com
feminism–
digest@ncar.ucar.edu
firearms–
request@cs.cmu.edu
gaynet–
request@queernet.org
hands@u.
washington.edu

info–aids@rainbow.uucp
karplus@ce.ucsc.edu
la–motss–
request@flash.usc.edu
libfem–
request@math.uio.no
listserv@idbsu.idbsu.edu
listserv
@mizzou1.missouri.edu
listserv@sjuvm.bitnet
listserv@vm.usc.edu
misc.activism.progressive
moms–request
@qiclab.scn.rain.com
oregon–news–request
@vector.intercon.com
soc.feminism
soc.rights.human
soc.women
talk.abortion
talk.rape
ysn–adm@zoyd.
ee.washington.edu
zita@ac.grin.edu

Architecture

alt.architecture
alt.architecture.
alternative
listserv@uci.com

Art

alt.artcom
alt.binaries.multimedia
alt.binaries.pictures
alt.binaries.pictures.d
alt.binaries.pictures.
    erotica
alt.binaries.pictures.
    erotica.blondes
alt.binaries.pictures.
    erotica.d
alt.binaries.pictures.
    erotica.female
alt.binaries.pictures.
    erotica.male
alt.binaries.pictures.
    erotica.orientals
alt.binaries.pictures.
    fine-art.d
alt.binaries.pictures.
    fine-art.digitized
alt.binaries.pictures.
    fine-art.graphics
alt.binaries.pictures.
    fractals
alt.binaries.pictures.misc
alt.binaries.pictures.
    supermodels
alt.binaries.pictures.
    tasteless
alt.binaries.pictures.
    utilities
alt.cascade
alt.fan.mike-jittlov
alt.postmodern
alt.sex.pictures
bit.listserv.ingrafx
clari.news.arts
glass–request
    @dixie.com
jhbercovitz@lbl.gov
k12.ed.art
minilist–
    request@cs.unc.edu

rec.arts.animation
rec.arts.anime
rec.arts.anime.info
rec.arts.anime.
    marketplace
rec.arts.anime.stories
rec.arts.bodyart
rec.arts.fine
rec.arts.theatre
relcom.comp.animation
sci.classics
stagecraft–request
    @jaguar.cs.utah.edu
theatre–
    request@world.std.com

Automotive

alt.autos.antique
alt.autos.rod-n-custom
alt.hotrod
autox–request
    @autox.team.net
bmw–request
    @balltown.cma.com
british–cars–request
    @autox.team.net
datsun–roadsters–
    request@autox.
    team.net
exotic–cars–request
    @sol.asl.hitachi.com
f–body–request
    @boogie.ebay.sun.com
harley–request
    @thinkage.on.ca
hotrod–
    request@dixie.com
htunca@ncsa.uiuc.edu
ihc–request
    @balltown.cma.com
info–honda–
    request@cs.ucla.edu
italian–cars–request
    @balltown.cma.com

kitcar–
    request@cs.usask.ca
listserv@sjsuvm1.sjsu.edu
lotus–adm%esprit.
    uucp@netcom.com
mazda–list–
    request@ms.uky.edu
miata–request
    @jhunix.hcf.jhu.edu
mr2–interest–
    request@validgh.com
mustangs–
    request@cup.hp.com
nedod–request
    @mbunix.mitre.org
pchaos!keithm
    @pail.rain.com
porschephiles–
    request@tta.com
quattro–request
    @aries.east.sun.com
racefab–request
    @pms706.pms.ford.com
rec.audio.car
rec.autos
rec.autos.antique
rec.autos.driving
rec.autos.rod-n-custom
rec.autos.sport
rec.autos.tech
rec.autos.vw
rec.motorcycles
rec.motorcycles.dirt
rec.motorcycles.harley
rec.motorcycles.racing
relcom.commerce.
    transport
rx7club@cbjjn.att.com
school–request
    @balltown.cma.com
stealth–request%jim.
    uucp@wupost.wustl.edu
swedishbricks–
    request@me.rochester.
    edu

todd@di.com
toyota–request
 @quack.kfu.com
vettes–
 request@compaq.com
wheeltowheel–
 request@abingdon.
 Eng.Sun.COM
z–car–request@dixie.com

Aviation

aeronautics–request
 @rascal.ics.utexas.edu
airplane–clubs–
 request@dg–rtp.
 dg.com
clari.news.aviation
clari.tw.aerospace
clari.tw.space
elements–
 request@telesoft.com
rec.aviation.announce
rec.aviation.answers
rec.aviation.homebuilt
rec.aviation.ifr
rec.aviation.military
rec.aviation.misc
rec.aviation.owning
rec.aviation.piloting
rec.aviation.products
rec.aviation.simulators
rec.aviation.soaring
rec.aviation.stories
rec.aviation.student
rec.travel.air
sci.aeronautics
sci.aeronautics.airliners
sci.space
sci.space.news
sci.space.shuttle
skunk–works–request
 @harbor.ecn.purdue.edu
talk.politics.space

Biology

alt.aquaria
alt.chinchilla
alt.cows.moo.moo.moo
alt.fan.furry
alt.fan.lemurs
alt.lemmings
alt.wolves
bionet.agroforestry
bionet.announce
bionet.biology.
 computational
bionet.biology.n2-
 fixation
bionet.biology.tropical
bionet.cellbiol
bionet.chlamydomonas
bionet.drosophila
bionet.general
bionet.genome.
 arabidopsis
bionet.genome.chrom22
bionet.genome.
 chromosomes
bionet.immunology
bionet.info-theory
bionet.jobs
bionet.journals.contents
bionet.journals.note
bionet.metabolic-reg
bionet.molbio.ageing
bionet.molbio.
 bio-matrix
bionet.molbio.
 embldatabank
bionet.molbio.evolution
bionet.molbio.gdb
bionet.molbio.genbank
bionet.molbio.genbank.
 updates
bionet.molbio.
 gene-linkage
bionet.molbio.genome-
 program

bionet.molbio.hiv
bionet.molbio.
 methds-reagnts
bionet.molbio.proteins
bionet.molbio.rapd
bionet.molbio.yeast
bionet.mycology
bionet.n2-fixation
bionet.neuroscience
bionet.photosynthesis
bionet.plants
bionet.population-bio
bionet.sci-resources
bionet.software
bionet.software.acedb
bionet.software.gcg
bionet.software.sources
bionet.users.addresses
bionet.virology
bionet.women-in-bio
bionet.xtallography
bit.listserv.biosph-l
clari.news.interest.animals
cogneuro–request
 @ptolemy.arc.nasa.gov
killie–request
 @mejac.paloalto.ca.us
listserv@bdt.ftpt.ansp.br
listserv@nic.surfnet.nl
sci.aquaria
sci.bio
sci.bio.technology
sci.engr.biomed
tout@genesys.cps.msu.edu
zaphod!pnwc!wildnet–
 request@access.usask.ca

Business

alt.business.multi-level
alt.fashion
balloon–
 request@lut.ac.uk
bbl7597@ritvax.isc.rit.edu

bionet.sci-resources
bit.listserv.buslib-l
bit.listserv.ioob-l
clari.biz.commodity
clari.biz.courts
clari.biz.economy
clari.biz.economy.world
clari.biz.features
clari.biz.finance
clari.biz.finance.earnings
clari.biz.finance.personal
clari.biz.finance.services
clari.biz.invest
clari.biz.labor
clari.biz.market
clari.biz.market.amex
clari.biz.market.dow
clari.biz.market.ny
clari.biz.market.otc
clari.biz.market.report
clari.biz.mergers
clari.biz.misc
clari.biz.products
clari.biz.top
clari.biz.urgent
clari.canada.biz
clari.nb.business
clari.news.consumer
clari.news.economy
clari.news.labor
clari.news.labor.strike
clari.tw.aerospace
clari.tw.computers
clari.tw.defense
clari.tw.electronics
clari.tw.health
clari.tw.misc
clari.tw.nuclear
clari.tw.stocks
domestic–request
  @tattoo.mti.sgi.com
info–request
  @tradent.wimsey.bc.ca
k12.ed.business

majordomo@csn.org
misc.entrepreneurs
misc.invest
misc.invest.canada
misc.invest.real-estate
misc.invest.technical
misc.taxes
relcom.commerce.estate
relcom.commerce.money
relcom.commerce.orgtech
relcom.commerce.stocks
relcom.currency
relcom.infomarket.quote
relcom.infomarket.talk
relcom.wtc
smi–request
  @world.std.com

Computers

386users–request
  @udel.edu
abc–list–request
  @cwi.nl
af–request
  @crl.dec.com
agenda–users–request
  @newcastle.ac.uk
alberta!oha!ctree–request
alife–request
  @cognet.ucla.edu
alpha–osf–managers–
  request@ornl.gov
alspa–users–request
  @ssyx.ucsc.edu
alt.1d
alt.3d
alt.aldus.pagemaker
alt.bbs
alt.bbs.ads
alt.bbs.allsysop
alt.bbs.first-class
alt.bbs.internet
alt.bbs.lists

alt.bbs.pcboard
alt.bbs.pcbuucp
alt.bbs.wildcat
alt.binaries.multimedia
alt.binaries.pictures
alt.binaries.pictures.d
alt.binaries.pictures.
  erotica
alt.binaries.pictures.
  erotica.blondes
alt.binaries.pictures.
  erotica.d
alt.binaries.pictures.
  erotica.female
alt.binaries.pictures.
  erotica.male
alt.binaries.pictures.
  erotica.orientals
alt.binaries.pictures.
  fine-art.d
alt.binaries.pictures.
  fine-art.digitized
alt.binaries.pictures.
  fine-art.graphics
alt.binaries.pictures.
  fractals
alt.binaries.pictures.
  misc
alt.binaries.pictures.
  supermodels
alt.binaries.pictures.
  tasteless
alt.binaries.pictures.
  utilities
alt.binaries.sounds.d
alt.binaries.sounds.misc
alt.binaries.sounds.music
alt.cad
alt.cad.autocad
alt.cd-rom
alt.cobol
alt.comp.databases.
  xbase.clipper
alt.comp.fsp

bit.listserv.innopac
bit.listserv.ipct-l
bit.listserv.isn
bit.listserv.jes2-l
bit.listserv.jnet-l
bit.listserv.l-vmctr
bit.listserv.liaison
bit.listserv.license
bit.listserv.linkfail
bit.listserv.lstsrv-l
bit.listserv.mail-l
bit.listserv.mailbook
bit.listserv.mbu-l
bit.listserv.netnws-l
bit.listserv.nettrain
bit.listserv.new-list
bit.listserv.next-l
bit.listserv.nodmgt-l
bit.listserv.notis-l
bit.listserv.novell
bit.listserv.os2-l
bit.listserv.ozone
bit.listserv.pacs-l
bit.listserv.page-l
bit.listserv.pagemakr
bit.listserv.pmdf-l
bit.listserv.power-l
bit.listserv.relusr-l
bit.listserv.rscs-l
bit.listserv.rscsmods
bit.listserv.s-comput
bit.listserv.script-l
bit.listserv.seds-l
bit.listserv.sfs-l
bit.listserv.simula
bit.listserv.snamgt-l
bit.listserv.sqlinfo
bit.listserv.tech-l
bit.listserv.test
bit.listserv.tex-l
bit.listserv.tn3270-l
bit.listserv.toolb-l
bit.listserv.trans-l
bit.listserv.tsorexx

bit.listserv.ucp-l
bit.listserv.ug-l
bit.listserv.uigis-l
bit.listserv.urep-l
bit.listserv.usrdir-l
bit.listserv.valert-l
bit.listserv.vfort-l
bit.listserv.vm-util
bit.listserv.vmesa-l
bit.listserv.vmslsv-l
bit.listserv.vmxa-l
bit.listserv.vnews-l
bit.listserv.win3-l
bit.listserv.wpcorp-l
bit.listserv.wpwin-l
bit.listserv.x400-l
bit.listserv.xedit-l
bit.listserv.xerox-l
bit.mailserv.
   word-mac
bit.mailserv.word-pc
bit.software.international
biz.clarinet
biz.clarinet.sample
biz.comp.hardware
biz.comp.services
biz.comp.software
biz.comp.telebit
biz.comp.telebit.netblazer
biz.config
biz.dec
biz.dec.decathena
biz.dec.decnews
biz.dec.ip
biz.dec.workstations
biz.digex.announce
biz.jobs.offered
biz.misc
biz.next.newprod
biz.oreilly.announce
biz.pagesat
biz.sco.announce
biz.sco.binaries
biz.sco.general
biz.sco.magazine

biz.sco.opendesktop
biz.sco.sources
biz.sco.wserver
biz.stolen
biz.tadpole.sparcbook
biz.test
biz.univel.misc
biz.zeos.announce
biz.zeos.general
bnnj–request
   @plts.org
brent@greatcircle.com
bugs–386bsd–request
   @ms.uky.edu
bunker!stpstn!objc–
   request
bx–talk–request
   @qiclab.scn.rain.com
c–ibm–370–request
   @dhw68k.cts.com
camz@dlogtech.cuc.ab.ca
cdpub–info
   @knex.via.mind.org
cisco–request
   @spot.colorado.edu
clari.biz.products
clari.nb.apple
clari.nb.general
clari.nb.govt
clari.nb.ibm
clari.nb.review
clari.net.admin
clari.net.announce
clari.net.newusers
clari.net.products
clari.net.talk
clari.tw.computers
commune–request
   @stealth.acf.nyu.edu
comp.admin.policy
comp.ai
comp.ai.fuzzy
comp.ai.genetic
comp.ai.jair.announce
comp.ai.jair.papers

comp.ai.nat-lang
comp.ai.neural-nets
comp.ai.nlang-know-rep
comp.ai.philosophy
comp.ai.shells
comp.answers
comp.apps.spreadsheets
comp.arch
comp.arch.bus.vmebus
comp.arch.storage
comp.archives
comp.archives.admin
comp.archives.
  msdos.announce
comp.archives.msdos.d
comp.bbs.misc
comp.bbs.waffle
comp.benchmarks
comp.binaries.acorn
comp.binaries.amiga
comp.binaries.apple2
comp.binaries.atari.st
comp.binaries.ibm.pc
comp.binaries.ibm.pc.d
comp.binaries.ibm.
  pc.wanted
comp.binaries.mac
comp.binaries.
  ms-windows
comp.binaries.os2
comp.bugs.2bsd
comp.bugs.4bsd
comp.bugs.4bsd.
  ucb-fixes
comp.bugs.misc
comp.bugs.sys5
comp.cad.cadence
comp.cad.compass
comp.cad.synthesis
comp.client-server
comp.cog-eng
comp.compilers
comp.compression
comp.compression.
  research

comp.databases
comp.databases.informix
comp.databases.ingres
comp.databases.
  ms-access
comp.databases.object
comp.databases.oracle
comp.databases.pick
comp.databases.sybase
comp.databases.theory
comp.databases.
  xbase.fox
comp.databases.
  xbase.misc
comp.dcom.cell-relay
comp.dcom.fax
comp.dcom.isdn
comp.dcom.lans.ethernet
comp.dcom.lans.fddi
comp.dcom.lans.
  hyperchannel
comp.dcom.lans.misc
comp.dcom.lans.
  token-ring
comp.dcom.modems
comp.dcom.servers
comp.dcom.sys.cisco
comp.dcom.sys.wellfleet
comp.dcom.telecom
comp.doc
comp.doc.techreports
comp.dsp
comp.editors
comp.edu
comp.edu.composition
comp.emacs
comp.fonts
comp.graphics
comp.graphics.algorithms
comp.graphics.animation
comp.graphics.avs
comp.graphics.data-
  explorer
comp.graphics.explorer

comp.graphics.gnuplot
comp.graphics.opengl
comp.graphics.research
comp.graphics.
  visualization
comp.groupware
comp.human-factors
comp.infosystems
comp.infosystems.gis
comp.ivideodisc
comp.lang.ada
comp.lang.apl
comp.lang.asm370
comp.lang.c
comp.lang.c++
comp.lang.clos
comp.lang.clu
comp.lang.dylan
comp.lang.eiffel
comp.lang.forth
comp.lang.forth.mac
comp.lang.fortran
comp.lang.functional
comp.lang.hermes
comp.lang.icon
comp.lang.idl
comp.lang.idl-pvwave
comp.lang.lisp
comp.lang.lisp.franz
comp.lang.lisp.mcl
comp.lang.misc
comp.lang.ml
comp.lang.modula2
comp.lang.modula3
comp.lang.oberon
comp.lang.objective-c
comp.lang.pascal
comp.lang.perl
comp.lang.pop
comp.lang.postscript
comp.lang.prolog
comp.lang.rexx
comp.lang.sather
comp.lang.scheme

comp.lang.scheme.c
comp.lang.sigplan
comp.lang.smalltalk
comp.lang.tcl
comp.lang.verilog
comp.lang.vhdl
comp.lang.visual
comp.laser-printers
comp.lsi
comp.lsi.cad
comp.lsi.testing
comp.mail.elm
comp.mail.headers
comp.mail.maps
comp.mail.mh
comp.mail.mime
comp.mail.misc
comp.mail.
   multi-media
comp.mail.mush
comp.mail.sendmail
comp.mail.uucp
comp.misc
comp.multimedia
comp.music
comp.networks.
   noctools.announce
comp.networks.
   noctools.bugs
comp.networks.
   noctools.d
comp.networks.
   noctools.submissions
comp.networks.
   noctools.tools
comp.networks.
   noctools.wanted
comp.newprod
comp.object
comp.object.logic
comp.org.eff.news
comp.org.eff.talk
comp.org.fidonet
comp.org.ieee
comp.org.isoc.interest

comp.org.issnnet
comp.org.sug
comp.org.usenix
comp.org.usenix.
   roomshare
comp.os.386bsd.
   announce
comp.os.386bsd.apps
comp.os.386bsd.bugs
comp.os.386bsd.
   development
comp.os.386bsd.misc
comp.os.386bsd.
   questions
comp.os.aos
comp.os.coherent
comp.os.cpm
comp.os.cpm.amethyst
comp.os.geos
comp.os.linux
comp.os.linux.admin
comp.os.linux.announce
comp.os.linux.
   development
comp.os.linux.help
comp.os.linux.misc
comp.os.mach
comp.os.minix
comp.os.misc
comp.os.ms-windows.
   advocacy
comp.os.ms-windows.
   announce
comp.os.ms-windows.
   apps
comp.os.ms-windows.
   misc
comp.os.ms-windows.
   nt.misc
comp.os.ms-windows.
   nt.setup
comp.os.ms-windows.
   programmer.misc
comp.os.ms-windows.
   programmer.tools

comp.os.ms-windows.
   programmer.win32
comp.os.ms-windows.
   setup
comp.os.msdos.4dos
comp.os.msdos.apps
comp.os.msdos.desqview
comp.os.msdos.
   mail-news
comp.os.msdos.misc
comp.os.msdos.pcgeos
comp.os.msdos.
   programmer
comp.os.msdos.
   programmer.turbovision
comp.os.os2.advocacy
comp.os.os2.announce
comp.os.os2.apps
comp.os.os2.beta
comp.os.os2.bugs
comp.os.os2.misc
comp.os.os2.multimedia
comp.os.os2.networking
comp.os.os2.programmer.
   misc
comp.os.os2.programmer.
   porting
comp.os.os2.setup
comp.os.os2.ver1x
comp.os.os9
comp.os.research
comp.os.rsts
comp.os.v
comp.os.vms
comp.os.vxworks
comp.os.xinu
comp.parallel
comp.parallel.pvm
comp.patents
comp.periphs
comp.periphs.printers
comp.periphs.scsi
comp.programming
comp.programming.
   literate

comp.sys.cdc
comp.sys.concurrent
comp.sys.convex
comp.sys.dec
comp.sys.dec.micro
comp.sys.encore
comp.sys.handhelds
comp.sys.harris
comp.sys.hp
comp.sys.hp48
comp.sys.ibm.pc.demos
comp.sys.ibm.pc.digest
comp.sys.ibm.pc.games.
    action
comp.sys.ibm.pc.games.
    adventure
comp.sys.ibm.pc.games.
    announce
comp.sys.ibm.pc.games.
    flight-sim
comp.sys.ibm.pc.games.
    misc
comp.sys.ibm.pc.games.
    rpg
comp.sys.ibm.pc.games.
    strategic
comp.sys.ibm.pc.
    hardware
comp.sys.ibm.pc.misc
comp.sys.ibm.pc.rt
comp.sys.ibm.pc.
    soundcard
comp.sys.ibm.ps2.
    hardware
comp.sys.intel
comp.sys.intel.ipsc310
comp.sys.laptops
comp.sys.m6809
comp.sys.m68k
comp.sys.m68k.pc
comp.sys.m88k
comp.sys.mac.advocacy
comp.sys.mac.announce
comp.sys.mac.apps

comp.sys.mac.comm
comp.sys.mac.databases
comp.sys.mac.digest
comp.sys.mac.games
comp.sys.mac.hardware
comp.sys.mac.hypercard
comp.sys.mac.misc
comp.sys.mac.oop.
    macapp3
comp.sys.mac.oop.misc
comp.sys.mac.oop.tcl
comp.sys.mac.portables
comp.sys.mac.
    programmer
comp.sys.mac.scitech
comp.sys.mac.system
comp.sys.mac.wanted
comp.sys.mentor
comp.sys.misc
comp.sys.ncr
comp.sys.newton.
    announce
comp.sys.newton.misc
comp.sys.newton.
    programmer
comp.sys.next.advocacy
comp.sys.next.announce
comp.sys.next.bugs
comp.sys.next.hardware
comp.sys.next.marketplace
comp.sys.next.misc
comp.sys.next.
    programmer
comp.sys.next.software
comp.sys.next.sysadmin
comp.sys.northstar
comp.sys.novell
comp.sys.nsc.32k
comp.sys.palmtops
comp.sys.pen
comp.sys.prime
comp.sys.proteon
comp.sys.pyramid
comp.sys.ridge

comp.sys.sequent
comp.sys.sgi.admin
comp.sys.sgi.announce
comp.sys.sgi.apps
comp.sys.sgi.bugs
comp.sys.sgi.graphics
comp.sys.sgi.hardware
comp.sys.sgi.misc
comp.sys.stratus
comp.sys.sun.admin
comp.sys.sun.announce
comp.sys.sun.apps
comp.sys.sun.hardware
comp.sys.sun.misc
comp.sys.sun.wanted
comp.sys.super
comp.sys.tahoe
comp.sys.tandy
comp.sys.ti.explorer
comp.sys.transputer
comp.sys.unisys
comp.sys.xerox
comp.sys.zenith
comp.sys.zenith.z100
comp.terminals
comp.terminals.bitgraph
comp.terminals.tty5620
comp.text
comp.text.desktop
comp.text.frame
comp.text.interleaf
comp.text.sgml
comp.text.tex
comp.theory
comp.theory.
    cell-automata
comp.theory.
    dynamic-sys
comp.theory.
    info-retrieval
comp.theory.
    self-org-sys
comp.unix.admin
comp.unix.aix
comp.unix.amiga

improv–request
@bmt.gun.com
impulse–users–
request@j.cc.purdue.
edu
info–encore–request
@cs–gw.d.umn.edu
info–encore–request
@umnd–cs.uucp
info–fortune–request
@csd4.csd.uwm.edu
info–gnu–request
@prep.ai.mit.edu
info–ingres–request
@math.ams.com
info–labview–request
@pica.army.mil
info–pgp–request
@lucpul.it.luc.edu
info–prime–request
@blx–a.prime.com
info–stratus–request
@mike.lrc.edu
info–tahoe–request
@uwm.edu
info–tandem–request
@zorch.sf–bay.org
info–vm–
request@uunet.uu.net
info.bind
info.brl-cad
info.bytecounters
info.convex
info.gated
info.grass.programmer
info.isode
info.labmgr
info.mach
info.nets
info.nsfnet.cert
info.nupop
info.nysersnmp
info.osf
info.ph

info.snmp
info.solbourne
info.unix-sw
informix–list–request
@rmy.emory.edu
informix_sig_nca–
request@adaclabs.com
interest–groups–
request@nisc.sri.com
intertxt@network.
ucsd.edu
irchat–request
@cc.tut.fi
istserv@research.
canon.oz.au
iti151–request
@oce.orst.edu
jargon–helpers–
request@snark.
thyrsus.com
jet@nas.nasa.gov
jhbercovitz@lbl.gov
k12.ed.comp.literacy
khoros–request
@chama.eece.unm.edu
lang–lucid–request
@csl.sri.com
linux–activists–
request@niksula.hut.fi
listmaster@germany.eu.net
listserv@archive.oit.unc.edu
listserv@bolis.sf–bay.
org
listserv@boxer.nas.nasa.gov
listserv@cis.vutbr.cz
listserv@eng.monash.edu.au
listserv@grot.starconn.com
listserv@pandora.sf.ca.us
listserv@vtvm1.cc.vt.edu
logo–friends–request
@aiai.ed.ac.uk
mac–security–request
@world.std.com

machten–request
@tenon.com
mail–bbones–request
@yorku.ca
mail–server
@knex.via.mind.org
majordomo@ornl.gov
majordomo@taskon.no
majordomo@theus.
rain.com
matlab–users–request
@mcs.anl.gov
medphys–request
@radonc.duke.edu
misc.forsale.computers.d
misc.forsale.computers.
mac
misc.forsale.computers.
pc-clone
misc.forsale.computers.
workstation
misc.kids.computer
misc.legal.computing
misc.test
mp–users–request
@thunder.mcrcim.
mcgill.
ms–access–request
@eunet.co.at
multicast–request
@arizona.edu
navnews@nctamslant.
navy.mil
neci–discuss–request
@pioneer.ci.net
netblazer–users–
request@telebit.com
neuron–request
@cattell.psych.
upenn.edu
nev@renews.
relcom.msk.su
news.admin.misc
news.admin.technical
news.config

sybase–request
@apple.com
tcad–request
@iec.ufl.edu
tcp–group–request
@ucsd.edu
teleusers–request
@telesoft.com
testing–research–
request@cs.uiuc.edu
think–c–request
@ics.uci.edu
tim@qedbbs.com   160
tinymuck–sloggers–
request@piggy.
ucsb.edu
tinymush–programmers–
request
@cygnus.com
transputer–request
@tcgould.tn.cornell.edu
u3b.config
u3b.misc
u3b.tech
u3b.test
umd5!grebyn!posix–ada–
request
unisys–request
@bcm.tmc.edu
univel–request
@telly.on.ca
usergroup–request
@mjolner.dk
utzoo!trigraph!oda–
request
uug–dist–request
@dsi.com
uunet!zardoz!security–
request
vmsnet.admin
vmsnet.alpha
vmsnet.announce.
newusers
vmsnet.databases.rdb
vmsnet.decus.journal

vmsnet.decus.lugs
vmsnet.infosystems.
gopher
vmsnet.infosystems.misc
vmsnet.internals
vmsnet.mail.misc
vmsnet.mail.mx
vmsnet.mail.pmdf
vmsnet.misc
vmsnet.networks.
desktop.misc
vmsnet.networks.
desktop.pathworks
vmsnet.networks.
management.decmcc
vmsnet.networks.
management.misc
vmsnet.networks.misc
vmsnet.networks.
tcp-ip.cmu-tek
vmsnet.networks.
tcp-ip.multinet
vmsnet.networks.
tcp-ip.tcpware
vmsnet.networks.
tcp-ip.ucx
vmsnet.networks.
tcp-ip.wintcp
vmsnet.pdp-11
vmsnet.sources
vmsnet.sources.d
vmsnet.sources.games
vmsnet.sysmgt
vmsnet.test
vmsnet.uucp
vmsnet.vms-posix
word–mac–request
@alsvid.une.edu.au
x–ada–request
@expo.lcs.mit.edu
xgks–request
@unidata.ucar.edu
xopen–testing–
request@uel.co.uk
zforum–request
@comlab.ox.ac.uk

Culture

alt.appalachian
alt.california
alt.culture.alaska
alt.culture.argentina
alt.culture.hawaii
alt.culture.indonesia
alt.culture.karnataka
alt.culture.kerala
alt.culture.ny-upstate
alt.culture.oregon
alt.culture.tuva
alt.culture.us.
asian-indian
alt.culture.us.southwest
alt.fashion
alt.folklore.urban
alt.india.progressive
alt.memetics
alt.native
alt.skinheads
alt.society.conservatism
alt.society.
generation-x
argentina–request
@ois.db.toronto.edu
bit.listserv.india-d
bit.listserv.slovak-l
bit.listserv.xcult-l
bras–net–request
@cs.ucla.edu
burkov@drfmc.ceng.cea.fr
clari.news.lifestyle
davep@acsu.buffalo.edu
dimitrije@buenga.bu.edu
elendil@mintir.
new–orleans.la.us
gst@gnosys.svle.ma.us
ibenko@maveric0.
uwaterloo.ca
krzystek@u.washington.
edu
lasnet–request
@emx.utexas.edu

Dancing

Disabilities

bit.listserv.autism
bit.listserv.blindnws
bit.listserv.deaf-l
bit.listserv.dsshe-l
k12.ed.special
listserv@n7kbt.rain.com
living–request
    @qiclab.scn.rain.com
misc.handicap
misc.health.diabetes
our–kids–request
    @oar.net
panic–request
    @gnu.ai.mit.edu
recovery@wvnvm.
    wvnet.edu
wtm@bunker.shel.
    isc–br.com

Education

alt.education.ib
alt.education.ib.tok
alt.folklore.college
alt.grad-student.
    tenured
alt.grad.skool.sux
bit.listserv.ashe-l
bit.listserv.dectei-l
bit.listserv.dsshe-l
bit.listserv.edpolyan
bit.listserv.edtech
bit.listserv.edusig-l
bit.listserv.erl-l
bit.listserv.ibm-hesc
bit.listserv.lawsch-l
bit.listserv.mba-l
bit.listserv.mbu-l
bit.listserv.mdphd-l
bit.listserv.medforum
bit.listserv.nettrain
bit.listserv.physhare
bit.listserv.psycgrad
bit.listserv.sganet

bit.listserv.slart-l
bit.listserv.tecmat-l
bit.listserv.ucp-l
cabot–request
    @sol.crd.ge.com
clari.tw.education
cogneuro–request
    @ptolemy.arc.nasa.gov
comp.ai.edu
comp.edu
comp.edu.composition
ctf–discuss–request
    @cis.upenn.edu
cussnet–request
    @stat.com
decnews@mr4dec.
    enet.dec.com
dont–tell–request
    @choice.princeton.edu
home–ed–politics–
    request@mainstream.
    com
home–ed–request
    @think.comrelcom.
    commerce.chemical
hreha@vax2.concordia.ca
info.nsf.grants
info.nsfnet.status
k12.chat.elementary
k12.chat.junior
k12.chat.senior
k12.chat.teacher
k12.ed.art
k12.ed.business
k12.ed.comp.literacy
k12.ed.health-pe
k12.ed.life-skills
k12.ed.math
k12.ed.music
k12.ed.science
k12.ed.soc-studies
k12.ed.special
k12.ed.tag
k12.ed.tech
k12.lang.art

k12.lang.deutsch-eng
k12.lang.esp-eng
k12.lang.francais
k12.lang.russian
k12.library
k12.sys.channel0
k12.sys.channel1
k12.sys.channel10
k12.sys.channel11
k12.sys.channel12
k12.sys.channel2
k12.sys.channel3
k12.sys.channel4
k12.sys.channel5
k12.sys.channel6
k12.sys.channel7
k12.sys.channel8
k12.sys.channel9
k12.sys.projects
learning–request
    @sea.east.sun.com
listserv@cornell.edu
misc.education
misc.education.
    language.english
misc.int-property
misc.legal
misc.writing
prog–pubs–request
    @fuggles.acc.
    virginia.edu
rec.aviation.student
sci.edu
sci.med.pharmacy
sci.op-research
sci.stat.edu
service@swi.psy.uva.nl
soc.college
soc.college.grad
soc.college.gradinfo
soc.college.
    teaching-asst
ups500@dbnrhrz1

Electrical

comp.org.fidonet
comp.org.ieee
ieee.announce
ieee.config
ieee.general
ieee.pcnfs
ieee.rab.announce
ieee.rab.general
ieee.region1
ieee.tab.announce
ieee.tab.general
ieee.tcos
ieee.usab.announce
ieee.usab.general

Electronics

bit.listserv.edi-l
bit.listserv.emusic-l
bit.listserv.vpiej-l
clari.tw.electronics
rec.video
rec.video.cable-tv
rec.video.releases
rec.video.satellite
relcom.commerce.
   audio-video
sci.electronics

Employment

bionet.jobs
biz.jobs.offered
cogneuro–request
   @ptolemy.arc.nasa.gov
employ–request
   @oti.disa.mil
listserv@jerusalem1.
   datasrv.co.il
listserv@pnfi.forestry.ca
misc.jobs.contract
misc.jobs.misc
misc.jobs.offered
misc.jobs.offered.entry

misc.jobs.resumes
relcom.commerce.jobs
sci.research.careers
vmsnet.employment

Engineering

comp.org.fidonet
comp.org.ieee
ieee.announce
ieee.config
ieee.general
ieee.pcnfs
ieee.rab.announce
ieee.rab.general
ieee.region1
ieee.tab.announce
ieee.tab.general
ieee.tcos
ieee.usab.general
info.ietf
info.ietf.hosts
info.ietf.njm
info.ietf.smtp
info.pem-dev
info.wisenet
sci.engr
sci.engr.advanced-tv
sci.engr.biomed
sci.engr.chem
sci.engr.civil
sci.engr.control
sci.engr.manufacturing
sci.engr.mech
sci.materials

Entertainment

alt.asian-movies
alt.comedy.
   firesgn-thtre
alt.commercial-hit-
   radio.must.die
alt.cult-movies
alt.cult-movies.
   rocky-horror
alt.drwho.creative

alt.elvis.king
alt.fan.dave_barry
alt.fan.disney.afternoon
alt.fan.dune
alt.fan.g-gordon-liddy
alt.fan.holmes
alt.fan.howard-stern
alt.fan.james-bond
alt.fan.mike-jittlov
alt.fan.monty-python
alt.fan.rush-limbaugh
alt.fan.woody-allen
alt.fandom.cons
alt.gothic
alt.horror
alt.horror.werewolves
alt.magic
alt.radio.networks.npr
alt.radio.pirate
alt.radio.scanner
alt.satellite.tv.europe
alt.sex.movies
alt.showbiz.gossip
alt.stagecraft
alt.startrek.creative
alt.supermodels
alt.vampyres
bit.listserv.cinema-l
bit.listserv.film-l
clari.news.entertain
clari.news.movies
clari.sfbay.entertain
equestrians–request
   @world.std.com
exhibitionists–request
   @jvnc.net
filmmakers–request
   @grissom.larc.nasa.gov
finewine–request
   @world.std.com
jeremy@stat.
   washington.edu
joe–bob–request
   @blkbox.com
kites–request

@harvard.harvard.edu
listserv@cornell.edu
listserv@suvm.acs.syr.edu
magic–request
@maillist.crd.ge.com
mikey@perch.nosc.mil
musicals–request
@world.std.com
mystery–request
@csd4.csd.uwm.edu
ranger–list–request
@taronga.com
rec.arts.animation
rec.arts.anime
rec.arts.anime.
marketplace
rec.arts.anime.stories
rec.arts.drwho
rec.arts.movies
rec.arts.movies.reviews
rec.arts.sf.movies
rec.arts.startrek.current
rec.arts.startrek.reviews
rec.arts.theatre
rec.audio
rec.audio.high-end
rec.games.video.classic
rec.video.production
rec.video.releases
rec.video.satellite
relcom.comp.animation
soundtracks–request
@ifi.unizh.ch
theatre–request
@world.std.com
see also Dancing; Music;
Television

Farming

alt.chinchilla
alt.cows.moo.moo.moo
alt.sustainable.agriculture
framers–request
@uunet.uu.net

Finance

bionet.sci-resources
clari.biz.economy
clari.biz.economy.world
clari.biz.finance
clari.biz.finance.earnings
clari.biz.finance.personal
clari.biz.finance.services
clari.biz.invest
clari.biz.market
clari.biz.market.amex
clari.biz.market.dow
clari.biz.market.ny
clari.biz.market.otc
clari.biz.market.report
clari.news.economy
clari.news.gov.budget
clari.news.gov.taxes
clari.tw.stocks
info.nsf.grants
info.nsfnet.status
misc.entrepreneurs
misc.invest
misc.invest.canada
misc.invest.real-estate
misc.invest.technical
misc.taxes
relcom.commerce.estate
relcom.commerce.money
relcom.commerce.stocks
relcom.currency
relcom.infomarket.quote
relcom.infomarket.talk
relcom.spbnews
relcom.wtc
sci.econ
smi–request
@world.std.com

Food

alt.beer
alt.cereal
alt.college.food

alt.folklore.herbs
alt.food.cocacola
alt.food.fat-free
alt.food.mcdonalds
alt.gourmand
alt.mcdonalds
alt.spam
fatfree–request
@hustle.rahul.net
homebrew–request
%hpfcmr@hplabs.
hp.com
hplabs!hpfcmr!homebrew–
request
kuharske–bukve
@krpan.arnes.si
listserv@gibbs.oit.unc.edu
rec.crafts.winemaking
rec.food.cooking
rec.food.drink
rec.food.historic
rec.food.recipes
rec.food.restaurants
rec.food.sourdough
rec.food.veg
relcom.commerce.food
relcom.commerce.
food.sweet

Fun

alt.callahans
alt.comedy.british
alt.dragons-inn
alt.kids-talk
alt.party
alt.pub.dragons-inn
alt.quotations
alt.shenanigans
clari.news.almanac
geiser@pictel.com
rec.games.trivia
rec.humor
rec.humor.d
rec.humor.funny

rec.humor.oracle
rec.humor.oracle.d
relcom.humor
talk.bizarre
talk.rumors

Games

alt.games.frp.dnd-util
alt.games.frp.
  live-action
alt.games.gb
alt.games.lynx
alt.games.mk
alt.games.omega
alt.games.sf2
alt.games.torg
alt.games.vga-planets
alt.games.xpilot
alt.netgames.bolo
appel@erzo.berkeley.edu
ars–magica–request
  @soda.berkeley.edu
bit.listserv.games-l
chessnews–request
  @tssi.com
comp.sys.ibm.pc.
  games.action
comp.sys.ibm.pc.
  games.adventure
comp.sys.ibm.pc.
  games.announce
comp.sys.ibm.pc.
  games.misc
comp.sys.ibm.pc.
  games.rpg
comp.sys.ibm.pc.
  games.strategic
crossfire–request
  @ifi.uio.no
cz–request@stsci.edu
flashlife–request
  @netcom.com
grass–server
  @wharton.upenn.edu

hcobb@fly2.berkeley.edu
jwisdom@gnu.ai.mit.edu
listserv@boxer.
  nas.nasa.gov
listserv@cornell.edu
listserv@hearn.bitnet
listserv@hearn.nic.
  surfnet.nl
lsonko@pearl.tuft.edu
owner–gurps–
  announceext
  @think.com
raven+request
  @drycas.club.cc.
  cmu.edu
rec.gambling
rec.games.abstract
rec.games.backgammon
rec.games.board
rec.games.board.ce
rec.games.bridge
rec.games.chess
rec.games.corewar
rec.games.design
rec.games.diplomacy
rec.games.empire
rec.games.frp.advocacy
rec.games.frp.announce
rec.games.frp.archives
rec.games.frp.dnd
rec.games.frp.marketplace
rec.games.frp.misc
rec.games.go
rec.games.hack
rec.games.int-fiction
rec.games.miniatures
rec.games.misc
rec.games.moria
rec.games.mud.admin
rec.games.mud.announce
rec.games.mud.diku
rec.games.mud.lp
rec.games.mud.misc
rec.games.mud.tiny
rec.games.netrek

rec.games.pbm
rec.games.pinball
rec.games.programmer
rec.games.rogue
rec.games.roguelike.
  announce
rec.games.roguelike.
  misc
rec.games.vectrex
rec.games.video.arcade
rec.games.video.classic
rec.games.video.
  marketplace
rec.games.video.misc
rec.games.video.nintendo
rec.games.video.sega
rec.games.xtank.play
rec.puzzles
rec.puzzles.crosswords
runequest–request
  @glorantha.holland.
  sun.com
tekumel–request
  @ssdc.honeywell.com
traveller–request
  @engrg.uwo.ca
vampire–request
  @math.ufl.edu
wfrp–request
  @morticia.cnns.unt.edu

Gardening

alt.folklore.herbs
listserv@cms.cc.wayne.edu
rec.gardens

General

adoption–request
  @think.com
alt.answers
alt.basement.graveyard
alt.bigfoot
alt.bitterness
alt.bogus.group

alt.co-ops
alt.conspiracy
alt.destroy.the.earth
alt.dev.null
alt.devilbunnies
alt.fandom.cons
alt.good.morning
alt.good.news
alt.life.sucks
alt.military.cadet
alt.necromicon
alt.non.sequitur
alt.pantyhose
alt.peeves
alt.personals
alt.personals.ads
alt.personals.bondage
alt.personals.misc
alt.personals.poly
alt.prisons
alt.shut.the.hell.up.geek
alt.spleen
alt.stupidity
alt.tasteless
alt.toys.hi-tech
alt.toys.lego
alt.toys.transformers
alt.wedding
alt.whine
altinst–request
  @cs.cmu.edu
bit.listserv.candle-l
bit.org.peace-corps
brewer@ace.enet.
  dec.com
clari.local.arizona
clari.local.california
clari.local.california.briefs
clari.local.chicago
clari.local.chicago.briefs
clari.local.florida
clari.local.florida.briefs
clari.local.georgia
clari.local.georgia.briefs
clari.local.headlines

clari.local.illinois
clari.local.illinois.briefs
clari.local.indiana
clari.local.indiana.briefs
clari.local.iowa
clari.local.iowa.briefs
clari.local.los_angeles
clari.local.louisiana
clari.local.maritimes.briefs
clari.local.maryland
clari.local.maryland.briefs
clari.local.massachusetts
clari.local.massachusetts.
  briefs
clari.local.michigan
clari.local.michigan.briefs
clari.local.minnesota
clari.local.minnesota.briefs
clari.local.missouri
clari.local.missouri.briefs
clari.local.nebraska
clari.local.nebraska.briefs
clari.local.nevada
clari.local.nevada.briefs
clari.local.new_england
clari.local.new_hampshire
clari.local.new_jersey
clari.local.new_jersey.briefs
clari.local.new_york
clari.local.new_york.briefs
clari.local.nyc
clari.local.nyc.briefs
clari.local.ohio
clari.local.ohio.briefs
clari.local.oregon
clari.local.oregon.briefs
clari.local.pennsylvania
clari.local.sfbay
clari.local.texas
clari.local.texas.briefs
clari.local.utah
clari.local.utah.briefs
clari.local.virginia+dc
clari.local.virginia+dc.
  briefs

clari.local.washington
clari.local.washington.
  briefs
clari.local.wisconsin
clari.local.wisconsin.
  briefs
clari.nb.top
clari.nb.trends
clari.news.briefs
clari.news.bulletin
clari.news.cast
clari.news.disaster
clari.news.features
clari.news.flash
clari.news.goodnews
clari.news.group
clari.news.group.blacks
clari.news.group.women
clari.news.headlines
clari.news.interest
clari.news.interest.history
clari.news.interest.people
clari.news.interest.quirks
clari.news.issues
clari.news.top
clari.news.trends
clari.news.trouble
clari.news.urgent
clari.sfbay.briefs
clari.sfbay.fire
clari.sfbay.general
clari.sfbay.misc
clari.sfbay.police
clari.sfbay.roads
clari.sfbay.short
dc–motss–request
  @vector.intercon.com
deviants–request
  @csv.warwick.ac.uk
geiser@pictel.com
gsp–list–request
  @ms.uky.edu
gsp–list–request
  @ukma.bitnet
info.firearms

info.firearms.politics
info@vm1.nodak.edu
k12.chat.elementary
k12.chat.junior
k12.chat.senior
k12.chat.teacher
libernet–request
    @dartmouth.edu
listserv@uci.com
listserv@ucsd.edu
liz@ai.mit.edu
misc.consumers
misc.consumers.house
misc.forsale
misc.forsale.computers.d
misc.forsale.computers.
    mac
misc.forsale.computers.
    other
misc.forsale.computers.
    pc-clone
misc.forsale.computers.
    workstation
misc.headlines
misc.int-property
misc.kids
misc.kids.computer
misc.rural
misc.wanted
nerdnosh–request
    @scruz.ucsc.edu
news.announce.
    conferences
news.announce.
    important
news.announce.
    newgroups
news.announce.
    newusers
news.config
news.lists
news.newsites
owner–twins
    @athena.mit.edu

partners–request
    @cs.cmu.edu
prion–request
    @stolaf.edu
qv–interest–request
    @swap.eng.sun.com
rec.arts.misc
rec.arts.wobegon
rec.folk-dancing
rec.gambling
rec.games.trivia
rec.heraldry
rec.mag.fsfnet
rec.nude
rec.org.sca
rec.parks.theme
rec.pyrotechnics
rec.roller-coaster
relcom.ads
relcom.archives
relcom.bbs
relcom.commerce.
    construction
relcom.commerce.
    consume
relcom.commerce.
    household
relcom.commerce.
    infoserv
relcom.commerce.
    machinery
relcom.commerce.metals
relcom.commerce.other
relcom.commerce.talk
relcom.expo
relcom.fido.flirt
relcom.fido.su.general
relcom.fido.su.magic
relcom.infomarket.quote
relcom.jusinf
relcom.kids
relcom.maps
relcom.netnews.big
relcom.newusers
relcom.talk

sca–request
    @mc.lcs.mit.edu
sca–west–request
    @ecst.csuchico.edu
sci.research
sci.skeptic
scoann–request
    @xenitec.on.ca
scogen–request
    @xenitec.on.ca
siege–request
    @bransle.ucs.mun.ca
soc.answers
soc.college
soc.couples
soc.libraries.talk
soc.misc
soc.net-people
soc.singles
societies–request
    @athena.mit.edu
talk.bizarre
talk.rumors
ups_alumni–request
    @stephsf.com
uruguay–request
    @eniac.seas.upenn.
    edu
utne–salon–request
    @netcom.com
vintage–request
    @presto.ig.com
vmsnet.announce
weather–users-
    request@zorch.
    sf–bay.org

Geography

alt.great-lakes
bit.listserv.india-d
bit.listserv.mideur-l
bit.listserv.seasia-l
bit.listserv.uigis-l
frabbani@epas.utoronto.
    ca

listserv@ukcc.uky.edu

migra–list–request
@cc.utah.edu

sstaton@deltos.com

Government

alt.dear.whitehouse

alt.politics.org.batf

alt.politics.org.cia

alt.politics.org.nsa

alt.president.clinton

bit.listserv.govdoc-l

bit.listserv.sganet

bottasini@cesi.it

clari.canada.gov

clari.nb.govt

clari.news.gov

clari.news.gov.agency

clari.news.gov.budget

clari.news.gov.corrupt

clari.news.gov.
   international

clari.news.gov.officials

clari.news.gov.state

clari.news.gov.taxes

clari.news.gov.usa

clari.news.law.supreme

clari.news.military

clari.tw.space

dont–tell–request
@choice.princeton.edu

fairness–request
@mainstream.com

sci.military

soc.veterans

subscribe@xamiga.
   linet.org

talk.politics.crypto

Health

alt.abuse.recovery

alt.angst

alt.backrubs

alt.drugs.caffeine

alt.hemp

alt.hypnosis

alt.med.cfs

alt.meditation

alt.mindcontrol

alt.recovery.
   codependency

bit.listserv.c+health

bit.listserv.cfs.newsletter

bit.listserv.mednews

clari.tw.health

clari.tw.health.aids

fatfree–request
@hustle.rahul.net

ibdlist–request
%mvac23@udel.edu

immune–request
@weber.ucsd.edu

info–aids
@rainbow.uucp

k12.ed.health-pe

listserv@dartcms1.
   dartmouth.edu

listserv@gibbs.oit.unc.edu

listserv@lehigh.edu

listserv@sjuvm.stjohns.edu

maynor@ra.msstate.edu

misc.emerg-services

misc.fitness

misc.health.alternative

misc.health.diabetes

pipes–request
@paul.rutgers.edu

rec.running

recovery@wvnvm.
   wvnet.edu

relcom.commerce.
   tobacco

weights–request
@mickey.disney.com

wtm@bunker.shel.
   isc–br.com

History

alt.conspiracy.jfk

alt.history.living

alt.history.what-if

alt.mythology

alt.revisionism

alt.war

alt.war.civil.usa

alt.war.vietnam

bit.listserv.c18-l

bit.listserv.history

bottasini@cesi.it

clari.news.interest.history

info–russ
@smarty.ece.jhu.edu

k12.ed.soc-studies

rec.food.historic

rec.heraldry

sci.classics

soc.culture.french

soc.culture.german

soc.culture.tamil

soc.history

soc.roots

soc.veterans

Hobbies

2strokes–request
@microunity.com

alt.aquaria

alt.collecting.autographs

alt.comics.batman

alt.comics.lnh

alt.comics.superman

alt.fishing

alt.history.living

alt.magic

alt.sewing

alt.skate-board

alt.surfing

bit.listserv.postcard

bit.listserv.scuba-l

brewer@ace.enet.
   dec.com

rec.scuba
rec.sport.paintball
rec.video.production
rec.woodworking
relcom.commerce.
    tobacco
relcom.penpals
rx7club@cbjjn.att.com
sf–lovers–request
    @rutgers.edu
soc.penpals
talk.politics.guns
tcp–group–request
    @ucsd.edu
todd@di.com
tx–firearms–request
    @frontier.lonestar.org
vintage–request
    @presto.ig.com
weather–users–
    request@zorch.
    sf–bay.org
wetleather–request
    @frigg.isc–br.com
wheeltowheel–
    request@abingdon.
    Eng.Sun.COM
wxsat–request
    @ssg.com

Human Sexuality

alt.binaries.pictures.
    erotica
alt.binaries.pictures.
    erotica.blondes
alt.binaries.pictures.
    erotica.d
alt.binaries.pictures.
    erotica.female
alt.binaries.pictures.
    erotica.male
alt.binaries.pictures.
    erotica.orientals
alt.feminism

alt.flame
alt.flame.net-cops
alt.flame.roommate
alt.homosexual
alt.personals
alt.personals.ads
alt.personals.bondage
alt.personals.misc
alt.personals.poly
alt.politics.
    homosexuality
alt.polyamory
alt.romance
alt.romance.chat
alt.sex
alt.sex.bestiality
alt.sex.bestiality.barney
alt.sex.bondage
alt.sex.exhibitionism
alt.sex.fetish.feet
alt.sex.fetish.orientals
alt.sex.masturbation
alt.sex.motss
alt.sex.movies
alt.sex.pictures
alt.sex.spanking
alt.sex.stories
alt.sex.stories.d
alt.sex.voyeurism
alt.sex.wanted
alt.sex.watersports
alt.sex.wizards
alt.transgendered
amazons–request
    @math.uio.no
ausgblf–request
    @minyos.xx.rmit.oz.au
ba–sappho–request
    @labrys.mti.sgi.com
bit.listserv.gaynet
c._louise_vigil.osbu_north
    @xerox.com
cd–request
    @valis.biocad.com

chorus–request
    @psych.toronto.edu
clari.news.group.gays
clari.news.group.women
clari.news.sex
dsa–lgb–request
    @midway.uchicago.edu
eagles–request
    @flash.usc.edu
el406010@brownvm.
    brown.edu
endorphins–request
    @taronga.com
ericg@indiana.edu
gaynet–request
    @queernet.org
glbpoc–request
    @geri.pa.dec.com
khush–request
    @husc3.harvard.edu
la–motss–request
    @flash.usc.edu
libfem–request
    @math.uio.no
listserv@american.edu
listserv@brownvm.
    brown.edu
listserv@ksuvm.ksu.edu
listserv@ukcc.uky.edu
listserv@vm.usc.edu
mail–men–request
    @usl.com
majordomo@cs.
    colorado.edu
majordomo@plts.org
majordomo@
    queernet.org
moms–request
    @qiclab.scn.rain.com
ne–social–motss–
    request@plts.org
noglstp–request
    @elroy.jpl.nasa.gov
oh–motss–request
    @cps.udayton.edu

esperanto–request
  @rand.org
ibenko@maveric0.
  uwaterloo.ca
info–russ
  @smarty.ece.jhu.edu
k12.lang.deutsch-eng
k12.lang.esp-eng
k12.lang.francais
k12.lang.russian
lojban–list–request
  @snark.thyrsus.com
misc.education.
  language.english
oglasna–deska
  @krpan.arnes.si
oglasna.deska
  @uni–lj.si
pisma–bralcev
  @krpan.arnes.si
relcom.bbs.list
rokpress@krpan.arnes.si
rokpress@uni–lj.si
romanians@sep.
  stanford.edu
sci.classics
sci.lang
sci.lang.japan
soc.culture.esperanto
soc.culture.tamil
tolkien–request
  @pub.vse.cz
tolklang–request
  @lfcs.ed.ac.uk
uruguay–request
  @eniac.seas.upenn.edu

Legal

alt.abortion.inequity
alt.adoption
alt.dads-rights
alt.law-enforcement
alt.missing-kids
bit.listserv.ada-law

biz.stolen
clari.biz.courts
clari.canada.law
clari.nb.govt
clari.news.gov.taxes
clari.news.law
clari.news.law.civil
clari.news.law.crime
clari.news.law.crime.sex
clari.news.law.crime.
  violent
clari.news.law.drugs
clari.news.law.
  investigation
clari.news.law.police
clari.news.law.prison
clari.news.law.supreme
clari.sfbay.police
firearms–request
  @cs.cmu.edu
misc.legal
misc.legal.computing
rec.autos
relcom.jusinf
talk.rape

Literature

alt.amateur-comp
alt.books.anne-rice
alt.books.deryni
alt.books.
  isaac-asimov
alt.books.reviews
alt.books.technical
alt.comics.batman
alt.comics.lnh
alt.comics.superman
alt.fan.douglas-adams
alt.fan.furry
alt.fan.holmes
alt.fan.james-bond
alt.fan.pern
alt.fan.piers-anthony
alt.fan.pratchett

alt.fan.tolkien
alt.fan.tom-robbins
alt.fan.wodehouse
alt.prose
alt.quotations
alt.society.ati
alt.wired
alt.zines
alt.znet.pc
amagyar@phoenix.
  princeton.edu
appel@erzo.berkeley.edu
bionet.journals.contents
bionet.journals.note
bit.lang.neder-l
bit.listserv.cfs.newsletter
bit.listserv.literary
bit.listserv.mednews
bit.listserv.rra-l
bit.listserv.xcult-l
biz.books.technical
biz.sco.magazine
cerebi-request
  @tomservo.b23b.
  ingr.com
clari.feature.dave_barry
clari.feature.mike_royko
clari.feature.miss_manners
clari.matrix_news
clari.nb.review
clari.news.books
clari.news.interest.
  people.column
clari.news.movies
clari.news.music
clari.news.tv
clari.sfbay.entertain
comp.ai.jair.announce
comp.ai.jair.papers
comp.answers
da1n@andrew.cmu.edu
decnews–pr–request
  @pa.dec.com
decnews–unix–
  request@pa.dec.com

Medicine

Music

alt.music.alternative
alt.music.canada
alt.music.enya
alt.music.filk
alt.music.hardcore
alt.music.jewish
alt.music.marillion
alt.music.prince
alt.music.progressive
alt.music.queen
alt.music.rush
alt.music.ska
alt.music.tmbg
alt.music.u2
alt.music.world
alt.rap
alt.rave
alt.rock-n-roll
alt.rock-n-roll.acdc
alt.rock-n-roll.classic
alt.rock-n-roll.hard
alt.rock-n-roll.metal
alt.rock-n-roll.
   metal.gnr
alt.rock-n-roll.
   metal.heavy
alt.rock-n-roll.
   metal.metallica
alt.rock-n-roll.
   metal.progressive
alt.rock-n-roll.oldies
alt.rock-n-roll.stones
backstreets–request
   @virginia.edu
barbershop–request
   @bigd.cray.com
bit.listserv.allmusic
bit.listserv.emusic-l
bit.listserv.mla-l
brass–request
   @geomag.gly.fsu.edu
bwoolf@pro–woolf.
   clark.net
chorus–request
   @psych.toronto.edu

clari.news.music
com@spacsun.rice.edu
comp.music
comp.sys.amiga.audio
concrete–blonde–
   request@piggy.ucsb.
   edu
costello–request
   @gnu.ai.mit.edu
dewy–fields–request
   @ifi.uio.no
dire–straits–request
   @merrimack.edu
echoes–request
   @fawnya.tcs.com
ecto–request
   @ns1.rutgers.edu
elo–list–request
   @andrew.cmu.edu
etheridge–request
   @krylov.cnd.mcgill.ca
fegmaniax–request
   @gnu.ai.mit.edu
freaks–request
   @bnf.com
funky–music–request
   @athena.mit.edu
fuzzy–ramblings–
   request@piggy.
   ucsb.edu
glocke@morgan.ucs.
   mun.ca
hey–joe–request
   @ms.uky.edu
indigo–girls–request
   @cgrg.ohio
   state.edu
info–high–audio–
   request@csd4.csd.
   uwm.edu
info.jethro-tull
inxs–list–request
   @iastate.edu
j.arnold@bull.com
janes–addiction–
   request@ms.uky.edu

jpop–request
   @ferkel.ucsb.edu
jtull–request
   @remus.rutgers.edu
jump–in–the–river–
   request@presto.ig.com
k12.ed.music
kiwimusic–request
   @athena.mit.edu
klf–request
   @asylum.sf.ca.us
kosmos–request
   @athena.mit.edu
larryn@csufres.csufresno.
   edu
level42–request
   @enterprise.bih.
   harvard.edu
life–talking–request
   @ferkel.ucsb.edu
listserv@brownvm.
   brown.edu
listserv@orbital.demon.
   co.uk
listserv@suvm.acs.syr.edu
loureed–request
   @cvi.hahnemann.edu
lute–request
   @sunapee.
   dartmouth.edu
middle–eastern–music–
   request
   @nic.funet.fi
mikey@perch.nosc.mil
mkwong@scf.nmsu.edu
murph@maine.bitnet
music–research–
   request@prg.
   oxford.ac.uk
musicals–request
   @world.std.com
ne–raves–request
   @silver.lcs.mit.edu
netjam–request
   @xcf.berkeley.edu

on–u–request
@connect.com.au
oysters–request
@blowfish.taligent.
com
ph7–request@bnf.com
pipes–request
@sunapee.
dartmouth.edu
police–request
@cindy.ecst.csuchico.
edu
prince–request
@icpsr.umich.edu
queensryche–request
@pilot.njin.net
really–deep–thoughts–
request
@gradient.cis.upenn
rec.arts.marching.
drumcorps
rec.arts.marching.misc
rec.audio
rec.audio.car
rec.audio.high-end
rec.audio.pro
rec.music.a-cappella
rec.music.afro-latin
rec.music.beatles
rec.music.bluenote
rec.music.cd
rec.music.celtic
rec.music.christian
rec.music.classical
rec.music.classical.guitar
rec.music.classical.
performing
rec.music.compose
rec.music.country.western
rec.music.dementia
rec.music.dylan
rec.music.early
rec.music.folk
rec.music.funky
rec.music.gaffa

rec.music.gdead
rec.music.indian.classical
rec.music.indian.misc
rec.music.industrial
rec.music.info
rec.music.makers
rec.music.makers.bass
rec.music.makers.guitar
rec.music.makers.guitar.
acoustic
rec.music.makers.guitar.
tablature
rec.music.makers.
marketplace
rec.music.makers.
percussion
rec.music.makers.synth
rec.music.marketplace
rec.music.misc
rec.music.newage
rec.music.phish
rec.music.reggae
rec.music.reviews
rec.music.video
relcom.music
rstewart@unex.ucla.edu
rtv1@cornell.edu
rush–request
@syrinx.umd.edu
smallmusic–request
@xcf.berkeley.edu
soundtracks–request
@ifi.unizh.ch
stormcock–request
@dcs.qmw.ac.uk
tadream–request
@vacs.uwp.edu
tears4–fears–request
@ms.uky.edu
they–might–be–
request@gnu.ai.
mit.edu
top–request
@cv.ruu.nl

undercover–request
@snowhite.cis.
uoguelph.ca
uwm!uwpvacs!tadream–
request
uwpvacs!tadream–
request@uwm.edu
valerie@athena.mit.edu
yello–request
@overpass.
calpoly.edu
zeppelin–l
@cornell.edu
see also Entertainment

Parapsychology

alt.alien.visitors
alt.astrology
alt.divination
alt.folklore.
ghost-stories
alt.magick
alt.meditation.
transcendental
alt.out-of-body
alt.paranet.abduct
alt.paranet.paranormal
alt.paranet.science
alt.paranet.skeptic
alt.paranet.ufo
alt.paranormal
comp.ai.edu
comp.ai.vision
listserv@jhuvm.hcf.
jhu.edu
relcom.fido.su.magic

Pets

equestrians–request
@world.std.com
ferret–request
@ferret.ocunix.on.ca
golden–request
@hobbes.ucsd.edu

rec.pets
rec.pets.birds
rec.pets.cats
rec.pets.dogs
rec.pets.herp
talk.politics.animals

Philosophy

alt.discordia
alt.evil
alt.individualism
alt.memetics
alt.philosophy.
   objectivism
ayurveda–request
   @netcom.com
bit.listserv.fnord-l
bit.listserv.xtropy-l
extropians–request
   @extropy.org
objectivism–request
   @vix.com
pagan–request
   @drycas.club.cc.
   cmu.edu
pruss@math.ubc.ca
sci.logic
sci.philosophy.meta
sci.philosophy.tech
solan@math.uio.no
talk.philosophy.misc
uus–l@info.
   terraluna.org

Politics

ae852@yfn.ysu.edu
aids–request
   @cs.ucla.edu
alt.dear.whitehouse
alt.fan.dan-quayle
alt.fan.ronald-reagan
alt.fan.rush-limbaugh
alt.politics.british
alt.politics.clinton
alt.politics.correct

alt.politics.economics
alt.politics.greens
alt.politics.
   homosexuality
alt.politics.libertarian
alt.politics.org.batf
alt.politics.org.cia
alt.politics.org.nsa
alt.politics.perot
alt.politics.radical-left
alt.politics.reform
alt.politics.sex
alt.politics.usa.
   constitution
alt.politics.usa.misc
alt.politics.usa.
   republican
alt.president.clinton
alt.slick.willy.tax.tax.tax
alt.society.anarchy
alt.society.
   civil-liberties
alt.society.civil-liberty
alt.society.conservatism
alt.society.resistance
alt.visa.us
alt.war
alt.war.vietnam
ba–firearms–request
   @shell.portal.com
bit.listserv.disarm-l
bit.listserv.govdoc-l
bit.listserv.politics
ca–firearms–request
   @shell.portal.com
clari.canada.politics
clari.news.election
clari.news.gov.officials
clari.news.politics
clari.news.politics.people
clari.news.sex
clari.tw.health.aids
dont–tell–request
   @choice.princeton.edu
dsa–lgb–request
   @midway.uchicago.edu

info.firearms.politics
karplus@ce.ucsc.edu
majordomo@cs.colorado.
   edu
rec.guns
relcom.politics
relcom.spbnews
soc.politics
soc.politics.arms-d
subscribe@xamiga.linet.
   org
talk.politics.animals
talk.politics.china
talk.politics.crypto
talk.politics.drugs
talk.politics.guns
talk.politics.medicine
talk.politics.mideast
talk.politics.misc
talk.politics.soviet
talk.politics.space
talk.politics.theory
talk.rape
tx–firearms–request
   @frontier.lonestar.org
ups500@dbnrhrz1

Professional

alt.computer.consultants
alt.law-enforcement
alt.locksmithing
bionet.users.addresses
clari.news.law.profession
cussnet–request
   @stat.com
exhibitionists–request
   @jvnc.net
majordomo@csn.org
misc.emerg-services
misc.jobs.misc
misc.jobs.offered
misc.jobs.offered.entry
misc.jobs.resumes
noglstp–request
   @elroy.jpl.nasa.gov

relcom.commerce.jobs
sci.med.dentistry
skuster@bingvmb.bitnet
vmsnet.employment

Psychology

alt.child-support
alt.consciousness
alt.dreams
alt.dreams.lucid
alt.mindcontrol
alt.parents-teens
alt.polyamory
alt.psychology.
  personality
alt.recovery
alt.recovery.
  codependency
alt.romance
alt.self-improve
alt.sexual.abuse.recovery
alt.suicide.holiday
alt.support
alt.support.
  abuse-partners
alt.support.big-folks
alt.support.cancer
alt.support.diet
alt.support.
  mult-sclerosis
alt.support.step-parents
bit.listserv.envbeh-l
bit.listserv.ioob-l
bit.listserv.psycgrad
bit.listserv.sportpsy
clari.news.children
clari.news.issues.family
immune–request
  @weber.ucsd.edu
listserv@ucsd.edu
mensatalk–request
  @psg.com
misc.kids
nadir@acca.nmsu.edu

our–kids–request
  @oar.net
owner–twins
  @athena.mit.edu
panic–request
  @gnu.ai.mit.edu
recovery@wvnvm.
  wvnet.edu
relcom.kids
sci.cognitive
sci.life-extension
sci.psychology
suhre@trwrb.dsd.
  trw.com
talk.politics.drugs
walkers–request
  @world.std.com

Reference

alt.usage.english
bit.listserv.advanc-l
bit.listserv.axslib-l
bit.listserv.buslib-l
bit.listserv.circplus
bit.listserv.cwis-l
bit.listserv.dectei-l
bit.listserv.libref-l
bit.listserv.libres
bit.listserv.medlib-l
bit.listserv.mla-l
comp.internet.library
misc.legal

Religion

alt.atheism
alt.atheism.moderated
alt.brother-jed
alt.buddha.short.fat.guy
alt.divination
alt.evil
alt.hindu
alt.magick
alt.messianic
alt.music.jewish
alt.pagan

alt.religion.emacs
alt.religion.kibology
alt.religion.monica
alt.religion.scientology
alt.satanism
bahai–faith–request
  @oneworld.wa.com
bit.listserv.catholic
bit.listserv.christia
bit.listserv.hindu-d
bit.listserv.uus-l
catholic–request
  @sarto.gaithersburg.
  md.us
clari.news.religion
cms@dragon.com
faigin@aerospace.
  aero.org
godlygraphics–
  request@acs.
  harding.edu
grass–server
  @wharton.upenn.edu
lds–request
  @decwrl.dec.com
listserv@american.edu
listserv@arizvm1.
  ccit.arizona.edu
listserv@israel.
  nysernet.org
pagan–request
  @drycas.club.cc.
  cmu.edu
pruss@math.ubc.ca
rec.music.christian
rfreeman@vpnet.chi.il.us
soc.culture.jewish
soc.religion.bahai
soc.religion.christian
soc.religion.christian.
  bible-study
soc.religion.eastern
soc.religion.islam
soc.religion.quaker
st0o+sda@andrew.
  cmu.edu

talk.origins
talk.religion.misc
talk.religion.newage
uus–l
  @info.terraluna.org

Science

931rowe@merlin.nlu.edu
alife–request
  @cognet.ucla.edu
alt.engr.explosives
alt.fan.dall-agata
alt.folklore.science
alt.psychoactives
alt.sci.physics.acoustics
alt.sci.physics.
  new-theories
alt.sci.planetary
alt.sci.sociology
bit.listserv.biosph-l
bit.listserv.ethology
bit.listserv.geodesic
bit.listserv.libres
bit.listserv.physhare
bit.listserv.qualrs-l
bit.listserv.sos-data
bit.listserv.wx-talk
clari.news.weather
clari.sfbay.weather
clari.tw.science
clari.tw.space
cogneuro–request
  @ptolemy.arc.nasa.gov
dinosaur–request
  @donald.wichitaks.
  ncr.com
em–request
  @decwd.ece.uiuc.edu
fusion–request
  @zorch.sf–bay.org
gps–request
  @esseye.si.com
gst@gnosys.svle.ma.us
hyperchem–request
  @autodesk.com

iams–request
  @quack.kfu.com
info.wisenet
k12.ed.math
k12.ed.science
kgs@csdec2.tuwien.ac.at
kqb@whscad1.att.com
medphys–request
  @radonc.duke.edu
na.join@na–net.
  ornl.gov
novice–mzt
  @krpan.arnes.si
novice.mzt@uni–lj.si
nqthm–users–request
  @inf.fu–berlin.de
nqthm–users–request
  @cli.com
nucmed–request
  @uwovax.uwo.ca
physics–request
  @qedqcd.rye.ny.us
rec.arts.sf.science
rec.aviation.announce
rec.aviation.answers
rec.aviation.homebuilt
rec.aviation.ifr
rec.aviation.military
rec.aviation.misc
rec.aviation.products
rec.aviation.simulators
rec.aviation.soaring
relcom.commerce.
  chemical
relcom.commerce.
  energy
rockhounds–request
  @infodyn.com
rwhit@cs.umu.se
saarikko@cc.helsinki.fi
sci.aeronautics
sci.aeronautics.airliners
sci.anthropology
sci.aquaria
sci.archaeology
sci.astro

sci.astro.fits
sci.astro.hubble
sci.astro.planetarium
sci.bio
sci.bio.ecology
sci.chem
sci.chem.organomet
sci.classics
sci.cognitive
sci.comp-aided
sci.cryonics
sci.crypt
sci.data.formats
sci.econ
sci.econ.research
sci.electronics
sci.energy
sci.energy.hydrogen
sci.engr
sci.engr.advanced-tv
sci.engr.biomed
sci.engr.chem
sci.environment
sci.fractals
sci.geo.fluids
sci.geo.geology
sci.geo.meteorology
sci.life-extension
sci.logic
sci.math
sci.math.num-analysis
sci.math.research
sci.math.stat
sci.math.symbolic
sci.med.physics
sci.misc
sci.nanotech
sci.nonlinear
sci.op-research
sci.optics
sci.philosophy.meta
sci.philosophy.tech
sci.physics
sci.physics.accelerators
sci.physics.fusion

sci.physics.research
sci.polymers
sci.research
sci.research.careers
sci.skeptic
sci.space
sci.space.news
sci.space.shuttle
sci.stat.consult
sci.stat.edu
sci.stat.math
sci.systems
siege–request
    @bransle.ucs.mun.ca
soc.culture.scientists
starkid@ddsw1.mcs.com
talk.environment
talk.origins
talk.politics.space
tout@genesys.cps.
    msu.edu
see also Aviation; Biology

Social Groups

eagles–request
    @flash.usc.edu
ptrei@mitre.org

Sports

ahl–news–request
    @andrew.cmu.edu
aj755@cleveland.
    freenet.edu
alt.archery
alt.college.
    college-bowl
alt.fishing
alt.skate-board
alt.sport.bowling
alt.sport.darts
alt.sport.foosball
alt.sport.lasertag
alt.sport.officiating

alt.sport.pool
alt.sports.baseball.
    atlanta-braves
alt.sports.baseball.
    balt-orioles
alt.sports.baseball.
    chicago-cubs
alt.sports.baseball.
    cinci-reds
alt.sports.baseball.
    col-rockies
alt.sports.baseball.
    houston-astros
alt.sports.baseball.
    la-dodgers
alt.sports.baseball.
    mke-brewers
alt.sports.baseball.
    mn-twins
alt.sports.baseball.
    montreal-expos
alt.sports.baseball.
    ny-mets
alt.sports.baseball.
    phila-phillies
alt.sports.baseball.
    pitt-pirates
alt.sports.baseball.
    sf-giants
alt.sports.baseball.
    stl-cardinals
alt.sports.football.
    mn-vikings
alt.sports.football.
    pro.wash-redskins
alt.surfing
autox–request
    @autox.team.net
balloon–request
    @lut.ac.uk
bikecommute–request
    @bike2work.
    eng.sun.com
bit.listserv.sportpsy

cards–request
    @tanstaafl.
    uchicago.edu
cavers–request
    @vlsi.bu.edu
clari.sports.baseball
clari.sports.baseball.
    games
clari.sports.basketball
clari.sports.basketball.
    college
clari.sports.features
clari.sports.football
clari.sports.football.
    college
clari.sports.hockey
clari.sports.misc
clari.sports.motor
clari.sports.olympic
clari.sports.tennis
clari.sports.top
dead–runners–request
    @unx.sas.com
derby–request
    @ekrl.com
echl–news–request
    @andrew.cmu.edu
equestrians–request
    @world.std.com
firearms–request
    @cs.cmu.edu
giants–request
    @medraut.apple.com
hang–gliding–request
    @virginia.edu
hockey3–request
    @hooville.mitre.org
huskers–request
    @tssi.com
jplee@cymbal.
    calpoly.edu
karplus@ce.ucsc.edu
listserv@psuvm.psu.edu
martial–arts–request
    @dragon.cso.uiuc.edu

minors–request
@medraut.apple.com
nordic–ski–request
@graphics.cornell.edu
nwu–sports–request
@tssi.com
offroad–request
@ai.gtri.gatech.edu
orienteering–request
@graphics.cornell.
edu
raiders–request
@super.org
rec.backcountry
rec.bicycles.marketplace
rec.bicycles.misc
rec.bicycles.racing
rec.bicycles.rides
rec.bicycles.soc
rec.bicycles.tech
rec.boats
rec.boats.paddle
rec.climbing
rec.collecting.cards
rec.folk-dancing
rec.guns
rec.hunting
rec.juggling
rec.martial-arts
rec.misc
rec.outdoors.fishing
rec.running
rec.scuba
rec.skate
rec.skiing
rec.skydiving
rec.sport.baseball
rec.sport.baseball.college
rec.sport.baseball.fantasy
rec.sport.basketball.
college
rec.sport.basketball.
misc
rec.sport.basketball.pro
rec.sport.cricket.scores

rec.sport.disc
rec.sport.fencing
rec.sport.football.
australian
rec.sport.football.
canadian
rec.sport.football.college
rec.sport.football.misc
rec.sport.football.pro
rec.sport.golf
rec.sport.hockey
rec.sport.hockey.field
rec.sport.misc
rec.sport.olympics
rec.sport.paintball
rec.sport.
pro-wrestling
rec.sport.rowing
rec.sport.rugby
rec.sport.soccer
rec.sport.swimming
rec.sport.table-tennis
rec.sport.tennis
rec.sport.triathlon
rec.sport.volleyball
rec.sport.waterski
rec.windsurfing
seattle–mariners–
request@kei.com
stlouis@unixg.ubc.ca
tandem–request
@hobbes.ucsd.edu
torg–request
@cool.vortech.com
uk–hockey–request
@cee.hw.ac.uk
waterski–request
@nda.com
weights–request
@mickey.disney.com
whitewater–request
@gynko.circ.upenn.edu
windsurfing–request
@gcm.com
wts@maine.maine.edu

Technology

2strokes–request
@microunity.com
alt.clearing.technology
alt.radio.scanner
alt.satellite.tv.europe
alt.sci.physics.acoustics
alt.sys.intergraph
alt.video.laserdisc
bit.listserv.devel-l
bit.listserv.edtech
bit.listserv.omrscan
bit.listserv.tecmat-l
brewer@ace.enet.dec.com
clari.tw.telecom
comp.ivideodisc
comp.laser-printers
fm–10–request
@dg–rtp.dg.com
icf–2010–request
@cup.hp.com
jhbercovitz@lbl.gov
k12.ed.tech
k12.library
listserv@orbital.demon.
co.uk
majordomo
@thumper.lerc.
nasa.gov
misc.books.technical
nedod–request
@mbunix.mitre.org
news.future
novice–mzt
@krpan.arnes.si
novice.mzt@uni–lj.si
nucmed–request
@uwovax.uwo.ca
racefab–request
@pms706.pms.
ford.com
rec.arts.cinema
rec.arts.startrek.tech
rec.autos.tech
rec.bicycles.tech

World Events

ae852@yfn.ysu.edu
alt.current-events.
  bosnia
alt.desert-storm
alt.india.progressive
alt.news.macedonia
alt.politics.british
bit.listserv.disarm-l
burkov@drfmc.ceng.cea.fr
clari.biz.economy.world
clari.canada.biz
clari.canada.briefs
clari.canada.briefs.ont
clari.canada.briefs.west
clari.canada.features
clari.canada.general
clari.canada.gov
clari.canada.law
clari.canada.newscast
clari.canada.politics
clari.canada.trouble
clari.local.alberta.briefs
clari.local.bc.briefs
clari.local.manitoba.briefs
clari.local.ontario.briefs
clari.local.saskatchewan.
  briefs
clari.news.canada
clari.news.demonstration
clari.news.election
clari.news.europe
clari.news.fighting
clari.news.gov.
  international

clari.news.headlines
clari.news.hot.east_europe
clari.news.hot.somalia
clari.news.hot.ussr
clari.news.issues.conflict
clari.news.terrorism
clari.news.top.world
cro-news-request
  @medphys.ucl.ac.uk
croatian-news-
  request@andrew.
  cmu.edu
ctn-editors
  @utcc.utoronto.ca
dimitrije
  @buenga.bu.edu
frabbani
  @epas.utoronto.ca
gst@gnosys.svle.ma.us
hozo@math.lsa.umich.
  edu
hrvatski-vjesnik-
  zamolbe@andrew.
  cmu.edu
info-russ
  @smarty.ece.jhu.edu
joe@mullara.
  met.unimelb.edu.au
listserv@oneb.almanac.
  bc.ca
listserv@orbital.demon.
  co.uk
misc.news.east-
  europe.rferl
misc.news.southasia

news.lists
novice-mzt
  @krpan.arnes.si
novice.mzt@uni-lj.si
oglasna-deska
  @krpan.arnes.si
oglasna.deska@uni-lj.si
owner@moumee.
  calstatela.edu
pkd@fed.frb.gov
przemek@ndcvx.cc.nd.edu
slnetad@ganu.colorado.
  edu
soc.culture.african
soc.culture.bangladesh
soc.culture.
  bosna-herzgvna
soc.culture.british
soc.culture.canada
soc.culture.caribbean
soc.culture.china
soc.culture.europe
soc.culture.french
soc.culture.hongkong
soc.culture.indian
soc.culture.iranian
soc.culture.japan
talk.politics.china
talk.politics.mideast
talk.politics.soviet
ujsagker@vuhepx.phy.
  vanderbilt.edu
vilo@cs.helsinki.fi

Chapter 20

USENET News Groups Descriptions

This chapter contains two lists. The first is a list of USENET group names, accompanied by a short description of the focus of group; the second identifies many of the available mailing lists, describes their focuses, and provides contact information.

Use the index in the preceding chapter to look up topics you are interested in. Then use the mailing list or news group name(s) mentioned in the index to look up the full description(s) in this chapter.

Alternatively, to find mailing lists and news groups of interest, use the disk that accompanies this book. The lists on the disk have been indexed electronically to allow you to search quickly on keywords. See Appendix A, "Using the Companion Disk," for more information.

USENET Groups List

The following list was compiled and maintained by Gene Spafford (spaf@cs.purdue.edu) until April 1993, when David Lawrence (tale@uunet.uu.net) took over the task. It is periodically posted to the following news groups:

```
news.lists
news.groups
news.announce.newusers
news.announce.newgroups
news.answers
```

Eight major group categories are available:

alt	"Alternative" discussion on a wide variety of topics
comp	Computer-related information and discussion
sci	Science news and information
misc	The ubiquitous "all other" category
news	Issues concerning USENET itself
rec	Recreational activities, such as golf and motorcycling
soc	Topics of interest for students of sociology and psychology
talk	USENET's version of talk radio

> **Note**
>
> The reader should be advised that some of the alt groups have names and discuss topics that are of questionable taste.

Also, a number of other news group categories exist for specific interest areas. The more popular of these include

bionet	Groups of interest for biologists
bit	Redistribution of BITNET LISTSERV mailing lists
biz	Product announcements, enhancements, and so on

`clari`	ClariNet commercial news service
`gnu`	GNU project of the Free Software Foundation
`hep`	Groups of interest for high-energy physics researchers
`ieee`	Groups distributed by the Institute of Electrical and Electronics Engineers
`inet`	Alternative means for distribution of high-volume groups. Names are preceded with (inet) to distinguish from normal distribution.
`info`	Redistribution of University of Illinois mailing lists
`k12`	Groups of interest for teachers of grades K-12
`relcom`	Groups of interest for Russian-language readers
`u3b`	Groups of interest for AT&T 3B computer users
`vmsnet`	Groups of interest for DEC VAX/VMS users

> **Note**
>
> Although the following list has come directly from the Internet, some of the descriptions have been edited for content and consistency.

News Group	Description
alt.1d	One-dimensional imaging.
alt.3d	Three-dimensional imaging.
alt.abortion.inequity	Paternal obligations of failing to abort unwanted child.
alt.abuse.recovery	Helping victims of abuse to recover.
alt.activism	Activities for activists.
alt.activism.d	A place to discuss issues in alt.activism.
alt.activism.death-penalty	For people opposed to capital punishment.
alt.adoption	For those involved with or contemplating adoption.
alt.aldus.pagemaker	Don't use expensive user support; come here instead.
alt.alien.visitors	Space Aliens on Earth! Abduction! Gov't Cover-Up!

V

Resource Reference

News Group	Description
alt.amateur-comp	Discussion and input for *Amateur Computerist Newsletter*.
alt.angst	Anxiety in the modern world.
alt.answers	As if anyone on alt has the answers. (Moderated)
alt.appalachian	Appalachian region awareness, events, and culture.
alt.aquaria	The aquarium (and related topics) as a hobby.
alt.archery	Robin Hood had the right idea.
alt.architecture	Building design/construction and related topics.
alt.architecture.alternative	Non-traditional building designs.
alt.artcom	Artistic community, arts and communication.
alt.asian-movies	Movies from Hong Kong, Taiwan, and the Chinese mainland.
alt.astrology	Twinkle, twinkle, little planet.
alt.atheism	Godless heathens.
alt.atheism.moderated	Focused Godless heathens. (Moderated)
alt.autos.antique	Discussion of all facets of older automobiles.
alt.autos.rod-n-custom	Vehicles with modified engines and/or appearance.
alt.backrubs	Lower...to the right...aaaah!
alt.barney.dinosaur.die.die.die	There's enough hatred of Barney for everyone!
alt.basement.graveyard	Another side of the do-it-yourself movement.
alt.bbs	Computer BBS systems and software.
alt.bbs.ads	Ads for various computer BBSs.
alt.bbs.allsysop	Sysop concerns of all networks and technologies.
alt.bbs.first-class	The First-Class Mac GUI BBS.
alt.bbs.internet	BBSs that are hooked up to the Internet.
alt.bbs.lists	Postings of regional BBS listings.
alt.bbs.pcboard	Technical support for the PCBoard BBS.
alt.bbs.pcbuucp	The commercial PCBoard gateway, PCB-UUCP.
alt.bbs.wildcat	WILDCAT! BBS from Mustang Software, Inc.
alt.beer	Good for what ales ya.
alt.best.of.internet	It was a time of sorrow, it was a time of joy.

News Group	Description
alt.bigfoot	Dr. Scholl's gone native.
alt.binaries.multimedia	Sound, text, and graphics data rolled in one.
alt.binaries.pictures	Additional volume in the form of huge image files.
alt.binaries.pictures.d	Discussions about picture postings.
alt.binaries.pictures.erotica	Gigabytes of copyright violations.
alt.binaries.pictures.erotica.blondes	Copyright violations featuring blondes.
alt.binaries.pictures.erotica.d	Discussing erotic copyright violations.
alt.binaries.pictures.erotica.female	Copyright violations featuring females.
alt.binaries.pictures.erotica.male	Copyright violations featuring males.
alt.binaries.pictures.erotica.orientals	Copyright violations featuring Asians.
alt.binaries.pictures.fine-art.d	Discussion of the fine-art binaries. (Moderated)
alt.binaries.pictures.fine-art.digitized	Art from conventional media. (Moderated)
alt.binaries.pictures.fine-art.graphics	Art created on computers. (Moderated)
alt.binaries.pictures.fractals	Cheaper just to send the program parameters.
alt.binaries.pictures.misc	Have we saturated the network yet?
alt.binaries.pictures.supermodels	Yet more copyright violations.
alt.binaries.pictures.tasteless	Eccchh, that last one was *sick*....
alt.binaries.pictures.utilities	Posting of picture-related utilities.
alt.binaries.sounds.d	Sounding off.
alt.binaries.sounds.misc	Digitized audio adventures.
alt.binaries.sounds.music	Music samples in MOD/669 format.
alt.bitterness	No matter what it's for, you know how it'll turn out.
alt.bogus.group	A paradox for its readers.
alt.books.anne-rice	The Vampire Thermostat.
alt.books.deryni	Katherine Kurtz's books, especially the Deryni series.
alt.books.isaac-asimov	Fans of the late sci-fi/science author Isaac Asimov.
alt.books.reviews	If you want to know how it turns out, read it!
alt.books.technical	Discussion of technical books.
alt.brother-jed	The born-again minister touring U.S. campuses.

(continues)

V

Resource Reference

News Group	Description
alt.buddha.short.fat.guy	Religion. And not religion. Both. Neither.
alt.business.multi-level	Multi-level (network) marketing businesses.
alt.cad	Computer-aided design.
alt.cad.autocad	CAD as practiced by customers of Autodesk.
alt.california	The state and the state of mind.
alt.callahans	Callahan's bar for puns and fellowship.
alt.cascade	Art or litter, you decide.
alt.cd-rom	Discussions of optical storage media.
alt.censorship	Discussion about restricting speech/press.
alt.cereal	Breakfast cereals and their (m)ilk.
alt.child-support	Raising children in a split family.
alt.chinchilla	The nature of chinchilla farming in America today.
alt.chinese.text	Postings in Chinese; Chinese-language software.
alt.chinese.text.big5	Posting in Chinese[BIG 5].
alt.clearing.technology	Renegades from the Church of Scientology.
alt.co-ops	Discussion about cooperatives.
alt.cobol	Relationship between programming and stone axes.
alt.collecting.autographs	WOW! You got Pete Rose's? What about Kibo's?
alt.college.college-bowl	Discussions of the college bowl competition.
alt.college.food	Dining halls, cafeterias, mystery meat, and more.
alt.comedy.british	Discussion of British comedy in a variety of media.
alt.comedy.firesgn-thtre	Firesign Theatre in all its flaming glory.
alt.comics.batman	Marketing mania.
alt.comics.lnh	Interactive net.madness in the superhero genre.
alt.comics.superman	No one knows it is also alt.clark.kent.
alt.commercial-hit-radio.must.die	Video killed the radio star.
alt.comp.acad-freedom.news	Academic freedom issues related to computers. (Moderated)
alt.comp.acad-freedom.talk	Academic freedom issues related to computers.
alt.comp.databases.xbase.clipper	The Clipper database language.

News Group	Description
alt.comp.fsp	A file transport protocol.
alt.comp.hardware.homebuilt	Designing devious devices in the den.
alt.computer.consultants	Geeks on patrol.
alt.config	Alternative subnet discussions and connectivity.
alt.consciousness	Discussions on the study of the human consciousness.
alt.conspiracy	Be paranoid—they're out to get you.
alt.conspiracy.jfk	The Kennedy assassination.
alt.cows.moo.moo.moo	Like cows would cluck or something.
alt.cult-movies	Movies with a cult following.
alt.cult-movies.rocky-horror	Virgin! Virgin! Virgin! Virgin!
alt.culture.alaska	Is this where the ice weasels come from?
alt.culture.argentina	Don't cry for me.
alt.culture.hawaii	Ua Mau Ke Ea O Ka 'Aina I Ka Pono.
alt.culture.indonesia	Indonesian culture, news, etc.
alt.culture.internet	The culture(s) of the Internet.
alt.culture.karnataka	Culture and language of the Indian state of Karnataka.
alt.culture.kerala	People of Keralite origin and the Malayalam language.
alt.culture.ny-upstate	New York State, above Westchester.
alt.culture.oregon	Discussion about the state of Oregon.
alt.culture.tuva	Topics related to the Republic of Tuva, South Siberia.
alt.culture.us.asian-indian	Asian Indians in the U.S. and Canada.
alt.culture.us.southwest	Basking in the sun of the U.S.'s lower left.
alt.culture.usenet	A self-referential oxymoron.
alt.current-events.bosnia	The strife of Bosnia-Herzegovina.
alt.cyberpunk	High-tech low-life.
alt.cyberpunk.chatsubo	Literary virtual reality in a cyberpunk hangout.
alt.cyberpunk.movement	Topics related to the cyberpunk movement.
alt.cyberpunk.tech	Cyberspace and cyberpunk technology.
alt.cyberspace	Cyberspace and how it should work.
alt.dads-rights	Rights of fathers trying to win custody in court.

(continues)

News Group	Description
alt.dcom.telecom	Discussion of telecommunications technology.
alt.dear.whitehouse	When Hints from Heloise aren't enough.
alt.decathena	Digital's DECathena product. (Moderated)
alt.desert-storm	Some wars never end.
alt.destroy.the.earth	Please leave the light on when you leave.
alt.dev.null	The ultimate in moderated news groups. (Moderated)
alt.devilbunnies	Probably better left undescribed.
alt.discordia	All hail Eris, etc.
alt.discrimination	Quotas, affirmative action, bigotry, persecution.
alt.divination	Divination techniques (e.g., I Ching, Tarot, runes).
alt.dragons-inn	Breathing fire tends to make one very thirsty.
alt.dreams	What do they mean?
alt.dreams.lucid	What do they *really* mean?
alt.drugs	Recreational pharmaceuticals and related flames.
alt.drugs.caffeine	All about the world's most-used stimulant drug.
alt.drwho.creative	Writing about long scarfs and time machines.
alt.education.ib	The International Baccalaureate Diploma Program.
alt.education.ib.tok	International Baccalaureates in Theory of Knowledge.
alt.elvis.king	A fat, dead king, but king nonetheless.
alt.engr.explosives	Building backyard bombs.
alt.ensign.wesley.die.die.die	We just can't get enough of him.
alt.evil	Tales from the dark side.
alt.exotic-music	Exotic music discussions.
alt.fan.bill-gates	Fans of the original micro-softie.
alt.fan.dall-agata	Michele Dall'Agata, famous physicist from Fermi Lab.
alt.fan.dan-quayle	For discussion of the former vice president.
alt.fan.dave_barry	Electronic fan club for humorist Dave Barry.
alt.fan.devo	Funny hats do not a band make.

News Group	Description
alt.fan.disney.afternoon	Disney afternoon characters and shows.
alt.fan.douglas-adams	Author of *The Meaning of Liff* and other fine works.
alt.fan.dune	Herbert's drinking buddies.
alt.fan.eddings	The works of writer David Eddings.
alt.fan.frank-zappa	Is that a Sears poncho?
alt.fan.furry	Fans of funny animals, a la Steve Gallacci's book.
alt.fan.g-gordon-liddy	Y'know, I saw him and Rush holding hands in a bar once.
alt.fan.goons	Careful, Neddy, it's that dastardly Moriarty again.
alt.fan.greaseman	Fans of Doug Tracht, the DJ.
alt.fan.hofstadter	Douglas Hofstadter and Godel, Escher, Bach.
alt.fan.holmes	Elementary, my dear Watson. Like he ever said that.
alt.fan.howard-stern	Fans of the abrasive radio and TV personality.
alt.fan.jai-maharaj	A contributor to alt.astrology and soc.culture.indian.
alt.fan.james-bond	On his Majesty's Secret Service (and secret linen too).
alt.fan.jen-coolest	Gosh, isn't she just wonderful?
alt.fan.jimmy-buffett	A white sports coat and a pink crustacean.
alt.fan.karla-homolka	Discussion of the Karla Homolka case.
alt.fan.lemurs	Little critters with *big* eyes.
alt.fan.letterman	One of the top 10 reasons to get the alt groups.
alt.fan.lightbulbs	A hardware problem.
alt.fan.madonna	The Material Girl.
alt.fan.mike-jittlov	Electronic fan club for animator Mike Jittlov.
alt.fan.monty-python	Electronic fan club for those wacky Brits.
alt.fan.oingo-boingo	Have you ever played Ping-Pong in Pago Pago?
alt.fan.pern	Anne McCaffery's sci-fi oeuvre.
alt.fan.piers-anthony	For fans of the sci-fi author Piers Anthony.

V

Resource Reference

(continues)

News Group	Description
alt.fan.pratchett	For fans of Terry Pratchett, sci-fi humor writer.
alt.fan.ronald-reagan	Jellybeans and all.
alt.fan.rush-limbaugh	Derogation of others for fun and profit.
alt.fan.spinal-tap	Down on the sex farm.
alt.fan.tolkien	Mortal Men doomed to die.
alt.fan.tom-robbins	31 flavors for readers.
alt.fan.u2	The Irish rock band U2.
alt.fan.warlord	The War Lord of the West Preservation Fan Club.
alt.fan.wodehouse	Discussion of the works of humor author P.G. Wodehouse.
alt.fan.woody-allen	The diminutive neurotic.
alt.fandom.cons	Announcements of conventions (sci-fi and others).
alt.fashion	All facets of the fashion industry discussed.
alt.feminism	Like soc.feminism, only different.
alt.fishing	Fishing as a hobby and sport.
alt.flame	Alternative, literate, pithy, succinct screaming.
alt.flame.net-cops	Our riot gear is better than yours.
alt.flame.roommate	Putting the pig on a spit.
alt.folklore.college	Collegiate humor.
alt.folklore.computers	Stories and anecdotes about computers (some true!).
alt.folklore.ghost-stories	Boo!
alt.folklore.herbs	Discussion of all aspects of herbs and their uses.
alt.folklore.science	The folklore of science, not the science of folklore.
alt.folklore.urban	Urban legends, ala Jan Harold Brunvand.
alt.food.cocacola	And Royal Crown, Pepsi, Dr Pepper, NEHI, etc.
alt.food.fat-free	Quest for thinness.
alt.food.mcdonalds	Carl Sagan's favorite burger place.
alt.fun.with.tob	An ego on parade.
alt.games.frp.dnd-util	Discussion and creation of utility programs for AD&D.
alt.games.frp.live-action	Discussion of all forms of live-action gaming.

News Group	Description
alt.games.gb	The Galactic Bloodshed conquest game.
alt.games.lynx	The Atari Lynx.
alt.games.mk	Struggling in Mortal Kombat!
alt.games.omega	The computer game Omega.
alt.games.sf2	The video game Street Fighter 2.
alt.games.torg	Gateway for TORG mailing list.
alt.games.vga-planets	Discussion of Tim Wisseman's VGA Planets.
alt.games.xpilot	Discussion on all aspects of the X11 game Xpilot.
alt.gathering.rainbow	For discussing the annual Rainbow Gathering.
alt.geek	To fulfill an observed need.
alt.good.morning	Would you like coffee with that?
alt.good.news	A place for some news that's good news.
alt.gopher	Discussion of the gopher information service.
alt.gothic	The gothic movement: things mournful and dark.
alt.gourmand	Recipes and cooking info. (Moderated)
alt.grad-student.tenured	Most prison terms are finished sooner.
alt.grad.skool.sux	Doctor, it hurts when I study this.
alt.graphics.pixutils	Discussion of pixmap utilities.
alt.great-lakes	Discussions of the Great Lakes and adjacent places.
alt.guitar	You axed for it, you got it.
alt.guitar.bass	Bass guitars.
alt.guitar.tab	Discussions about guitar tablature music.
alt.hackers	Descriptions of projects currently under development. (Moderated)
alt.hemp	It's about knot-tying with rope. Knot!
alt.hindu	The Hindu religion. (Moderated)
alt.history.living	A forum for discussing the hobby of living history.
alt.history.what-if	What would the net have been like without this group?
alt.homosexual	Same as alt.sex.homosexual.
alt.horror	The horror genre.

(continues)

News Group	Description
alt.horror.cthulhu	Campus Crusade for Cthulhu, Ctulhu, Ctulu, and the rest.
alt.horror.werewolves	They were wolves, now they're something to be wary of.
alt.hotrod	High-speed automobiles. (Moderated)
alt.humor.best-of-usenet	What the moderator thinks is funnlest. (Moderated)
alt.humor.best-of-usenet.d	Why everyone else doesn't think it's funny.
alt.hypertext	Discussion of hypertext—uses, transport, etc.
alt.hypnosis	When you awaken, you will forget about this news group.
alt.illuminati	See alt.cabal. Fnord.
alt.image.medical	Medical image exchange discussions.
alt.india.progressive	Progressive politics in the Indian subcontinent. (Moderated)
alt.individualism	Philosophies where individual rights are paramount.
alt.internet.access.wanted	Oh, OK, how about just an MX record for now?
alt.internet.services	Not available in the UUCP world, even via e-mail.
alt.irc	Internet Relay Chat material.
alt.ketchup	*Whak Whak...shake...Whak*–Damn, all over my tie.
alt.kids-talk	A place for the precollege set on the net.
alt.lang.asm	Assembly languages of various flavors.
alt.lang.basic	The Language That Would Not Die.
alt.law-enforcement	No, ossifer, there's nothing illegal going on in alt.
alt.lemmings	Rodents with a death wish.
alt.life.sucks	And then you shrivel up.
alt.locksmithing	You locked your keys in *where?*
alt.lucid-emacs.bug	Bug reports about Lucid Emacs.
alt.lucid-emacs.help	Q & A and general discussion of Lucid Emacs.
alt.magic	For discussion about stage magic.
alt.magick	For discussion about supernatural arts.
alt.mcdonalds	Can I get fries with that?

News Group	Description
alt.med.cfs	Chronic fatigue syndrome information.
alt.meditation	General discussion of meditation.
alt.meditation.transcendental	Contemplation of states beyond the teeth.
alt.memetics	The evolution of ideas in societies.
alt.messianic	Messianic traditions.
alt.military.cadet	Preparing for the coming apocalypse.
alt.mindcontrol	NothREADing inTHISteresting goiGROUPng on here.
alt.missing-kids	Locating missing children.
alt.msdos.programmer	For the serious MS-DOS programmer (no for sale ads).
alt.mud	Same as rec.games.mud.
alt.music.a-cappella	Voice only, no /dev/sound.
alt.music.alternative	For groups having two or less platinum-selling albums.
alt.music.canada	Oh, Canada, eh?
alt.music.enya	Gaelic set to spacey music.
alt.music.filk	Sci-fi/fantasy-related folk music.
alt.music.hardcore	Could be porno set to music.
alt.music.jewish	Jewish music.
alt.music.marillion	A progressive band. *The Silmarillion* is a book.
alt.music.prince	Prince.
alt.music.progressive	Yes, Marillion, Asia, King Crimson, etc.
alt.music.queen	He's dead, Jim.
alt.music.rush	For Rushheads.
alt.music.ska	Discussions of ska (skank) music, bands, and the like.
alt.music.tmbg	They Might Be Giants.
alt.music.u2	Another group for the band U2. See also alt.fan.u2.
alt.music.world	Discussion of music from around the world.
alt.mythology	Zeus rules.
alt.native	People indigenous to an area before modern colonization.
alt.necromicon	Yet another sign of the coming apocalypse.

(continues)

V

Resource Reference

News Group	Description
alt.netgames.bolo	A multiplayer tank game for the Macintosh.
alt.news-media	Don't believe the hype.
alt.news.macedonia	News concerning Macedonia in the Balkan Region.
alt.nick.sucks	Probably.
alt.non.sequitur	Richard Nixon.
alt.online-service	Large commercial on-line services and the Internet.
alt.os.multics	30 years old and going strong.
alt.out-of-body	Out-of-body experiences.
alt.pagan	Discussions about paganism and religion.
alt.pantyhose	Stockings are sexier.
alt.paranet.abduct	They replaced Jim-Bob with a look-alike!
alt.paranet.paranormal	If it exists, how can supernatural be beyond natural?
alt.paranet.science	Maybe if we dissect the psychic....
alt.paranet.skeptic	I don't believe they turned you into a newt.
alt.paranet.ufo	Heck, I guess naming it *UFO* identifies it.
alt.paranormal	Phenomena that are not scientifically explicable.
alt.parents-teens	Parent-teenager relationships.
alt.party	Parties, celebration, and general debauchery.
alt.peeves	Discussion of peeves and related info.
alt.personals	Do you really want to meet someone this way?
alt.personals.ads	Geek seeks Dweeb. Object: low-level interfacing.
alt.personals.bondage	Are you tied up this evening?
alt.personals.misc	Dweeb seeks Geek. Object: low-level interfacing.
alt.personals.poly	Hi there, do you multiprocess?
alt.philosophy.objectivism	A product of the Ayn Rand Corporation.
alt.pixar.typestry	Pixar's Typestry type-styling software package.
alt.politics.british	Politics and a Queen, too.

News Group	Description
alt.politics.clinton	Discussing Clinton.
alt.politics.correct	A Neil Bush fan club.
alt.politics.economics	War==Poverty, and other discussions.
alt.politics.greens	Green party politics and activities worldwide.
alt.politics.homosexuality	Homosexual topics.
alt.politics.libertarian	The libertarian ideology.
alt.politics.org.batf	Politics of the U.S. Bureau of Alcohol, Tobacco, and Firearms.
alt.politics.org.cia	Politics of the U.S. Central Intelligence Agency.
alt.politics.org.misc	Political organizations.
alt.politics.org.nsa	Politics of the U.S. National Security Agency.
alt.politics.perot	Discussion of the non-candidate.
alt.politics.radical-left	Who remains after the radicals left?
alt.politics.reform	Political reform.
alt.politics.sex	Not a good idea to mix them, sez Marilyn and Profumo.
alt.politics.usa.constitution	U.S. Constitutional politics.
alt.politics.usa.misc	Miscellaneous U.S. politics.
alt.politics.usa.republican	Discussions of the U.S. Republican Party.
alt.polyamory	For those who maintain multiple love relationships.
alt.postmodern	Postmodernism, semiotics, deconstruction, and the like.
alt.president.clinton	Will the CIA undermine his efforts?
alt.prisons	Can I get an alt.* feed in the slammer?
alt.privacy	Privacy issues in cyberspace.
alt.privacy.anon-server	Technical and policy matters of anonymous contact servers.
alt.prose	Postings of original writings, fictional and otherwise.
alt.psychoactives	Better living through chemistry.
alt.psychology.personality	Personality taxonomy, such as Myers-Briggs.
alt.pub.dragons-inn	Fantasy virtual reality pub similar to alt.callahans.
alt.punk	Burning them keeps insects away.
alt.ql.creative	The *Quantum Leap* TV show.

V

Resource Reference

(continues)

News Group	Description
alt.quotations	Quotations, quips, .sig lines, witticisms, et. al.
alt.radio.networks.npr	Discussion of anything related to U.S. National Public Radio: shows, stories, personalities.
alt.radio.pirate	Hide the gear, here comes the magic station wagons.
alt.radio.scanner	Discussion of scanning radio receivers.
alt.rap	For fans of rap music.
alt.rave	Techno-culture: music, dancing, drugs, dancing.
alt.recovery	For people in recovery programs (such as AA, ACA, GA).
alt.recovery.codependency	Recovering from the disease of codependency.
alt.religion.emacs	Emacs. Umacs. We all macs.
alt.religion.kibology	He's Fred, Jim.
alt.religion.monica	Discussion about net-venus Monica and her works.
alt.religion.scientology	He's dead, Jim.
alt.revisionism	It can't be that way 'cause here's the facts.
alt.revolution.counter	Discussions of counterrevolutionary issues.
alt.rock-n-roll	Counterpart to alt.sex and alt.drugs.
alt.rock-n-roll.acdc	Dirty deeds done dirt cheap.
alt.rock-n-roll.classic	Classic rock, both the music and its marketing.
alt.rock-n-roll.hard	Music where stance is everything.
alt.rock-n-roll.metal	For the headbangers on the net.
alt.rock-n-roll.metal.gnr	For Guns 'n' Roses fans.
alt.rock-n-roll.metal.heavy	Non-sissyboy metal bands.
alt.rock-n-roll.metal.ironmaiden	Sonic torture methods.
alt.rock-n-roll.metal.metallica	Sort of like Formica with more hair.
alt.rock-n-roll.metal.progressive	Slayer teams up with Tom Cora.
alt.rock-n-roll.oldies	Discussion of rock and roll music from 1950-1970.
alt.rock-n-roll.stones	Gathering plenty of moss by now.
alt.romance	Discussion about the romantic side of love.
alt.romance.chat	Talk about no sex.

News Group	Description
News Group	Descriptionalt.rush-limbaugh Fans of the conservative activist radio announcer.
alt.satanism	Not such a bad dude once you get to know him.
alt.satellite.tv.europe	All about European satellite TV.
alt.save.the.earth	Environmentalist causes.
alt.sb.programmer	Programming the Sound Blaster PC sound card.
alt.sci.physics.acoustics	Sound advice.
alt.sci.physics.new-theories	Scientific theories you won't find in journals.
alt.sci.planetary	Studies in planetary science.
alt.sci.sociology	People are really interesting when you watch them.
alt.security	Security issues on computer systems.
alt.security.index	Pointers to good stuff in alt.security. (Moderated)
alt.security.pgp	The Pretty Good Privacy package.
alt.sega.genesis	Another addiction.
alt.self-improve	Self-improvement in less than 14 characters.
alt.sewing	A group that is not as it seams.
alt.sex	Postings of a prurient nature.
alt.sex.bestiality	Happiness is a warm puppy.
alt.sex.bestiality.barney	For people with big, purple newt fetishes.
alt.sex.bondage	Tie me, whip me, make me read the net!
alt.sex.exhibitionism	So you want to be a star.
alt.sex.fetish.feet	Kiss them! Now!
alt.sex.fetish.orientals	The mysteries of Asia are a potent lure.
alt.sex.masturbation	Where one's SO is oneself.
alt.sex.motss	Jesse Helms would not subscribe to this group.
alt.sex.movies	Discussing the ins and outs of certain movies.
alt.sex.pictures	Gigabytes of copyright violations.
alt.sex.spanking	Who's been lighting the Grail light again?
alt.sex.stories	For those who need it *NOW*.

V

Resource Reference

(continues)

News Group	Description
alt.sex.stories.d	For those who talk about needing it *NOW*.
alt.sex.voyeurism	You do it, I'll just sit here and watch.
alt.sex.wanted	Requests for erotica, either literary or in the flesh.
alt.sex.watersports	Fun in the shower.
alt.sex.wizards	Questions for only true sex wizards.
alt.sexual.abuse.recovery	Helping others deal with traumatic experiences.
alt.shenanigans	Practical jokes, pranks, randomness, etc.
alt.showbiz.gossip	A misguided attempt to centralize gossip.
alt.shut.the.hell.up.geek	Group for USENET motto.
alt.skate-board	Discussion of all aspects of skate-boarding.
alt.skinheads	The skinhead culture/anticulture.
alt.slack	Posting relating to the Church of the Subgenius.
alt.slick.willy.tax.tax.tax	Not just for rich people anymore.
alt.snail-mail	Mail sent on paper. Some people still do that.
alt.society.anarchy	Societies without rulers.
alt.society.ati	The Activist Times Digest. (Moderated)
alt.society.civil-liberties	Individual rights.
alt.society.civil-liberty	Same as alt.society.civil-liberties.
alt.society.conservatism	Social, cultural, and political conservatism.
alt.society.generation-x	Discussion of lifestyles of those born 1960-early 1970s.
alt.society.resistance	Resistance against governments.
alt.sources	Alternative source code, unmoderated. Caveat Emptor.
alt.sources.amiga	Source code for the Amiga.
alt.sources.d	Discussion of posted sources.
alt.sources.index	Pointers to source code in alt.sources.*. (Moderated)
alt.sources.wanted	Requests for source code.
alt.spam	What is that stuff that doth jiggle in the breeze?
alt.spleen	Venting as a biological function.

News Group	Description
alt.sport.bowling	In the gutter again.
alt.sport.darts	Look what you've done to the wall!
alt.sport.foosball	Table soccer and dizzy little men.
alt.sport.lasertag	Indoor splatball with infrared lasers.
alt.sport.officiating	Discussion of problems related to officiating athletic contests.
alt.sport.pool	Knock your balls into your pockets for fun.
alt.sports.baseball.atlanta-braves	Atlanta Braves baseball talk.
alt.sports.baseball.balt-orioles	Baltimore Orioles baseball talk.
alt.sports.baseball.chicago-cubs	Chicago Cubs baseball talk.
alt.sports.baseball.cinci-reds	Cincinnati Reds baseball talk.
alt.sports.baseball.col-rockies	Colorado Rockies baseball talk.
alt.sports.baseball.houston-astros	Houston Astros baseball talk.
alt.sports.baseball.la-dodgers	Los Angeles Dodgers baseball talk.
alt.sports.baseball.mke-brewers	Milwaukee Brewers baseball talk.
alt.sports.baseball.mn-twins	Minnesota Twins baseball talk.
alt.sports.baseball.montreal-expos	Montreal Expos baseball talk.
alt.sports.baseball.ny-mets	New York Mets baseball talk.
alt.sports.baseball.phila-phillies	Philadelphia Phillies baseball talk.
alt.sports.baseball.pitt-pirates	Pittsburgh Pirates baseball talk.
alt.sports.baseball.sf-giants	San Francisco Giants baseball talk.
alt.sports.baseball.stl-cardinals	St. Louis Cardinals baseball talk.
alt.sports.football.mn-vikings	Minnesota Vikings football talk.
alt.sports.football.pro.wash-redskins	Washington Redskins football talk.
alt.stagecraft	Technical theatre issues.
alt.startrek.creative	Stories and parodies related to *Star Trek*.
alt.stupidity	Discussion about stupid news groups.
alt.suicide.holiday	Talk of why suicides increase at holidays.
alt.supermodels	Discussing famous and beautiful models.
alt.support	Dealing with emotional situations and experiences.
alt.support.abuse-partners	Partners of people who were abused.
alt.support.big-folks	Sizeism can be as awful as sexism or racism.
alt.support.cancer	Emotional aid for people with cancer.

(continues)

News Group	Description
alt.support.diet	Seeking enlightenment through weight loss.
alt.support.mult-sclerosis	Discussion about living with multiple sclerosis.
alt.support.step-parents	Difficulties of being a stepparent.
alt.surfing	Riding the ocean waves.
alt.sustainable.agriculture	Such as the Mekong delta before Agent Orange.
alt.swedish.chef.bork.bork.bork	The beginning of the end.
alt.sys.amiga.demos	Code and talk to show off the Amiga.
alt.sys.amiga.uucp	AmigaUUCP.
alt.sys.intergraph	Support for Intergraph machines.
alt.sys.pc-clone.gateway2000	A PC clone vendor.
alt.sys.sun	Technical discussion of Sun Microsystems products.
alt.tasteless	Truly disgusting.
alt.tasteless.jokes	Sometimes insulting rather than disgusting or humorous.
alt.test	Alternative subnetwork testing.
alt.test.test	More from the people who brought you "BBS systems."
alt.thrash	Thrashlife.
alt.toolkits.xview	The X Windows XView toolkit.
alt.toys.hi-tech	Optimus Prime is my hero.
alt.toys.lego	Snap 'em together.
alt.toys.transformers	From robots to vehicles and back again.
alt.transgendered	Boys will be girls, and vice versa.
alt.tv.animaniacs	Steven Spielberg's Animaniacs!
alt.tv.babylon-5	Casablanca in space.
alt.tv.barney	He's everywhere. Now appearing in several alt groups.
alt.tv.beakmans-world	Some sort of science and comedy show.
alt.tv.beavis-n-butthead	Uh huh huh huh uh uh huh uh huh.
alt.tv.bh90210	Fans of *Beverly Hills 90210* TV show.
alt.tv.dinosaurs.barney.die.die.die	Squish the saccharine newt.
alt.tv.la-law	For the folks out in la-law land.
alt.tv.liquid-tv	A BBC/MTV animation showcase program.

News Group	Description
alt.tv.mash	Nothing like a good comedy about war and dying.
alt.tv.melrose-place	Cat fights and sleaziness, Wednesdays on FOX.
alt.tv.mst3k	Hey, you robots! Down in front!
alt.tv.muppets	Miss Piggy on the tube.
alt.tv.mwc	*Married... With Children.*
alt.tv.northern-exp	For the TV show with moss growing on it.
alt.tv.prisoner	*The Prisoner* television series from years ago.
alt.tv.red-dwarf	The British sci-fi/comedy show.
alt.tv.ren-n-stimpy	Some change from *Lassie*, eh?
alt.tv.rockford-files	But he won't do windows.
alt.tv.seinfeld	A funny guy.
alt.tv.simpsons	Don't have a cow, man!
alt.tv.tiny-toon	Discussion about the *Tiny Toon Adventures* show.
alt.tv.tiny-toon.fandom	Apparently one fan group could not bind them all.
alt.tv.twin-peaks	Discussion about the popular (and unusual) TV show.
alt.usage.english	English grammar, word usage, and related topics.
alt.usenet.offline-reader	Getting your fix off-line.
alt.uu.future	Does Usenet University have a viable future?
alt.vampyres	Discussion of vampires and related writings, films, etc.
alt.video.laserdisc	LD players and selections available for them.
alt.visa.us	Discussion and information on visas pertaining to U.S.
alt.war	Not just collateral damage.
alt.war.civil.usa	Discussion of the U.S. Civil War (1861-1865).
alt.war.vietnam	Discussion of all aspects of the Vietnam War.
alt.wedding	Til death or our lawyers do us part.
alt.whine	Why me?
alt.whistleblowing	Whistleblowing on fraud, abuse, and other corruption.
alt.winsock	Windows Sockets.

(continues)

News Group	Description
alt.wired	*Wired* magazine.
alt.wolves	Discussing wolves and wolf-mix dogs.
alt.zima	Not to be confused with zuma.
alt.zines	Small magazines, mostly non-commercial.
alt.znet.aeo	*Atari Explorer Online* magazine. (Moderated)
alt.znet.pc	Z*NET International ASCII magazines (weekly). (Moderated)
bionet.agroforestry	Discussion of agroforestry.
bionet.announce	Announcements of widespread interest to biologists. (Moderated)
bionet.biology.computational	Computer and mathematical applications. (Moderated)
bionet.biology.n2-fixation	Research issues on biological nitrogen fixation.
bionet.biology.tropical	Discussions about tropical biology.
bionet.cellbiol	Discussions about cell biology.
bionet.chlamydomonas	Discussions about the green alga chlamydomonas.
bionet.drosophila	Discussions about the biology of fruit flies.
bionet.general	General BIOSCI discussion.
bionet.genome.arabidopsis	Information about the Arabidopsis project.
bionet.genome.chrom22	Discussion of Chromosome 22.
bionet.genome.chromosomes	Mapping and sequencing of eucaryote chromosomes.
bionet.immunology	Discussions about research in immunology.
bionet.info-theory	Discussions about biological information theory.
bionet.jobs	Scientific job opportunities.
bionet.journals.contents	Contents of biology journal publications. (Moderated)
bionet.journals.note	Advice on dealing with journals in biology.
bionet.metabolic-reg	Kinetics and thermodynamics at the cellular level.
bionet.molbio.ageing	Discussions of cellular and organismal ageing.
bionet.molbio.bio-matrix	Computer applications to biological databases.

News Group	Description
bionet.molbio.embldatabank	Information about the EMBL nucleic acid database.
bionet.molbio.evolution	How genes and proteins have evolved.
bionet.molbio.gdb	Messages to and from the GDB database staff.
bionet.molbio.genbank	Info about the GenBank nucleic acid database.
bionet.molbio.genbank.updates	Hot off the presses! (Moderated)
bionet.molbio.gene-linkage	Discussions about genetic linkage analysis.
bionet.molbio.genome-program	Discussion of Human Genome Project issues.
bionet.molbio.hiv	Discussions about the molecular biology of HIV.
bionet.molbio.methds-reagnts	Requests for information and lab reagents.
bionet.molbio.proteins	Research on proteins and protein databases.
bionet.molbio.rapd	Research on Randomly Amplified Polymorphic DNA.
bionet.molbio.yeast	The molecular biology and genetics of yeast.
bionet.mycology	Discussions about filamentous fungi.
bionet.n2-fixation	Research issues on biological nitrogen fixation.
bionet.neuroscience	Research issues in the neurosciences.
bionet.photosynthesis	Discussions about research on photosynthesis.
bionet.plants	Discussion about all aspects of plant biology.
bionet.population-bio	Technical discussions about population biology.
bionet.sci-resources	Information about funding agencies and so on. (Moderated)
bionet.software	Information about software for biology.
bionet.software.acedb	Discussions by users of genome DBs using ACEDB.
bionet.software.gcg	Discussions about using the ACEDB software.
bionet.software.sources	Software source relating to biology. (Moderated)
bionet.users.addresses	Who's who in biology.

(continues)

Resource Reference

V

News Group	Description
bionet.virology	Discussions about research in virology.
bionet.women-in-bio	Discussions about women in biology.
bionet.xtallography	Discussions about protein crystallography.
bit.admin	bit.* news group discussions.
bit.general	Discussions relating to BITNET/USENET.
bit.lang.neder-l	Dutch language and literature list. (Moderated)
bit.listserv.3com-l	3Com products discussion list.
bit.listserv.9370-l	IBM 9370 and VM/IS specific topics list.
bit.listserv.ada-law	ADA law discussions.
bit.listserv.advanc-l	Geac advanced integrated library system users.
bit.listserv.advise-l	User services list.
bit.listserv.aix-l	IBM AIX discussion list.
bit.listserv.allmusic	Discussions on all forms of music.
bit.listserv.appc-l	APPC discussion list.
bit.listserv.apple2-l	Apple II list.
bit.listserv.applicat	Applications under BITNET.
bit.listserv.arie-l	RLG Ariel document transmission group.
bit.listserv.ashe-l	Higher education policy and research.
bit.listserv.asm370	IBM 370 assembly programming discussions.
bit.listserv.autism	Autism and developmental disabilities list.
bit.listserv.axslib-l	Library access for people with disabilities.
bit.listserv.banyan-l	Banyan Vines network software discussions.
bit.listserv.big-lan	Campus-size LAN discussion group. (Moderated)
bit.listserv.billing	Chargeback of computer resources.
bit.listserv.biosph-l	Biosphere, ecology discussion list.
bit.listserv.bitnews	BITNET news.
bit.listserv.blindnws	Blindness issues and discussions. (Moderated)
bit.listserv.buslib-l	Business libraries list.
bit.listserv.c+health	Computers and health discussion list.

News Group	Description
bit.listserv.c18-l	18th century interdisciplinary discussion.
bit.listserv.c370-l	C/370 discussion list.
bit.listserv.candle-l	Candle products discussion list.
bit.listserv.catala	Catalan discussion list.
bit.listserv.catholic	Free Catholics mailing list.
bit.listserv.cdromlan	CD-ROM on local area networks.
bit.listserv.cfs.newsletter	Chronic fatigue syndrome newsletter. (Moderated)
bit.listserv.christia	Practical Christian life. (Moderated)
bit.listserv.cics-l	CICS discussion list.
bit.listserv.cinema-l	Discussions on all forms of cinema.
bit.listserv.circplus	Circulation reserve and related library issues.
bit.listserv.cmspip-l	VM/SP CMS pipelines discussion list.
bit.listserv.csg-l	Control system group network.
bit.listserv.cumrec-l	CUMREC-L administrative computer use. (Moderated)
bit.listserv.cw-email	Campus-wide e-mail discussion list.
bit.listserv.cwis-l	Campus-wide information systems.
bit.listserv.cyber-l	CDC computer discussion.
bit.listserv.dasig	Database administration.
bit.listserv.db2-l	DB2 database discussion list.
bit.listserv.dbase-l	Discussion on the use of dBASE IV.
bit.listserv.deaf-l	Deaf list.
bit.listserv.decnews	Digital Equipment Corporation news list.
bit.listserv.dectei-l	DECUS education software library discussions.
bit.listserv.devel-l	Technology transfer in international development.
bit.listserv.disarm-l	Disarmament discussion list.
bit.listserv.domain-l	Domains discussion group.
bit.listserv.dsshe-l	Disabled student services in higher education.
bit.listserv.earntech	EARN technical group.
bit.listserv.edi-l	Electronic data interchange issues.
bit.listserv.edpolyan	Professionals and students discuss education.
bit.listserv.edtech	EDTECH—educational technology. (Moderated)

V

Resource Reference

(continues)

News Group	Description
bit.listserv.edusig-l	EDUSIG discussions.
bit.listserv.emusic-l	Electronic music discussion list.
bit.listserv.endnote	Bibsoft endnote discussions.
bit.listserv.envbeh-l	Forum on environment and human behavior.
bit.listserv.erl-l	Educational research list.
bit.listserv.ethics-l	Discussion of ethics in computing.
bit.listserv.ethology	Ethology list.
bit.listserv.euearn-l	Computers in Eastern Europe.
bit.listserv.film-l	Film making and reviews list.
bit.listserv.fnord-l	New ways of thinking list.
bit.listserv.frac-l	Fractal discussion list.
bit.listserv.free-l	Fathers' rights and equality discussion list.
bit.listserv.games-l	Computer games list.
bit.listserv.gaynet	GayNet discussion list. (Moderated)
bit.listserv.gddm-l	The GDDM discussion list.
bit.listserv.geodesic	List for the discussion of Buckminster Fuller.
bit.listserv.gguide	BITNIC GGUIDE list.
bit.listserv.govdoc-l	Discussion of government document issues.
bit.listserv.gutnberg	GUTNBERG discussion list.
bit.listserv.hellas	The Hellenic discussion list. (Moderated)
bit.listserv.help-net	Help on BITNET and the Internet.
bit.listserv.hindu-d	Hindu digest. (Moderated)
bit.listserv.history	History list.
bit.listserv.hp3000-l	HP-3000 computer systems discussion list.
bit.listserv.hytel-l	hytelnet discussions. (Moderated)
bit.listserv.i-amiga	Info-Amiga list.
bit.listserv.ibm-hesc	IBM higher education consortium.
bit.listserv.ibm-main	IBM mainframe discussion list.
bit.listserv.ibm-nets	BITNIC IBM-NETS list.
bit.listserv.ibm7171	Protocol converter list.
bit.listserv.ibmtcp-l	IBM TCP/IP list.
bit.listserv.india-d	India interest group. (Moderated)
bit.listserv.ingrafx	Information graphics.

News Group	Description
bit.listserv.innopac	Innovative interfaces on-line public access.
bit.listserv.ioob-l	Industrial psychology.
bit.listserv.ipct-l	Interpersonal computing and technology list. (Moderated)
bit.listserv.isn	ISN data switch technical discussion group.
bit.listserv.jes2-l	JES2 discussion group.
bit.listserv.jnet-l	BITNIC JNET-L list.
bit.listserv.l-hcap	Handicap list. (Moderated)
bit.listserv.l-vmctr	VMCENTER components discussion list.
bit.listserv.lawsch-l	Law school discussion list.
bit.listserv.liaison	BITNIC LIAISON.
bit.listserv.libref-l	Library reference issues. (Moderated)
bit.listserv.libres	Library and information science research. (Moderated)
bit.listserv.license	Software licensing list.
bit.listserv.linkfail	Link failure announcements.
bit.listserv.literary	Discussions about literature.
bit.listserv.lstsrv-l	Forum on LISTSERV.
bit.listserv.mail-l	BITNIC MAIL-L list.
bit.listserv.mailbook	MAIL/MAILBOOK subscription list.
bit.listserv.mba-l	MBA student curriculum discussion.
bit.listserv.mbu-l	Megabyte University—computers and writing.
bit.listserv.mdphd-l	Dual degree programs discussion list.
bit.listserv.medforum	Medical student discussions. (Moderated)
bit.listserv.medlib-l	Medical libraries discussion list.
bit.listserv.mednews	Health Info-Com network newsletter. (Moderated)
bit.listserv.mideur-l	Middle Europe discussion list.
bit.listserv.mla-l	Music library association.
bit.listserv.netnws-l	NETNWS-L netnews list.
bit.listserv.nettrain	Network trainers list.
bit.listserv.new-list	NEW-LIST—new list announcements. (Moderated)
bit.listserv.next-l	NeXT computer list.
bit.listserv.nodmgt-l	Node management.
bit.listserv.notabene	Nota Bene list.

(continues)

News Group	Description
bit.listserv.notis-l	NOTIS/DOBIS discussion group list.
bit.listserv.novell	Novell LAN interest group.
bit.listserv.omrscan	OMR scanner discussion.
bit.listserv.os2-l	OS/2 discussion.
bit.listserv.ozone	OZONE discussion list.
bit.listserv.pacs-l	Public-Access computer system forum. (Moderated)
bit.listserv.page-l	IBM 3812/3820 tips and problems discussion list.
bit.listserv.pagemakr	PageMaker for desktop publishers.
bit.listserv.physhare	K-12 physics list.
bit.listserv.pmdf-l	PMDF distribution list.
bit.listserv.politics	Forum for the discussion of politics.
bit.listserv.postcard	Postcard collectors' discussion group.
bit.listserv.power-l	POWER-L IBM RS/6000 POWER family.
bit.listserv.powerh-l	PowerHouse discussion list.
bit.listserv.psycgrad	Psychology grad student discussions.
bit.listserv.qualrs-l	Qualitative research of the human sciences.
bit.listserv.relusr-l	Relay users forum.
bit.listserv.rra-l	Romance readers anonymous. (Moderated)
bit.listserv.rscs-l	VM/RSCS mailing list.
bit.listserv.rscsmods	The RSCS modifications list.
bit.listserv.s-comput	SuperComputers list.
bit.listserv.script-l	IBM vs. Waterloo SCRIPT discussion group.
bit.listserv.scuba-l	Scuba diving discussion list.
bit.listserv.seasia-l	Southeast Asia discussion list.
bit.listserv.seds-l	Interchapter SEDS communications.
bit.listserv.sfs-l	VM shared file system discussion list.
bit.listserv.sganet	Student government global mail network.
bit.listserv.simula	The SIMULA language list.
bit.listserv.slart-l	SLA research and teaching.
bit.listserv.slovak-l	Slovak discussion list.
bit.listserv.snamgt-l	SNA network management discussion.
bit.listserv.sos-data	Social science data list.
bit.listserv.spires-l	SPIRES conference list.

News Group	Description
bit.listserv.sportpsy	Exercise and sports psychology.
bit.listserv.sqlinfo	Forum for SQL/DS and related topics.
bit.listserv.tech-l	BITNIC TECH-L list.
bit.listserv.techwr-l	Technical writing list.
bit.listserv.tecmat-l	Technology in secondary math.
bit.listserv.test	Test news group.
bit.listserv.tex-l	The TeXnical topics list.
bit.listserv.tn3270-l	tn3270 protocol discussion list.
bit.listserv.toolb-l	Asymetrix toolbook list.
bit.listserv.trans-l	BITNIC TRANS-L list.
bit.listserv.travel-l	Tourism discussions.
bit.listserv.tsorexx	REXX for TSO list.
bit.listserv.ucp-l	University computing project mailing list.
bit.listserv.ug-l	Usage guidelines.
bit.listserv.uigis-l	User interface for geographical info systems.
bit.listserv.urep-l	UREP-L mailing list.
bit.listserv.usrdir-l	User directory list.
bit.listserv.uus-l	Unitarian-Universalist list.
bit.listserv.valert-l	Virus Alert list. (Moderated)
bit.listserv.vfort-l	VS-FORTRAN discussion list.
bit.listserv.vm-util	VM utilities discussion list.
bit.listserv.vmesa-l	VM/ESA mailing list.
bit.listserv.vmslsv-l	VAX/VMS LISTSERV discussion list.
bit.listserv.vmxa-l	VM/XA discussion list.
bit.listserv.vnews-l	VNEWS discussion list.
bit.listserv.vpiej-l	Electronic publishing discussion list.
bit.listserv.win3-l	Microsoft Windows Version 3 forum.
bit.listserv.words-l	English language discussion group.
bit.listserv.wpcorp-l	WordPerfect Corporation product discussions.
bit.listserv.wpwin-l	WordPerfect for Windows.
bit.listserv.wx-talk	Weather issues discussions.
bit.listserv.x400-l	x.400 protocol list.
bit.listserv.xcult-l	International intercultural newsletter.
bit.listserv.xedit-l	VM system editor list.
bit.listserv.xerox-l	The Xerox discussion list.
bit.listserv.xmailer	Crosswell mailer.

V

Resource Reference

(continues)

News Group	Description
bit.listserv.xtropy-l	Extopian list.
bit.mailserv.word-mac	Word processing on the Macintosh.
bit.mailserv.word-pc	Word processing on the IBM PC.
bit.org.peace-corps	International volunteers discussion group.
bit.software.international	International software list. (Moderated)
biz.americast	AmeriCast announcements.
biz.americast.samples	Samples of AmeriCast. (Moderated)
biz.books.technical	Technical bookstore and publisher advertising and info.
biz.clarinet	Announcements about ClariNet.
biz.clarinet.sample	Samples of ClariNet news groups for the outside world.
biz.comp.hardware	Generic commercial hardware postings.
biz.comp.services	Generic commercial service postings.
biz.comp.software	Generic commercial software postings.
biz.comp.telebit	Support of the Telebit modem.
biz.comp.telebit.netblazer	The Telebit Netblazer.
biz.config	Biz Usenet configuration and administration.
biz.dec	DEC equipment and software.
biz.dec.decathena	DECathena discussions.
biz.dec.decnews	The DECNews newsletter. (Moderated)
biz.dec.ip	IP networking on DEC machines.
biz.dec.workstations	DEC workstation discussions and info.
biz.digex.announce	Announcements from Digex. (Moderated)
biz.jobs.offered	Position announcements.
biz.misc	Miscellaneous postings of a commercial nature.
biz.next.newprod	New product announcements for the NeXT.
biz.oreilly.announce	New product announcements from O'Reilly and Associates. (Moderated)
biz.pagesat	For discussion of the Pagesat Satellite Usenet Newsfeed.
biz.sco.announce	SCO and related product announcements. (Moderated)

News Group	Description
biz.sco.binaries	Binary packages for SCO Xenix, UNIX, or ODT. (Moderated)
biz.sco.general	Q & A, discussions and comments on SCO products.
biz.sco.magazine	To discuss SCO Magazine and its contents.
biz.sco.opendesktop	ODT environment and applications tech info, Q & A.
biz.sco.sources	Source code ported to an SCO operating environment. (Moderated)
biz.sco.wserver	SCO widget server questions, answers, and discussion.
biz.stolen	Postings about stolen merchandise.
biz.tadpole.sparcbook	Discussions on the Sparcbook portable computer.
biz.test	Biz news group test messages.
biz.univel.misc	Discussions and comments on Univel products.
biz.zeos.announce	Zeos product announcements. (Moderated)
biz.zeos.general	Zeos technical support and general information.
clari.biz.commodity	Commodity news and price reports. (Moderated)
clari.biz.courts	Lawsuits and business-related legal matters. (Moderated)
clari.biz.economy	Economic news and indicators. (Moderated)
clari.biz.economy.world	Economy stories for non-U.S. countries. (Moderated)
clari.biz.features	Business feature stories. (Moderated)
clari.biz.finance	Finance, currency, corporate finance. (Moderated)
clari.biz.finance.earnings	Earnings and dividend reports. (Moderated)
clari.biz.finance.personal	Personal investing and finance. (Moderated)
clari.biz.finance.services	Banks and financial industries. (Moderated)
clari.biz.invest	News for investors. (Moderated)
clari.biz.labor	Strikes, unions, and labor relations. (Moderated)
clari.biz.market	General stock market news. (Moderated)

(continues)

V

Resource Reference

News Group	Description
clari.biz.market.amex	American Stock Exchange reports and news. (Moderated)
clari.biz.market.dow	Dow Jones NYSE reports. (Moderated)
clari.biz.market.ny	NYSE reports. (Moderated)
clari.biz.market.otc	NASDAQ reports. (Moderated)
clari.biz.market.report	General market reports, S & P, etc. (Moderated)
clari.biz.mergers	Mergers and acquisitions. (Moderated)
clari.biz.misc	Other business news. (Moderated)
clari.biz.products	Important new products and services. (Moderated)
clari.biz.top	Top business news. (Moderated)
clari.biz.urgent	Breaking business news. (Moderated)
clari.canada.biz	Canadian business summaries. (Moderated)
clari.canada.briefs	Regular updates of Canadian news in brief. (Moderated)
clari.canada.briefs.ont	News briefs for Ontario and Toronto. (Moderated)
clari.canada.briefs.west	News briefs for Alberta, the Prairies, and B.C. (Moderated)
clari.canada.features	Almanac, Ottawa Special, Arts. (Moderated)
clari.canada.general	Short items on Canadian news stories. (Moderated)
clari.canada.gov	Government-related news (all levels). (Moderated)
clari.canada.law	Crimes, the courts, and the law. (Moderated)
clari.canada.newscast	Regular newscast for Canadians. (Moderated)
clari.canada.politics	Political and election items. (Moderated)
clari.canada.trouble	Mishaps, accidents, and serious problems. (Moderated)
clari.feature.dave_barry	Columns of humorist Dave Barry. (Moderated)
clari.feature.mike_royko	Chicago opinion columnist Mike Royko. (Moderated)
clari.feature.miss_manners	Judith Martin's humorous etiquette advice. (Moderated)
clari.local.alberta.briefs	Local news briefs. (Moderated)

News Group	Description
clari.local.arizona	Local news. (Moderated)
clari.local.arizona.briefs	Local news briefs. (Moderated)
clari.local.bc.briefs	Local news briefs. (Moderated)
clari.local.california	Local news. (Moderated)
clari.local.california.briefs	Local news briefs. (Moderated)
clari.local.chicago	Local news. (Moderated)
clari.local.chicago.briefs	Local news briefs. (Moderated)
clari.local.florida	Local news. (Moderated)
clari.local.florida.briefs	Local news briefs. (Moderated)
clari.local.georgia	Local news. (Moderated)
clari.local.georgia.briefs	Local news briefs. (Moderated)
clari.local.headlines	Various local headline summaries. (Moderated)
clari.local.illinois	Local news. (Moderated)
clari.local.illinois.briefs	Local news briefs. (Moderated)
clari.local.indiana	Local news. (Moderated)
clari.local.indiana.briefs	Local news briefs. (Moderated)
clari.local.iowa	Local news. (Moderated)
clari.local.iowa.briefs	Local news briefs. (Moderated)
clari.local.los_angeles	Local news. (Moderated)
clari.local.los_angeles.briefs	Local news briefs. (Moderated)
clari.local.louisiana	Local news. (Moderated)
clari.local.manitoba.briefs	Local news briefs. (Moderated)
clari.local.maritimes.briefs	Local news briefs. (Moderated)
clari.local.maryland	Local news. (Moderated)
clari.local.maryland.briefs	Local news briefs. (Moderated)
clari.local.massachusetts	Local news. (Moderated)
clari.local.massachusetts.briefs	Local news briefs. (Moderated)
clari.local.michigan	Local news. (Moderated)
clari.local.michigan.briefs	Local news briefs. (Moderated)
clari.local.minnesota	Local news. (Moderated)
clari.local.minnesota.briefs	Local news briefs. (Moderated)
clari.local.missouri	Local news. (Moderated)
clari.local.missouri.briefs	Local news briefs. (Moderated)
clari.local.nebraska	Local news. (Moderated)
clari.local.nebraska.briefs	Local news briefs. (Moderated)
clari.local.nevada	Local news. (Moderated)
clari.local.nevada.briefs	Local news briefs. (Moderated)
clari.local.new_england	Local news. (Moderated)

(continues)

Resource Reference

V

News Group	Description
clari.local.new_hampshire	Local news. (Moderated)
clari.local.new_jersey	Local news. (Moderated)
clari.local.new_jersey.briefs	Local news briefs. (Moderated)
clari.local.new_york	Local news. (Moderated)
clari.local.new_york.briefs	Local news briefs. (Moderated)
clari.local.nyc	Local news (New York City). (Moderated)
clari.local.nyc.briefs	Local news briefs. (Moderated)
clari.local.ohio	Local news. (Moderated)
clari.local.ohio.briefs	Local news briefs. (Moderated)
clari.local.ontario.briefs	Local news briefs. (Moderated)
clari.local.oregon	Local news. (Moderated)
clari.local.oregon.briefs	Local news briefs. (Moderated)
clari.local.pennsylvania	Local news. (Moderated)
clari.local.pennsylvania.briefs	Local news briefs. (Moderated)
clari.local.saskatchewan.briefs	Local news briefs. (Moderated)
clari.local.sfbay	Stories datelined San Francisco Bay Area. (Moderated)
clari.local.texas	Local news. (Moderated)
clari.local.texas.briefs	Local news briefs. (Moderated)
clari.local.utah	Local news. (Moderated)
clari.local.utah.briefs	Local news briefs. (Moderated)
clari.local.virginia+dc	Local news. (Moderated)
clari.local.virginia+dc.briefs	Local news briefs. (Moderated)
clari.local.washington	Local news. (Moderated)
clari.local.washington.briefs	Local news briefs. (Moderated)
clari.local.wisconsin	Local news. (Moderated)
clari.local.wisconsin.briefs	Local news briefs. (Moderated)
clari.matrix_news	Monthly journal on the Internet. (Moderated)
clari.nb.apple	Newsbytes Apple/Macintosh news. (Moderated)
clari.nb.business	Newsbytes business and industry news. (Moderated)
clari.nb.general	Newsbytes general computer news. (Moderated)
clari.nb.govt	Newsbytes legal and government computer news. (Moderated)
clari.nb.ibm	Newsbytes IBM PC World coverage. (Moderated)
clari.nb.review	Newsbytes new product reviews. (Moderated)

News Group	Description
clari.nb.telecom	Newsbytes telecom and on-line industry news. (Moderated)
clari.nb.top	Newsbytes top stories (crossposted). (Moderated)
clari.nb.trends	Newsbytes new developments and trends. (Moderated)
clari.nb.unix	Newsbytes UNIX news. (Moderated)
clari.net.admin	Announcements for news administration at ClariNet sites. (Moderated)
clari.net.announce	Announcements for all ClariNet readers. (Moderated)
clari.net.newusers	On-line information about ClariNet. (Moderated)
clari.net.products	New ClariNet products. (Moderated)
clari.net.talk	Discussion of ClariNet—only unmoderated group.
clari.news.almanac	Daily almanac—quotes, "this date in history," etc. (Moderated)
clari.news.arts	Stage, drama, and other fine arts. (Moderated)
clari.news.aviation	Aviation industry and mishaps. (Moderated)
clari.news.books	Books and publishing. (Moderated)
clari.news.briefs	Regular news summaries. (Moderated)
clari.news.bulletin	Major breaking stories of the week. (Moderated)
clari.news.canada	News related to Canada. (Moderated)
clari.news.cast	Regular U.S. news summary. (Moderated)
clari.news.children	Stories related to children and parenting. (Moderated)
clari.news.consumer	Consumer news, car reviews, etc. (Moderated)
clari.news.demonstration	Demonstrations around the world. (Moderated)
clari.news.disaster	Major problems, accidents, and natural disasters. (Moderated)
clari.news.economy	General economic news. (Moderated)
clari.news.election	News regarding both U.S. and international elections. (Moderated)
clari.news.entertain	Entertainment industry news and features. (Moderated)

(continues)

V

Resource Reference

News Group	Description
clari.news.europe	News related to Europe. (Moderated)
clari.news.features	Unclassified feature stories. (Moderated)
clari.news.fighting	Clashes around the world. (Moderated)
clari.news.flash	Ultra-important, once-a-year news flashes. (Moderated)
clari.news.goodnews	Stories of success and survival. (Moderated)
clari.news.gov	General government-related stories. (Moderated)
clari.news.gov.agency	Government agencies, FBI, etc. (Moderated)
clari.news.gov.budget	Budgets at all levels. (Moderated)
clari.news.gov.corrupt	Government corruption, kickbacks, etc. (Moderated)
clari.news.gov.international	International government-related stories. (Moderated)
clari.news.gov.officials	Government officials and their problems. (Moderated)
clari.news.gov.state	State government stories of national importance. (Moderated)
clari.news.gov.taxes	Tax laws, trials, etc. (Moderated)
clari.news.gov.usa	U.S. federal government news. (High volume, moderated)
clari.news.group	Special interest groups not covered in their own group. (Moderated)
clari.news.group.blacks	News of interest to black people. (Moderated)
clari.news.group.gays	Homosexuality and gay rights. (Moderated)
clari.news.group.jews	Jews and Jewish interests. (Moderated)
clari.news.group.women	Women's issues and abortion. (Moderated)
clari.news.headlines	Hourly list of the top U.S./World headlines. (Moderated)
clari.news.hot.east_europe	News from Eastern Europe. (Moderated)
clari.news.hot.somalia	News from Somalia. (Moderated)
clari.news.hot.ussr	News from the Soviet Union. (Moderated)
clari.news.interest	Human interest stories. (Moderated)

News Group	Description
clari.news.interest.animals	Animals in the news. (Moderated)
clari.news.interest.history	Human-interest stories and history in the making. (Moderated)
clari.news.interest.people	Famous people in the news. (Moderated)
clari.news.interest.people.column	Daily *People* column—tidbits on celebrities. (Moderated)
clari.news.interest.quirks	Unusual or funny news stories. (Moderated)
clari.news.issues	Stories on major issues not covered in their own group. (Moderated)
clari.news.issues.civil_rights	Freedom, racism, civil rights issues. (Moderated)
clari.news.issues.conflict	Conflict between groups around the world. (Moderated)
clari.news.issues.family	Family, child abuse, etc. (Moderated)
clari.news.labor	Unions, strikes. (Moderated)
clari.news.labor.strike	Strikes. (Moderated)
clari.news.law	General group for law-related issues. (Moderated)
clari.news.law.civil	Civil trials and litigation. (Moderated)
clari.news.law.crime	Major crimes. (Moderated)
clari.news.law.crime.sex	Sex crimes and trials. (Moderated)
clari.news.law.crime.trial	Trials for criminal actions. (Moderated)
clari.news.law.crime.violent	Violent crime and criminals. (Moderated)
clari.news.law.drugs	Drug-related crimes and drug stories. (Moderated)
clari.news.law.investigation	Investigation of crimes. (Moderated)
clari.news.law.police	Police and law enforcement. (Moderated)
clari.news.law.prison	Prisons, prisoners, and escapes. (Moderated)
clari.news.law.profession	Lawyers, judges, etc. (Moderated)
clari.news.law.supreme	U.S. Supreme court rulings and news. (Moderated)
clari.news.lifestyle	Fashion, leisure, etc. (Moderated)
clari.news.military	Military equipment, people, and issues. (Moderated)
clari.news.movies	Reviews, news, and stories on movie stars. (Moderated)

V

Resource Reference

(continues)

News Group	Description
clari.news.music	Reviews and issues concerning music and musicians. (Moderated)
clari.news.politics	Politicians and politics. (Moderated)
clari.news.politics.people	Politicians and political personalities. (Moderated)
clari.news.religion	Religion, religious leaders, televangelists. (Moderated)
clari.news.sex	Sexual issues, sex-related political stories. (Moderated)
clari.news.terrorism	Terrorist actions and related news around the world. (Moderated)
clari.news.top	Top U.S. news stories. (Moderated)
clari.news.top.world	Top international news stories. (Moderated)
clari.news.trends	Surveys and trends. (Moderated)
clari.news.trouble	Less major accidents, problems, and mishaps. (Moderated)
clari.news.tv	TV news, reviews, and stars. (Moderated)
clari.news.urgent	Major breaking stories of the day. (Moderated)
clari.news.weather	Weather and temperature reports. (Moderated)
clari.sfbay.briefs	Twice daily news roundups for San Francisco Bay Area. (Moderated)
clari.sfbay.entertain	Reviews and entertainment news for San Francisco Bay Area. (Moderated)
clari.sfbay.fire	Stories from fire departments of the San Francisco Bay Area. (Moderated)
clari.sfbay.general	Main stories for San Francisco Bay Area. (Moderated)
clari.sfbay.misc	Shorter general items for San Francisco Bay Area. (Moderated)
clari.sfbay.police	Stories from police departments of the San Francisco Bay Area. (Moderated)
clari.sfbay.roads	Reports from Caltrans and the CHP. (Moderated)
clari.sfbay.short	Very short items for San Francisco Bay Area. (Moderated)
clari.sfbay.weather	San Francisco Bay and California weather reports. (Moderated)
clari.sports.baseball	Baseball scores, stories, stats. (Moderated)
clari.sports.baseball.games	Baseball games and box scores. (Moderated)

News Group	Description
clari.sports.basketball	Basketball coverage. (Moderated)
clari.sports.basketball.college	College basketball coverage. (Moderated)
clari.sports.features	Sports feature stories. (Moderated)
clari.sports.football	Pro football coverage. (Moderated)
clari.sports.football.college	College football coverage. (Moderated)
clari.sports.football.games	Coverage of individual pro games. (Moderated)
clari.sports.hockey	NHL coverage. (Moderated)
clari.sports.misc	Other sports, plus general sports news. (Moderated)
clari.sports.motor	Racing, motor sports. (Moderated)
clari.sports.olympic	The Olympic Games. (Moderated)
clari.sports.tennis	Tennis news and scores. (Moderated)
clari.sports.top	Top sports news. (Moderated)
clari.tw.aerospace	Aerospace industry and companies. (Moderated)
clari.tw.computers	Computer industry, applications, and developments. (Moderated)
clari.tw.defense	Defense industry issues. (Moderated)
clari.tw.education	Stories involving universities and colleges. (Moderated)
clari.tw.electronics	Electronics makers and sellers. (Moderated)
clari.tw.environment	Environmental news, hazardous waste, forests. (Moderated)
clari.tw.health	Disease, medicine, health care, sick celebrities. (Moderated)
clari.tw.health.aids	AIDS stories, research, political issues. (Moderated)
clari.tw.misc	General technical industry stories. (Moderated)
clari.tw.nuclear	Nuclear power and waste. (Moderated)
clari.tw.science	General science stories. (Moderated)
clari.tw.space	NASA, astronomy, space flight. (Moderated)
clari.tw.stocks	Regular reports on computer and technology stock prices. (Moderated)
clari.tw.telecom	Phones, satellites, media, and general Telecom. (Moderated)

V

Resource Reference

(continues)

News Group	Description
comp.admin.policy	Discussions of site administration policies.
comp.ai	Artificial intelligence discussions.
comp.ai.fuzzy	Fuzzy set theory, a.k.a. fuzzy logic.
comp.ai.genetic	Genetic algorithms in computing.
comp.ai.jair.announce	Announcements and abstracts of the *Journal of AI Research*. (Moderated)
comp.ai.jair.papers	Papers published by the *Journal of AI Research*. (Moderated)
comp.ai.nat-lang	Natural language processing by computers.
comp.ai.neural-nets	All aspects of neural networks.
comp.ai.nlang-know-rep	Natural language and knowledge representation. (Moderated)
comp.ai.philosophy	Philosophical aspects of artificial intelligence.
comp.ai.shells	Artificial intelligence applied to shells.
comp.answers	Repository for periodic USENET articles. (Moderated)
comp.apps.spreadsheets	Spreadsheets on various platforms.
comp.arch	Computer architecture.
comp.arch.bus.vmebus	Hardware and software for VMEbus systems.
comp.arch.storage	Storage system issues, both hardware and software.
comp.archives	Descriptions of public-access archives. (Moderated)
comp.archives.admin	Issues relating to computer archive administration.
comp.archives.msdos.announce	Announcements about MS-DOS archives. (Moderated)
comp.archives.msdos.d	Discussion of materials available in MS-DOS archives.
comp.bbs.misc	All aspects of computer bulletin board systems.
comp.bbs.waffle	The Waffle BBS and USENET system on all platforms.
comp.benchmarks	Discussion of benchmarking techniques and results.
comp.binaries.acorn	Binary-only postings for Acorn machines. (Moderated)
comp.binaries.amiga	Encoded public-domain programs in binary. (Moderated)

News Group	Description
comp.binaries.apple2	Binary-only postings for the Apple II computer.
comp.binaries.atari.st	Binary-only postings for the Atari ST. (Moderated)
comp.binaries.ibm.pc	Binary-only postings for IBM PC/ MS-DOS. (Moderated)
comp.binaries.ibm.pc.d	Discussions about IBM PC binary postings.
comp.binaries.ibm.pc.wanted	Requests for IBM PC and compatible programs.
comp.binaries.mac	Encoded Macintosh programs in binary. (Moderated)
comp.binaries.ms-windows	Binary programs for Microsoft Windows. (Moderated)
comp.binaries.os2	Binaries for use under the OS/2 ABI. (Moderated)
comp.bugs.2bsd	Reports of UNIX* version 2BSD related bugs.
comp.bugs.4bsd	Reports of UNIX version 4BSD related bugs.
comp.bugs.4bsd.ucb-fixes	Bug reports/fixes for BSD UNIX. (Moderated)
comp.bugs.misc	General UNIX bug reports and fixes (including V7, UUCP).
comp.bugs.sys5	Reports of USG (System III, V, etc.) bugs.
comp.cad.cadence	Users of Cadence Design Systems products.
comp.cad.compass	Compass Design Automation EDA tools.
comp.cad.pro-engineer	Parametric Technology's Pro/ Engineer design package.
comp.cad.synthesis	Research and production in the field of logic synthesis.
comp.client-server	Topics relating to client/server technology.
comp.cog-eng	Cognitive engineering.
comp.compilers	Compiler construction, theory, etc. (Moderated)
comp.compression	Data compression algorithms and theory.
comp.compression.research	Discussions about data compression research.
comp.databases	Database and data management issues and theory.

V

Resource Reference

(continues)

News Group	Description
comp.databases.informix	Informix database management software discussions.
comp.databases.ingres	Issues relating to INGRES products.
comp.databases.ms-access	MS Windows' relational database system, Access.
comp.databases.object	Object-oriented paradigms in database systems.
comp.databases.oracle	The SQL database products of the Oracle Corporation.
comp.databases.pick	Pick-like, postrelational database systems.
comp.databases.sybase	Implementations of the SQL server.
comp.databases.theory	Discussing advances in database technology.
comp.databases.xbase.fox	Fox Software's xBase system and compatibles.
comp.databases.xbase.misc	Discussion of xBase (dBASE-like) products.
comp.dcom.cell-relay	Forum for discussion of Cell Relay-based products.
comp.dcom.fax	Fax hardware, software, and protocols.
comp.dcom.isdn	The Integrated Services Digital Network (ISDN).
comp.dcom.lans.ethernet	Discussions of the EtherNet/IEEE 802.3 protocols.
comp.dcom.lans.fddi	Discussions of the FDDI protocol suite.
comp.dcom.lans.misc	Local area network hardware and software.
comp.dcom.lans.token-ring	Installing and using token-ring networks.
comp.dcom.modems	Data communications hardware and software.
comp.dcom.servers	Selecting and operating data communications servers.
comp.dcom.sys.cisco	Info on Cisco routers and bridges.
comp.dcom.sys.wellfleet	Wellfleet bridge and router systems hardware and software.
comp.dcom.telecom	Telecommunications digest. (Moderated)
comp.doc	Archived public-domain documentation. (Moderated)
comp.doc.techreports	Lists of technical reports. (Moderated)

News Group	Description
comp.dsp	Digital Signal Processing using computers.
comp.edu	Computer science education.
comp.emacs	Emacs editors of different flavors.
comp.fonts	Typefonts—design, conversion, use, etc.
comp.graphics	Computer graphics, art, animation, image processing.
comp.graphics.algorithms	Algorithms used in producing computer graphics.
comp.graphics.animation	Technical aspects of computer animation.
comp.graphics.avs	The Application Visualization System.
comp.graphics.data-explorer	IBM's Visualization Data Explorer, a.k.a. DX.
comp.graphics.explorer	The Explorer Modular Visualisation Environment (MVE).
comp.graphics.gnuplot	The GNUPLOT interactive function plotter.
comp.graphics.opengl	The OpenGL 3-D application programming interface.
comp.graphics.research	Highly technical computer graphics discussion. (Moderated)
comp.graphics.visualization	Info on scientific visualization.
comp.groupware	Software and hardware for shared interactive environments.
comp.human-factors	Issues related to human-computer interaction (HCI).
comp.infosystems	Any discussion about information systems.
comp.infosystems.gis	All aspects of Geographic Information Systems.
comp.infosystems.gopher	Discussion of the Gopher information service.
comp.infosystems.wais	The Z39.50-based WAIS full-text search system.
comp.infosystems.www	The World Wide Web information system.
comp.internet.library	Discussing electronic libraries. (Moderated)
comp.ivideodisc	Interactive videodiscs—uses, potential, etc.
comp.lang.ada	Discussion about Ada.
comp.lang.apl	Discussion about APL.

(continues)

Resource Reference

V

News Group	Description
comp.lang.c	Discussion about C.
comp.lang.c++	The object-oriented C++ language.
comp.lang.clos	Common Lisp Object System discussions.
comp.lang.dylan	For discussion of the Dylan language.
comp.lang.eiffel	The object-oriented Eiffel language.
comp.lang.forth	Discussion about Forth.
comp.lang.fortran	Discussion about FORTRAN.
comp.lang.functional	Discussion about functional languages.
comp.lang.hermes	The Hermes language for distributed applications.
comp.lang.idl-pvwave	IDL and PV-Wave language discussions.
comp.lang.lisp	Discussion about LISP.
comp.lang.lisp.mcl	Discussing Apple's Macintosh Common Lisp.
comp.lang.logo	The Logo teaching and learning language.
comp.lang.misc	Different computer languages not specifically listed.
comp.lang.ml	ML languages, including Standard ML, CAML, Lazy ML, etc. (Moderated)
comp.lang.modula2	Discussion about Modula-2.
comp.lang.modula3	Discussion about the Modula-3 language.
comp.lang.oberon	The Oberon language and system.
comp.lang.objective-c	The Objective-C language and environment.
comp.lang.pascal	Discussion about Pascal.
comp.lang.perl	Discussion of Larry Wall's Perl system.
comp.lang.pop	Pop11 and the Plug user group.
comp.lang.postscript	The PostScript page description language.
comp.lang.prolog	Discussion about PROLOG.
comp.lang.sather	The object-oriented computer language Sather.
comp.lang.scheme	The Scheme programming language.
comp.lang.sigplan	Info and announcements from ACM SIGPLAN. (Moderated)

News Group	Description
comp.lang.smalltalk	Discussion about Smalltalk 80.
comp.lang.tcl	The Tcl programming language and related tools.
comp.lang.verilog	Discussing Verilog and PLI.
comp.lang.vhdl	VHSIC Hardware Description Language, IEEE 1076/87.
comp.laser-printers	Laser printers, hardware, and software. (Moderated)
comp.lsi	Large-scale integrated circuits.
comp.lsi.testing	Testing of electronic circuits.
comp.mail.elm	Discussion and fixes for the ELM mail system.
comp.mail.headers	Gatewayed from the Internet header-people list.
comp.mail.maps	Various maps, including UUCP maps. (Moderated)
comp.mail.mh	The UCI version of the Rand Message Handling system.
comp.mail.mime	Multipurpose Internet Mail Extensions of RFC 1341.
comp.mail.misc	General discussions about computer mail.
comp.mail.mush	The Mail User's Shell (MUSH).
comp.mail.sendmail	Configuring and using the BSD sendmail agent.
comp.mail.uucp	Mail in the UUCP network environment.
comp.misc	General topics about computers not covered elsewhere.
comp.multimedia	Interactive multimedia technologies of all kinds.
comp.newprod	Announcements of new products of interest. (Moderated)
comp.object	Object-oriented programming and languages.
comp.object.logic	Integrating object-oriented and logic programming.
comp.org.acm	Topics about the Association for Computing Machinery.
comp.org.decus	Digital Equipment Computer Users' Society news group.
comp.org.eff.news	News from the Electronic Frontier Foundation. (Moderated)
comp.org.eff.talk	Discussion of EFF goals, strategies, etc.

V

Resource Reference

(continues)

News Group	Description
comp.org.fidonet	FidoNews digest, official news of FidoNet Assoc. (Moderated)
comp.org.ieee	Issues and announcements about the IEEE and its members.
comp.org.issnnet	The International Student Society for Neural Networks.
comp.org.sug	Talk about/for the The Sun User's Group.
comp.org.usenix	USENIX Association events and announcements.
comp.org.usenix.roomshare	Finding lodging during USENIX conferences.
comp.os.386bsd.announce	Announcements relating to the 386bsd operating system. (Moderated)
comp.os.386bsd.apps	Applications that run under 386bsd.
comp.os.386bsd.bugs	Bugs and fixes for the 386bsd OS and its clients.
comp.os.386bsd.development	Working on 386bsd internals.
comp.os.386bsd.misc	General aspects of 386bsd not covered by other groups.
comp.os.386bsd.questions	General questions about 386bsd.
comp.os.coherent	Discussion and support of the Coherent operating system.
comp.os.cpm	Discussion about the CP/M operating system.
comp.os.geos	The GEOS operating system by GeoWorks for PC clones.
comp.os.linux	The free UNIX clone for the 386/486, LINUX.
comp.os.linux.admin	Installing and administering LINUX systems.
comp.os.linux.announce	Announcements important to the LINUX community. (Moderated)
comp.os.linux.development	Ongoing work on the LINUX operating system.
comp.os.linux.help	Questions and advice about LINUX.
comp.os.linux.misc	LINUX-specific topics not covered by other groups.
comp.os.mach	The MACH OS from CMU and other places.
comp.os.minix	Discussion of Tanenbaum's MINIX system.
comp.os.misc	General OS-oriented discussion not carried elsewhere.

News Group	Description
comp.os.ms-windows.advocacy	Speculation and debate about Microsoft Windows.
comp.os.ms-windows.announce	Announcements relating to Windows. (Moderated)
comp.os.ms-windows.apps	Applications in the Windows environment.
comp.os.ms-windows.misc	General discussions about Windows issues.
comp.os.ms-windows.nt.misc	General discussion about Windows NT.
comp.os.ms-windows.nt.setup	Configuring Windows NT systems.
comp.os.ms-windows.programmer.misc	Programming Microsoft Windows.
comp.os.ms-windows.programmer.tools	Development tools in Windows.
comp.os.ms-windows.programmer.win32	32-bit Windows programming interfaces.
comp.os.ms-windows.setup	Installing and configuring Microsoft Windows.
comp.os.msdos.apps	Discussion of applications that run under MS-DOS.
comp.os.msdos.desqview	QuarterDeck's DESQview and related products.
comp.os.msdos.mail-news	Administering mail and network news systems under MS-DOS.
comp.os.msdos.misc	Miscellaneous topics about MS-DOS machines.
comp.os.msdos.pcgeos	GeoWorks PC/GEOS and PC/GEOS-based packages.
comp.os.msdos.programmer	Programming MS-DOS machines.
comp.os.msdos.programmer.turbovision	Borland's text application libraries.
comp.os.os2.advocacy	Supporting and flaming OS/2.
comp.os.os2.announce	Notable news and announcements related to OS/2. (Moderated)
comp.os.os2.apps	Discussions of applications under OS/2.
comp.os.os2.beta	All aspects of beta releases of OS/2 systems software.
comp.os.os2.bugs	OS/2 system bug reports, fixes, and workarounds.
comp.os.os2.misc	Miscellaneous topics about the OS/2 system.
comp.os.os2.multimedia	Multimedia on OS/2 systems.
comp.os.os2.networking	Networking in OS/2 environments.
comp.os.os2.programmer.misc	Programming OS/2 machines.
comp.os.os2.programmer.porting	Porting software to OS/2 machines.

V

Resource Reference

(continues)

News Group	Description
comp.os.os2.setup	Installing and configuring OS/2 systems.
comp.os.os2.ver1x	All aspects of OS/2 versions 1.0 through 1.3.
comp.os.os9	Discussions about the OS9 operating system.
comp.os.research	Operating systems and related areas. (Moderated)
comp.os.vms	DEC's VAX-* line of computers and VMS.
comp.os.vxworks	The VxWorks real-time operating system.
comp.os.xinu	The XINU operating system from Purdue (D. Comer).
comp.parallel	Massively parallel hardware/software. (Moderated)
comp.parallel.pvm	The PVM system of multicomputer parallelization.
comp.patents	Discussing patents of computer technology. (Moderated)
comp.periphs	Peripheral devices.
comp.periphs.scsi	Discussion of SCSI-based peripheral devices.
comp.programming	Programming issues that transcend languages and OSs.
comp.programming.literate	Literate programs and programming tools.
comp.protocols.appletalk	Applebus hardware and software.
comp.protocols.dicom	Digital Imaging and Communications in Medicine.
comp.protocols.ibm	Networking with IBM mainframes.
comp.protocols.iso	The ISO protocol stack.
comp.protocols.kerberos	The Kerberos authentication server.
comp.protocols.kermit	Info about the Kermit package. (Moderated)
comp.protocols.misc	Various forms and types of protocol.
comp.protocols.nfs	Discussion about the Network File System protocol.
comp.protocols.ppp	Discussion of the Internet Point-to-Point Protocol.
comp.protocols.tcp-ip	TCP and IP network protocols.
comp.protocols.tcp-ip.ibmpc	TCP/IP for IBM(-like) personal computers.
comp.publish.cdrom.hardware	Hardware used in publishing with CD-ROM.

News Group	Description
comp.publish.cdrom.multimedia	Software for multimedia authoring and publishing.
comp.publish.cdrom.software	Software used in publishing with CD-ROM.
comp.realtime	Issues related to real-time computing.
comp.research.japan	The nature of research in Japan. (Moderated)
comp.risks	Risks to the public from computers and users. (Moderated)
comp.robotics	All aspects of robots and their applications.
comp.security.misc	Security issues of computers and networks.
comp.simulation	Simulation methods, problems, uses. (Moderated)
comp.society	The impact of technology on society. (Moderated)
comp.society.cu-digest	The Computer Underground Digest. (Moderated)
comp.society.development	Computer technology in developing countries.
comp.society.folklore	Computer folklore and culture, past and present. (Moderated)
comp.society.futures	Events in technology affecting future computing.
comp.society.privacy	Effects of technology on privacy. (Moderated)
comp.soft-sys.khoros	The Khoros X11 visualization system.
comp.soft-sys.matlab	The MathWorks calculation and visualization package.
comp.soft-sys.sas	The SAS statistics package.
comp.soft-sys.shazam	The SHAZAM econometrics computer program.
comp.soft-sys.spss	The SPSS statistics package.
comp.software-eng	Software engineering and related topics.
comp.software.licensing	Software licensing technology.
comp.software.testing	All aspects of testing computer systems.
comp.sources.3b1	Source code-only postings for the AT&T 3b1. (Moderated)
comp.sources.acorn	Source code-only postings for the Acorn. (Moderated)

(continues)

V

Resource Reference

News Group	Description
comp.sources.amiga	Source code-only postings for the Amiga. (Moderated)
comp.sources.apple2	Source code and discussion for the Apple II. (Moderated)
comp.sources.atari.st	Source code-only postings for the Atari ST. (Moderated)
comp.sources.bugs	Bug reports, fixes, discussion for posted sources.
comp.sources.d	For any discussion of source postings.
comp.sources.games	Postings of recreational software. (Moderated)
comp.sources.games.bugs	Bug reports and fixes for posted game software.
comp.sources.hp48	Programs for the HP48 and HP28 calculators. (Moderated)
comp.sources.mac	Software for the Apple Macintosh. (Moderated)
comp.sources.misc	Posting of software. (Moderated)
comp.sources.postscript	Source code for programs written in PostScript. (Moderated)
comp.sources.reviewed	Source code evaluated by peer review. (Moderated)
comp.sources.sun	Software for Sun workstations. (Moderated)
comp.sources.testers	Finding people to test software.
comp.sources.unix	Postings of complete, UNIX-oriented sources. (Moderated)
comp.sources.wanted	Requests for software and fixes.
comp.sources.x	Software for the X Windows system. (Moderated)
comp.specification	Languages and methodologies for formal specification.
comp.specification.z	Discussion about the formal specification notation Z.
comp.speech	Research and applications in speech science and technology.
comp.std.c	Discussion about C language standards.
comp.std.c++	Discussion about C++ language, library, standards.
comp.std.internat	Discussion about international standards.
comp.std.misc	Discussion about various standards.

News Group	Description
comp.std.mumps	Discussion for the X11.1 Committee on Mumps. (Moderated)
comp.std.unix	Discussion for the P1003 Committee on UNIX. (Moderated)
comp.std.wireless	Examining standards for wireless network technology. (Moderated)
comp.sw.components	Software components and related technology.
comp.sys.3b1	Discussion and support of AT&T 7300/3B1/UnixPC.
comp.sys.acorn	Discussion on Acorn and ARM-based computers.
comp.sys.acorn.advocacy	Why Acorn computers and programs are better.
comp.sys.acorn.announce	Announcements for Acorn and ARM users. (Moderated)
comp.sys.acorn.tech	Software and hardware aspects of Acorn and ARM products.
comp.sys.alliant	Info and discussion about Alliant computers.
comp.sys.amiga.advocacy	Why an Amiga is better than XYZ.
comp.sys.amiga.announce	Announcements about the Amiga. (Moderated)
comp.sys.amiga.applications	Miscellaneous applications.
comp.sys.amiga.audio	Music, MIDI, speech synthesis, other sounds.
comp.sys.amiga.datacomm	Methods of getting bytes in and out.
comp.sys.amiga.emulations	Various hardware and software emulators.
comp.sys.amiga.games	Discussion of games for the Commodore Amiga.
comp.sys.amiga.graphics	Charts, graphs, pictures, etc.
comp.sys.amiga.hardware	Amiga computer hardware, Q & A, reviews, etc.
comp.sys.amiga.introduction	Group for newcomers to Amigas.
comp.sys.amiga.marketplace	Where to find it, prices, etc.
comp.sys.amiga.misc	Discussions not falling in another Amiga group.
comp.sys.amiga.multimedia	Animations, video, and multimedia.
comp.sys.amiga.programmer	Developers and hobbyists discuss code.
comp.sys.amiga.reviews	Reviews of Amiga software, hardware. (Moderated)
comp.sys.apollo	Apollo computer systems.

V

Resource Reference

(continues)

News Group	Description
comp.sys.apple2	Discussion about Apple II micros.
comp.sys.apple2.comm	Apple II data communications.
comp.sys.apple2.gno	The AppleIIgs GNO multitasking environment.
comp.sys.apple2.marketplace	Buying, selling, and trading Apple II equipment.
comp.sys.apple2.programmer	Programming on the Apple II.
comp.sys.apple2.usergroups	All about Apple II users' groups.
comp.sys.atari.8bit	Discussion about 8-bit Atari micros.
comp.sys.atari.advocacy	Attacking and defending Atari computers.
comp.sys.atari.st	Discussion about 16-bit Atari micros.
comp.sys.atari.st.tech	Technical discussions of Atari ST hard/software.
comp.sys.att	Discussions about AT&T microcomputers.
comp.sys.cbm	Discussion about Commodore micros.
comp.sys.concurrent	The Concurrent/Masscomp line of computers. (Moderated)
comp.sys.convex	Convex computer systems hardware and software.
comp.sys.dec	Discussions about DEC computer systems.
comp.sys.dec.micro	DEC Micros (Rainbow, Professional 350/380).
comp.sys.encore	Encore's MultiMax computers.
comp.sys.harris	Harris computer systems, especially real-time systems.
comp.sys.hp	Discussion about Hewlett-Packard equipment.
comp.sys.hp48	Hewlett-Packard's HP48 and HP28 calculators.
comp.sys.ibm.pc.demos	Demonstration programs that showcase programmer skill.
comp.sys.ibm.pc.digest	The IBM PC, PC-XT, and PC-AT. (Moderated)
comp.sys.ibm.pc.games.action	Arcade-style games on PCs.
comp.sys.ibm.pc.games.adventure	Adventure (non-rpg) games on PCs.
comp.sys.ibm.pc.games.announce	Announcements for all PC gamers. (Moderated)
comp.sys.ibm.pc.games.flight-sim	Flight simulators on PCs.
comp.sys.ibm.pc.games.misc	Games not covered by other PC groups.

News Group	Description
comp.sys.ibm.pc.games.rpg	Role-playing games on the PC.
comp.sys.ibm.pc.games.strategic	Strategy/planning games on PCs.
comp.sys.ibm.pc.hardware	XT/AT/EISA hardware, any vendor.
comp.sys.ibm.pc.misc	Discussion about IBM personal computers.
comp.sys.ibm.pc.rt	Topics related to IBM's RT computer.
comp.sys.ibm.pc.soundcard	Hardware and software aspects of PC sound cards.
comp.sys.ibm.ps2.hardware	Microchannel hardware, any vendor.
comp.sys.intel	Discussions about Intel systems and parts.
comp.sys.isis	The ISIS distributed system from Cornell.
comp.sys.laptops	Laptop (portable) computers.
comp.sys.m6809	Discussion about 6809s.
comp.sys.m68k	Discussion about 68k's.
comp.sys.m68k.pc	Discussion about 68k-based PCs. (Moderated)
comp.sys.m88k	Discussion about 88k-based computers.
comp.sys.mac.advocacy	The Macintosh computer family compared to others.
comp.sys.mac.announce	Important notices for Macintosh users. (Moderated)
comp.sys.mac.apps	Discussions of Macintosh applications.
comp.sys.mac.comm	Discussion of Macintosh communications.
comp.sys.mac.databases	Database systems for the Apple Macintosh.
comp.sys.mac.digest	Apple Macintosh: info and uses, but no programs. (Moderated)
comp.sys.mac.games	Discussions of games on the Macintosh.
comp.sys.mac.hardware	Macintosh hardware issues and discussions.
comp.sys.mac.hypercard	The Macintosh HyperCard: info and uses.
comp.sys.mac.misc	General discussions about the Apple Macintosh.
comp.sys.mac.oop.macapp3	Version 3 of the MacApp object-oriented system.
comp.sys.mac.oop.misc	Object-oriented programming issues on the Mac.

(continues)

News Group	Description
comp.sys.mac.oop.tcl	Symantec's THINK Class Library for object programming.
comp.sys.mac.portables	Discussion particular to laptop Macintoshes.
comp.sys.mac.programmer	Discussion by people programming the Apple Macintosh.
comp.sys.mac.scitech	Using the Macintosh in scientific and technological work.
comp.sys.mac.system	Discussions of Macintosh system software.
comp.sys.mac.wanted	Postings of "I want XYZ for my Mac."
comp.sys.mentor	Mentor Graphics products and the Silicon Compiler System.
comp.sys.mips	Systems based on MIPS chips.
comp.sys.misc	Discussion about computers of all kinds.
comp.sys.ncr	Discussion about NCR computers.
comp.sys.newton.announce	Newton information posts. (Moderated)
comp.sys.newton.misc	Miscellaneous discussion about Newton systems.
comp.sys.newton.programmer	Discussion of Newton software development.
comp.sys.next.advocacy	The NeXT religion.
comp.sys.next.announce	Announcements related to the NeXT computer system. (Moderated)
comp.sys.next.bugs	Discussion and solutions for known NeXT bugs.
comp.sys.next.hardware	Discussing the physical aspects of NeXT computers.
comp.sys.next.marketplace	NeXT hardware, software, and jobs.
comp.sys.next.misc	General discussion about the NeXT computer system.
comp.sys.next.programmer	NeXT-related programming issues.
comp.sys.next.software	Function, use, and availability of NeXT programs.
comp.sys.next.sysadmin	Discussions related to NeXT system administration.
comp.sys.novell	Discussion of Novell NetWare products.
comp.sys.nsc.32k	National Semiconductor 32000 series chips.
comp.sys.palmtops	Super-powered calculators in the palm of your hand.

News Group	Description
comp.sys.pen	Interacting with computers through pen gestures.
comp.sys.prime	Prime Computer products.
comp.sys.proteon	Proteon gateway products.
comp.sys.pyramid	Pyramid 90x computers.
comp.sys.ridge	Ridge 32 computers and ROS.
comp.sys.sequent	Sequent systems (Balance and Symmetry).
comp.sys.sgi.admin	System administration on Silicon Graphics's Irises.
comp.sys.sgi.announce	Announcements for the SGI community. (Moderated)
comp.sys.sgi.apps	Applications that run on the Iris.
comp.sys.sgi.bugs	Bugs found in the IRIX operating system.
comp.sys.sgi.graphics	Graphics packages and issues on SGI machines.
comp.sys.sgi.hardware	Base systems and peripherals for Iris computers.
comp.sys.sgi.misc	General discussion about Silicon Graphics's machines.
comp.sys.stratus	Stratus products, including System/88, CPS-32, VOS, and FTX.
comp.sys.sun.admin	Sun system administration issues and questions.
comp.sys.sun.announce	Sun announcements and Sunergy mailings. (Moderated)
comp.sys.sun.apps	Software applications for Sun computer systems.
comp.sys.sun.hardware	Sun Microsystems hardware.
comp.sys.sun.misc	Miscellaneous discussions about Sun products.
comp.sys.sun.wanted	People looking for Sun products and support.
comp.sys.tahoe	CCI 6/32, Harris HCX/7, and Sperry 7000 computers.
comp.sys.tandy	Discussion about Tandy computers: new and old.
comp.sys.ti	Discussion about Texas Instruments.
comp.sys.transputer	The Transputer computer and OCCAM language.
comp.sys.unisys	Sperry, Burroughs, Convergent, and Unisys systems.

(continues)

V

Resource Reference

News Group	Description
comp.sys.xerox	Xerox 1100 workstations and protocols.
comp.sys.zenith.z100	The Zenith Z-100 (Heath H-100) family of computers.
comp.terminals	All sorts of terminals.
comp.text	Text processing issues and methods.
comp.text.desktop	Technology and techniques of desktop publishing.
comp.text.frame	Desktop publishing with FrameMaker.
comp.text.interleaf	Applications and use of Interleaf software.
comp.text.sgml	ISO 8879 SGML, structured documents, markup languages.
comp.text.tex	Discussion about the TeX and LaTeX systems and macros.
comp.theory.info-retrieval	Information Retrieval topics. (Moderated)
comp.unix.admin	Administering a UNIX-based system.
comp.unix.aix	IBM's version of UNIX.
comp.unix.amiga	Minix, SYSV4, and other *nix on an Amiga.
comp.unix.aux	The version of UNIX for Apple Macintosh II computers.
comp.unix.bsd	Discussion of Berkeley Software Distribution UNIX.
comp.unix.dos-under-unix	MS-DOS running under UNIX by whatever means.
comp.unix.internals	Discussions on hacking UNIX internals.
comp.unix.large	UNIX on mainframes and in large networks.
comp.unix.misc	Various topics that don't fit other groups.
comp.unix.osf.misc	Various aspects of Open Software Foundation products.
comp.unix.osf.osf1	The Open Software Foundation's OSF/1.
comp.unix.pc-clone.16bit	UNIX on 286 architectures.
comp.unix.pc-clone.32bit	UNIX on 386 and 486 architectures.
comp.unix.programmer	Q & A for people programming under UNIX.
comp.unix.questions	UNIX neophytes group.
comp.unix.shell	Using and programming the UNIX shell.

News Group	Description
comp.unix.sys3	System III UNIX discussions.
comp.unix.sys5.misc	Versions of System V that predate Release 3.
comp.unix.sys5.r3	Discussing System V Release 3.
comp.unix.sys5.r4	Discussing System V Release 4.
comp.unix.ultrix	Discussions about DEC's Ultrix.
comp.unix.wizards	Questions for only true UNIX wizards.
comp.unix.xenix.misc	General discussions regarding XENIX (except SCO).
comp.unix.xenix.sco	XENIX versions from the Santa Cruz Operation.
comp.virus	Computer viruses and security. (Moderated)
comp.windows.garnet	The Garnet user interface development environment.
comp.windows.interviews	The InterViews object-oriented windowing system.
comp.windows.misc	Various issues about windowing systems.
comp.windows.news	Sun Microsystems' NeWS window system.
comp.windows.open-look	Discussion about the Open Look GUI.
comp.windows.suit	The SUIT user-interface toolkit.
comp.windows.x	Discussion about the X Windows system.
comp.windows.x.apps	Getting and using, not programming, applications for X.
comp.windows.x.i386unix	The XFree86 window system and others.
comp.windows.x.intrinsics	Discussion of the X toolkit.
comp.windows.x.pex	The PHIGS extension of the X Windows system.
gnu.announce	Status and announcements from the project. (Moderated)
gnu.bash.bug	Bourne Again SHell bug reports and suggested fixes. (Moderated)
gnu.chess	Announcements about the GNU Chess program.
gnu.emacs.announce	Announcements about GNU Emacs. (Moderated)
gnu.emacs.bug	GNU Emacs bug reports and suggested fixes. (Moderated)

V

Resource Reference

(continues)

News Group	Description
gnu.emacs.gnews	News reading under GNU Emacs using Weemba's Gnews.
gnu.emacs.gnus	News reading under GNU Emacs using GNUS (in English).
gnu.emacs.help	User queries and answers.
gnu.emacs.sources	Only (*please!*) C and Lisp source code for GNU Emacs.
gnu.emacs.vm.bug	Bug reports on the Emacs VM mail package.
gnu.emacs.vm.info	Information about the Emacs VM mail package.
gnu.emacs.vms	VMS port of GNU Emacs.
gnu.epoch.misc	The Epoch X11 extensions to Emacs.
gnu.g++.announce	Announcements about the GNU C++ Compiler. (Moderated)
gnu.g++.bug	g++ bug reports and suggested fixes. (Moderated)
gnu.g++.help	GNU C++ compiler (g++) user queries and answers.
gnu.g++.lib.bug	g++ library bug reports/suggested fixes. (Moderated)
gnu.gcc.announce	Announcements about the GNU C Compiler. (Moderated)
gnu.gcc.bug	GNU C Compiler bug reports/ suggested fixes. (Moderated)
gnu.gcc.help	GNU C Compiler (gcc) user queries and answers.
gnu.gdb.bug	gcc/g++ DeBugger bugs and suggested fixes. (Moderated)
gnu.ghostscript.bug	GNU Ghostscript interpreter bugs. (Moderated)
gnu.gnusenet.config	GNU's Not Usenet administration and configuration.
gnu.gnusenet.test	GNU's Not Usenet alternative hierarchy testing.
gnu.groff.bug	Bugs in the GNU roff programs. (Moderated)
gnu.misc.discuss	Serious discussion about GNU and freed software.
gnu.smalltalk.bug	Bugs in GNU Smalltalk. (Moderated)
gnu.utils.bug	GNU utilities bugs (e.g., make, gawk, ls). (Moderated)
hepnet.admin	Discussions among hepnet.* netnews administrators.

News Group	Description
hepnet.announce	Announcement of general interest.
hepnet.conferences	Discussions of conference and workshops.
hepnet.freehep	Discussions about the freehep archives.
hepnet.general	Discussions of general interest.
hepnet.hepix	Discussions on the use of UNIX.
hepnet.heplib	Discussions about HEPLIB.
hepnet.jobs	Job announcements and discussions.
hepnet.lang.c++	Discussions of the use of C++.
hepnet.test	Test postings.
hepnet.videoconf	Discussions on the use of videoconferencing.
ieee.announce	General announcements for IEEE community.
ieee.config	Postings about managing the ieee.* groups.
ieee.general	IEEE—general discussion.
ieee.pcnfs	Discussion and tips on PC-NFS.
ieee.rab.announce	Regional Activities Board—announcements.
ieee.rab.general	Regional Activities Board—general discussion.
ieee.region1	Region 1 announcements.
ieee.tab.announce	Technical Activities Board—announcements.
ieee.tab.general	Technical Activities Board—general discussion.
ieee.tcos	The Technical Committee on Operating Systems. (Moderated)
ieee.usab.announce	USAB—announcements.
ieee.usab.general	USAB—general discussion.
(inet) comp.ai.edu	Applications of artificial intelligence to education.
(inet) comp.ai.vision	Artificial intelligence vision research. (Moderated)
(inet) comp.dcom.lans.hyperchannel	Hyperchannel networks within an IP network.
(inet) comp.editors	Topics related to computerized text editing.
(inet) comp.edu.composition	Writing instruction in computer-based classrooms.

V

Resource Reference

(continues)

News Group	Description
(inet) comp.lang.asm370	Programming in IBM System/370 assembly language.
(inet) comp.lang.clu	The CLU language and related topics.
(inet) comp.lang.forth.mac	The CSI MacForth programming environment.
(inet) comp.lang.icon	Topics related to the ICON programming language.
(inet) comp.lang.idl	IDL (Interface Description Language) related topics.
(inet) comp.lang.lisp.franz	The Franz Lisp programming language.
(inet) comp.lang.lisp.x	The XLISP language system.
(inet) comp.lang.rexx	The REXX command language.
(inet) comp.lang.scheme.c	The Scheme language environment.
(inet) comp.lang.visual	Visual programming languages.
(inet) comp.lsi.cad	Electrical computer aided design.
(inet) comp.mail.multi-media	Multimedia mail.
(inet) comp.music	Applications of computers in music research.
(inet) comp.networks.noctools.announce	Info and announcements about NOC tools. (Moderated)
(inet) comp.networks.noctools.bugs	Bug reports and fixes for NOC tools.
(inet) comp.networks.noctools.d	Discussion about NOC tools.
(inet) comp.networks.noctools.submissions	New NOC tools submissions.
(inet) comp.networks.noctools.tools	Descriptions of available NOC tools. (Moderated)
(inet) comp.networks.noctools.wanted	Requests for NOC software.
(inet) comp.org.isoc.interest	Discussion about the Internet Society.
(inet) comp.os.aos	Topics related to Data General's AOS/VS.
(inet) comp.os.cpm.amethyst	Discussion of Amethyst, CP/M-80 software package.
(inet) comp.os.msdos.4dos	The 4DOS command processor for MS-DOS.
(inet) comp.os.rsts	Topics related to the PDP-11 RSTS/E operating system.
(inet) comp.os.v	The V distributed operating system from Stanford.
(inet) comp.periphs.printers	Information on printers.
(inet) comp.protocols.iso.dev-environ	The ISO Development Environment.
(inet) comp.protocols.iso.x400	X400 mail protocol discussions.

News Group	Description
(inet) comp.protocols.iso.x400.gateway	X400 mail gateway discussions. (Moderated)
(inet) comp.protocols.pcnet	Topics related to PCNET (a personal computer network).
(inet) comp.protocols.snmp	The Simple Network Management Protocol.
(inet) comp.protocols.tcp-ip.domains	Topics related to Domain Style names.
(inet) comp.protocols.time.ntp	The network time protocol.
(inet) comp.security.announce	Announcements from the CERT about security. (Moderated)
(inet) comp.soft-sys.andrew	The Andrew system from CMU.
(inet) comp.soft-sys.nextstep	The NeXTstep computing environment.
(inet) comp.std.announce	Announcements about standards activities. (Moderated)
(inet) comp.sys.cdc	Control Data Corporation computers (e.g., Cybers).
(inet) comp.sys.handhelds	Hand-held computers and programmable calculators.
(inet) comp.sys.intel.ipsc310	Anything related to the Intel 310.
(inet) comp.sys.northstar	Northstar microcomputer users.
(inet) comp.sys.super	Supercomputers.
(inet) comp.sys.ti.explorer	The Texas Instruments Explorer.
(inet) comp.sys.zenith	Heath terminals and related Zenith products.
(inet) comp.terminals.bitgraph	The BB&N BitGraph Terminal.
(inet) comp.terminals.tty5620	AT&T Dot-mapped display terminals (5620 and BLIT).
(inet) comp.theory	Theoretical computer science.
(inet) comp.theory.cell-automata	Discussion of all aspects of cellular automata.
(inet) comp.theory.dynamic-sys	Ergodic theory and dynamical systems.
(inet) comp.theory.self-org-sys	Topics related to self-organization.
(inet) comp.unix.cray	Cray computers and their operating systems.
(inet) comp.unix.solaris	Discussions about the Solaris operating system.
(inet) comp.windows.x.announce	X Consortium announcements. (Moderated)
(inet) comp.windows.x.motif	The Motif GUI for the X Window System.

V

Resource Reference

(continues)

News Group	Description
(inet) ddn.mgt-bulletin	The DDN management bulletin from nic.ddn.mil. (Moderated)
(inet) ddn.newsletter	The DDN newsletter from nic.ddn.mil. (Moderated)
(inet) news.software.nntp	The Network News Transfer Protocol.
(inet) rec.games.vectrex	The Vectrex game system.
(inet) rec.mag.fsfnet	A science fiction "fanzine." (Moderated)
(inet) sci.bio.technology	Any topic relating to biotechnology.
(inet) sci.math.num-analysis	Numerical analysis.
(inet) sci.philosophy.meta	Discussions within the scope of "metaphilosophy."
(inet) soc.culture.esperanto	The neutral international language Esperanto.
info.admin	Administrative messages regarding info* groups (usenet@ux1.cso.uiuc.edu). (Moderated)
info.big-internet	*Issues facing a huge Internet (big-internet@munnari.oz.au). (Moderated)
info.bind	*The Berkeley BIND server (bind@arpa.berkeley.edu). (Moderated)
info.brl-cad	BRL's Solid Modeling CAD system (cad@brl.mil). (Moderated)
info.bytecounters	*NSstat network analysis program. (bytecounters@venera.isi.edu). (Moderated)
info.convex	Convex Corp machines (info-convex@pemrac.space.swri.edu). (Moderated)
info.firearms	Non-political firearms discussions (firearms@cs.cmu.edu). (Moderated)
info.firearms.politics	Political firearms discussions (firearms-politics@cs.cmu.edu). (Moderated)
info.gated	*Cornell's GATED program (gated-people@devvax.tn.cornell.edu). (Moderated)
info.grass.programmer	GRASS geographic information system programmer issues (grassp-list@moon.cecer.army.mil). (Moderated)
info.grass.user	GRASS geographic information system user issues (grassu-list@moon.cecer.army.mil). (Moderated)

News Group	Description
info.ietf	*Internet Engineering Task Force (IETF) discussions (ietf@venera.isi.edu). (Moderated)
info.ietf.hosts	*IETF host requirements discussions (ietf-hosts@nnsc.nsf.net). (Moderated)
info.ietf.isoc	*Internet Society discussions (isoc-interest@relay.sgi.com). (Moderated)
info.ietf.njm	*Jo-MAAN—The Joint Monitoring Access between Adjacent Networks IETF working group (njm@merit.edu). (Moderated)
info.ietf.smtp	*IETF SMTP extension discussions (ietf-smtp@dimacs.rutgers.edu). (Moderated)
info.isode	*The ISO Development Environment package (isode@nic.ddn.mil). (Moderated)
info.jethro-tull	Discussions about Jethro Tull's music (jtull@remus.rutgers.edu). (Moderated)
info.labmgr	Computer lab managers' list (labmgr@ukcc.uky.edu). (Moderated)
info.mach	The Mach operating system (info-mach@cs.cmu.edu). (Moderated)
info.mh.workers	*MH development discussions (mh-workers@ics.uci.edu). (Moderated)
info.nets	Inter-network connectivity (info-nets@think.com).
info.nsf.grants	*NSF grant notes (grants@note.nsf.gov). (Moderated)
info.nsfnet.cert	*Computer Emergency Response Team announcements (nsfnet-cert@merit.edu). (Moderated)
info.nsfnet.status	NSFnet status reports. (Moderated)
info.nupop	Northwestern University's POP for PCs (nupop@casbah.acns.nwu.edu). (Moderated)
info.nysersnmp	*The SNMP software distributed by PSI (nysersnmp@nisc.nyser.net). (Moderated)

(continues)

V

Resource Reference

News Group	Description
info.osf	*OSF Electronic Bulletin mailings (roma@uiuc.edu). (Moderated)
info.pem-dev	*IETF privacy enhanced mail discussions (pem-dev@tis.com). (Moderated)
info.ph	Qi, ph, sendmail/phquery discussions (info-ph@uxc.cso.uiuc.edu). (Moderated)
info.rfc	*Announcements of newly released RFCs (rfc-request@nic.ddn.mil). (Moderated)
info.slug	Care and feeding of Symbolics Lisp machines (slug@iu.ai.sri.com). (Moderated)
info.snmp	*SNMP—Simple Gateway/ Network Monitoring Protocol (snmp@nisc.nyser.net). (Moderated)
info.solbourne	Discussions and info about Solbourne computers (info-solbourne@acsu.buffalo.edu). (Moderated)
info.sun-managers	*Sun-managers digest (sun-managers@rice.edu). (Moderated)
info.sun-nets	*Sun-nets (nee Sun Spots) digest (sun-nets@umiacs.umd.edu). (Moderated)
info.theorynt	Theory list (theorynt@vm1.nodak.edu). (Moderated)
info.unix-sw	Software available for anonymous ftp (unix-sw-request@wsmr-simtel20.army.mil). (Moderated)
info.wisenet	Women in Science and Engineering NETwork (wisenet@uicvm.uic.edu). (Moderated)
k12.ed.art	Arts and crafts curricula in K-12 education.
k12.ed.business	Business education curricula in grades K-12.
k12.ed.comp.literacy	Teaching computer literacy in grades K-12.
k12.ed.health-pe	Health and physical education curricula in grades K-12.
k12.ed.life-skills	Home economics, career education, and school counseling.
k12.ed.math	Mathematics curriculum in K-12 education.

News Group	Description
k12.ed.music	Music and performing arts curriculum in K-12 education.
k12.ed.science	Science curriculum in K-12 education.
k12.ed.soc-studies	Social studies and history curriculum in K-12 education.
k12.ed.special	Educating students with handicaps and/or special needs.
k12.ed.tag	K-12 education for gifted and talented students.
k12.ed.tech	Industrial arts and vocational education in grades K-12.
k12.library	Implementing info technologies in school libraries.
k12.lang.art	The art of teaching language skills in grades K-12.
k12.lang.deutsch-eng	Bilingual German/English practice with native speakers.
k12.lang.esp-eng	Bilingual Spanish/English practice with native speakers.
k12.lang.francais	French practice with native speakers.
k12.lang.russian	Bilingual Russian/English practice with native speakers.
k12.sys.projects	Discussion of potential projects.
k12.sys.channel0	Current projects.
k12.sys.channel1	Current projects.
k12.sys.channel2	Current projects.
k12.sys.channel3	Current projects.
k12.sys.channel4	Current projects.
k12.sys.channel5	Current projects.
k12.sys.channel6	Current projects.
k12.sys.channel7	Current projects.
k12.sys.channel8	Current projects.
k12.sys.channel9	Current projects.
k12.sys.channel10	Current projects.
k12.sys.channel11	Current projects.
k12.sys.channel12	Current projects.
k12.chat.elementary	Casual conversation for elementary students, grades K-5.
k12.chat.junior	Casual conversation for students in grades 6-8.
k12.chat.senior	Casual conversation for high school students.

Resource Reference

(continues)

News Group	Description
k12.chat.teacher	Casual conversation for teachers of grades K-12.
misc.activism.progressive	Information for Progressive activists. (Moderated)
misc.answers	Repository for periodic USENET articles. (Moderated)
misc.books.technical	Discussion of books about technical topics.
misc.consumers	Consumer interests, product reviews, etc.
misc.consumers.house	Discussion about owning and maintaining a house.
misc.education	Discussion of the educational system.
misc.education.language.english	Teaching English to speakers of other languages.
misc.emerg-services	Forum for paramedics and other first responders.
misc.entrepreneurs	Discussion on operating a business.
misc.fitness	Physical fitness, exercise, etc.
misc.forsale	Short, tasteful postings about items for sale.
misc.forsale.computers.d	Discussion of misc.forsale.computers.*.
misc.forsale.computers.mac	Apple Macintosh-related computer items.
misc.forsale.computers.other	Selling miscellaneous computer stuff.
misc.forsale.computers.pc-clone	IBM PC-related computer items.
misc.forsale.computers.workstation	Workstation-related computer items.
misc.handicap	Items of interest for/about the handicapped. (Moderated)
misc.headlines	Current interest: drug testing, terrorism, etc.
misc.health.alternative	Alternative, complementary, and holistic health care.
misc.health.diabetes	Discussion of diabetes management in day-to-day life.
misc.int-property	Discussion of intellectual property rights.
misc.invest	Investments and the handling of money.
misc.invest.canada	Investing in Canadian financial markets.
misc.invest.real-estate	Property investments.
misc.invest.technical	Analyzing market trends with technical methods.

News Group	Description
misc.jobs.contract	Discussions about contract labor.
misc.jobs.misc	Discussion about employment, workplaces, careers.
misc.jobs.offered	Announcements of positions available.
misc.jobs.offered.entry	Job listings only for entry-level positions.
misc.jobs.resumes	Postings of resumes and "situation-wanted" articles.
misc.kids	Children, their behavior and activities.
misc.kids.computer	The use of computers by children.
misc.legal	Legalities and the ethics of law.
misc.legal.computing	Discussing the legal climate of the computing world.
misc.misc	Various discussions not fitting in any other group.
misc.news.east-europe.rferl	Radio Free Europe/Radio Liberty Daily Report. (Moderated)
misc.news.southasia	News from Bangladesh, India, Nepal, etc. (Moderated)
misc.rural	Devoted to issues concerning rural living.
misc.taxes	Tax laws and advice.
misc.test	For testing of network software. Very boring.
misc.wanted	Requests for things that are needed (*not* software).
misc.writing	Discussion of writing in all of its forms.
news.admin.misc	General topics of network news administration.
news.admin.policy	Policy issues of USENET.
news.admin.technical	Technical aspects of maintaining network news. (Moderated)
news.announce.conferences	Calls for papers and conference announcements. (Moderated)
news.announce.important	General announcements of interest to all. (Moderated)
news.announce.newgroups	Calls for news groups and announcements of same. (Moderated)
news.announce.newusers	Explanatory postings for new users. (Moderated)

(continues)

Resource Reference

V

News Group	Description
news.answers	Repository for periodic USENET articles. (Moderated)
news.config	Postings of system down times and interruptions.
news.future	The future technology of network news systems.
news.groups	Discussions and lists of news groups.
news.lists	News-related statistics and lists. (Moderated)
news.lists.ps-maps	Maps relating to USENET traffic flows. (Moderated)
news.misc	Discussions of USENET itself.
news.newsites	Postings of new site announcements.
news.newusers.questions	Q & A for users new to the USENET.
news.software.anu-news	VMS B-news software from Australian National University.
news.software.b	Discussion about B-news-compatible software.
news.software.nn	Discussion about the "nn" news reader package.
news.software.notes	Notesfile software from the University of Illinois.
news.software.readers	Discussion of software used to read network news.
rec.answers	Repository for periodic USENET articles. (Moderated)
rec.antiques	Discussing antiques and vintage items.
rec.aquaria	Keeping fish and aquaria as a hobby.
rec.arts.animation	Discussion of various kinds of animation.
rec.arts.anime	Japanese animation fan discussion.
rec.arts.anime.info	Announcements about Japanese animation. (Moderated)
rec.arts.anime.marketplace	Things for sale in the Japanese animation world.
rec.arts.anime.stories	All about Japanese comic fanzines. (Moderated)
rec.arts.bodyart	Tattoos and body decoration discussions.
rec.arts.bonsai	Dwarfish trees and shrubbery.
rec.arts.books	Books of all genres, and the publishing industry.
rec.arts.books.tolkien	The works of J.R.R. Tolkien.

News Group	Description
rec.arts.cinema	Discussion of the art of cinema. (Moderated)
rec.arts.comics.info	Reviews, convention information, and other comics news. (Moderated)
rec.arts.comics.marketplace	The exchange of comics and comic-related items.
rec.arts.comics.misc	Comic books, graphic novels, sequential art.
rec.arts.comics.strips	Discussion of short-form comics.
rec.arts.comics.xbooks	The Mutant Universe of Marvel Comics.
rec.arts.dance	Any aspects of dance not covered in another news group.
rec.arts.disney	Discussion of any Disney-related subjects.
rec.arts.drwho	Discussion about Dr. Who.
rec.arts.erotica	Erotic fiction and verse. (Moderated)
rec.arts.fine	Fine arts and artists.
rec.arts.int-fiction	Discussions about interactive fiction.
rec.arts.manga	All aspects of the Japanese storytelling art form.
rec.arts.marching.drumcorps	Drum and bugle corps.
rec.arts.marching.misc	Marching-related performance activities.
rec.arts.misc	Discussions about the arts not in other groups.
rec.arts.movies	Discussions of movies and movie making.
rec.arts.movies.reviews	Reviews of movies. (Moderated)
rec.arts.poems	For the posting of poems.
rec.arts.prose	Short works of prose fiction and follow-up discussion.
rec.arts.sf.announce	Major announcements of the sci-fi world. (Moderated)
rec.arts.sf.fandom	Discussions of sci-fi fan activities.
rec.arts.sf.marketplace	Personal for-sale notices of sci-fi materials.
rec.arts.sf.misc	Science fiction lovers' news group.
rec.arts.sf.movies	Discussing sci-fi motion pictures.
rec.arts.sf.reviews	Reviews of science fiction/fantasy/horror works. (Moderated)
rec.arts.sf.science	Real and speculative aspects of sci-fi science.

(continues)

V

Resource Reference

News Group	Description
rec.arts.sf.starwars	Discussion of the *Star Wars* universe.
rec.arts.sf.tv	Discussing general television science fiction.
rec.arts.sf.written	Discussion of written science fiction and fantasy.
rec.arts.startrek.current	New *Star Trek* shows, movies, and books.
rec.arts.startrek.fandom	*Star Trek* conventions and memorabilia.
rec.arts.startrek.info	Information about the universe of *Star Trek*. (Moderated)
rec.arts.startrek.misc	General discussions of *Star Trek*.
rec.arts.startrek.reviews	Reviews of *Star Trek* books, episodes, films, etc. (Moderated)
rec.arts.startrek.tech	*Star Trek*'s depiction of future technologies.
rec.arts.theatre	Discussion of all aspects of stage work and theatre.
rec.arts.tv	The boob tube, its history, and past and current shows.
rec.arts.tv.soaps	Postings about soap operas.
rec.arts.tv.uk	Discussions of telly shows from the U.K.
rec.arts.wobegon	*A Prairie Home Companion* radio show discussion.
rec.audio	High-fidelity audio.
rec.audio.car	Discussions of automobile audio systems.
rec.audio.high-end	High-end audio systems. (Moderated)
rec.audio.pro	Professional audio recording and studio engineering.
rec.autos	Automobiles, automotive products, and laws.
rec.autos.antique	Discussing all aspects of automobiles over 25 years old.
rec.autos.driving	Driving automobiles.
rec.autos.rod-n-custom	High-performance automobiles.
rec.autos.sport	Discussion of organized, legal auto competitions.
rec.autos.tech	Technical aspects of automobiles and so on.
rec.autos.vw	Issues pertaining to Volkswagen products.

News Group	Description
rec.aviation.announce	Events of interest to the aviation community. (Moderated)
rec.aviation.answers	Frequently asked questions about aviation. (Moderated)
rec.aviation.homebuilt	Selecting, designing, building, and restoring aircraft.
rec.aviation.ifr	Flying under Instrument Flight Rules.
rec.aviation.military	Military aircraft of the past, present, and future.
rec.aviation.misc	Miscellaneous topics in aviation.
rec.aviation.owning	Information on owning airplanes.
rec.aviation.piloting	General discussion for aviators.
rec.aviation.products	Reviews and discussion of products useful to pilots.
rec.aviation.simulators	Flight simulation on all levels.
rec.aviation.soaring	All aspects of sailplanes and hang-gliders.
rec.aviation.stories	Anecdotes of flight experiences. (Moderated)
rec.aviation.student	Learning to fly.
rec.backcountry	Activities in the great outdoors.
rec.bicycles.marketplace	Buying, selling, and reviewing items for cycling.
rec.bicycles.misc	General discussion of bicycling.
rec.bicycles.racing	Bicycle racing techniques, rules, and results.
rec.bicycles.rides	Discussions of tours and training or commuting routes.
rec.bicycles.soc	Societal issues of bicycling.
rec.bicycles.tech	Cycling product design, construction, maintenance, etc.
rec.birds	Hobbyists interested in bird watching.
rec.boats	Hobbyists interested in boating.
rec.boats.paddle	Talk about any boats with oars, paddles, etc.
rec.climbing	Climbing techniques, competition announcements, etc.
rec.collecting	Discussion among collectors of many things.
rec.collecting.cards	Collecting all sorts of sport and non-sport cards.
rec.crafts.brewing	The art of making beers and meads.

(continues)

News Group	Description
rec.crafts.metalworking	All aspects of working with metal.
rec.crafts.misc	Handiwork arts not covered elsewhere.
rec.crafts.quilting	All about quilts and other quilted items.
rec.crafts.textiles	Sewing, weaving, knitting, and other fiber arts.
rec.crafts.winemaking	The tasteful art of making wine.
rec.equestrian	Discussion of things equestrian.
rec.folk-dancing	Folk dances, dancers, and dancing.
rec.food.cooking	Food, cooking, cookbooks, and recipes.
rec.food.drink	Wines and spirits.
rec.food.historic	The history of food-making arts.
rec.food.recipes	Recipes for interesting food and drink. (Moderated)
rec.food.restaurants	Discussion of dining out.
rec.food.sourdough	Making and baking with sourdough.
rec.food.veg	Vegetarians.
rec.gambling	Articles on games of chance and betting.
rec.games.abstract	Perfect information, pure strategy games.
rec.games.backgammon	Discussion of the game of backgammon.
rec.games.board	Discussion and hints on board games.
rec.games.board.ce	The Cosmic Encounter board game.
rec.games.bridge	Hobbyists interested in bridge.
rec.games.chess	Chess and computer chess.
rec.games.corewar	The Core War computer challenge.
rec.games.design	Discussion of game-design-related issues.
rec.games.diplomacy	The conquest game Diplomacy.
rec.games.empire	Discussion and hints about Empire.
rec.games.frp.advocacy	Flames and rebuttals about various role-playing systems.
rec.games.frp.announce	Announcements of happenings in the role-playing world. (Moderated)
rec.games.frp.archives	Archivable fantasy stories and other projects. (Moderated)
rec.games.frp.cyber	Discussions of cyberpunk-related role-playing games.

News Group	Description
rec.games.frp.dnd	Fantasy role-playing with TSR's Dungeons and Dragons.
rec.games.frp.marketplace	Role-playing game materials wanted and for sale.
rec.games.frp.misc	General discussions of role-playing games.
rec.games.go	Discussion about Go.
rec.games.hack	Discussion, hints, etc., about the Hack game.
rec.games.int-fiction	All aspects of interactive fiction games.
rec.games.mecha	Giant robot games.
rec.games.miniatures	Tabletop wargaming.
rec.games.misc	Games and computer games.
rec.games.moria	Comments, hints, and info about the Moria game.
rec.games.mud.admin	Administrative issues of multiuser dungeons.
rec.games.mud.announce	Informational articles about multiuser dungeons. (Moderated)
rec.games.mud.diku	All about DikuMuds.
rec.games.mud.lp	Discussions of the LPMUD computer role-playing game.
rec.games.mud.misc	Various aspects of multiuser computer games.
rec.games.mud.tiny	Discussion about Tiny muds, like MUSH, MUSE, and MOO.
rec.games.netrek	Discussion of the X Windows system game Netrek (XtrekII).
rec.games.pbm	Discussion about Play by Mail games.
rec.games.pinball	Discussing pinball-related issues.
rec.games.programmer	Discussion of adventure-game programming.
rec.games.rogue	Discussion and hints about Rogue.
rec.games.roguelike.announce	Major info about rogue-styled games. (Moderated)
rec.games.roguelike.misc	Rogue-style dungeon games without other groups.
rec.games.trivia	Discussion about trivia.
rec.games.video.arcade	Discussions about coin-operated video games.
rec.games.video.classic	Older home video entertainment systems.

V

Resource Reference

(continues)

News Group	Description
rec.games.video.marketplace	Home video game stuff for sale or trade.
rec.games.video.misc	General discussion about home video games.
rec.games.video.nintendo	All Nintendo video game systems and software.
rec.games.video.sega	All Sega video game systems and software.
rec.games.xtank.play	Strategy and tactics for the distributed game Xtank.
rec.games.xtank.programmer	Coding the Xtank game and its robots.
rec.gardens	Gardening, methods and results.
rec.guns	Discussions about firearms. (Moderated)
rec.heraldry	Discussion of coats of arms.
rec.humor	Jokes and the like. May be somewhat offensive.
rec.humor.d	Discussions on the content of rec.humor articles.
rec.humor.funny	Jokes that are funny (in the moderator's opinion). (Moderated)
rec.humor.oracle	Sagacious advice from the USENET Oracle. (Moderated)
rec.humor.oracle.d	Comments about the USENET Oracle's comments.
rec.hunting	Discussions about hunting. (Moderated)
rec.juggling	Juggling techniques, equipment, and events.
rec.kites	Talk about kites and kiting.
rec.mag	Magazine summaries, tables of contents, etc.
rec.martial-arts	Discussion of the various martial art forms.
rec.misc	General topics about recreational/participant sports.
rec.models.railroad	Model railroads of all scales.
rec.models.rc	Radio-controlled models for hobbyists.
rec.models.rockets	Model rockets for hobbyists.
rec.models.scale	Construction of models.
rec.motorcycles	Motorcycles and related products and laws.

News Group	Description
rec.motorcycles.dirt	Riding motorcycles and ATVs off-road.
rec.motorcycles.harley	All aspects of Harley-Davidson motorcycles.
rec.motorcycles.racing	Discussion of all aspects of racing motorcycles.
rec.music.a-cappella	Vocal music without instrumental accompaniment.
rec.music.afro-latin	Music with Afro-Latin, African, and Latin influences.
rec.music.beatles	Postings about the Fab Four and their music.
rec.music.bluenote	Discussion of jazz, blues, and related types of music.
rec.music.cd	CDs—availability and other discussions.
rec.music.celtic	Traditional and modern music with a Celtic flavor.
rec.music.christian	Christian music, both contemporary and traditional.
rec.music.classical	Discussion about classical music.
rec.music.classical.guitar	Classical music performed on guitar.
rec.music.classical.performing	Performing classical (including early) music.
rec.music.compose	Creating musical and lyrical works.
rec.music.country.western	C & W music, performers, performances, etc.
rec.music.dementia	Discussion of comedy and novelty music.
rec.music.dylan	Discussion of Bob's works and music.
rec.music.early	Discussion of preclassical European music.
rec.music.folk	Folks discussing folk music of various sorts.
rec.music.funky	Funk, rap, hip-hop, house, soul, R & B, and related topics.
rec.music.gaffa	Discussion of Kate Bush and other alternative music. (Moderated)
rec.music.gdead	A group for (Grateful) Dead-heads.
rec.music.indian.classical	Hindustani and Carnatic Indian classical music.
rec.music.indian.misc	Discussing Indian music in general.
rec.music.industrial	Discussion of all industrial-related music styles.

(continues)

News Group	Description
rec.music.info	News and announcements on musical topics. (Moderated)
rec.music.makers	For performers and their discussions.
rec.music.makers.bass	Upright bass and bass guitar techniques and equipment.
rec.music.makers.guitar	Electric and acoustic guitar techniques and equipment.
rec.music.makers.guitar.acoustic	Discussion of acoustic guitar playing.
rec.music.makers.guitar.tablature	Guitar tablature/chords.
rec.music.makers.marketplace	Buying and selling used music-making equipment.
rec.music.makers.percussion	Drum and other percussion techniques and equipment.
rec.music.makers.synth	Synthesizers and computer music.
rec.music.marketplace	Records, tapes, and CDs: wanted, for sale, etc.
rec.music.misc	Music lovers' group.
rec.music.newage	"New Age" music discussions.
rec.music.phish	Discussing the musical group Phish.
rec.music.reggae	Roots, Rockers, Dancehall Reggae.
rec.music.reviews	Reviews of music of all genres and mediums. (Moderated)
rec.music.video	Discussion of music videos and music video software.
rec.nude	Hobbyists interested in naturist/nudist activities.
rec.org.mensa	Talking with members of the high IQ society Mensa.
rec.org.sca	Society for Creative Anachronism.
rec.outdoors.fishing	All aspects of sport and commercial fishing.
rec.parks.theme	Entertainment theme parks.
rec.pets	Pets, pet care, and household animals in general.
rec.pets.birds	The culture and care of indoor birds.
rec.pets.cats	Discussion about domestic cats.
rec.pets.dogs	Any and all subjects relating to dogs as pets.
rec.pets.herp	Reptiles, amphibians, and other exotic vivarium pets.
rec.photo	Hobbyists interested in photography.
rec.puzzles	Puzzles, problems, and quizzes.
rec.puzzles.crosswords	Making and playing gridded word puzzles.

News Group	Description
rec.pyrotechnics	Fireworks, rocketry, safety, and other topics.
rec.radio.amateur.antenna	Antennas: theory, techniques, and construction.
rec.radio.amateur.digital.misc	Packet radio and other digital radio modes.
rec.radio.amateur.equipment	All about production amateur radio hardware.
rec.radio.amateur.homebrew	Amateur radio construction and experimentation.
rec.radio.amateur.misc	Amateur radio practices, contests, events, rules, etc.
rec.radio.amateur.policy	Radio use and regulation policy.
rec.radio.amateur.space	Amateur radio transmissions through space.
rec.radio.broadcasting	Local area broadcast radio. (Moderated)
rec.radio.cb	Citizen-band radio.
rec.radio.info	Informational postings related to radio. (Moderated)
rec.radio.noncomm	Topics relating to non-commercial radio.
rec.radio.scanner	"Utility" broadcasting traffic above 30 MHz.
rec.radio.shortwave	Shortwave radio enthusiasts.
rec.radio.swap	Offers to trade and swap radio equipment.
rec.railroad	For fans of real trains, ferroequinologists.
rec.roller-coaster	Roller coasters and other amusement park rides.
rec.running	Running for enjoyment, sport, exercise, etc.
rec.scouting	Scouting youth organizations worldwide.
rec.scuba	Hobbyists interested in SCUBA diving.
rec.skate	Ice skating and roller skating.
rec.skiing	Hobbyists interested in snow skiing.
rec.skydiving	Hobbyists interested in skydiving.
rec.sport.baseball	Discussion about baseball.
rec.sport.baseball.college	Baseball on the collegiate level.
rec.sport.baseball.fantasy	Rotisserie (fantasy) baseball play.
rec.sport.basketball.college	Hoops on the collegiate level.

(continues)

News Group	Description
rec.sport.basketball.misc	Discussion about basketball.
rec.sport.basketball.pro	Talk of professional basketball.
rec.sport.cricket	Discussion about the sport of cricket.
rec.sport.cricket.scores	Scores from cricket matches around the globe. (Moderated)
rec.sport.disc	Discussion of flying-disc-based sports.
rec.sport.fencing	All aspects of swordplay.
rec.sport.football.australian	Discussion of Australian (rules) football.
rec.sport.football.canadian	All about Canadian rules football.
rec.sport.football.college	U.S.-style college football.
rec.sport.football.misc	Discussion about U.S.-style football.
rec.sport.football.pro	U.S.-style professional football.
rec.sport.golf	Discussion about all aspects of golfing.
rec.sport.hockey	Discussion about ice hockey.
rec.sport.hockey.field	Discussion of the sport of field hockey.
rec.sport.misc	Spectator sports.
rec.sport.olympics	All aspects of the Olympic Games.
rec.sport.paintball	Discussing all aspects of the survival game Paintball.
rec.sport.pro-wrestling	Discussion about professional wrestling.
rec.sport.rowing	Crew for competition or fitness.
rec.sport.rugby	Discussion about the game of rugby.
rec.sport.soccer	Discussion about soccer (Association Football).
rec.sport.swimming	Training for and competing in swimming events.
rec.sport.table-tennis	Things related to table tennis (a.k.a. Ping-Pong).
rec.sport.tennis	Things related to the sport of tennis.
rec.sport.triathlon	Discussing all aspects of multievent sports.
rec.sport.volleyball	Discussion about volleyball.
rec.sport.waterski	Waterskiing and other boat-towed activities.
rec.travel	Traveling all over the world.
rec.travel.air	Airline travel around the world.
rec.travel.marketplace	Tickets and accommodations wanted and for sale.

News Group	Description
rec.video	Video and video components.
rec.video.cable-tv	Technical and regulatory issues of cable television.
rec.video.production	Making professional-quality video productions.
rec.video.releases	Prerecorded video releases on laserdisc and videotape.
rec.video.satellite	Getting shows via satellite.
rec.windsurfing	Riding the waves as a hobby.
rec.woodworking	Hobbyists interested in woodworking.
relcom.ads	Non-commercial ads. (Moderated)
relcom.archives	Messages about new items on archive sites.
relcom.archives.d	Discussions on file servers, archives.
relcom.bbs	BBS news.
relcom.bbs.list	Lists of Russian-language BBSs. (Moderated)
relcom.commerce.audio-video	Audio and video equipment.
relcom.commerce.chemical	Chemical production.
relcom.commerce.computers	Computer hardware.
relcom.commerce.construction	Construction materials and equipment.
relcom.commerce.consume	Cosmetics, perfumes, dresses, shoes.
relcom.commerce.energy	Gas, coal, oil, fuel, generators, etc.
relcom.commerce.estate	Real estate.
relcom.commerce.food	Food and drinks (including alcoholic).
relcom.commerce.food.drinks	Spirits and soft drinks.
relcom.commerce.food.sweet	Sweets and sugar.
relcom.commerce.household	All for house—furniture, freezers, ovens, etc.
relcom.commerce.infoserv	Information services.
relcom.commerce.jobs	Jobs offered/wanted.
relcom.commerce.machinery	Machinery, plant equipment.
relcom.commerce.medicine	Medical services, equipment, drugs.
relcom.commerce.metals	Metals and metal products.
relcom.commerce.money	Credits, deposits, currency.
relcom.commerce.orgtech	Office equipment.
relcom.commerce.other	Miscellanea.
relcom.commerce.software	Software.

Resource Reference

(continues)

News Group	Description
relcom.commerce.stocks	Stocks and bonds.
relcom.commerce.talk	Discussions about commercial groups.
relcom.commerce.tobacco	Cigarettes and tobacco.
relcom.commerce.tour	Tourism, leisure, and entertainment opportunities.
relcom.commerce.transport	Vehicles and spare parts.
relcom.comp.animation	Discussions on computer animation programs. (Moderated)
relcom.comp.binaries	Binary codes of computer programs. (Moderated)
relcom.comp.dbms.foxpro	FoxPro database development system.
relcom.comp.demo	Demo versions of various software. (Moderated)
relcom.comp.demo.d	Discussions on demonstration programs.
relcom.comp.lang.pascal	Using Pascal programming language.
relcom.comp.os.os2	FidoNet area, OS/2 operational system.
relcom.comp.os.vms	VMS operational system.
relcom.comp.os.windows	FidoNet area, MS Windows operational system.
relcom.comp.os.windows.prog	FidoNet area, programming under MS Windows.
relcom.comp.sources.d	Discussions on sources.
relcom.comp.sources.misc	Software sources. (Moderated)
relcom.currency	Money matters in the ex-USSR.
relcom.exnet	Discussions on ExNet electronic exchange.
relcom.exnet.quote	ExNet quotes.
relcom.expo	Exhibitions and fairs announcements and reviews. (Moderated)
relcom.fido.flirt	FidoNet, just talking of love.
relcom.fido.ru.hacker	FidoNet, hackers and crackers (legal!).
relcom.fido.ru.modem	Internetwork discussion on modems.
relcom.fido.ru.networks	Internetwork discussion of global nets.
relcom.fido.ru.strack	FidoNet, digitized sound.
relcom.fido.ru.unix	Internetwork challenge to OS UNIX.
relcom.fido.su.books	FidoNet, for book readers and lovers.

News Group	Description
relcom.fido.su.c-c++	FidoNet, C and C++ languages.
relcom.fido.su.dbms	FidoNet, database management systems.
relcom.fido.su.general	FidoNet, about everything and nothing.
relcom.fido.su.hardw	FidoNet, computer hardware.
relcom.fido.su.magic	FidoNet, magic and occult sciences.
relcom.fido.su.softw	FidoNet, software in general.
relcom.fido.su.tolkien	FidoNet, creations of J.R.R Tolkien.
relcom.fido.su.virus	FidoNet, viruses and vaccines.
relcom.humor	Ha-ha-ha. Jokes, you know them, funny.
relcom.infomarket.quote	Ex-USSR exchanges' quotes /ASMP/. (Moderated)
relcom.infomarket.talk	Discussion on market development /ASMP/. (Moderated)
relcom.jusinf	Information on laws by "Justicinform." (Moderated)
relcom.kids	About kids.
relcom.lan	Internetwork discussion on local area networks.
relcom.maps	Relcom maps.
relcom.msdos	MS-DOS software.
relcom.music	Music lovers.
relcom.netnews	Announcements and articles important for all netters.
relcom.netnews.big	General BIG articles.
relcom.newusers	Q & A of new Relcom users.
relcom.penpals	To find friends, colleagues, etc.
relcom.politics	Political discussions.
relcom.postmasters	For RELCOM postmasters, official. (Moderated)
relcom.postmasters.d	Discussion of postmaster's troubles and bright ideas.
relcom.relarn.general	Scientific academic subnet RELARN: general issues. (Moderated)
relcom.renews	Net magazine RENEWS. (Moderated)
relcom.spbnews	Political and economic news digest by SPB-News Agency. (Moderated)
relcom.talk	Unfettered talk.
relcom.tcpip	TCP/IP protocols and their implementation.

(continues)

News Group	Description
relcom.terms	Discussion of various terms and terminology.
relcom.test	Wow, does it really work?
relcom.wtc	Commercial proposals of World Trade Centers.
relcom.x	X Windows discussion.
sci.aeronautics	The science of aeronautics and related technology. (Moderated)
sci.aeronautics.airliners	Airliner technology. (Moderated)
sci.answers	Repository for periodic USENET articles. (Moderated)
sci.anthropology	All aspects of studying humankind.
sci.aquaria	Only scientifically oriented postings about aquaria.
sci.archaeology	Studying antiquities of the world.
sci.astro	Astronomy discussions and information.
sci.astro.fits	Issues related to the Flexible Image Transport System.
sci.astro.hubble	Processing Hubble Space Telescope data. (Moderated)
sci.astro.planetarium	Discussion of planetariums.
sci.bio	Biology and related sciences.
sci.bio.ecology	Ecological research.
sci.chem	Chemistry and related sciences.
sci.chem.organomet	Organometallic chemistry.
sci.classics	Studying classical history, languages, art, and more.
sci.cognitive	Perception, memory, judgment, and reasoning.
sci.comp-aided	The use of computers as tools in scientific research.
sci.cryonics	Theory and practice of biostasis, suspended animation.
sci.crypt	Different methods of data en-/decryption.
sci.data.formats	Modeling, storage, and retrieval of scientific data.
sci.econ	The science of economics.
sci.econ.research	Research in all fields of economics. (Moderated)
sci.edu	The science of education.
sci.electronics	Circuits, theory, electrons, and discussions.
sci.energy	Discussions about energy, science, and technology.

News Group	Description
sci.energy.hydrogen	All about hydrogen as an alternative fuel.
sci.engr	Technical discussions about engineering tasks.
sci.engr.advanced-tv	HDTV/DATV standards, formats, equipment, practices.
sci.engr.biomed	Discussing the field of biomedical engineering.
sci.engr.chem	All aspects of chemical engineering.
sci.engr.civil	Topics related to civil engineering.
sci.engr.control	The engineering of control systems.
sci.engr.manufacturing	Manufacturing technology.
sci.engr.mech	The field of mechanical engineering.
sci.environment	Discussions about the environment and ecology.
sci.fractals	Objects of non-integral dimension and other chaos.
sci.geo.fluids	Discussion of geophysical fluid dynamics.
sci.geo.geology	Discussion of solid earth sciences.
sci.geo.meteorology	Discussion of meteorology and related topics.
sci.image.processing	Scientific image processing and analysis.
sci.lang	Natural languages, communication, etc.
sci.lang.japan	The Japanese language, both spoken and written.
sci.life-extension	Slowing, stopping, or reversing the aging process.
sci.logic	Logic—math, philosophy, and computational aspects.
sci.materials	All aspects of materials engineering.
sci.math	Mathematical discussions and pursuits.
sci.math.research	Discussion of current mathematical research. (Moderated)
sci.math.stat	Statistics discussion.
sci.math.symbolic	Symbolic algebra discussion.
sci.med	Medicine and its related products and regulations.
sci.med.aids	AIDS: treatment, pathology/biology of HIV, prevention. (Moderated)
sci.med.dentistry	Dentally related topics; all about teeth.

(continues)

News Group	Description
sci.med.nutrition	Physiological impacts of diet.
sci.med.occupational	Preventing, detecting, and treating occupational injuries.
sci.med.pharmacy	The teaching and practice of pharmacy.
sci.med.physics	Issues of physics in medical testing/care.
sci.med.telemedicine	Clinical consulting through computer networks.
sci.military	Discussion about science and the military. (Moderated)
sci.misc	Short-lived discussions on subjects in the sciences.
sci.nanotech	Self-reproducing molecular-scale machines. (Moderated)
sci.nonlinear	Chaotic systems and other non-linear scientific study.
sci.op-research	Research, teaching, and application of operations research.
sci.optics	Discussion relating to the science of optics.
sci.philosophy.tech	Technical philosophy: math, science, logic, etc.
sci.physics	Physical laws, properties, etc.
sci.physics.accelerators	Particle accelerators and the physics of beams.
sci.physics.fusion	Info on fusion, especially "cold" fusion.
sci.physics.research	Current physics research. (Moderated)
sci.polymers	All aspects of polymer science.
sci.psychology	Topics related to psychology.
sci.psychology.digest	PSYCOLOQUY: Refereed Psychology Journal and Newsletter. (Moderated)
sci.research	Research methods, funding, ethics, and whatever.
sci.research.careers	Issues relevant to careers in scientific research.
sci.skeptic	Skeptics discussing pseudoscience.
sci.space	Space, space programs, space-related research, etc.
sci.space.news	Announcements of space-related news items. (Moderated)
sci.space.shuttle	The space shuttle and the STS program.
sci.stat.consult	Statistical consulting.

News Group	Description
sci.stat.edu	Statistics education.
sci.stat.math	Statistics from a strictly mathematical viewpoint.
sci.systems	The theory and application of systems science.
sci.virtual-worlds	Virtual Reality—technology and culture. (Moderated)
sci.virtual-worlds.apps	Current and future uses of virtual-worlds technology. (Moderated)
soc.answers	Repository for periodic USENET articles. (Moderated)
soc.bi	Discussions of bisexuality.
soc.college	College, college activities, campus life, etc.
soc.college.grad	General issues related to graduate schools.
soc.college.gradinfo	Information about graduate schools.
soc.college.teaching-asst	Issues affecting collegiate teaching assistants.
soc.couples	Discussions for couples (cf. soc.singles).
soc.culture.afghanistan	Discussion of the Afghan society.
soc.culture.african	Discussions about Africa and things African.
soc.culture.african.american	Discussions about Afro-American issues.
soc.culture.arabic	Technological and cultural issues, not politics.
soc.culture.argentina	All about life in Argentina.
soc.culture.asean	Countries of the Association of SE Asian Nations.
soc.culture.asian.american	Issues and discussion about Asian-Americans.
soc.culture.australian	Australian culture and society.
soc.culture.austria	Austria and its people.
soc.culture.baltics	People of the Baltic states.
soc.culture.bangladesh	Issues and discussion about Bangladesh.
soc.culture.bosna-herzgvna	The independent state of Bosnia and Herzegovina.
soc.culture.brazil	Talking about the people and country of Brazil.
soc.culture.british	Issues about Britain and those of British descent.

(continues)

V

Resource Reference

News Group	Description
soc.culture.bulgaria	Discussing Bulgarian society.
soc.culture.canada	Discussions of Canada and its people.
soc.culture.caribbean	Life in the Caribbean.
soc.culture.celtic	Irish, Scottish, Breton, Cornish, Manx, and Welsh.
soc.culture.china	About China and Chinese culture.
soc.culture.croatia	The lives of people of Croatia.
soc.culture.czecho-slovak	Bohemian, Slovak, Moravian, and Silesian life.
soc.culture.europe	Discussing all aspects of all-European society.
soc.culture.filipino	Group about the Filipino culture.
soc.culture.french	French culture, history, and related discussions.
soc.culture.german	Discussions about German culture and history.
soc.culture.greek	Group about Greeks.
soc.culture.hongkong	Discussions pertaining to Hong Kong.
soc.culture.indian	Group for discussion about India and things Indian.
soc.culture.indian.telugu	The culture of the Telugu people of India.
soc.culture.indonesia	All about the Indonesian nation.
soc.culture.iranian	Discussions about Iran and things Iranian/Persian.
soc.culture.italian	The Italian people and their culture.
soc.culture.japan	Everything Japanese, except the Japanese language.
soc.culture.jewish	Jewish culture and religion. (cf. talk.politics.mideast)
soc.culture.korean	Discussions about Korea and things Korean.
soc.culture.latin-america	Topics about Latin America.
soc.culture.lebanon	Discussion about things Lebanese.
soc.culture.maghreb	North African society and culture.
soc.culture.magyar	The Hungarian people and their culture.
soc.culture.malaysia	All about Malaysian society.
soc.culture.mexican	Discussion of Mexico's society.
soc.culture.misc	Group for discussion about other cultures.
soc.culture.native	Aboriginal people around the world.

News Group	Description
soc.culture.nepal	Discussion of people and things in and from Nepal.
soc.culture.netherlands	People from the Netherlands and Belgium.
soc.culture.new-zealand	Discussion of topics related to New Zealand.
soc.culture.nordic	Discussion about culture up north.
soc.culture.pakistan	Topics of discussion about Pakistan.
soc.culture.peru	All about the people of Peru.
soc.culture.polish	Polish culture, Polish past, and Polish politics.
soc.culture.portuguese	Discussion of the people of Portugal.
soc.culture.romanian	Discussion of Romanian and Moldavian people.
soc.culture.scientists	Cultural issues about scientists and scientific projects.
soc.culture.singapore	The past, present, and future of Singapore.
soc.culture.soviet	Topics relating to Russian or Soviet culture.
soc.culture.spain	Discussion of culture on the Iberian peninsula.
soc.culture.sri-lanka	Things and people from Sri Lanka.
soc.culture.taiwan	Discussion about things Taiwanese.
soc.culture.tamil	Tamil language, history, and culture.
soc.culture.thai	Thai people and their culture.
soc.culture.turkish	Discussion about things Turkish.
soc.culture.ukrainian	The lives and times of the Ukrainian people.
soc.culture.usa	The culture of the United States of America.
soc.culture.venezuela	Discussion of topics related to Venezuela.
soc.culture.vietnamese	Issues and discussions of Vietnamese culture.
soc.culture.yugoslavia	Discussions of Yugoslavia and its people.
soc.feminism	Discussion of feminism and feminist issues. (Moderated)
soc.history	Discussions of things historical.
soc.libraries.talk	Discussing all aspects of libraries.
soc.men	Issues related to men, their problems, and relationships.

Resource Reference

V

(continues)

News Group	Description
soc.misc	Socially oriented topics not in other groups.
soc.motss	Issues pertaining to homosexuality.
soc.net-people	Announcements, requests, etc., about people on the net.
soc.penpals	In search of net.friendships.
soc.politics	Political problems, systems, solutions. (Moderated)
soc.politics.arms-d	Arms discussion digest. (Moderated)
soc.religion.bahai	Discussion of the Baha'i faith. (Moderated)
soc.religion.christian	Christianity and related topics. (Moderated)
soc.religion.christian.bible-study	Examining the Holy Bible. (Moderated)
soc.religion.eastern	Discussions of Eastern religions. (Moderated)
soc.religion.islam	Discussions of the Islamic faith. (Moderated)
soc.religion.quaker	The Religious Society of Friends.
soc.rights.human	Human rights and activism (e.g., Amnesty International).
soc.roots	Discussing genealogy and genealogical matters.
soc.singles	News group for single people, their activities, etc.
soc.veterans	Social issues relating to military veterans.
soc.women	Issues related to women, their problems, and relationships.
talk.abortion	All sorts of discussions and arguments on abortion.
talk.answers	Repository for periodic USENET articles. (Moderated)
talk.bizarre	The unusual, bizarre, curious, and often stupid.
talk.environment	Discussion of the state of the environment and what to do.
talk.origins	Evolution versus creationism (sometimes hot!).
talk.philosophy.misc	Philosophical musings on all topics.
talk.politics.animals	The use and/or abuse of animals.
talk.politics.china	Discussion of political issues related to China.

News Group	Description
talk.politics.crypto	The relation between cryptography and government.
talk.politics.drugs	The politics of drug issues.
talk.politics.guns	The politics of firearm ownership and (mis)use.
talk.politics.medicine	The politics and ethics involved with health care.
talk.politics.mideast	Discussion and debate over Middle Eastern events.
talk.politics.misc	Political discussions and ravings of all kinds.
talk.politics.soviet	Discussion of Soviet politics, domestic and foreign.
talk.politics.space	Non-technical issues affecting space exploration.
talk.politics.theory	Theory of politics and political systems.
talk.rape	Discussions on stopping rape; not to be crossposted.
talk.religion.misc	Religious, ethical, and moral implications.
talk.religion.newage	Esoteric and minority religions and philosophies.
talk.rumors	For the posting of rumors.
u3b.config	3B distribution configuration.
u3b.misc	3B miscellaneous discussions.
u3b.sources	Sources for AT&T 3B systems.
u3b.tech	3B technical discussions.
u3b.test	3B distribution testing.
vmsnet.admin	Administration of the VMSnet news groups.
vmsnet.alpha	Discussion about Alpha AXP architecture, systems, porting, etc.
vmsnet.announce	General announcements of interest to all. (Moderated)
vmsnet.announce.newusers	Orientation info for new users. (Moderated)
vmsnet.databases.rdb	DEC's Rdb relational DBMS and related topics.
vmsnet.decus.journal	The DECUServe Journal. (Moderated)
vmsnet.decus.lugs	Discussion of DECUS Local User Groups and related issues.
vmsnet.employment	Jobs sought/offered, workplace- and employment-related issues.

V

Resource Reference

(continues)

News Group	Description
vmsnet.infosystems.gopher	Gopher software for VMS, gatewayed to VMSGopher-L.
vmsnet.infosystems.misc	Miscellaneous infosystem software for VMS (e.g., WAIS, WWW).
vmsnet.internals	VMS internals, MACRO-32, Bliss, etc., gatewayed to MACRO32 list.
vmsnet.mail.misc	Other electronic mail software.
vmsnet.mail.mx	MX e-mail system, gatewayed to the MX mailing list.
vmsnet.mail.pmdf	PMDF e-mail system, gatewayed to the ipmdf mailing list.
vmsnet.misc	General VMS topics not covered elsewhere.
vmsnet.networks.desktop.misc	Other desktop integration software.
vmsnet.networks.desktop.pathworks	DEC Pathworks desktop integration software.
vmsnet.networks.management.decmcc	DECmcc and related software.
vmsnet.networks.management.misc	Other network management solutions.
vmsnet.networks.misc	General networking topics not covered elsewhere.
vmsnet.networks.tcp-ip.cmu-tek	CMU-TEK TCP/IP package, gatewayed to cmu-tek-tcp+@andrew.cmu.edu.
vmsnet.networks.tcp-ip.misc	Other TCP/IP solutions for VMS.
vmsnet.networks.tcp-ip.multinet	TGV's Multinet TCP/IP, gatewayed to info-multinet.
vmsnet.networks.tcp-ip.tcpware	Discussion of Process Software's TCPWARE TCP/IP software.
vmsnet.networks.tcp-ip.ucx	DEC's VMS/Ultrix Connection (or TCP/IP services for VMS) product.
vmsnet.networks.tcp-ip.wintcp	The Wollongong Group's WIN-TCP TCP/IP software.
vmsnet.pdp-11	PDP-11 hardware and software, gatewayed to info-pdp11.
vmsnet.sources	Source code postings only. (Moderated)
vmsnet.sources.d	Discussion about or requests for sources.
vmsnet.sources.games	Recreational software postings.
vmsnet.sysmgt	VMS system management.
vmsnet.test	Test messages.
vmsnet.tpu	TPU language and applications, gatewayed to info-tpu.
vmsnet.uucp	DECUS UUCP software, gatewayed to vmsnet mailing list.
vmsnet.vms-posix	Discussion about VMS POSIX.

Mailing Lists

The following compilation of mailing lists is maintained by Stephanie da Silva (`arielle@taronga.com`) and Chuq Von Rospach (`chuq@apple.com`). The on-line version of this list is periodically posted to

    news.lists

    news.announce.newusers

    news.answers

Many addresses and messages included in the following list contain place-holders (set in a special *italic* typeface)—for example, *yourfullname*. When entering such an address or message, replace the placeholder with the appropriate information.

> **Note**
>
> Although the following list has come directly from the Internet, some of the descriptions have been edited for content and consistency.

V

Resource Reference

12step
Contact: `suhre@trwrb.dsd.trw.com` (Maurice Suhre)

Purpose: To discuss/share experiences about 12-step programs such as Alcoholics Anonymous, Overeaters Anonymous, Al-Anon, and ACA. Questions are answered. Please include a phone number in case of trouble establishing an e-mail path.

30something
Contact: `30something-request@fuggles.acc.virginia.edu` (Marc Rouleau)

Purpose: To discuss the TV show by the same name, including actors, episodes, plots, characters, etc.

386users
Contact: `386users-request@udel.edu` (William Davidsen Jr.)

Purpose: To discuss 80386-based computers and all hardware and software that is either 386-specific or that has special interest on the 386.

3d
Contact: `jhbercovitz@lbl.gov` (John Bercovitz)

Purpose: To discuss 3-D (stereo) photography. General info, hints, experiences, equipment, techniques, and stereo "happenings." Anyone interested is welcome to join.

900#
Contact: `bbl7597@ritvax.isc.rit.edu` (Bruce B. LeRoy)

Purpose: To discuss issues in running a 900 telephone number business. Membership restricted to `900#` information providers.

90210
Contact: `90210-request@ferkel.ucsb.edu` (Jim Lick)

Purpose: Discussion of the Fox TV show *Beverly Hills, 90210.*

ABC
Contact: `abc-list-request@cwi.nl` (Steven Pemberton)

Purpose: To discuss the ABC Programming Language and its implementations. Information on ABC is available in *The ABC Programmer's Handbook*, Leo Geurts, et.al., Prentice Hall 1990; "An Alternative Simple Language and Environment for PCs," Steven Pemberton, *IEEE Software*, Vol. 4, No. 1, January 1987, pp. 56-64; by ftp from `mcsun.eu.net` in file `programming/languages/abc/abc.intro`; and by mail-server from `info-server@hp4nl.nluug.nl`: send two-line message: `request programming/languages/abc topic abc.intro`.

Accordion
Contact: `accordion@marie.stat.uga.edu`

Purpose: For individuals with an interest in accordions and accordion music to communicate over the Internet. This is an unmoderated mailing list accessible to everyone with a connected computer. All aspects of acquiring, playing, collecting, repairing, and discography of the accordion are fair topics of conversation. Accordions of all types and designs, including concertinas and button accordions, are discussed. The general philosophy is that we can all learn a great deal if we each share what we know with the other members of the e-mail list.

ACTION-ALERT

Contact: `action-alert-request@vector.intercon.com` (Ron Buckmire)
(David Casti)

Purpose: To provide the LGBTF community a resource by which we can respond to attacks on our community that are occurring anywhere.

ACTION-ALERT is moderated and accepts only postings that include a brief summary of the situation requiring the ACTION along with contact information that members of the ACTION-ALERT distribution list can use to take ACTION! Be sure to include fax numbers and e-mail addresses if at all possible. Messages that do not address a specific issue for ACTION will be returned to the sender.

ACTIV-L

Contact: `listserv@mizzou1.missouri.edu`

Purpose: Concerned with peace, empowerment, justice, and environmental issues. To subscribe, send the message `SUB ACTIV-L` *yourfullname* to `listserv@mizzou1.missouri.edu`.

Act-Up

Contact: `act-up-request@world.std.com` (Lenard Diggins)

Purpose: To discuss the work being done by the various act-up chapters worldwide, to announce events, to exchange ideas related to AIDS activism, and, more broadly, to discuss the politics of AIDS and health care.

Add-Parents

Contact: `listserv@n7kbt.rain.com`

Purpose: For providing support and information to parents of children with Attention Deficit/Hyperactivity Disorder. To subscribe, send mail to `listserv@n7kbt.rain.com` with a message body of this form: `subscribe add-parents` *yourfullname*.

Adoptees

Contact: `listserv@ucsd.edu`

Purpose: A forum for discussion among adult adoptees of any topic related to adoption. It is not intended to be a general discussion forum for adoption among non-adoptees.

To subscribe, mail to `listserv@ucsd.edu` with `subscribe` `youraccount@yoursubdomain.yourdomain` adoptees in the body of the text.

Adoption
Contact: `adoption-request@think.com`

Purpose: To discuss anything and everything connected with adoption.

AFRICA-N
Contact: `frabbani@epas.utoronto.ca` (Faraz Rabbani)

Purpose: A moderated mailing list dedicated to the exchange of news and information on Africa from many sources.

To subscribe, e-mail `listserv@utoronto.bitnet`, and send the following one-line message (the subject header is ignored):

```
SUBSCRIBE AFRICA-N yourfullname
```

Aeronautics
Contact: `aeronautics-request@rascal.ics.utexas.edu`

Purpose: A news-to-mail feed of the `sci.aeronautics` news group, which has a charter of

> A moderated discussion-group dealing with atmospheric flight, specifically: aerodynamics, flying qualities, simulation, structures, systems, propulsion, and design human factors.

Subscribers can participate in real time with the main group.

AF
Contact: `af-request@crl.dec.com`

Purpose: Discussion of AudioFile, a client/server, network-transparent, device-independent audio system.

Agenda-Users
Contact: `agenda-users-request@newcastle.ac.uk`

Purpose: A new mailing list for users of the Microwriter Agenda hand-held computer.

AIDS

Contact: `aids-request@cs.ucla.edu` (Daniel R. Greening)

Purpose: A distribution list for people who can't read `sci.med.aids`. This list covers predominantly medical issues of AIDS, with some discussion of political and social issues. Postings to AIDSNEWS and Health InfoCom News mailing lists are also carried.

Unlike `info-aids`, postings to `aids@cs.ucla.edu` are *non-confidential*. The average number of postings to `aids` is about two per day. The average size of articles is very large (statistics, news summaries, etc.). `sci.med.aids` and `aids@cs.ucla.edu` are moderated. (See also the `info-aids` mailing list.)

Aikido-L

Contact: `listserv@psuvm.psu.edu` (Gerry Santoro)

Purpose: Discussion and information exchange regarding the Japanese martial art Aikido.

Send subscription requests to `listserv@psuvm.psu.edu` as electronic mail with the following in the body of the mail:

```
// JOB SUBSCRIBE AIKIDO-L yourfullname// EOJ
```

This is based on an IBM LISTSERV.

Airplane-Clubs

Contact: `airplane-clubs-request@dg-rtp.dg.com` (Matthew Waugh)

Purpose: To discuss all matters relating to the management and operation of groups operating aircraft.

Ajax Amsterdam

Contact: `vdpoll@fwi.uva.nl`

Purpose: For fans or anyone else who's interested.

Alife

Contact: `alife-request@cognet.ucla.edu`

Purpose: For communications regarding artificial life, a formative inter-disciplinary field involving computer science, the natural sciences, mathematics, medicine, and others. The recent book *Artificial Life*, Christopher Langton, ed., Addison Wesley, 1989, introduces the scope of artificial life as a field of study.

Alife was chartered in February 1990 at the Second Artificial Life Workshop, held in Santa Fe and organized by the Center for Nonlinear Studies at the Los Alamos National Laboratory and the Santa Fe Institute. The list is intended primarily for low-volume, high-content scientific correspondence and as a publicly accessible forum for interested members of the public. Membership as of July 1990 includes more than 1,200 addresses on four continents. There is an ftp-accessible archives/repository of past traffic, software, and papers.

The list is maintained by the Artificial Life Research Group, Computer Science Department, Lindley Hall 101, Indiana University, Bloomington, IN 47405. Redistribution of the list is conditional to minimize any misunderstanding or exaggeration concerning this new area of study.

Allman

Contact: `allman—request@world.std.com` (Eric Budke)

Purpose: The discussion of the Allman Brothers Band and its derivatives. Some tape trading, tour info, and whatever else happens to pop up.

Alpha-OSF-Managers

Contact: `alpha-osf-managers-request@ornl.gov`

`majordomo@ornl.gov`

Purpose: Fast-turnaround troubleshooting tool for managers of DEC Alpha AXP systems running OSF/1.

Alspa

Contact: `alspa—users—request@ssyx.ucsc.edu` (Brad Allen)

Purpose: Discussion by owners/users of the CP/M machines made by (the now defunct) Alspa Computer, Inc.

Alternates

Contact: `alternates—request@ns1.rutgers.edu`

Purpose: For people who advocate and/or practice an open sexual lifestyle. Its members are primarily bisexual men and women and their SOs. `Mail.alternates` is intended as a forum and support group for adult men and women who espouse their freedom of choice and imagination in human sexual relations, no matter what their orientations. Those who are offended by frank and uninhibited discussions relating to sexual issues should not subscribe.

AltInst

Contact: `altinst—request@cs.cmu.edu` (Robin Hanson)

Purpose: You are invited to joint AltInst, a new e-mail list on Alternative Institutions. AltInst is solely for proposing and critiquing alternative institutions for various walks of life. Alternative ways to run conversations, countries, households, markets, offices, romances, schools, etc., are all fair game.

AltInst is open to folks from any political persuasion, but general political flaming/discussion is forbidden. Skip the theory and just tell us your vision of how something could be different and how that would work. Many of us are truly excited to hear about creative, well-considered suggestions, no matter what the source, but quickly bored by both ideological is-to/is-not flaming and partisan rah-rahs for anything "politically correct" in some camp.

Amazons International

Contact: `amazons—request@math.uio.no` (Thomas Gramstad)

Purpose: An electronic digest newsletter for and about Amazons (physically and psychologically strong, assertive women who are not afraid to break free from traditional ideas about gender roles, femininity, and the female physique) and their friends and lovers. Amazons International is dedicated to the image of the female hero in fiction and, in fact, as it is expressed in art and literature, in the physiques and feats of female athletes, and in sexual values and practices, and provides information, discussion, and a supportive environment for these values and issues. Gender-role traditionalists and others who are opposed to Amazon ideals should not subscribe.

Amend2-Discuss, Amend2-Info

Contact: `majordomo@cs.colorado.edu`

Purpose: Colorado voted in an amendment to its state constitution that revokes any existing gay/lesbian/bisexual civil rights legislation and prohibits the drafting of any new legislation. The amendment was spearheaded by a right-wing organization named Colorado Family Values (CFV). It is our understanding that they have no intention of stopping their campaign here.

Two mail/news groups have been created in response to this discriminatory amendment.

> `Amend2-discuss` is for people who are discussing the implications and issues surrounding the passing of amendment 2.

> `Amend2-info` is a moderated mailing list for people interested in information on the implication and issues of amendment 2.

Sending mail to either mailing list has the effect of also posting the message to the corresponding shadow news group. We encourage people to use the mailing list address when disseminating information so that those people who are on the mailing list but who do not have access to news can benefit from the discussion/information.

To subscribe to either list, send mail to `majordomo@cs.colorado.edu`, where the body of the message is `subscribe` *listname*.

America
Contact: `subscribe@xamiga.linet.org`

Purpose: For people interested in how the United States is dealing with foreign trade policies, congressional status, and other inside information about the government that is freely distributable. This list has monthly postings that are generally in large batches, with posts exceeding a few hundred lines. America tends to receive mail only a few times per month and is a moderated group. An unmoderated group is also available.

Send subscription requests to `subscribe@xamiga.linet.org`, using this format:

> `#america` *youraccount@yoursubdomain.yourdomain*;

American Hockey League
Contact: `ahl-news-request@andrew.cmu.edu`

Purpose: For people interested in discussing and following the American Hockey League.

AM/FM

Contact: `listserv@orbital.demon.co.uk`

Purpose: For the AM/FM Online Edition, a monthly compilation of news stories concerning the U.K. radio industry.

To subscribe to the list, write to `listserv@orbital.demon.co.uk` with `subscribe amfm yourfullname` as the first line in the message body, replacing *yourfullname* with your real name, not your e-mail address.

AMOS

Contact: `subscribe@xamiga.linet.org`

Purpose: For the AMOS programming language on Amiga computers. Features source, bug reports, and help from users around the world, but mainly European users. Most posts will be in English, but there are no limitations to the language used, since AMOS is very popular in most European countries.

Send subscription requests to `subscribe@xamiga.linet.org`, using this format:

```
#amos youraccount@yoursubdomain.yourdomain;
```

Anneal

Contact: `anneal–request@cs.ucla.edu` (Daniel R. Greening)

Purpose: Discussion of simulated annealing techniques and analysis, as well as other related issues (stochastic optimization, Boltzmann machines, metricity of NP-complete move spaces, etc.).

Membership is restricted to those doing active research in simulated annealing or related areas. Current membership is international, and about half of the members are published authors. The list itself is unmoderated.

APC-Open

Contact: `apc–open–request@uunet.uu.net` (Fred Rump)

> `fred@compu.com`

Purpose: To interchange information relevant to SCO Advanced Product Centers. Membership restricted to APC OPEN members or those specifically invited.

Resource Reference

V

apE-Info

Contact: `ape—info—request@ferkel.ucsb.edu` (Jim Lick)

Purpose: Discussion of the scientific visualization software package apE.

Argentina

Contact: `argentina—request@ois.db.toronto.edu` (Carlos G. Mendioroz)

Purpose: Mailing list for general discussion and information. By joining, you can learn about how to make those patties (*empanadas*) that you miss so much, discuss how to *cebar un buen mate*, and of course, discuss how to solve Argentina's most outstanding problems. We don't have a regular news service yet, but some members send a briefing every now and then. To join, send name, e-mail, phone number, address, and topics of interest. List contents are primarily in Spanish.

AR-News

Contact: `Ar-news-request@cygnus.com` (Ian Lance Taylor)
(Chip Roberson)

Purpose: A public news wire for items relating to animal rights and welfare.

Appropriate postings to AR-News include posting a news item, requesting information on some event, or responding to a request for information. Discussions on AR-News will *not* be allowed, and we ask that any commentary be taken either to AR-Talk or to private e-mail.

Currently, no resources are available for archiving this list.

Ars Magica

Contact: `ars—magica—request@soda.berkeley.edu`

Purpose: A mailing list for the discussion of White Wolf's Role Playing Game, Ars Magica. Also available as a nightly digest, on request.

AR-Talk

Contact: `ar-talk-request@cygnus.com` (Chip Roberson)
(Ian Lance Taylor)

Purpose: An unmoderated list for the discussion of animal rights. Peter Singer's book *Animal Liberation* proposes a "New Ethics for our Treatment of Animals," and many activist groups, such as PETA (People for the

Ethical Treatment of Animals), regard this as the "Bible of the Animal Rights movement." Consumers and researchers alike are facing new questions concerning the human animals' treatment of the rest of the animal kingdom. The purpose of this list is to provide students, researchers, and activists with a forum for discussing issues like the following:

Animal rights	Animal liberation
Consumer product testing	Cruelty-free products
Vivasection/dissection	Medical testing
Animals in laboratories	Research using animals
Hunting/trapping/fishing	Animals in entertainment
Factory farming	Fur
Ecology	Environmental protection
Vegetarianism	Vegan lifestyles
Christian perspectives	Other perspectives

Currently, no resources are available for archiving this list.

Artist-Users

Contact: `artist-users-request@uicc.com` (Jeff Putsch)

Purpose: Discussion group for users and potential users of the software tools from Cadence Design Systems. This can be used to

- Discuss current problems and their solutions/workarounds

- Discuss usage of the product

- Discuss enhancements and product improvements

- Anything else regarding these products in an analog circuit design environment

All users or potential users of the Cadence Design Systems tools are encouraged to join. (The name is a holdover from pre-`comp.cad.cadence` days—when the group was specifically for users of Cadence's Analog Artist product.)

This mailing list is bidirectionally gatewayed to the USENET news group `comp.cad.cadence`.

ATT-PC+
Contact: `bill@ssbn.wlk.com`

> `...!{att,cs.utexas.edu,sun!daver}!ssbn!bill` (Bill Kennedy)

Purpose: For people interested in the AT&T PC 63xx series of systems. Sublists are maintained for MS-DOS-only and Simul-Task mailings, as well as the full list for items of general interest. Membership must be requested and mail path verification is required before membership is granted.

AUC-TeX
Contact: `auc-tex-request@iesd.auc.dk` (Kresten Krab Thorup)

Purpose: Discussion and information exchange about the AUC TeX package, which runs under GNU Emacs.

AUGLBC-L
Contact: `listserv@american.edu` (Erik G. Paul)

Purpose: The American University Gay, Lesbian, and Bisexual Community is a support group for lesbian, gay, bisexual, transgender, and supportive students. The group is open to all. The group is also connected with the International Lesbian, Gay Youth organization (known as IGLYO).

To subscribe, send a message with one line containing `SUB AUGLBC-L` *yourfullname* to `listserv@american.edu`.

AusGBLF
Contact: `ausgblf-request@minyos.xx.rmit.oz.au`

Purpose: Welcome to AusGBLF, an Australian-based mailing list for gays, bisexuals, lesbians, and friends. The mailing list is maintained from `zglc@minyos.xx.rmit.oz.au`, an account belonging to RMIT's Gay and Lesbian Collective.

Autox
Contact: `autox-request@autox.team.net`

> `autox-request@hoosier.cs.utah.edu`

Purpose: Discussion of autocrossing, SCCA Solo events. Also available as a digest. Many of the list's members are SCCA (Sports Car Club of America).

Aviator

Contact: `aviator-request@icdwest.teradyne.com` (Jim Hickstein)

Purpose: A mailing list of, by, and for users of Aviator, the flight simulation program from Artificial Horizons, Inc. Aviator runs on Sun workstations with the GX graphics accelerator option. The list is unmoderated at present and is unaffiliated with AHI.

Its charter is simply to facilitate communication among users of Aviator. It is *not* intended to communicate with the *providers* of Aviator. All mail received at the submission address is reflected to all the subscribers of the list.

Ayurveda

Contact: `ayurveda-request@netcom.com`

Purpose: Ayurveda is the ancient science of life originating in India. This mailing list is used to help people find out more about ayurveda such as lectures, workshops, stores that sell ayurvedic herbs, and so on.

Backstreets

Contact: `backstreets-request@virginia.edu` (Marc Rouleau)

Purpose: Our purpose is to discuss any and all issues likely to be of interest to people who enjoy Bruce Springsteen's music.

Bagpipe

Contact: `pipes-request@sunapee.dartmouth.edu`

Purpose: Any topic related to bagpipes, most generally defined as any instrument where air is forced manually from a bellows or bag through drones and/or over reeds. All manner of Scottish, Irish, English, and other instruments are discussed. Anyone with an interest is welcome.

Bahai-Faith

Contact: `bahai-faith-request@oneworld.wa.com` (Charles W. Cooper II)

Purpose: A non-threatening forum for discussing and sharing information about the tenets, history, and texts of the Baha'i Faith. This mailing list is gatewayed into the USENET news group `soc.religion.bahai`.

V

Resource Reference

Balloon
Contact: `balloon-request@lut.ac.uk` (Phil Herbert)

Purpose: This is a list for balloonists of any sort, be they hot air or gas, commercial or sport. Currently the number of subscribers is low. Discussion topics include just about anything related to ballooning.

Ballroom
Contact: `ballroom-request@athena.mit.edu` (Shahrukh Merchant)

Purpose: Discussion of any aspect of ballroom dancing. For instance, places to dance, announcements of special events (e.g., inter-university competitions), exchange of information about clubs, ballroom dance music, discussion of dances, steps, etc.

Anyone may join; please send *all* of the following information: (1) full name; (2) Internet-compatible e-mail address; (3) affiliation with any ballroom dance organization or group, if any; (4) ZIP or postal code, and country if other than the U.S.; (5) whether you have access to netnews (Yes/No/Don't know/Yes but don't use).

BA-Poker-List
Contact: `ba-poker-request@netcom.com` (Martin Veneroso)

Purpose: Discussion of poker as it is available to residents of and visitors to the San Francisco Bay Area (broadly defined), in home games as well as in licensed card rooms. Topics include upcoming events, unusual games, strategies, comparisons of various venues, and player "networking."

Barbershop
Contact: `barbershop-request@bigd.cray.com` (David Bowen)

Purpose: Discussion about barbershop harmony, quartets, and choruses and the activities of organizations promoting barbershop singing such as the S.P.E.B.S.Q.S.A., Sweet Adelines, and Harmony, Inc.

BA-Sappho
Contact: `ba-sappho-request@labrys.mti.sgi.com`

Purpose: A Bay Area lesbian mailing list intended for local networking and announcements. BA-Sappho is *not* a discussion group. To maintain its effectiveness as a networking tool and ensure that as many women as possible can participate, it is important for the volume to remain low.

Basic Programming

Contact: `basic-request@ireq.hydro.qc.ca` (Robert Meunier)

Purpose: Discussion and exchange on using BASIC as a programming language.

BBLISA

Contact: `bblisa-request@cs.umb.edu`

Purpose: Discussion about system administration issues, and announcements concerning Back Bay LISA (Large Installation Systems Administration (Boston MA/New England)) activities, meetings, etc.

BBLISA-Announce

Contact: `bblisa-announce-request@cs.umb.edu`

Purpose: Announcements list for Back Bay LISA (Large Installation Systems Administration (Boston MA/New England)) activities, meetings, etc.

Bbones

Contact: `mail-bbones-request@yorku.ca`

Purpose: A list discussing the construction of mail backbones for organizations and campuses. Bbones was created as a followup to a discussion to the 1992 spring Inetrop hosted by Einger Stefferud.

Bears

Contact: `bears-request@spdcc.com` (Steve Dyer and Brian Gollum)

```
...!{harvard,ima,linus,mirror}!spdcc!bears-request
```

Purpose: A mailing list in digest format for gay and bisexual men who are bears themselves and for those who enjoy the company of bears. The exact definition of a "bear" seems to be a personal one, but it encompasses men who are variously cuddly, furry, perhaps stocky, or bearded. `mail.bears` is designed to be a forum to bring together folks with similar interests for conversation, friendship, and sharing of experiences. The tone of `mail.bears` is determined by its members, but people uncomfortable with discussing sexually explicit topics via electronic mail should not subscribe.

Bel Canto
Contact: dewy–fields–request@ifi.uio.no

Purpose: A list open to all discussion regarding the music, lyrics, shows of the group, or the group members' solo projects, or even related artists if appropriate.

BETA
Contact: usergroup–request@mjolner.dk (Elmer Soerensen Sandvad)

Purpose: A discussion forum for BETA users. BETA is a modern object-oriented programming language with powerful abstraction mechanisms including class, subclass, virtual class, class variable, procedure, sub-procedure, virtual procedure, procedure variable, coroutine, subcoroutine, virtual coroutine, coroutine variable, and many more, all unified to the ultimate abstraction mechanism: the pattern. Other features include general block structure, coroutines, concurrency, strong typing, part objects, separate objects, and classless objects.

Between the Lines
Contact: mkwong@scf.nmsu.edu (Myra Wong)

Purpose: To share information and discuss Debbie Gibson and her music.

BiAct-L
Contact: el406010@brownvm.brown.edu (Elaine Brennan)

Purpose: Bisexual activists' discussion list. Directions for posting to the list will be sent to you when you are added to the list.

BiFem-L
Contact: listserv@brownvm.brown.edu (Elaine Brennan)

Purpose: A mailing list for Bi women and Bi-friendly women. To subscribe, send a message to listserv@brownvm.brown.edu with no subject line and the following message body:

```
SUBSCRIBE BIFEM-L *yourfullname*
```

You will receive an acknowledgment of your message and will later receive a message welcoming you to the list and explaining how to post messages. The list volume is 80-100 messages per day.

Big-DB
Contact: `big-db@midway.uchicago.edu` (Fareed Asad-Harooni)

Purpose: Discussions pertaining to large databases (generally greater than 1 million records) and large database management systems such as IMS, DB2, and CCA's Model/204. Anyone having interests in large database issues is welcome.

Bikecommute
Contact: `bikecommute-request@bike2work.eng.sun.com`

Purpose: Mainly Silicon Valley folk. The discussion centers around bicycle transportation and the steps necessary for improved bicycling conditions in (sub)urban areas.

We do have several folks from around the area, as well as a few national organizations (the League of American Wheelmen, Bikecentennial, and the Bicycle Federation of America).

Bikepeople
Contact: `karplus@ce.ucsc.edu` (Kevin Karplus)

Purpose: An area group of bicycle activists, mainly in Santa Cruz County, CA. We discuss bicycle issues: local, state, and national. Public hearings and government meetings are announced and reported on. Messages are occasionally cross-posted with the bikecommute mailing list.

BiNet New Jersey
Contact: `bnnj-request@plts.org`

Purpose: Local BiNet New Jersey mailing list; mostly announcements.

Biodiv-L
Contact: `listserv@bdt.ftpt.ansp.br`

Purpose: To discuss technical opportunities, administrative and economic issues, practical limitations, and scientific goals, leading to recommendations for the establishment of a biodiversity network.

Individual contributions are requested, not only as to network capabilities, but also as to existing databases of interest to biodiversity.

For those interested in receiving a summary of all contributions that have been sent to this list, please send the following message to `listserv@bdt.ftpt.ansp.br`: get biodiv-1 readme.first.

To subscribe, send a message containing `subscribe biodiv-1` *yourfullname, institution* to `listserv@bdt.ftpt.ansp.br`.

Biomch-L
Contact: `listserv@nic.surfnet.nl` (Ton van den Bogert)

Purpose: For members of the International, European, American, Canadian, and other Societies of Biomechanics, ISEK (International Society of Electrophysiological Kinesiology), and for all others with an interest in the general field of biomechanics and human or animal movement. For the scope of this list, see, e.g., the *Journal of Biomechanics* (Pergamon Press), the *Journal of Biomechanical Engineering* (ASME), or *Human Movement Science* (North-Holland).

Biomch-L is operated under the patronage of the International Society of Biomechanics.

Technical help can be obtained by sending the command `send biomch-1 guide` to `listserv@hearn` or `listserv@nic.surfnet.nl`, or by contacting one of the list owners.

Subscribe by sending `subscribe biomch-1` *yourfirstname yourlastname* to `listserv@hearn` (BITNET) or `listserv@nic.surfnet.nl` (Internet and others).

Biosym
Contact: `dibug-request@comp.bioz.unibas.ch` (Reinhard Doelz)

Purpose: For users of Biosym Technologies software. This includes the products InsightII, Discover, Dmol, Homology, Delphi, and Polymer. The list is not run by Biosym.

Birthmother
Contact: `nadir@acca.nmsu.edu`

Purpose: For any birthmother who has relinquished a child for adoption. To join the mailing list, send mail to `nadir@acca.nmsu.edu` with your e-mail address and brief information about your situation (e.g., bmom who relinquished *x* years ago, and does/does not have contact, has/has not been reunited).

Bisexu-L
Contact: `listserv@brownvm.brown.edu` (Bill Sklar)

Purpose: For discussion of issues of bisexuality. Cordial and civilized exchange of relevant ideas, opinions, and experiences between members of all orientations is encouraged—we do not discriminate on the basis of orientation, religion, gender, race, etc.

This list is not intended in the spirit of separatism from any other lists devoted to lesbian, gay, and bisexual issues, but as an additional resource for discussion of bisexual concerns in particular; by the same token, the existence of Bisexu-L should not imply in any way that other discussion lists are no longer appropriate forums for discussion of bisexuality.

BITNET users can subscribe by sending the following command to `listserv@browvm`: `subscribe bisexu-l` *yourfullname*, where *yourfullname* is your real name, not your login ID. Internet users can subscribe by sending the above command in the text/body of a message to `listserv@brownvm.brown.edu`.

BITHRY-L
Contact: `listserv@brownvm.brown.edu` (Elaine Brennan)

Purpose: For the theoretical discussion of bisexuality and gender issues. It is neither a social group, nor a support group, nor an announcement or news forum. There are many other lists that serve those purposes on the networks. Cross-postings from other groups are strongly discouraged.

To subscribe, send the message `SUB BITHRY-L` *yourfullname* to `listserv@brownvm.brown.edu`.

BIVERSITY
Contact: `liz@ai.mit.edu`

Purpose: For announcement of Boston-area events and organizing (not a discussion-type list).

V

Resource Reference

BLUES-L

Contact: `listserv@brownvm.brown.edu`

Purpose: For everyone who can't get enough of the blues, there is a mailing list for blues.

To subscribe, send e-mail to `listserv@brownvm.brown.edu` with the message (no subject) `SUBSCRIBE BLUES-L`, followed by your first and last name.

Also, do not include a .sig, as this seems to confuse the mailer. If you have trouble getting through to `listserv@brownvm.brown.edu`, try `listserv@brownvm.bitnet` or `listserv at brownvm`.

There is an option to receive it in digest form if you desire. Once you get acknowledgment from the listserver that you are on the list, send another message to the listserver (not the list!) with the message `SET BLUES-L DIG`. This should get you on with digest form.

If you send the command `help` to the listserver, you will get a list of useful commands and pointers to other help documents.

BMW

Contact: `bmw-request@balltown.cma.com` (Richard Welty)

Purpose: Discussion of cars made by BMW. Both regular and digest forms are available.

Bolton

Contact: `bwoolf@pro-woolf.clark.net` (Beverly Woolf)

Purpose: To discuss Michael Bolton and his music. To subscribe, send e-mail to `bwoolf@pro-woolf.clark.net` in this form: `subscribe bolton` *yourfullname* (and) *youraccount@yoursubdomain.yourdomain*. A digest form of the list is forthcoming; write for information.

Bonsai

Contact: `listserv@cms.cc.wayne.edu` (Dan@foghorn.pass.wayne.edu)

Purpose: To facilitate discussion of the art and craft of Bonsai and related art forms. Bonsai is the Oriental Art (Craft?) of miniaturizing trees and plants into forms that mimic nature. Everyone interested, whether novice or professional, is invited to subscribe.

BosNet

Contact: `hozo@math.lsa.umich.edu` (Hozo Iztok)

Purpose: A moderated mailing list published daily, covering news and discussions mainly about Bosnia and Hercegovina. The service is run by volunteers. Language is English and Bosnian, whichever the contributor is most comfortable with. It includes also news from international press and important announcements related to Bosnia and Hecegovina. Readers are encouraged to send original contributions.

Brasil

Contact: `bras-net-request@cs.ucla.edu` (B. R. Araujo Neto)

Purpose: Mailing list for general discussion and information. To join, send name, e-mail, phone number, address, and topics of interest. Portuguese is the main language of discussion.

Brass

Contact: `brass-request@geomag.gly.fsu.edu` (Ted Zateslo)

Purpose: A discussion group for people interested in brass musical performance and related topics, especially small musical ensembles of all kinds.

Brit-Iron

Contact: `brit-iron@indiana.edu`

　　　　　`cstringe@indiana.edu`

Purpose: To provide a friendly forum for riders, owners, and admirers of British motorcycles to share information and experiences. We maintain a list of parts sources and shops that repair these classic machines. All marques are welcome from AJS to Vellocette.

British-Cars

Contact: `british-cars-request@autox.team.net` (Mark Bradakis)

　　　　　`british-cars-request@hoosier.cs.utah.edu`

Purpose: Discussion of owning, repairing, racing, cursing, and loving

British cars, predominantly sports cars, some Land Rover and sedan stuff. Also available as a digest.

BTHS-ENews-L
Contact: `listserv@cornell.edu`

Purpose: For providing an open forum for students, teachers, and alumni of Brooklyn Technical High School. To subscribe, send mail to `listserv@cornell.edu` with a message body of this form: `subscribe BTHS-ENews-L` *yourfullname*

Bugs-386bsd
Contact: `bugs-386bsd-request@ms.uky.edu`

Purpose: For 386bsd bugs, patches, and ports. Requirements to join: interest in actively working on 386bsd to improve the operating system for use by yourself and others.

BX-Talk
Contact: `bx-talk-request@qiclab.scn.rain.com` (Darci L. Chapman)

Purpose: For users of Builder Xcessory (BX) to discuss problems (and solutions!) and ideas for using BX.

BX is a graphical user interface builder for Motif applications, sold by ICS. Please note that this list is not associated with ICS (the authors of BX) in any way. This list is unmoderated.

Cabot
Contact: `cabot-request@sol.crd.ge.com` (Richard Welty)

Purpose: Official mailing list of the New York State Institute for Sebastian Cabot Studies.

CA-Firearms
Contact: `ca-firearms-request@shell.portal.com` (Jeff Chan)

BA-Firearms
Contact: `ba-firearms-request@shell.portal.com` (Jeff Chan)

Purpose: Announcement and discussion of firearms legislation and related issues.

The `ca-` list is for California statewide issues; the `ba-` list is for the San Francisco Bay Area and gets all messages sent to the `ca-` list. You subscribe to one or the other, generally depending on whether you're in the San Francisco Bay Area.

CA-Liberty
Contact: `ca–liberty–request@shell.portal.com` (Jeff Chan)

BA-Liberty
Contact: `ba–liberty–request@shell.portal.com` (Jeff Chan)

Purpose: Announcement of local libertarian meetings, events, activities, etc.

The `ca–` list is for California statewide issues; the `ba–` list is for the San Francisco Bay Area and gets all messages sent to the `ca–` list. You subscribe to one or the other, generally depending on whether you're in the San Francisco Bay Area.

Cards
Contact: `cards–request@tanstaafl.uchicago.edu` (Keane Arase)

Purpose: For people interested in collection, speculation, and investing in baseball, football, basketball, hockey, and other trading cards and/or memorabilia. Discussion and want/sell lists are welcome. Open to anyone.

Catholic
Contact: `listserv@american.edu` (Cindy Smith)

> `cms@dragon.com`

Purpose: A forum for Catholics who want to discuss their discipleship to Jesus Christ in terms of the Catholic approach to Christianity. "Catholic" is loosely defined as anyone embracing the Catholic approach to Christianity, whether Roman Catholic, Anglo-Catholic, or Orthodox. Protestants or non-Christians are invited to listen in on discussions, but full-blown debates between Catholics and Protestants are best carried out in Internet's `soc.religion.christian` or `talk.religion.misc` news groups. Discussions on ecumenism are encouraged.

To subscribe, send a one-line message body (not subject) to the subscription address:

```
SUBSCRIBE CATHOLIC yourfullname
```

This list is also bidirectionally forwarded to the news group `bit.listserv.catholic`.

Catholic-Action

Contact: `rfreeman@vpnet.chi.il.us` (Richard Freeman)

Purpose: A moderated list concerned with Catholic evangelism, church revitalization, and preservation of Catholic teachings, traditions and values, and the vital effort to decapitate modernist heresy.

Catholic Doctrine

Contact: `catholic-request@sarto.gaithersburg.md.us`

Purpose: For discussions of orthodox Catholic theology by everyone under the jurisdiction of the Holy Father, John Paul II. Moderated. No attacks on the Catholic Church here, please. There is an archive server (containing Catholic art and magisterial documents) associated with this list. Send mail to the above address to subscribe or to get details about the archive server.

Cavers

Contact: `cavers-request@vlsi.bu.edu` (John D. Sutter)

Purpose: Information resource and forum for all interested in exploring caves. To join, send a note to the above address, including your geographical location as well as e-mail address; details of caving experience and locations where you've caved; NSS number, if you have one; and any other information that might be useful.

CD-Forum

Contact: `cd-request@valis.biocad.com` (Valerie)

Purpose: To provide support/discuss/share experiences about gender-related issues; crossdressing, transvestism, transsexualism, etc. This list is in digest format.

CDPub

Contact: `cdpub-info@knex.via.mind.org`

Purpose: An electronic mailing list for folks engaged or interested in CD-ROM publishing in general and desktop CD-ROM recorders and publishing systems in particular.

Topics of interest to the list include information on the various desktop publishing systems for premastering using CD-ROM media and tapes (DAT, e.g.), replication services, various standards of interest to publishers (ISO9660, RockRidge, and so forth), retrieval engines, platform independence issues, and so on.

Discussions on all platforms are welcome, be it MS-DOS-based PCs, Apple, UNIX, Amiga, etc. Also of interest will be publishing for platforms such as CD-I, 3DO, et. al.

In short, if it relates to CD-ROM publishing, we want to talk about it, exchange information, inform, and be informed.

To subscribe, send to `mail-server@knex.via.mind.org` the following command:

```
SUBSCRIBE CDPub yourfirstname yourlastname
```

Cerebi
Contact: `cerebi-request@tomservo.b23b.ingr.com` (Christian Walters)

Purpose: About the Cerebus comic book by Dave Sim. Anything relating to Cerebus or Sim is welcome. It's just an echo list, so anything that gets mailed is bounced to everyone.

Chalkhills
Contact: `chalkhills-request@presto.ig.com` (John M. Relph)

Purpose: A mailing list for the discussion of the music and records of XTC (the band). Chalkhills is moderated and is distributed in a digest format.

The Chaosium Digest
Contact: `appel@erzo.berkeley.edu`

Purpose: A weekly digest for the discussion of Chaosium's many games, including Call of Cthulhu, Elric!, Elfquest, and Pendragon.

Chem-Eng
Contact: `trayms@cc.curtin.edu.au` (Dr. Martyn Ray)

Purpose: An electronic newsletter on chemical engineering.

V

Resource Reference

Chem-Talk
Contact: ...!{ames,cbosgd}!pacbell!unicom!manus (Dr. Manus Monroe)

Purpose: As chemists, dialogue and conversation with other scientists are essential to stimulating or provoking new ideas. As teachers and researchers, we can find the demands of our profession extensive, which may lead to a reduction in our ability to keep abreast of new data and changes in theories. Sometimes, conversation helps to clarify articles, illuminate new perceptions of theories, and sustain us through our precarious journey in chemistry. A solution to this problem or concern is the creation of efficient communication network using this mailing list.

Chessnews
Contact: chessnews-request@tssi.com (Michael Nolan)

Purpose: A repeater for the USENET news group rec.games.chess. This is a bidirectional repeater. Postings originating from USENET are sent to the list, and those originating from the list are sent to rec.games.chess.

Chorus
Contact: chorus-request@psych.toronto.edu

Purpose: Lesbian and gay chorus mailing list, formed November 1991 by John Schrag (jschrag@alias.com) and Brian Jarvis (jarvis@psych.toronto.edu). Membership includes artistic directors, singers, chorus officers, interpreters, support staff, and friends. Topics of discussion include repertoire, arrangements, staging, costuming, management, fundraising, music, events, concerts, and much more.

Christian
Contact: ames!elroy!grian!mailjc-request

       mailjc-request@grian.cps.altadena.ca.us

Purpose: To provide a non-hostile environment for discussion among Christians. Non-Christians may join the list and "listen-in," but full-blown debates between Christians and non-Christians are best carried out in talk.religion.misc or soc.religion.christian.

C-IBM-370
Contact: {spsd,zardoz,felix,elroy}!dhw68k!C-ibm-370-request

       c-ibm-370-request@dhw68k.cts.com (David Wolfskill)

Purpose: A place to discuss aspects of using the C programming language on s/370-architecture computers—especially under IBM's operating systems for that environment.

Cisco

Contact: `cisco-request@spot.colorado.edu` (David Wood)

Purpose: For discussion of the network products from Cisco Systems, Inc.; primarily the AGS gateway, but also the ASM terminal multiplexor and any other relevant products. Discussions about operation, problems, features, topology, configuration, protocols, routing, loading, serving, etc., are all encouraged. Other topics include vendor relations, new product announcements, availability of fixes and new features, and discussion of new requirements and desirables.

CJI

Contact: `listserv@jerusalem1.datasrv.co.il` (Jacob Richman)

Purpose: A one-way list that will automatically send you the monthly updated computer jobs document. The Computer Jobs in Israel (CJI) list will also send you other special documents/announcements regarding finding computer work in Israel.

During the first 2-3 months (startup), please do not send any requests to the list owner regarding "I have this experience, who should I contact?" Eventually this list will be an open, moderated list for everyone to exchange information about computer jobs in Israel.

To subscribe, send mail to `listserv@jerusalem1.datasrv.co.il` with the following text:

```
sub cji yourfirstname yourlastname
```

Clarissa

Contact: `clarissa-request@tcp.com` (Jim Lick)

Purpose: Discussion of the Nickelodeon TV show *Clarissa Explains It All*.

Cleveland Sports

Contact: `aj755@cleveland.freenet.edu` (Richard Kowicki)

Purpose: Provides a forum for people to discuss their favorite Cleveland sports teams/personalities, and provides news and information about those teams that most out-of-towners couldn't get otherwise.

V

Resource Reference

Teams discussed include the Cleveland Indians, the Cleveland Browns, the Cleveland Cavaliers, and the teams from Ohio State University. Topics of discussion have included local high school teams, local Olympic personalities, other local college teams, and other local professional teams. Anything related to the Cleveland sports scene is fair game here.

CM5-Managers
Contact: `listserv@boxer.nas.nasa.gov` (machine)

`jet@nas.nasa.gov` (human) (J. Eric Townsend)

Purpose: Discussion of administrating the Thinking Machines CM5 parallel supercomputer. To subscribe, send a message to `listserv@boxer.nas.nasa.gov` with a body of `subscribe cm5-managers` *yourfullname.*

CoCo
Contact: `pecampbe@mtus5.bitnet` (Paul E. Campbell)

Purpose: Discussion related to the Tandy Color Computer (any model), OS-9 Operating System, and any other topics relating to the "CoCo," as this computer is affectionately known.

Anyone wanting to be on the list should send me mail. UUCP users, please note that I need a nearby Internet or BITNET node to get things through to you reliably, so please send me a path in the following form: `zeus!yourhost!yourid@sun.com`

Cogneuro
Contact: `cogneuro-request@ptolemy.arc.nasa.gov`

Purpose: An informal, relatively low-volume way to discuss matters at the interface of cognitive science and neuroscience.

The discussion will be scientific and academic, covering biological aspects of behavior and cognitive issues in neuroscience. Also discussable are curricula, graduate programs, and jobs in the field.

To use the list, please follow these examples exactly so that my software works.

To subscribe, send mail like this:

> To: `cogneuro-request@ptolemy.arc.nasa.gov`
> Subject: `cogneuro: subscribe`

To unsubscribe, send mail like this:

> To: `cogneuro-request@ptolemy.arc.nasa.gov`
> Subject: `cogneuro: unsubscribe`

You don't need to put anything in the body of the message. There will be no automatic confirmation, but you might get a note from me.

To change your e-mail address (also very polite to do if you know that your machine will go down for a while, or in case you leave the net), simply unsubscribe from your old address and resubscribe from your new address. This prevents error messages and prevents me from having to verify your address manually.

To post (send a message to everybody on the list), send mail to `cogneuro@ptolemy.arc.nasa.gov`, or follow up to an existing message. For example,

> To: `cogneuro@ptolemy.arc.nasa.gov`
> Subject: `corpus callsosum`

To ask a *metaquestion*, send it to `cogneuro-request@ptolemy.arc.nasa.gov`. Suggestions for improving this announcement or the list are welcome.

The following are the list guidelines:

- The language of the list is English.

- The list is meant to be low in volume and high in s/n ratio.

- Controversy and speculation are welcome, as are lack of controversy and rigor. Since the emphasis is scientific and academic, participants are expected to be extremely tolerant of other participants' opinions and choice of words. Since cogneuro is such a huge field, submission shouldn't be too off-topic or otherwise not essentially scientific or academic.

V

Resource Reference

- The list is initially open to anybody who is interested. Although I don't expect ever to need to exercise it, I reserve the right to remove anybody from the list if there are problems. I want to keep a spirit of free exchange of cognitive neuroscience.

- Other than this, the list is moderated and informal.

COHOUSING-L
Contact: `listserv@uci.com`

Purpose: A list for discussion of *cohousing*, the name of a type of collaborative housing that has been developed primarily in Denmark since 1972 where it is known as *bofoellesskaber* (English approximation).

Cohousing is housing designed to foster community and cooperation while preserving independence. Private residences are clustered near shared facilities. The members design and manage all aspects of their community.

For automated subscription, send e-mail message to `listserv@uci.com` with the following command in the message body (no subject):

```
SUBSCRIBE COHOUSING-L yourfullname (no logins, please)
```

In response, an informative introduction will be sent. E-mail to `fholson@uci.com` for more information.

Coins
Contact: `coins-request@iscsvax.uni.edu` (Daniel J. Power)

Purpose: To provide a forum for discussions on numismatic topics including U.S. and world coins, paper money, tokens, medals, etc. The list is growing and new members are welcome.

Comix
Contact: `comix-request@world.std.com` (Elizabeth Lear Newman)

Purpose: Intended for talking about non-mainstream and independent comic books. We generally don't talk about superheroes much, and we don't talk about Marvel Mutants at all.

Commodore-Amiga

Contact: `subscribe@xamiga.linet.org`

Purpose: For Commodore Amiga computer users. Weekly postings of hardware reviews, news briefs, system information, company progress, and information for finding out more about the Commodore and Amiga.

Send subscription requests to `subscribe@xamiga.linet.org` using this format:

```
#commodore youraccount@yoursubdomain.yourdomain;
```

COMMUNE

Contact: `commune-request@stealth.acf.nyu.edu` (Dan Bernstein)

Purpose: To discuss the COMMUNE protocol, a telnet replacement. The list is a mail reflector, `commune-list@stealth.acf.nyu.edu`.

Concrete-Blonde

Contact: `concrete-blonde-request@piggy.ucsb.edu` (Robert Earl)

Purpose: Discussion of the rock group Concrete Blonde and related artists and issues.

Counterev-L

Contact: `ae852@yfn.ysu.edu` (Jovan Weismiller)

Purpose: A list under the aegis of l'Alliance Monarchists and is dedicated to promoting the cause of traditional monarchy and the Counter Revolution. We believe in government based on natural law principles, decentralization, subsidiarity, an economy based on the principles of distributive justice, and the defense of traditional Western values.

We believe in a Europe, united, traditional, and free from the Atlantic to the Urals, but we oppose the centralizing bureaucracy of the Maastricht Treaty. While we are based in the U.S., we are affiliated with L'Alliance pour la maintenance de la France en Europe, and we have members, as well as fraternal relations, with the monarchist organizations in most Western European countries.

We work for the strengthening of existing monarchies, the restoration in those countries with a monarchist tradition, and the building up of an infrastructure appropriate to the instauration of monarchy in those countries without a living monarchist tradition.

CP

Contact: `listserv@hpl-opus.hpl.hp.com` (Rick Walker)

Purpose: Topics of interest to the group include

1. Cultivation and propagation of CPs (carniverous plants)

2. Field observations of CPs

3. Sources of CP material

4. CP trading between members

The discussion is not moderated and usually consists of short messages offering plants for trade, asking CP questions and advice, relating experiences with plant propagation, etc. The group also maintains archives of commercial plant sources and member's growing lists.

To subscribe, send a one-line message

```
SUB CP yourfirstname yourlastname
```

(substituting your own name for *yourfirstname yourlastname*) to the address `listserv@hpl-opus.hpl.hp.com`.

Please direct all system-related questions to Rick Walker at `walker@hpl-opus.hpl.hp.com`.

Croatian-News/Hrvatski-Vjesnik

Contact: `croatian-news-request@andrew.cmu.edu`

`hrvatski-vjesnik-zamolbe@andrew.cmu.edu`

Purpose: News from and related to Croatia, run by volunteers. These are actually two news distributions: one in Croatian (occasionally an article can be in some other South Slavic language) and one in English.

For subscription, please send a message with the following information: your name, your e-mail address, state/country where your account is. Please put the state/country information in the Subject line of your letter. If you would like to receive the news in Croatian as well, please indicate that in your message. If you would prefer to receive the news in Croatian *only*, please send a message to `hrvatski-vjesnik-zamolbe@andrew.cmu.edu`.

Cro-News/SCYU-Digest

Contact: `cro-news-request@medphys.ucl.ac.uk` (Nino Margetic)

Purpose: *Cro-News*—A non-moderated list that is the distribution point for the news coming from Croatia. At the time of writing (Aug. 1992), the list carries articles from Novi Vjesnik, Vecernji List, Croatia Monitor, Slobodna Dalmacija, Novi Danas, Radio Free Europe/Radio Luxemburg bulletins, UPI reports, etc. The volume of news is relatively high. The languages are Croatian, English, and occasionally Slovene. For application *only*, e-mail address is required. Please send requests for subscription to the aforementioned address.

SCCro-Digest/SCYU-Digest—Two moderated mailing lists that enable people without access to the USENET news groups `soc.culture.croatia` and `soc.culture.yugoslavia` to receive messages published on those forums in a digested form. The volume of the material depends on the traffic on the respective news group, but usually there are at least 700-800 lines of text daily (on each list). The topics cover wide-ranging subjects and on occasion one can witness *very* heated discussions between the participants. Language is mostly English. The interaction is possible through the gateway at Berkeley.

> **Note**
>
> These two lists are *completely* separate, and one can subscribe to one, the other, or both of them.

Crossfire

Contact: `crossfire-request@ifi.uio.no` (Frank Tore Johansen)

Purpose: To discuss the development of the game Crossfire. The official anonymous ftp site is `ftp.ifi.uio.no` in the directory `/pub/crossfire`. Old mails to the list are archived there. Crossfire is a multiplayer graphical arcade and adventure game made for the X Windows environment.

Cro-Views

Contact: `joe@mullara.met.unimelb.edu.au` (Joe Stojsic)

Purpose: An opinion service that consists of discussions relating to Croatia and other former-Yugoslav republics. The main objective is to give people who cannot access the news network (e.g., via the `rn` command in UNIX) a chance to read and voice their own opinions about these issues. Cro-Views is a non-moderated service.

Crowes

Contact: `rstewart@unex.ucla.edu`

Purpose: To provide a forum for discussion about the rock band the Black Crowes. Topics could include the group's music and lyrics, but could also include topics such as the band's participation with NORML, concert dates and playlists, bootlegs (audio and video), etc.

To subscribe, mail to the address shown above with the command `subscribe` in the first line. Discussion is encouraged.

Cryonics

Contact: `...att!whscad1!kqb` (Kevin Q. Brown)

      `kqb@whscad1.att.com`

Purpose: Cryonic suspension is an experimental procedure whereby patients who can no longer be kept alive with today's medical abilities are preserved at low temperatures for treatment in the future. This list is a forum for topics related to cryonics, which include biochemistry of memory, low-temperature biology, legal status of cryonics and cryonically suspended people, nanotechnology and cell repair machines, philosophy of identity, mass media coverage of cryonics, new research and publications, conferences, and local cryonics group meetings.

CSAA

Contact: `announce-request@cs.ucdavis.edu` (Carlos Amezaga)

Purpose: For those folks who have no access to USENET. I provide the gate between the USENET CSAA (`comp.sys.amiga.announce`) news group and mail.

This group distributes announcements of importance to people using the Commodore brand Amiga computers. Announcements may contain any important information, but most likely will deal with new products, disk library releases, software updates, reports of major bugs or dangerous viruses, notices of meetings or upcoming events, and so forth. A large proportion of posts announce the upload of software packages to anonymous ftp archive sites.

To subscribe, unsubscribe, or send comments on this mailing list, send mail to announce-request@cs.ucdavis.edu, and your request will be taken care of.

CTF-Discuss
Contact: ctf-discuss-request@cis.upenn.edu (Dave Farber)

Purpose: This mailing list is targeted at stimulating discussion of issues critical to the computer science community in the United States (and, by extension, the world). The Computer Science and Telecommunications Board (CSTB) of the National Research Council (NRC) is charged with identifying and initiating studies in areas critical to the health of the field. Recently, one such study—"Computing the Future"—has generated a major discussion in the community and has motivated the establishment of this mailing list in order to involve broader participation. This list will be used in the future to report and discuss the activities of the CSTB and to solicit opinions in a variety of areas.

CTN News
Contact: ctn-editors@utcc.utoronto.ca

Purpose: A list covering news on Tibet.

Ctree
Contact: alberta!oha!ctree-request (Tony Olekshy)

Purpose: To provide a forum for the discussion of FairCom's C-Tree, R-Tree, and D-Tree products. This mailing list is not associated with FairCom. We have over three dozen members and cover virtually all hardware and operating system ports.

V

Resource Reference

CUSSNET
Contact: `cussnet-request@stat.com`

Purpose: Computer Users in the Social Sciences is a discussion group devoted to issues of interest to social workers, counselors, and human service workers of all disciplines. The discussion frequently involves computer applications in treatment, agency administration, and research. Students, faculty, community-based professionals, and just good ol' plain folks join in the discussion. Software, hardware, and ethical issues associated with their use in the human service generate lively and informative discussions. Please join us. Bill Allbritten, Ph.D., Moderator (Director, Counseling and Testing Center, Murray State University, Murray, KY 42071).

To join the list, send e-mail to `listserv@stat.com`. The first line of text should be

    subscribe cussnet

CZ
Contact: `cz-request@stsci.edu` (Tom Comeau)

Purpose: To discuss the Harpoon naval wargame series and related topics. This includes Harpoon, Captain's Edition Harpoon, Computer Harpoon, Harpoon SITREP, and various supplements for print and computer versions. Naval topics are discussed insofar as they are related to the game or provide useful background. Discussion is moderated. The Convergence Zone (or CZ for short) is packaged in a digest format. Listeners as well as contributors are welcome.

Dark-Shadows
Contact: `shadows-request@sunee.waterloo.ca` (Bernie Roehl)

Purpose: *Dark Shadows* was a daily soap opera that ran on ABC in the late '60s (ending in 1971). It had a Gothic feel to it and featured storylines involving witchcraft, vampires, werewolves, and the supernatural. It was (appropriately enough) "brought back from the dead" by NBC for a single season last year. It also spawned two feature films, a series of paperback novels, and lots more; the series is celebrating its 25th anniversary this year. There are a number of international fan clubs for the series, but so far there has been no news group or (electronic) mailing list devoted to it. Now there is.

Data-Exp

Contact: `stein@watson.ibm.com`

Purpose: An open forum for users to discuss the Visualization Data Explorer Package. It contains three files at the moment:

`faq`	Frequently asked questions
`summary`	A summary of the software, user interface, executive, data architecture
`forum`	Continuing forum of questions and answers about the software

Additionally, internal forum questions and answers are also posted to it by me.

The mail server understands the following commands:

`index`	Send an index of available files
`faq`	Send the faq file
`forum`	Send the forum file

Each of the above commands can be preceded with `send`

Additional commands:

`subscribe`	Subscribe to any appends that are made to the forum
`add`	Add this mail file to the forum
`remove`	Remove the subscribe to the forum
`help`	Send help on this mail server

This has been set up to quickly disseminate information about the software. We are in the process of setting up an unmoderated USENET forum too.

Datsun-Roadsters

Contact: `datsun—roadsters—request@autox.team.net` (Mark J. Bradakis)

`datsun—roadsters—request@hoosier.utah.edu`

Purpose: To discuss any and all aspects of owning, showing, repairing, driving, etc., Datsun roadsters.

DC-MOTSS

Contact: `dc—motss—request@vector.intercon.com`

Purpose: A social mailing list for the GLBO folks who live in the Washington Metropolitan Area—everything within approximately 50 miles of the Mall.

DDTs-Users

Contact: `ddts—users—request@bigbird.bu.edu` (automated help reply)

Purpose: For discussions of issues related to the DDTs defect tracking software from QualTrak, including (but not limited to) software, methods, mechanisms, techniques, general usage tips, policies, bugs, and bug workarounds. It is intended primarily for DDTs administrators, but that does not necessarily preclude other topics.

"DDTs" and "QualTrak" are probably both trademarks of QualTrak.

Dead-Runners

Contact: `dead—runners—request@unx.sas.com` (Christopher Mark Conn)

Purpose: The Dead Runners Society—a mailing list for runners who like to talk about the psychological, philosophical, and personal aspects of running. We really like to talk about anything that has to do with running, but we tend to be more interested in how it affects our lives and our brains rather than our 10K times. The group is very diverse in experience—there are marathoners and there are people who just jog around the block.

Decision Power

Contact: `dp—friends—request@aiai.ed.ac.uk` (Ken Johnson)

Purpose: Decision Power is a product of ICL Computers Limited comprising a logic programming language Prolog, a constraint handling system Chip, a database interface Seduce (runs on top of Ingres), a development environment Kegi (runs on X), and an end-user graphical display environment KHS (also runs on X). It is in use for various purposes at a dozen or so sites around the United Kingdom and Ireland.

DECnews-EDU

Contact: `decnews@mr4dec.enet.dec.com` (Anne Marie McDonald)

Purpose: DECNEWS for Education and Research—a monthly electronic publication from Digital Equipment Corporation's Education Business Unit for the education and research communities worldwide.

To subscribe, send a message to `listserv@ubvm.cc.buffalo.edu` or `listserv@ubvm.bitnet`. The message should be this command: `SUB DECNEWS` *`yourfirstname yourlastname`* (e.g., `SUB DECNEWS John Jones`). The command is the text of your message; the subject is ignored by LISTSERV.

DECnews-PR

Contact: `decnews-pr-request@pa.dec.com` (Russ Jones)

Purpose: DECnews for Press and Analysts—an Internet-based distribution of all Digital press releases. It is provided as a courtesy to analysts, members of the press, and the consulting community. This is a one-way mailing list. Approximately eight press releases per week.

To subscribe, send mail to `decnews-pr@pa.dec.com` with a subject line of `subscribe`. Please include your name and telephone number in the body of the subscription request.

DECnews-UNIX

Contact: `decnews-unix-request@pa.dec.com` (Russ Jones)

Purpose: DECnews for UNIX—published electronically by Digital Equipment Corporation for Internet distribution every three weeks and contains product and service information of interest to the Digital UNIX community.

To subscribe, send mail to `decnews-unix@pa.dec.com` with a subject line of `subscribe abstract`. Please include your name and telephone number in the body of the subscription request.

V

Resource Reference

DECstation-Managers
Contact: `decstation-managers-request@ornl.gov`

`majordomo@ornl.gov`

Purpose: Fast-turnaround troubleshooting tool for managers of RISC DECstations.

DECUServe-Journal
Contact: `frey@eisner.decus.org` (Sharon Frey)

Purpose: An alternate method of distribution for the *DECUServe Journal*, a monthly digest of technical discussions that take place on the DECUS conferencing system. The Journal (and list) is open to anyone who is interested in Digital Equipment topics, third-party topics, and connectivity topics.

Derby
Contact: `derby-request@ekrl.com` (John Wilkes)

Purpose: To discuss various aspects and strategies of horse racing, primarily dealing with, but not limited to, handicapping. Anyone is free to join.

Deryni-L
Contact: `mail-server@mintir.new-orleans.la.us`

`elendil@mintir.new-orleans.la.us` (Edward J. Branley)

Purpose: A list for readers and fans of Katherine Kurtz' novels and other works. While primary focus is on the Deryni universe, discussion of Kurtz' other works (the Adept series, for example) is also encouraged. To join the list, send a message to `mail-server@mintir.new-orleans.la.us` with the following in the body:

    SUBSCRIBE DERYNI-L

Deviants
Contact: `deviants-request@csv.warwick.ac.uk`

Purpose: To discuss the workings of the Great Wok and all things deviant from accepted social norm. Occasionally disgusting, but not always, it is the home of ranting, experimental reports, news clippings, and other related items. Medical curiosities, cults, murders, and other phenomena are well in place here.

DG-Users

Contact: dg–users–request@ilinx.wimsey.com

Purpose: The technical details of Data General, its OSs, and the cornucopia of hardware it supplies and supports.

The administrator e-mail address is brian@ilinx.wimsey.com or uunet!van–bc!ilinx!brian.

Dinosaur

Contact: dinosaur–request@donald.wichitaks.ncr.com (John Matrow)

Purpose: Discussion of dinosaurs and other archosaurs.

Direct

Contact: direct–request@ctsx.celtech.com (Keith Gregoire)

Purpose: Discussion of the work of the musical artist Vangelis. Both "bounce" and daily digest modes are available, so you might want to specify your preference when subscribing.

Dire-Straits

Contact: dire–straits–request@merrimack.edu (Rand P. Hall)

Purpose: Discussion of the musical group Dire Straits and associated side projects.

To subscribe, send mail with a message body of this form: subscribe

Dirt-Users

Contact: dirt–users–request@ukc.ac.uk

Purpose: An X11-based UIMS.

Disney-Afternoon

Contact: ranger–list–request@taronga.com (Stephanie da Silva)

Purpose: Discussion of the Disney Afternoon and other related topics. This is a very high-volume, low-noise mailing list. It is moderated and is also available as a digest.

Disney-Comics

Contact: disney–comics–request@student.docs.uu.se (Per Starb{ck)

Purpose: Discussion of Disney comics.

Dist-Users
Contact: `shigeya@foretune.co.jp` (Shigeya Suzuki)

`ram@acri.fr` (Raphael Manfredi)

Purpose: This list is for discussions of issues related to the dist 3.0 package and its components: metaconfig, jmake, patch tools, etc. The dist package was posted on `comp.sources.misc` (August 1993).

To subscribe, send mail to `majordomo@foretune.co.jp` saying

```
subscribe dist-users youraccount@yoursubdomain.yourdomain
```

or optionally specifying your e-mail address if you are not on the Internet or if the addresses in your mail headers cannot be relied upon.

Dodge Stealth/Mitsubishi 3000GT
Contact: `stealth-request%jim.uucp@wupost.wustl.edu`

Purpose: Discussion of anything related to these cars.

Dokken/Lynch Mob
Contact: `kydeno00@ukpr.uky.edu` (Kirsten DeNoyelles)

`kydeno00@mik.uky.edu`

Purpose: Articles, questions, and discussions on Dokken and Lynch Mob.

Domestic
Contact: `domestic-request@tattoo.mti.sgi.com`

Purpose: For the discussion of workplace-related issues concerning domestic partners. Topics of discussion include methods for obtaining benefits at one's place of work, methods that did not work, cost of benefits, and other related topics. University students are welcome, as are people from countries other than the U.S.A. (though most of the discussions are U.S.A.-centric). Flame wars are not allowed on this low-volume list.

Donosy
Contact: `przemek@ndcvx.cc.nd.edu` (Przemek Klosowski)

Purpose: Distribution of a news bulletin from Poland. English and Polish versions are both available.

Dont-Tell

Contact: `dont—tell—request@choice.princeton.edu`

Purpose: An e-mail distribution list for people concerned about the effects that the new military policy known as "don't ask/don't tell" will have at academic institutions. This new policy forbids students at the nation's service academies or enrolled in campus ROTC programs from revealing truthful information about themselves.

DSA-LGB

Contact: `dsa—lgb—request@midway.uchicago.edu`

Purpose: A mailing list for members of the Lesbian/Gay/Bisexual Commission of the Democratic Socialists of America, and for other people interested in discussing connections between sexual identity and the democratic socialist movement in the U.S. and other nations. The list is neither archived nor moderated.

Dual-Personalities

Contact: `dual—personalities—request@darwin.uucp`

Purpose: Discussion, maintenance/survival tips, and commercial offerings for the System/83 UNIX box made by the now-defunct DUAL Systems Corporation of Berkeley, as well as similar machines using the IEEE-696 bus (such as the CompuPro 8/16E with Root/Unisoft UNIX).

DVI-list

Contact: `dvi—list—request@calvin.dgbt.doc.ca` (Andrew Patrick)

Purpose: For discussions about Intel's DVI (Digital Video Interactive) system. These discussions cover both applications and programming with DVI.

Eagles

Contact: `eagles—request@flash.usc.edu`

Purpose: To provide a forum for Scouts, Scouters, and former Scouts who are gay/lesbian/bisexual to discuss how they can apply pressure to the BSA to change their homophobic policies. All others who are interested are also welcome.

V

Resource Reference

East Coast Hockey League
Contact: `echl-news-request@andrew.cmu.edu`

Purpose: For people interested in discussing and following the East Coast Hockey League.

Echoes
Contact: `echoes-request@fawnya.tcs.com` (H. W. Neff)

Purpose: Information and commentary on the musical group Pink Floyd, as well as other projects members of the group have been involved with.

Econ-Dev
Contact: `majordomo@csn.org`

Purpose: To share information and network with professionals either in economic development or who are pursuing some of the same informational goals.

We here at the economic development department in Littleton, Colorado, use information as the cornerstone of our program. Littleton's New Economy Project works primarily with small, innovative companies, trying to give them the sophisticated tools they need to compete in the new global environment. Rather than "hunt" for faraway companies and offer incentives to try to get them to locate in Littleton, we concentrate on adding value to existing local companies, or "gardening." Services include using commercial databases to provide a variety of strategic information.

We are also actively interested in systems thinking, chaos, and complexity as they apply to economics. We look forward to hearing from those of you out there who use information, and who are involved with businesses. To subscribe, send the following to `majordomo@csn.org`:

```
subscribe econ-dev
```

This should be sent in the body of the message. The subject is ignored.

ECTL
Contact: `ectl-request@snowhite.cis.uoguelph.ca` (David Leip)

Purpose: A list dedicated to researchers interested in Computer Speech Interfaces.

Ecto

Contact: `ecto-request@ns1.rutgers.edu` (Jessica Dembski)

Purpose: Information and discussion about singer/songwriter Happy Rhodes, and other music, art, books, films of common (or singular) interest.

Eerie, Indiana

Contact: `owner-eerie-indiana@sfu.ca` (Corey Kirk)

Purpose: The list is for the discussion of the critically acclaimed but short-lived TV series *Eerie, Indiana*, which originally aired on NBC in 1991-1992 and is now distributed internationally. The show is a strange mix of humor, fantasy, and science fiction—sort of *"The Wonder Years* meets *Twin Peaks* with a dash of Gary Larson's comic strip *The Far Side"* (*TV Guide*).

Electric Light Orchestra

Contact: `elo-list-request@andrew.cmu.edu`

Purpose: Discussion of the music of Electric Light Orchestra and later solo efforts by band members and former members.

Electric Vehicles

Contact: `listserv@sjsuvm1.sjsu.edu` (Clyde Visser)

Purpose: General list for discussion of all aspects of electric vehicles. (Flamers will be drenched.)

For additions, send mail to `listserv@sjsuvm1.bitnet` with a message text consisting of the line SUBSCRIBE EV *yourfirstname yourlastname*

For digest format, subscribe as above, but with the second line being SET EV DIGEST

Electromagnetics

Contact: `em-request@decwd.ece.uiuc.edu`

Purpose: Discussion of issues relating to electromagnetics. This may take the form of book reviews, code problems, techniques, etc.

V

Resource Reference

Elements
Contact: `elements-request@telesoft.com` (Gary Morris KK6YB)

Purpose: The Shuttle Elements mailing list—to get Keplerian Elements out as quickly as possible during flights. We send out prelaunch elements and postlaunch elements based on either Flight Dynamics Office predictions, Shuttle computer state vector data, or on NORAD radar tracking data. Anyone may subscribe, but prior approval is required before sending submissions to the list.

E-List
Contact: `vilo@cs.helsinki.fi` (Jaak Vilo)

Purpose: News and discussion on Estonia.

ELP
Contact: `j.arnold@bull.com` (John Arnold)

Purpose: To share news, opinions, and other discussions about the musical group Emerson, Lake & Palmer, and related topics.

Elvis Costello
Contact: `costello-request@gnu.ai.mit.edu` (Danny Hernandez)

Purpose: For the discussion and dissemination of information of Declan Patrick Aloysius MacManus, better known as Elvis Costello. Everyone is welcome.

Embedded Digest
Contact: `embed-request@synchro.com` (Chuck Cox)

Purpose: A forum for the discussion of embedded computer system engineering. Suitable topics include embedded hardware and software design techniques, development and testing tool reviews, product announcements, etc.

Empire-List
Contact: `empire-list-request@bbn.com`

Purpose: Discussion of design and implementation issues of BSD Empire among authors and interested parties.

Emplant
Contact: `subscribe@xamiga.linet.org`

Purpose: For the Emplant Macintosh Hardware Emulator. Emplant is a hardware board that allows Amiga users to run any Macintosh programs, in color. The mailing list will provide any compatibility info and info on software upgrades.

Send subscription requests to `subscribe@xamiga.linet.org` using this format:

    #emplant *youraccount@yoursubdomain.yourdomain*;

EMPLOY
Contact: `employ-request@oti.disa.mil` (Jeff Roth)

Purpose: An electronic informational forum to assist federal employees and others in the sharing of job opportunities as well as ideas on gaining employment. Problems confronting personnel seeking employment are complex and require insight, experience, and alternative perspectives to reach realistic solutions. Electronic communications provides a convenient, cost-effective, timely method of contacting valuable resources without the restraints of conventional communication.

emTeX-User
Contact: `emtex@chemie.fu-berlin.de` (Vera Heinau and Heiko Schlichting)

    emtex-user-request@chemie.fu-berlin.de

Purpose: Information about emTeX, an implementation of TeX for MS-DOS and OS/2. This list is meant for everyone who wants to discuss problems concerning installation and/or use of the emTeX package and to be informed about bugs, fixes, and new releases. It sometimes has a traffic of about 5-10 mails per day, so if you (or your host) can't handle such a quantity of mail, please don't sign on. The list is maintained "by hand," so please be patient if a request is not answered immediately.

Conversation language: English

Endorphins

Contact: `endorphins-request@taronga.com` (Stephanie da Silva)

Purpose: For people who love to attain that elusive endorphin high, whether it be by long-distance running, eating red-hot chili peppers, or being paddled on the bottom. If you feel you may be offended by discussion in the last category, then please do not subscribe.

Episcopal (Anglican)

Contact: `listserv@american.edu`

   `cms@dragon.com` (Cindy Smith)

Purpose: To provide a non-hostile environment for discussion among Christians who are members of the Holy Catholic Church in the Anglican Communion, or who are simply interested in Episcopal beliefs and practices. Non-Anglicans and non-Christians may join the list and listen in, but full-blown debates between Anglicans and Protestants/Roman Catholics/non-Christians are best carried out in the `soc.religion.christian` and `talk.religion.misc` news groups. It is hoped that the availability of this list will not diminish the contributions Christians make there. Discussions on ecumenism are encouraged.

To subscribe, send a one-line message body (not subject) to the subscription address:

   `SUBSCRIBE ANGLICAN` *yourfullname*

Epoch Users Forum

Contact: `epuf-request@mcs.anl.gov`

Purpose: An ideas exchange mechanism for users of Epoch fileservers. Comments, questions, and feedback are encouraged.

es

Contact: `es-request@hawkwind.utcs.toronto.edu` (Chris Siebenmann)

Purpose: Discussion of the *es* shell. es is both simple and highly programmable. By exposing many of the internals and adopting constructs from functional programming languages, Paul Haahr and Byron Rakitzis have created a shell that supports new paradigms for programmers. The es shell and the mailing list archives are available on `ftp.sys.utoronto.ca`, directory `/pub/es`.

Esperanto

Contact: `esperanto-request@rand.org` (Mike Urban)

Purpose: A forum for people interested in the neutral international language Esperanto. Discussions about the language itself, the Esperanto movement, publications, and news is encouraged; of course, discussion *in* the language itself are especially encouraged, although English translations may be advisable when the material is of interest to beginners or non-Esperantists.

Ethology

Contact: `saarikko@cc.helsinki.fi` (Jarmo Saarikko)

Purpose: An unmoderated mailing list for the discussion of animal behavior and behavioral ecology. Possible topics could be, for example, new or controversial theories, new research methods, and equipment. Announcements of books, papers, conferences, new software for behavioral analysis, etc., with possible experiences, are also encouraged.

Excelsior!

Contact: `subscribe@xamiga.linet.org`

Purpose: For users of the Amiga Excelsior! BBS system. Used for transferring small binaries, update notices, bug reports, and suggestions.

Send subscription requests to `subscribe@xamiga.linet.org` using this format:

```
#excelsior youraccount@yoursubdomain.yourdomain;
```

Exhibitionists

Contact: `exhibitionists-request@jvnc.net`

Purpose: Primarily for managers and/or projectionists, but open also to anyone working in a cinema or film society, etc. Anyone's welcome to join, but the conversation is mainly about things that only cinema workers (and, in some cases, only projectionists) would be interested in, so if this isn't you, think twice about joining. In short, a forum where someone can ask "So, how was work at the theater today?" and then actually understand what you're talking about.

Exotic-Cars
Contact: `exotic-cars-request@sol.asl.hitachi.com` (Joe Augenbraun)

Purpose: Discussion about exotic and limited-production automobiles, including maintenance, driving impressions, artistic nits, and any other aspect of the world's rarest and most desirable cars.

Extropians
Contact: `extropians-request@extropy.org`

Purpose: Discussion and development of Extropian ideas. The term "Extropian" was coined by the publishers of the journal *Extropy*, which is devoted to Extropian philosophy. This list is a spinoff of the journal. Extropians may be roughly described as those simultaneously interested in anarchocapitalist politics, cryonics (and other life-extension techniques), the technological extension of human intelligence and perception, nanotechnology, spontaneous orders, and a number of other related ideas. If you are an Extropian, the concept that these are all related topics will seem natural.

All Extropians (and those who suspect that they are Extropians) are invited to join.

For more information on the Extropy Institute, Inc., a not-for-profit educational foundation, send mail to `exi-info@extropy.org` or write Max More, c/o Extropy Institute, 11860 Magnolia Avenue, Suite R, Riverside, CA 92503.

Fairness
Contact: `fairness-request@mainstream.com` (automated—Craig Peterson)

Purpose: Monitoring issues of "fairness" with respect to the government. Press releases from the White House, articles from papers and journals, and opinions from individuals are included.

Fall
Contact: `fall-request@wg.estec.esa.nl`

Purpose: Any discussion concerning the Fall and the various offspring of it, plus any related subjects.

FASE

Contact: fase@cs.uh.edu

Purpose: FASE (Forum for Academic Software Engineering)—A forum for communication among academic educators who teach software engineering. Submissions are compiled and mailed to subscribers approximately monthly.

FATFREE

Contact: `fatfree-request@hustle.rahul.net` (Michelle R. Dick)

Purpose: FATFREE, the McDougall/Ornish mailing list—for discussion about extremely low-fat vegetarianism. For this list, "very low-fat" indicates diets with less than 15 percent of calories as fat. Vegetarian includes milk, eggs, and honey, but excludes all meat, fish, and poultry. Two main proponents of this style of diet are John McDougall and Dean Ornish.

Members are encouraged to contribute recipes, testimonials, food news, requests, tips on dealing with family and friends, anecdotes, jokes, and questions of any sort at least mildly related to low-fat vegetarianism and living a healthy lifestyle (both McDougall and Ornish emphasize mild exercise and relaxation activities as part of a healthy lifestyle). This is not a moderated list.

This is a high-volume list; we generally get between 5 and 30 messages per day. There are two ways to receive the list: regular and digest. Regular members receive each message individually throughout the day. Digest members receive just one e-mail each day containing all the previous day's traffic. There is no difference in content.

To join, send e-mail to `fatfree-request@hustle.rahul.net`, using one of the following subjects:

`add`	To join as a regular member
`add digest`	To join as a digest member

F-Body

Contact: `f-body-request@boogie.ebay.sun.com` (Richard Koch)

Purpose: Discussion of Camaros and Firebirds.

Fegmaniax

Contact: `fegmaniax—request@gnu.ai.mit.edu`

Purpose: Discussion, news, and information regarding that English eccentric and musician, Robyn Hitchcock.

Femail

Contact: `femail—request@lucerne.eng.sun.com` (Ellen Eades)

Purpose: To provide a forum for discussion of issues of interest to women, in a friendly atmosphere. The basic tenets of feminism and the day-to-day experiences of women do not have to be explained or defended. Men and women can join, but everyone requesting to be added to the mailing list must provide the moderator with the following:

- A full name

- A complete UUCP path to a well-known host or a fully specified Internet address

- The correspondent's gender (for records and statistics only). *No* exceptions.

Feminism-Digest

Contact: `feminism—digest@ncar.ucar.edu` (Cindy Tittle Moore)

Purpose: A digest version of `soc.feminism`. It is intended for those who have difficulty getting `soc.feminism`, or who prefer to read it all at once or whatever.

Ferrets

Contact: `ferret—request@ferret.ocunix.on.ca` (Chris Lewis)

> `{utzoo,utai,uunet}!cunews!latour!ecicrl!ferret—request`

Purpose: For people who have or are merely interested in ferrets (Mustela Furo). Discussions are welcome on any subject relating to ferrets—suitability as pets, health information, funny ferret stories, etc.

Filmmakers

Contact: `filmmakers—request@grissom.larc.nasa.gov`

Purpose: Deals with all aspects of motion picture production, with an emphasis on technical issues. Heavily stressed are construction and design issues for those working on tight budgets. It should be emphasized that the subject is film, and not video.

Finewine

Contact: `finewine-request@world.std.com` (Eric Budke)

Purpose: A news group dedicated to the rock music group God Street Wine.

Firearms

Contact: `firearms-request@cs.cmu.edu` (Karl Kleinpaste)

Purpose: To provide an environment in which sportsmen can discuss issues of concern to them. Topics include but are not limited to hunting, firearms safety, legal issues, reloading tips, maintenance suggestions, target shooting, and dissemination of general information. Anyone is welcome to join—note that we do *not* intend to discuss the merits of gun control.

Flags

Contact: `bottasini@cesi.it` (Giuseppe Bottasini)

Purpose: The creation of worldwide, real-time updated database about all kind of flags: (inter)national, (un)official, ethnical, political, religious, movements' flags. Discussion of symbols or colors used on flags, in order to find common and/or unique meanings of them. Gathering information about flags' histories.

Flamingo

Contact: `flamingo-request@lenny.corp.sgi.com`

Purpose: The list is for unmoderated discussion among fans of the series *Parker Lewis* (formerly *Parker Lewis Can't Lose*) on the Fox television network. It is available both as a mail reflector and as a digest. The two formats distribute the same material; please state your preference when you subscribe.

Flashlife

Contact: `flashlife-request@netcom.com` (Carl Rigney)

Purpose: A mailing list for GMs of Shadowrun and other cyberpunk role-playing games to discuss rules and scenarios, ask questions, make up answers, and similar fasfax.

FL-MOTSS

Contact: `fl-motss-request@pts.mot.com`

Purpose: Discussion of LGB issues in Florida. Anyone can join and participate. Please include full name and e-mail address on all requests.

FM-10

Contact: `fm-10-request@dg-rtp.dg.com`

Purpose: To talk about modifications, enhancements, and uses of the Ramsey FM-10, other BA-1404-based FM Stereo broadcasters, also some discussion of the FM pirate radio.

Fogelberg

Contact: `bwoolf@pro-woolf.clark.net` (Beverly Woolf)

Purpose: To discuss Dan Fogelberg and his music. To subscribe, send e-mail to `bwoolf@pro-woolf.clark.net` in this form:

```
subscribe fogelberg yourfullname (and)
youraccount@yoursubdomain.yourdomain
```

A digest form of the list is forthcoming; write for information.

Folk-Dancing

Contact: `tjw+@pitt.edu` (Terry J. Wood)

```
tjw@pittvms.bitnet
```

Purpose: Any discussion of folk dancing. Areas of dance would include but not be limited to international, contra, square, Western square morris, Cajun, and barn dancing.

Please feel free to discuss such things as touring groups, artists, camps, workshops, styling, equipment, recordings, and so on. This mailing list also welcomes queries about where to find dance groups and how to get started dancing.

Please note that the Folk Dancing Mailing List (FDML) operates in conjunction with the USENET news group `rec.folk-dancing`. Material in `rec.folk-dancing` appears in the FDML. This mailing list is primarily for people who cannot (or do not want to) receive USENET.

When subscribing to the FDML, please include several computer mail addresses *and* a postal mail address (or phone number) as a last resort.

Forest Management DSS

Contact: `listserv@pnfi.forestry.ca` (Tom Moore)

Purpose: The discussion group is a forum for rapid exchange of information, ideas, and opinions related to the topics of decision support systems and information systems for forest management planning. Also welcome are announcements of meetings, calls for papers, calls for proposals, help wanted, employment wanted, resumes, book reviews, and copies of papers or speeches.

Although this is being sponsored as part of a Canadian research program, participation from the international community is welcome. Please pass this information on to your colleagues.

To subscribe to the list, send an e-mail to `listserv@pnfi.forestry.ca` with the message `SUBSCRIBE FMDSS-L` *yourfirstname yourlastname*

FoxPro

Contact: `fileserv@polarbear.rankin-inlet.nt.ca` (Chris O'Neill)

Purpose: To foster information sharing between users of the FoxPro database development environment now owned and distributed by Microsoft Corporation. Both new and experienced users of FoxPro are welcome to join in the discussions.

Topics that may be discussed in the foxpro-l mailing list include (but are not necessarily limited to) the following: ideas for applications, exchanging code snippets, problem solving, product news, and just about anything else related to the FoxPro development environment.

> **Note**
>
> The foxpro-l mailing list is not affiliated with Microsoft Corporation in any way.

To subscribe to the foxpro-l mailing list, send an e-mail message to `fileserv@polarbear.rankin-inlet.nt.ca` with the following in the body:

```
JOIN FOXPRO-L
QUIT
```

Framers

Contact: `framers-request@uunet.uu.net` (Mark Lawrence)

Purpose: A user' forum for sharing experiences and information about the FrameMaker desktop publishing package from Frame Technology.

Freaks

Contact: `freaks-request@bnf.com`

Purpose: A list which talks about Marillion and related rock groups. To subscribe, send a message containing: `subscribe freaks yourfullname`

FREEDOM

Contact: `listserv@idbsu.idbsu.edu`

Purpose: Mailing list of people organizing against the Idaho Citizens Alliance anti-gay ballot initiative.

To subscribe, send a message to `listserv@idbsu.idbsu.edu` with one line: `SUB FREEDOM yourfullname`.

FSP-Discussion

Contact: `listmaster@germany.eu.net`

Purpose: Discussion of the new FSP protocol. FSP is a set of programs that implements a public-access archive similar to an anonymous ftp archive. The difference is that FSP is connectionless and virtually stateless. This list is open for everybody.

FSUUCP

Contact: `fsuucp-request@polyslo.calpoly.edu` (Christopher J. Ambler)

Purpose: For the discussion, bug hunting, feature proposing, and announcements of the availability and release dates of FSUUCP, an MS-DOS UUCP/mail/news package. FSUUCP is shareware, and includes uucico/uuxqt (with support for rmail and rnews—single, batched, and compressed batch), as well as readnews, postnews, mail, expire, uuq, uusnap, uulog, and a host of utilities.

Funky-Music

Contact: `funky-music-request@athena.mit.edu`

Purpose: The discussion of funk music, as well as rap, hip-hop, soul, R & B, and related varieties. Discussions of zydeco, reggae, salsa, soca, and similar gutsy street music are also welcome.

Funk music is based on the rhythmic innovations pioneered by James Brown. Other notable artists in the genre are Parliament, Funkadelic, War, Earth Wind and Fire, the Meters, and Mandrill.

Funky music has a danceable beat to it, a soulful feel, and an underlying intelligence. All the varieties of music mentioned above are funky.

Fusion

Contact: `fusion-request@zorch.sf-bay.org`

Purpose: E-mail redistribution of USENET `sci.physics.fusion` news group, for sites/users that don't have access to USENET.

Futurebus+ Users

Contact: `majordomo@theus.rain.com`

Purpose: A discussion group for users of Futurebus+. Topics include the design, implementation, integration, and operation of the hardware and software that are related to Futurebus+.

To subscribe, mail to `majordomo@theus.rain.com` with `subscribe fbus_users` *youraccount@yoursubdomain.yourdomain* in the body of the text.

Fuzzy-Ramblings

Contact: `fuzzy-ramblings-request@piggy.ucsb.edu` (Robert Earl)

Purpose: Discussion of the British girl group We've Got a Fuzzbox and We're Going to Use It!!!.

GAY-LIBN

Contact: `listserv@vm.usc.edu`

Purpose: Gay/Lesbian/Bisexual Librarians Network. To join the list and receive mailings from GAY-LIBN,

- At BITNET nodes, send mail or an interactive message to `listserv@uscvm` with the text `SUB GAY-LIBN` *YOURFIRSTNAME YOURLASTNAME* (no punctuation, no other text).

- At other nodes, send mail to `listserv@vm.usc.edu` with the text `SUB GAY-LIBN` *YOURFIRSTNAME YOURLASTNAME* (no punctuation, no other text).

GayNet
Contact: `gaynet-request@queernet.org` (Roger B.A. Klorese)

Purpose: A list about gay, lesbian, and bisexual concerns (with a focus on college campuses), including (but not limited to) outreach programs, political action, AIDS education, dealing with school administrations, social programs, and just finding out what other support groups are doing. Items of general gay/lesbian interest are also welcome.

The list is not moderated.

Subscription/unsubscription requests are managed by an automated server called Majordomo.

To subscribe, send a mail message to

`majordomo@queernet.org`

The first (not subject) line of the message should be

`subscribe gaynet`

Other administrative questions and requests should be sent to the e-mail address `gaynet-approval@queernet.org`.

GEGSTAFF
Contact: `listserv@ukcc.uky.edu` (Jeff Jones)

Purpose: The discussion of all topics relating to sexuality and gender in geography. Discussions of theoretical and empirical work/issues are welcome, as are book reviews, calls for papers, and information on conferences.

To subscribe, send mail to `listserv@ukcc`, or on the Internet to `listserv@ukcc.uky.edu`, with the body containing the command SUB GEGSTAFF *yourfirstname yourlastname*

Gender
Contact: `ericg@indiana.edu` (Eric Garrison)

Purpose: A list created for the purpose of discussing gender issues. The intent is to provide an open-minded forum for discussion of gender stereotypes versus individuality, gender roles, and particularly how people can get beyond these restrictions. Any related topic is fair game: I won't presume to dictate the subject matter of the list, I want everyone on the list to do that. Anonymous "posting" is available.

To join, mail `ericg@indiana.edu` with `add me mail.gender` in the subject line.

GL-ASB

Contact: `majordomo@queernet.org` (Roger B.A. Klorese)

Purpose: For discussion of bondage and S & M topics for gay men and lesbians. It is intended to provide a forum for discussion and stories with an atmosphere of gay and lesbian culture perceived by some as being less prevalent in the `alt.sex.bondage` news group than they want.

The gl-asb list is administered with the assistance of an automated mailing list server called Majordomo, written by Brent Chapman. In order to be added to the list, please send a message to one of the following addresses:

```
*majordomo@queernet.org
```

`wellconnectedsite!unpc!majordomo` (if you support only UUCP paths)

with the following content in the message:

```
subscribe gl-asb
end
```

Any administrative questions should be addressed to

```
gl-asb-approval@queernet.org
```
`wellconnectedsite!unpc!gl-asb-approval` (if you support only UUCP paths)

Glass Arts

Contact: `glass-request@dixie.com`

Purpose: For stained/hot glass artists.

GLBPOC

Contact: `glbpoc-request@geri.pa.dec.com`

Purpose: A mailing list for lesbian, gay, and bisexual people of color. To be added to the list, you must provide your full name and a complete Internet address.

Glove-List
Contact: `listserv@boxer.nas.nasa.gov` (machine)

`jet@nas.nasa.gov` (human) (J. Eric Townsend)

Purpose: Discussion of the Nintendo PowerGlove, a less than $100 dataglove available on the remaindered racks of Toys 'R Us and other big toy stores. To subscribe, send e-mail to `listserv@boxer.nas.nasa.gov` with a body of `subscribe glove—list` *yourfullname*.

GNU-Manual
Contact: `gnu—manual—request@a.cs.uiuc.edu` (Internet)

Purpose: GNU-manual members are volunteers who write, proofread, and comment on documents for a GNU Emacs Lisp programmers' manual.

GodlyGraphics
Contact: `godlygraphics—request@acs.harding.edu` (Ron Pacheco)

Purpose: The GodlyGraphics mailing list is for the discussion of Christian uses of computer graphics and animations, especially using the Amiga computer, and for related trading of ideas, objects, images, and even joint projects, such as the design of a Christian computer game. The possibilities for innovative uses of computer graphics, animations, multimedia applications, and video productions in support of various Christian ministries and other endeavors are *wide open*. What better use of your technical skills or creative talents than to serve The One who gave them to you? Any interested or curious Christian is welcome to join.

Golden
Contact: `golden—request@hobbes.ucsd.edu`

Purpose: A mailing list for Golden Retriever enthusiasts. Suitable topics include questions and answers regarding the Golden Retriever breed in general, news bits, article summaries, discussions of particular lines and breeders, shows, activities (CCI, therapy dogs, guide dogs), show bragging, summaries of local GR club activities or newsletters, other items which might be too Golden-introverted for `rec.pets.dogs`, cooperation on a breed-specific FAQ for r.p.d, etc.

GPS Digest
Contact: `gps-request@esseye.si.com`

Purpose: A forum for the discussion of topics related to the USAF Global Positioning System (GPS) and other satellite navigation positioning systems. The digest is moderated.

GRASS
Contact: `grass-server@wharton.upenn.edu`

Purpose: The Generic Religions and Secret Societies mailing list—a forum for the development of religions and secret societies for use in role-playing games. Both real-world and fictional religions and secret societies are covered. GRASS is an erratic volume, high signal-to-noise mailing list.

To subscribe, send mail to the contact address with a subject of SUBSCRIBE *yourfullname*.

Grunge-L
Contact: `listserv@ubvm.cc.buffalo.edu` (Jon Hilgreen)

Purpose: This list is intended for the discussion of any and all topics related to the form of music known as "grunge rock" (not just Seattle-based or Sub Pop bands). It is an open, unmoderated list with a frequently high level of traffic.

As a general guideline, the following talk is encouraged:

- Recording/concert reviews and recommendations

- Band tour dates

- Local scene reviews and news

- Record store and mail-order company recommendations

- Nose-picking techniques

- Interviews and articles, original or otherwise

- Quotes, band gossip, and insider information

- Anything else one would typically find in a music magazine

People who find "adult language and references" offensive will not want to join this list. It is also a good idea to read the grunge list with an extra dose of patience, perverse humor, and sarcasm.

To subscribe, send a message containing

```
subscribe grunge-l complete real name
```

to `listserv@ubvm` (BITNET), *or* `listserv@ubvm.cc.buffalo.edu` (Internet).

GSP-List
Contact: `gsp-list-request@ms.uky.edu` (David W. Rankin Jr.)

```
gsp-list-request@ukma.bitnet

{uunet, gatech, rutgers}!ukma!gsp-list-request
```

Purpose: To allow "alumni" (as defined by the GSPAA) of the Kentucky Governor's Scholars Program to participate in intellectual discussions on various topics, while also promoting the spirit of "community" fostered by GSP. The list maintainer requests that only GSPeople request to join the list, and that when they do, they send at least two good e-mail addresses (if possible) and the year and campus at which they attended GSP.

Gug-Sysadmins
Contact: `gug-sysadmins-request@vlsivie.tuwien.ac.at`

Purpose: Distributions of rumors, bug fixes, and workarounds concerning the CAD-Tool genesil and related tools to members of the Eurochip project and other interested parties.

Gunk'I'Dunk
Contact: `jeremy@stat.washington.edu` (Jeremy York)

Purpose: A forum for discussing and promoting *Tales of the Beanworld*, an unusual black-and-white comic published by Eclipse comics. It is a moderated newsletter that occasionally receives input from the creator of the Beanworld, Larry Marder.

GURPS-Announce-Ext
Contact: `owner-gurps-announce-ext@think.com` (Laird Popkin)

Purpose: Low-bandwidth list for announcements relating to the Generic Universal Role Playing System from Steve Jackson Games. Announcements include the availability of playtest drafts of material, new products, and assorted occasional updates.

GURPS-Ext

Contact: owner—gurps—announce—ext@think.com (Laird Popkin).

Purpose: General discussion of the Generic Universal Role Playing System from Steve Jackson Games. All of the announcements are also sent to this list, so you don't need to be on both lists.

Gymn

Contact: raek@athena.mit.edu (Robyn Kozierok)

Purpose: For the discussion of all aspects of gymnastics.

Handicap

Contact: wtm@bunker.shel.isc—br.com

Purpose: The Handicap Digest—information/discussion exchange for issues dealing with the physically/mentally handicapped. Topics include but are not limited to medical, education, legal, technological aids, and the handicapped in society.

> **Note**
>
> The articles from the Handicap Digest are also posted in the USENET news group misc.handicap.

HANDS

Contact: hands@u.washington.edu

Purpose: A list compiled by Hands Off Washington-University of Washington chapter. This list tells people when our next meetings are, provides information on upcoming events such as rallies and speakers, and provides a chance for people to read selected forwarded newsbriefs from Washington state as well as other parts of the country.

V

Resource Reference

The main purpose is to keep people up to date on activities planned by HOW-UW and to inform people about the agenda of the Citizen's Alliance of Washington (CAW) and other discriminatory organizations.

Hang-Gliding

Contact: `hang-gliding-request@virginia.edu` (Galen Hekhuis)

Purpose: Topics covering all aspects of hang-gliding and ballooning, for ultra-light and lighter-than-air enthusiasts.

Harleys

Contact: `harley-request@thinkage.on.ca` (Ken Dykes)

   `harley-request@thinkage.com`

   `uunet!thinkage!harley-request`

Purpose: Discussion about the bikes, politics, lifestyles, and anything else of interest to Harley-Davidson motorcycle lovers. The list is an automated digest format scheduled for twice a day Monday through Friday. Members may access an e-mail archive server for back issues and other items of interest.

Hey-Joe

Contact: `hey-joe-request@ms.uky.edu` (Joel Abbott)

Purpose: Discussion and worship of Jimi Hendrix and his music. Although Jimi has been dead for about two decades, we feel that his music is still worthy to be recognized. Prerequisite to joining: appreciation for his music.

Hindu Digest

Contact: `listserv@arizvm1.ccit.arizona.edu`

Purpose: Hindu dharma (religious philosophy and way of life) is followed by more than 650 million people in the world. Prominent among its teaching are the acceptance of various religious paths and the spirit of universal family.

The Hindu Digest is a forum to discuss various Hindu doctrines as they are applicable to day-to-day living. We also discuss various issues that affect the Hindu perspective, such as war and peace and human rights, and the participation of Hindus in political processes to promote the universal ideals mentioned above. It is also a forum for cultural news about Hindus from around the world.

To subscribe, send mail to `listserv@arizvm1.ccit.arizona.edu` in this form: `SUB HINDU–D` *Full Name* (*Full Name* must be at least two words).

HIX

Contact: `amagyar@phoenix.princeton.edu`

Purpose: Hollosi Information Exchange—a mail server containing information about Hungarian electronic resources, i.e., discussion lists, newsletters, etc. Information is in Hungarian.

In the subject field, write only `HIX`, and make the text of the letter `HELP all`.

HOCKEY-L

Contact: `listserv@maine.maine.edu`

`wts@maine.maine.edu` (Wayne Smith)

Purpose: The discussion of collegiate ice hockey, including scores, team info, schedules, etc., allowing fans to become more involved and knowledgeable about the game.

Substantial information is available via HOCKEY-L subscription, including current year Division I team and composite schedules and scores, and other college and Olympic hockey information as assembled or created by the subscribers. In-season postings include all Division I scores and descriptions of most games. Division II, III, and Club hockey discussions are welcome.

See also `hockey3–request@hooville.mitre.org` for a list devoted to Division III college hockey.

To subscribe to HOCKEY-L, send a one-line message body (not subject) to the subscription address as follows:

```
SUBSCRIBE HOCKEY-L your name and college team(s) of interest
```

V

Resource Reference

Holocaust Information
Contact: `listserv@oneb.almanac.bc.ca`

Purpose: For Holocaust research and the refutation of those who deny the event. It is currently an unmoderated, public list, but I reserve the right to change status to private/moderated if the need arises.

Topics within the scope of the list include: worldwide racial supremacy organizations and activities; worldwide neo-nazi organizations and activities; Holocaust denial via electronic networking, including but not limited to FidoNet, USENET, Internet, Prodigy, GEnie, CompuServe, etc.; and the notification of all list members when a new bulletin board, fax forwarding, or voice-mail organization is identified as representing the views of the various organizations noted above, including The Institute for Historical Review (IHR), Christian Identity, Aryan Nation, America First Committee, Liberty Lobby, and activities of well-known folks like Willy Carto, David Irving, and many, many others.

To subscribe to the list, send the following command to `listserv@oneb.almanac.bc.ca` in this form:

```
subscribe hlist yourfirstname yourlastname
```

Example: `subscribe hlist ken mcvay`

If you do not receive confirmation from the server within 24 hours, please let me know and I will add you to the list manually.

Homebrew
Contact: `homebrew-request%hpfcmr@hplabs.hp.com`

`hplabs!hpfcmr!homebrew-request` (Rob Gardner)

Purpose: Forum on beer, homebrewing, and related issues. Though mainly intended for discussion of beer making, also welcome are discussions on making cider, mead, wine, or any other fermented (but not distilled) beverage. Beginners are welcome, as well as experienced brewers.

Home-Ed
Contact: `home-ed-request@think.com` (David Mankins)

Purpose: For the discussion of all aspects and methods of home education. These include the "unschooling" approach, curricula-based homeschooling, and others. The list is currently unmoderated and welcomes everyone interested in educating their children at home, whatever the reasons.

Home-Ed-Politics
Contact: `home-ed-politics-request@mainstream.com` (Craig Peterson)

Purpose: Discussion of home education (typically by home educators) techniques and issues. Many of the discussions are politically oriented (as in monitoring of government programs).

Horse
Contact: `equestrians-request@world.std.com` (David C. Kovar)

Purpose: Discussion of things equestrian. Horse enthusiasts of all disciplines and levels of experience are welcome. Articles are distributed periodically in digest format, and also appear individually in the USENET news group `rec.equestrian`.

Hotrod
Contact: `hotrod-request@dixie.com` (Include on the Subject line the
          keyword `subscribe` and a return path to your site.)

Purpose: To provide a forum for people interested in high-performance vehicles to exchange ideas and discuss topics of current interest. This list is chartered as broadly as possible, consistent with noise suppression. Explicitly acceptable is any discussion regarding increasing the performance of any vehicle with more than three wheels.

HP Patch
Contact: `hpux-patch-request@cv.ruu.nl`

Purpose: The HP Patch Descriptions Mailing List—in short, the purpose of the mailing list is this:

1. If somebody receives a patch from HP, he/she can post the *description* of that patch to the mailing list.

2. Other members now know that a patch exists and can ask HP for "patch *xxxx*" if they think they have a problem.

3. The patches themselves are *never* posted!!!!!!!!

4. This list exists only as long as HP itself doesn't supply a list of available patches.

To reach all members of the list, send e-mail to `hpux–patch@cv.ruu.nl`. This is what you might want to do if you receive a new patch.

To subscribe, send e-mail to `hpux–patch–request@cv.ruu.nl`. Please include your e-mail address in the message. Not all mailers generate proper return addresses.

Problems, questions, suggestions, and the like should go to this address too. To ease searching for a patch to a specific problem, I've started to write a set of tools which I loosely call "pltools." Currently, there's one script (written in PERL) called plfind that searches through an unofficial list of patch descriptions according to user-supplied queries. Updates to this list and to the tools are posted on a semiregular base. Also, each new member of the list receives the current distribution upon subscription.

Huskers
Contact: `huskers–request@tssi.com` (Michael Nolan)

Purpose: To provide coverage of University of Nebraska sports. The major in-season sports (football, basketball) will likely make up the majority of posts, but other sports are likely to be mentioned from time to time, depending on the interest. Other items likely to be of interest to NU alums or Cornhusker fans may also appear.

Hyperami
Contact: `listserv@archive.oit.unc.edu`

Purpose: For informal product discussion and mutual assistance concerning AmigaVision, CanDo, DeluxeVideo III, Director 2, Foundation, Hyperbook, InterActor, PILOT, ShowMaker, TACL, Thinker, and VIVA.

To join, send a mail request to `listserv@archive.oit.unc.edu` and give a one-line message, asking `subscribe hyperami`.

This list is separate from the USENET news group `comp.sys.amiaga.multimedia`, but material from the list may occasionally be posted to the news group.

Hyperbole, Hyperbole-Announce

Contact: `hyperbole—request@cs.brown.edu` (Bob Weiner)

Purpose: For discussion of the Hyperbole systems and the related topics of hypertext and information retrieval.

Hyperbole-announce announces new releases and bug fixes for Hyperbole. Anyone on hyperbole is automatically subscribed to Hyperbole-announce, so you should request subscription to only one of the two lists.

Hyperbole is a flexible hypertext manager developed at Brown University that sits atop of GNU Emacs and provides efficient point-and-click information access and full customizability in GNU Emacs Lisp. Hyperbole allows hypertext buttons to be embedded within unstructured and structured files, mail messages and news articles. It also provides point-and-click access to ftp archives, Wide Area Information Servers (WAIS), and the World Wide Web (WWW) hypertext system.

Use the following format on your Subject line to execute requests, (include the period at the end of the line):

```
Add yourfirstname-yourlastname <youraccount@yoursubdomain.yourdomain>
to mail-list-name-without-domain.
```

Example: `Add Joe Smith <joe@mot.com> to hyperbole.`

HyperChem

Contact: `hyperchem—request@autodesk.com` (Mark Davies)

Purpose: Designed for but not limited to HyperChem users. Any and all scientific and technical issues related to the use of HyperChem are appropriate for discussion on this group.

The group is unmoderated, so any message sent to the group is sent automatically to all other members of the group. Any information on this group is to be taken "as is" without representation or warranty of any kind, either express or implied. The entire risk as to the use of this information is assumed by the user.

IAMS (Internet Amateur Mathematics Society)
Contact: `iams-request@quack.kfu.com`

Purpose: For discussion of math puzzles and problems.

IB
Contact: `hreha@vax2.concordia.ca` (Dr. Steve Hreha)

Purpose: To provide a forum for teachers, IB coordinators, and administrators involved with the International Baccalaureate Diploma Program. Discussion of all aspects of the IB program is welcome.

IBDlist
Contact: `ibdlist-request%mvac23@udel.edu` (Thomas Lapp)

    ...!udel!mvac23!IBDlist-request

Purpose: A moderated mailing list that discusses all aspects of Inflammatory Bowel Diseases, with particular emphasis on Crohn's disease and Ulcerative Colitis. Anyone with an interest in these diseases, whether direct or indirect, is welcome. This list will also act as a clearinghouse for information and discussion of current treatments, research, and other information related to IBDs. This list is open to any interested party and is not restricted to those with a direct link to IBD.

ICF-2010
Contact: `icf-2010-request@cup.hp.com` (Gary Gitzen)

    {hplabs, uunet}!cup.hp.com!icf-2010-request

Purpose: A low-volume mutual support group to discuss/share technical issues, problems, solutions, performance, and modifications related to the Sony ICF-2010 and 2001D shortwave radios.

ICI
Contact: `listserv@research.canon.oz.au`

Purpose: Discussion of Tim Long's ICI language and its interpreter. Also acts as an archive for the interpreter source, patches, and documentation.

ICLInfo
Contact: `{obdient,tfd}!tons61!iclinfo`

Purpose: To update and relay information regarding the CCI/ICL processors. Includes information on product updates, product problems, service problems and information, system options, and information on CCI/ICL from "off-line" sources (i.e., inside "scoops" direct from "hidden" CCI/ICL sources).

IDOL

Contact: `idol-group-request@luvthang.ori-cal.com` (David Talmage)

Purpose: An unmoderated mailing list for people interested in the Idol language. Idol, an "icon-derived object language," is "an object-oriented extension and environment for the Icon programming language." The idol-group is a forum for discussing Idol programming, object-oriented programming, and Idol implementation issues. It is also a place to exchange Idol classes and programs, contributing to the library of useful Idol code.

Igor

Contact: `igor-request@pica.army.mil` (Tom Coradeschi)

Purpose: To provide an easy means for users of Igor to share problems and solutions, as well as for potential users to seek opinions on the utility and performance of the application.

Imagen-L

Contact: `listserv@bolis.sf-bay.org`

Purpose: A discussion forum for all aspects of Imagen laser printers. Any discussion pertaining to Imagen printers is welcome, including software compatibility, hardware interfacing, LAN attachment capabilities, imPRESS programming, or methods used to create spooling and accounting software.

To subscribe, send an Internet e-mail message to `listserv@bolis.sf-bay.org` that contains the following:

```
subscribe Imagen-L
```

and you will be added to the list.

V

Resource Reference

Imagine

Contact: `imagine-request@email.sp.paramax.com` (Dave Wickard)

Purpose: Dedicated to the 3-D computer rendering package "Imagine" by Impulse, Inc. Currently, this package is available on the Amiga computer and for MS-DOS. Subject matter spans most areas and packages in 3-D rendering, but mostly in comparison to Imagine. There are many professional artists using the IML, and the tone is light and friendly. All levels of knowledge and experience are welcome here, and everyone is encouraged to participate. We have held contests, and a frequently asked questions list and full archives since the list's inception in January 1991 are available upon request. Merely send a note to the above address with the word `subscribe` in the subject line.

> **Note**
>
> Bang-style addressing is not supported, so please include your Internet-style address in subscription request (e.g., *somebody@someplace*`.edu`).

Immune

Contact: `immune-request@weber.ucsd.edu` (Cyndi Norman)

Purpose: A support group for people with immune-system breakdowns (and their symptoms), such as Chronic Fatigue Syndrome, Lupus, Candida, Hypoglycemia, multiple allergies, learning disabilities, etc., and their SOs, medical caretakers, etc. The group is unmoderated and open to anyone, anywhere in the world. (No arguments about whether these disabilities exist.)

Improv

Contact: `improv-request@bmt.gun.com` (Timothy Reed)

Purpose: Questions, comments, and bug-reports relating to the Improv spreadsheet for NeXTSTEP and Windows, published by Lotus Corporation. Some mail includes attachments that may be read with mail readers compatible with the NeXT Computer's NeXTmail format.

Impulse

Contact: `impulse-users-request@j.cc.purdue.edu` (Kevin Braunsdorf)

Purpose: A low-volume list for users of the LPC Mpulse line of computers. The moderator does filter and journalize submissions.

INDEX-L

Contact: `skuster@bingvmb.bitnet` (Charlotte Skuster)

Purpose: Discussion of good indexing practice by providing a forum through which professional and aspiring indexers can share information and ideas relating to the intellectual, philosophical, and technical aspects of index preparation. Some recent participants include professional indexers, members of the American Society of Indexers (ASI), librarians, library school faculty and students, information access professionals, hypertext and database developers, and authors indexing their own work.

Indigo-Girls

Contact: `indigo–girls–request@cgrg.ohio–state.edu` (Stephen Spencer)

Purpose: Discussion of Indigo Girls and related artists' music, tour dates, concert reviews, etc. Both regular and digest formats are available—please specify when sending a `subscribe me` message. The digest format gets you one message a day; regular gets you each message as it is sent to the list.

Info-Aids

Contact: `info–aids@rainbow.uucp`

> `{pacbell,apple,hoptoad,ucbvax}!well!rainbow!info–aids`
> (Ken Davis)

Purpose: To act as a clearinghouse for information and discussion about AIDS, including alternative treatments, political implications, etc. Exchanges files with `aidnews@rutvm1.bitnet`. Open to anyone with the time and inclination to participate. Mailing list will be confidential and known only to the members. Anonymous postings will be accepted. (See also "Aids" mailing list.)

Info-CCC

Contact: `uunet!xurilka!info–ccc–request` (Luigi Perrotta)

Purpose: Devoted to the Concurrent C and Concurrent C++ programming languages. However, discussions can be anything relevant to concurrent programming.

INFOCD
Contact: `mikey@perch.nosc.mil` (Michael Pawka)

Purpose: For the exchange of subjective comments about the compact audio disc medium and related hardware. Topics of discussion may include CD reviews, players, portables, import CDs, etc. Occasionally the threads even drift off onto lyrics, video discs, etc.

Info-Encore
Contact: `info–encore–request@cs–gw.d.umn.edu`

`info–encore–request@umnd–cs.uucp` (Dan Burrows)

Purpose: Mailing list for discussion of issues involving hardware and software issues of Encore computers and EtherNet terminal servers.

This mailing list is also gatewayed into the inet list `comp.sys.encore`.

Info-Fortune
Contact: `info–fortune–request@csd4.csd.uwm.edu` (Thomas Krueger)

Purpose: For users of UNIX-based microcomputers produced by Fortune Systems. Any subject pertaining to Fortune computers is allowed.

Info-GNU
Contact: `info–gnu–request@prep.ai.mit.edu`

`ucbvax!prep.ai.mit.edu!info–gnu–request`

Purpose: To distribute progress reports on the GNU Project, headed by Richard Stallman, and to ask members for various kinds of help. The list is gated both ways with the alternative news group `gnu.announce`, and is filtered (weakly moderated) by Leonard H. Tower Jr. GNU, which stands for *Gnu's Not Unix*, is the name for a complete UNIX-compatible software system whose sources can be given away free to everyone. Major parts have already been written; major parts still remain undone. Project GNU has additional mailing lists to distribute information about specific GNU programs and to report bugs in them. Contact us at the above address for details.

Info-High-Audio
Contact: `info–high–audio–request@csd4.csd.uwm.edu` (Thomas Krueger)

Purpose: This list is for the exchange of subjective comments about high-end audio equipment and modifications performed to high-end pieces. Techniques used to modify equipment—especially, but not limited to, vacuum tube electronics—are exchanged. Some comments may be subjective or intuitive and may not yet have a measurable basis. Other topics of discussion include turntables, arms, and cartridges; preamplifiers, headamps, and cartridge matching; speakers, amplifiers, and matching; placement of speakers; and room treatments. Any comments that prevent an open exchange of ideas and techniques are not encouraged.

Archives of projects will be maintained on `csd4.csd.uwm.edu` and available via anonymous ftp. Info-High-Audio is bidirectionally gatewayed with the USENET news group `rec.audio.high-end`.

Info-Honda
Contact: `info-honda-request@cs.ucla.edu` (Rich Wales)

Purpose: Discussion of Honda and Acura automobiles.

Info-Ingres
Contact: `info-ingres-request@math.ams.com`

Purpose: To discuss the commercial version of Ingres.

Info-LabVIEW
Contact: `info-labview-request@pica.army.mil`

Purpose: Discussion of the use of National Instruments' LabVIEW package for Macintosh, Windows, and Sparcstation environments.

LabVIEW is a graphical software system for developing high-performance scientific and engineering applications. LabVIEW acquires data from IEEE-488 (GPIB), RS-232/422, and modular (VXI or CAMAC) instruments and plug-in data acquisition boards.

LabVIEW programs, called *virtual instruments* (VIs), are created using icons instead of conventional, text-based code. A VI consists of a front panel and a block diagram. The front panel (with knobs, switches, graphs, and so on) is the user interface. The block diagram, which is the executable code, consists of icons that operate on data connected by wires that pass data between them.

Resource Reference

The list is being run as a simple redistribution of all submitted messages. ftp archives are on `ftp.pica.army.mil`, directory `/pub/labview`.

Info-PGP

Contact: `info-pgp-request@lucpul.it.luc.edu`

Purpose: Discussion of Phil Zimmerman & Co.'s Pretty Good Privacy (PGP) public key encryption program for MS-DOS, UNIX, SPARC, VMS, Atari, Amiga, and other platforms. Mirror of `alt.security.pgp` and related articles on `sci.crypt`.

Info-Prime

Contact: `info-prime-request@blx-a.prime.com`

Purpose: The discussion group/mailing list for users and administrators of Prime Computer equipment: 50-series (PRIMOS) and EXL series (UNIX). This mailing list is gatewayed to the USENET news group `comp.sys.prime`.

Informix-List

Contact: `informix-list-request@rmy.emory.edu` (Walt Hultgren)

Purpose: An unmoderated list for the discussion of Informix software and related subjects. Topics include all Informix offerings, from C-ISAM to WingZ, plus third-party products. Membership is open to anyone, including end users, vendors, and employees of Informix Software, Inc. An optional gateway service of Informix-related articles from `comp.databases` is offered. Not affiliated with Informix Software, Inc.

INFORMIX_SIG_NCA

Contact: `informix_sig_nca-request@adaclabs.com`

Purpose: For the INFORMIX User Group of Northern California. The purpose of this mailing list is two-fold. It is the voice for the INFORMIX User Group of Northern California. Also, it is a method of information exchange for users of Informix products. Group activities will be advertised in this mailing list and posted to `comp.databases.informix`.

Info-Russ

Contact: `info-russ@smarty.ece.jhu.edu` (Aleksander Kaplan)

Purpose: Informal communication in Russian-speaking (or having related interests) community.

Info-Solbourne

Contact: `info–solbourne–request@acsu.buffalo.edu` (Paul Graham)

Purpose: Discussions and information about Solbourne computers.

Info-Stratus

Contact: `info–stratus–request@mike.lrc.edu` (Richard Shuford)

Purpose: A user-centered and user-conducted forum for discussing the fault-tolerant machines produced by Stratus Computer Corporation and also their cousins, the IBM System/88 and Olivetti CPS-32.

Info-Stratus is not intended to replace the vendor-provided support channels but to complement them. Subscribers to Info-Stratus will exchange technical information and tap the collective experience of a host of other professionals who use or develop software on Stratus architecture systems, or who configure and maintain hardware in the Stratus environment.

Info-Tahoe

Contact: `info–tahoe–request@uwm.edu`

> `uwm!info–tahoe–request` (Jim Lowe)

Purpose: Discussions pertaining to the Tahoe type of CPU. These include the CCI Power 6/32, the Harris HCX/7, and the Sperry 7000 series computers.

The info-tahoe mailing list is set up as a mail reflector.

This mailing list is also gatewayed into the inet list, `comp.sys.tahoe`.

Info-Tandem

Contact: `info–tandem–request@zorch.sf–bay.org`

Purpose: Discussion of systems from Tandem Computers, Inc. Includes both open and proprietary lines.

Info-VM

Contact: `info-vm-request@uunet.uu.net` (Kyle Jones and others)

Purpose: Discussion and information exchange about the VM mail reader, which runs under GNU Emacs.

INSOFT-L

Contact: `listserv@cis.vutbr.cz`

> `insoft-l-request@cis.vutbr.cz`

Purpose: Internationalized software relates to software that is written so a user can easily change the language of the interface and versions of software, such as Czech WordPerfect, whose interface language differs from the original product.

Topics discussed on this list will include:

- Techniques for developing new software

- Techniques for converting existing software

- Internationalization tools

- Announcements of internationalized public domain software

- Announcements of foreign-language versions of commercial software

- Calls for papers

- Conference announcements

- References to documentation related to the internationalization of software

This list is moderated.

To subscribe to this list, send an electronic mail message to `listserv@cis.vutbr.cz`, with the body containing the following command:

```
SUB INSOFT-L yourfirstname yourlastname
```

Interest-Groups

Contact: `interest-groups-request@nisc.sri.com`

Purpose: A document that can be obtained by anonymous ftp from `ftp.nisc.sri.com`. The document contains a listing of many of the current mailing lists.

Intergraph

Contact: `nik@ingr.ingr.com`

Purpose: Discussion of all Intergraph CADCAM software and hardware. This mailing list is a bidirectional gateway to `alt.sys.intergraph`.

International Harvester

Contact: `ihc-request@balltown.cma.com` (Richard Welty)

Purpose: Discussion of Scouts, pickups, etc.

International Trade & Commerce

Contact: `info-request@tradent.wimsey.bc.ca`

Purpose: Discussions of international trade and commerce and the global economy, including postings of company profiles, trade leads, and topics pertaining to entrepreneurial ventures.

Internet Radio Journal

Contact: `rrb@airwaves.chi.il.us`

Purpose: A repeater for the news group `rec.radio.broadcasting` and, on occasion, carries independent material as well. The list is mailed as news warrants, and covers any subject related to domestic radio broadcasting. "Domestic," in this case, refers to radio that is broadcast primarily for reception within the same country from which it originates. The news group and mailing list are international and frequently cover matters pertaining to nations other than the U.S. or in North America. Any subject pertaining to the group's charter is encouraged, including but not limited to programming, engineering and technical matters, new trends in the field, laws and regulations, DXing, pirate radio, community and public radio, and much more. Subscriptions are open to anyone who desires one and has an Internet-compatible e-mail account. Individuals and non-commercial systems are eligible.

InterText

Contact: `intertxt@network.ucsd.edu` (Jason Snell)

Purpose: A bimonthly fiction magazine with more than 1,000 subscribers worldwide. InterText publishes in two formats: straight ASCII and PostScript (for PostScript-compatible laser printers). For more information, to ask about subscribing, or for submission guidelines, mail `intertxt@network.ucsd.edu`. Back issues may be ftp-ed from `network.ucsd.edu`, in the `/intertext` directory.

INXS

Contact: `inxs-list-request@iastate.edu`

Purpose: An unmoderated forum for the discussion of the Australian rock group INXS.

iPSC-Managers

Contact: `listserv@boxer.nas.nasa.gov` (machine)

`jet@nas.nasa.gov` (human) (J. Eric Townsend)

Purpose: Discussion of administrating the Intel iPSC line of parallel computers. To subscribe, send a message to `listserv@boxer.nas.nasa.gov` with a body of subscribe ipsc-managers *yourfullname*.

IRChat

Contact: `irchat-request@cc.tut.fi` (Kai "Kaizzu" Keinnen)

Purpose: Discussion on irchat.el, a GNU Emacs interface to IRC, the Internet Relay Chat.

Italian-Cars

Contact: `italian-cars-request@balltown.cma.com` (Richard Welty)

Purpose: Discussion of Italian-made automobiles. Both regular and digest forms are available.

ITI151

Contact: `iti151-request@oce.orst.edu` (John Stanley)

`{tektronix, hplabs!hp-pcd}!orstcs!oce.orst.edu!iti151-request`

Purpose: For users of Imaging Technology's series 150 and 151 image processing systems and ITEX151 software. The goal is to share algorithms, code, tricks, pitfalls, advice, etc., in an effort to decrease development time and increase functionality for the users of these systems.

Janes-Addiction

Contact: `janes-addiction-request@ms.uky.edu` (Joel Abbot)

Purpose: Discussion of the defunct music group Jane's Addiction and its former members' current projects.

Jargon-Helpers

Contact: `jargon-helpers-request@snark.thyrsus.com`

Purpose: An e-mail reflector that supplements the ongoing public discussions of hacker jargon, `net.culture`, and the Jargon File on `alt.folklore.computers`. If you have a continuing interest in these topics, you are welcome to join. The list owner is the current Jargon File editor. Members get to see new entries "in the raw" and have a hand in editorial policy.

Jewish

Contact: `listserv@israel.nysernet.org` (machine)

> `mljewish@israel.nysernet.org` (human) (Avi Feldblum)

Purpose: A non-abusive forum for discussion of Jewish topics with an emphasis on Jewish law, within the framework of the validity of the Halakhic system. Debates between Jews and non-Jews, or between various factions of Judaism should be posted to `talk.religion.misc`.

Distributions are generally on a daily basis at irregular times (when contribution load is sufficient to send, or relating to the urgency of the material to be sent).

To make a subscription request, send e-mail to `listserv@israel.nysernet.org` with the following message body:

```
subscribe mail-jewish yourfirstname yourlastname
```

For any other correspondence, send e-mail to the editor:

`mljewish@israel.nysernet.org` (Avi Feldblum)

Joe-Bob
Contact: `joe-bob-request@blkbox.com`

Purpose: Dedicated to the humor, writings, TV and movie performances, and movie reviews of the infamous Joe Bob Briggs, b-movie critic of the Movie Channel and publisher of The Joe Bob Report, a biweekly rag about everything from Americana to slasher flicks.

JPop
Contact: `jpop-request@ferkel.ucsb.edu` (Jim Lick)

Purpose: Discussion of Japanese popular music.

JTull
Contact: `jtull-request@remus.rutgers.edu` (Dave Steiner)

Purpose: A mailing list for discussions about the music group Jethro Tull, including ex-members and related artists.

JudgeNet
Contact: `judge-request@synchro.com` (Chuck Cox—BJCP Master Judge)

Purpose: Discussion of beer judging and competition organization. Please include your name, Internet address, and judging rank (if any) in your subscription request.

Jugo
Contact: `dimitrije@buenga.bu.edu` (Dimitrije Stamenovic)

Purpose: To distribute news and provide a forum for discussions about the current events in the former Yugoslavia. Also, they originate public actions related to these events.

Jump-in-the-River
Contact: `jump-in-the-river-request@presto.ig.com` (Michael C. Berch)

`{apple,ames,rutgers}!bionet!ig!jump-in-the-river-request`

Purpose: For the discussion of the music and recordings of Sinéad O'Connor and related matters, such as lyrics and tour information. Unmoderated.

KAW

Contact: `service@swi.psy.uva.nl`

Purpose: For information exchange between people participating and/or interested in the knowledge acquisition workshops (EKAW, JKAW, Banff KAW, etc.) and related activities (Sisyphus, problem-solving methods workshops).

To subscribe, send mail to `service@swi.psy.uva.nl` with the following message:

```
subscribe kaw yourfullname
```

Khoros

Contact: `khoros-request@chama.eece.unm.edu`

Purpose: To discuss the Khoros software package, developed by Dr. Rasure, his staff, and his students at the University of New Mexico. Khoros is an integrated software development environment for information processing and visualization, based on X11R4.

Killifish

Contact: `killie-request@mejac.palo-alto.ca.us`

Purpose: For people who keep and are interested in killifish (family Cyprinodontidae).

Kitcar

Contact: `kitcar-request@cs.usask.ca` (John Punshon)

Purpose: To discuss purchasing, building, driving, and anything else to do with kit cars. That is, cars built using body/chassis from one source (kit manufacturer) and engine/mechanicals from another (usually a *donor* production car). List is archived and archives can be anon ftp-ed from `ece.rutgers.edu`.

Kites

Contact: `kites-request@harvard.harvard.edu`

`harvard!kites-request` (U.S.A./Canada/Europe)

`koscvax.keio.junet!kites-request` (Japan)

Purpose: This mailing list is for people interested in making, flying, or just talking about all kinds of kites. Topics will (I hope) include kite plans and construction techniques, reviews of commercially available kites and plans, timely (or otherwise) human interest notes, and talk about flying.

Kiwimusic

Contact: `kiwimusic-request@athena.mit.edu` (Katie Livingston)

Purpose: Discussion of New Zealand pop bands, particularly those on the Flying Nun, Failsafe, and Xpressway labels. Example groups include The Chills, The Bats, The Clean, Tall Dwarfs, Straitjacket Fits, and so on.

All requests for addition or deletion, or correspondence with the moderator should go to `kiwimusic-request@athena.mit.edu`

Khush

Contact: `khush-request@husc3.harvard.edu`

Purpose: A mailing list for gay, lesbian, bisexual South Asians and their friends. We define South Asian as people from or descending from countries such as Bangladesh, Bhutan, India, Maldives, Nepal, Pakistan, and Sri-Lanka. The purpose of this list is to discuss South Asian gay culture/experiences/issues, as well as to form a social and support network. Currently the list is unmoderated, and anybody can join or leave the list at any time.

You can join the list by sending mail to `khush-request@husc3.harvard.edu`. The first line in your mail *must* be of the following form:

`subscribe khush youraccount@yoursubdomain.yourdomain`

Please send any questions about the list or any other administrative stuff to `khush-help@husc3.harvard.edu`.

KLF/Orb & Co.

Contact: `klf-request@asylum.sf.ca.us` (Lazlo Nibble)

Purpose: Discussion of the KLF, the Orb, and related bands (the JAMs, the Timelords, System 7/777, Fortran 5, et al.). Moderator maintains a complete discography. ftp archives available on asylum.

Kosmos
Contact: kosmos—request@athena.mit.edu

Purpose: Want to know the latest up-to-date news about the solo career of Paul "The Mod God" Weller from his foremost fanzine writers from the U.K. and the U.S.? Want to discuss his previous bands with people who actually know whom you're talking about? Just want to meet some cool people who like good music? Join Kosmos, the Paul Weller mailing list!

Previous postings are stored in monthly files and are available to all subscribers. They can be obtained from dlodge@mcs.dundee.ac.uk.

Kuharske Bukve
Contact: kuharske—bukve@krpan.arnes.si (Polona Novak and Andrej
Brodnik)

kuharske.bukve@uni—lj.si

Purpose: A moderated mailing list published weekly. Each issue brings one recipe previously tested by a member of editorial board. The recipes are formatted. Language in them is Slovene only. The editors are happy to receive readers' opinions.

Kundera-List
Contact: kundera—request@anat3d1.anatomy.upenn.edu

Purpose: The discussion of the works of Milan Kundera, the internationally renowned contemporary writer whose originality of imagination and clarity of prose have moved and enlightened many readers and serious writers. New subscribers will automatically receive past articles sent to the list.

Kurt Goedel Society
Contact: kgs@csdec2.tuwien.ac.at

Purpose: For members and people interested in the activities of the Kurt Goedel Society. Information about the Goedel Colloquia, Calls for Papers, the Collegium Logicum Lecture Series, the newsletter, and information from sister societies will be distributed. If you would like to be included in the mailing list, or have any questions, send an e-mail to `kgs@csdec2.tuwien.ac.at`.

Labrys
Contact: `c._louise_vigil.osbu_north@xerox.com`

Purpose: To provide a safe space for lesbians to discuss topics of interest. The membership is restricted in order to provide a space for lesbians. The forum is free form, with the exception of occasional moderation, should the charter be violated.

All administrative requests should be sent to

> `c._louise_vigil.osbu_north@xerox.com`

Please include the word `labrys` in the subject line.

LAMBDA
Contact: `listserv@ukcc.uky.edu` (Jeff Jones)

Purpose: This list is open to the discussion of all topics relating to gays/lesbians/bisexuals and their issues with specific focus on issues at the University of Kentucky, Lexington, and Kentucky communities.

To subscribe, send mail to `listserv@ukcc` or on the Internet to `listserv@ukcc.uky.edu` with the body containing the command `sub lambda` *yourfirstname yourlastname*.

LA-MOTSS, LA-MOTSS-ANNOUNCE
Contact: `la-motss-request@flash.usc.edu`

Purpose: On-line social and political forum for gay, lesbian, and bisexual issues in the Los Angeles and Southern California area.

Anything posted to the announcements list is automatically forwarded to the discussion list. You may choose to receive announcements only, or receive both announcements and general discussion.

Lang-Lucid
Contact: `lang-lucid-request@csl.sri.com` (R. Jagannathan)

Purpose: Discussions on all aspects related to the language Lucid, including (but not restricted to) language design issues, implementations for personal computers, implementations for parallel machines, language extensions, programming environments, products, bug reports, bug fixes/workarounds.

Lasnet

Contact: `lasnet-request@emx.utexas.edu` (Langston James Goree VI)

Purpose: To facilitate the exchange of information among scholars doing research related to Latin America.

LDS

Contact: `lds-request@decwrl.dec.com`

```
decwrl!lds-request
```

Purpose: A forum for members of the Church of Jesus Christ of Latter-day Saints (Mormons) to discuss church doctrine, Mormon culture and life in general. Non-Mormons are welcome to join, but we're not interested in flame wars.

The Learning List

Contact: `learning-request@sea.east.sun.com` (Rowan Hawthorne)

Purpose: An electronic forum for discussing child-centered learning. It is intended to provide a meeting place in cyberspace in which to advance our understanding of the processes of learning and to share personal experiences and practical suggestions to help in the great adventure we share with our children.

Members must agree with the Charter of the Learning list to subscribe. A copy of the Charter is available from the above address.

Level 42

Contact: `level42-request@enterprise.bih.harvard.edu`

Purpose: To support discussions of the musical artist Level 42.

Liberal-Judaism

Contact: `faigin@aerospace.aero.org` (Daniel Faigin)

Purpose: Non-judgmental discussions of liberal Judaism (Reform, Reconstructionist, Conservative, Secular Humanist, etc.) and liberal Jewish issues, its practices, opinions, and beliefs.

This list is moderated and is in digest format.

Libernet
Contact: libernet–request@dartmouth.edu (Barry S. Fagin)

Purpose: A Libertarian mailing list. The list is available in two modes: as a mail reflector and as a digest.

Life-Talking
Contact: life–talking–request@ferkel.ucsb.edu (Jim Lick)

Purpose: Discussion of the musical group Life Talking.

LIBFEM
Contact: libfem–request@math.uio.no (Thomas Gramstad)

Purpose: Focuses on the classical liberty and individual rights perspective as applied to feminist issues, such as issues regarding ideology, politics, culture, gender, etc., in order to establish a network for information, discourse, cooperation, encouragement, and consciousness raising. There has always been an element of individualism in the various women and feminist movements, although this element seems to have been somewhat neglected in recent movements.

Lightwave
Contact: subscribe@xamiga.linet.org

Purpose: For Video Toaster users, supporting the NewTek 3D object modeler/ray tracer and hardware involved in video editing, such as time base correcters and VCR equipment. This mail is echoed from another site.

Send subscription requests to subscribe@xamiga.linet.org using this format:

```
#lightwave youraccount@yoursubdomain.yourdomain;
```

Linda
Contact: linda–users–request@cs.yale.edu

linda–users–request@yalecs.bitnet

{cmcl2,decvax,harvard}!yale!linda–users–request

Purpose: Discussion group for users and potential users of Linda-based parallel programming systems. Linda is a set of operators that are added to various conventional programming languages to produce a parallel programming language.

Linux-Activists

Contact: `linux—activists—request@niksula.hut.fi` (Ari Lemmke)

Purpose: LINUX operating system hacking. LINUX is now on a hackers only stage. More information is available by ftp from `nic.funet.fi`, directory `/pub/OS/Linux/README`.

LIS (Lesbians in Science)

Contact: `zita@ac.grin.edu`

Purpose: A forum for discussions, a resource for professional and personal information sharing, and a social network and support group. (Womyn only.)

List-Managers

Contact: `brent@greatcircle.com` (Brent Chapman)

Purpose: There was a "Mailing Lists" workshop session at the USENIX System Administration Conference (LISA VI) in Long Beach, CA, on October 22, 1992. The participants in that workshop expressed a desire for a mailing list for discussions of issues related to managing Internet mailing lists, including (but not limited to) software, methods, mechanisms, techniques, and policies.

I've created the list as `list—managers@greatcircle.com`. That address is a direct mail reflector: all messages sent to that address are immediately forwarded to the list. There is a digest version of the list available as `list—managers—digest@greatcircle.com`. The digest version has exactly the same messages as the direct version; the messages are simply bundled into digests daily (or more frequently, if traffic warrants). Both lists are unmoderated.

To join the List-Mangers mailing list, send the command

```
subscribe list-managers
```

in the body of a message to `majordomo@greatcircle.com`. If you want to subscribe something other than the account the mail is coming from, such as a local redistribution list, then append that address to the `subscribe` command; for example, to subscribe "local-list-managers," send the following:

```
subscribe list-managers local-list-managers@your.domain.net
```

V

Resource Reference

To subscribe to the digest version, substitute `list-managers-digest` for `list-managers` in the examples above.

Living
Contact: `living-request@qiclab.scn.rain.com`

Purpose: A list for women with some sort of physical handicap. It is not limited to women in wheelchairs, but is meant to be a support list for women to talk about any sort of physically challenging situation that they are living in at the moment, be it temporary or permanent. (Women only.)

Llajta
Contact: `readingj@cerf.net` (John Reading)

Purpose: For the discussion of any and all topics relating to Bolivia. All communication regarding the list is sent to `readingj@cerf.net`, and messages are redistributed manually as needed.

Logo
Contact: `logo-friends-request@aiai.ed.ac.uk`

Purpose: Discuss the Logo computer language.

Lojban
Contact: `lojban-list-request@snark.thyrsus.com` (John Cowan)

Purpose: To use, discuss, and contribute to the development of the constructed human language called Lojban (known in earlier versions as Loglan). Lojban has a grammar based on predicate logic and vocabulary built from the six most widely spoken human languages. It is intended as a tool for experimental linguistics, as a medium for communication with computers, and as a possible international auxiliary language.

Lojban-list is an unmoderated mail reflector. New subscribers are asked to send their postal mailing addresses as well, so that they can be placed on the mailing list of The Logical Language Group, Inc., a non-profit organization. The postal mailing list provides materials that are useful in learning about the language. Lojban-list and LLG, Inc. are in no way affiliated with The Loglan Institute, Inc., or with James Cooke Brown, the founder of Loglan.

Lotus-Cars

Contact: `lotus-adm%esprit.uucp@netcom.com` (Alan F. Perry)

Purpose: For anyone interested in cars made by Lotus, now or in the past.

Loureed

Contact: `loureed-request@cvi.hahnemann.edu` (Sylvia)

Purpose: Mailing list for discussion of music, etc., related to the 30-years-and-running career of Mr. Lou Reed, including Velvet Underground matters. No digest format currently available. Unmoderated, but owner is reached at `sylvia@cvi.hahnemann.edu`.

Lute

Contact: `lute-request@sunapee.dartmouth.edu` (Wayne B. Cripps)

Purpose: For lute players and researchers of lute music.

LymeNet-L

Contact: `listserv@lehigh.edu`

`mcg2@lehigh.edu` (Marc Gabriel)

Purpose: The LymeNet Newsletter provides timely information on the many aspects of the Lyme disease epidemic. Published about once every 10-15 days, it includes the latest medical abstracts, support group info, and political events. Subscribers may submit questions and opinions to the newsletter for publication.

Macgyver

Contact: `shari@cc.gatech.edu` (Shari Feldman)

Purpose: To discuss current and previous *MacGyver* episodes. We also discuss what is currently happening with the main and recurring actors on the show.

MachTen

Contact: `machten-request@tenon.com` (Leonard Cuff)

Purpose: Discuss topics of interest to users of MachTen, a Mach/BSD UNIX for all Macintoshes, from Tenon Intersystems. This includes programming tips and examples, configuration questions, and discussion of problems and workarounds. People not currently using MachTen and wanting either general information or specific questions answered should not subscribe, but write to `info@tenon.com`.

Mac-Security

Contact: `mac-security-request@world.std.com` (David C. Kovar)

Purpose: This mailing list is for people interested in Macintosh security. This can be used to

- Discuss existing security problems in various Macintosh applications

- Discuss security applications, hardware, and solutions

- Discuss potential problems and their solutions

- Just about anything else related to Macintosh security and access control.

With the arrival of System 7.0 and its wealth of information-sharing facilities, Macintosh security has entered a new era. Originally, you only had to worry about someone getting into your Macintosh via the keyboard or stealing it outright. Now it's much easier to browse through information on someone else's Macintosh over the network.

MAGIC

Contact: `magic-request@maillist.crd.ge.com` (Bruce Barnett)

Purpose: For the discussion of sleight of hand and the art of magic. Membership to the list is restricted, as people who are merely curious are not encouraged to join. You must fill out a questionnaire to qualify.

Mailing-Lists

Contact: `mailing-lists@krpan.arnes.si`

Purpose: Information on mailing lists from South Slavic countries.

Mail-Men

Contact: `mail-men-request@usl.com` (Marcel Franck Simon)

Purpose: Discusses "men's issues." Both women and men may join. Mail-men is a place where men and women can discuss men's issues in an atmosphere of openness and support. Men's issues are those problems and experiences that affect male humans.

MAK-NEWS
Contact: `listserv@uts.edu.au`

Purpose: A news group for following the developments in the Republic of Macedonia. Both the Macedonian and the English languages are used, whichever the original source is usually in, or whichever the contributors feel most comfortable with. Discussions and submissions are primarily from contributors who inform subscribers of events, usually in their local areas, but often further. Sources of articles from which some users extract documents are wide and varied.

MAK-NEWS is run entirely by volunteers and is reasonably well connected with outside regular sources. Translations of articles are also possible. The Macedonian Information Liaison Service (M.I.L.S.) in Brussels sends daily bulletins to MAK-NEWS from Monday to Friday. We also have individual news bulletins arriving from Skopje through a link that is fragile, but that has lately been holding up well and is improving all the time.

MAK-NEWS recently converted to run as a listserv mail group (`mak-news@uts.edu.au`) with the usual listserv mail commands applying. Distributions are generally on a daily basis at irregular times (when contribution load is sufficient to send, or relating to the urgency of the material to be sent), and is about 200-300 kilobytes per week.

To make subscription requests, send e-mail to `listserv@uts.edu.au` with the following message body:

```
subscribe MAK-NEWS yourfirstname yourlastname
```

For other correspondence, send e-mail to the current editors:

`shopov@tartarus.ccsd.uts.edu.au` (Sacha Shopov)

`sk@sunbim.be` (Sasa Konecni) [M.I.L.S.]

Martial-Arts
Contact: `martial-arts-request@dragon.cso.uiuc.edu` (Steven Miller)

Purpose: For discussion on various aspects of the martial arts. This includes teaching and training techniques, martial arts philosophy, self-defense, and traditional and non-traditional styles, among other topics.

V

Resource Reference

Masonic Digest
Contact: `ptrei@mitre.org` (Peter Trei)

Purpose: A moderated forum for discussion of Free Masonry, affiliated groups, and other fraternal orders. As moderator, I do not pass on any message that contains or purports to contain material I am obliged to conceal, or which I believe members of other orders are obliged to conceal. Within that restriction, I am as liberal as possible. Postings from non-Masons are welcome. So is criticism, as long as it is reasoned and in good taste.

MasPar
Contact: `mp-users-request@thunder.mcrcim.mcgill.edu` (Lee Iverson)

Purpose: We have no restrictive charter, so are open to any and all discussions of hardware/software issues surrounding the use of the MasPar MP-1 class of parallel SIMD machines. These machines have a full-featured data-parallel instruction set and are programmable in Fortran90 and MPL, a K&R C with parallel data types.

MATLAB
Contact: `matlab-users-request@mcs.anl.gov` (Chris Bischof)

Purpose: Discussion group for users and potential users of the MATLAB numeric computation software from The MathWorks. MATLAB is an interactive matrix-oriented product for linear algebra, digital signal processing, equation solving, control system design, and other engineering and scientific applications. This mail group is administered by the independent MATLAB User Group.

Mayberry
Contact: `listserv@bolis.sf-bay.org`

Purpose: For discussion of TV shows featuring Andy Griffith, including *The Andy Griffith Show* and *Mayberry RFD*.

To subscribe, send an e-mail message to `listserv@bolis.sf-bay.org` containing the following:

```
subscribe Mayberry
```

and you will be added to the list.

Mazda-List

Contact: `mazda-list-request@ms.uky.edu` (Joel Abbott)

Purpose: Technical correspondence and discussion of Mazda-designed vehicles.

MEDGAY-L

Contact: `listserv@ksuvm.ksu.edu` (Robert Clark)

Purpose: The official list of the Society for the Study of Homosexuality in the Middle Ages, an affiliated society of the Medieval Institute of Western Michigan University.

To subscribe, send a one-line message, `SUB MEDGAY-L` *yourfullname*, to `listserv@ksuvm.ksu.edu`.

Medphys

Contact: `medphys-request@radonc.duke.edu`

Purpose: An attempt to foster electronic communication between medical physicists, open to interested others. Medical physics is a somewhat opaque but widely used synonym for radiological physics—the physics of the diagnostic and therapeutic use of radiation in medicine. At present, most of the subscribers are involved in radiotherapy.

Melissa Etheridge

Contact: `etheridge-request@krylov.cnd.mcgill.ca`

Purpose: To discuss Melissa Etheridge and her music.

Melrose-Place

Contact: `melrose-place-request@ferkel.ucsb.edu` (Jim Lick)

Purpose: Discussion of the Fox TV show *Melrose Place*.

Mensatalk

Contact: `mensatalk-request@psg.com` (Ed Wright)

Purpose: For members of Mensa only.

V

Resource Reference

MetaCard-List
Contact: `listserv@grot.starconn.com`

Purpose: Discussion of the MetaCard product from MetaCard Corporation. MetaCard is an application development system that is similar to Apple's HyperCard product and runs on a variety of popular platforms in a UNIX/X11/Motif environment.

To subscribe to the MetaCard-list, send mail to `listserv@grot.starconn.com` with the following commands in the body of the message:

```
subscribe metacard-list yourfirstname yourlastname
quit
```

Replace *yourfirstname yourlastname* with your name, not your e-mail address.

Administrative messages other than subscription and unsubscription should be sent to `metacard-list-owner@grot.starconn.com`.

Meteorology Students
Contact: `dennis@metw3.met.fu-berlin.de`

Purpose: A new mailing list, open to everyone, but particularly intended as a communication facility for meteorology students. At the moment there are 20 people from three continents subscribed to the list.

Beside the usual chatting, subjects of discussion could be student-related topics such as scholarships, summer schools, conferences, and conditions of studying meteorology at a particular university. There is also the option to ask the community for help in meteorology-related questions. There are freshman, as well as graduate students, who will be available to answer your questions in this field.

If there are enough people interested, we could organize a kind of project, too.

To come to know each other, there is a short questionnaire available. Though no obligation exists to fill it out, it would be nice if all new subscribers would at least answer the basic questions about their name, address, and university. New answered forms are posted to the list; old ones are available upon request.

Administrative mail such as subscription or questionnaire requests should be sent to

```
dennis@metw3.met.fu-berlin.de
```

Though the list is situated in Germany, the language is English. I hope for strong participation.

Miata

Contact: `miata-request@jhunix.hcf.jhu.edu` (Andy S. Poling)

Purpose: Formed when it became evident that there was a growing body of enthusiastic Mazda Miata owners. There are no rules governing what you can and cannot post to the list—it is an open forum.

Middle-Eastern Music

Contact: `middle-eastern-music-request@nic.funet.fi` (Juhana Kouhia)

Purpose: Discussion of the music originating in the Middle East.

Migra-List

Contact: `migra-list-request@cc.utah.edu`

`moliva@cc.utah.edu` (Maurizio Oliva)

Purpose: Mailing list on international migration.

Miniatures

Contact: `minilist-request@cs.unc.edu`

Purpose: An archived mailing list for discussion of painting, sculpting, converting, and displaying of miniature figurines, generally for wargaming or fantasy role-playing games and in the smaller scales (15mm-30mm).

Minor-League Baseball

Contact: `minors-request@medraut.apple.com` (Chuq von Rospach)

Purpose: Issues affecting the minor leagues, including new stadium standards, minor-league franchise status and changes, road trips and groups, schedules, team and league status, players and teams to watch, collectibles, and anything else of importance about minor-league baseball.

Miracles
Contact: `perry.sills@ebay`

   `perrys@spiritlead.sun.com`

Purpose: To provide daily readings from A Course in Miracles, and other selected readings from teachers, lecturers, and A Course in Miracles centers to provide additional reflection, inspiration, and avenues of practical application.

Through the above contact address, one may also subscribe to a discussion list for A Course in Miracles, as well as a list for receiving the daily lessons from the course.

MLB Scores and Standings
Contact: `jplee@cymbal.calpoly.edu` (Jason Lee)

Purpose: A distributive list for people who want daily updates of scores and standings of major league baseball.

MMOS2-l
Contact: `mail-server@knex.via.mind.org`

Purpose: The list's primary goal is to discuss programming of multimedia elements under IBM's OS/2, authoring tools, and multimedia peripherals such as audio boards, motion video subsystems, and devices such as CD-ROM, videodiscs, etc. The list welcomes the participation of and contribution from programmers, multimedia designers, and presentation experts and novices, as well as content creators such as CBT authors, computer musicians, animators, etc. Users of multimedia programs and publications are also welcome.

MMOS2-l redistributes submissions as they come in as individual articles.

To subscribe to the list, send mail to `mail-server@knex.via.mind.org`, where the body of the message is `subscribe mmos2-L` *yourfirstname yourlastname.*

Model-Horse
Contact: `model-horse-request@qiclab.scn.rain.com` (Darci L. Chapman)

Purpose: Discussion of the model horse hobby. All aspects of showing (live and photo), collecting, remaking/repainting for all breeds and makes are discussed. All ages and levels of experience welcome.

Modesty Blaise

Contact: `modesty-blaise-request@math.uio.no` (Thomas Gramstad)

Purpose: Discussion and information exchange centered on Peter O'Donnell's Modesty Blaise books and comics, such as characters, plot, artists, relevant articles, etc.

Moms

Contact: `moms-request@qiclab.scn.rain.com`

Purpose: A list for lesbian mothers. (Women only.)

Morris Dancing Discussion List

Contact: `listserv@suvm.acs.syr.edu`

Purpose: Discussion of all things Morris. This includes Cotswold, Border, NorthWest, Rapper, LongSword, Abbots Bromley, Garland, and similar forms of English dance, along with the accompanying music and traditions. To subscribe, send mail with a message body containing

```
SUBSCRIBE MORRIS yourfullname (your-team-name)
```

If on BITNET, send this message to `listserv@suvm`. If on Internet, send this message to `listserv@suvm.acs.syr.edu`.

MR2-Interest

Contact: `mr2-interest-request@validgh.com` (David Hough)

Purpose: Discussion of Toyota MR2s, old and new.

MS-Access

Contact: `ms-access-request@eunet.co.at` (Martin Hilger)

Purpose: An unmoderated list for MS Access topics, including Access Basic questions, reviews, rumors, etc. Open to owners, users, prospective users, and the merely curious.

All requests to be added to or deleted from this list, problems, questions, etc., should be sent to `ms-access-request@eunet.co.at`.

Mtxinu-Users

Contact: `dunike!mtxinu—users—request`

> `mtxinu—users—request@nike.cair.du.edu`

Purpose: Discussion and bug fixes for users of the 4.3+NFS release from the Mt. Xinu folks.

MUD

Contact: `jwisdom@gnu.ai.mit.edu` (Joseph Wisdom)

Purpose: If you are new in the MUD world, or are simply looking for new places to get into, try subscribing to Internet Games MUD-List today! Make sure to include the string `mud list` in the subject header.

Multicast

Contact: `multicast—request@arizona.edu` (Joel Snyder)

Purpose: For discussion of multicast and broadcast issues in an OSI environment. Archives of the list and a database of contributed documents are also available on `arizona.edu`.

Musicals

Contact: `musicals—request@world.std.com` (Elizabeth Lear Newman)

Purpose: For the general discussion of musical theater, in whatever form it make take, but related non-musical theater topics are welcome too. 90 percent of the traffic is the musicals-related flow from the news group `rec.arts.theatre`.

Music-Research

Contact: `music—research—request@prg.oxford.ac.uk` (Stephen Page)

Purpose: Established after a suggestion made at a meeting at Oxford in July 1986 to provide an effective and fast means of bringing together musicologists, music analysts, computer scientists, and others working on applications of computers in music research.

As with any forum for discussion, there are certain subject areas that are of particular interest to the group of people on this list. Initially, the list was established for people whose chief interests concern computers and their applications to music representation systems, information retrieval systems for musical scores, music printing, music analysis, musicology and ethnomusicology, and tertiary music education. The following areas are not the principal concern of this list, although overlapping subjects may well be interesting: primary and secondary education, sound generation techniques, and composition. Articles on electronic music, synthesizers, MIDI, etc., will be rejected at the request of the readers of the list.

Mustangs

Contact: `mustangs-request@cup.hp.com` (Gary Gitzen)

> `{hplabs, uunet}!cup.hp.com!mustangs-request`

Purpose: To discuss/share technical issues, problems, solutions, and modifications relating to late-model (~1980+) Ford Mustangs. Some issues may also be relevant to other Fords. Flames and "my car is faster than your car" mailings are discouraged.

> **Note**
>
> List "noise level" is actively controlled.

Mystery

Contact: `mystery-request@csd4.csd.uwm.edu` (Thomas Krueger)

Purpose: A mailing list for mystery and detective fiction. Reviews of works and discussions of plot, characterization, and other aspects will be discussed. The medium, whether novel, movie, or television series, is unimportant.

NA-NET

Contact: `na.join@na-net.ornl.gov`

Purpose: Numerical analysis discussions. To join the NA-NET, send mail and, in the message body, specify the following three fields in any order: Lastname:, Firstname:, E-mail:.

V

Resource Reference

NativeNet

Contact: `gst@gnosys.svle.ma.us` (Gary S. Trujillo)

Purpose: To provide information about and to discuss issues relating to indigenous people around the world and current threats to their cultures and habitats (e.g., rainforests).

NAVNEWS

Contact: `navnews@nctamslant.navy.mil`

Purpose: E-mail distribution list for the weekly Navy News Service (NAVNEWS), published by the Navy Internal Relations Activity in Washington. NAVNEWS contains official news and information about fleet operations and exercises, personnel policies, budget actions, and more. This is the same news service that is distributed through Navy circuits to ships at sea and to shore commands around the world. Subscriptions to NAVNEWS by e-mail are available at no charge to anyone with a mailbox on any network reachable through the Internet.

NCUBE

Contact: `ncube-users-request@cs.tufts.edu` (David Krumme)

Purpose: Exchange of information among people using NCUBE parallel computers.

NECI-Discuss

Contact: `neci-discuss-request@pioneer.ci.net`

Purpose: The general discussion forum of New England Community Internet, an organization dedicated to making USENET and Internet accessible to the public without barriers of economics or technical expertise. The group is developing ways to bring IP connectivity at low cost into homes and non-profit organizations.

To get a daily digest version, subscribe to `neci-digest`. To receive organizational announcements only, subscribe to `neci-announce`.

nedod

Contact: `nedod-request@mbunix.mitre.org` (automated LISTSERV)

   `cookson@mbunix.mitre.org`

Purpose: The discussion of events, technical issues, and just plain socializing related to motorcycling in the New England area of the U.S.

To subscribe, mail a single-line message to `nedod-request@mbunix.mitre.org` consisting of `subscribe nedod` *yourfullname* (not e-mail address).

Plain reflected and digest-type subscriptions are available. To subscribe in digest format, append `set nedod mail digest` to your subscription request.

NERaves
Contact: `ne-raves-request@silver.lcs.mit.edu` (John Adams)

Purpose: Started as a North Eastern United States/Canada equivalent of SFRaves. The list provides a forum for people to discuss the "rave" music/ club/dance scene. For the purposes of the list, "North Eastern" is loosely defined as from Chicago east, and from Washington D.C. north, including Ontario, Quebec, and the maritime provinces. People from outside this area are welcome, too! NERaves is an unmoderated list.

Nerdnosh
Contact: `nerdnosh-request@scruz.ucsc.edu` (Tim Bowden)

Purpose: Begun as a breakfast club for local nerds and writers in Santa Cruz, CA, it has expanded into an international forum about where, how, and why we live where we do. Think of it as a universal camp town meeting in M.F.K. Fisher shades and Jack Kerouac tones. Frivolous, friendly, and informative, in roughly that order.

NERO NY
Contact: `lsonko@pearl.tuft.edu`

Purpose: NERO is a live-action medieval role-playing game with chapters in New York, Georgia, and Massachusetts. This mailing list is for In-Game and Out-of-Game announcements about NERO NY/Ashbury. To subscribe to the list or just get information about NERO NY/Ashbury, write to `lsonko@pearl.tuft.edu`.

NE-Social-MOTSS
Contact: `ne-social-motss-request@plts.org`

Purpose: Announcements of social and other events and happenings in the North East (of the continental United States) of interest to lesbians, gay men, and bisexuals.

V

Resource Reference

NetBlazer-Users

Contact: `netblazer-users-request@telebit.com`

Purpose: To provide an unmoderated forum for discussions among users of Telebit NetBlazer products. Topics include known problems and workarounds, features discussions, and configuration advice.

NetJam

Contact: `netjam-request@xcf.berkeley.edu` (Craig Latta)

Purpose: A means for people to collaborate on musical compositions by sending Musical Instrument Digital Interface (MIDI) and other files (such as MAX patchers and notated scores) to each other, mucking about with them, and resending them. All those with MIDI-compatible (and other interesting) equipment, access to e-mailing and compression facilities and to the Internet, and an interest in making music are encouraged to participate. Please e-mail `netjam-request@xcf.berkeley.edu` with the subject line `request for info`.

Network-Audio-Bits

Contact: `murph@maine.bitnet` (Michael A. Murphy)

Purpose: Network Audio Bits & Audio Software Review—a bimonthly electronic magazine that features reviews of and information about current rock, pop, new age, jazz, funk, folk, and other musical genres. A mixture of major label artists and independent recording artists can be found reviewed in these pages.

Neuron

Contact: `neuron-request@cattell.psych.upenn.edu` (Peter Marvit)

Purpose: The Neuron Digest—a moderated list (in digest form) dealing with all aspects of neural networks (and any type of network or neuromorphic system). Topics include both connectionist models (artificial neural networks) and biological systems ("wetware"). Back issues and limited software are available via ftp from `cattell.psych.upenn.edu`. The Digest is gatewayed to USENET's `comp.ai.neural-nets`.

Newlists

Contact: info@vm1.nodak.edu (Marty Hoag)

Purpose: A mailing list "clearinghouse" for new mailing lists. Subscribers will get announcements of new lists that are mailed to this list.

Neworl-Dig

Contact: mail—server@mintir.new—orleans.la.us

　　　　　elendil@mintir.new—orleans.la.us (Edward J. Branley)

Purpose: A digest version of the New Orleans mailing list (new—orleans@mintir.new—orleans.la.us). This digest will be distributed on a monthly basis and will include articles from the New Orleans list, minus the "noise." To subscribe, send a message to mail—server@mintir.new—orleans.la.us, with SUBSCRIBE NEW—ORLEANS in the body.

New-Orleans

Contact: mail—server@mintir.new—orleans.la.us

　　　　　elendil@mintir.new—orleans.la.us (Edward J. Branley)

Purpose: A list for discussing any and all aspects of the city of New Orleans. History, politics, culture, food, restaurants, music, entertainment, Mardi Gras, etc., are all fair game. To subscribe, send a message to mail—server@mintir.new—orleans.la.us, with SUBSCRIBE NEW—ORLEANS in the body.

NewsCom

Contact: starkid@ddsw1.mcs.com (Lance Sanders)

Purpose: To make available synergies discerned in, and created from, print news media (up to a 12-year time span). Many "facts," particularly scientific ones, have a habit of changing with time. NewsCommando shows extreme prejudice toward those articles whose contents exhibit "legs." The depth of insight possible using the information mosaic method can be staggering. A form of electronic magazine, NewsCommando can serve as a reference tool, offer unique jump-off points for Medline, PaperChase, or other searches, and, in many ways, is the "poor-man's IdeaFisher/IdeaBank." Vol. 1 will contain the following articles:

"ChemTao: Synergies In the Life Sciences"

"EarthWatch1: Defining the Scope of Environmental Destruction"

"Why Euthanasia Must Never Be Legalized"

Use `NewsCom request` in the Subject field of message headers. Indicate article title(s) desired or `all` in the body of the message. Articles will be deposited in your mailbox with a `NewsCom/Vol.#` Subject header. Most will be in excess of 20K. Please group-save them to a file for later reading.

NeXT-GIS
Contact: `sstaton@deltos.com` (Steven R. Staton)

`listserv@deltos.com`

Purpose: Discussion of GIS- and cartographic-related topics on the NeXT and other workstation computers. Some moderated reposting of `comp.infosys.gis` occurs as well.

To join, send a `SUBSCRIBE` *yourfullname* message.

NeXT-Icon
Contact: `next-icon-request@bmt.gun.com` (Timothy Reed)

Purpose: Distribute and receive 64-by-64 or 48-by-48 pixel icons, (2-, 12-, 24-, and/or 32-bit), compatible with NeXT Computer's NeXTStep software. Nearly all mail is in NeXTmail format.

NeXT-Med
Contact: `next-med-request@ms.uky.edu`

Purpose: Open to end users and developers interested in medical solutions using NeXT computers and/or 486 systems running NEXTStep. Discussions on any topic related to NeXT use in the medical industry or relating to health care is encouraged.

NJ-MOTSS, NJ-MOTSS-ANNOUNCE
Contact: `majordomo@plts.org`

Purpose: *NJ-MOTSS*—Mailing list for gay, lesbian, and bisexual issues, etc., in New Jersey.

NJ-MOTSS-ANNOUNCE—announcements of interest to New Jersey's finest 10 percent. Messages sent here also go to NJ-MOTSS; do *not* crosspost!

To subscribe to either list, send the message

```
subscribe nj-motss
```

or

```
subscribe nj-motss-announce
```

to `majordomo@plts.org`.

NOGLSTP
Contact: `noglstp–request@elroy.jpl.nasa.gov`

Purpose: A national organization of lesbigay people employed or interested in scientific or high-technology fields.

Non Serviam
Contact: `solan@math.uio.no` (Svein Olav Nyberg)

Purpose: An electronic newsletter centered on the philosophy of Max Stirner, author of *Der Einzige und Sein Eigentum* (*The Ego and Its Own*), and his dialectical egoism. The contents, however, are decided by the individual contributors and the censoring eye of the editor. The aim is to have somewhat more elaborate and carefully reasoned articles than are usually found on the news groups and lists.

Nordic-Skiing
Contact: `nordic–ski–request@graphics.cornell.edu` (Mitch Collinsworth)

Purpose: Discussion of Nordic skiing sports. This includes cross-country, biathlon, ski-orienteering, ski jumping, Nordic combined, telemark, and back-country.

Novice MZT
Contact: `novice–mzt@krpan.arnes.si`

```
novice.mzt@uni–lj.si
```

Purpose: News of the Ministry for Science and Technology of the Republic of Slovenia. Provides easy access to news from science, development, universities, and innovative activities to individuals and institutions in research and development areas. The news includes the following parts:

Resource Reference

V

Part	Description
Presentation	Brief information about individual institutions, their areas of work, departments, etc.
Achievements	Important research results, development applications, international awards and prizes, new books, etc.
Problems	Different authors present their proposals, critiques, and questions
Announcements	About seminars, symposia, conferences, different advertisements, scholarships, etc.
Exchange of Services and Projects	Offers of and searches for research help, equipment, projects, services, etc.

The language of publishing is Slovene. News is published at least once monthly and at most once in ten days. The volume varies.

NQTHM-Users
Contact: `nqthm—users—request@cli.com`

`nqthm—users—request@inf.fu—berlin.de`

Purpose: Discussion of theorem proving, using the Boyler-Moore theorem prover, NQTHM. Offers lore, advice, information, discussion, help, and a few flames.

NTP
Contact: `ntp—request@trantor.umd.edu`

Purpose: Discussion of the Network Time Protocol.

NPLC
Contact: `tout@genesys.cps.msu.edu` (Walid Tout)

Purpose: To establish this network for rapid communication among researchers in the field of plant lipids. This network can serve as a means to make announcements (such as post-doctoral positions) to the field.

Additionally, it can be used to query co-workers regarding techniques, resources, etc. Also, we hope that research results will be disseminated more rapidly by the posting of abstracts for publications that have been accepted and are "in press." Finally, the NPLC newsletter and announcements regarding NPLC meetings, business, etc., will be posted on the network. The NPLC welcomes plant lipid researchers from anywhere in the world to make use of this network.

To subscribe, send the following message:

```
SUB NPLC yourfullname
```

to `listproc@genesys.cps.msu.edu`.

Nucmed

Contact: `nucmed-request@uwovax.uwo.ca`

`trevorc@uwovax.uwo.ca` (Trevor Cradduck)

Purpose: A discussion of nuclear medicine and related issues. Of particular concern is the format of digital images.

Numeric-Interest

Contact: `numeric-interest-request@validgh.com` (David Hough)

Purpose: Discussion of issues of floating-point correctness and performance with respect to hardware, operating systems, languages, and standard libraries.

NWU-Sports

Contact: `nwu-sports-request@tssi.com` (Michael Nolan)

Purpose: Information on Northwestern University Wildcats sports. Send requests to the contact address.

Objc

Contact: `bunker!stpstn!objc-request` (Anthony A. Datri)

Purpose: The Objective-C mailing list—for the discussion of Stepstone's Objective-C language, Objective-C compiler, Objective-C interpreter, and the ICPak-201 user interface library.

V

Resource Reference

Objectivism
Contact: `objectivism-request@vix.com` (Paul Vixie)

Purpose: A mailing list where students of Objectivism can discuss their ideas, concrete issues, exchange news, etc. Any issue that may have some relevance to Objectivists is appropriate here.

The Observer
Contact: `rwhit@cs.umu.se` (Randall Whitaker)

Purpose: The central scope of the group covers the following:

- The theory of *autopoiesis* (Humberto Maturana and Francisco Varela)

- "Enactive Cognitive Science" (Varela, et al., 1991, *The Embodied Mind*)

The extended scope includes applications of the above theoretical work and linkages to other relevant work in, for example, systems theory, cognitive science, phenomenology, artificial life, etc. Started February 1993. Current format: *The Observer*, an edited electronic newsletter issued (approximately) twice monthly. ASCII research resources (e.g., bibliographies) available on request.

ODA
Contact: `utzoo!trigraph!oda-request` (Les Gondor)

Purpose: A mailing list for topics related to the ISO 8613 standard for Office Document Architecture, and ODIF (Office Document Interchange Format).

Offroad
Contact: `offroad-request@ai.gtri.gatech.edu` (Stefan Roth)

Purpose: To discuss and share experiences about 4x4 and off-road adventures, driving tips, vehicle modifications, and anything else related to four-wheeling. This list is specifically designed for owners, users, or enthusiasts of four-wheel-drive vehicles. Discussions center around technical and mechanical matters, driving techniques, and trip reports. The list is unmoderated. This list is available as a real-time option (default) or as a digest option.

Oglasna Deska

Contact: `oglasna–deska@krpan.arnes.si` (Dean Mozetic and Marjeta
Cedilnik)

   `oglasna.deska@uni–lj.si`

Purpose: *Oglasna Deska* (bulletin board)—transcripts taken from
SLON, which is a nickname for Decnet connecting several computers in
Slovenia. There is a conference similar to USENET running under SLON,
and the articles and replies are occasionally saved and sent to the world.
The topics cover a wide area; the language used is Slovene, Croatian, or
Serbian, but some articles are in English. At the moment, interaction is
limited to some "news groups" (others can only be read), but in the
near future it should be possible to send articles using the mail `reply`
command. The topics covered are equivalent to USENET groups
`talk.politics.misc`, `rec.cars`, `rec.humor`, `comp.networks.*`, `rec.climbing`,
and `misc.invest`.

OH-MOTSS

Contact: `oh–motss–request@cps.udayton.edu`

Purpose: The Ohio Members Of The Same Sex mailing list—for open
discussion of lesbian, gay, and bisexual issues in and affecting Ohio. The
mailing list is not moderated and is open to all, regardless of location or
sexuality. Further, participation on the list does not necessarily indicate a
person's sexual preference or orientation. The subscriber list is known
only to the list owner.

On-This-Day

Contact: `geiser@pictel.com` (Wayne Geiser)

Purpose: Provides a daily listing of interesting birthdays, events, religious holidays, astronomical events, etc. The messages are sent out in the
wee hours of the morning, so you should have it for your morning coffee.

On-U

Contact: `on–u–request@connect.com.au` (Ben Golding)

Purpose: The On-U Sound mailing list—discussions related to the Adrian
Sherwood's On-U Sound label and the artists that record on it. This in-
cludes Tack>>Head, Gary Clail, the Dub Syndicate, African Head Charge,
Bim Sherman, Mark Stewart, etc.

V

Resource Reference

Operlist
Contact: `operlist-request@eff.org` (Helen Trillian Rose)

Purpose: A discussion list for *everything* having to do with IRC. Its main purpose is IRC routing discussions, protocol discussions, and announcements of new versions (of IRC clients and servers).

Oregon-News
Contact: `oregon-news-request@vector.intercon.com`

Purpose: Mailing list of people organizing against the Oregon Citizens' Alliance. This list will carry news of lawsuits, rallies, events, votes, etc., that take place in the state of Oregon.

To subscribe: send a message to `oregon-news-request@vector.intercon.com` with one line: `SUBSCRIBE OREGON-NEWS` *yourfullname*.

Orienteering
Contact: `orienteering-request@graphics.cornell.edu` (Mitch Collinsworth)

Purpose: Discuss all aspects of the sport of orienteering.

Origami
Contact: `origami-l-request@nstn.ns.ca`

Purpose: An unmoderated mailing list for discussion of all facets of origami, the Japanese art of paper folding. Topics include bibliographies, folding techniques, display ideas, descriptions of new folds, creativity, materials, organizations, computer representations of folds, etc.

Archives are available by anonymous ftp from `rugcis.rug.nl`:

1. To start ftp, enter **ftp rugcis.rug.nl**.

2. Log in as `anonymous`.

3. As your password, enter your IP-address.

4. To change the directory, enter **cd origami**.

All requests to be added to or deleted from this list, problems, questions, etc., should be sent to `origami-l-request@nstn.ns.ca`.

Our-Kids

Contact: our-kids-request@oar.net

Purpose: Support for parents and others regarding care, diagnoses, and therapy for young children with developmental delays, whether or not otherwise diagnosed (e.g., CP, PDD, sensory integrative dysfunction). The name our-kids avoids labelling those who are, first and foremost, the special little ones in our lives.

OUTIL (Out in Linguistics)

Contact: outil-request@csli.stanford.edu (Arnold Zwicky)

Purpose: A list open to lesbian, gay, bisexual, dyke, queer, homosexual, etc., linguists and their friends. The only requirement is that you be willing to be out to everyone on the list as glb(-friendly); it's sort of like wearing a pink triangle.

The only official purposes of the group are to be visible and gather occasionally to enjoy one another's company; but we are all welcome to engage in any activity we can arouse interest in.

Oysters

Contact: oysters-request@blowfish.taligent.com

Purpose: For discussion of the British folk-rock band the Oyster and related topics.

Pagan

Contact: pagan-request@drycas.club.cc.cmu.edu (Stacey Greenstein)

Purpose: To discuss the religions, philosophy, etc., of paganism.

Panic

Contact: panic-request@gnu.ai.mit.edu

Purpose: A support group for panic disorders. Discussion involving phobias resulting from panic (agoraphobia and others). Also, a place to meet other people who have gone through the disorder.

Papa

Contact: dgross@polyslo.calpoly.edu (Dave Gross)

Purpose: To discuss the life and works of Ernest Hemingway.

ParNET
Contact: `parnet—list—request@ben.com` (Ben Jackson)

Purpose: To discuss the installation, use, and modification of ParNET, an Amiga-to-Amiga networking program. Please direct comments and questions to `parnet—list—owner@ben.com`.

Partners
Contact: `partners—request@cs.cmu.edu`

Purpose: To advise the administration of Carnegie Mellon University, through the Vice President of Human Resources (who reads the list) of developments in Domestic Partnership benefits and make recommendations on CMU policy regarding benefits.

PBL
Contact: `listserv@eng.monash.edu.au` (Roger Hadgraft)

Purpose: Announcing an e-mail list for those interested in PBL.

The list is an automatic way of keeping in touch with other PBLers in several countries around the world. It is an informal network that allows you to read contributions from others and to respond to their questions and comments. It is not an archive of published papers. It is most like a conversation between many participants, and consequently, it depends on enthusiastic contributions from all subscribers.

Currently, there are more than 100 subscribers from the U.S.A. (50%), Australia (28%), Canada (16%), N.Z., the U.K., etc. (the rest).

To subscribe, send the following one-line e-mail message (as the body of the message, not the Subject line):

```
sub pbl-list
```

to `listserv@eng.monash.edu.au`.

After you are subscribed (it'll take a few minutes), send messages to

```
pbl-list@eng.monash.edu.au
```

Send problems to me:

```
roger.hadgraft@eng.monash.edu.au
```

pc532

Contact: `pc532-request@bungi.com` (Dave Rand)

Purpose: A mailing list for people interested in the pc532 project. This is a National Semiconductor NS32532 based system, offered for a very low cost.

PCGEOS-List

Contact: `listserv@pandora.sf.ca.us`

Purpose: Discussion forum for users or potential users of PC/GEOS products, including GeoWorks Ensemble, GeoWorks Pro, GeoWorks POS, and third-party products. Topics include general information, tips, techniques, applications, experiences, etc.

PDP8-Lovers

Contact: `pdp8-lovers-request@mc.lcs.mit.edu` (Robert E. Seastrom)

Purpose: To facilitate communication and cooperation between owners of vintage DEC computers, specifically, but not limited to, the PDP-8 series of minicomputers. Discussions of all manner of hardware, software, programming techniques are invited. Ownership of an "antique" computer is not required for membership, but flames from people who feel that anything that is not cutting-edge technology is worthless are discouraged.

PDX-MOTSS

Contact: `pdx-motss-request@agora.rain.com`

Purpose: Discussion of LGB issues in the Portland, Oregon, metro area.

PERQ-Fanatics

Contact: `perq-fanatics-request@alchemy.com`

Purpose: For users of PERQ graphics workstations. To subscribe to the list, users should post a message to `perq-fanatics-request@alchemy.com`. There is also an associated news group that was recently started: `alt.sys.perq`.

Peru

Contact: `owner-peru@cs.sfsu.edu` (Herbert Koller)

Purpose: For discussion of Peruvian culture and other issues. This mailing list is simply an echo site, so all posts get bounced from that address to all the people subscribed.

PH7

Contact: `ph7-request@bnf.com`

Purpose: To talk about Peter Hammill and related rock groups. To subscribe, send a message containing `subscribe ph7` *yourfullname*.

Physics

Contact: `physics-request@qedqcd.rye.ny.us` (Mike Miskulin)

Purpose: A newly created digest to cover current developments in theoretical and experimental physics. Typical topics might include particle physics, plasmaphysics, astrophysics. Discussions related to all branches (large and small) of physics are welcome.

Picasso-Users

Contact: `picasso-users@postgres.berkeley.edu`

Purpose: For users of the Picasso graphical User Interface Development System.

Pigulka

Contact: `zielinski@acfcluster.nyu.edu` (Marek Zielinski)

   `davep@acsu.buffalo.edu` (Dave Phillips)

Purpose: Digest on the netnews from Poland, in English. Irregular.

Pipes

Contact: `pipes-request@paul.rutgers.edu` (Steve Masticola)

Purpose: For all those who enjoy smoking, collecting, or sharing information on pipes, tobacco, and related topics. Flames aren't allowed (except for the purpose of lighting up :-).)

Pisma Bralcev

Contact: `pisma-bralcev@krpan.arnes.si` (Andrej Brodnik and Srecko
                                        Vidmar)

   `pisma.bralcev@uni-lj.si`

Purpose: An edited (not moderated) mailing list that provides the possibility of publishing readers' opinions, questions, inquiries for help, answers, etc. There are also published travel tips and book reviews. Anybody can send the letter to the editor, and it will be published on the list under his name. The author can request anonymity, and it will be respected entirely. The frequency of publishing is about one issue per day or less. The language is originally Slovene, but other languages appear as well.

PKD-List

Contact: `pkd-list-request@wang.com`

Purpose: The discussion of the works and life of Philip K. Dick (1928-1982), one of the world's most unusual science fiction writers. Topics include his books and stories, and books and stories about him and his life; however, discussion can (of necessity) branch out into the nature of reality, consciousness, and religious experience.

POET

Contact: `poet-request@scruz.ucsc.edu` (Jon Luini)

Purpose: A workshop/critique forum for poetic works of all descriptions in progress.

Police

Contact: `police-request@cindy.ecst.csuchico.edu` (Pete Ashdown)

Purpose: Dedicated as a service to keep fans of the Police and its members—Sting, Stewart Copeland, and Andy Summers—informed and connected.

To subscribe, mail to `police-request@cindy.ecst.csuchico.edu`, with the command `subscribe` in the first line. For help, send the command `help` to the same address.

POP

Contact: `pop-request@jhunix.hcf.jhu.edu` (Andy S. Poling)

Purpose: To discuss the Post Office Protocol (POP2 and POP3—described in RFCs 918, 937, 1081, and 1082) and implementations thereof.

The driving interest was lack of easily obtained knowledge of available POP2 and POP3 servers and clients. This mailing list is meant to provide this information. Anyone, whether consumer or product provider, is invited to participate.

Porschephiles
Contact: `porschephiles-request@tta.com`

Purpose: This list is for people who own, operate, work on, or simply lust after various models and years of Porsche automobiles. It's a good place to ask questions, talk about features and functionality, get advice on what to buy—or for how much—and, in general, sort of have a little electronic fellowship around the "driving passion" in our lives. Much like a PCA meeting, only distributed and real time.

This list is currently being run as a mail reflector, sending incoming messages to the whole list, which is currently more than 350 people from all over the world. The participants include people with a variety of backgrounds, some very technical, some race/autocross/performance drivers and constructors, some owners, some admiring non-owners.

POSCIM
Contact: `ups500@dbnrhrz1` (Markus Schlegel)

Purpose: The Political Sciences mailing list—a forum of those researching, teaching, or studying the subject, as well as the practitioners of politics.

Being a private list, POSCIM tries to be free of the "noises" common to public lists or news groups related to politics. Exchange over research programs and their results and one's own projects, and the arrangement of special events or congresses are only a few of the various options of communication via POSCIM.

To join POSCIM, please contact

    `ups500@dbnrhrz1 ups500@ibm.rhrz.uni-bonn.de markus@uni-bonn.de`

POSIX-Ada
Contact: `umd5!grebyn!posix-ada-request`

    `posix-ada-request@grebyn.com` (Karl Nyberg)

Purpose: To discuss the Ada binding of the POSIX standard. This is the IEEE P1003.5 working group.

POSIX-Testing
Contact: `posix-testing-request@mindcraft.com` (Chuck Karish)

Purpose: To provide a forum for discussion of issues related to testing operating systems for conformance to the various POSIX standards and proposed standards (IEEE 1003.x and whatever derivative standards may emerge from the NIST, ANSI, ISO, and so on).

These issues include problems related to test suites in general, testability of various features of the standards, and portability of the test suites to the many very different POSIX implementations we expect to see in the near future. We'll focus on the test suites themselves, rather than on the standards to which they test (notably POSIX p1003.3).

Prince
Contact: `prince-request@icpsr.umich.edu`

Purpose: To discuss the musician Prince and related artists.

Prion
Contact: `prion-request@stolaf.edu` (Chris Swanson)

Purpose: To provide a resource for researchers working with prions and interested bystanders; however, all are welcome. All articles posted will be included in the next digest. If a poster feels that his or her posting is of an urgent nature, it may be distributed sooner than the regular digest.

PRL
Contact: `brewer@ace.enet.dec.com` (John Brewer)

Purpose: The Pirate Radio SWL list—for the distribution of questions, answers, information, and loggings of pirate radio stations. This includes SW stations, MW (AM broadcast), and FM pirates.

PROG-PUBS
Contact: `prog-pubs-request@fuggles.acc.virginia.edu`

Purpose: For people interested in progressive and/or alternative publications and other media.

PROG-PUBS was originally created to facilitate and encourage communication among people interested in and active with the "alternative student press" movement. However, the list's scope is now broader than this; we welcome and encourage participation from people involved in all kinds of small-scale, independent, progressive, and/or alternative media, including newspapers, newsletters, and radio and video shows, whether campus-based or not.

Progress
Contact: `progress-list-request@math.niu.edu`

Purpose: Discussion of the Progress RDBMS.

Proof-Users
Contact: `proof-request@xcf.berkeley.edu` (Craig Latta)

Purpose: To discuss the left-associative natural language parser "proof." To join, e-mail `proof-request@xcf.berkeley.edu` with the subject line `add me`.

Pubnet
Contact: `pubnet-request@chinacat.unicom.com` (Chip Rosenthal)

Purpose: The administration and use of public access computer systems—primarily UNIX systems. The list membership includes a large number of people who run sites listed in the world-famous NIXPUB listing. If you have questions about setting up or running a public-access system, this is the place to be.

Python
Contact: `python-list-request@cwi.nl` (Guido van Rossum)

Purpose: For discussion of and questions about all aspects of design and use of the Python programming language. This is an object-oriented, interpreted, extensible programming language. The source of the latest Python release is always available by anonymous ftp from `ftp.cwi.nl`, in directory `/pub/python`. To subscribe, send e-mail to `python-list-request@cwi.nl`; put your name and Internet e-mail address in the body. The list is not moderated.

QN
Contact: `qn-request@queernet.org` (Roger Klorese)

Purpose: A mailing list for Queer Nation activists and for all interested in Queer Nation, an activist group devoted to furthering gay rights. The purpose of QN is to network among various Queer Nation chapters, to discuss actions and tactics, and for general discussion of how to bring about Queer Liberation.

QNX2, QNX4
Contact: `camz@dlogtech.cuc.ab.ca` (Martin Zimmerman)

Purpose: To discuss all aspects of the QNX real-time operating systems. There are separate discussion lists for 2.15/2.20 and the 4.x POSIX versions.

Topics include compatible hardware, available third-party software, software reviews, available PD/free software, QNX platform-specific programming discussions, QNX and FLEET networking, fault-tolerance, distributed processing, process control, SCADA, and other QNX-related topics.

To subscribe, send a message to one of the following:

```
qnx2-request@dlogtech.cuc.ab.ca
qnx4-request@dlogtech.cuc.ab.ca
```

depending on which group you are interested in. The subject or body of the message should contain:

```
subscribe yourfulladdress
```

You also can send `help` in the subject field to get a more detailed description of how to use the list and how to post messages.

Quadraverb
Contact: `qv-interest-request@swap.eng.sun.com` (Bob Page)

Purpose: Discussion of the Alesis Quadraverb family of effects boxes. Unmoderated mail reflector; very light traffic.

Quanta
Contact: `da1n@andrew.cmu.edu`

Purpose: An electronically distributed magazine of science fiction. Published monthly, each issue contains short fiction, articles, and editorials by authors around the world and across the net. Quanta publishes in two formats: straight ASCII and PostScript for PostScript-compatible printers. To subscribe to Quanta, or just to get more info, send mail.

Quattro
Contact: `quattro-request@aries.east.sun.com` (David Tahajian)

Purpose: To disuss Audi cars, and especially the AWD quattro models. All Audi-related discussion is welcome, including news, opinions, maintenance procdures, and parts sources.

Queen

Contact: com@spacsun.rice.edu (Christopher Owen Miller)

Purpose: Discussion about the rock group Queen. Please include the word SUBSCRIBE as your subject.

Race

Contact: majordomo@thumper.lerc.nasa.gov

Purpose: To discuss motorcycle racing (primarily on asphalt tracks) and associated technologies. This is a fairly broad interest group, with experience spanning motojournalism, roadracing from the perspective of the pit crew and racers, and engineering.

To subscribe to race, send the following in an e-mail message to majordomo@thumper.lerc.nasa.gov:

    subscribe race

If you feel you need to reach a human, send e-mail to

    race-approval@thumper.lerc.nasa.gov

Racefab

Contact: racefab-request@pms706.pms.ford.com

Purpose: To discuss racing fabrication and engineering. Suitable topics include suspension geometry and configurations, anti-drive, anti-squat, control arm placement, shock and strut valving, spindle design, floating rear ends, pan-hard bars and watts linkages, cage construction, chassis reinforcement, bearing specs, sources for information and materials, etc.

Please include the type of racing you're involved in (autox, circle track, road race) and the type of race cars/bikes you work/race on in your subscription request.

Raiders

Contact: raiders-request@super.org (Adam Fox)

Purpose: Unmoderated list; all Raider fans are welcome.

Ravenloft

Contact: raven+request@drycas.club.cc.cmu.edu

Purpose: Discussion of Gothic Horror with respect to the Ravenloft Accessory to Advanced Dungeons & Dragons.

rc

Contact: `rc-request@hawkwind.utcs.toronto.edu` (Chris Siebenmann)

Purpose: Discussion of the rc shell. rc is a shell designed by Tom Duff to replace the venerable Bourne shell in Plan 9. It provides similar facilities to sh, with some small additions and mostly less idiosyncratic syntax. Most of the discussion on the list is about Byron Rakitzis' free reimplementation of the shell. See the rc FAQ for more details; get it from `rtfm.mit.edu` as `/pub/usenet/comp.unix.shell/rc-FAQ`.

Really-Deep-Thoughts

Contact: `really-deep-thoughts-request@gradient.cis.upenn.edu`

`rdt-request@gradient.cis.upenn.edu` (Anthony Kosky)

Purpose: Information and discussion on Tori Amos, her music, and other subjects that are relevant or of interest.

Recovery

Contact: `recovery@wvnvm.wvnet.edu` (Jeff Brooks)

Purpose: A forum and support group for survivors of childhood sexual abuse/incest and/or their SOs. Postings are published in digest format and contributors may post anonymously. The emphasis is on healing and recovery through the use of the Twelve Steps of Alcoholics Anonymous as adapted for our purpose.

REGAYN

Contact: `regayn-request@csd4.csd.uwm.edu`

`uunet!csd4.csd.uwm.edu!regayn-request`

Purpose: To serve as a contact point for discussions, opinions, meetings, personal experience sharing of addictions and recovery issues for gay, lesbian, bisexual, and transsexual people.

Any comments or suggestions are greatly appreciated. This is not a moderated mail group.

V

Resource Reference

REM

Contact: `valerie@athena.mit.edu` (Valerie Ohm)

Purpose: Discussion of the music and lyrics by the music group R.E.M.

REND386

Contact: `rend386-request@sunee.uwaterloo.ca`

Purpose: Discussion by and for users of the REND386 software package (fast polygon-based graphics on 386 and 486 systems).

RENDANCE

Contact: `listserver@morgan.ucs.mun.ca`

Purpose: For discussion of Renaissance dance. The intended focus is dance reconstruction and related research, but discussion on any relevant topic is welcome.

RENews

Contact: `nev@renews.relcom.msk.su`

Purpose: Monthly digest on networking and computing in Russia.

Rockhounds

Contact: `rockhounds-request@infodyn.com` (Tom Corson)

Purpose: To exchange ideas, collecting sites, tips, and other information of general interest to gem and mineral collectors.

RokPress

Contact: `ibenko@maveric0.uwaterloo.ca` (Igor Benko)

`rokpress@krpan.arnes.si`

`rokpress@uni-lj.si`

Purpose: A moderated mailing list, intended primarily for news from Slovenia. Slovene is the principal language, although the articles in other languages are often included. It also covers news from international press and important announcements, related to Slovenia and Slovenes. The volume is kept as low as possible.

Role Modeling

Contact: `majordomo@taskon.no`

Purpose: Concerned with the use of roles as a concept in object-oriented systems design.

Topics include:

- Role modeling in OO software development

- Role models in business process modeling

- Methodologies based on role modeling, such as the following:

    The OOram methodology, an object-oriented software development method that uses role modeling

    Using state machines to describe and/or specify certain aspects of an object's behavior

- Related subjects

The list is managed by `cepe@taskon.no`.

To subscribe to the list, send mail to `majordomo@taskon.no`. The body of the message should contain the line `subscribe role-modeling`.

If you need to get in touch with a human, send mail to `role-modeling-owner@taskon.no`.

Romanians

Contact: `romanians@sep.stanford.edu` (Mihai Popovici)

Purpose: Mailing list for discussion, news, and information in the Romanian language.

Rune-Quest

Contact: `runequest-request@glorantha.holland.sun.com` (Henk Langevald)

Purpose: The RuneQuest Digest—A collection of articles, discussion, and source material for use with Chaosium's Runequest fantasy role-playing game. A courtesy of Andrew Bell.

Rush

Contact: `rush-request@syrinx.umd.edu`

Purpose: For fans of the Canadian rock group Rush, to discuss things about the group and its music.

RX7Net E-Mail Club

Contact: `rx7club@cbjjn.att.com`

Purpose: An e-mail list of members who own Mazda RX7s or who are interested in gaining technical or general information about RX7s. You do not need to own an RX7 to join the list, just a love for the only rotary-powered sports car in the world. The RX7Net contains many knowledge-able people who have a lot of technical and historical information on the three generations of RX7s. The RX7Net currently has 190 members.

sam-Fans

Contact: `sam-fans-request@hawkwind.utcs.toronto.edu` (Chris
Siebenmann)

Purpose: Discussion of Rob Pike's sam editor. sam is an interactive multifile text editor intended for bitmap displays. A textual command language supplements the mouse-driven, cut-and-paste interface to make complex or repetitive editing tasks easy to specify. The language is charac-terized by the composition of regular expressions to describe the structure of the text being modified. sam can be ftp-ed from `research.att.com`, directory `/dist/sam`; the mailing list itself is archived on `ftp.sys.utoronto.ca` in `/pub/sam`.

San Francisco Giants

Contact: `giants-request@medraut.apple.com` (Chuq Von Rospach)

Purpose: Discussion and information exchange on the San Francisco Giants baseball team.

San Jose Sharks

Contact: `sharks-request@medraut.apple.com` (Laurie Sefton)

Purpose: Discussion and information exchange on the San Jose Sharks hockey team.

Sappho
Contact: `sappho-request@mc.lcs.mit.edu` (Regis M. Donovan)

Purpose: A forum and support group for gay and bisexual women. The list is not moderated, but may become so if the volume and/or content begins to warrant it. A digest version is available; if you want it, be sure to mention it in your addition request. Men who want to "listen in," for whatever reason, are requested to use the feminist and alternates mailing lists instead; sappho membership is limited to women.

SATNEWS
Contact: `listserv@orbital.demon.co.uk`

Purpose: The mailing list for *Satnews*, a biweekly report of events in the satellite television industry worldwide.

To subscribe to the list, write to `listserv@orbital.demon.co.uk` with `subscribe satnews` *yourfullname* as the first line in the message body, replacing *yourfullname* with your real name, not your e-mail address.

SCA
Contact: `sca-request@mc.lcs.mit.edu` (Danulf Donaldson, MKA Dana Groff)

Purpose: To discuss anything relating to the Society for Creative Anachronism, a world-wide medievalist organization. Anyone in the society (or interested in it) is welcome to join. Those with basic questions about the society should direct them to `justin@inmet.com` (Justin du Coeur, MKA Mark Waks), who will be happy to answer them. (Please note that the mailing list is not officially related to the SCA in any way; it is simply a group of talkative members.)

The SCA mailing list is gatewayed into the `rec.org.sca` news group.

SCA-West
Contact: `sca-west-request@ecst.csuchico.edu`

Purpose: To serve those persons who have a desire to discuss, share, etc., items of interest to the Society of Creative Anachronism members in the West and thereby reduce traffic on the Rialto (`rec.org.sca`) of subjects that might be considered too local; but there is really no restriction on any subject.

V

Resource Reference

It is for those members that are in the West Kingdom, which includes northern and central California, northern Nevada, Alaska, Australia, and Japan. Anyone is welcome to join, though. This is strictly a mail list; there is no echo to a news group.

To subscribe, send a message with `subscribe` *yourfullname* on the first line of the message to `sca-west-request@ecst.csuchico.edu`.

School
Contact: `school-request@balltown.cma.com` (Richard Welty)

Purpose: Discussion of high-performance driving schools.

Scoann
Contact: `scoann-request@xenitec.on.ca` (Ed Hew)

Purpose: The SCO Announce mailing list—a moderated announcements list providing product update and new product announcements supplied by SCO or by developers offering SCO-based products.

Submissions for the list should be addressed to `scoannmod@xenitec.on.ca`.

The scoann mail list is bidirectionally gatewayed with the USENET `biz.sco.annouce` news group.

Scogen
Contact: `scogen-request@xenitec.on.ca` (Geoff Scully)

Purpose: For anyone interested in or currently using Santa Cruz Operation products. This mailing list is a single area where discussions and information can be exchanged regarding *all* SCO products.

The scogen mail list is bidirectionally gatewayed with the USENET `biz.sco.general` news group.

Scoodt
Contact: `scoodt-request@xenitec.on.ca` (Ed Hew)

Purpose: The SCO Open Desktop electronic mailing list—to provide a communications vehicle for interested parties to provide, request, submit, and exchange information regarding the configuration, implementation, and use of the SCO Open Desktop operating system as available from the Santa Cruz Operation.

All submissions will be posted as received with appropriate author attribution. Questions are welcome. Someone may even answer them.

The scoodt mail list is bidirectionally gatewayed with the USENET `biz.sco.opendesktop` news group.

Screaming in Digital

Contact: `queensryche-request@pilot.njin.net`

Purpose: Discussion of the band Queensryche and related topics. Caveats: Available only in weekly digest form, hand-edited.

Scribe

Contact: `scribe-hacks-request@decwrl.dec.com`

Purpose: For persons who perform the role of Scribe Database Administrator at their installation. Discussion will be about Scribe features, bugs, enhancements, performance, support, and other topics of interest to Scribe DBAs. The list will not be moderated, but will simply consist of a mail reflector—that is, if you send a message to the list, it will be rebroadcast to everyone on the list. Discussion at the level of "How do I get a paragraph to indent 5 spaces instead of 3?" is specifically discouraged.

SDAnet

Contact: `st0o+sda@andrew.cmu.edu` (Steve Timm)

Purpose: A list for and about Seventh-Day Adventists. It is a moderated list. Anyone may post or subscribe.

Seattle-Mariners

Contact: `seattle-mariners-request@kei.com`

Purpose: The discussion of the Seattle Mariners baseball club, criticism included.

Security

Contact: `uunet!zardoz!security-request` (Neil Gorsuch)

          `security-request@cpd.com`

Purpose: To notify of UNIX security flaws *before* they become public knowledge, and to provide UNIX security-enhancement programs and information. Most postings are explanations of specific UNIX security

Resource Reference

"holes," including fixes or workarounds to prevent their usage. This list is not intended for discussions of general and/or theoretical security issues. It is joined at the pleasure of the applicant's system administrator and the list administrator.

Requests to join must be mailed from a system administration account and must specify the following:

1. The full name of the recipient

2. The address to send the list to

3. The address of the contact person for that site (if different from 2)

4. Whether you want moderated digests or reflected postings

SF-LOVERS

Contact: `sf-lovers-request@rutgers.edu` (Saul Jaffe)

Purpose: For discussions of many topics, all of them related in some way to the theme of science fiction and fantasy. Topics have ranged very widely from rewritten stories, sci-fi and fantasy books, sci-fi movies, and sci-fi conventions to reviews of books, movies, and television shows. Anyone is welcome to submit material on these or other topics of interest in this general area.

The digest has a very large number of readers, and trivial messages are strongly discouraged due to the heavy load SF-LOVERS puts on the host's CPU and disk space. Messages to SF-LOVERS are batched and broadcast periodically. Please be sure to read the file `SFLOVERS.POLICY` available from the archives.

For Internet subscribers, all requests to be added to or deleted from this list should be sent to `sf-lovers-request@rutgers.edu`. BITNET subscribers may issue the following command:

```
tell listserv at rutvm1 command sflovers yourfullname
```

where *command* is either `subscribe` or `unsubscribe`, as appropriate. Problems and administrative questions should always be sent to `sf-lovers-request@rutgers.edu`.

SFRaves
Contact: `sfraves-request@soda.berkeley.edu` (Brian Behlendorf)

Purpose: About the "rave" club scene in San Francisco. Even though it's locally focused, people from all over the world are on SFRaves. It is an unmoderated list.

Shadows-Updates
Contact: `shadows-update-request@sunee.uwaterloo.ca`

Purpose: Regular synopses of the episodes of the television series *Dark Shadows*, currently being show on the "Sci-Fi" cable channel. (See also Dark-Shadows in the list.)

ShadowTalk
Contact: `listserv@hearn.bitnet`

  `listserv@hearn.nic.surfnet.nl` (Robert Hayden)

Purpose: A listserv devoted to the role-playing game Shadowrun, which is published by FASA. Shadowrun takes place in the year 2054 and centers in the city of Seattle. ShadowTalk is an attempt to emulate the public communications networks presented in the game.

Contact the list owner (`aq650@slc4.ins.cwru.edu`) for a copy of the FAQ, which will outline many more of the details for this list, including instructions on how to subscribe.

Siege
Contact: `siege-request@bransle.ucs.mun.ca`

Purpose: For the discussion of pre-black powder methods of attack and defence of fortified positions. While the discussion of the downfall of the great siege engines caused by the advent of portable and powerful cannon is important, I would like this to be somewhat minimized.

Topics appropriate for discussion include physics, mechanics, materials, construction, transportation, terminology, historic evidence of use, historical reconstruction, common myths and misconceptions, and so on.

To subscribe, send mail to `siege-request@bransle.ucs.mun.ca` and include a single line saying `subscribe siege` *yourfullname*.

V

Resource Reference

Sierra Club
Contact: 931rowe@merlin.nlu.edu (Eddie Rowe)

Purpose: Discussion of environmental topics, with a focus on the Sierra Club's campaigns, news, and outings. A mirror of the FidoNet Sierra Club Conference (SIERRAN).

SII
Contact: owner@moumee.calstatela.edu

Purpose: To distribute news and provide a forum for discussions about the current events in the former Yugoslavia, centered around those involving or affecting Serbs. Also, they originate public actions related to these events.

SKEPTIC
Contact: listserv@jhuvm.hcf.jhu.edu

Purpose: A mailing list devoted to critical discussion of extraordinary claims. Among the paranormal topics that are commonly examined are parapsychology and psychic claims, creationism, cult archaeology, UFOs, cryptozoology, reincarnation/survival, quackery, the occult, and divination; but the discussion is not limited to any predetermined set of magical beliefs or alleged pseudosciences.

In connection with paranormal claims, issues involving science and philosophy in general are often raised. There is no policy of excluding any topic from consideration. While the common point of view expressed is skepticism about claims that go against current scientific pictures, critical approaches to science itself are also encouraged.

To subscribe, send a mail message to listserv@jhuvm.hcf.jhu.edu @jhuvm, with the line subscribe skeptic *yourfullname*.

SkillsBank
Contact: sun!kass!richard (Richard Karasik)

Purpose: To share skills with others—not just the computist ones, although those are handy to know, but some of the oddball ones that we all seem to have acquired.

Ground rules: The list is not going to be publicly available, but requests to the list for specific skills will be passed on to the people who have them, and they can decide about the level of participation they want to have. The only public piece that will be mailed around is the new skills that have been added, and the new requests for assistance.

I am open to any other suggestions for how to make this work.

Skunk-Works

Contact: `skunk-works-request@harbor.ecn.purdue.edu`

Purpose: To discuss Lockheed special project planes and current aviation news. We cover the Blackbird family (A-12, YF-12, and SR-71), the U-2 series, the F-117A, the B-2 (even though that's Northrop), and "Aurora."

smail3-Users

Contact: `smail3-users-request@cs.athabascau.ca` (Lyndon Nerenberg)

Purpose: Targeted towards those who administer smail3.X-based mailers. Discussion of operational problems and fixes, specialized configurations, and other topics related to the day-to-day operation of smail3.X are found here. The list does not discuss smail 2.5 issues. (smail 2.5 is an unrelated piece of software that appeared in the `comp.sources.unix` archives under the archive name "smail3.") Questions about smail 2.5 should be directed to the news group `comp.mail.misc`. smail3-users deals primarily with operational issues. If you're interested in technical discussions on smail3 internals, consider joining smail3-wizards.

smail3-Wizards

Contact: `smail3-wizards-request@cs.athabascau.ca` (Lyndon Nerenberg)

Purpose: A discussion forum for people who are actively porting, debugging, and extending smail3.X. Discussion should be limited to topics concerning smail3 internals. Questions about smail3 installation and operation should be directed to the smail3-users list.

Smallmusic

Contact: `smallmusic-request@xcf.berkeley.edu` (Craig Latta)

Purpose: To discuss and develop an object-oriented software system for music. The current environment is Smalltalk 80. If you are interested in joining the discussion, e-mail `smallmusic-request@xcf.berkeley.edu` with the subject line `add me`.

Smiths-Fans
Contact: `larryn@csufres.csufresno.edu`

Purpose: A mailing list dedicated to the music of the rock group the Smiths. Though the group is no longer together, we feel there is a substantial enough body of work to keep a list such as this going. Topics include discussion/interpretation of lyrics, work being done currently by members, and other intellectual concerns.

Smoke-Free
Contact: `maynor@ra.msstate.edu`

Purpose: A support list for people recovering from addiction to cigarettes. To subscribe to the list, send the following command to `listserv@ra.msstate.edu`:

```
subscribe smoke-free yourfullname
```

The list is running on UNIX listserv.

S-News
Contact: `s-news-request@stat.wisc.edu` (Douglas Bates)

Purpose: Information and discussion about the S language for data analysis and graphics.

Societies
Contact: `societies-request@athena.mit.edu`

Purpose: Discussion of Greek letter societies of all sorts, primarily those that are at American colleges. Flamage not encouraged by list owners; no affiliation with one is required. Currently unmoderated. Please include your most reliable Internet-accessible address in your subscription request.

Software Entrepreneurs
Contact: `softpub-request%toolz.uucp@mathcs.emory.edu` (Todd Merriman)

```
...!emory!slammer!toolz!softpub-request
```

Purpose: Devoted to the interests of entrepreneurial software publishing, including (but not limited to) shareware. The forum is completely open.

SOLN
Contact: `soln-request@gynko.circ.upenn.edu`

Purpose: SOLN (Satellite of Love News)—a moderated mailing list for fans of the television show *Mystery Science Theater 3000*, which is shown on the Comedy Channel (available on various cable networks in North America). Requests to be added/deleted should be sent to the address listed above. Archives of the list are maintained and may be accessed via anonymous ftp at `gynko.circ.upenn.edu`; look in the directory `pub/rsk/mst3k/soln`.

SONIC-LIFE-L
Contact: `rtv1@cornell.edu`

Purpose: The discussion of the music and other work of Sonic Youth. It is a private mailing list with restricted membership determined by the list owner.

To subscribe to SONIC-LIFE-L, send the following command in the body of a message via electronic mail to `listserv@cornell.edu`:

```
SUB SONIC-LIFE-L yourfirstname yourlastname
```

Please use your real first and last name. Nicknames and aliases may not be accepted. Lurkers (people who do not post on a regular basis) are always welcome.

If you have any questions about SONIC-LIFE-L, contact Rob Vaughn, the list owner, at `rtv1@cornell.ed`.

If you have any questions about listserv, contact the listserv manager at `listmgr@cornell.edu`.

Soundtracks
Contact: `soundtracks-request@ifi.unizh.ch` (Michel Hafner)

Purpose: For people with general soundtrack interests; the list includes the following:

- Discussions and reviews of new and older soundtracks (musical and technical aspects)

- Information about availability of specific soundtracks on different formats in different parts of the world

- Publication of trading lists so members can swap stuff and complete their collections

- Compiling of lists on different subjects with entries collected via the list (for example, passages in soundtracks "lifted" from other soundtracks, classical compositions with detailed data, discographies, etc.)

- Discussions and reviews of books, fanzines, etc., about soundtracks/music for films

- Discussions and reviews of hardware for (film) music reproduction

Please don't join if you are just looking for some soundtrack(s) but have no general interest in the field!

Sovokinform
Contact: burkov@drfmc.ceng.cea.fr

Purpose: CIS news, events, general information; usually in transliterated Russian. To subscribe, send the message SUB SOVOKINFORM *yourfullname*.

Space: 1999
Contact: space–1999–request@quack.kfu.com

Purpose: For discussion on almost any subject of interest to fans of the 1975-1976 TV show *Space: 1999*.

Spojrzenia
Contact: krzystek@u.washington.edu (Jerzy Krzystek)

Purpose: A weekly e-journal, devoted to Polish culture, history, politics, etc. In Polish.

Sports-Cards
Contact: cards–request@tanstaafl.uchicago.edu (Keane Arase)

Purpose: For people interested in collecting, speculating, and investing in baseball, football, basketball, hockey, and other trading cards and/or memorabilia. Discussion and want/sell lists are welcome. Open to anyone.

SQL-Sybase

Contact: sybase-request@apple.com

Purpose: A semi-unmoderated mailing list for sharing information about the Sybase SQL server and related products.

Sri Lanka Net (SLNet)

Contact: pkd@fed.frb.gov

slnetad@ganu.colorado.edu

Purpose: A moderated mailing list that carries news and other articles about Sri Lanka. Wire service (AP, UPI, Reuters, etc.) news is obtained for exclusive use of SLNet members. Newspaper clippings from Sri Lanka are also carried (in electronic form) on a regular basis. SLNet is not a discussion group. Members may request for information from others.

Stagecraft

Contact: stagecraft-request@jaguar.cs.utah.edu (Brad Davis)

Purpose: For the discussion of all aspects of stage work, including (but not limited to) special effects, sound effects, sound reinforcement, stage management, set design and building, lighting design, company management, hall management, hall design, and show production. This is not a forum for the discussion of various stage productions (unless the discussion pertains to the stagecraft of a production), acting or directing methods (unless you know of ways to get actors to stand in the right spots), or film or video production (unless the techniques can be used on the stage). The list will not be moderated unless problems crop up. Archives will be kept of the discussion (send mail to stagecraft-request for copies).

Star Fleet Battles

Contact: hcobb@fly2.berkeley.edu (Henry J. Cobb)

Purpose: The SFB Tacticsline—for discussion of tactics of the SFB game, and as a contact point for SFB PBeM games.

Starserver

Contact: starserver-request@engr.uky.edu (Wes Morgan)

Purpose: For owners, operators, and administrators of AT&T StarServer systems. While all interested parties are invited to join, the list is dedicated to matters of system administration/operation; many "UNIX

Resource Reference

V

questions and answers" resources are available, and we ask that you utilize them. Several ATT/NCR technical support personnel participate in the discussion. The list is not currently moderated.

Stock Market Secrets
Contact: `smi–request@world.std.com`

Purpose: A stock-market-related daily comment. In addition, we answer questions on a wide variety of investment and financial topics.

This is a moderated list in order to keep confidential information.

Stonewall25
Contact: `stonewall25–request@queernet.org`

`wellconnectedsite!unpc!stonewall25–request`

Purpose: For discussion and planning of the "Stonewall 25" international gay/lesbian/bi rights march in New York City on Sunday, June 26, 1994, and the events accompanying it.

Stormcock
Contact: `stormcock–request@dcs.qmw.ac.uk` (Paul Davison)

Purpose: For general discussion and news concerning the music of Roy Harper, a folk-rock musician with a conscience. Recommendations and news concerning similar artists are encouraged. The list is set up as a mail reflector.

> **Note**
>
> Some Internet sites may have to route mail through the U.K. Internet gateway `nsfnet–relay.ac.uk`. Also, in some exceptional circumstances, we may have to refuse membership because we get charged for mail to certain addresses in the UUCP domain.

Strathspey
Contact: `strathspey–request@math.uni–frankfurt.de`

Purpose: A forum for the discussion of all aspects of Scottish Country Dancing, e.g., dance descriptions, dancing technique, the history of dances and dancing, learning or teaching how to dance. We also welcome descriptions of new dances, announcements of events like courses or balls, or anything the subscribers might find interesting.

The mailing list is unmoderated, i.e., everything that is submitted is forwarded directly to the subscribers of the list. We hope to be able to offer an archive of past traffic if the demand should arise.

Subscription/unsubscription/info requests should be directed to

```
strathspey-request@math.uni-frankfurt.de
```

Just send a message with the word subscribe in the Subject header to subscribe to the list. Similarly, send a Subject of unsubscribe to unsubscribe, or a Subject of help to get a copy of the help message (which is very much like this posting).

Most (un)subscription requests are processed automatically without human intervention. To reach a human for special requests or problems, send mail to owner-strathspey@math.uni-frankfurt.de.

ST Viruses
Contact: r.c.karsmakers@stud.let.ruu.nl

Purpose: To provide fast and efficient help where infection with computer viruses is concerned—Atari ST/TT/Falcon only, no MS-DOS or compatibles! Also, it's the electronic helpline for registered users of the "Ultimate Virus Killer" program. Questions about virus symptoms or any other general questions of Atari 16/32-bit viral nature may be directed to the above address. No digest format available (at least not yet).

The Sugarcubes
Contact: glocke@morgan.ucs.mun.ca (Gord Locke)

Purpose: The blue-eyed-pop mailing list—for discussion of the now-defunct (though-not-necessarily-for-good) Icelandic band the Sugarcubes. Also acceptable fodder for discussion: the solo career of their lead singer, Bjork Gudmundsdottir; other Icelandic bands; trading/selling of sundry paraphernalia; what you like to take with your tea;...you get the idea.

To subscribe to this list, send a message to listserver@morgan.ucs.mun.ca, with the message body consisting only of

```
subscribe blue-eyed-pop yourfullname
```

(*yourfullname* is not your e-mail address, just your name—like Gord Locke.) The account you send this message from determines where mail from the list will be sent.

There is no blue-eyed-pop-request address; mail administrative stuff to the list owner (me, Gord Locke): glocke@morgan.ucs.mun.ca.

Sun-386i
Contact: sun-386i-request@ssg.com (Rick Emerson)

Purpose: Discussion and information about the 386i-based Sun machines.

Sunflash (aka The Florida SunFlash)
Contact: flash@sun.com (John J. McLaughlin)

Purpose: To keep Sun users informed about Sun via press releases, product announcements, and technical articles. This is a one-way mailing list. 25 to 35 articles are posted each month. More than 110,000 Sun users subscribe. Requests to be added to the list should go to sunflash-request@sun.com. For more information, send mail to info-sunflash@sun.com.

Sun-Managers
Contact: sun-managers-request@eecs.nwu.edu

Purpose: Information of special interest to managers of sites with Sun workstations or servers.

Sun-Nets
Contact: sun-nets-request@umiacs.umd.edu

Purpose: Discussion and information on networks using Sun hardware and/or software.

SupraFAX
Contact: subscribe@xamiga.linet.org (David Tiberio)

Purpose: To help people who have been having trouble using the SupraFAX v.32bis modem. Topics include what some common problems are, where to get support, what bugs are found in the current ROM revisions, and how to follow basic setup and usage of the Supra command set (Hayes compatible).

To subscribe to the list, send e-mail to `subscribe@xamiga.linet.org`, with a line in the body of the text like:

    #supra username@domain

where your *username* is the name mail is sent to and *domain* is your ip address for your machine. For example, I would subscribe by writing `#supra dtiberio@xamiga.linet.org` in the body. We run multiple lists, and users may subscribe to multiple lists in one posting. Upon receipt of your welcome letter, please respond to become an activated subscriber.

Sysops

Contact: `{harpo,bellcore,cmcl2}!cucard!dasys1!sysops-request`

`{allegra,cmcl2,philabs}!phri!dasys1!sysops-request`

Purpose: To facilitate communication among operators of computerized bulletin board systems. Topics will include, but are certainly not limited to, applications, security, legal issues, and software.

Szemle

Contact: `ujsagker@vuhepx.phy.vanderbilt.edu`

Purpose: Discussion and distribution of news about Hungary, in digest form. Information is mainly in Hungarian.

To receive the digest, write to the contact address, with the Subject KELL.

Tadream

Contact: `tadream-request@vacs.uwp.edu` (Dave Datta)

`...uwm!uwpvacs!tadream-request`

`uwpvacs!tadream-request@uwm.edu`

Purpose: A forum for discussions about Tangerine Dream and related artists. The discussions are not moderated, but discussions should have some small relation to Tangerine Dream (solo works and instrumentation discussions are welcome). The list is set up both as a mail relay and a daily digest.

V

Resource Reference

Talon-Eclipse-Laser

Contact: todd@di.com (Todd Day)

Purpose: For owners and admirers of Talon, Eclipse, or Laser automobiles.

Tandem

Contact: tandem-request@hobbes.ucsd.edu

Purpose: A mailing list for tandem bicycle enthusiasts. Suitable topics include questions and answers related to tandem componentry, riding technique, brands and equipment selection, prices, clubs, rides, and other activities; cooperating on a section on tandems for the rec.bicycles.* FAQ, etc.

Tandy4k

Contact: ...!{psu-cs,reed,ogcvax}!qiclab!tandy4k-users (Steven
Neighorn)

Purpose: A mailing list for owners, users, and other interested parties of the Intel 80386-based Tandy 4000 Microcomputer. The list will contain problems encountered, hints, program source code, and anything else related to the operation of Tandy's newest entry into the world of microcomputers.

TBI-Sprt

Contact: listserv@sjuvm.stjohns.edu

Purpose: The St. Johns University Traumatic Brain Injury Support List— for the exchange of information by survivors, supporters, and professionals concerned with traumatic brain injury and other neurological impairments that currently lack a forum. We know from our own experience that one of the difficulties people dealing with TBI face is that their time is often dominated by the survivor's recovery process. Accessing support groups or networking of any kind can seem like one more thing to add to an already packed schedule. A forum such as this is available at all hours of the day or night and does not need to become one more event that must be scheduled.

The postings to the list are archived and made available monthly through the listserv. A file containing introductions submitted by subscribers is also available along with files relevant to topics of the list. Additions to these resources are welcome.

To subscribe to tbi-sprt, send mail to `listserv@sjuvm.bitnet` or `listserv@sjuvm.stjohns.edu`. Leave the subject line blank and in the body of the message put the line `tbi-sprt` *yourfullname*.

List owners: Len Burns (`lburns@cats.ucsc.edu`) and Tapati Amber Sarasvati (`labyris@gorn.echo.com`).

TCAD
Contact: `tcad-request@iec.ufl.edu` (Mark Law)

Purpose: To serve the needs of users and software developers of TCAD (technology computer-aided design) codes. These codes typically aid the IC process designer in developing, debugging, and optimizing new and old processes. The group discusses software such as PISCES, SUPREM, FABRICS, SAMPLE, SIMPL, and MINIMOS.

TCP-Group
Contact: `tcp-group-request@ucsd.edu`

Purpose: Discussion about promoting TCP/IP use on Ham packet radio.

Tears4-Fears
Contact: `tears4-fears-request@ms.uky.edu` (Joel Abbot)

Purpose: Discussion of the music group Tears For Fears.

Tekumel
Contact: `tekumel-request@ssdc.honeywell.com` (Brett Slocum)

Purpose: To discuss the world of Tekumel, the fantasy world invented by M.A.R. Barker in the role-playing games Empire of the Petal Throne and Swords and Glory, and the DAW novels *Man of Gold* and *Flamesong*.

Anything related to Tekumel is welcome: game modifications, accounts of campaigns, questions, fiction, tables, NPCs, tips for converting to new game systems, etc. Listeners as well as contributors are welcome. This list is in digest format and is mailed when submissions warrant it (weekly, if possible).

TeleUSErs
Contact: `teleusers-request@telesoft.com` (Charlie Counts)

Purpose: To promote the interchange of technical information, examples, tips, etc., among the users of TeleUSE. The TeleUSErs mailing list is unmoderated. (Mail for TeleSoft TeleUSE Technical Support should *not* be sent to the list; technical support e-mail should be sent to `guisupport@telesoft.com`).

Testing-Research
Contact: `testing-research-request@cs.uiuc.edu` (Brian Marick)

Purpose: A forum for testing researchers to discuss current and future research. Since testing is one of the most down-to-earth kinds of software engineering research, testing practitioners are welcome. Messages about practice should be the kind that can guide or improve research; messages that can improve practice should go in `comp.software-eng`. This list is unmoderated.

Theatre
Contact: `theatre-request@world.std.com` (Elizabeth Lear Newman)

Purpose: For the general discussion of theater, in whatever form it may take. This list is primarily a gateway for the traffic in the news group `rec.arts.theatre`.

They-Might-Be
Contact: `they-might-be-request@gnu.ai.mit.edu`

Purpose: Discussion of the musical group They Might Be Giants.

Think-C
Contact: `think-c-request@ics.uci.edu` (Mark Nagel)

Purpose: To discuss the Think C compiler for the Macintosh. Acceptable topics include discussion of compiler problems and solutions/workarounds, discussion of object-oriented programming and Macintosh programming, and the sharing of source code. Associated with this list is an archive stored on `ics.uci.edu` accessible via ftp and a mail archive server (`archive-server@ics.uci.edu`). Submissions to the archive should go to `think-c-request`.

Thunderbird
Contact: `htunca@ncsa.uiuc.edu` (Han Tunca)

Purpose: To discuss all aspects of Ford Thunderbird automobiles. The mailing list is not limited to any model year.

TinyMUCK-Sloggers
Contact: `tinymuck-sloggers-request@piggy.ucsb.edu` (Robert Earl)

Purpose: Forum for programmers, wizards, and users of the extensible, programmable TinyMUD derivative known as TinyMUCK (current version: 2.2).

TinyMUSH-Programmers
Contact: `tinymush-programmers-request@cygnus.com`

Purpose: Discussion devoted to the programming language integral to the TinyMUSH subfamily of mud servers. (See the `rec.games.mud` FAQ for more general information about muds.)

Tolkien-Czech
Contact: `tolkien-request@pub.vse.cz`

Purpose: Discussion, held in Czech and Slovak languages only, concerning works of J.R.R. Tolkien, especially their Czech (and Slovak) translations.

To subscribe, send `SUBSCRIBE TOLKIEN` *yourfirstname yourlastname* mail to `listserver@pub.vse.cz`.

TolkLang
Contact: `tolklang-request@lfcs.ed.ac.uk` (Julian Bradfield)

Purpose: Discussions of the linguistic aspects of J.R.R. Tolkien's works. This covers everything from Elvish vocabulary and grammar to his use of Old English. The list is (lightly) moderated.

TOP
Contact: `top-request@cv.ruu.nl` (Ger Timmens)

Purpose: Discussion of the musical group Tower of Power and associated side projects.

Torg
Contact: `torg-request@cool.vortech.com` (Clay Luther)

Purpose: The mailing list dedicated to the infiniverse of West End Game's Torg, the Possibility Wars role-playing game. Please put `HELP` on the subject line, as this is an automated request.

Toronto Blue Jays
Contact: `stlouis@unixg.ubc.ca` (Phill St-Louis)

Purpose: Discussion of the Toronto Blue Jays baseball club, including player transactions, predictions, game commentary, etc. Everyone welcome!

Towers
Contact: `bill@wrangler.wlk.com` (Bill Kennedy)

Purpose: General discussion on the subject of NCR tower computers. Gatewayed with `comp.sys.ncr`.

Toyota
Contact: `toyota-request@quack.kfu.com`

Purpose: The discussion of almost any subject for owners and prospective owners of all models of Toyota consumer passenger vehicles and light trucks.

Toyota Corolla
Contact: `pchaos!keithm@pail.rain.com`

Purpose: The discussion of Toyota Corollas. From 1970-1994 models, all engines, even the Chevy Nova and Geo Prism twins.

TRANSGEN
Contact: `listserv@brownvm.brown.edu`

Purpose: A list specifically for and about people who are transsexual, transgendered, and/or transvestites. The list is open to the public.

TRANSGEN may be received in two formats. For setting TRANSGEN to post by post format, the proper command is SET TRANSGEN MAIL. For setting it to digest format, the command is SET TRANSGEN DIGEST. The proper address to which to send these commands is one of the following:

> `listserv@brownvm.brown.edu`
>
> `listserv@brownvm.bitnet`

Transputer
Contact: `transputer-request@tcgould.tn.cornell.edu`

Purpose: To enhance the communication among those who are interested in the Transputer and Transputer-based systems.

Submissions should be of nonproprietary nature and be concerned with, but not limited to, the following:

- Algorithms

- Current development efforts (hardware and software)

- INMOS and third-party systems (Meiko, FPS, etc.)

- Interfaces

- Dedicated computational resources

- Occam and non-Occam language development

Archives of submissions are available by anonymous ftp from the host `tcgould.tn.cornell.edu` (user ID anonymous; password is of the form *user@host*) and through UUCP on a per-request basis.

The list is maintained as a mail reflector. Submissions are therefore sent out as they are received.

Traveller
Contact: `traveller-request@engrg.uwo.ca` (James T. Perkins)

Purpose: To discuss the Traveller science fiction role-playing game, published by Game Designers' Workshop. All variants of Traveller (Traveller 2300, MegaTraveller) and Traveller games (Snapshot, Trillion Credit Squadron, etc.) are included, too. Discussion is unmoderated and open to all facets and levels of Traveller discussion. Listeners as well as contributors are welcome.

TREK-REVIEW-L
Contact: `listserv@cornell.edu` (Michael Scott Shappe)

Purpose: A noise-free forum for reviews of *Star Trek* material. This category includes, but is not limited to, television programs, feature films, novels and novelizations, comic books, games, and parodies of *Star Trek*.

The list is not rooted in any specific generation of *Trek*. Original Series, Animated Series, Movie Era, *Next Generation*, and *Deep Space Nine* materials are all valid.

To subscribe to the list, send the following command in mail to
`listserv@cornell.edu`:

    SUBSCRIBE TREK-REVIEW-L *yourfirstname yourlastname*

Triples
Contact: `triples-request@hal.com` (Howard A. Landman)

Purpose: To discuss non-monogamous relationships, polyfidelity, and
group marriage, and the various issues that arise in that context, like
jealousy, shared housing, marriage laws, sex, etc. Not moderated.

TurboVision
Contact: `listserv@vtvm1.cc.vt.edu`

Purpose: For TurboVision programmers (a library that comes with
Borland C++ and Pascal compilers). Both languages are discussed. You
can subscribe by sending the message `subscribe turbvis` *yourfullname* to
`listserv@vtvm1.cc.vt.edu`.

Twilight Zone
Contact: `r.c.karsmakers@stud.let.ruu.nl`

Purpose: A fiction-only on-line magazine. It's published quarterly and is
available only in ASCII. Fiction featured in it is primarily fantasy, science
fiction, and (hopefully) humor. Subscriptions may be acquired by sending
mail. Writers welcome, as long as they don't like carnivorous plants.

Twins
Contact: `owner-twins@athena.mit.edu`

Purpose: Even though the term "twins" is used, it is meant to represent
twins, triplets, etc. The purpose of this mailing list is to provide an open
forum for the discussion of issues related to twins. This might include
research on twin-related issues, parenting issues, and issues concerning
adult twins.

To join, send mail to `owner-twins@athena.mit.edu`, with `Twins
Subscription` on the subject line, and a brief note asking to be added to
(or deleted from) the list.

Two-Strokes

Contact: `2strokes-request@microunity.com`

Purpose: For the discussion of two-stroke motorcycle technology, maintenance, and riding. It is primarily oriented toward street and road-racing two-strokes, but discussion about two-stroke dirt bikes is fine.

TX-Firearms

Contact: `tx-firearms-request@frontier.lonestar.org`

Purpose: To keep interested parties aware of Texas firearms laws, hunting seasons, and regulations, pending legislation, group meetings, competition schedules—basically anything related to firearms in the State of Texas. The list is not moderated and is available to anyone.

UK-DANCE

Contact: `listserv@orbital.demon.co.uk`

Purpose: For discussion about all aspects of dance music culture in the U.K.: clubs, raves, record shops, radio, records, and anything else to do with the underground dance music scene.

To subscribe to the list, write to `listserv@orbital.demon.co.uk` with `subscribe uk-dance` *yourfullname* as the first line in the message body, replacing *yourfullname* with your real name, not your e-mail address.

UK-Hockey

Contact: `uk-hockey-request@cee.hw.ac.uk` (Steve Salvini)

Purpose: This is an open invitation to followers of hockey in the U.K. to join a mailing list dedicated to the discussion of (ice!) hockey in Britain. At present, we are mailing out news, gossip, league tables, match reports, and results on a fairly regular basis.

UK-MOTSS

Contact: `uk-motss-request@pyra.co.uk` (Internet)

   `uk-motss-request@uk.co.pyra` (JANet)

   `uk-motss-request%pyrltd.uknet` (Brain-dead JANet mailers)

V

Resource Reference

Purpose: For gay people in the U.K., or those who are interested in the U.K. gay scene/politics. It is a supportive environment for those unwilling or unable to read the `soc.motss` news group, and confidentiality is assured. Anonymous posting is available.

UltraLite-List
Contact: `listserv@grot.starconn.com`

Purpose: Discussion forum for users or potential users of the original NEC UltraLite PC1701 and PC1702 computers (the V30-based notebook computer with a 1M or 2M silicon hard disk, not the newer 80X86-based models). Topics include general information, tips, techniques, applications, experiences, and sources for hardware, software, accessories, and information.

To subscribe, send a message to `listserv@grot.starconn.com` with the following commands in the body of the message:

```
subscribe ultralite-list yourfirstname yourlastname
quit
```

Replace *yourfirstname yourlastname* with your name, not your e-mail address.

Administrative messages other than subscription and unsubscription may be sent to `ultralite-list-owner@grot.starconn.com`.

Undercover
Contact: `undercover-request@snowhite.cis.uoguelph.ca` (Steve Portigal)

Purpose: An unmoderated mailing list for the discussion of the Rolling Stones. Discussion topics may include bootleg trading; how-to guitar-playing advice; information about recent books, such as Wyman's *Stone Alone* and others; perspectives on recent solo albums by Watts, Richards, and Wood; and the upcoming album by Jagger (and the rarely released "Stuff" by Wyman).

To be added to (or removed from) the list, send mail to `undercover-request@snowhite.cis.uoguelph.ca`. Note that this is a human (me), so requests like `SUB LIST JOHN@TOADY` are kind of annoying. Please include your e-mail address in the message. If you don't get any messages, please get back in touch because I will drop bouncing addresses from the list.

This list (Rolling Stones discussion) is now a digest.

Unisys

Contact: `unisys-request@bcm.tmc.edu` (Richard H. Miller)

Purpose: Discussion of all Unisys products and equipment.

Univel

Contact: `univel-request@telly.on.ca`

Purpose: To provide a forum for users, developers, and others interested in the products of Univel, the Novell subsidiary that produces UNIX system software for PC-architecture systems. This list is gatewayed to/from the news group `biz.univel.misc`.

To subscribe, send mail to `univel-request@telly.on.ca` with a message body of this form:

```
subscribe univel yourfullname
```

UPS-Alumni

Contact: `ups_alumni-request@stephsf.com` (Bill England)

Purpose: Ostensibly for the purpose of linking graduates of the University of Puget Sound. This list will also help those interested keep abreast of current events and changes at the university. Commercial postings are prohibited.

Uruguay

Contact: `uruguay-request@eniac.seas.upenn.edu` (Raul Polakof)

Purpose: A mailing list for general discussions and information. To subscribe, please send name, e-mail, topics of interest, and (optionally) address and phone number. Spanish is the dominant language in this group.

Usenet-Oracle

Contact: `oracle-admin@cs.indiana.edu` (Steve Kinzler)

Purpose: An active, cooperative effort for creative humor. The Usenet Oracle answers any questions posed to it. Send mail to `oracle@cs.indiana.edu` with the word `help` in the subject line for complete details on how to participate.

A distribution list is available for receiving compilations of the best Usenet Oracle answers (the Usenet Oracularities, also posted to `rec.humor.oracle`).

V

Resource Reference

> **Note**
>
> This is wholly unrelated to the Oracle database software or company.

Utne-Salon-List

Contact: `utne-salon-request@netcom.com` (Bill Sheppard)

Purpose: Discussion relating to the Utne Reader Neighborhoood Salon Association, a group facilitating community discussion groups around the country where interested citizens can meet with other neighbors and community members to discuss any topics of interest, be they deeply philosophical or trivially important.

UUG-Dist

Contact: `uug-dist-request@dsi.com` (Syd Weinstein)

Purpose: Discussion of Unify Corporations Database products, including Unify, Accell/IDS, Accell/SQl, and Accell/"generic database engine."

UUs-L

Contact: `uus-l@info.terraluna.org` (Automated Info Server)

`uus-lman@terraluna.org` (Steve Traugott)

Purpose: A global meeting place for Unitarian Universalists and anyone going our way. The list's intent is to provide a forum for sharing of UU-related information across district and regional boundaries, to bring into contact people and ideas who normally would never have met, and to foster discussion of functional and structural innovations that we can make in our organizations and world.

To subscribe to UUs-L, send the following in the body of a message to `listserv@ubvm.cc.buffalo.edu`:

`SUBSCRIBE UUs-L` *yourfullname*

Vampire

Contact: `vampire-request@math.ufl.edu`

Purpose: A mailing list dedicated to the White Wolf role-playing game, Vampire.

Those who may be interested in the subject but are not familiar with the game itself are also invited to join. To subscribe, send `sub vampire` as the first line of a message to `vampire-request@math.ufl.edu`.

VEGGIE

Contact: `listserv@gibbs.oit.unc.edu`

Purpose: If you are interested in vegetarianism, veganism, fruitarianism, macrobiotics, whole/natural foods, health/fitness, cooking, etc., this new mailing list may be for you. (We are a "dissident" spin-off of Granola, another vegetarian mailing list.) Our list is called VEGGIE to be inclusive of vegans, fruitarians, lacto-, ovo-, ovo-lacto-vegetarians, vegetable-lovers, those simply interested in vegetarianism or veggie recipes, etc. You do not have to be a vegetarian to join.

Articles, recipes, discussions, your thoughts, etc., on vegetarianism or veganism are warmly welcomed. Flames are not.

Here's how to join—it's so easy! Send a message to `listserv@gibbs.oit.unc.edu` with this line:

```
SUB VEGGIE yourfirstname yourlastname
```

That's all!

For more information about VEGGIE (why we began an alternative to Granola, or anything else), feel free to contact any of the following people:

Penny Ward (`crunchy@gibbs.oit.unc.edu`)

Michael Blackmore (`michaelb@ksgrsch.harvard.edu`)

Johnn Tan (`atan@cc.weber.edu`)

Vettes

Contact: `vettes-request@compaq.com`

Purpose: For Corvette owners and enthusiasts to share their ideas and experiences about their cars.

V

Resource Reference

Vintage
Contact: `vintage-request@presto.ig.com`

Purpose: Vintage clothing and costume jewelry.

Vision
Contact: `pruss@math.ubc.ca`

Purpose: To discuss, in a charitable and Christian context, visions, prophecies, and spiritual gifts; to discuss any visions, dreams, and other manifestations that people may have received, to seek their significance in the spirit of truth. Non-Christians are invited, though it should be noted that the moderator may well not post any postings that are offensive. Postings may be done anonymously upon request, and efforts will be taken in the future to ensure anonymity in the membership.

Vizantija
Contact: `dimitrije@buenga.bu.edu` (Dimitrije Stamenovic)

Purpose: To distribute news and provide a forum for discussions about the current events in the former Yugoslavia, centered around those involving or affecting Serbs. Also, they originate public actions related to these events.

VMEbus
Contact: `att!houxl!mlh` (Marc Harrison)

Purpose: A users' group for the AT&T VMEbus products to provide a two-way USENET conduit for the open exchange of information, both within and outside of AT&T. There's very little data that's proprietary about the products (other than the source code for UNIX System V/VME), so the list is open to suggestions as to items of interest.

If you're interested, please send your name, e-mail path (via att preferred), affiliation, and use of WE 321SB (if you have one). Suggestions for items of interest are also encouraged.

Volvo
Contact: `swedishbricks-request@me.rochester.edu` (Tim Takahashi)

Purpose: A meeting place for Volvo automotive enthusiasts around the world. It is an open forum for discussion of Volvo-related topics, such as, but not limited to, ownership, maintenance, repairs, mechanics, fix-it yourself, competition driving, and preparation.

Vreme

Contact: `dimitrije@buenga.bu.edu` (Dimitrije Stamenovic)

Purpose: Carries *Vreme* and VND (selected articles from *Vreme* translated into English). Since the fall of 1989, *Vreme* has been the major independent newspaper in Yugoslavia and neighboring countries. It is published weekly on Monday, and the electronic mail edition of VND is usually available on the same day. Please keep in mind that due to the situation in the country, the distribution of VND is not always smooth. Further, VND is published by a professional news agency, which makes this material available to us by a special agreement. The proper credit to VND should be given whenever this material is cited or used in any way.

Vreme News Digest

Contact: `dimitrije@buenga.bu.edu` (Dimitrije Stamenovic)

Purpose: Vreme News Digest (VND) is an English-language newsletter published by the Vreme News Digest Agency (VNDA) from Belgrade.

WAIS-Discussion

Contact: `wais-discussion-request@think.com`

Purpose: WAIS stands for Wide Area Information Servers, an electronic publishing project lead by Thinking Machines.

The WAIS-discussion is a digested, moderated list on electronic publishing issues in general and Wide Area Information Servers in particular. There are postings every week or two.

WAIS-Talk

Contact: `wais-talk-request@think.com`

Purpose: WAIS stands for Wide Area Information Servers, an electronic publishing project lead by Thinking Machines.

WAIS-talk is an open list (interactive, not moderated) for implementors and developers. This is a techie list that is not meant as a support list. Please use the `alt.wais` news group for support, and send bug fixes and the like to `bug-wais@think.com`.

Walkers-in-Darkness
Contact: `walkers-request@world.std.com` (David Harmon)

Purpose: For sufferers from depression and/or bipolar disorder, and affected friends. This includes both "novices" and those who have learned to cope.

Warhammer
Contact: `wfrp-request@morticia.cnns.unt.edu`

Purpose: For the discussion of Games Workshop's Warhammer Universe, the Old World, Warhammer Fantasy Role Play, and Warhammer Fantasy Battle.

The Warhammer mailing list is running ListMan 1.0b List Manager software. To subscribe, send e-mail to the above request address and as the first word on the subject line or any line in the text of the message put the word `sub`. You may also include a parameter with the `sub` command. This parameter will be treated as your real name, not your address (which is determined from your mail headers). You may also send wfrp-request other commands, not the least of which is `help`.

Waterski
Contact: `waterski-request@nda.com`

Purpose: Discussion topics open to anything of interest to water-skiers, from absolute beginners to competitors. This includes any activity that involves being pulled behind a boat, such as barefooting, kneeboarding, wakeboarding, and even tubing. Discussion of boats, equipment, techniques, safety, courtesy, rules of competition, tournament results, site negotiation, and club organization are encouraged.

Weather-Users
Contact: `weather-users-request@zorch.sf-bay.org`

Purpose: Updates from the maintainer of the Weather Underground at the University of Michigan, exchange of programming hints and tips among weather client developers, and related discussion.

Weights
Contact: `weights-request@mickey.disney.com` (Michael Sullivan)

Purpose: The discussion of all aspects of using weights in exercise. Includes body-building (competitive and non-competitive), sport-related weight training, "stay in shape" weight training; basically anything to do with lifting weights.

Wetleather

Contact: `wetleather-request@frigg.isc-br.com` (automated LISTSERV)

`carlp@mail.isc-br.com` (Carl Paukstis)

Purpose: For discussion, chatter, ride reports, socializing, and announcements of upcoming motorcycle events in the Greater Pacific Northwest. The definition of that geographic term is flexible, but is generally taken to include the Cascadia subduction zone and all areas within a one-day ride from it, which naturally includes southwestern Canada. Anyone is free to subscribe, and topic limitations are not enforced. The list is not moderated, but is intended for socialization among the area riders—not to supplant `rec.motorcycles`.

Automated subscription information: send a single-line mail message to `wetleather-request@frigg.isc-br.com` consisting only of `subscribe WETLEATHER` *yourfullname*.

Wheel-to-Wheel

Contact: `wheeltowheel-request@abingdon.Eng.Sun.COM` (Andy Banta)

Purpose: For people interested in participation in auto racing as driver, worker, or crew. People interested in all types of wheel-to-wheel racing are welcome, but the majority of the discussion centers on road courses.

Whitewater

Contact: `whitewater-request@gynko.circ.upenn.edu`

Purpose: To discuss whitewater sports, experiences, and information. Includes kayak and canoeing enthusiasts. Please note that this mailing list is partially bidirectionally gatewayed to the USENET group `rec.boats.paddle`. Whitewater-specific postings are culled and sent to the mailing list, and mailing list traffic is sent to the news group. This mailing list is moderated and is probably only useful to those who do not receive `rec.boats.paddle`, or are only interested in the whitewater traffic in that group.

Tip
We're running LISTSERV 5.5, and `wetleather-request` is just aliased to `listserv`, so those familiar with LISTSERV services may use any of the usual commands. Both reflected and digest subscription modes are available, along with a small set of archive files.

V

Resource Reference

Wildnet

Contact: `zaphod!pnwc!wildnet-request@access.usask.ca`

   `wildnet-request@access.usask.ca` (Eric Woodsworth)

Purpose: Concerned with computing and statistics in fisheries and wildlife biology. Relevant topics include G.I.S., ecological modeling, software, etc.

Windsurfing

Contact: `windsurfing-request@gcm.com`

   `...uunet!gcm!windsurfing-request`

Purpose: To provide a discussion forum for boardsailing enthusiasts all over the world. While non-windsurfers are welcome to join, the primary purpose is to enhance the enjoyment of our sport by discussing windsurfing-related topics such as equipment, technique, sailing spots, weather, competition, etc. We welcome you to join and share your windsurfing experiences and thoughts. The list is unmoderated.

WITSENDO

Contact: `listserv@dartcms1.dartmouth.edu`

Purpose: A moderated mailing list that discusses all aspects of endometriosis, with particular emphasis on coping with the disease and its treatment. Anyone with an interest in this disease is welcome to participate, whether or not they actually suffer from the disease. The list will act as a clearinghouse for information exchange and to promote discussion of current treatments, research, and educational literature. Professional (medical) comments are, of course, most welcome. However, the list is primarily dedicated to the women who suffer from this painful and often demoralizing disease; therefore, any information should be expressed in lay terms and attempt to exclude professional jargon (or at the very least provide adequate references and/or definitions of terms).

To subscribe to the list, send mail to `listserv@dartcms1.bitnet` or `listserv@dartcms1.dartmouth.edu` with the body of the mail (*not* subject) containing the following command:

   `SUB WITSENDO `*`yourfullname`*

Owner: David Avery (`david.avery@dartmouth.edu`)

Word-Mac

Contact: word–mac–request@alsvid.une.edu.au (Roger Debreceny)

Purpose: To serve users of the Microsoft Word package in its various versions on the Apple Macintosh platform. The list is available in digest form, and archives of all digests are available by anonymous ftp from / pub/archives/word–mac/digests on alsvid.une.edu.au. Gopher access is also available by pointing your Gopher to alsvid.une.edu.au (port 70).

To subscribe, mail to listserv@alsvid.une.edu.au with the text subscribe word–mac *yourfirstname yourlastname* in the body of the e-mail.

Wxsat

Contact: wxsat–request@ssg.com (Richard B. Emerson)

Purpose: Two functions: The primary function is the distribution of NOAA status and prediction bulletins for the GOES and polar weather satellites. This data is the same data available via SCIENCEnet NOAA.SAT bulletin board area. The mail list also acts as a reflector for subscribers' comments and discussion of matters related to weather satellites, ground stations, and associated topics.

X-Ada

Contact: x–ada–request@expo.lcs.mit.edu

Purpose: To discuss the interfaces and bindings for an Ada interface to the X Windows system.

XGKS

Contact: xgks–request@unidata.ucar.edu (Steve Emmerson)

Purpose: A mailing-list for the maintenance, enhancement, and evolution of the XGKS package, created by the University of Illinois under contract with IBM and distributed as part of X11R4. The XGKS package is a full 2C GKS implementation and allows GKS applications to operate in an X Windows system environment.

V

Resource Reference

XOPEN-Testing

Contact: xopen–testing–request@uel.co.uk (Andrew Josey)

Purpose: A forum for discussion of issues related to testing operating systems for conformance to the X/OPEN Portability Guide (XPG), including Issue 3 (XPG3) and later.

The scope of this newsletter is the discussion of items associated with the testing of the X/Open Portability Guide—including, but not limited to, test suite technology (X/Open's VSX and other third-party test suites for the XPG), latest news on X/Open Branding, and other related issues. These issues can include problems related to test suites in general, testability of various features of the XPG, and portability of the test suites.

XPress-List

Contact: listserv@grot.starconn.com

Purpose: Discussion of the X*Press X*Change data service, which is available on some cable television systems in the U.S. and Canada and on some satellite television channels.

To subscribe to the xpress-list, send mail to listserv@grot.starconn.com with the following commands in the body of the message:

```
subscribe xpress-list yourfirstname yourlastname
quit
```

Replace *yourfirstname yourlastname* with your name, not your e-mail address.

Administrative messages other than subscription and unsubscription should be sent to xpress–list–owner@grot.starconn.com.

XVT

Contact: tim@qedbbs.com (Tim Capps)

Purpose: XVT is a multiplatform window environment development tool. Interested parties should send mail with HELP XVTDEV as the body of the letter to listserv@qedbbs.com.

Yello

Contact: yello–request@overpass.calpoly.edu (Cliff Tuel)

Purpose: A forum for discussing anything about the group Yello, or any solo works by the band's members. An extensive discography is available, as are several other files of interest.

Y-RIGHTS

Contact: `listserv@sjuvm.bitnet`

Purpose: Discussion group on the rights of kids and teens. Broad spectrum of discussion topics, with individual liberty being one of the main focuses. Open to kids, teens, young adults, adults, senior citizens, teachers, students, grade schools, middle schools, high schools, colleges, and university networks, gatewaying to other networks.

Digest/notebook version available, as well as past discussions. E-mail to `listserv@sjuvm.bitnet`, using the following commands as needed:

- To subscribe to the list, use SUB Y-RIGHTS *yourfirstname yourlastname*.

- To receive the weekly digest of the list, use AFD Y–RIGHTS DIGEST.

- To receive a list of previous discussion logs, use GET Y–RIGHTS FILELIST.

List owner: Kenneth Udut (`kudut@hamp.hampshire.edu`)

YSN

Contact: `ysn–adm@zoyd.ee.washington.edu` (John Sahr)

Purpose: Activism on employment issues for scientists just beginning their careers. The Young Scientists' Network attempts to inform the press, the public, and government officials that there is no shortage of scientists; we hope to find traditional and non-traditional employment for scientists. Stories about the Young Scientists' Network have appeared in *Science*, in *Physics Today*, and on National Public Radio; we've met with officials from the National Science Foundation and other agencies.

Zang Tuum Tumb

Contact: `ztt–request@asylum.sf.ca.us` (Lazlo Nibble)

Purpose: Discussion of artists, releases, and other issues related to Trevor Horn's U.K. record label Zang Tuum Tumb. (Frankie Goes to Hollywood, Art of Noise, Propaganda, 808 State, Seal, and others.) Moderator maintains a complete discography. ftp archives available on `asylum`.

V

Resource Reference

Z-Cars
Contact: `z-car-request@dixie.com` (John De Armond)

Purpose: For those interested in Datsun/Nissan Z cars. The interest base is primarily for the original Z, though all discussion regarding the Z line of cars is welcome.

Zeppelin
Contact: `zeppelin-l@cornell.edu`

Purpose: For fans of the rock group Led Zeppelin. For further information about this list, send e-mail to `listserv@cornell.edu` with `info zeppelin-l` as the body of the message.

ZForum
Contact: `zforum-request@comlab.ox.ac.uk` (Jonathan Bowen)

Purpose: To handle messages concerned with the formal specification notation Z. Based on set theory and first order predicate logic, Z has been developed at the Programming Research Group (PRG) at Oxford University for well over a decade. It is now used by industry as part of the software (and hardware) development process in both the U.K. and the U.S. It is currently undergoing standardization. ZForum provides a convenient forum for messages and queries concerned with recent developments and the use of Z. ZForum is gatewayed to the USENET news group `comp.specification.z`.

Zoomer-List
Contact: `listserv@grot.starconn.com` (Brian Smithson)

Purpose: Discussion forum for users or potential users of the Zoomer personal digital assistant products from Casio, Tandy, and others. Topics include general information, tips, techniques, applications, experiences, and sources for hardware, software, accessories, and information. To subscribe, send mail to the LISTSERV address with the following commands in the message body:

```
subscribe zoomer-list yourfirstname yourlastname
quit
```

Chapter 21

Indexes to RFC, FYI, and STD Documents

This chapter contains complete indexes to the RFC, FYI, and STD series of documents, current as of the time this book was published. All three indexes were obtained through anonymous ftp to host `ftp.nisc.sri.com` and were located in directory `/rfc`. See Chapter 4, "Finding and Using Internet Resources," for a thorough description of these document series.

> **Note**
>
> Keep in mind that the network is changing. If this site becomes un-available to you or is no longer a repository for these files, try one of the other sites given in Chapter 4.

RFC Index

Original Source: File `/rfc/rfc-index.txt` on host `ftp.nisc.sri.com`

```
                    RFC INDEX
                    ---------

This file contains citations for all RFCs in reverse numeric order.  RFC
citations appear in this format:

####   Title of RFC.  Author 1.; Author 2.; Author 3.   Issue date;
       ## p.  (Format: PS=xxx TXT=zzz bytes)  (Also FYI ##)
       (Obsoletes xxx; Obsoleted by xxx; Updates xxx; Updated by xxx)
```

Key to citations:

> #### is the RFC number; ## p. is the total number of pages.

> The format and byte information follows the page information in
> parenthesis. The format, either ASCII text (TXT) or PostScript
> (PS) or both, is noted, followed by an equals sign and the number
> of bytes for that version. (PostScript is a registered trademark
> of Adobe Systems Incorporated.) The example (Format: PS=xxx
> TXT=zzz bytes) shows that the PostScript version of the RFC
> is xxx bytes and the ASCII text version is zzz bytes.

> The (Also FYI ##) phrase gives the equivalent FYI number if
> the RFC was also issued as an FYI document.

> "Obsoletes xxx" refers to other RFCs that this one replaces;
> "Obsoleted by xxx" refers to RFCs that have replaced this one.
> "Updates xxx" refers to other RFCs that this one merely updates
> (but does not replace); "Updated by xxx" refers to RFCs that have
> been updated by this one (but not replaced). Only immediately
> succeeding and/or preceding RFCs are indicated, not the entire
> history of each related earlier or later RFC in a related series.

For example:

1129   Internet time synchronization: The Network Time
        Protocol. Mills, D.L. 1989 October; 29 p.
        (Format: PS=551697 bytes)

Many RFCs are available online; if not, this is indicated by (Not
online). Paper copies of all RFCs are available from SRI, either
individually or on a subscription basis (for more information contact
nisc@nisc.sri.com or call 1-415-859-6387). Online copies are
available via FTP from ftp.nisc.sri.com as rfc/rfc####.txt or
rfc/rfc####.ps (#### is the RFC number without leading zeroes).

Additionally, RFCs may be requested through electronic mail from SRI's
automated mail server by sending a message to mail-server@nisc.sri.com.
In the body of the message, indicate the RFC to be sent, e.g. "send rfcNNNN"
where NNNN is the number of the RFC. For PostScript RFCs, specify
the extension, e.g. "send rfcNNNN.ps". Multiple requests can be sent
in a single message by specifying each request on a separate line.
The RFC Index can be requested by typing "send rfc-index".

RFC INDEX

1500   Internet Official Protocol Standards. Postel, J.,ed. 1993 August; 36 p.
       (Format: TXT=79558 bytes) (Obsoletes RFC 1410, RFC 1360, RFC 1280, RFC
       1250, RFC 1100, RFC 1083, RFC 1130, RFC 1140, RFC 1200)

1499   Not yet issued.

1498   On the Naming and Binding of Network Destinations. Saltzer, J. 1993
       August; 10 p. (Format: TXT=24698 bytes)

1497 BOOTP Vendor Information Extensions. Reynolds, J.K. 1993 August; 8 p.
      (Format: TXT=16805 bytes) (Obsoletes RFC 1395, RFC 1084, RFC 1048;
      Updates RFC 951)

1496 Rules for Downgrading Messages from X.400/88 to X.400/84 When MIME
      Content-Types are Present in the Messages. Alvestrand, H.; Romaguera,
      J.; Jordan, K. 1993 August; 5 p. (Format: TXT=8411 bytes) (Updates RFC
      1328)

1495 Mapping between X.400 and RFC-822 Message Bodies. Alvestrand, H.; Kille,
      S.; Miles, R.; Rose, M.T.; Thompson, S. 1993 August; 11 p. (Format:
      TXT=20071 bytes) (Updates RFC 1327)

1494 Equivalences between 1988 X.400 and RFC-822 Message Bodies. Alvestrand,
      H.; Thompson, S. 1993 August; 19 p. (Format: TXT=37275 bytes)

1493 Definitions of Managed Objects for Bridges. Decker, E.; Langille, P.;
      Rijsinghani, A.; McCloghrie, K. 1993 July; 34 p. (Format: TXT=74493
      bytes) (Obsoletes RFC 1286)

1492 An Access Control Protocol, Sometimes Called TACACS. Finseth, C. 1993
      July; 21 p. (Format: TXT=41880 bytes)

1491 A Survey of Advanced Usages of X.500. Weider, C.; Wright, R. 1993 July;
      18 p. (Format: TXT=34883 bytes) (Also FYI 21)

1490 Multiprotocol Interconnect over Frame Relay. Bradley, T.; Brown, C.;
      Malis, A. 1993 July; 35 p. (Format: TXT=75206 bytes) (Obsoletes RFC
      1294)

1489 Registration of a Cyrillic Character Set. Chernov, A. 1993 July; 5 p.
      (Format: TXT=10495 bytes)

1488 The X.500 String Representation of Standard Attribute Syntaxes. Howes,
      T.; Kille, S.; Yeong, W.; Robbins, C. 1993 July; 11 p. (Format:
      TXT=17185 bytes)

1487 X.500 Lightweight Directory Access Protocol. Yeong, W.; Howes, T.;
      Kille, S. 1993 July; 21 p. (Format: TXT=10495 bytes)

1486 An Experiment in Remote Printing. Rose, M.T.; Malmud, C. 1993 July;
      12 p. (Format: TXT=26373 bytes)

1485 A String Representation of Distinguished Names (OSI-DS 23 (v5)).
      Hardcastle-Kille, S. 1993 July; 7 p. (Format: TXT=11158 bytes)

1484 Using the OSI Directory to achieve User Friendly Naming (OSI-DS 24
      (v1.2)). Hardcastle-Kille, S. 1993 July; 25 p. (Format: TXT=48973
      bytes)

1483 Multiprotocol Encapsulation over ATM Adaptation Layer 5. Heinanen, J.
      1993 July; 16 p. (Format: TXT=35192 bytes)

1482 Aggregation Support in the NSFNET Policy-Based Routing Database.
      Knopper, M.; Richardson, S.J. 1993 June; 11 p. (Format: TXT=25330
      bytes)

1481   IAB Recommendation for an Intermediate Strategy to Address the Issue of Scaling. Huitema, C.   1993 July; 2 p. (Format: TXT=3502 bytes)

1480   The US Domain. Cooper, A.; Postel, J.   1993 June; 47 p. (Format: TXT=100556 bytes)

1479   Inter-Domain Policy Routing Protocol Specification: Version 1. Steenstrup, M.   1993 July; 108 p. (Format: TXT=275823 bytes)

1478   An Architecture for Inter-Domain Policy Routing. Steenstrup, M.   1993 June; 35 p. (Format: TXT=90673 bytes)

1477   IDPR as a Proposed Standard. Steenstrup, M.   1993 July; 13 p. (Format: TXT=32238 bytes)

1476   RAP: Internet Route Access Protocol. Ullmann, R.   1993 June; 20 p. (Format: TXT=45560 bytes)

1475   TP/IX: The Next Internet. Ullmann, R.   1993 June; 35 p. (Format: TXT=77854 bytes)

1474   The Definitions of Managed Objects for the Bridge Network Control Protocol of the Point-to-Point Protocol. Kastenholz, F.   1993 June; 15 p. (Format: TXT=31846 bytes)

1473   The Definitions of Managed Objects for the IP Network Control Protocol of the Point-to-Point Protocol. Kastenholz, F.   1993 June; 9 p. (Format: TXT=20484 bytes)

1472   The Definitions of Managed Objects for the Security Protocols of the Point-to-Point Protocol. Kastenholz, F.   1993 June; 12 p. (Format: TXT=27152 bytes)

1471   The Definitions of Managed Objects for the Link Control Protocol of the Point-to-Point Protocol. Kastenholz, F.   1993 June; 25 p. (Format: TXT=53558 bytes)

1470   FYI on a Network Management Tool Catalog: Tools for Monitoring and Debugging TCP/IP Internets and Interconnected Devices. Enger, R.; Reynolds, J.K.,eds.   1993 June; 192 p. (Format: TXT=308528 bytes) (Also FYI 2)   (Obsoletes RFC 1147)

1469   IP Multicast over Token-Ring Local Area Networks. Pusateri, T.   1993 June; 4 p. (Format: TXT=8189 bytes)

1468   Japanese Character Encoding for Internet Messages. Murai, J.; Crispin, M.; van der Poel, E.   1993 June; 6 p. (Format: TXT=10970 bytes)

1467   Status of CIDR Deployment in the Internet. Topolcic, C.   1993 August; 9 p. (Format: TXT=20720 bytes)   (Obsoletes RFC 1367)

1466   Guidelines for Management of IP Address Space. Gerich, E.   1993 May; 10 p. (Format: TXT=22262 bytes)   (Obsoletes RFC 1366)

1465   Routing Coordination for X.400 MHS Services Within a Multi Protocol / Multi Network Environment Table Format V3 for Static Routing. Eppenberger, D.   1993 May; 31 p. (Format: TXT=66833 bytes)

1464 Using the Domain Name System To Store Arbitrary String Attributes. Rosenbaum, R. 1993 May; 4 p. (Format: TXT=7953 bytes)

1463 FYI on Introducing the Internet -- A Short Bibliography of Introductory Internetworking Readings for the Network Novice. Hoffman, E.; Jackson, L. 1993 May; 4 p. (Format: TXT=7116 bytes) (Also FYI 19)

1462 FYI on "What is the Internet?". Krol, E.; Hoffman, E. 1993 May; 11 p. (Format: TXT=27811 bytes) (Also FYI 20)

1461 SNMP MIB extension for Multiprotocol Interconnect over X.25. Throop, D. 1993 May; 21 p. (Format: TXT=47945 bytes)

1460 Post Office Protocol - Version 3. Rose, M.T. 1993 May; 17 p. (Format: TXT=38827 bytes)   (Obsoletes RFC 1081, RFC 1225)

1459 Internet Relay Chat Protocol. Oikarinen, J.; Reed, D. 1993 May; 65 p. (Format: TXT=138964 bytes)

1458 Requirements for Multicast Protocols. Braudes, R.; Zabele, S. 1993 May; 19 p. (Format: TXT=48106 bytes)

1457 Security Label Framework for the Internet. Housley, R. 1993 May; 14 p. (Format: TXT=35802 bytes)

1456 Conventions for Encoding the Vietnamese Language; VISCII: VIetnamese Standard Code for Information Interchange; VIQR: VIetnamese Quoted-Readable Specification; Revision 1.1. Nguyen, C.T.; Ngo, H.D.; Bui, C.M.; Nguyen, T.V. 1993 May; 7 p. (Format: TXT=14732 bytes)

1455 Physical Link Security Type of Service. Eastlake, D. 1993 May; 6 p. (Format: TXT=12391 bytes)

1454 Comparison of Proposals for Next Version of IP. Dixon, T. 1993 May; 15 p. (Format: TXT=35046 bytes)

1453 Comment on packet video conferencing and the transport/network layers. Chimiak, W.J. 1993 April; 10 p. (Format: TXT=23563 bytes)

1452 Coexistence between version 1 and version 2 of the Internet-standard Network Management Framework. Case, J.D.; McCloghrie, K.; Rose, M.T.; Waldbusser, S. 1993 April; 17 p. (Format: TXT=32176 bytes)

1451 Manager-to-Manager Management Information Base. Case, J.D.; McCloghrie, K.; Rose, M.T.; Waldbusser, S. 1993 April; 36 p. (Format: TXT=62935 bytes)

1450 Management Information Base for version 2 of the Simple Network Management Protocol (SNMPv2). Case, J.D.; McCloghrie, K.; Rose, M.T.; Waldbusser, S. 1993 April; 27 p. (Format: TXT=42172 bytes)

1449 Transport Mappings for version 2 of the Simple Network Management Protocol (SNMPv2). Case, J.D.; McCloghrie, K.; Rose, M.T.; Waldbusser, S. 1993 April; 25 p. (Format: TXT=41161 bytes)

1448 Protocol Operations for version 2 of the Simple Network Management Protocol (SNMPv2). Case, J.D.; McCloghrie, K.; Rose, M.T.; Waldbusser, S. 1993 April; 36 p. (Format: TXT=74224 bytes)

V

Resource Reference

1447 Party MIB for version 2 of the Simple Network Management Protocol (SNMPv2). McCloghrie, K.; Galvin, J.M. 1993 April; 50 p. (Format: TXT=80762 bytes)

1446 Security Protocols for version 2 of the Simple Network Management Protocol (SNMPv2). Galvin, J.M.; McCloghrie, K. 1993 April; 52 p. (Format: TXT=108733 bytes)

1445 Administrative Model for version 2 of the Simple Network Management Protocol (SNMPv2). Galvin, J.M.; McCloghrie, K. 1993 April; 47 p. (Format: TXT=99443 bytes)

1444 Conformance Statements for version 2 of the Simple Network Management Protocol (SNMPv2). Case, J.D.; McCloghrie, K.; Rose, M.T.; Waldbusser, S. 1993 April; 33 p. (Format: TXT=57744 bytes)

1443 Textual Conventions for version 2 of the Simple Network Management Protocol (SNMPv2). Case, J.D.; McCloghrie, K.; Rose, M.T.; Waldbusser, S. 1993 April; 31 p. (Format: TXT=60947 bytes)

1442 Structure of Management Information for version 2 of the Simple Network Management Protocol (SNMPv2). Case, J.D.; McCloghrie, K.; Rose, M.T.; Waldbusser, S. 1993 April; 54 p. (Format: TXT=95779 bytes)

1441 SMTP Introduction to version 2 of the Internet-standard Network Management Framework. Case, J.D.; McCloghrie, K.; Rose, M.T.; Waldbusser, S. 1993 April; 13 p. (Format: TXT=25386 bytes)

1440 SIFT/UFT: Sender-Initiated/Unsolicited File Transfer. Troth, R. 1993 July; 9 p. (Format: TXT=17366 bytes)

1439 Uniqueness of unique identifiers. Finseth, C. 1993 March; 11 p. (Format: TXT=20477 bytes)

1438 Internet Engineering Task Force Statements of Boredom (SOBs). Chapin, A.L.; Huitema, C. 1993 April 1; 2 p. (Format: TXT=3044 bytes)

1437 Extension of MIME content-types to a new medium. Borenstein, N.; Linimon, M. 1993 April 1; 6 p. (Format: TXT=13356 bytes)

1436 Internet Gopher Protocol (a distributed document search and retrieval protocol). Anklesaria, F.; McCahill, M.; Linder, P.; Johnson, D.; Torrey, D.; Alberti, B. 1993 March; 16 p. (Format: TXT=36493 bytes)

1435 IESG advice from experience with Path MTU Discovery. Knowles, S. 1993 March; 2 p. (Format: TXT=2708 bytes)

1434 Data Link Switching: Switch-to-Switch Protocol. Dixon, R.C.; Kushi, D.M. 1993 March; 33 p. (Format: TXT=80182 bytes)

1433 Directed ARP. Garrett, J.; Hagan, J.D.; Wong, J.A. 1993 March; 18 p. (Format: TXT=41028 bytes)

1432 Recent Internet books. Quarterman, J. 1993 March; 15 p. (Format: TXT=27089 bytes)

1431 DUA metrics. Barker, P. 1993 February; 19 p. (Format: TXT=42240 bytes)

1430 Strategic plan for deploying an Internet X.500 directory service. Hardcastle-Kille, S.; Huizer, E.; Cerf, V.; Hobby, R.; Kent, S. 1993 February; 20 p. (Format: TXT=47887 bytes)

1429 Listserv Distribute Protocol. Thomas, E. 1993 February; 8 p. (Format: TXT=17759 bytes)

1428 Transition of Internet Mail from Just-Send-8 to 8bit-SMTP/MIME. Vaudreuil, G.M. 1993 February; 6 p. (Format: TXT=12064 bytes)

1427 SMTP Service Extension for Message Size Declaration. Klensin, J.; Freed, N.; Moore, K. 1993 February; 8 p. (Format: TXT=17856 bytes)

1426 SMTP Service Extension for 8bit-MIME Transport. Klensin, J.; Freed, N.; Rose, M.T.; Stefferud, E.A.; Crocker, D. 1993 February; 6 p. (Format: TXT=11661 bytes)

1425 SMTP Service Extension. Klensin, J.; Freed, N.; Rose, M.T.; Stefferud, E.A.; Crocker, D. 1993 February; 10 p. (Format: TXT=20932 bytes)

1424 Privacy Enhancement for Internet Electronic Mail: Part IV: Key Certification and Related Services. Kaliski, B.S. 1993 February; 9 p. (Format: TXT=17537 bytes)

1423 Privacy Enhancement for Internet Electronic Mail: Part III: Algorithms, Modes, and Identifiers. Balenson, D. 1993 February; 14 p. (Format: TXT=33277 bytes) (Obsoletes RFC 1115)

1422 Privacy Enhancement for Internet Electronic Mail: Part II: Certificate-Based Key Management. Kent, S.T. 1993 February; 32 p. (Format: TXT=86085 bytes) (Obsoletes RFC 1114)

1421 Privacy Enhancement for Internet Electronic Mail: Part I: Message Encryption and Authentication Procedures. Linn, J. 1993 February; 42 p. (Format: TXT=103894 bytes) (Obsoletes RFC 1113)

1420 SNMP over IPX. Bostock, S. 1993 March; 4 p. (Format: TXT=6762 bytes)

1419 SNMP over AppleTalk. Minshall, G.; Ritter, M. 1993 March; 7 p. (Format: TXT=16470 bytes)

1418 SNMP over OSI. Rose, M.T. 1993 March; 4 p. (Format: TXT=7721 bytes) (Obsoletes RFC 1161, RFC 1283)

1417 NADF Standing Documents: A Brief Overview. North American Directory Forum. 1993 February; 4 p. (Format: TXT=7270 bytes) (Obsoletes RFC 1295, RFC 1255, RFC 1218)

1416 Telnet Authentication Option. Borman, D.A.,ed. 1993 February; 7 p. (Format: TXT=13270 bytes) (Obsoletes RFC 1409)

1415 FTP-FTAM Gateway Specification. Mindel, J.L.; Slaski, R.L. 1993 January; 58 p. (Format: TXT=128261 bytes)

V

Resource Reference

1414 Identification MIB. St. Johns, M.; Rose, M.T. 1993 February; 7 p.
      (Format: TXT=14165 bytes)

1413 Identification Protocol. St. Johns, M. 1993 February; 8 p. (Format:
      TXT=16291 bytes) (Obsoletes RFC 931)

1412 Telnet Authentication: SPX. Alagappan, K. 1993 January; 4 p. (Format:
      TXT=6952 bytes)

1411 Telnet Authentication: Kerberos Version 4. Borman, D.A.,ed. 1993
      January; 4 p. (Format: TXT=7967 bytes)

1410 IAB Official Protocol Standards. Postel, J.,ed. 1993 March; 35 p.
      (Format: TXT=76524 bytes) (Obsoletes RFC 1360, RFC 1280, RFC 1250, RFC
      1100, RFC 1083, RFC 1130, RFC 1140, RFC 1200)

1409 Telnet Authentication Option. Borman, D.A.,ed. 1993 January; 7 p.
      (Format: TXT=13119 bytes) (Obsoleted by RFC 1416)

1408 Telnet Environment Option. Borman, D.A.,ed. 1993 January; 7 p. (Format:
      TXT=13936 bytes)

1407 Definitions of Managed Objects for the DS3/E3 Interface Type. Cox, T.A.;
      Tesink, K.,eds. 1993 January; 43 p. (Format: TXT=90682 bytes)
      (Obsoletes RFC 1233)

1406 Definitions of Managed Objects for the DS1 and E1 Interface Types.
      Baker, F.; Watt, J.,eds. 1993 January; 50 p. (Format: TXT=97559 bytes)
      (Obsoletes RFC 1232)

1405 Mapping between X.400 (1984/1988) and Mail-11 (DECnet mail). Allocchio,
      C. 1993 January; 19 p. (Format: TXT=33885 bytes)

1404 A Model for Common Operational Statistics. Stockman, B. 1993 January;
      27 p. (Format: TXT=52814 bytes)

1403 BGP OSPF Interaction. Varadhan, K. 1993 January; 17 p. (Format:
      TXT=36173 bytes) (Obsoletes RFC 1364)

1402 There's Gold in them thar Networks! or Searching for Treasure in all the
      Wrong Places. Martin, J. 1993 January; 39 p. (Format: TXT=71176 bytes)
      (Also FYI 10)   (Obsoletes RFC 1290)

1401 Correspondence between the IAB and DISA on the use of DNS throughout the
      Internet. Chapin, A.L. 1993 January; 8 p. (Format: TXT=12528 bytes)

1400 Transition and Modernization of the Internet Registration Service.
      Williamson, S. 1993 March; 7 p. (Format: TXT=13008 bytes)

1399 Not yet issued.

1398 Definitions of Managed Objects for the Ethernet-like Interface Types.
      Kastenholz, F. 1993 January; 17 p. (Format: TXT=36685 bytes)
      (Obsoletes RFC 1284)

1397 Default Route Advertisement In BGP2 And BGP3 Versions of the Border
      Gateway Protocol. Haskin, D. 1993 January; 2 p. (Format: TXT=4124
      bytes)

1396   The Process for Organization of Internet Standards Working Group
        (POISED). Crocker, S.D.   1993 January; 10 p. (Format: TXT=22096 bytes)

1395   BOOTP Vendor Information Extensions. Reynolds, J.K.   1993 January; 8 p.
        (Format: TXT=16314 bytes)   (Obsoletes RFC 1084, RFC 1048; Obsoleted by
        RFC 1497; Updates RFC 951)

1394   Relationship of Telex Answerback Codes to Internet Domains. Robinson, P.
        1993 January; 17 p. (Format: TXT=43776 bytes)

1393   Traceroute Using an IP Option. Malkin, G.S.   1993 January; 7 p. (Format:
        TXT=13140 bytes)

1392   Internet Users' Glossary. Malkin, G.S.; Parker, T.L.,eds.   1993 January;
        53 p. (Format: TXT=104624 bytes) (Also FYI 18)

1391   The Tao of IETF: A Guide for New Attendees of the Internet Engineering
        Task Force. Malkin, G.S.   1993 January; 19 p. (Format: TXT=23569 bytes)
        (Also FYI 17)

1390   Transmission of IP and ARP over FDDI Networks. Katz, D.   1993 January;
        11 p. (Format: TXT=22077 bytes)

1389   RIP Version 2 MIB Extension. Malkin, G.S.; Baker, F.   1993 January;
        13 p. (Format: TXT=23569 bytes)

1388   RIP Version 2: Carrying Additional Information. Malkin, G.S.   1993
        January; 7 p. (Format: TXT=16227 bytes)   (Updates RFC 1058)

1387   RIP Version 2 Protocol Analysis. Malkin, G.S.   1993 January; 3 p.
        (Format: TXT=5598 bytes)

1386   The US Domain. Cooper, A.; Postel, J.B.   1992 December; 31 p. (Format:
        TXT=62310 bytes)

1385   EIP: The Extended Internet Protocol: A framework for maintaining
        background compatibility Wang, Z.   1992 November; 17 p. (Format:
        TXT=39166 bytes)

1384   Naming Guidelines for Directory Pilots. Barker, P.; Hardcastle-Kille,
        S.E.   1993 January; 12 p. (Format: TXT=25870, PS=175044 bytes)

1383   Mapping between X.400 and RFC-822 Message Bodies. Huitema, C.   1992
        December; 14 p. (Format: TXT=32680 bytes)

1382   SNMP MIB extensions for the X.25 packet layer. Throop, D.D.,ed.   1992
        November; 69 p. (Format: TXT=153877 bytes)

1381   SNMP MIB extension for X.25 LAPB. Throop, D.D.; Baker, F.   1992
        November; 33 p. (Format: TXT=71253 bytes)

1380   IESG deliberations on routing and addressing. Gross, P.G.; Almquist, P.
        1992 November; 22 p. (Format: TXT=49415 bytes)

1379   Extending TCP for transactions -- Concepts. Braden, R.T.   1992 November;
        38 p. (Format: TXT=91353 bytes)

V

Resource Reference

1378   PPP AppleTalk Control Protocol (ATCP). Parker, B. 1992 November; 16 p.
       (Format: TXT=28496 bytes)

1377   PPP OSI Network Layer Control Protocol (OSINLCP). Katz, D. 1992
       November; 10 p. (Format: TXT=22109 bytes)

1376   PPP DECnet Phase IV Control Protocol (DNCP). Senum, S.J. 1992 November;
       6 p. (Format: TXT=12448 bytes)

1375   Suggestion for new classes of IP addresses. Robinson, P. 1992 October;
       7 p. (Format: TXT=16990 bytes)

1374   IP and ARP on HIPPI. Renwick, J.K.; Nicholson, A. 1992 October; 43 p.
       (Format: TXT=100903 bytes)

1373   Portable DUAs. Tignor, T. 1992 October; 12 p. (Format: TXT=19931 bytes)

1372   Telnet remote flow control option. Hedrick, C.L.; Borman, D. 1992
       October; 6 p. (Format: TXT=11098 bytes) (Obsoletes RFC 1080)

1371   Choosing a "common IGP" for the IP Internet (The IESG's recommendation
       to the IAB). Gross, P.G.,ed. 1992 October; 9 p. (Format: TXT=18168
       bytes)

1370   Applicability statement for OSPF. Chapin, A. Lyman 1992 October; 2 p.
       (Format: TXT=4303 bytes)

1369   Implementation notes and experience for the Internet Ethernet MIB.
       Kastenholz, F.J. 1992 October; 7 p. (Format: TXT=13961 bytes)

1368   Definitions of managed objects for IEEE 802.3 repeater devices.
       McMaster, D.; McCloghrie, K. 1992 October; 40 p. (Format: TXT=83905
       bytes)

1367   Schedule for address space management guidelines. Topolcic, C. 1992
       October; 3 p. (Format: TXT=4780 bytes) (Obsoleted by RFC 1467)

1366   Guidelines for management of IP address space. Gerich, E. 1992 October;
       8 p. (Format: TXT=17793 bytes) (Obsoleted by RFC 1466)

1365   IP address extension proposal. Siyan, K. 1992 September; 6 p. (Format:
       TXT=12790 bytes)

1364   BGP OSPF interaction. Varadhan, K. 1992 September; 14 p. (Format:
       TXT=32121 bytes) (Obsoleted by RFC 1403)

1363   Proposed flow specification. Partridge, C. 1992 September; 20 p.
       (Format: TXT=50214 bytes)

1362   Novell IPX over various WAN media (IPXWAN). Allen, M. 1992 September;
       13 p. (Format: TXT=30219 bytes)

1361   Simple Network Time Protocol (SNTP). Mills, D. 1992 August; 10 p.
       (Format: TXT=23812 bytes)

1360   IAB official protocol standards. Postel, J.B.,ed. 1992 September; 33 p.
       (Format: TXT=71860 bytes) (Obsoletes RFC 1280; Obsoleted by RFC 1410)

1359 Connecting to the Internet: What connecting institutions should anticipate. ACM SIGUCCS Networking Task Force 1992 August; 25 p. (Format: TXT=53449 bytes) (Also FYI 16)

1358 Charter of the Internet Architecture Board (IAB). Chapin, A.L. 1992 August; 5 p. (Format: TXT=11328 bytes)

1357 Format for e-mailing bibliographic records. Cohen, D. 1992 July; 13 p. (Format: TXT=25021 bytes)

1356 Multiprotocol interconnect on X.25 and ISDN in the packet mode. Malis, A.; Robinson, D.; Ullmann, R. 1992 August; 14 p. (Format: TXT=32043 bytes) (Obsoletes RFC 877)

1355 Privacy and accuracy issues in network information center databases. Curran, J.; Marine, A.N. 1992 August; 4 p. (Format: TXT=8858 bytes) (Also FYI 15)

1354 IP forwarding table MIB. Baker, F. 1992 July; 12 p. (Format: TXT=24905 bytes)

1353 Definitions of managed objects for administration of SNMP parties. McCloghrie, K.; Davin, J.R.; Galvin, J.M. 1992 July; 26 p. (Format: TXT=59556 bytes)

1352 SNMP security protocols. Galvin, J.M.; McCloghrie, K.; Davin, J.R. 1992 July; 41 p. (Format: TXT=95732 bytes)

1351 SNMP administrative model. Davin, J.R.; Galvin, J.M.; McCloghrie, K. 1992 July; 35 p. (Format: TXT=80721 bytes)

1350 TFTP protocol (revision 2). Sollins, K.R. 1992 July; 11 p. (Format: TXT=24599 bytes) (Obsoletes RFC 783)

1349 Type of Service in the Internet protocol suite. Almquist, P. 1992 July; 28 p. (Format: TXT=68949 bytes) (Updates RFC 1248, RFC 1247, RFC 1195, RFC 1123, RFC 1122, RFC 1060, RFC 791)

1348 DNS NSAP RRs. Manning, B. 1992 July; 4 p. (Format: TXT=6871 bytes) (Updates RFC 1034, RFC 1035)

1347 TCP and UDP with Bigger Addresses (TUBA), A simple proposal for Internet addressing and routing. Callon, R.W. 1992 June; 7 p. (Format: TXT=26562 , PS=42398 bytes)

1346 Resource allocation, control, and accounting for the use of network resources. Jones, P. 1992 June; 6 p. (Format: TXT=13084 bytes)

1345 Character mnemonics and character sets. Simonsen, K. 1992 June; 103 p. (Format: TXT=249737 bytes)

1344 Implications of MIME for Internet mail gateways. Borenstein, N. 1992 June; 8 p. (Format: TXT=25872, PS=51812 bytes)

1343 User agent configuration mechanism for multimedia mail format information. Borenstein, N. 1992 June; 10 p. (Format: TXT=29295, PS=59978 bytes)

Resource Reference

1342   Representation of non-ASCII text in Internet message headers. Moore, K. 1992 June; 7 p. (Format: TXT=15845 bytes)

1341   MIME (Multipurpose Internet Mail Extensions): Mechanisms for specifying and describing the format of Internet message bodies. Borenstein, N.; Freed, N. 1992 June; 69 p. (Format: TXT=211117, PS=347082 bytes)

1340   Assigned Numbers. Reynolds, J.K.; Postel, J.B. 1992 July; 138 p. (Format: TXT=232974 bytes) (Obsoletes RFC 1060)

1339   Remote mail checking protocol. Dorner, S.; Resnick, P. 1992 June; 5 p. (Format: TXT=13115 bytes)

1338   Supernetting: An address assignment and aggregation strategy. Fuller, V.; Li, T.; Yu, J.Y.; Varadhan, K. 1992 June; 20 p. (Format: TXT=47975 bytes)

1337   TIME-WAIT assassination hazards in TCP. Braden, R.T. 1992 May; 11 p. (Format: TXT=22887 bytes)

1336   Who's who in the Internet: Biographies of IAB, IESG and IRSG members. Malkin, G.S. 1992 May; 33 p. (Format: TXT=92119 bytes) (Also FYI 9) (Obsoletes RFC 1251)

1335   Two-tier address structure for the Internet: A solution to the problem of address space exhaustion. Wang, Z.; Crowcroft, J. 1992 May; 7 p. (Format: TXT=15418 bytes)

1334   PPP authentication protocols. Lloyd, B.; Simpson, W.A. 1992 October; 16 p. (Format: TXT=33248 bytes)

1333   PPP link quality monitoring. Simpson, W.A. 1992 May; 15 p. (Format: TXT=29965 bytes)

1332   PPP Internet Protocol Control Protocol (IPCP). McGregor, G. 1992 May; 12 p. (Format: TXT=17613 bytes) (Obsoletes RFC 1172)

1331   Point-to-Point Protocol (PPP) for the transmission of multi-protocol datagrams over point-to-point links. Simpson, W.A. 1992 May; 66 p. (Format: TXT=129892 bytes) (Obsoletes RFC 1171, RFC 1172)

1330   Recommendations for the phase I deployment of OSI Directory Services (X.500) and OSI Message Handling Services (X.400) within the ESnet community. ESnet Site Coordinating Committee, X.500/X.400 Task Force. 1992 May; 87 p. (Format: TXT=192925 bytes)

1329   Thoughts on address resolution for dual MAC FDDI networks. Kuehn, P. 1992 May; 28 p. (Format: TXT=58150 bytes)

1328   X.400 1988 to 1984 downgrading. Hardcastle-Kille, S.E. 1992 May; 5 p. (Format: TXT=10006 bytes) (Updated by RFC 1496)

1327   Mapping between X.400(1988)/ISO 10021 and RFC 822. Hardcastle-Kille, S.E. 1992 May; 113 p. (Format: TXT=228598 bytes) (Obsoletes RFC 1148, RFC 1138, RFC 1026, RFC 987; Updates RFC 822; Updated by RFC 1495)

1326 Mutual encapsulation considered dangerous. Tsuchiya, P.F. 1992 May;
5 p. (Format: TXT=11241 bytes)

1325 FYI on questions and answers: Answers to commonly asked "new Internet
user" questions. Malkin, G.S.; Marine, A.N. 1992 May; 42 p. (Format:
TXT=91884 bytes) (Also FYI 4)   (Obsoletes RFC 1206)

1324 Discussion on computer network conferencing. Reed, D. 1992 May; 11 p.
(Format: TXT=24988 bytes)

1323 TCP extensions for high performance. Jacobson, V.; Braden, R.T.; Borman,
D.A. 1992 May; 37 p. (Format: TXT=84558 bytes)   (Obsoletes RFC 1072,
RFC 1185)

1322 Unified approach to inter-domain routing. Estrin, D.; Rekhter, Y.; Hotz,
S. 1992 May; 38 p. (Format: TXT=96934 bytes)

1321 MD5 Message-Digest algorithm. Rivest, R.L. 1992 April; 21 p. (Format:
TXT=35222 bytes)

1320 MD4 Message-Digest algorithm. Rivest, R.L. 1992 April; 20 p. (Format:
TXT=32407 bytes)   (Obsoletes RFC 1186)

1319 MD2 Message-Digest algorithm. Kaliski, B.S. 1992 April; 17 p. (Format:
TXT=25661 bytes)   (Updates RFC 1115)

1318 Definitions of managed objects for parallel-printer-like hardware
devices. Stewart, B.,ed. 1992 April; 11 p. (Format: TXT=19570 bytes)

1317 Definitions of managed objects for RS-232-like hardware devices.
Stewart, B.,ed. 1992 April; 17 p. (Format: TXT=30442 bytes)

1316 Definitions of managed objects for character stream devices. Stewart,
B.,ed. 1992 April; 17 p. (Format: TXT=35143 bytes)

1315 Management Information Base for frame relay DTEs. Brown, C.; Baker, F.;
Carvalho, C. 1992 April; 19 p. (Format: TXT=33825 bytes)

1314 File format for the exchange of images in the Internet. Katz, A.R.;
Cohen, D. 1992 April; 23 p. (Format: TXT=54072 bytes)

1313 Today's programming for KRFC AM 1313 Internet talk radio. Partridge, C.
1992 April 1; 3 p. (Format: TXT=5444 bytes)

1312 Message Send Protocol 2. Nelson, R.; Arnold, G. 1992 April; 8 p.
(Format: TXT=18037 bytes)   (Obsoletes RFC 1159)

1311 Introduction to the STD notes. Postel, J.B.,ed. 1992 March; 5 p.
(Format: TXT=11308 bytes)

1310 Internet standards process. Chapin, A.L. 1992 March; 23 p. (Format:
TXT=54738 bytes)

1309 Technical overview of directory services using the X.500 protocol.
Weider, C.; Reynolds, J.K.; Heker, S. 1992 March; 16 p. (Format:
TXT=35694 bytes) (Also FYI 14)

1308 Executive introduction to directory services using the X.500 protocol. Weider, C.; Reynolds, J.K. 1992 March; 4 p. (Format: TXT=9392 bytes) (Also FYI 13)

1307 Dynamically switched link control protocol. Nicholson, A.; Young, J. 1992 March; 13 p. (Format: TXT=24145 bytes)

1306 Experiences supporting by-request circuit-switched T3 networks. Nicholson, A.; Young, J. 1992 March; 10 p. (Format: TXT=25788 bytes)

1305 Network Time Protocol (Version 3): Specification, implementation, and analysis. Mills, D.L. 1992 March; 113 p. (Format: TXT=307085, tar.Z=815759 bytes) (Obsoletes RFC 1119)

1304 Definitions of managed objects for the SIP interface type. Cox, T.A.; Tesink, K.,eds. 1992 February; 25 p. (Format: TXT=5241 bytes)

1303 Convention for describing SNMP-based agents. McCloghrie, K.; Rose, M.T. 1992 February; 12 p. (Format: TXT=22915 bytes)

1302 Building a network information services infrastructure. Sitzler, D.D.; Smith, P.G.; Marine, A.N. 1992 February; 13 p. (Format: TXT=29135 bytes) (Also FYI 12)

1301 Multicast Transport Protocol. Armstrong, S.M.; Freier, A.O.; Marzullo, K.A. 1992 February; 38 p. (Format: TXT=91976 bytes)

1300 Remembrances of things past. Greenfield, S.R. 1992 February; 4 p. (Format: TXT=4963 bytes)

1299 Not yet issued.

1298 SNMP over IPX. Wormley, R.B.; Bostock, S. 1992 February; 5 p. (Format: TXT=7878 bytes)

1297 NOC integrated trouble ticket system: Functional specification wish list ("NOC TT requirements"). Johnson, D.S. 1992 January; 12 p. (Format: TXT=32964 bytes)

1296 Internet Growth (1981-1991). Lottor, M. 1992 January; 9 p. (Format: TXT=20103 bytes)

1295 User bill of rights for entries and listing in the public directory. North American Directory Forum. 1992 January; 2 p. (Format: TXT=3502 bytes) (Obsoleted by RFC 1417)

1294 Multiprotocol interconnect over Frame Relay. Bradley, T.; Brown, C.; Malis, A.G. 1992 January; 28 p. (Format: TXT=54992 bytes) (Obsoleted by RFC 1490)

1293 Inverse Address Resolution Protocol. Bradely, T.; Brown, C. 1992 January; 6 p. (Format: TXT=11368 bytes)

1292 Catalog of Available X.500 Implementations. Lang, R.; Wright, R. 1991 December; 103 p. (Format: TXT=129468 bytes) (Also FYI 11)

1291   Mid-Level networks: Potential technical services. Aggarwal, V. 1991
       December; 10 p. (Format: TXT=24314, PS=218918 bytes)

1290   There's gold in them thar networks! or searching for treasure in all the
       wrong places. Martin, J. 1991 December; 27 p. (Format: TXT=46997 bytes)
       (Also FYI 10)   (Obsoleted by RFC 1402)

1289   DECnet phase IV MIB extensions. Saperia, J. 1991 December; 64 p.
       (Format: TXT=122272 bytes)

1288   Finger User Information Protocol. Zimmerman, D.P. 1991 December; 12 p.
       (Format: TXT=25161 bytes)   (Obsoletes RFC 1196)

1287   Towards the future Internet architecture. Clark, D.D.; Chapin, L.A.;
       Cerf, V.G.; Braden, R.T.; Hobby, R. 1991 December; 29 p. (Format:
       TXT=59812 bytes)

1286   Definitions of managed objects for bridges. Decker, E.; Langille, P.;
       Rijsinghani, A.; McCloghrie, K. 1991 December; 40 p. (Format: txt=79104
       bytes)   (Obsoleted by RFC 1493)

1285   FDDI Management Information Base. Case, J.D. 1992 January; 46 p.
       (Format: TXT=99747 bytes)

1284   Definitions of managed objects for the Ethernet-like interface types.
       Cook, J.,ed. 1991 December; 21 p. (Format: TXT=43225 bytes)
       (Obsoleted by RFC 1398)

1283   SNMP over OSI. Rose, M.T. 1991 December; 8 p. (Format: TXT=16814 bytes)
       (Obsoletes RFC 1161; Obsoleted by RFC 1418)

1282   BSD rlogin. Kantor, B. 1991 December; 5 p. (Format: TXT=10704 bytes)
       (Obsoletes RFC 1258)

1281   Guidelines for the secure operations of the Internet. Pethia, R.D.;
       Crocker, S.D.; Fraser, B.Y. 1991 November; 10 p. (Format: TXT=22618
       bytes)

1280   IAB official protocol standards. Postel, J.B.,ed. 1992 March; 32 p.
       (Format: TXT=70458 bytes)   (Obsoletes RFC 1250; Obsoleted by RFC 1410)

1279   X.500 and domains. Hardcastle-Kille, S.E. 1991 November; 13 p. (Format:
       TXT=26669, PS=170029 bytes)

1278   String encoding of presentation address. Hardcastle-Kille, S.E. 1991
       November; 5 p. (Format: TXT=10256, PS=128696 bytes)

1277   Encoding network addresses to support operations over non-OSI lower
       layers. Hardcastle-Kille, S.E. 1991 November; 10 p. (Format: TXT=22254,
       PS=176169 bytes)

1276   Replication and distributed operations extensions to provide an Internet
       directory using X.500. Hardcastle-Kille, S.E. 1991 November; 17 p.
       (Format: TXT=33731, PS=217170 bytes)

V

Resource Reference

1275 Replication requirements to provide an Internet directory using X.500. Hardcastle-Kille, S.E. 1991 November; 2 p. (Format: TXT=4616, PS=83736 bytes)

1274 COSINE and Internet X.500 schema. Kille, S.E.; Barker, P. 1991 November; 60 p. (Format: TXT=92827 bytes)

1273 Measurement study of changes in service-level reachability in the global TCP/IP Internet: Goals, experimental design, implementation, and policy considerations. Schwartz, M.F. 1991 November; 8 p. (Format: TXT=19949 bytes)

1272 Internet accounting: Background. Mills, C.; Hirsh, D.; Ruth, G.R. 1991 November; 19 p. (Format: TXT=46562 bytes)

1271 Remote network monitoring Management Information Base. Waldbusser, S. 1991 November; 81 p. (Format: TXT=184111 bytes)

1270 SNMP communications services. Kastenholz, F.J.,ed. 1991 October; 11 p. (Format: TXT=26167 bytes)

1269 Definitions of managed objects for the Border Gateway Protocol: Version 3. Willis, S.; Burruss, J.W. 1991 October; 13 p. (Format: TXT=25717 bytes)

1268 Application of the Border Gateway Protocol in the Internet. Rekhter, Y.; Gross, P.G.,eds. 1991 October; 13 p. (Format: TXT=31102 bytes) (Obsoletes RFC 1164)

1267 Border Gateway Protocol 3 (BGP-3). Lougheed, K.; Rekhter, Y. 1991 October; 35 p. (Format: TXT=80724 bytes) (Obsoletes RFC 1163)

1266 Experience with the BGP protocol. Rekhter, Y.,ed. 1991 October; 9 p. (Format: TXT=21938 bytes)

1265 BGP protocol analysis. Rekhter, Y.,ed. 1991 October; 8 p. (Format: TXT=20728 bytes)

1264 Internet Engineering Task Force internet routing protocol standardization criteria. Hinden, R.M. 1991 October; 8 p. (Format: TXT=17016 bytes)

1263 TCP extensions considered harmful. O'Malley, S.; Peterson, L.L. 1991 October; 19 p. (Format: TXT=54078 bytes)

1262 Guidelines for internet measurement activities. Cerf, V.G.,ed. 1991 October; 3 p. (Format: TXT=6381 bytes)

1261 Transiton of NIC services. Williamson, S.; Nobile, L. 1991 September; 3 p. (Format: TXT=4488 bytes)

1260 Not yet issued.

1259 Building the open road: The NREN as test-bed for the national public network. Kapor, M. 1991 September; 23 p. (Format: TXT=62944 bytes)

1258   BSD Rlogin. Kantor, B.   1991 September; 5 p. (Format: TXT=10763 bytes)
(Obsoleted by RFC 1282)

1257   Isochronous applications do not require jitter-controlled networks.
Partridge, C.   1991 September; 5 p. (Format: TXT=11075 bytes)

1256   ICMP router discovery messages. Deering, S.E.,ed.   1991 September; 19 p.
(Format: TXT=44628 bytes)

1255   Naming scheme for c=US. North American Directory Forum.   1991 September;
25 p. (Format: TXT=53783 bytes)   (Obsoletes RFC 1218; Obsoleted by RFC
1417)

1254   Gateway congestion control survey. Mankin, A.; Ramakrishnan, K.K.,eds.
1991 August; 25 p. (Format: TXT=69793 bytes)

1253   OSPF version 2: Management Information Base. Baker, F.; Coltun, R.   1991
August; 42 p. (Format: TXT=77232 bytes)   (Obsoletes RFC 1252)

1252   OSPF version 2: Management Information Base. Baker, F.; Coltun, R.   1991
August; 42 p. (Format: TXT=77250 bytes)   (Obsoletes RFC 1248;
Obsoleted by RFC 1253)

1251   Who's who in the internet: Biographies of IAB, IESG and IRSG members.
Malkin, G.S.   1991 August; 26 p. (Format: TXT=72721 bytes) (Also FYI 9)
(Obsoleted by RFC 1336)

1250   IAB official protocol standards. Postel, J.B.,ed.   1991 August; 28 p.
(Format: TXT=65279 bytes)   (Obsoletes RFC 1200; Obsoleted by RFC 1410)

1249   DIXIE protocol specification. Howes, T.; Smith, M.; Beecher, B.   1991
August; 10 p. (Format: TXT=20693 bytes)

1248   OSPF version 2: Management Information Base. Baker, F.; Coltun, R.   1991
July; 42 p. (Format: TXT=77126 bytes)   (Obsoleted by RFC 1252;
Updated by RFC 1349)

1247   OSPF version 2. Moy, J.   1991 July; 189 p. (Format: PS=1063028,
TXT=443917 bytes)   (Obsoletes RFC 1131; Updated by RFC 1349)

1246   Experience with the OSPF protocol. Moy, J.,ed.   1991 July; 31 p.
(Format: PS=146913, TXT=72180 bytes)

1245   OSPF protocol analysis. Moy, J.,ed.   1991 July; 12 p. (Format: PS=64094,
TXT=27492 bytes)

1244   Site Security Handbook. Holbrook, J.P.; Reynolds, J.K.,eds.   1991 July;
101 p. (Format: TXT=259129 bytes) (Also FYI 8)

1243   Appletalk Management Information Base. Waldbusser, S.,ed.   1991 July;
29 p. (Format: TXT=61985 bytes)

1242   Benchmarking terminology for network interconnection devices. Bradner,
S.,ed.   1991 July; 12 p. (Format: TXT=22817 bytes)

1241   Scheme for an internet encapsulation protocol: Version 1. Woodburn,
R.A.; Mills, D.L.   1991 July; 17 p. (Format: TXT=42468, PS=128921 bytes)

V

Resource Reference

1240 OSI connectionless transport services on top of UDP: Version 1. Shue,
      C.; Haggerty, W.; Dobbins, K. 1991 June; 8 p. (Format: TXT=18140 bytes)

1239 Reassignment of experimental MIBs to standard MIBs. Reynolds, J.K. 1991
      June; 2 p. (Format: TXT=3656 bytes) (Updates RFC 1229, RFC 1230, RFC
      1231, RFC 1232, RFC 1233)

1238 CLNS MIB for use with Connectionless Network Protocol (ISO 8473) and End
      System to Intermediate System (ISO 9542). Satz, G. 1991 June; 32 p.
      (Format: TXT=65159 bytes) (Obsoletes RFC 1162)

1237 Guidelines for OSI NSAP allocation in the internet. Collela, R.;
      Gardner, E.P.; Callon, R.W. 1991 July; 38 p. (Format: PS=162808,
      TXT=119962 bytes)

1236 IP to X.121 address mapping for DDN. Morales, L.F., Jr.; Hasse, P.R.
      1991 June; 7 p. (Format: TXT=12626 bytes)

1235 Coherent File Distribution Protocol. Ioannidis, J.; Maguire, G.Q., Jr.
      1991 June; 12 p. (Format: TXT=29345 bytes)

1234 Tunneling IPX traffic through IP networks. Provan, D. 1991 June; 6 p.
      (Format: TXT=12333 bytes)

1233 Definitions of managed objects for the DS3 Interface type. Cox, T.A.;
      Tesink, K.,eds. 1991 May; 23 p. (Format: TXT=49559 bytes)
      (Obsoleted by RFC 1407; Updated by RFC 1239)

1232 Definitions of managed objects for the DS1 Interface type. Baker, F.;
      Kolb, C.P.,eds. 1991 May; 28 p. (Format: TXT=60757 bytes)
      (Obsoleted by RFC 1406; Updated by RFC 1239)

1231 IEEE 802.5 Token Ring MIB. McCloghrie, K.; Fox, R.; Decker, E. 1991
      May; 23 p. (Format: TXT=53542 bytes) (Updated by RFC 1239)

1230 IEEE 802.4 Token Bus MIB. McCloghrie, K.; Fox, R. 1991 May; 23 p.
      (Format: TXT=53100 bytes) (Updated by RFC 1239)

1229 Extensions to the generic-interface MIB. McCloghrie, K.,ed. 1991 May;
      16 p. (Format: TXT=36022 bytes) (Updated by RFC 1239)

1228 SNMP-DPI: Simple Network Management Protocol Distributed Program
      Interface. Carpenter, G.; Wijnen, B. 1991 May; 50 p. (Format: TXT=96972
      bytes)

1227 SNMP MUX protocol and MIB. Rose, M.T. 1991 May; 13 p. (Format:
      TXT=25868 bytes)

1226 Internet protocol encapsulation of AX.25 frames. Kantor, B. 1991 May;
      2 p. (Format: TXT=2573 bytes)

1225 Post Office Protocol: Version 3. Rose, M.T. 1991 May; 16 p. (Format:
      TXT=37340 bytes) (Obsoletes RFC 1081; Obsoleted by RFC 1460)

1224 Techniques for managing asynchronously generated alerts. Steinberg, L.
      1991 May; 22 p. (Format: TXT=54303 bytes)

1223 OSI CLNS and LLC1 protocols on Network Systems HYPERchannel. Halpern, J.M. 1991 May; 12 p. (Format: TXT=29601 bytes)

1222 Advancing the NSFNET routing architecture. Braun, H.W.; Rekhter, Y. 1991 May; 6 p. (Format: TXT=15067 bytes)

1221 Host Access Protocol (HAP) specification: Version 2. Edmond, W. 1991 April; 68 p. (Format: TXT=156550 bytes)   (Updates RFC 907)

1220 Point-to-Point Protocol extensions for bridging. Baker, F.,ed. 1991 April; 18 p. (Format: TXT=38165 bytes)

1219 On the assignment of subnet numbers. Tsuchiya, P.F. 1991 April; 13 p. (Format: TXT=30609 bytes)

1218 Naming scheme for c=US. North American Directory Forum. 1991 April; 23 p. (Format: TXT=42698 bytes)   (Obsoleted by RFC 1417)

1217 Memo from the Consortium for Slow Commotion Research (CSCR). Cerf, V.G. 1991 April 1; 5 p. (Format: TXT=11079 bytes)

1216 Gigabit network economics and paradigm shifts. Richard, P.; Kynikos, P. 1991 April 1; 4 p. (Format: TXT=8130 bytes)

1215 Convention for defining traps for use with the SNMP. Rose, M.T.,ed. 1991 March; 9 p. (Format: TXT=19336 bytes)

1214 OSI internet management: Management Information Base. LaBarre, L.,ed. 1991 April; 83 p. (Format: TXT=172564 bytes)

1213 Management Information Base for network management of TCP/IP-based internets: MIB-II. McCloghrie, K.; Rose, M.T.,eds. 1991 March; 70 p. (Format: TXT=146080 bytes)   (Obsoletes RFC 1158)

1212 Concise MIB definitions. Rose, M.T.; McCloghrie, K.,eds. 1991 March; 19 p. (Format: TXT=43579 bytes)

1211 Problems with the maintenance of large mailing lists. Westine, A.; Postel, J.B. 1991 March; 54 p. (Format: TXT=96167 bytes)

1210 Network and infrastructure user requirements for transatlantic research collaboration: Brussels, July 16-18, and Washington July 24-25, 1990. Cerf, V.G.; Kirstein, P.T.; Randell, B.,eds. 1991 March; 36 p. (Format: TXT=79048 bytes)

1209 Transmission of IP datagrams over the SMDS Service. Piscitello, D.M.; Lawrence, J. 1991 March; 11 p. (Format: TXT=25280 bytes)

1208 Glossary of networking terms. Jacobsen, O.J.; Lynch, D.C. 1991 March; 18 p. (Format: TXT=41156 bytes)

1207 FYI on Questions and Answers: Answers to commonly asked "experienced Internet user" questions. Malkin, G.S.; Marine, A.N.; Reynolds, J.K. 1991 February; 15 p. (Format: TXT=33385 bytes) (Also FYI 7)

V

Resource Reference

1206 FYI on Questions and Answers: Answers to commonly asked "new Internet
      user" questions. Malkin, G.S.; Marine, A.N. 1991 February; 32 p.
      (Format: TXT=72479 bytes) (Also FYI 4)   (Obsoletes RFC 1177;
      Obsoleted by RFC 1325)

1205 5250 Telnet interface. Chmielewski, P. 1991 February; 12 p. (Format:
      TXT=27179 bytes)

1204 Message Posting Protocol (MPP). Yeh, S.; Lee, D. 1991 February; 6 p.
      (Format: TXT=11371 bytes)

1203 Interactive Mail Access Protocol: Version 3. Rice, J. 1991 February;
      49 p. (Format: TXT=123325 bytes)   (Obsoletes RFC 1064)

1202 Directory Assistance service. Rose, M.T. 1991 February; 11 p. (Format:
      TXT=21645 bytes)

1201 Transmitting IP traffic over ARCNET networks. Provan, D. 1991 February;
      7 p. (Format: TXT=16959 bytes)   (Obsoletes RFC 1051)

1200 IAB official protocol standards. Defense Advanced Research Projects
      Agency, Internet Activities Board. 1991 April; 31 p. (Format: TXT=67069
      bytes)   (Obsoletes RFC 1140; Obsoleted by RFC 1410)

1199 Request for Comments Summary: RFC Numbers 1100-1199. Reynolds, J.K.
      1991 December; 22 p. (Format: TXT=46443 bytes)

1198 FYI on the X window system. Scheifler, R.W. 1991 January; 3 p. (Format:
      TXT=3629 bytes) (Also FYI 6)

1197 Using ODA for translating multimedia information. Sherman, M. 1990
      December; 2 p. (Format: TXT=3620 bytes)

1196 Finger User Information Protocol. Zimmerman, D.P. 1990 December; 12 p.
      (Format: TXT=24799 bytes)   (Obsoletes RFC 1194; Obsoleted by RFC 1288)

1195 Use of OSI IS-IS for routing in TCP/IP and dual environments. Callon,
      R.W. 1990 December; 65 p. (Format: PS=381799, TXT=192628 bytes)
      (Updated by RFC 1349)

1194 Finger User Information Protocol. Zimmerman, D.P. 1990 November; 12 p.
      (Format: TXT=24626 bytes)   (Obsoletes RFC 742; Obsoleted by RFC 1196)

1193 Client requirements for real-time communication services. Ferrari, D.
      1990 November; 24 p. (Format: TXT=61540 bytes)

1192 Commercialization of the Internet summary report. Kahin, B.,ed. 1990
      November; 13 p. (Format: TXT=35253 bytes)

1191 Path MTU discovery. Mogul, J.C.; Deering, S.E. 1990 November; 19 p.
      (Format: TXT=47936 bytes)   (Obsoletes RFC 1063)

1190 Experimental Internet Stream Protocol: Version 2 (ST-II). Topolcic, C.,
      ed. 1990 October; 148 p. (Format: TXT=386909 bytes)   (Obsoletes IEN
      119)

1189 Common Management Information Services and Protocols for the Internet
(CMOT and CMIP). Warrier, U.S.; Besaw, L.; LaBarre, L.; Handspicker,
B.D. 1990 October; 15 p. (Format: TXT=32928 bytes) (Obsoletes RFC
1095)

1188 Proposed standard for the transmission of IP datagrams over FDDI
networks. Katz, D. 1990 October; 11 p. (Format: TXT=22424 bytes)
(Obsoletes RFC 1103)

1187 Bulk table retrieval with the SNMP. Rose, M.T.; McCloghrie, K.; Davin,
J.R. 1990 October; 12 p. (Format: TXT=27220 bytes)

1186 MD4 message digest algorithm. Rivest, R.L. 1990 October; 18 p. (Format:
TXT=35391 bytes) (Obsoleted by RFC 1320)

1185 TCP extension for high-speed paths. Jacobson, V.; Braden, R.T.; Zhang,
L. 1990 October; 21 p. (Format: TXT=49508 bytes) (Obsoleted by RFC
1323)

1184 Telnet Linemode option. Borman, D.A.,ed. 1990 October; 23 p. (Format:
TXT=53085 bytes) (Obsoletes RFC 1116)

1183 New DNS RR definitions. Everhart, C.F.; Mamakos, L.A.; Ullmann, R.;
Mockapetris, P.V. 1990 October; 11 p. (Format: TXT=23788 bytes)
(Updates RFC 1034, RFC 1035)

1182 Not yet issued.

1181 RIPE terms of reference. Blokzijl, R. 1990 September; 2 p. (Format:
TXT=2523 bytes)

1180 TCP/IP tutorial. Socolofsky, T.J.; Kale, C.J. 1991 January; 28 p.
(Format: TXT=65494 bytes)

1179 Line printer daemon protocol. McLaughlin, L. 1990 August; 14 p.
(Format: TXT=24324 bytes)

1178 Choosing a name for your computer. Libes, D. 1990 August; 8 p. (Format:
TXT=18472 bytes) (Also FYI 5)

1177 FYI on Questions and Answers: Answers to commonly asked "new internet
user" questions. Malkin, G.S.; Marine, A.N.; Reynolds, J.K. 1990
August; 24 p. (Format: TXT=52852 bytes) (Also FYI 4) (Obsoleted by RFC
1206)

1176 Interactive Mail Access Protocol: Version 2. Crispin, M.R. 1990 August;
30 p. (Format: TXT=67330 bytes) (Obsoletes RFC 1064)

1175 FYI on where to start: A bibliography of internetworking information.
Bowers, K.L.; LaQuey, T.L.; Reynolds, J.K.; Roubicek, K.; Stahl, M.K.;
Yuan, A. 1990 August; 42 p. (Format: TXT=67330 bytes) (Also FYI 3)

1174 IAB recommended policy on distributing internet identifier assignment
and IAB recommended policy change to internet "connected" status. Cerf,
V.G. 1990 August; 9 p. (Format: TXT=21321 bytes)

V

Resource Reference

1173   Responsibilities of host and network managers: A summary of the "oral tradition" of the Internet. VanBokkelen, J. 1990 August; 5 p. (Format: TXT=12527 bytes)

1172   Point-to-Point Protocol (PPP) initial configuration options. Perkins, D.; Hobby, R. 1990 July; 38 p. (Format: TXT=76132 bytes) (Obsoleted by RFC 1331, RFC 1332)

1171   Point-to-Point Protocol for the transmission of multi-protocol datagrams over Point-to-Point links. Perkins, D. 1990 July; 48 p. (Format: TXT=92321 bytes) (Obsoletes RFC 1134; Obsoleted by RFC 1331)

1170   Public key standards and licenses. Fougner, R.B. 1991 January; 2 p. (Format: TXT=3144 bytes)

1169   Explaining the role of GOSIP. Cerf, V.G.; Mills, K.L. 1990 August; 15 p. (Format: TXT=30255 bytes)

1168   Intermail and Commercial Mail Relay services. Westine, A.; DeSchon, A.L.; Postel, J.B.; Ward, C.E. 1990 July; 23 p. (Format: PS=149816 bytes)

1167   Thoughts on the National Research and Education Network. Cerf, V.G. 1990 July; 8 p. (Format: TXT=20682 bytes)

1166   Internet numbers. Kirkpatrick, S.; Stahl, M.K.; Recker, M. 1990 July; 182 p. (Format: TXT=566778 bytes) (Obsoletes RFC 1117, RFC 1062, RFC 1020)

1165   Network Time Protocol (NTP) over the OSI Remote Operations Service. Crowcroft, J.; Onions, J.P. 1990 June; 10 p. (Format: TXT=18277 bytes)

1164   Application of the Border Gateway Protocol in the Internet. Honig, J.C.; Katz, D.; Mathis, M.; Rekhter, Y.; Yu, J.Y. 1990 June; 23 p. (Format: TXT=56278 bytes) (Obsoleted by RFC 1268)

1163   Border Gateway Protocol (BGP). Lougheed, K.; Rekhter, Y. 1990 June; 29 p. (Format: TXT=69404 bytes) (Obsoletes RFC 1105; Obsoleted by RFC 1267)

1162   Connectionless Network Protocol (ISO 8473) and End System to Intermediate System (ISO 9542) Management Information Base. Satz, G. 1990 June; 70 p. (Format: TXT=109893 bytes) (Obsoleted by RFC 1238)

1161   SNMP over OSI. Rose, M.T. 1990 June; 8 p. (Format: TXT=16036 bytes) (Obsoleted by RFC 1283, RFC 1418)

1160   Internet Activities Board. Cerf, V. 1990 May; 11 p. (Format: TXT=28182 bytes) (Obsoletes RFC 1120)

1159   Message Send Protocol. Nelson, R. 1990 June; 2 p. (Format: TXT=3957 bytes) (Obsoleted by RFC 1312)

1158   Management Information Base for network management of TCP/IP-based internets: MIB-II. Rose, M.T.,ed. 1990 May; 133 p. (Format: TXT=212152 bytes) (Obsoleted by RFC 1213)

1157   Simple Network Management Protocol (SNMP). Case, J.D.; Fedor, M.;
       Schoffstall, M.L.; Davin, C. 1990 May; 36 p. (Format: TXT=74894 bytes)
       (Obsoletes RFC 1098)

1156   Management Information Base for network management of TCP/IP-based
       internets. McCloghrie, K.; Rose, M.T. 1990 May; 91 p. (Format:
       TXT=138781 bytes)   (Obsoletes RFC 1066)

1155   Structure and identification of management information for TCP/IP-based
       internets. Rose, M.T.; McCloghrie, K. 1990 May; 22 p. (Format:
       TXT=40927 bytes)   (Obsoletes RFC 1065)

1154   Encoding header field for internet messages. Robinson, D.; Ullmann, R.
       1990 April; 7 p. (Format: TXT=12214 bytes)

1153   Digest message format. Wancho, F.J. 1990 April; 4 p. (Format: TXT=6632
       bytes)

1152   Workshop report: Internet research steering group workshop on
       very-high-speed networks. Partridge, C. 1990 April; 23 p. (Format:
       TXT=64003 bytes)

1151   Version 2 of the Reliable Data Protocol (RDP). Partridge, C.; Hinden,
       R.M. 1990 April; 4 p. (Format: TXT=8293 bytes)   (Updates RFC 908)

1150   F.Y.I. on F.Y.I.: Introduction to the F.Y.I. notes. Malkin, G.S.;
       Reynolds, J.K. 1990 March; 4 p. (Format: TXT=7867 bytes) (Also FYI 1)

1149   Standard for the transmission of IP datagrams on avian carriers.
       Waitzman, D. 1990 April 1; 2 p. (Format: TXT=3329 bytes)

1148   Mapping between X.400(1988) / ISO 10021 and RFC 822. Kille, S.E. 1990
       March; 94 p. (Format: TXT=194292 bytes)   (Obsoleted by RFC 1327; Updates
       RFC 1138)

1147   FYI on a network management tool catalog: Tools for monitoring and
       debugging TCP/IP internets and interconnected devices. Stine, R.H.,ed.
       1990 April; 126 p. (Format: TXT=336906, PS=555225 bytes) (Also FYI 2)
       (Obsoleted by RFC 1470)

1146   TCP alternate checksum options. Zweig, J.; Partridge, C. 1990 March;
       5 p. (Format: TXT=10955 bytes)   (Obsoletes RFC 1145)

1145   TCP alternate checksum options. Zweig, J.; Partridge, C. 1990 February;
       5 p. (Format: TXT=11052 bytes)   (Obsoleted by RFC 1146)

1144   Compressing TCP/IP headers for low-speed serial links. Jacobson, V.
       1990 February; 43 p. (Format: TXT=120959, PS=534729 bytes)

1143   Q method of implementing Telnet option negotiation. Bernstein, D.J.
       1990 February; 10 p. (Format: TXT=23331 bytes)

1142   OSI IS-IS Intra-domain routing protocol. Oran, D.,ed. 1990 February;
       157 p. (Format: PS=1204297, TXT=425379 bytes)

1141   Incremental updating of the Internet checksum. Mallory, T.; Kullberg, A.
       1990 January; 2 p. (Format: TXT=3587 bytes)   (Updates RFC 1071)

V

Resource Reference

1140   IAB official protocol standards. Defense Advanced Research Projects
       Agency, Internet Activities Board.   1990 May; 27 p. (Format: TXT=60501
       bytes)   (Obsoletes RFC 1130; Obsoleted by RFC 1410)

1139   Echo function for ISO 8473. Hagens, R.A.   1990 January; 6 p. (Format:
       TXT=14229 bytes)

1138   Mapping between X.400(1988) / ISO 10021 and RFC 822. Kille, S.E.   1989
       December; 92 p. (Format: TXT=191029 bytes)   (Obsoleted by RFC 1327;
       Updates RFC 1026; Updated by RFC 1148)

1137   Mapping between full RFC 822 and RFC 822 with restricted encoding.
       Kille, S.E.   1989 December; 3 p. (Format: TXT=6436 bytes)   (Updates RFC
       976)

1136   Administrative Domains and Routing Domains: A model for routing in the
       Internet. Hares, S.; Katz, D.   1989 December; 10 p. (Format: TXT=22158
       bytes)

1135   Helminthiasis of the Internet. Reynolds, J.K.   1989 December; 33 p.
       (Format: TXT=77033 bytes)

1134   Point-to-Point Protocol: A proposal for multi-protocol transmission of
       datagrams over Point-to-Point links. Perkins, D.   1989 November; 38 p.
       (Format: TXT=87352 bytes)   (Obsoleted by RFC 1171)

1133   Routing between the NSFNET and the DDN. Yu, J.Y.; Braun, H.W.   1989
       November; 10 p. (Format: TXT=23169 bytes)

1132   Standard for the transmission of 802.2 packets over IPX networks.
       McLaughlin, L.J.   1989 November; 4 p. (Format: TXT=8128 bytes)

1131   OSPF specification. Moy, J.   1989 October; 107 p. (Format: PS=857280
       bytes)   (Obsoleted by RFC 1247)

1130   IAB official protocol standards. Defense Advanced Research Projects
       Agency, Internet Activities Board.   1989 October; 17 p. (Format:
       TXT=33858 bytes)   (Obsoletes RFC 1100; Obsoleted by RFC 1410)

1129   Internet time synchronization: The Network Time Protocol. Mills, D.L.
       1989 October; 29 p. (Format: PS=551697 bytes)

1128   Measured performance of the Network Time Protocol in the Internet
       system. Mills, D.L.   1989 October; 20 p. (Format: PS=633742 bytes)

1127   Perspective on the Host Requirements RFCs. Braden, R.T.   1989 October;
       20 p. (Format: TXT=41267 bytes)

1126   Goals and functional requirements for inter-autonomous system routing.
       Little, M.   1989 October; 25 p. (Format: TXT=62725 bytes)

1125   Policy requirements for inter Administrative Domain routing. Estrin, D.
       1989 November; 18 p. (Format: TXT=55248, PS=282123 bytes)

1124   Policy issues in interconnecting networks. Leiner, B.M.   1989 September;
       54 p. (Format: PS=315692 bytes)

1123 Requirements for Internet hosts – application and support. Braden, R.T., ed. 1989 October; 98 p. (Format: TXT=245503 bytes) (Updated by RFC 1349)

1122 Requirements for Internet hosts – communication layers. Braden, R.T.,ed. 1989 October; 116 p. (Format: TXT=295992 bytes) (Updated by RFC 1349)

1121 Act one – the poems. Postel, J.B.; Kleinrock, L.; Cerf, V.G.; Boehm, B. 1989 September; 6 p. (Format: TXT=10644 bytes)

1120 Internet Activities Board. Cerf, V. 1989 September; 11 p. (Format: TXT=26123 bytes) (Obsoleted by RFC 1160)

1119 Network Time Protocol (version 2) specification and implementation. Mills, D.L. 1989 September; 64 p. (Format: PS=535202 bytes) (Obsoletes RFC 1059, RFC 958; Obsoleted by RFC 1305)

1118 Hitchhikers guide to the Internet. Krol, E. 1989 September; 24 p. (Format: TXT=62757 bytes)

1117 Internet numbers. Romano, S.; Stahl, M.K.; Recker, M. 1989 August; 109 p. (Format: TXT=324666 bytes) (Obsoletes RFC 1062, RFC 1020, RFC 997; Obsoleted by RFC 1166)

1116 Telnet Linemode option. Borman, D.A.,ed. 1989 August; 21 p. (Format: TXT=47473 bytes) (Obsoleted by RFC 1184)

1115 Privacy enhancement for Internet electronic mail: Part III – algorithms, modes, and identifiers [Draft]. Linn, J. 1989 August; 8 p. (Format: TXT=18226 bytes) (Obsoleted by RFC 1423; Updated by RFC 1319)

1114 Privacy enhancement for Internet electronic mail: Part II – certificate-based key management [Draft]. Kent, S.T.; Linn, J. 1989 August; 25 p. (Format: TXT=69661 bytes) (Obsoleted by RFC 1422)

1113 Privacy enhancement for Internet electronic mail: Part I – message encipherment and authentication procedures [Draft]. Linn, J. 1989 August; 34 p. (Format: TXT=89293 bytes) (Obsoletes RFC 989, RFC 1040; Obsoleted by RFC 1421)

1112 Host extensions for IP multicasting. Deering, S.E. 1989 August; 17 p. (Format: TXT=39904 bytes) (Obsoletes RFC 988, RFC 1054)

1111 Request for comments on Request for Comments: Instructions to RFC authors. Postel, J.B. 1989 August; 6 p. (Format: TXT=11793 bytes) (Obsoletes RFC 825)

1110 Problem with the TCP big window option. McKenzie, A.M. 1989 August; 3 p. (Format: TXT=5778 bytes)

1109 Report of the second Ad Hoc Network Management Review Group. Cerf, V.G. 1989 August; 8 p. (Format: TXT=20642 bytes)

1108 U.S. Department of Defense security options for the Internet Protocol. Kent, S.T. 1991 November; 17 p. (Format: TXT=41791 bytes) (Obsoletes RFC 1038)

1107   Plan for Internet directory services. Sollins, K.R.   1989 July; 19 p.
        (Format: TXT=51773 bytes)

1106   TCP big window and NAK options. Fox, R.   1989 June; 13 p. (Format:
        TXT=37105 bytes)

1105   Border Gateway Protocol (BGP). Lougheed, K.; Rekhter, Y.   1989 June;
        17 p. (Format: TXT=37644 bytes)   (Obsoleted by RFC 1163)

1104   Models of policy based routing. Braun, H.W.   1989 June; 10 p. (Format:
        TXT=25468 bytes)

1103   Proposed standard for the transmission of IP datagrams over FDDI
        Networks. Katz, D.   1989 June; 9 p. (Format: TXT=19439 bytes)
        (Obsoleted by RFC 1188)

1102   Policy routing in Internet protocols. Clark, D.D.   1989 May; 22 p.
        (Format: TXT=59664 bytes)

1101   DNS encoding of network names and other types. Mockapetris, P.V.   1989
        April; 14 p. (Format: TXT=28677 bytes)   (Updates RFC 1034, RFC 1035)

1100   IAB official protocol standards. Defense Advanced Research Projects
        Agency, Internet Activities Board.   1989 April; 14 p. (Format: TXT=30101
        bytes)   (Obsoletes RFC 1083; Obsoleted by RFC 1410)

1099   Request for comments summary: RFC numbers 1000-1099. Reynolds, J.K.
        1991 December; 22 p. (Format: TXT=49108 bytes)

1098   Simple Network Management Protocol (SNMP). Case, J.D.; Fedor, M.;
        Schoffstall, M.L.; Davin, C.   1989 April; 34 p. (Format: TXT=71563
        bytes)   (Obsoletes RFC 1067; Obsoleted by RFC 1157)

1097   Telnet subliminal-message option. Miller, B.   1989 April 1; 3 p.
        (Format: TXT=5490 bytes)

1096   Telnet X display location option. Marcy, G.A.   1989 March; 3 p. (Format:
        TXT=4634 bytes)

1095   Common Management Information Services and Protocol over TCP/IP (CMOT).
        Warrier, U.S.; Besaw, L.   1989 April; 67 p. (Format: TXT=157506 bytes)
        (Obsoleted by RFC 1189)

1094   NFS: Network File System Protocol specification. Sun Microsystems, Inc.
        1989 March; 27 p. (Format: TXT=51454 bytes)

1093   NSFNET routing architecture. Braun, H.W.   1989 February; 9 p. (Format:
        TXT=20629 bytes)

1092   EGP and policy based routing in the new NSFNET backbone. Rekhter, J.
        1989 February; 5 p. (Format: TXT=11865 bytes)

1091   Telnet terminal-type option. VanBokkelen, J.   1989 February; 7 p.
        (Format: TXT=13439 bytes)   (Obsoletes RFC 930)

1090   SMTP on X.25. Ullmann, R.   1989 February; 4 p. (Format: TXT=6141 bytes)

1089   SNMP over Ethernet. Schoffstall, M.L.; Davin, C.; Fedor, M.; Case, J.D.
       1989 February; 3 p. (Format: TXT=4458 bytes)

1088   Standard for the transmission of IP datagrams over NetBIOS networks.
       McLaughlin, L.J. 1989 February; 3 p. (Format: TXT=5749 bytes)

1087   Ethics and the Internet. Defense Advanced Research Projects Agency,
       Internet Activities Board. 1989 January; 2 p. (Format: TXT=4582 bytes)

1086   ISO-TP0 bridge between TCP and X.25. Onions, J.P.; Rose, M.T. 1988
       December; 9 p. (Format: TXT=19934 bytes)

1085   ISO presentation services on top of TCP/IP based internets. Rose, M.T.
       1988 December; 32 p. (Format: TXT=64643 bytes)

1084   BOOTP vendor information extensions. Reynolds, J.K. 1988 December; 8 p.
       (Format: TXT=16327 bytes) (Obsoletes RFC 1048; Obsoleted by RFC 1497)

1083   IAB official protocol standards. Defense Advanced Research Projects
       Agency, Internet Activities Board. 1988 December; 12 p. (Format:
       TXT=27128 bytes) (Obsoleted by RFC 1410)

1082   Post Office Protocol: Version 3: Extended service offerings. Rose, M.T.
       1988 November; 11 p. (Format: TXT=25423 bytes)

1081   Post Office Protocol: Version 3. Rose, M.T. 1988 November; 16 p.
       (Format: TXT=37009 bytes) (Obsoleted by RFC 1225)

1080   Telnet remote flow control option. Hedrick, C.L. 1988 November; 4 p.
       (Format: TXT=6688 bytes) (Obsoleted by RFC 1372)

1079   Telnet terminal speed option. Hedrick, C.L. 1988 December; 3 p.
       (Format: TXT=4942 bytes)

1078   TCP port service Multiplexer (TCPMUX). Lottor, M. 1988 November; 2 p.
       (Format: TXT=3248 bytes)

1077   Critical issues in high bandwidth networking. Leiner, B.M.,ed. 1988
       November; 46 p. (Format: TXT=116464 bytes)

1076   HEMS monitoring and control language. Trewitt, G.; Partridge, C. 1988
       November; 42 p. (Format: TXT=98774 bytes) (Obsoletes RFC 1023)

1075   Distance Vector Multicast Routing Protocol. Waitzman, D.; Partridge, C.;
       Deering, S.E. 1988 November; 24 p. (Format: TXT=54731 bytes)

1074   NSFNET backbone SPF based Interior Gateway Protocol. Rekhter, J. 1988
       October; 5 p. (Format: TXT=10872 bytes)

1073   Telnet window size option. Waitzman, D. 1988 October; 4 p. (Format:
       TXT=7639 bytes)

1072   TCP extensions for long-delay paths. Jacobson, V.; Braden, R.T. 1988
       October; 16 p. (Format: TXT=36000 bytes) (Obsoleted by RFC 1323)

V

Resource Reference

1071   Computing the Internet checksum. Braden, R.T.; Borman, D.A.; Partridge,
       C. 1988 September; 24 p. (Format: TXT=54941 bytes) (Updated by RFC
       1141)

1070   Use of the Internet as a subnetwork for experimentation with the OSI
       network layer. Hagens, R.A.; Hall, N.E.; Rose, M.T. 1989 February;
       17 p. (Format: TXT=37354 bytes)

1069   Guidelines for the use of Internet-IP addresses in the ISO
       Connectionless-Mode Network Protocol. Callon, R.W.; Braun, H.W. 1989
       February; 10 p. (Format: TXT=24268 bytes) (Obsoletes RFC 986)

1068   Background File Transfer Program (BFTP). DeSchon, A.L.; Braden, R.T.
       1988 August; 27 p. (Format: TXT=51004 bytes)

1067   Simple Network Management Protocol. Case, J.D.; Fedor, M.; Schoffstall,
       M.L.; Davin, J.R. 1988 August; 33 p. (Format: TXT=69592 bytes)
       (Obsoleted by RFC 1098)

1066   Management Information Base for network management of TCP/IP-based
       internets. McCloghrie, K.; Rose, M.T. 1988 August; 90 p. (Format:
       TXT=135177 bytes) (Obsoleted by RFC 1156)

1065   Structure and identification of management information for TCP/IP-based
       internets. McCloghrie, K.; Rose, M.T. 1988 August; 21 p. (Format:
       TXT=38858 bytes) (Obsoleted by RFC 1155)

1064   Interactive Mail Access Protocol: Version 2. Crispin, M.R. 1988 July;
       26 p. (Format: TXT=57813 bytes) (Obsoleted by RFC 1176, RFC 1203)

1063   IP MTU discovery options. Mogul, J.C.; Kent, C.A.; Partridge, C.;
       McCloghrie, K. 1988 July; 11 p. (Format: TXT=27121 bytes)
       (Obsoleted by RFC 1191)

1062   Internet numbers. Romano, S.; Stahl, M.K.; Recker, M. 1988 August;
       65 p. (Format: TXT=198729 bytes) (Obsoletes RFC 1020; Obsoleted by RFC
       1117)

1061   Not yet issued.

1060   Assigned numbers. Reynolds, J.K.; Postel, J.B. 1990 March; 86 p.
       (Format: TXT=177923 bytes) (Obsoletes RFC 1010; Obsoleted by RFC 1340;
       Updated by RFC 1349)

1059   Network Time Protocol (version 1) specification and implementation.
       Mills, D.L. 1988 July; 58 p. (Format: TXT=140890 bytes) (Obsoleted by
       RFC 1119)

1058   Routing Information Protocol. Hedrick, C.L. 1988 June; 33 p. (Format:
       TXT=93285 bytes) (Updated by RFC 1388)

1057   RPC: Remote Procedure Call Protocol specification: Version 2. Sun
       Microsystems, Inc. 1988 June; 25 p. (Format: TXT=52462 bytes)
       (Obsoletes RFC 1050)

1056   PCMAIL: A distributed mail system for personal computers. Lambert, M.L.
       1988 June; 38 p. (Format: TXT=85368 bytes) (Obsoletes RFC 993)

1055 Nonstandard for transmission of IP datagrams over serial lines: SLIP.
Romkey, J.L. 1988 June; 6 p. (Format: TXT=12911 bytes)

1054 Host extensions for IP multicasting. Deering, S.E. 1988 May; 19 p.
(Format: TXT=45465 bytes) (Obsoletes RFC 988; Obsoleted by RFC 1112)

1053 Telnet X.3 PAD option. Levy, S.; Jacobson, T. 1988 April; 21 p.
(Format: TXT=48952 bytes)

1052 IAB recommendations for the development of Internet network management
standards. Cerf, V.G. 1988 April; 14 p. (Format: TXT=30569 bytes)

1051 Standard for the transmission of IP datagrams and ARP packets over
ARCNET networks. Prindeville, P.A. 1988 March; 4 p. (Format: TXT=7779
bytes) (Obsoleted by RFC 1201)

1050 RPC: Remote Procedure Call Protocol specification. Sun Microsystems,
Inc. 1988 April; 24 p. (Format: TXT=51540 bytes) (Obsoleted by RFC
1057)

1049 Content-type header field for Internet messages. Sirbu, M.A. 1988
March; 8 p. (Format: TXT=18923 bytes)

1048 BOOTP vendor information extensions. Prindeville, P.A. 1988 February;
7 p. (Format: TXT=15423 bytes) (Obsoleted by RFC 1084, RFC 1395, RFC
1497)

1047 Duplicate messages and SMTP. Partridge, C. 1988 February; 3 p. (Format:
TXT=5888 bytes)

1046 Queuing algorithm to provide type-of-service for IP links. Prue, W.;
Postel, J.B. 1988 February; 11 p. (Format: TXT=30106 bytes)

1045 VMTP: Versatile Message Transaction Protocol: Protocol specification.
Cheriton, D.R. 1988 February; 123 p. (Format: TXT=272058 bytes)

1044 Internet Protocol on Network System's HYPERchannel: Protocol
specification. Hardwick, K.; Lekashman, J. 1988 February; 43 p.
(Format: TXT=103241 bytes)

1043 Telnet Data Entry Terminal option: DODIIS implementation. Yasuda, A.;
Thompson, T. 1988 February; 26 p. (Format: TXT=59478 bytes) (Updates
RFC 732)

1042 Standard for the transmission of IP datagrams over IEEE 802 networks.
Postel, J.B.; Reynolds, J.K. 1988 February; 15 p. (Format: TXT=35201
bytes) (Obsoletes RFC 948)

1041 Telnet 3270 regime option. Rekhter, Y. 1988 January; 6 p. (Format:
TXT=11608 bytes)

1040 Privacy enhancement for Internet electronic mail: Part I: Message
encipherment and authentication procedures. Linn, J. 1988 January;
29 p. (Format: TXT=76276 bytes) (Obsoletes RFC 989; Obsoleted by RFC
1113)

V

Resource Reference

1039 DoD statement on Open Systems Interconnection protocols. Latham, D.
1988 January; 3 p. (Format: TXT=6194 bytes) (Obsoletes RFC 945)

1038 Draft revised IP security option. St. Johns, M. 1988 January; 7 p.
(Format: TXT=15879 bytes) (Obsoleted by RFC 1108)

1037 NFILE - a file access protocol. Greenberg, B.; Keene, S. 1987 December;
86 p. (Format: TXT=197312 bytes)

1036 Standard for interchange of USENET messages. Horton, M.R.; Adams, R.
1987 December; 19 p. (Format: TXT=46891 bytes) (Obsoletes RFC 850)

1035 Domain names - implementation and specification. Mockapetris, P.V. 1987
November; 55 p. (Format: TXT=125626 bytes) (Obsoletes RFC 973, RFC 882,
RFC 883; Updated by RFC 1101, RFC 1183, RFC 1348)

1034 Domain names - concepts and facilities. Mockapetris, P.V. 1987
November; 55 p. (Format: TXT=129180 bytes) (Obsoletes RFC 973, RFC 882,
RFC 883; Updated by RFC 1101, RFC 1183, RFC 1348)

1033 Domain administrators operations guide. Lottor, M. 1987 November; 22 p.
(Format: TXT=37263 bytes)

1032 Domain administrators guide. Stahl, M.K. 1987 November; 14 p. (Format:
TXT=29454 bytes)

1031 MILNET name domain transition. Lazear, W.D. 1987 November; 10 p.
(Format: TXT=20137 bytes)

1030 On testing the NETBLT Protocol over divers networks. Lambert, M.L. 1987
November; 16 p. (Format: TXT=40964 bytes)

1029 More fault tolerant approach to address resolution for a Multi-LAN
system of Ethernets. Parr, G. 1988 May; 17 p. (Format: TXT=44019 bytes)

1028 Simple Gateway Monitoring Protocol. Davin, J.R.; Case, J.D.; Fedor, M.;
Schoffstall, M.L. 1987 November; 38 p. (Format: TXT=82440 bytes)

1027 Using ARP to implement transparent subnet gateways. Carl-Mitchell, S.;
Quarterman, J.S. 1987 October; 8 p. (Format: TXT=21297 bytes)

1026 Addendum to RFC 987: (Mapping between X.400 and RFC-822). Kille, S.E.
1987 September; 4 p. (Format: TXT=7117 bytes) (Obsoleted by RFC 1327;
Updates RFC 987; Updated by RFC 1138)

1025 TCP and IP bake off. Postel, J.B. 1987 September; 6 p. (Format:
TXT=11648 bytes)

1024 HEMS variable definitions. Partridge, C.; Trewitt, G. 1987 October;
74 p. (Format: TXT=126536 bytes)

1023 HEMS monitoring and control language. Trewitt, G.; Partridge, C. 1987
October; 17 p. (Format: TXT=40992 bytes) (Obsoleted by RFC 1076)

1022 High-level Entity Management Protocol (HEMP). Partridge, C.; Trewitt, G.
1987 October; 12 p. (Format: TXT=25348 bytes)

1021   High-level Entity Management System (HEMS). Partridge, C.; Trewitt, G.
        1987 October; 5 p. (Format: TXT=12993 bytes)

1020   Internet numbers. Romano, S.; Stahl, M.K.   1987 November; 51 p. (Format:
        TXT=146864 bytes)   (Obsoletes RFC 997; Obsoleted by RFC 1062, RFC 1117)

1019   Report of the Workshop on Environments for Computational Mathematics.
        Arnon, D.   1987 September; 8 p. (Format: TXT=21151 bytes)

1018   Some comments on SQuID. McKenzie, A.M.   1987 August; 3 p. (Format:
        TXT=7931 bytes)

1017   Network requirements for scientific research: Internet task force on
        scientific computing. Leiner, B.M.   1987 August; 19 p. (Format:
        TXT=49512 bytes)

1016   Something a host could do with source quench: The Source Quench
        Introduced Delay (SQuID). Prue, W.; Postel, J.B.   1987 July; 18 p.
        (Format: TXT=47922 bytes)

1015   Implementation plan for interagency research Internet. Leiner, B.M.
        1987 July; 24 p. (Format: TXT=63159 bytes)

1014   XDR: External Data Representation standard. Sun Microsystems, Inc.   1987
        June; 20 p. (Format: TXT=39316 bytes)

1013   X Window System Protocol, version 11: Alpha update April 1987.
        Scheifler, R.W.   1987 June; 101 p. (Format: TXT=244905 bytes)

1012   Bibliography of Request For Comments 1 through 999. Reynolds, J.K.;
        Postel, J.B.   1987 June; 64 p. (Format: TXT=129194 bytes)

1011   Official Internet protocols. Reynolds, J.K.; Postel, J.B.   1987 May;
        52 p. (Format: TXT=74593 bytes)   (Obsoletes RFC 991)

1010   Assigned numbers. Reynolds, J.K.; Postel, J.B.   1987 May; 44 p. (Format:
        TXT=78179 bytes)   (Obsoletes RFC 990; Obsoleted by RFC 1060)

1009   Requirements for Internet gateways. Braden, R.T.; Postel, J.B.   1987
        June; 55 p. (Format: TXT=128173 bytes)   (Obsoletes RFC 985)

1008   Implementation guide for the ISO Transport Protocol. McCoy, W.   1987
        June; 73 p. (Format: TXT=204664 bytes)

1007   Military supplement to the ISO Transport Protocol. McCoy, W.   1987 June;
        23 p. (Format: TXT=51280 bytes)

1006   ISO transport services on top of the TCP: Version 3. Rose, M.T.; Cass,
        D.E.   1987 May; 17 p. (Format: TXT=31935 bytes)   (Obsoletes RFC 983)

1005   ARPANET AHIP-E Host Access Protocol (enhanced AHIP). Khanna, A.; Malis,
        A.G.   1987 May; 31 p. (Format: TXT=69957 bytes)

1004   Distributed-protocol authentication scheme. Mills, D.L.   1987 April;
        8 p. (Format: TXT=21402 bytes)

V

Resource Reference

1003   Issues in defining an equations representation standard. Katz, A.R.
       1987 March; 7 p. (Format: TXT=19816 bytes)

1002   Protocol standard for a NetBIOS service on a TCP/UDP transport: Detailed
       specifications. Defense Advanced Research Projects Agency, Internet
       Activities Board, End-to-End Services Task Force, NetBIOS Working Group.
       1987 March; 85 p. (Format: TXT=170262 bytes)

1001   Protocol standard for a NetBIOS service on a TCP/UDP transport: Concepts
       and methods. Defense Advanced Research Projects Agency, Internet
       Activities Board, End-to-End Services Task Force, NetBIOS Working Group.
       1987 March; 68 p. (Format: TXT=158437 bytes)

1000   Request For Comments reference guide. Reynolds, J.K.; Postel, J.B. 1987
       August; 149 p. (Format: TXT=323960 bytes)   (Obsoletes RFC 999)

999   Requests For Comments summary notes: 900-999. Westine, A.; Postel, J.B.
       1987 April; 22 p. (Format: TXT=62877 bytes)   (Obsoleted by RFC 1000)

998   NETBLT: A bulk data transfer protocol. Clark, D.D.; Lambert, M.L.;
       Zhang, L. 1987 March; 21 p. (Format: TXT=57147 bytes)   (Obsoletes RFC
       969)

997   Internet numbers. Reynolds, J.K.; Postel, J.B. 1987 March; 42 p.
       (Format: TXT=123919 bytes)   (Obsoleted by RFC 1020, RFC 1117; Updates
       RFC 990)

996   Statistics server. Mills, D.L. 1987 February; 3 p. (Format: TXT=6127
       bytes)

995   End System to Intermediate System Routing Exchange Protocol for use in
       conjunction with ISO 8473. International Organization for
       Standardization. 1986 April; 41 p. (Format: TXT=94069 bytes)

994   Final text of DIS 8473, Protocol for Providing the Connectionless-mode
       Network Service. International Organization for Standardization. 1986
       March; 52 p. (Format: TXT=129006 bytes)   (Obsoletes RFC 926)

993   PCMAIL: A distributed mail system for personal computers. Clark, D.D.;
       Lambert, M.L. 1986 December; 28 p. (Format: TXT=71725 bytes)
       (Obsoletes RFC 984; Obsoleted by RFC 1056)

992   On communication support for fault tolerant process groups. Birman,
       K.P.; Joseph, T.A. 1986 November; 18 p. (Format: TXT=52313 bytes)

991   Official ARPA-Internet protocols. Reynolds, J.K.; Postel, J.B. 1986
       November; 46 p. (Format: TXT=65205 bytes)   (Obsoletes RFC 961;
       Obsoleted by RFC 1011)

990   Assigned numbers. Reynolds, J.K.; Postel, J.B. 1986 November; 75 p.
       (Format: TXT=174784 bytes)   (Obsoletes RFC 960; Obsoleted by RFC 1010;
       Updated by RFC 997)

989   Privacy enhancement for Internet electronic mail: Part I: Message
       encipherment and authentication procedures. Linn, J. 1987 February;
       23 p. (Format: TXT=63934 bytes)   (Obsoleted by RFC 1040, RFC 1113)

988   Host extensions for IP multicasting. Deering, S.E.   1986 July; 20 p.
       (Format: TXT=45220 bytes)   (Obsoletes RFC 966; Obsoleted by RFC 1054,
       RFC 1112)

987   Mapping between X.400 and RFC 822. Kille, S.E.   1986 June; 69 p.
       (Format: TXT=127540 bytes)   (Obsoleted by RFC 1327; Updated by RFC 1026)

986   Guidelines for the use of Internet-IP addresses in the ISO
       Connectionless-Mode Network Protocol [Working draft]. Callon, R.W.;
       Braun, H.W.   1986 June; 7 p. (Format: TXT=13950 bytes)   (Obsoleted by
       RFC 1069)

985   Requirements for Internet gateways – draft. National Science Foundation,
       Network Technical Advisory Group.   1986 May; 23 p. (Format: TXT=59221
       bytes)   (Obsoleted by RFC 1009)

984   PCMAIL: A distributed mail system for personal computers. Clark, D.D.;
       Lambert, M.L.   1986 May; 31 p. (Format: TXT=69333 bytes)   (Obsoleted by
       RFC 993)

983   ISO transport arrives on top of the TCP. Cass, D.E.; Rose, M.T.   1986
       April; 27 p. (Format: TXT=59819 bytes)   (Obsoleted by RFC 1006)

982   Guidelines for the specification of the structure of the Domain Specific
       Part (DSP) of the ISO standard NSAP address. Braun, H.W.   1986 April;
       11 p. (Format: TXT=22595 bytes)

981   Experimental multiple-path routing algorithm. Mills, D.L.   1986 March;
       22 p. (Format: TXT=59069 bytes)

980   Protocol document order information. Jacobsen, O.J.; Postel, J.B.   1986
       March; 12 p. (Format: TXT=24416 bytes)

979   PSN End-to-End functional specification. Malis, A.G.   1986 March; 15 p.
       (Format: TXT=39472 bytes)

978   Voice File Interchange Protocol (VFIP). Reynolds, J.K.; Gillman, R.;
       Brackenridge, W.A.; Witkowski, A.; Postel, J.B.   1986 February; 5 p.
       (Format: TXT=9223 bytes)

977   Network News Transfer Protocol. Kantor, B.; Lapsley, P.   1986 February;
       27 p. (Format: TXT=55062 bytes)

976   UUCP mail interchange format standard. Horton, M.R.   1986 February;
       12 p. (Format: TXT=26814 bytes)

975   Autonomous confederations. Mills, D.L.   1986 February; 10 p. (Format:
       TXT=28010 bytes)

974   Mail routing and the domain system. Partridge, C.   1986 January; 7 p.
       (Format: TXT=18581 bytes)

973   Domain system changes and observations. Mockapetris, P.V.   1986 January;
       10 p. (Format: TXT=22364 bytes)   (Obsoleted by RFC 1034, RFC 1035;
       Updates RFC 882, RFC 883)

972   Password Generator Protocol. Wancho, F.J.   1986 January; 2 p. (Format:
       TXT=3890 bytes)

971   Survey of data representation standards. DeSchon, A.L.   1986 January;
       9 p. (Format: TXT=22883 bytes)

970   On packet switches with infinite storage. Nagle, J.   1985 December; 9 p.
       (Format: TXT=24970 bytes)

969   NETBLT: A bulk data transfer protocol. Clark, D.D.; Lambert, M.L.;
       Zhang, L.   1985 December; 15 p. (Format: TXT=40894 bytes)   (Obsoleted by
       RFC 998)

968   Twas the night before start-up. Cerf, V.G.   1985 December; 2 p. (Format:
       TXT=2573 bytes)

967   All victims together. Padlipsky, M.A.   1985 December; 2 p. (Format:
       TXT=4820 bytes)

966   Host groups: A multicast extension to the Internet Protocol. Deering,
       S.E.; Cheriton, D.R.   1985 December; 27 p. (Format: TXT=61006 bytes)
       (Obsoleted by RFC 988)

965   Format for a graphical communication protocol. Aguilar, L.   1985
       December; 51 p. (Format: TXT=108361 bytes)

964   Some problems with the specification of the Military Standard
       Transmission Control Protocol. Sidhu, D.P.   1985 November; 10 p.
       (Format: TXT=21542 bytes)

963   Some problems with the specification of the Military Standard Internet
       Protocol. Sidhu, D.P.   1985 November; 19 p. (Format: TXT=45102 bytes)

962   TCP-4 prime. Padlipsky, M.A.   1985 November; 2 p. (Format: TXT=2885
       bytes)

961   Official ARPA-Internet protocols. Reynolds, J.K.; Postel, J.B.   1985
       December; 38 p. (Format: TXT=54874 bytes)   (Obsoletes RFC 944;
       Obsoleted by RFC 991)

960   Assigned numbers. Reynolds, J.K.; Postel, J.B.   1985 December; 60 p.
       (Format: TXT=129292 bytes)   (Obsoletes RFC 943; Obsoleted by RFC 990)

959   File Transfer Protocol. Postel, J.B.; Reynolds, J.K.   1985 October;
       69 p. (Format: TXT=151249 bytes)   (Obsoletes RFC 765 [IEN 149])

958   Network Time Protocol (NTP). Mills, D.L.   1985 September; 14 p. (Format:
       TXT=31520 bytes)   (Obsoleted by RFC 1119)

957   Experiments in network clock synchronization. Mills, D.L.   1985
       September; 27 p. (Format: TXT=70490 bytes)

956   Algorithms for synchronizing network clocks. Mills, D.L.   1985
       September; 26 p. (Format: TXT=68868 bytes)

955   Towards a transport service for transaction processing applications.
       Braden, R.T.   1985 September; 10 p. (Format: TXT=23066 bytes)

954   NICNAME/WHOIS. Harrenstien, K.; Stahl, M.K.; Feinler, E.J.   1985
October; 4 p. (Format: TXT=7623 bytes)   (Obsoletes RFC 812)

953   Hostname Server. Harrenstien, K.; Stahl, M.K.; Feinler, E.J.   1985
October; 5 p. (Format: TXT=8588 bytes)   (Obsoletes RFC 811)

952   DoD Internet host table specification. Harrenstien, K.; Stahl, M.K.;
Feinler, E.J.   1985 October; 6 p. (Format: TXT=12728 bytes)   (Obsoletes
RFC 810)

951   Bootstrap Protocol. Croft, W.J.; Gilmore, J.   1985 September; 12 p.
(Format: TXT=29038 bytes)   (Updated by RFC 1497)

950   Internet standard subnetting procedure. Mogul, J.C.; Postel, J.B.   1985
August; 18 p. (Format: TXT=39010 bytes)   (Updates RFC 792)

949   FTP unique-named store command. Padlipsky, M.A.   1985 July; 2 p.
(Format: TXT=4130 bytes)

948   Two methods for the transmission of IP datagrams over IEEE 802.3
networks. Winston, I.   1985 June; 5 p. (Format: TXT=11843 bytes)
(Obsoleted by RFC 1042)

947   Multi-network broadcasting within the Internet. Lebowitz, K.; Mankins,
D.   1985 June; 5 p. (Format: TXT=12854 bytes)

946   Telnet terminal location number option. Nedved, R.   1985 May; 4 p.
(Format: TXT=6513 bytes)

945   DoD statement on the NRC report. Postel, J.B.   1985 May; 2 p. (Format:
TXT=5131 bytes)   (Obsoleted by RFC 1039)

944   Official ARPA-Internet protocols. Reynolds, J.K.; Postel, J.B.   1985
April; 40 p. (Format: TXT=63693 bytes)   (Obsoletes RFC 924; Obsoleted by
RFC 961)

943   Assigned numbers. Reynolds, J.K.; Postel, J.B.   1985 April; 50 p.
(Format: TXT=108133 bytes)   (Obsoletes RFC 923; Obsoleted by RFC 960)

942   Transport protocols for Department of Defense data networks. National
Research Council.   1985 February; 68 p. (Format: TXT=222477 bytes)

941   Addendum to the network service definition covering network layer
addressing. International Organization for Standardization.   1985 April;
34 p. (Format: TXT=70706 bytes)

940   Toward an Internet standard scheme for subnetting. Gateway Algorithms
and Data Structures Task Force.   1985 April; 3 p. (Format: TXT=7061
bytes)

939   Executive summary of the NRC report on transport protocols for
Department of Defense data networks. National Research Council.   1985
February; 20 p. (Format: TXT=43485 bytes)

938   Internet Reliable Transaction Protocol functional and interface
specification. Miller, T.   1985 February; 16 p. (Format: TXT=40561
bytes)

V

Resource Reference

937   Post Office Protocol: Version 2. Butler, M.; Postel, J.B.; Chase, D.;
        Goldberger, J.; Reynolds, J.K.   1985 February; 24 p. (Format: TXT=43762
        bytes)   (Obsoletes RFC 918)

936   Another Internet subnet addressing scheme. Karels, M.J.   1985 February;
        4 p. (Format: TXT=10407 bytes)

935   Reliable link layer protocols. Robinson, J.G.   1985 January; 13 p.
        (Format: TXT=32335 bytes)

934   Proposed standard for message encapsulation. Rose, M.T.; Stefferud, E.A.
        1985 January; 10 p. (Format: TXT=22340 bytes)

933   Output marking Telnet option. Silverman, S.   1985 January; 4 p. (Format:
        TXT=6943 bytes)

932   Subnetwork addressing scheme. Clark, D.D.   1985 January; 4 p. (Format:
        TXT=9509 bytes)

931   Authentication server. St. Johns, M.   1985 January; 4 p. (Format:
        TXT=9259 bytes)   (Obsoletes RFC 912; Obsoleted by RFC 1413)

930   Telnet terminal type option. Solomon, M.; Wimmers, E.   1985 January;
        4 p. (Format: TXT=6805 bytes)   (Obsoletes RFC 884; Obsoleted by RFC
        1091)

929   Proposed Host-Front End Protocol. Lilienkamp, J.; Mandell, R.;
        Padlipsky, M.A.   1984 December; 52 p. (Format: TXT=138234 bytes)

928   Introduction to proposed DoD standard H-FP. Padlipsky, M.A.   1984
        December; 21 p. (Format: TXT=61658 bytes)

927   TACACS user identification Telnet option. Anderson, B.A.   1984 December;
        4 p. (Format: TXT=5702 bytes)

926   Protocol for providing the connectionless mode network services.
        International Organization for Standardization.   1984 December; 101 p.
        (Format: TXT=172024 bytes)   (Obsoleted by RFC 994)

925   Multi-LAN address resolution. Postel, J.B.   1984 October; 15 p. (Format:
        TXT=31992 bytes)

924   Official ARPA-Internet protocols for connecting personal computers to
        the Internet. Reynolds, J.K.; Postel, J.B.   1984 October; 35 p. (Format:
        TXT=50543 bytes)   (Obsoletes RFC 901; Obsoleted by RFC 944)

923   Assigned numbers. Reynolds, J.K.; Postel, J.B.   1984 October; 47 p.
        (Format: TXT=99193 bytes)   (Obsoletes RFC 900; Obsoleted by RFC 943)

922   Broadcasting Internet datagrams in the presence of subnets. Mogul, J.C.
        1984 October; 12 p. (Format: TXT=24832 bytes)

921   Domain name system implementation schedule - revised. Postel, J.B.   1984
        October; 13 p. (Format: TXT=24059 bytes)   (Updates RFC 897)

920   Domain requirements. Postel, J.B.; Reynolds, J.K.   1984 October; 14 p.
        (Format: TXT=28621 bytes)

919   Broadcasting Internet datagrams. Mogul, J.C. 1984 October; 8 p. (Format: TXT=16838 bytes)

918   Post Office Protocol. Reynolds, J.K. 1984 October; 5 p. (Format: TXT=10166 bytes)   (Obsoleted by RFC 937)

917   Internet subnets. Mogul, J.C. 1984 October; 22 p. (Format: TXT=48326 bytes)

916   Reliable Asynchronous Transfer Protocol (RATP). Finn, G.G. 1984 October; 54 p. (Format: TXT=113815 bytes)

915   Network mail path service. Elvy, M.A.; Nedved, R. 1984 December; 11 p. (Format: TXT=22262 bytes)

914   Thinwire protocol for connecting personal computers to the Internet. Farber, D.J.; Delp, G.; Conte, T.M. 1984 September; 22 p. (Format: TXT=58586 bytes)

913   Simple File Transfer Protocol. Lottor, M. 1984 September; 15 p. (Format: TXT=21784 bytes)

912   Authentication service. St. Johns, M. 1984 September; 3 p. (Format: TXT=4715 bytes)   (Obsoleted by RFC 931)

911   EGP Gateway under Berkeley UNIX 4.2. Kirton, P. 1984 August 22; 22 p. (Format: TXT=57043 bytes)

910   Multimedia mail meeting notes. Forsdick, H.C. 1984 August; 11 p. (Format: TXT=25553 bytes)

909   Loader Debugger Protocol. Welles, C.; Milliken, W. 1984 July; 127 p. (Format: TXT=217583 bytes)

908   Reliable Data Protocol. Velten, D.; Hinden, R.M.; Sax, J. 1984 July; 56 p. (Format: TXT=101185 bytes)   (Updated by RFC 1151)

907   Host Access Protocol specification. Bolt Beranek and Newman, Inc. 1984 July; 75 p. (Format: TXT=134566 bytes)   (Updated by RFC 1221)

906   Bootstrap loading using TFTP. Finlayson, R. 1984 June; 4 p. (Format: TXT=10329 bytes)

905   ISO Transport Protocol specification ISO DP 8073. McKenzie, A.M. 1984 April; 154 p. (Format: TXT=258729 bytes)   (Obsoletes RFC 892)

904   Exterior Gateway Protocol formal specification. Mills, D.L. 1984 April; 30 p. (Format: TXT=65226 bytes)   (Updates RFC 827, RFC 888)

903   Reverse Address Resolution Protocol. Finlayson, R.; Mann, T.; Mogul, J.C.; Theimer, M. 1984 June; 4 p. (Format: TXT=9572 bytes)

902   ARPA Internet Protocol policy. Reynolds, J.K.; Postel, J.B. 1984 July; 5 p. (Format: TXT=11317 bytes)

901 Official ARPA-Internet protocols. Reynolds, J.K.; Postel, J.B. 1984
June; 28 p. (Format: TXT=42682 bytes) (Obsoletes RFC 880; Obsoleted by
RFC 924)

900 Assigned Numbers. Reynolds, J.K.; Postel, J.B. 1984 June; 43 p.
(Format: TXT=84610 bytes) (Obsoletes RFC 870; Obsoleted by RFC 923)

899 Request For Comments summary notes: 800-899. Postel, J.B.; Westine, A.
1984 May; 18 p. (Format: TXT=41028 bytes)

898 Gateway special interest group meeting notes. Hinden, R.M.; Postel,
J.B.; Muuss, M.; Reynolds, J.K. 1984 April; 24 p. (Format: TXT=43504
bytes)

897 Domain name system implementation schedule. Postel, J.B. 1984 February;
8 p. (Format: TXT=16139 bytes) (Updates RFC 881; Updated by RFC 921)

896 Congestion control in IP/TCP internetworks. Nagle, J. 1984 January 6;
9 p. (Format: TXT=27294 bytes)

895 Standard for the transmission of IP datagrams over experimental Ethernet
networks. Postel, J.B. 1984 April; 3 p. (Format: TXT=5156 bytes)

894 Standard for the transmission of IP datagrams over Ethernet networks.
Hornig, C. 1984 April; 3 p. (Format: TXT=5868 bytes)

893 Trailer encapsulations. Leffler, S.; Karels, M.J. 1984 April; 3 p.
(Format: TXT=13695 bytes)

892 ISO Transport Protocol specification [Draft]. International Organization
for Standardization. 1983 December; 82 p. (Format: TXT=162564 bytes)
(Obsoleted by RFC 905)

891 DCN local-network protocols. Mills, D.L. 1983 December; 26 p. (Format:
TXT=66769 bytes)

890 Exterior Gateway Protocol implementation schedule. Postel, J.B. 1984
February; 3 p. (Format: TXT=6070 bytes)

889 Internet delay experiments. Mills, D.L. 1983 December; 12 p. (Format:
TXT=27812 bytes)

888 "STUB" Exterior Gateway Protocol. Seamonson, L.; Rosen, E.C. 1984
January; 38 p. (Format: TXT=55585 bytes) (Updated by RFC 904)

887 Resource Location Protocol. Accetta, M. 1983 December; 16 p. (Format:
TXT=37683 bytes)

886 Proposed standard for message header munging. Rose, M.T. 1983 December
15; 16 p. (Format: TXT=31546 bytes)

885 Telnet end of record option. Postel, J.B. 1983 December; 2 p. (Format:
TXT=3346 bytes)

884 Telnet terminal type option. Solomon, M.; Wimmers, E. 1983 December;
5 p. (Format: TXT=8166 bytes) (Obsoleted by RFC 930)

883   Domain names: Implementation specification. Mockapetris, P.V.   1983
      November; 73 p. (Format: TXT=179416 bytes)   (Obsoleted by RFC 1034, RFC
      1035; Updated by RFC 973)

882   Domain names: Concepts and facilities. Mockapetris, P.V.   1983 November;
      31 p. (Format: TXT=81574 bytes)   (Obsoleted by RFC 1034, RFC 1035;
      Updated by RFC 973)

881   Domain names plan and schedule. Postel, J.B.   1983 November; 10 p.
      (Format: TXT=24070 bytes)   (Updated by RFC 897)

880   Official protocols. Reynolds, J.K.; Postel, J.B.   1983 October; 26 p.
      (Format: TXT=38840 bytes)   (Obsoletes RFC 840; Obsoleted by RFC 901)

879   TCP maximum segment size and related topics. Postel, J.B.   1983
      November; 11 p. (Format: TXT=22662 bytes)

878   ARPANET 1822L Host Access Protocol. Malis, A.G.   1983 December; 48 p.
      (Format: TXT=77784 bytes)   (Obsoletes RFC 851)

877   Standard for the transmission of IP datagrams over public data networks.
      Korb, J.T.   1983 September; 2 p. (Format: TXT=3385 bytes)   (Obsoleted by
      RFC 1356)

876   Survey of SMTP implementations. Smallberg, D.   1983 September; 13 p.
      (Format: TXT=38529 bytes)

875   Gateways, architectures, and heffalumps. Padlipsky, M.A.   1982
      September; 8 p. (Format: TXT=23380 bytes)

874   Critique of X.25. Padlipsky, M.A.   1982 September; 13 p. (Format:
      TXT=37259 bytes)

873   Illusion of vendor support. Padlipsky, M.A.   1982 September; 8 p.
      (Format: TXT=23673 bytes)

872   TCP-on-a-LAN. Padlipsky, M.A.   1982 September; 8 p. (Format: TXT=22994
      bytes)

871   Perspective on the ARPANET reference model. Padlipsky, M.A.   1982
      September; 25 p. (Format: TXT=76037 bytes)

870   Assigned numbers. Reynolds, J.K.; Postel, J.B.   1983 October; 26 p.
      (Format: TXT=57563 bytes)   (Obsoletes RFC 820; Obsoleted by RFC 900)

869   Host Monitoring Protocol. Hinden, R.M.   1983 December; 70 p. (Format:
      TXT=98720 bytes)

868   Time Protocol. Postel, J.B.; Harrenstien, K.   1983 May; 2 p. (Format:
      TXT=3140 bytes)

867   Daytime Protocol. Postel, J.B.   1983 May; 2 p. (Format: TXT=2405 bytes)

866   Active users. Postel, J.B.   1983 May; 1 p. (Format: TXT=2087 bytes)

865   Quote of the Day Protocol. Postel, J.B.   1983 May; 1 p. (Format:
      TXT=1734 bytes)

V

Resource Reference

864   Character Generator Protocol. Postel, J.B.   1983 May; 3 p. (Format: TXT=7016 bytes)

863   Discard Protocol. Postel, J.B.   1983 May; 1 p. (Format: TXT=1297 bytes)

862   Echo Protocol. Postel, J.B.   1983 May; 1 p. (Format: TXT=1294 bytes)

861   Telnet extended options: List option. Postel, J.B.; Reynolds, J.K.   1983 May; 1 p. (Format: TXT=3181 bytes)   (Obsoletes NIC 16239)

860   Telnet timing mark option. Postel, J.B.; Reynolds, J.K.   1983 May; 4 p. (Format: TXT=8108 bytes)   (Obsoletes NIC 16238)

859   Telnet status option. Postel, J.B.; Reynolds, J.K.   1983 May; 3 p. (Format: TXT=4443 bytes)   (Obsoletes RFC 651)

858   Telnet Suppress Go Ahead option. Postel, J.B.; Reynolds, J.K.   1983 May; 3 p. (Format: TXT=3825 bytes)   (Obsoletes NIC 15392)

857   Telnet echo option. Postel, J.B.; Reynolds, J.K.   1983 May; 5 p. (Format: TXT=11143 bytes)   (Obsoletes NIC 15390)

856   Telnet binary transmission. Postel, J.B.; Reynolds, J.K.   1983 May; 4 p. (Format: TXT=9192 bytes)   (Obsoletes NIC 15389)

855   Telnet option specifications. Postel, J.B.; Reynolds, J.K.   1983 May; 4 p. (Format: TXT=6218 bytes)   (Obsoletes NIC 18640)

854   Telnet Protocol specification. Postel, J.B.; Reynolds, J.K.   1983 May; 15 p. (Format: TXT=39371 bytes)   (Obsoletes RFC 764, NIC 18639)

853   Not issued.

852   ARPANET short blocking feature. Malis, A.G.   1983 April; 13 p. (Format: TXT=17151 bytes)

851   ARPANET 1822L Host Access Protocol. Malis, A.G.   1983 April 18; 44 p. (Format: TXT=72042 bytes)   (Obsoletes RFC 802; Obsoleted by RFC 878)

850   Standard for interchange of USENET messages. Horton, M.R.   1983 June; 18 p. (Format: TXT=43871 bytes)   (Obsoleted by RFC 1036)

849   Suggestions for improved host table distribution. Crispin, M.R.   1983 May; 2 p. (Format: TXT=5290 bytes)

848   Who provides the "little" TCP services?. Smallberg, D.   1983 March 14; 5 p. (Format: TXT=11280 bytes)

847   Summary of Smallberg surveys. Smallberg, D.; Westine, A.; Postel, J.B.   1983 February; 2 p. (Format: TXT=3906 bytes)   (Obsoletes RFC 846)

846   Who talks TCP? - survey of 22 February 1983. Smallberg, D.   1983 February 23; 14 p. (Format: TXT=46421 bytes)   (Obsoletes RFC 845; Obsoleted by RFC 847)

845   Who talks TCP? - survey of 15 February 1983. Smallberg, D. 1983
       February 17; 14 p. (Format: TXT=46806 bytes) (Obsoletes RFC 843;
       Obsoleted by RFC 846)

844   Who talks ICMP, too? - Survey of 18 February 1983. Clements, R. 1983
       February 18; 5 p. (Format: TXT=9323 bytes) (Updates RFC 843)

843   Who talks TCP? - survey of 8 February 83. Smallberg, D. 1983 February
       9; 14 p. (Format: TXT=47023 bytes) (Obsoletes RFC 842; Obsoleted by RFC
       845; Updated by RFC 844)

842   Who talks TCP? - survey of 1 February 83. Smallberg, D. 1983 February
       3; 14 p. (Format: TXT=46784 bytes) (Obsoletes RFC 839; Obsoleted by RFC
       843)

841   Specification for message format for Computer Based Message Systems.
       National Bureau of Standards. 1983 January 27; 110 p. (Format:
       TXT=238774 bytes) (Obsoletes RFC 806)

840   Official protocols. Postel, J.B. 1983 April 13; 23 p. (Format:
       TXT=34868 bytes) (Obsoleted by RFC 880)

839   Who talks TCP?. Smallberg, D. 1983 January 26; 14 p. (Format: TXT=45987
       bytes) (Obsoletes RFC 838; Obsoleted by RFC 842)

838   Who talks TCP?. Smallberg, D. 1983 January 20; 14 p. (Format: TXT=45844
       bytes) (Obsoletes RFC 837; Obsoleted by RFC 839)

837   Who talks TCP?. Smallberg, D. 1983 January 12; 14 p. (Format: TXT=45627
       bytes) (Obsoletes RFC 836; Obsoleted by RFC 838)

836   Who talks TCP?. Smallberg, D. 1983 January 5; 13 p. (Format: TXT=44397
       bytes) (Obsoletes RFC 835; Obsoleted by RFC 837)

835   Who talks TCP?. Smallberg, D. 1982 December 29; 13 p. (Format:
       TXT=43713 bytes) (Obsoletes RFC 834; Obsoleted by RFC 836)

834   Who talks TCP?. Smallberg, D. 1982 December 22; 13 p. (Format:
       TXT=43512 bytes) (Obsoletes RFC 833; Obsoleted by RFC 835)

833   Who talks TCP?. Smallberg, D. 1982 December 14; 13 p. (Format:
       TXT=43728 bytes) (Obsoletes RFC 832; Obsoleted by RFC 834)

832   Who talks TCP?. Smallberg, D. 1982 December 7; 13 p. (Format: TXT=43518
       bytes) (Obsoleted by RFC 833)

831   Backup access to the European side of SATNET. Braden, R.T. 1982
       December; 5 p. (Format: TXT=12090 bytes)

830   Distributed system for Internet name service. Su, Z. 1982 October;
       16 p. (Format: TXT=32585 bytes)

829   Packet satellite technology reference sources. Cerf, V.G. 1982
       November; 5 p. (Format: TXT=10919 bytes)

828   Data communications: IFIP's international "network" of experts. Owen, K.
       1982 August; 11 p. (Format: TXT=29922 bytes)

827   Exterior Gateway Protocol (EGP). Rosen, E.C. 1982 October; 44 p.
      (Format: TXT=68436 bytes) (Updated by RFC 904)

826   Ethernet Address Resolution Protocol: Or converting network protocol
      addresses to 48.bit Ethernet address for transmission on Ethernet
      hardware. Plummer, D.C. 1982 November; 10 p. (Format: TXT=22026 bytes)

825   Request for comments on Requests For Comments. Postel, J.B. 1982
      November; 2 p. (Format: TXT=4255 bytes) (Obsoleted by RFC 1111)

824   CRONUS Virtual Local Network. MacGregor, W.I.; Tappan, D.C. 1982 August
      25; 41 p. (Format: TXT=58732 bytes)

823   DARPA Internet gateway. Hinden, R.M.; Sheltzer, A. 1982 September;
      33 p. (Format: TXT=62620 bytes) (Updates IEN 109, IEN 30)

822   Standard for the format of ARPA Internet text messages. Crocker, D.
      1982 August 13; 47 p. (Format: TXT=109200 bytes) (Obsoletes RFC 733;
      Updated by RFC 1327)

821   Simple Mail Transfer Protocol. Postel, J.B. 1982 August; 58 p. (Format:
      TXT=124482 bytes) (Obsoletes RFC 788)

820   Assigned numbers. Postel, J.B. 1982 August 14; 1 p. (Format: TXT=54213
      bytes) (Obsoletes RFC 790; Obsoleted by RFC 870)

819   Domain naming convention for Internet user applications. Su, Z.; Postel,
      J.B. 1982 August; 18 p. (Format: TXT=36358 bytes)

818   Remote User Telnet service. Postel, J.B. 1982 November; 2 p. (Format:
      TXT=3809 bytes)

817   Modularity and efficiency in protocol implementation. Clark, D.D. 1982
      July; 26 p. (Format: TXT=47319 bytes)

816   Fault isolation and recovery. Clark, D.D. 1982 July; 12 p. (Format:
      TXT=20754 bytes)

815   IP datagram reassembly algorithms. Clark, D.D. 1982 July; 9 p. (Format:
      TXT=15028 bytes)

814   Name, addresses, ports, and routes. Clark, D.D. 1982 July; 14 p.
      (Format: TXT=25426 bytes)

813   Window and acknowlegement strategy in TCP. Clark, D.D. 1982 July; 22 p.
      (Format: TXT=39277 bytes)

812   NICNAME/WHOIS. Harrenstien, K.; White, V. 1982 March 1; 3 p. (Format:
      TXT=5562 bytes) (Obsoleted by RFC 954)

811   Hostnames Server. Harrenstien, K.; White, V.; Feinler, E.J. 1982 March
      1; 5 p. (Format: TXT=8007 bytes) (Obsoleted by RFC 953)

810   DoD Internet host table specification. Feinler, E.J.; Harrenstien, K.;
      Su, Z.; White, V. 1982 March 1; 9 p. (Format: TXT=14659 bytes)
      (Obsoletes RFC 608; Obsoleted by RFC 952)

809   UCL facsimile system. Chang, T.   1982 February; 96 p. (Format: TXT=171153 bytes)

808   Summary of computer mail services meeting held at BBN on 10 January 1979. Postel, J.B.   1982 March 1; 8 p. (Format: TXT=15930 bytes)

807   Multimedia mail meeting notes. Postel, J.B.   1982 February 9; 6 p. (Format: TXT=11633 bytes)

806   Proposed Federal Information Processing Standard: Specification for message format for computer based message systems. National Bureau of Standards.   1981 September; 99 p. (Format: TXT=216377 bytes) (Obsoleted by RFC 841)

805   Computer mail meeting notes. Postel, J.B.   1982 February 8; 6 p. (Format: TXT=12522 bytes)

804   CCITT draft recommendation T.4 [Standardization of Group 3 facsimile apparatus for document transmission]. International Telecommunication Union, International Telegraph and Telephone Consultative Committee. 1981; 12 p. (Format: TXT=17025 bytes)

803   Dacom 450/500 facsimile data transcoding. Agarwal, A.; O'Connor, M.J.; Mills, D.L.   1981 November 2; 14 p. (Format: TXT=33826 bytes)

802   ARPANET 1822L Host Access Protocol. Malis, A.G.   1981 November; 43 p. (Format: TXT=62470 bytes)   (Obsoleted by RFC 851)

801   NCP/TCP transition plan. Postel, J.B.   1981 November; 21 p. (Format: TXT=42041 bytes)

800   Request For Comments summary notes: 700-799. Postel, J.B.; Vernon, J. 1982 November; 10 p. (Format: TXT=18354 bytes)

799   Internet name domains. Mills, D.L.   1981 September; 6 p. (Format: TXT=14189 bytes)

798   Decoding facsimile data from the Rapicom 450. Katz, A.R.   1981 September; 17 p. (Format: TXT=39853 bytes)

797   Format for Bitmap files. Katz, A.R.   1981 September; 2 p. (Format: TXT=3183 bytes)

796   Address mappings. Postel, J.B.   1981 September; 7 p. (Format: TXT=11645 bytes)   (Obsoletes IEN 115)

795   Service mappings. Postel, J.B.   1981 September; 7 p. (Format: TXT=5460 bytes)

794   Pre-emption. Cerf, V.G.   1981 September; 4 p. (Format: TXT=6022 bytes) (Updates IEN 125)

793   Transmission Control Protocol. Postel, J.B.   1981 September; 85 p. (Format: TXT=177957 bytes)

792   Internet Control Message Protocol. Postel, J.B.   1981 September; 21 p. (Format: TXT=30404 bytes)   (Obsoletes RFC 777; Updated by RFC 950)

Resource Reference

V

791   Internet Protocol. Postel, J.B.   1981 September; 45 p. (Format:
      TXT=97779 bytes)   (Obsoletes RFC 760; Updated by RFC 1349)

790   Assigned numbers. Postel, J.B.   1981 September; 15 p. (Format: TXT=36186
      bytes)   (Obsoletes RFC 776; Obsoleted by RFC 820)

789   Vulnerabilities of network control protocols: An example. Rosen, E.C.
      1981 July; 15 p. (Format: TXT=26440 bytes)

788   Simple Mail Transfer Protocol. Postel, J.B.   1981 November; 62 p.
      (Format: TXT=112698 bytes)   (Obsoletes RFC 780; Obsoleted by RFC 821)

787   Connectionless data transmission survey/tutorial. Chapin, A.L.   1981
      July; 41 p. (Format: TXT=86362 bytes)

786   Mail Transfer Protocol: ISI TOPS20 MTP-NIMAIL interface. Sluizer, S.;
      Postel, J.B.   1981 July; 2 p. (Format: TXT=3245 bytes)

785   Mail Transfer Protocol: ISI TOPS20 file definitions. Sluizer, S.;
      Postel, J.B.   1981 July; 3 p. (Format: TXT=7206 bytes)

784   Mail Transfer Protocol: ISI TOPS20 implementation. Sluizer, S.; Postel,
      J.B.   1981 July; 3 p. (Format: TXT=6030 bytes)

783   TFTP Protocol (revision 2). Sollins, K.R.   1981 June; 18 p. (Format:
      TXT=23522 bytes)   (Obsoletes IEN 133; Obsoleted by RFC 1350)

782   Virtual Terminal management model. Nabielsky, J.; Skelton, A.P.   1981;
      20 p. (Format: TXT=44887 bytes)

781   Specification of the Internet Protocol (IP) timestamp option. Su, Z.
      1981 May; 2 p. (Format: TXT=4100 bytes)

780   Mail Transfer Protocol. Sluizer, S.; Postel, J.B.   1981 May; 43 p.
      (Format: TXT=82951 bytes)   (Obsoletes RFC 772; Obsoleted by RFC 788)

779   Telnet send-location option. Killian, E.   1981 April; 2 p. (Format:
      TXT=2680 bytes)

778   DCNET Internet Clock Service. Mills, D.L.   1981 April 18; 5 p. (Format:
      TXT=9689 bytes)

777   Internet Control Message Protocol. Postel, J.B.   1981 April; 14 p.
      (Format: TXT=80232 bytes)   (Obsoletes RFC 760; Obsoleted by RFC 792)

776   Assigned numbers. Postel, J.B.   1981 January; 13 p. (Format: TXT=31065
      bytes)   (Obsoletes RFC 770; Obsoleted by RFC 790)

775   Directory oriented FTP commands. Mankins, D.; Franklin, D.; Owen, A.D.
      1980 December; 6 p. (Format: TXT=9822 bytes)

774   Internet Protocol Handbook: Table of contents. Postel, J.B.   1980
      October; 3 p. (Format: TXT=3625 bytes)   (Obsoletes RFC 766)

773   Comments on NCP/TCP mail service transition strategy. Cerf, V.G.   1980
      October; 11 p. (Format: TXT=22818 bytes)

772   Mail Transfer Protocol. Sluizer, S.; Postel, J.B.   1980 September; 31 p.
       (Format: TXT=62858 bytes)   (Obsoleted by RFC 780)

771   Mail transition plan. Cerf, V.G.; Postel, J.B.   1980 September; 9 p.
       (Format: TXT=19154 bytes)

770   Assigned numbers. Postel, J.B.   1980 September; 15 p. (Format: TXT=27117
       bytes)   (Obsoletes RFC 762; Obsoleted by RFC 776)

769   Rapicom 450 facsimile file format. Postel, J.B.   1980 September 26; 2 p.
       (Format: TXT=4194 bytes)

768   User Datagram Protocol. Postel, J.B.   1980 August 28; 3 p. (Format:
       TXT=6069 bytes)

767   Structured format for transmission of multi-media documents. Postel,
       J.B.   1980 August; 33 p. (Format: TXT=62316 bytes)

766   Internet Protocol Handbook: Table of contents. Postel, J.B.   1980 July;
       1 p. (Format: TXT=3585 bytes)   (Obsoleted by RFC 774)

765   File Transfer Protocol specification. Postel, J.B.   1980 June; 70 p.
       (Format: TXT=150771 bytes)   (Obsoletes RFC 542; Obsoleted by RFC 959)

764   Telnet Protocol specification. Postel, J.B.   1980 June; 15 p. (Format:
       TXT=40874 bytes)   (Obsoleted by RFC 854)

763   Role mailboxes. Abrams, M.D.   1980 May 7; 1 p. (Format: TXT=965 bytes)

762   Assigned numbers. Postel, J.B.   1980 January; 13 p. (Format: TXT=25421
       bytes)   (Obsoletes RFC 758; Obsoleted by RFC 770)

761   DoD standard Transmission Control Protocol. Postel, J.B.   1980 January;
       84 p. (Format: TXT=172234 bytes)

760   DoD standard Internet Protocol. Postel, J.B.   1980 January; 41 p.
       (Format: TXT=84214 bytes)   (Obsoletes IEN 123; Obsoleted by RFC 791, RFC
       777)

759   Internet Message Protocol. Postel, J.B.   1980 August; 71 p. (Format:
       TXT=127948 bytes)

758   Assigned numbers. Postel, J.B.   1979 August; 12 p. (Format: TXT=23606
       bytes)   (Obsoletes RFC 755; Obsoleted by RFC 762)

757   Suggested solution to the naming, addressing, and delivery problem for
       ARPANET message systems. Deutsch, D.P.   1979 September 10; 17 p.
       (Format: TXT=36773 bytes)

756   NIC name server - a datagram-based information utility. Pickens, J.R.;
       Feinler, E.J.; Mathis, J.E.   1979 July; 11 p. (Format: TXT=24172 bytes)

755   Assigned numbers. Postel, J.B.   1979 May 3; 12 p. (Format: TXT=22734
       bytes)   (Obsoletes RFC 750; Obsoleted by RFC 758)

754   Out-of-net host addresses for mail. Postel, J.B.   1979 April 6; 10 p.
       (Format: TXT=19791 bytes)

753   Internet Message Protocol. Postel, J.B.   1979 March; 62 p. (Format:
       TXT=97006 bytes)

752   Universal host table. Crispin, M.R.   1979 January 2; 13 p. (Format:
       TXT=34560 bytes)

751   Survey of FTP mail and MLFL. Lebling, P.D.   1978 December 10; 5 p.
       (Format: TXT=10363 bytes)

750   Assigned numbers. Postel, J.B.   1978 September 26; 10 p. (Format:
       TXT=20686 bytes)   (Obsoletes RFC 739; Obsoleted by RFC 755)

749   Telnet SUPDUP-Output option. Greenberg, B.   1978 September 18; 4 p.
       (Format: TXT=9160 bytes)

748   Telnet randomly-lose option. Crispin, M.R.   1978 April 1; 2 p. (Format:
       TXT=2858 bytes)

747   Recent extensions to the SUPDUP Protocol. Crispin, M.R.   1978 March 21;
       3 p. (Format: TXT=2928 bytes)

746   SUPDUP graphics extension. Stallman, R.   1978 March 17; 15 p. (Format:
       TXT=31081 bytes)

745   JANUS interface specifications. Beeler, M.   1978 March 30; 10 p.
       (Format: TXT=(22042 bytes)

744   MARS - a Message Archiving and Retrieval Service. Sattley, J.   1978
       January 8; 6 p. (Format: TXT=11337 bytes)

743   FTP extension: XRSQ/XRCP. Harrenstien, K.   1977 December 30; 8 p.
       (Format: TXT=16720 bytes)

742   NAME/FINGER Protocol. Harrenstien, K.   1977 December 30; 7 p. (Format:
       TXT=12733 bytes)   (Obsoleted by RFC 1194)

741   Specifications for the Network Voice Protocol (NVP). Cohen, D.   1977
       November 22; 30 p. (Format: TXT=59582 bytes)

740   NETRJS Protocol. Braden, R.T.   1977 November 22; 19 p. (Format:
       TXT=39953 bytes)   (Obsoletes RFC 599)

739   Assigned numbers. Postel, J.B.   1977 November 11; 11 p. (Format:
       TXT=16983 bytes)   (Obsoletes RFC 604, RFC 503; Obsoleted by RFC 750)

738   Time server. Harrenstien, K.   1977 October 31; 1 p. (Format: TXT=1909
       bytes)

737   FTP extension: XSEN. Harrenstien, K.   1977 October 31; 1 p. (Format:
       TXT=2185 bytes)

736   Telnet SUPDUP option. Crispin, M.R.   1977 October 31; 2 p. (Format:
       TXT=3200 bytes)

735   Revised Telnet byte macro option. Crocker, D.; Gumpertz, R.H.   1977
       November 3; 5 p. (Format: TXT=10879 bytes)   (Obsoletes RFC 729)

734   SUPDUP Protocol. Crispin, M.R. 1977 October 7; 14 p. (Format: TXT=33920 bytes)

733   Standard for the format of ARPA network text messages. Crocker, D.; Vittal, J.; Pogran, K.T.; Henderson, D.A. 1977 November 21; 38 p. (Format: TXT=75001 bytes) (Obsoletes RFC 724; Obsoleted by RFC 822)

732   Telnet Data Entry Terminal option. Day, J.D. 1977 September 12; 30 p. (Format: TXT=58929 bytes) (Obsoletes RFC 731; Updated by RFC 1043)

731   Telnet Data Entry Terminal option. Day, J.D. 1977 June 27; 28 p. (Format: TXT=63300 bytes) (Obsoleted by RFC 732)

730   Extensible field addressing. Postel, J.B. 1977 May 20; 5 p. (Format: TXT=9812 bytes)

729   Telnet byte macro option. Crocker, D. 1977 May 13; 4 p. (Format: TXT=6695 bytes) (Obsoleted by RFC 735)

728   Minor pitfall in the Telnet Protocol. Day, J.D. 1977 April 27; 1 p. (Format: TXT=2265 bytes)

727   Telnet logout option. Crispin, M.R. 1977 April 27; 3 p. (Format: TXT=5850 bytes)

726   Remote Controlled Transmission and Echoing Telnet option. Postel, J.B.; Crocker, D. 1977 March 8; 16 p. (Format: TXT=39594 bytes)

725   RJE protocol for a resource sharing network. Day, J.D.; Grossman, G.R. 1977 March 1; 26 p. (Format: TXT=45604 bytes)

724   Proposed official standard for the format of ARPA Network messages. Crocker, D.; Pogran, K.T.; Vittal, J.; Henderson, D.A. 1977 May 12; 33 p. (Format: TXT=77423 bytes) (Obsoleted by RFC 733)

723   Not issued.

722   Thoughts on interactions in distributed services. Haverty, J. 1976 September 16; 20 p. (Format: TXT=30278 bytes)

721   Out-of-band control signals in a Host-to-Host Protocol. Garlick, L.L. 1976 September 1; 7 p. (Format: TXT=13978 bytes)

720   Address specification syntax for network mail. Crocker, D. 1976 August 5; 4 p. (Format: TXT=6835 bytes)

719   Discussion on RCTE. Postel, J.B. 1976 July 22; 2 p. (Format: TXT=4823 bytes)

718   Comments on RCTE from the Tenex implementation experience. Postel, J.B. 1976 June 30; 2 p. (Format: TXT=3944 bytes)

717   Assigned network numbers. Postel, J.B. 1976 July 1; 2 p. (Format: TXT=2430 bytes)

716   Interim revision to Appendix F of BBN 1822. Walden, D.C.; Levin, J. 1976 May 24; 2 p. (Format: TXT=3451 bytes)

715   Not issued.

714   Host-Host Protocol for an ARPANET-type network (Not online) McKenzie, A.M. 1976 April 21; 43 p.

713   MSDTP-Message Services Data Transmission Protocol. Haverty, J. 1976 April 6; 29 p. (Format: TXT=42452 bytes)

712   Distributed Capability Computing System (DCCS) (Not online) Donnelley, J.E. 1976 February 5; 38 p.

711   Not issued.

710   Not issued.

709   Not issued.

708   Elements of a distributed programming system. White, J.E. 1976 January 28; 29 p. (Format: TXT=59595 bytes)

707   High-level framework for network-based resource sharing. White, J.E. 1975 December 23; 27 p. (Format: TXT=58900 bytes)

706   On the junk mail problem. Postel, J.B. 1975 November 8; 1 p. (Format: TXT=2131 bytes)

705   Front-end Protocol B6700 version. Bryan, R.F. 1975 November 5; 40 p. (Format: TXT=73143 bytes)

704   IMP/Host and Host/IMP Protocol change. Santos, P.J. 1975 September 15; 3 p. (Format: TXT=7676 bytes) (Obsoletes RFC 687)

703   July, 1975, survey of New-Protocol Telnet Servers (Not online) Dodds, D.W. 1975 July 11; 2 p.

702   September, 1974, survey of New-Protocol Telnet servers (Not online) Dodds, D.W. 1974 September 25; 2 p.

701   August, 1974, survey of New-Protocol Telnet servers. Dodds, D.W. 1974 August; 2 p. (Format: TXT=3662 bytes)

700   Protocol experiment. Mader, E.; Plummer, W.W.; Tomlinson, R.S. 1974 August; 6 p. (Format: TXT=14931 bytes)

699   Request For Comments summary notes: 600-699. Postel, J.B.; Vernon, J. 1982 November; 9 p. (Format: TXT=15219 bytes)

698   Telnet extended ASCII option. Mock, T. 1975 July 23; 4 p. (Format: TXT=5307 bytes)

697   CWD command of FTP (Not online) Lieb, J. 1975 July 14; 2 p.

696   Comments on the IMP/Host and Host/IMP Protocol changes   (Not online)
       Cerf, V.G.   1975 July 13; 2 p.

695   Official change in Host-Host Protocol. Krilanovich, M.   1975 July 5;
       2 p. (Format: TXT=3527 bytes)

694   Protocol information   (Not online) Postel, J.B.   1975 June 18; 36 p.

693   Not issued.

692   Comments on IMP/Host Protocol changes (RFCs 687 and 690)   (Not online)
       Wolfe, S.M.   1975 June 20; 2 p.   (Updates RFC 690)

691   One more try on the FTP. Harvey, B.   1975 May 28; 13 p. (Format:
       TXT=33535 bytes)

690   Comments on the proposed Host/IMP Protocol changes   (Not online) Postel,
       J.B.   1975 June 6; 4 p.   (Updates RFC 687; Updated by RFC 692)

689   Tenex NCP finite state machine for connections. Clements, R.   1975 May
       23; 6 p. (Format: TXT=13378 bytes)

688   Tentative schedule for the new Telnet implementation for the TIP   (Not
       online) Walden, D.C.   1975 June 4; 1 p.

687   IMP/Host and Host/IMP Protocol changes. Walden, D.C.   1975 June 2; 3 p.
       (Format: TXT=6183 bytes)   (Obsoleted by RFC 704; Updated by RFC 690)

686   Leaving well enough alone   (Not online) Harvey, B.   1975 May 10; 9 p.

685   Response time in cross network debugging. Beeler, M.   1975 April 16;
       4 p. (Format: TXT=7084 bytes)

684   Commentary on procedure calling as a network protocol. Schantz, R.   1975
       April 15; 7 p. (Format: TXT=21575 bytes)

683   FTPSRV - Tenex extension for paged files. Clements, R.   1975 April 3;
       9 p. (Format: TXT=8981 bytes)

682   Not issued.

681   Network UNIX. Holmgren, S.   1975 March 18; 6 p. (Format: TXT=19305
       bytes)

680   Message Transmission Protocol   (Not online) Myer, T.H.; Henderson, D.A.
       1975 April 30; 6 p.   (Updates RFC 561)

679   February, 1975, survey of New-Protocol Telnet servers   (Not online)
       Dodds, D.W.   1975 February 21; 2 p.

678   Standard file formats. Postel, J.B.   1974 December 19; 8 p. (Format:
       TXT=12865 bytes)

677   Maintenance of duplicate databases   (Not online) Johnson, P.R.; Thomas,
       R.   1975 January 27; 9 p.

V

Resource Reference

676   Not issued.

675   Specification of Internet Transmission Control Program (Not online)
      Cerf, V.G.; Dalal, Y.K.; Sunshine, C.A. 1974 December; 70 p.

674   Procedure call documents: Version 2. Postel, J.B.; White, J.E. 1974
      December 12; 4 p. (Format: TXT=12475 bytes)

673   Not issued.

672   Multi-site data collection facility. Schantz, R. 1974 December 6; 10 p.
      (Format: TXT=26279 bytes)

671   Note on Reconnection Protocol (Not online) Schantz, R. 1974 December
      6; 8 p.

670   Not issued.

669   November, 1974, survey of New-Protocol Telnet servers (Not online)
      Dodds, D.W. 1974 December 4; 4 p.

668   Not issued.

667   BBN host ports (Not online) Chipman, S.G. 1974 December 17; 1 p.

666   Specification of the Unified User-Level Protocol (Not online)
      Padlipsky, M.A. 1974 November 26; 17 p.

665   Not issued.

664   Not issued.

663   Lost message detection and recovery protocol. Kanodia, R. 1974 November
      29; 17 p. (Format: TXT=45956 bytes)

662   Performance improvement in ARPANET file transfers from Multics. Kanodia,
      R. 1974 November 26; 3 p. (Format: TXT=9048 bytes)

661   Protocol information (Not online) Postel, J.B. 1974 November 23; 23 p.

660   Some changes to the IMP and the IMP/Host interface. Walden, D.C. 1974
      October 23; 2 p. (Format: TXT=5106 bytes)

659   Announcing additional Telnet options (Not online) Postel, J.B. 1974
      October 18; 1 p.

658   Telnet output linefeed disposition. Crocker, D. 1974 October 25; 4 p.
      (Format: TXT=6603 bytes)

657   Telnet output vertical tab disposition option. Crocker, D. 1974 October
      25; 4 p. (Format: TXT=5871 bytes)

656   Telnet output vertical tabstops option. Crocker, D. 1974 October 25;
      3 p. (Format: TXT=4952 bytes)

655   Telnet output formfeed disposition option. Crocker, D. 1974 October 25;
       4 p. (Format: TXT=6105 bytes)

654   Telnet output horizontal tab disposition option. Crocker, D. 1974
       October 25; 4 p. (Format: TXT=6270 bytes)

653   Telnet output horizontal tabstops option. Crocker, D. 1974 October 25;
       3 p. (Format: TXT=4782 bytes)

652   Telnet output carriage-return disposition option. Crocker, D. 1974
       October 25; 3 p. (Format: TXT=7165 bytes)

651   Revised Telnet status option. Crocker, D. 1974 October 25; 3 p.
       (Format: TXT=4446 bytes)   (Obsoleted by RFC 859)

650   Not issued.

649   Not issued.

648   Not issued.

647   Proposed protocol for connecting host computers to ARPA-like networks
       via front end processors (Not online) Padlipsky, M.A. 1974 November
       12; 20 p.

646   Not issued.

645   Network Standard Data Specification syntax (Not online) Crocker, D.
       1974 June 26; 9 p.

644   On the problem of signature authentication for network mail. Thomas, R.
       1974 July 22; 6 p. (Format: TXT=9728 bytes)

643   Network Debugging Protocol. Mader, E. 1974 July; 8 p. (Format:
       TXT=12959 bytes)

642   Ready line philosophy and implementation (Not online) Burchfiel, J.D.
       1974 July 5; 5 p.

641   Not issued.

640   Revised FTP reply codes. Postel, J.B. 1974 June 5; 16 p. (Format:
       TXT=40431 bytes)

639   Not issued.

638   IMP/TIP preventive maintenance schedule (Not online) McKenzie, A.M.
       1974 April 25; 4 p.   (Obsoletes RFC 633)

637   Change of network address for SU-DSL (Not online) McKenzie, A.M. 1974
       April 23; 1 p.

636   TIP/Tenex reliability improvements. Burchfiel, J.D.; Cosell, B.;
       Tomlinson, R.S.; Walden, D.C. 1974 June 10; 9 p. (Format: TXT=20360
       bytes)

V

Resource Reference

635   Assessment of ARPANET protocols (Not online) Cerf, V.G. 1974 April 22; 21 p.

634   Change in network address for Haskins Lab (Not online) McKenzie, A.M. 1974 April 10; 1 p.

633   IMP/TIP preventive maintenance schedule (Not online) McKenzie, A.M. 1974 March 18; 4 p. (Obsoleted by RFC 638)

632   Throughput degradations for single packet messages (Not online) Opderbeck, H. 1974 May 20; 6 p.

631   International meeting on minicomputers and data communication: Call for papers (Not online) Danthine, A. 1974 April 17; 1 p.

630   FTP error code usage for more reliable mail service (Not online) Sussmann, J. 1974 April 10; 2 p.

629   Scenario for using the Network Journal (Not online) North, J.B. 1974 March 27; 2 p.

628   Status of RFC numbers and a note on pre-assigned journal numbers (Not online) Keeney, M.L. 1974 March 27; 1 p.

627   ASCII text file of hostnames (Not online) Kudlick, M.D.; Feinler, E.J. 1974 March 25; 1 p.

626   On a possible lockup condition in IMP subnet due to message sequencing. Kleinrock, L.; Opderbeck, H. 1974 March 14; 6 p. (Format: TXT=13484 bytes)

625   On-line hostnames service (Not online) Kudlick, M.D.; Feinler, E.J. 1974 March 7; 1 p.

624   Comments on the File Transfer Protocol. Krilanovich, M.; Gregg, G.; Hathaway, W.; White, J.E. 1974 February 28; 4 p. (Format: TXT=10335 bytes) (Obsoletes RFC 607)

623   Comments on on-line host name service (Not online) Krilanovich, M. 1974 February 22; 2 p.

622   Scheduling IMP/TIP down time (Not online) McKenzie, A.M. 1974 March 13; 3 p.

621   NIC user directories at SRI ARC (Not online) Kudlick, M.D. 1974 March 6; 1 p.

620   Request for monitor host table updates. Ferguson, B. 1974 March 1; 2 p. (Format: TXT=1995 bytes)

619   Mean round-trip times in the ARPANET (Not online) Naylor, W.; Opderbeck, H. 1974 March 7; 13 p.

618   Few observations on NCP statistics. Taft, E.A. 1974 February 19; 4 p. (Format: TXT=5155 bytes)

617   Note on socket number assignment. Taft, E.A.   1974 February 19; 4 p.
      (Format: TXT=8281 bytes)

616   Latest network maps   (Not online) Walden, D.C.   1973 February 11; 3 p.

615   Proposed Network Standard Data Pathname syntax. Crocker, D.   1974 March
      1; 6 p. (Format: TXT=9735 bytes)

614   Response to RFC 607: "Comments on the File Transfer Protocol". Pogran,
      K.T.; Neigus, N.   1974 January 28; 5 p. (Format: TXT=11641 bytes)
      (Updates RFC 607)

613   Network connectivity: A response to RFC 603   (Not online) McKenzie, A.M.
      1974 January 21; 1 p.   (Updates RFC 603)

612   Traffic statistics (December 1973)   (Not online) McKenzie, A.M.   1974
      January 16; 5 p.

611   Two changes to the IMP/Host Protocol to improve user/network
      communications   (Not online) Walden, D.C.   1974 February 14; 4 p.

610   Further datalanguage design concepts   (Not online) Winter, R.; Hill, J.;
      Greiff, W.   1973 December 15; 79 p.

609   Statement of upcoming move of NIC/NLS service   (Not online) Ferguson, B.
      1974 January 10; 1 p.

608   Host names on-line   (Not online) Kudlick, M.D.   1974 January 10; 3 p.
      (Obsoleted by RFC 810)

607   Comments on the File Transfer Protocol. Krilanovich, M.; Gregg, G.   1974
      January 7; 4 p. (Format: TXT=8826 bytes)   (Obsoleted by RFC 624;
      Updated by RFC 614)

606   Host names on-line. Deutsch, L.P.   1973 December 29; 3 p. (Format:
      TXT=7027 bytes)

605   Not issued.

604   Assigned link numbers   (Not online) Postel, J.B.   1973 December 26; 2 p.
      (Obsoletes RFC 317; Obsoleted by RFC 739)

603   Response to RFC 597: Host status   (Not online) Burchfiel, J.D.   1973
      December 31; 1 p.   (Updates RFC 597; Updated by RFC 613)

602   "The stockings were hung by the chimney with care". Metcalfe, R.M.   1973
      December 27; 2 p. (Format: TXT=2035 bytes)

601   Traffic statistics (November 1973)   (Not online) McKenzie, A.M.   1973
      December 14; 5 p.

600   Interfacing an Illinois plasma terminal to the ARPANET   (Not online)
      Berggreen, A.   1973 November 26; 4 p.

599   Update on NETRJS. Braden, R.T.   1973 December 13; 8 p. (Format:
      TXT=17120 bytes)   (Obsoletes RFC 189; Obsoleted by RFC 740)

Resource Reference

V

598   RFC index - December 5, 1973 (Not online) Stanford Research Inst., Network Information Center. 1973 December 5; 8 p.

597   Host status (Not online) Neigus, N.; Feinler, E.J. 1973 December 12; 9 p. (Updated by RFC 603)

596   Second thoughts on Telnet Go-Ahead (Not online) Taft, E.A. 1973 December 8; 6 p.

595   Second thoughts in defense of the Telnet Go-Ahead (Not online) Hathaway, W. 1973 December 12; 5 p.

594   Speedup of Host-IMP interface (Not online) Burchfiel, J.D. 1973 December 10; 3 p.

593   Telnet and FTP implementation schedule change (Not online) McKenzie, A.M.; Postel, J.B. 1973 November 29; 1 p.

592   Some thoughts on system design to facilitate resource sharing (Not online) Watson, R.W. 1973 November 20; 5 p.

591   Addition to the Very Distant Host specifications (Not online) Walden, D.C. 1973 November 29; 1 p.

590   MULTICS address change (Not online) Padlipsky, M.A. 1973 November 19; 1 p.

589   CCN NETRJS server messages to remote user (Not online) Braden, R.T. 1973 November 26; 4 p.

588   London node is now up (Not online) Stokes, A.V. 1973 October 29; 3 p.

587   Announcing new Telnet options (Not online) Postel, J.B. 1973 November 13; 1 p.

586   Traffic statistics (October 1973) (Not online) McKenzie, A.M. 1973 November 8; 4 p.

585   ARPANET users interest working group meeting (Not online) Crocker, D.; Neigus, N.; Feinler, E.J.; Iseli, J. 1973 November 6; 9 p.

584   Charter for ARPANET Users Interest Working Group (Not online) Iseli, J.; Crocker, D.; Neigus, N. 1973 November 6; 2 p.

583   Not issued.

582   Comments on RFC 580: Machine readable protocols (Not online) Clements, R. 1973 November 5; 1 p. (Updates RFC 580)

581   Corrections to RFC 560: Remote Controlled Transmission and Echoing Telnet option (Not online) Crocker, D.; Postel, J.B. 1973 November 2; 4 p.

580   Note to protocol designers and implementers. Postel, J.B. 1973 October 25; 1 p. (Format: TXT=1492 bytes) (Updated by RFC 582)

579   Traffic statistics (September 1973)   (Not online) McKenzie, A.M.   1973
       November 26; 4 p.

578   Using MIT-Mathlab MACSYMA from MIT-DMS Muddle   (Not online) Bhushan,
       A.K.; Ryan, N.D.   1973 October 29; 13 p.

577   Mail priority   (Not online) Crocker, D.   1973 October 18; 2 p.

576   Proposal for modifying linking   (Not online) Victor, K.   1973 September
       26; 2 p.

575   Not issued.

574   Announcement of a mail facility at UCSB   (Not online) Krilanovich, M.
       1973 September 26; 1 p.

573   Data and file transfer: Some measurement results. (Not online) Bhushan,
       A.K.   1973 September 14; 12 p.

572   Not issued.

571   Tenex FTP problem   (Not online) Braden, R.T.   1973 November 15; 1 p.

570   Experimental input mapping between NVT ASCII and UCSB On Line System
       (Not online) Pickens, J.R.   1973 October 30; 10 p.

569   NETED: A common editor for the ARPA network. Padlipsky, M.A.   1973
       October 15; 7 p. (Format: TXT=18090 bytes)

568   Response to RFC 567 - cross country network bandwidth   (Not online)
       McQuillan, J.M.   1973 September 18; 2 p.   (Updates RFC 567)

567   Cross country network bandwidth. Deutsch, L.P.   1973 September 6; 1 p.
       (Format: TXT=1572 bytes)   (Updated by RFC 568)

566   Traffic statistics (August 1973)   (Not online) McKenzie, A.M.   1973
       September 4; 4 p.

565   Storing network survey data at the datacomputer   (Not online) Cantor, D.
       1973 August 28; 6 p.

564   Not issued.

563   Comments on the RCTE Telnet option   (Not online) Davidson, J.   1973
       August 28; 4 p.

562   Modifications to the Telnet specification   (Not online) McKenzie, A.M.
       1973 August 28; 1 p.

561   Standardizing network mail headers. Bhushan, A.K.; Pogran, K.T.;
       Tomlinson, R.S.; White, J.E.   1973 September 5; 2 p. (Format: TXT=6484
       bytes)   (Updated by RFC 680)

560   Remote Controlled Transmission and Echoing Telnet option   (Not online)
       Crocker, D.; Postel, J.B.   1973 August 18; 11 p.

V

Resource Reference

559   Comments on the new Telnet Protocol and its implementation (Not online)
       Bhushan, A.K. 1973 August 15; 5 p.

558   Not issued.

557   Revelations in network host measurements (Not online) Wessler, B.D.
       1973 August 30; 2 p.

556   Traffic statistics (July 1973) (Not online) McKenzie, A.M. 1973 August
       13; 4 p.

555   Responses to critiques of the proposed mail protocol (Not online)
       White, J.E. 1973 July 30; 14 p.

554   Not issued.

553   Draft design for a text/graphics protocol (Not online) Irby, C.H.;
       Victor, K. 1973 July 14; 17 p.

552   Single access to standard protocols (Not online) Owen, A.D. 1973 July
       13; 1 p.

551   [Letter from Feinroth re: NYU, ANL, and LBL entering the net, and FTP
       protocol] (Not online) Feinroth, Y.; Fink, R. 1973 August 27; 1 p.

550   NIC NCP experiment (Not online) Deutsch, L.P. 1973 August 24; 2 p.

549   Minutes of Network Graphics Group meeting, 15-17 July 1973 (Not online)
       Michener, J.C. 1973 July 17; 13 p.

548   Hosts using the IMP Going Down message (Not online) Walden, D.C. 1973
       August 16; 1 p.

547   Change to the Very Distant Host specification (Not online) Walden, D.C.
       1973 August 13; 4 p.

546   Tenex load averages for July 1973 (Not online) Thomas, R. 1973 August
       10; 4 p.

545   Of what quality be the UCSB resources evaluators? (Not online) Pickens,
       J.R. 1973 July 23; 2 p.

544   Locating on-line documentation at SRI-ARC (Not online) Meyer, N.D.;
       Kelley, K. 1973 July 13; 1 p.

543   Network journal submission and delivery (Not online) Meyer, N.D. 1973
       July 24; 8 p.

542   File Transfer Protocol. Neigus, N. 1973 July 12; 52 p. (Format:
       TXT=10340 bytes) (Obsoletes RFC 354; Obsoleted by RFC 765)

541   Not issued.

540   Not issued.

539 Thoughts on the mail protocol proposed in RFC 524 (Not online) Crocker, D.; Postel, J.B. 1973 July 7; 3 p.

538 Traffic statistics (June 1973) (Not online) McKenzie, A.M. 1973 July 5; 4 p.

537 Announcement of NGG meeting July 16-17 (Not online) Bunch, S. 1973 June 27; 2 p.

536 Not issued.

535 Comments on File Access Protocol (Not online) Thomas, R. 1973 July 25; 6 p.

534 Lost message detection (Not online) Walden, D.C. 1973 July 17; 2 p.

533 Message-ID numbers (Not online) Walden, D.C. 1973 July 17; 1 p.

532 UCSD-CC Server-FTP facility (Not online) Merryman, R.G. 1973 July 12; 3 p.

531 Feast or famine? A response to two recent RFC's about network information (Not online) Padlipsky, M.A. 1973 June 26; 2 p.

530 Report on the Survey project (Not online) Bhushan, A.K. 1973 June 22; 9 p.

529 Note on protocol synch sequences (Not online) McKenzie, A.M.; Thomas, R.; Tomlinson, R.S.; Pogran, K.T. 1973 June 29; 6 p.

528 Software checksumming in the IMP and network reliability (Not online) McQuillan, J.M. 1973 June 20; 11 p.

527 ARPAWOCKY. Covill, D.L. 1973 May; 1 p. (Format: TXT=1901 bytes)

526 Technical meeting: Digital image processing software systems (Not online) Pratt, W.K. 1973 June 25; 3 p.

525 MIT-MATHLAB meets UCSB-OLS -an example of resource sharing (Not online) Parrish, W.; Pickens, J.R. 1973 June 1; 10 p.

524 Proposed Mail Protocol (Not online) White, J.E. 1973 June 13; 44 p.

523 SURVEY is in operation again (Not online) Bhushan, A.K. 1973 June 5; 1 p.

522 Traffic statistics (May 1973) (Not online) McKenzie, A.M. 1973 June 5; 4 p.

521 Restricted use of IMP DDT (Not online) McKenzie, A.M. 1973 May 30; 2 p.

520 Memo to FTP group: Proposal for File Access Protocol (Not online) Day, J.D. 1973 June 25; 8 p.

V

Resource Reference

519   Resource evaluation   (Not online) Pickens, J.R.   1973 June; 6 p.

518   ARPANET accounts   (Not online) Vaughan, N.; Feinler, E.J.   1973 June 19;
      7 p.

517   Not issued.

516   Lost message detection   (Not online) Postel, J.B.   1973 May 18; 2 p.

515   Specifications for datalanguage: Version 0/9   (Not online) Winter, R.
      1973 June 6; 35 p.

514   Network make-work   (Not online) Kantrowitz, W.   1973 June 5; 3 p.

513   Comments on the new Telnet specifications   (Not online) Hathaway, W.
      1973 May 30; 3 p.

512   More on lost message detection   (Not online) Hathaway, W.   1973 May 23;
      1 p.

511   Enterprise phone service to NIC from ARPANET sites   (Not online) North,
      J.B.   1973 May 23; 4 p.

510   Request for network mailbox addresses   (Not online) White, J.E.   1973
      May 30; 3 p.

509   Traffic statistics (April 1973)   (Not online) McKenzie, A.M.   1973 April
      7; 3 p.

508   Real-time data transmission on the ARPANET   (Not online) Pfeifer, L.;
      McAfee, J.   1973 May 7; 11 p.

507   Not issued.

506   FTP command naming problem   (Not online) Padlipsky, M.A.   1973 June 26;
      1 p.

505   Two solutions to a file transfer access problem   (Not online) Padlipsky,
      M.A.   1973 June 25; 3 p.

504   Distributed resources workshop announcement   (Not online) Thomas, R.
      1973 April 30; 4 p.

503   Socket number list   (Not online) Neigus, N.; Postel, J.B.   1973 April
      12; 9 p.   (Obsoletes RFC 433; Obsoleted by RFC 739)

502   Not issued.

501   Un-muddling "free file transfer"   (Not online) Pogran, K.T.   1973 May
      11; 5 p.

500   Integration of data management systems on a computer network   (Not
      online) Shoshani, A.; Spiegler, I.   1973 April 16; 6 p.

499   Harvard's network RJE   (Not online) Reussow, B.R.   1973 April 1; 7 p.

498   On mail service to CCN   (Not online) Braden, R.T.   1973 April 17; 2 p.

497   Traffic statistics (March 1973)   (Not online) McKenzie, A.M.   1973 April 10; 4 p.

496   TNLS quick reference card is available   (Not online) Auerbach, M.F. 1973 April 5; 2 p.

495   Telnet Protocol specifications   (Not online) McKenzie, A.M.   1973 May 1; 3 p.   (Obsoletes RFC 158)

494   Availability of MIX and MIXAL in the Network   (Not online) Walden, D.C. 1973 April 20; 1 p.

493   Graphics Protocol   (Not online) Michener, J.C.; Cotton, I.W.; Kelley, K.C.; Liddle, D.E.; Meyer, E.W., Jr.   1973 April 26; 30 p.

492   Response to RFC 467   (Not online) Meyer, E.W., Jr.   1973 April 18; 9 p. (Updates RFC 467)

491   What is "Free"?   (Not online) Padlipsky, M.A.   1973 April 12; 2 p.

490   Surrogate RJS for UCLA-CCN   (Not online) Pickens, J.R.   1973 March 6; 5 p.

489   Comment on resynchronization of connection status proposal   (Not online) Postel, J.B.   1973 March 26; 1 p.

488   NLS classes at network sites   (Not online) Auerbach, M.F.   1973 March 23; 2 p.

487   Free file transfer   (Not online) Bressler, R.D.   1973 April 6; 2 p.

486   Data transfer revisited   (Not online) Bressler, R.D.   1973 March 20; 2 p.

485   MIX and MIXAL at UCSB   (Not online) Pickens, J.R.   1973 March 19; 1 p.

484   Not issued.

483   Cancellation of the resource notebook framework meeting   (Not online) Kudlick, M.D.   1973 March 14; 1 p.

482   Traffic statistics (February 1973)   (Not online) McKenzie, A.M.   1973 March 12; 4 p.

481   Not issued.

480   Host-dependent FTP parameters   (Not online) White, J.E.   1973 March 8; 1 p.

479   Use of FTP by the NIC Journal   (Not online) White, J.E.   1973 March 8; 6 p.

478   FTP server-server interaction - II   (Not online) Bressler, R.D.; Thomas,
      R.   1973 March 26; 2 p.

477   Remote Job Service at UCSB   (Not online) Krilanovich, M.   1973 May 23;
      18 p.

476   IMP/TIP memory retrofit schedule (rev. 2)   (Not online) McKenzie, A.M.
      1973 March 7; 2 p.   (Obsoletes RFC 447)

475   FTP and network mail system   (Not online) Bhushan, A.K.   1973 March 6;
      8 p.

474   Announcement of NGWG meeting: Call for papers   (Not online) Bunch, S.
      1973 March; 1 p.

473   MIX and MIXAL?   (Not online) Walden, D.C.   1973 February 28; 1 p.

472   Illinois' reply to Maxwell's request for graphics information (NIC
      14925)   (Not online) Bunch, S.   1973 March; 2 p.

471   Workshop on multi-site executive programs   (Not online) Thomas, R.   1973
      March 13; 2 p.

470   Change in socket for TIP news facility   (Not online) Thomas, R.   1973
      March 13; 1 p.

469   Network mail meeting summary   (Not online) Kudlick, M.D.   1973 March 8;
      9 p.

468   FTP data compression   (Not online) Braden, R.T.   1973 March 8; 5 p.

467   Proposed change to Host-Host Protocol: Resynchronization of connection
      status   (Not online) Burchfiel, J.D.; Tomlinson, R.S.   1973 February 20;
      13 p.   (Updated by RFC 492)

466   Telnet logger/server for host LL-67   (Not online) Winett, J.M.   1973
      February 27; 8 p.

465   Not issued.

464   Resource notebook framework   (Not online) Kudlick, M.D.   1973 February
      27; 2 p.

463   FTP comments and response to RFC 430   (Not online) Bhushan, A.K.   1973
      February 21; 3 p.

462   Responding to user needs   (Not online) Iseli, J.; Crocker, D.   1973
      February 22; 2 p.

461   Telnet Protocol meeting announcement   (Not online) McKenzie, A.M.   1973
      February 14; 1 p.

460   NCP survey   (Not online) Kline, C.   1973 February 13; 7 p.

459   Network questionnaires   (Not online) Kantrowitz, W.   1973 February 26;
      1 p.

458 Mail retrieval via FTP (Not online) Bressler, R.D.; Thomas, R. 1973 February 20; 2 p.

457 TIPUG (Not online) Walden, D.C. 1973 February 15; 1 p.

456 Memorandum: Date change of mail meeting (Not online) Kudlick, M.D. 1973 February 13; 1 p.

455 Traffic statistics (January 1973) (Not online) McKenzie, A.M. 1973 February 12; 4 p.

454 File Transfer Protocol – meeting announcement and a new proposed document (Not online) McKenzie, A.M. 1973 February 16; 38 p.

453 Meeting announcement to discuss a network mail system (Not online) Kudlick, M.D. 1973 February 7; 3 p.

452 Not issued.

451 Tentative proposal for a Unified User Level Protocol (Not online) Padlipsky, M.A. 1973 February 22; 3 p.

450 MULTICS sampling timeout change (Not online) Padlipsky, M.A. 1973 February 8; 1 p.

449 Current flow-control scheme for IMPSYS (Not online) Walden, D.C. 1973 January 6; 1 p. (Updates RFC 442)

448 Print files in FTP (Not online) Braden, R.T. 1973 February 27; 4 p.

447 IMP/TIP memory retrofit schedule (Not online) McKenzie, A.M. 1973 January 29; 2 p. (Obsoletes RFC 434; Obsoleted by RFC 476)

446 Proposal to consider a network program resource notebook (Not online) Deutsch, L.P. 1973 January 25; 1 p.

445 IMP/TIP preventive maintenance schedule (Not online) McKenzie, A.M. 1973 January 22; 3 p.

444 Not issued.

443 Traffic statistics (December 1972) (Not online) McKenzie, A.M. 1973 January 18; 3 p.

442 Current flow-control scheme for IMPSYS (Not online) Cerf, V.G. 1973 January 24; 7 p. (Updated by RFC 449)

441 Inter-Entity Communication – an experiment (Not online) Bressler, R.D.; Thomas, R. 1973 January 19; 10 p.

440 Scheduled network software maintenance (Not online) Walden, D.C. 1973 January; 1 p.

439 PARRY encounters the DOCTOR (Not online) Cerf, V.G. 1973 January 21; 5 p.

V

Resource Reference

438 FTP server-server interaction (Not online) Thomas, R.; Clements, R.
1973 January 15; 5 p.

437 Data Reconfiguration Service at UCSB (Not online) Faeh, E. 1973 June
30; 9 p.

436 Announcement of RJS at UCSB (Not online) Krilanovich, M. 1973 January
10; 2 p.

435 Telnet issues (Not online) Cosell, B.; Walden, D.C. 1973 January 5;
14 p. (Updates RFC 318)

434 IMP/TIP memory retrofit schedule (Not online) McKenzie, A.M. 1973
January 4; 2 p. (Obsoleted by RFC 447)

433 Socket number list (Not online) Postel, J.B. 1972 December 22; 8 p.
(Obsoletes RFC 349; Obsoleted by RFC 503)

432 Network logical map (Not online) Neigus, N. 1972 December 29; 2 p.

431 Update on SMFS login and logout (Not online) Krilanovich, M. 1972
December 15; 3 p. (Obsoletes RFC 399)

430 Comments on File Transfer Protocol (Not online) Braden, R.T. 1973
February 7; 8 p.

429 Character generator process (Not online) Postel, J.B. 1972 December
12; 1 p.

428 Not issued.

427 Not issued.

426 Reconnection Protocol (Not online) Thomas, R. 1973 January 26; 16 p.

425 "But my NCP costs $500 a day". Bressler, R.D. 1972 December 19; 1 p.
(Format: TXT=1817 bytes)

424 Not issued.

423 UCLA Campus Computing Network liaison staff for ARPANET (Not online)
Noble, B. 1972 December 12; 1 p. (Obsoletes RFC 389)

422 Traffic statistics (November 1972) (Not online) McKenzie, A.M. 1972
December 11; 4 p.

421 Software consulting service for network users (Not online) McKenzie,
A.M. 1972 November 27; 1 p.

420 CCA ICCC weather demo (Not online) Murray, H. 1973 January 4; 11 p.

419 To: Network liaisons and station agents (Not online) Vezza, A. 1972
December 12; 1 p.

418 Server file transfer under TSS/360 at NASA Ames (Not online) Hathaway,
W. 1972 November 27; 10 p.

417   Link usage violation   (Not online) Postel, J.B.; Kline, C.   1972
      December 6; 1 p.

416   ARC system will be unavailable for use during Thanksgiving week   (Not
      online) Norton, J.C.   1972 November 7; 1 p.

415   Tenex bandwidth   (Not online) Murray, H.   1972 November 29; 2 p.

414   File Transfer Protocol (FTP) status and further comments   (Not online)
      Bhushan, A.K.   1972 December 29; 5 p.   (Updates RFC 385)

413   Traffic statistics (October 1972)   (Not online) McKenzie, A.M.   1972
      November 13; 8 p.

412   User FTP documentation   (Not online) Hicks, G.   1972 November 27; 10 p.

411   New MULTICS network software features   (Not online) Padlipsky, M.A.
      1972 November 14; 1 p.

410   Removal of the 30-second delay when hosts come up   (Not online)
      McQuillan, J.M.   1972 November 10; 2 p.

409   Tenex interface to UCSB's Simple-Minded File System   (Not online) White,
      J.E.   1972 December 8; 8 p.

408   NETBANK   (Not online) Owen, A.D.; Postel, J.B.   1972 October 25; 1 p.

407   Remote Job Entry Protocol. Bressler, R.D.; Guida, R.; McKenzie, A.M.
      1972 October 16; 24 p. (Format: TXT=48770 bytes)   (Obsoletes RFC 360)

406   Scheduled IMP software releases   (Not online) McQuillan, J.M.   1972
      October 10; 2 p.

405   Correction to RFC 404   (Not online) McKenzie, A.M.   1972 October 10;
      1 p.   (Obsoletes RFC 404)

404   Host address changes involving Rand and ISI   (Not online) McKenzie, A.M.
      1972 October 5; 1 p.   (Obsoleted by RFC 405)

403   Desirability of a network 1108 service   (Not online) Hicks, G.   1973
      January 10; 5 p.

402   ARPA Network mailing lists   (Not online) North, J.B.   1972 October 26;
      8 p.   (Obsoletes RFC 363)

401   Conversion of NGP-0 coordinates to device specific coordinates   (Not
      online) Hansen, J.   1972 October 23; 2 p.

400   Traffic statistics (September 1972)   (Not online) McKenzie, A.M.   1972
      October 18; 3 p.

399   SMFS login and logout   (Not online) Krilanovich, M.   1972 September 26;
      2 p.   (Obsoleted by RFC 431; Updates RFC 122)

398   ICP sockets   (Not online) Pickens, J.R.; Faeh, E.   1972 September 22;
      2 p.

397   Not issued.

396   Network Graphics Working Group meeting - second iteration   (Not online)
       Bunch, S.   1972 November 13; 1 p.

395   Switch settings on IMPs and TIPs   (Not online) McQuillan, J.M.   1972
       October 3; 1 p.

394   Two proposed changes to the IMP-Host Protocol   (Not online) McQuillan,
       J.M.   1972 September 27; 3 p.

393   Comments on Telnet Protocol changes   (Not online) Winett, J.M.   1972
       October 3; 5 p.

392   Measurement of host costs for transmitting network data   (Not online)
       Hicks, G.; Wessler, B.D.   1972 September 20; 9 p.

391   Traffic statistics (August 1972)   (Not online) McKenzie, A.M.   1972
       September 15; 3 p.   (Obsoletes RFC 378)

390   TSO scenario   (Not online) Braden, R.T.   1972 September 12; 3 p.

389   UCLA Campus Computing Network liaison staff for ARPA Network   (Not
       online) Noble, B.   1972 August 30; 2 p.   (Obsoleted by RFC 423)

388   NCP statistics   (Not online) Cerf, V.G.   1972 August 23; 4 p.   (Updates
       RFC 323)

387   Some experiences in implementing Network Graphics Protocol Level 0   (Not
       online) Kelley, K.C.; Meir, J.   1972 August 10; 6 p.

386   Letter to TIP users-2   (Not online) Cosell, B.; Walden, D.C.   1972
       August 16; 7 p.

385   Comments on the File Transfer Protocol   (Not online) Bhushan, A.K.   1972
       August 18; 5 p.   (Updates RFC 354; Updated by RFC 414)

384   Official site idents for organizations in the ARPA Network   (Not online)
       North, J.B.   1972 August 28; 5 p.   (Obsoletes RFC 289)

383   Not issued.

382   Mathematical software on the ARPA Network   (Not online) McDaniel, L.
       1972 August 3; 1 p.

381   Three aids to improved network operation   (Not online) McQuillan, J.M.
       1972 July 26; 4 p.

380   Not issued.

379   Using TSO at CCN   (Not online) Braden, R.T.   1972 August 11; 5 p.

378   Traffic statistics (July 1972)   (Not online) McKenzie, A.M.   1972 August
       10; 3 p.   (Obsoleted by RFC 391)

377   Using TSO via ARPA Network Virtual Terminal   (Not online) Braden, R.T.
       1972 August 10; 8 p.

376   Network host status   (Not online) Westheimer, E.   1972 August 8; 3 p.
        (Obsoletes RFC 370)

375   Not issued.

374   IMP system announcement   (Not online) McKenzie, A.M.   1972 July 19; 2 p.

373   Arbitrary character sets   (Not online) McCarthy, J.   1972 July 14; 4 p.

372   Notes on a conversation with Bob Kahn on the ICCC   (Not online) Watson,
        R.W.   1972 July 12; 3 p.

371   Demonstration at International Computer Communications Conference   (Not
        online) Kahn, R.E.   1972 July 12; 2 p.

370   Network host status   (Not online) Westheimer, E.   1972 July 31; 3 p.
        (Obsoletes RFC 367; Obsoleted by RFC 376)

369   Evaluation of ARPANET services January-March, 1972   (Not online)
        Pickens, J.R.   1972 July 25; 14 p.

368   Comments on "Proposed Remote Job Entry Protocol"   (Not online) Braden,
        R.T.   1972 July 21; 2 p.

367   Network host status   (Not online) Westheimer, E.   1972 July 19; 3 p.
        (Obsoletes RFC 366; Obsoleted by RFC 370)

366   Network host status   (Not online) Westheimer, E.   1972 July 11; 3 p.
        (Obsoletes RFC 362; Obsoleted by RFC 367)

365   Letter to all TIP users   (Not online) Walden, D.C.   1972 July 11; 5 p.

364   Serving remote users on the ARPANET   (Not online) Abrams, M.D.   1972
        July 11; 7 p.

363   ARPA Network mailing lists   (Not online) Stanford Research Inst.,
        Network Information Center.   1972 August 8; 6 p.   (Obsoletes RFC 329;
        Obsoleted by RFC 402)

362   Network host status   (Not online) Westheimer, E.   1972 June 28; 3 p.
        (Obsoletes RFC 353; Obsoleted by RFC 366)

361   Deamon processes on host 106   (Not online) Bressler, R.D.   1972 July 5;
        1 p.

360   Proposed Remote Job Entry Protocol   (Not online) Holland, C.   1972 June
        24; 16 p.   (Obsoleted by RFC 407)

359   Status of the release of the new IMP System (2600)   (Not online) Walden,
        D.C.   1972 June 22; 1 p.   (Obsoletes RFC 343)

358   Not issued.

357   Echoing strategy for satellite links   (Not online) Davidson, J.   1972
        June 26; 15 p.

356   ARPA Network Control Center   (Not online) Alter, R.   1972 June 21; 1 p.

355   Response to NWG/RFC 346   (Not online) Davidson, J.   1972 June 9; 2 p.

354   File Transfer Protocol   (Not online) Bhushan, A.K.   1972 July 8; 29 p.
(Obsoletes RFC 264, RFC 265; Obsoleted by RFC 542; Updated by RFC 385)

353   Network host status   (Not online) Westheimer, E.   1972 June 12; 3 p.
(Obsoletes RFC 344; Obsoleted by RFC 362)

352   TIP site information form   (Not online) Crocker, D.   1972 June 5; 3 p.

351   Graphics information form for the ARPANET graphics resources notebook
(Not online) Crocker, D.   1972 June 5; 3 p.

350   User accounts for UCSB On-Line System   (Not online) Stoughton, R.   1972
May 18; 3 p.

349   Proposed standard socket numbers   (Not online) Postel, J.B.   1972 May
30; 1 p.   (Obsoleted by RFC 433)

348   Discard process   (Not online) Postel, J.B.   1972 May 30; 1 p.

347   Echo process   (Not online) Postel, J.B.   1972 May 30; 1 p.

346   Satellite considerations   (Not online) Postel, J.B.   1972 May 30; 1 p.

345   Interest in mixed integer programming (MPSX on NIC 360/91 at CCN)   (Not
online) Kelley, K.C.   1972 May 26; 1 p.

344   Network host status   (Not online) Westheimer, E.   1972 May 22; 3 p.
(Obsoletes RFC 342; Obsoleted by RFC 353)

343   IMP System change notification   (Not online) McKenzie, A.M.   1972 May
19; 2 p.   (Obsoletes RFC 331; Obsoleted by RFC 359)

342   Network host status   (Not online) Westheimer, E.   1972 May 15; 3 p.
(Obsoletes RFC 332; Obsoleted by RFC 344)

341   Not issued.

340   Proposed Telnet changes   (Not online) O'Sullivan, T.C.   1972 May 15;
1 p.

339   MLTNET: A "Multi Telnet" subsystem for Tenex   (Not online) Thomas, R.
1972 May 5; 8 p.

338   EBCDIC/ASCII mapping for network RJE   (Not online) Braden, R.T.   1972
May 17; 6 p.

337   Not issued.

336   Level 0 Graphic Input Protocol   (Not online) Cotton, I.W.   1972 May 5;
2 p.

335   New interface - IMP/360   (Not online) Bryan, R.F.   1972 May 1; 1 p.

334   Network use on May 8 (Not online) McKenzie, A.M. 1972 May 1; 1 p.

333   Proposed experiment with a Message Switching Protocol (Not online)
       Bressler, R.D.; Murphy, D.; Walden, D.C. 1972 May 15; 52 p.

332   Network host status (Not online) Westheimer, E. 1972 April 25; 3 p.
       (Obsoletes RFC 330; Obsoleted by RFC 342)

331   IMP System change notification (Not online) McQuillan, J.M. 1972 April
       19; 1 p. (Obsoleted by RFC 343)

330   Network host status (Not online) Westheimer, E. 1972 April 13; 3 p.
       (Obsoletes RFC 326; Obsoleted by RFC 332)

329   ARPA Network mailing lists (Not online) Stanford Research Inst.,
       Network Information Center. 1972 May 17; 7 p. (Obsoletes RFC 303;
       Obsoleted by RFC 363)

328   Suggested Telnet Protocol changes (Not online) Postel, J.B. 1972 April
       29; 1 p.

327   Data and File Transfer workshop notes (Not online) Bhushan, A.K. 1972
       April 27; 7 p.

326   Network host status (Not online) Westheimer, E. 1972 April 3; 3 p.
       (Obsoletes RFC 319; Obsoleted by RFC 330)

325   Network Remote Job Entry program - NETRJS (Not online) Hicks, G. 1972
       April 6; 9 p.

324   RJE Protocol meeting (Not online) Postel, J.B. 1972 April 3; 1 p.

323   Formation of Network Measurement Group (NMG) (Not online) Cerf, V.G.
       1972 March 23; 9 p. (Updated by RFC 388)

322   Well known socket numbers (Not online) Cerf, V.G.; Postel, J.B. 1972
       March 26; 1 p.

321   CBI networking activity at MITRE (Not online) Karp, P.M. 1972 March
       24; 13 p.

320   Workshop on hard copy line printers (Not online) Reddy, R. 1972 March
       27; 4 p.

319   Network host status (Not online) Westheimer, E. 1972 March 21; 3 p.
       (Obsoletes RFC 315; Obsoleted by RFC 326)

318   [Ad hoc Telnet Protocol] (Not online) Postel, J.B. 1972 April 3; 23 p.
       (Updates RFC 158; Updated by RFC 435)

317   Official Host-Host Protocol modification: Assigned link numbers (Not
       online) Postel, J.B. 1972 March 20; 1 p. (Obsoleted by RFC 604)

316   ARPA Network Data Management Working Group (Not online) McKay, D.B.;
       Mullery, A.P. 1972 February 23; 10 p.

315   Network host status (Not online) Westheimer, E. 1972 March 8; 3 p.
       (Obsoletes RFC 306; Obsoleted by RFC 319)

314   Network Graphics Working Group meeting (Not online) Cotton, I.W. 1972
      March 14; 1 p.

313   Computer based instruction (Not online) O'Sullivan, T.C. 1972 March 6;
      9 p.

312   Proposed change in IMP-to-Host Protocol (Not online) McKenzie, A.M.
      1972 March 22; 2 p.

311   New console attachments to the USCB host (Not online) Bryan, R.F. 1972
      February 29; 2 p.

310   Another look at Data and File Transfer Protocols (Not online) Bhushan,
      A.K. 1972 April 3; 7 p.

309   Data and File Transfer workshop announcement (Not online) Bhushan, A.K.
      1972 March 17; 5 p.

308   ARPANET host availability data (Not online) Seriff, M. 1972 March 13;
      3 p.

307   Using network Remote Job Entry (Not online) Harslem, E. 1972 February
      24; 6 p.

306   Network host status (Not online) Westheimer, E. 1972 February 15; 3 p.
      (Obsoletes RFC 298; Obsoleted by RFC 315)

305   Unknown host numbers (Not online) Alter, R. 1972 February 23; 1 p.

304   Data management system proposal for the ARPA network (Not online)
      McKay, D.B. 1972 February 17; 12 p.

303   ARPA Network mailing lists (Not online) Stanford Research Inst.,
      Network Information Center. 1972 February 23; 6 p. (Obsoletes RFC 300;
      Obsoleted by RFC 329)

302   Exercising the ARPANET (Not online) Bryan, R.F. 1972 February 8; 3 p.

301   BBN IMP (#5) and NCC schedule March 4, 1971 (Not online) Alter, R.
      1972 February 11; 1 p.

300   ARPA Network mailing lists (Not online) North, J.B. 1972 January 25;
      6 p. (Obsoletes RFC 211; Obsoleted by RFC 303)

299   Information management system (Not online) Hopkin, D. 1972 February
      11; 1 p.

298   Network host status (Not online) Westheimer, E. 1972 February 11; 3 p.
      (Obsoletes RFC 293; Obsoleted by RFC 306)

297   TIP message buffers (Not online) Walden, D.C. 1972 January 31; 5 p.

296   DS-1 display system (Not online) Liddle, D.E. 1972 January 27; 23 p.

295   Report of the Protocol Workshop, 12 October 1971 (Not online) Postel,
      J.B. 1972 January 2; 4 p.

294   On the use of "set data type" transaction in File Transfer Protocol
       (Not online) Bhushan, A.K. 1972 January 25; 2 p. (Updates RFC 265)

293   Network host status (Not online) Westheimer, E. 1972 January 18; 3 p.
       (Obsoletes RFC 288; Obsoleted by RFC 298)

292   Graphics Protocol: Level 0 only (Not online) Michener, J.C.; Cotton,
       I.W.; Kelley, K.C.; Liddle, D.E.; Meyer, E.W., Jr. 1972 January 12;
       9 p.

291   Data management meeting announcement (Not online) McKay, D.B. 1972
       January 14; 2 p.

290   Computer networks and data sharing: A bibliography (Not online)
       Mullery, A.P. 1972 January 11; 15 p. (Obsoletes RFC 243)

289   What we hope is an official list of host names (Not online) Watson,
       R.W. 1971 December 21; 3 p. (Obsoleted by RFC 384)

288   Network host status (Not online) Westheimer, E. 1972 January 6; 6 p.
       (Obsoletes RFC 287; Obsoleted by RFC 293)

287   Status of network hosts (Not online) Westheimer, E. 1971 December 22;
       3 p. (Obsoletes RFC 267; Obsoleted by RFC 288)

286   Network library information system (Not online) Forman, E. 1971
       December 21; 1 p.

285   Network graphics (Not online) Huff, D. 1971 December 15; 13 p.

284   Not issued.

283   NETRJT: Remote Job Service Protocol for TIPS (Not online) Braden, R.T.
       1971 December 20; 9 p. (Updates RFC 189)

282   Graphics meeting report (Not online) Padlipsky, M.A. 1971 December 8;
       8 p.

281   Suggested addition to File Transfer Protocol (Not online) McKenzie,
       A.M. 1971 December 8; 5 p.

280   Draft of host names (Not online) Watson, R.W. 1971 November 17; 4 p.

279   Not issued.

278   Revision of the Mail Box Protocol (Not online) Bhushan, A.K.; Braden,
       R.T.; Harslem, E.; Heafner, J.F.; McKenzie, A.M.; Melvin, J.T.;
       Sundberg, R.L.; Watson, R.W.; White, J.E. 1971 November 17; 4 p.
       (Obsoletes RFC 221)

277   Not issued.

276   NIC course (Not online) Watson, R.W. 1971 November 8; 2 p.

275   Not issued.

V

Resource Reference

274 Establishing a local guide for network usage (Not online) Forman, E.
     1971 November 1; 5 p.

273 More on standard host names (Not online) Watson, R.W. 1971 October 18;
     3 p. (Obsoletes RFC 237)

272 Not issued.

271 IMP System change notifications (Not online) Cosell, B. 1972 January
     3; 2 p.

270 Correction to BBN Report No. 1822 (NIC NO 7958) (Not online) McKenzie,
     A.M. 1972 January 1; 3 p. (Updates NIC 7959)

269 Some experience with file transfer (Not online) Brodie, H. 1971
     December 6; 3 p. (Updates RFC 122, RFC 238)

268 Graphics facilities information (Not online) Postel, J.B. 1971
     November 24; 1 p.

267 Network host status (Not online) Westheimer, E. 1971 November 22; 3 p.
     (Obsoletes RFC 266; Obsoleted by RFC 287)

266 Network host status (Not online) Westheimer, E. 1971 November 8; 2 p.
     (Obsoletes RFC 255; Obsoleted by RFC 267)

265 File Transfer Protocol (Not online) Bhushan, A.K.; Braden, R.T.;
     Crowther, W.R.; Harslem, E.; Heafner, J.F.; McKenzie, A.M.; Melvin,
     J.T.; Sundberg, R.L.; Watson, R.W.; White, J.E. 1971 November 17; 11 p.
     (Obsoletes RFC 172; Obsoleted by RFC 354; Updated by RFC 294)

264 Data Transfer Protocol (Not online) Bhushan, A.K.; Braden, R.T.;
     Crowther, W.R.; Harslem, E.; Heafner, J.F.; McKenzie, A.M.; Melvin,
     J.T.; Sundberg, R.L.; Watson, R.W.; White, J.E. 1971 December 15; 8 p.
     (Obsoletes RFC 171; Obsoleted by RFC 354)

263 "Very Distant" Host interface (Not online) McKenzie, A.M. 1971
     December 17; 2 p.

262 Not issued.

261 Not issued.

260 Not issued.

259 Not issued.

258 Not issued.

257 Not issued.

256 IMPSYS change notification (Not online) Cosell, B. 1971 November 3;
     1 p.

255 Status of network hosts (Not online) Westheimer, E. 1971 October 26;
     2 p. (Obsoletes RFC 252; Obsoleted by RFC 266)

254   Scenarios for using ARPANET computers   (Not online) Bhushan, A.K.   1971
       October 29; 32 p.

253   Second Network Graphics meeting details   (Not online) Moorer, J.A.   1971
       October 19; 1 p.

252   Network host status   (Not online) Westheimer, E.   1971 October 8; 3 p.
       (Obsoletes RFC 240; Obsoleted by RFC 255)

251   Weather data   (Not online) Stern, D.   1971 October 13; 2 p.

250   Some thoughts on file transfer   (Not online) Brodie, H.   1971 October 7;
       1 p.

249   Coordination of equipment and supplies purchase   (Not online) Borelli,
       R.F.   1971 October 8; 2 p.

248   Not issued.

247   Proffered set of standard host names   (Not online) Karp, P.M.   1971
       October 12; 4 p.   (Obsoletes RFC 226)

246   Network Graphics meeting   (Not online) Vezza, A.   1971 October 5; 1 p.

245   Reservations for Network Group meeting   (Not online) Falls, C.   1971
       October 5; 1 p.

244   Not issued.

243   Network and data sharing bibliography   (Not online) Mullery, A.P.   1971
       October 5; 6 p.   (Obsoleted by RFC 290)

242   Data descriptive language for shared data   (Not online) Haibt, L.;
       Mullery, A.P.   1971 July 19; 12 p.

241   Connecting computers to MLC ports   (Not online) McKenzie, A.M.   1971
       September 29; 2 p.

240   Site status   (Not online) McKenzie, A.M.   1971 September 30; 5 p.
       (Obsoletes RFC 235; Obsoleted by RFC 252)

239   Host mnemonics proposed in RFC 226 (NIC 7625)   (Not online) Braden, R.T.
       1971 September 23; 1 p.

238   Comments on DTP and FTP proposals   (Not online) Braden, R.T.   1971
       September 29; 1 p.   (Updates RFC 171, RFC 172; Updated by RFC 269)

237   NIC view of standard host names   (Not online) Watson, R.W.   1971
       September 29; 1 p.   (Obsoleted by RFC 273)

236   Standard host names   (Not online) Postel, J.B.   1971 September 27; 2 p.
       (Obsoletes RFC 229)

235   Site status   (Not online) Westheimer, E.   1971 September 27; 4 p.
       (Obsoleted by RFC 240)

234 Network Working Group meeting schedule (Not online) Vezza, A. 1971
     October 5; 1 p. (Updates RFC 222, RFC 204)

233 Standardization of host call letters (Not online) Bhushan, A.K.;
     Metcalfe, R.M. 1971 September 28; 1 p.

232 Postponement of network graphics meeting (Not online) Vezza, A. 1971
     September 23; 1 p.

231 Service center standards for remote usage: A user's view (Not online)
     Heafner, J.F.; Harslem, E. 1971 September 21; 5 p.

230 Toward reliable operation of minicomputer-based terminals on a TIP (Not
     online) Pyke, T.N., Jr. 1971 September 24; 3 p.

229 Standard host names (Not online) Postel, J.B. 1971 September 22; 2 p.
     (Obsoleted by RFC 236)

228 Clarification (Not online) Walden, D.C. 1971 September 22; 1 p.
     (Updates RFC 70)

227 Data transfer rates (Rand/UCLA) (Not online) Heafner, J.F.; Harslem, E.
     1971 September 17; 2 p. (Updates RFC 113)

226 Standardization of host mnemonics (Not online) Karp, P.M. 1971
     September 20; 1 p. (Obsoleted by RFC 247)

225 Rand/UCSB network graphics experiment (Not online) Harslem, E.;
     Stoughton, R. 1971 September 13; 6 p. (Updates RFC 74)

224 Comments on Mailbox Protocol (Not online) McKenzie, A.M. 1971
     September 14; 2 p.

223 Network Information Center schedule for network users (Not online)
     Melvin, J.T.; Watson, R.W. 1971 September 14; 3 p.

222 Subject: System programmer's workshop (Not online) Metcalfe, R.M. 1971
     September 13; 2 p. (Updates RFC 212; Updated by RFC 234)

221 Mail Box Protocol: Version 2 (Not online) Watson, R.W. 1971 August 27;
     5 p. (Obsoletes RFC 196; Obsoleted by RFC 278)

220 Not issued.

219 User's view of the datacomputer (Not online) Winter, R. 1971 September
     3; 10 p.

218 Changing the IMP status reporting facility (Not online) Cosell, B.
     1971 September 8; 1 p.

217 Specifications changes for OLS, RJE/RJOR, and SMFS (Not online) White,
     J.E. 1971 September 8; 2 p. (Updates RFC 74, RFC 105, RFC 122)

216 Telnet access to UCSB's On-Line System (Not online) White, J.E. 1971
     September 8; 27 p.

215   NCP, ICP, and Telnet: The Terminal IMP implementation   (Not online)
McKenzie, A.M.   1971 August 30; 7 p.

214   Network checkpoint   (Not online) Harslem, E.   1971 August 21; 2 p.
(Obsoletes RFC 198)

213   IMP System change notification   (Not online) Cosell, B.   1971 August 20;
1 p.

212   NWG meeting on network usage   (Not online) University of Southern
California, Information Sciences Inst.   1971 August 23; 2 p.   (Obsoletes
RFC 207; Updated by RFC 222)

211   ARPA Network mailing lists   (Not online) North, J.B.   1971 August 18;
5 p.   (Obsoletes RFC 168; Obsoleted by RFC 300)

210   Improvement of flow control   (Not online) Conrad, W.   1971 August 16;
3 p.

209   Host/IMP interface documentation   (Not online) Cosell, B.   1971 August
13; 2 p.

208   Address tables   (Not online) McKenzie, A.M.   1971 August 9; 4 p.

207   September Network Working Group meeting   (Not online) Vezza, A.   1971
August 9; 2 p.   (Obsoleted by RFC 212)

206   User Telnet - description of an initial implementation   (Not online)
White, J.E.   1971 August 9; 17 p.

205   NETCRT - a character display protocol   (Not online) Braden, R.T.   1971
August 6; 14 p.

204   Sockets in use   (Not online) Postel, J.B.   1971 August 5; 1 p.
(Updated by RFC 234)

203   Achieving reliable communication   (Not online) Kalin, R.B.   1971 August
10; 14 p.

202   Possible deadlock in ICP   (Not online) Wolfe, S.M.; Postel, J.B.   1971
July 26; 2 p.

201   Not issued.

200   RFC list by number   (Not online) North, J.B.   1971 August 1; 2 p.
(Obsoletes RFC 170, RFC 160; Obsoleted by NIC 7724)

199   Suggestions for a network data-tablet graphics protocol   (Not online)
Williams, T.   1971 July 15; 13 p.

198   Site certification - Lincoln Labs 360/67   (Not online) Heafner, J.F.
1971 July 20; 1 p.   (Obsoletes RFC 193; Obsoleted by RFC 214)

197   Initial Connection Protocol - Reviewed   (Not online) Shoshani, A.;
Harslem, E.   1971 July 14; 4 p.

V

Resource Reference

196   Mail Box Protocol (Not online) Watson, R.W. 1971 July 20; 4 p.
(Obsoleted by RFC 221)

195   Data computers-data descriptions and access language (Not online)
Mealy, G.H. 1971 July 16; 4 p.

194   Data Reconfiguration Service - compiler/interpreter implementation notes
(Not online) Cerf, V.G.; Harslem, E.; Heafner, J.F.; Metcalfe, R.M.;
White, J.E. 1971 July; 22 p.

193   Network checkout (Not online) Harslem, E.; Heafner, J.F. 1971 July 14;
2 p. (Obsoleted by RFC 198)

192   Some factors which a Network Graphics Protocol must consider (Not
online) Watson, R.W. 1971 July 12; 21 p.

191   Graphics implementation and conceptualization at Augmentation Research
Center (Not online) Irby, C.H. 1971 July 13; 4 p.

190   DEC PDP-10-IMLAC communications system (Not online) Deutsch, L.P. 1971
July 13; 15 p.

189   Interim NETRJS specifications. Braden, R.T. 1971 July 15; 19 p.
(Format: TXT=37862 bytes) (Obsoletes RFC 88; Obsoleted by RFC 599;
Updated by RFC 283)

188   Data management meeting announcement (Not online) Karp, P.M.; McKay,
D.B. 1971 January 28; 2 p.

187   Network/440 protocol concept (Not online) McKay, D.B.; Karp, D.P. 1971
July; 15 p.

186   Network graphics loader (Not online) Michener, J.C. 1971 July 12;
21 p.

185   NIC distribution of manuals and handbooks (Not online) North, J.B.
1971 July 7; 1 p.

184   Proposed graphic display modes (Not online) Kelley, K.C. 1971 July 6;
7 p.

183   EBCDIC codes and their mapping to ASCII (Not online) Winett, J.M. 1971
July 21; 15 p.

182   Compilation of list of relevant site reports (Not online) North, J.B.
1971 June 25; 1 p.

181   Modifications to RFC 177 (Not online) McConnell, J. 1971 July 21; 2 p.
(Updates RFC 177)

180   File system questionnaire (Not online) McKenzie, A.M. 1971 June 25;
8 p.

179   Link number assignments. McKenzie, A.M. 1971 June 22; 1 p. (Format:
TXT=810 bytes) (Updates RFC 107)

178   Network graphic attention handling   (Not online) Cotton, I.W.   1971 June 27; 18 p.

177   Device independent graphical display description   (Not online) McConnell, J.   1971 June 15; 10 p.   (Updates RFC 125; Updated by RFC 181)

176   Comments on "Byte size for connections"   (Not online) Bhushan, A.K.; Kanodia, R.; Metcalfe, R.M.; Postel, J.B.   1971 June 14; 5 p.

175   Comments on "Socket conventions reconsidered"   (Not online) Harslem, E.; Heafner, J.F.   1971 June 11; 1 p.

174   UCLA - computer science graphics overview   (Not online) Postel, J.B.; Cerf, V.G.   1971 June 8; 3 p.

173   Network data management committee meeting announcement   (Not online) Karp, P.M.; McKay, D.B.   1971 June 4; 3 p.

172   File Transfer Protocol   (Not online) Bhushan, A.K.; Braden, R.T.; Crowther, W.R.; Harslem, E.; Heafner, J.F.; McKenzie, A.M.; Melvin, J.T.; Sundberg, R.L.; Watson, R.W.; White, J.E.   1971 June 23; 15 p. (Obsoleted by RFC 265; Updates RFC 114; Updated by RFC 238)

171   Data Transfer Protocol   (Not online) Bhushan, A.K.; Braden, R.T.; Crowther, W.R.; Harslem, E.; Heafner, J.F.; McKenzie, A.M.; Melvin, J.T.; Sundberg, R.L.; Watson, R.W.; White, J.E.   1971 June 23; 13 p. (Obsoleted by RFC 264; Updates RFC 114; Updated by RFC 238)

170   RFC list by number   (Not online) Stanford Research Inst., Network Information Center.   1971 June 1; 2 p.   (Obsoleted by RFC 200)

169   Computer networks   (Not online) Crocker, S.D.   1971 May 27; 5 p.

168   ARPA Network mailing lists   (Not online) North, J.B.   1971 May 26; 5 p. (Obsoletes RFC 155; Obsoleted by RFC 211)

167   Socket conventions reconsidered   (Not online) Bhushan, A.K.; Metcalfe, R.M.; Winett, J.M.   1971 May 24; 7 p.

166   Data Reconfiguration Service: An implementation specification   (Not online) Anderson, R.H.; Cerf, V.G.; Harslem, E.; Heafner, J.F.; Madden, J.; Metcalfe, R.M.; Shoshani, A.; White, J.E.; Wood, D.C.M.   1971 May 25; 24 p.

165   Proffered official Initial Connection Protocol   (Not online) Postel, J.B.   1971 May 25; 6 p.   (Obsoletes RFC 145, RFC 143, RFC 123; Updated by NIC 7101)

164   Minutes of Network Working Group meeting, 5/16 through 5/19/71   (Not online) Heafner, J.F.   1971 May 25; 38 p.

163   Data transfer protocols   (Not online) Cerf, V.G.   1971 May 19; 3 p.

162   NETBUGGER3   (Not online) Kampe, M.   1971 May 22; 1 p.

V

Resource Reference

161   Solution to the race condition in the ICP   (Not online) Shoshani, A.
       1971 May 19; 2 p.

160   RFC brief list   (Not online) Stanford Research Inst., Network
       Information Center. 1971 May 18; 4 p. (Obsoleted by RFC 200; Updates
       NIC 6716)

159   Not issued.

158   Telnet Protocol: A proposed document   (Not online) O'Sullivan, T.C.
       1971 May 19; 11 p. (Obsoleted by RFC 495; Updates RFC 139; Updated by
       RFC 318)

157   Invitation to the Second Symposium on Problems in the Optimization of
       Data Communications Systems   (Not online) Cerf, V.G. 1971 May 12; 1 p.

156   Status of the Illinois site: Response to RFC 116   (Not online)
       Bouknight, J. 1971 April 26; 1 p. (Updates RFC 116)

155   ARPA Network mailing lists   (Not online) North, J.B. 1971 May; 5 p.
       (Obsoletes RFC 95; Obsoleted by RFC 168)

154   Exposition style   (Not online) Crocker, S.D. 1971 May 12; 1 p.
       (Obsoletes RFC 132)

153   SRI ARC-NIC status   (Not online) Melvin, J.T.; Watson, R.W. 1971 May
       15; 4 p.

152   SRI Artificial Intelligence status report   (Not online) Wilber, M. 1971
       May 10; 1 p.

151   Comments on a proffered official ICP: RFCs 123, 127   (Not online)
       Shoshani, A. 1971 May 10; 3 p. (Updates RFC 127)

150   Use of IPC facilities: A working paper   (Not online) Kalin, R.B. 1971
       May 5; 16 p.

149   Best laid plans. Crocker, S.D. 1971 May 10; 1 p. (Format: TXT=713
       bytes) (Updates RFC 140)

148   Comments on RFC 123   (Not online) Bhushan, A.K. 1971 May 7; 1 p.
       (Updates RFC 123)

147   Definition of a socket   (Not online) Winett, J.M. 1971 May 7; 2 p.
       (Updates RFC 129)

146   Views on issues relevant to data sharing on computer networks   (Not
       online) Karp, P.M.; McKay, D.B.; Wood, D.C.M. 1971 May 12; 7 p.

145   Initial Connection Protocol control commands   (Not online) Postel, J.B.
       1971 May 4; 1 p. (Obsoletes RFC 127; Obsoleted by RFC 165)

144   Data sharing on computer networks   (Not online) Shoshani, A. 1971 April
       30; 8 p.

143   Regarding proffered official ICP   (Not online) Naylor, W.; Wong, J.;
       Kline, C.; Postel, J.B.   1971 May 3; 4 p.   (Obsoleted by RFC 165)

142   Time-out mechanism in the Host-Host Protocol   (Not online) Kline, C.;
       Wong, J.   1971 May 3; 3 p.

141   Comments on RFC 114: A File Transfer Protocol   (Not online) Harslem, E.;
       Heafner, J.F.   1971 April 29; 2 p.   (Updates RFC 114)

140   Agenda for the May NWG meeting   (Not online) Crocker, S.D.   1971 May 4;
       3 p.   (Updated by RFC 149)

139   Discussion of Telnet Protocol   (Not online) O'Sullivan, T.C.   1971 May
       7; 11 p.   (Updates RFC 137; Updated by RFC 158)

138   Status report on proposed Data Reconfiguration Service   (Not online)
       Anderson, R.H.; Cerf, V.G.; Harslem, E.; Heafner, J.F.; Madden, J.;
       Metcalfe, R.M.; Shoshani, A.; White, J.E.; Wood, D.C.M.   1971 April 28;
       30 p.

137   Telnet Protocol - a proposed document   (Not online) O'Sullivan, T.C.
       1971 April 30; 6 p.   (Updated by RFC 139)

136   Host accounting and administrative procedures   (Not online) Kahn, R.E.
       1971 April 29; 6 p.

135   Response to NWG/RFC 110   (Not online) Hathaway, W.   1971 April 29; 2 p.
       (Updates RFC 110)

134   Network Graphics meeting   (Not online) Vezza, A.   1971 April 29; 2 p.

133   File transfer and recovery   (Not online) Sundberg, R.L.   1971 April 27;
       5 p.

132   Typographical error in RFC 107   (Not online) White, J.E.   1971 April 28;
       1 p.   (Obsoleted by RFC 154; Updates RFC 107)

131   Response to RFC 116: May NWG meeting   (Not online) Harslem, E.; Heafner,
       J.F.   1971 April 22; 4 p.   (Updates RFC 116)

130   Response to RFC 111: Pressure from the chairman   (Not online) Heafner,
       J.F.   1971 April 22; 2 p.   (Updates RFC 111)

129   Request for comments on socket name structure   (Not online) Harslem, E.;
       Heafner, J.F.; Meyer, E.W., Jr.   1971 April 22; 6 p.   (Updated by RFC
       147)

128   Bytes   (Not online) Postel, J.B.   1971 April 21; 2 p.

127   Comments on RFC 123   (Not online) Postel, J.B.   1971 April 20; 1 p.
       (Obsoleted by RFC 145; Updates RFC 123; Updated by RFC 151)

126   Graphics facilities at Ames Research Center   (Not online) McConnell, J.
       1971 April 18; 2 p.

125   Response to RFC 86: Proposal for network standard format for a graphics data stream (Not online) McConnell, J. 1971 April 18; 4 p. (Updates RFC 86; Updated by RFC 177)

124   Typographical error in RFC 107 (Not online) Melvin, J.T. 1971 April 19; 1 p. (Updates RFC 107)

123   Proffered official ICP (Not online) Crocker, S.D. 1971 April 20; 4 p. (Obsoletes RFC 66, RFC 80; Obsoleted by RFC 165; Updates RFC 98, RFC 101; Updated by RFC 127, RFC 148)

122   Network specifications for UCSB's Simple-Minded File System (Not online) White, J.E. 1971 April 26; 21 p. (Updated by RFC 217, RFC 269, RFC 399)

121   Network on-line operators (Not online) Krilanovich, M. 1971 April 21; 14 p.

120   Network PL1 subprograms (Not online) Krilanovich, M. 1971 April 21; 16 p.

119   Network Fortran subprograms (Not online) Krilanovich, M. 1971 April 21; 17 p.

118   Recommendations for facility documentation (Not online) Watson, R.W. 1971 April 16; 3 p.

117   Some comments on the official protocol (Not online) Wong, J. 1971 April 7; 5 p.

116   Structure of the May NWG meeting (Not online) Crocker, S.D. 1971 April 12; 1 p. (Updates RFC 99; Updated by RFC 131, RFC 156)

115   Some Network Information Center policies on handling documents (Not online) Watson, R.W.; North, J.B. 1971 April 16; 12 p.

114   File Transfer Protocol (Not online) Bhushan, A.K. 1971 April 10; 24 p. (Updated by RFC 141, RFC 172, RFC 171)

113   Network activity report: UCSB Rand (Not online) Harslem, E.; Heafner, J.F.; White, J.E. 1971 April 5; 2 p. (Updated by RFC 227)

112   User/Server Site Protocol: Network host questionnaire responses (Not online) O'Sullivan, T.C. 1971 April 1; 3 p.

111   Pressure from the chairman (Not online) Crocker, S.D. 1971 March 31; 2 p. (Updates RFC 107; Updated by RFC 130)

110   Conventions for using an IBM 2741 terminal as a user console for access to network server hosts (Not online) Winett, J.M. 1971 March 25; 4 p. (Updated by RFC 135)

109   Level III Server Protocol for the Lincoln Laboratory NIC 360/67 Host (Not online) Winett, J.M. 1971 March 24; 12 p.

108   Attendance list at the Urbana NWG meeting, February 17-19, 1971   (Not
       online) Watson, R.W.   1971 March 25; 3 p.   (Updates RFC 101)

107   Output of the Host-Host Protocol glitch cleaning committee   (Not online)
       Bressler, R.D.; Crocker, S.D.; Crowther, W.R.; Grossman, G.R.;
       Tomlinson, R.S.; White, J.E.   1971 March 23; 11 p.   (Updates RFC 102;
       Updated by RFC 179, RFC 132, RFC 124, RFC 111, NIC 7147)

106   User/Server Site Protocol network host questionnaire   (Not online)
       O'Sullivan, T.C.   1971 March 3; 3 p.

105   Network specifications for Remote Job Entry and Remote Job Output
       Retrieval at UCSB   (Not online) White, J.E.   1971 March 22; 8 p.
       (Updated by RFC 217)

104   Link 191   (Not online) Postel, J.B.; Crocker, S.D.   1971 February 25;
       1 p.

103   Implementation of interrupt keys   (Not online) Kalin, R.B.   1971
       February 24; 3 p.

102   Output of the Host-Host Protocol glitch cleaning committee   (Not online)
       Crocker, S.D.   1971 February 22; 6 p.   (Updated by RFC 107)

101   Notes on the Network Working Group meeting, Urbana, Illinois, February
       17, 1971   (Not online) Watson, R.W.   1971 February 23; 14 p.
       (Updated by RFC 108, RFC 123)

100   Categorization and guide to NWG/RFCs   (Not online) Karp, P.M.   1971
       February 26; 43 p.

99   Network meeting   (Not online) Karp, P.M.   1971 February 22; 1 p.
       (Updated by RFC 116)

98   Logger Protocol proposal   (Not online) Meyer, E.W., Jr.; Skinner, T.P.
       1971 February 11; 12 p.   (Updated by RFC 123)

97   First cut at a proposed Telnet Protocol   (Not online) Melvin, J.T.;
       Watson, R.W.   1971 February 15; 10 p.

96   Interactive network experiment to study modes of access to the Network
       Information Center   (Not online) Watson, R.W.   1971 February 12; 4 p.

95   Distribution of NWG/RFC's through the NIC   (Not online) Crocker, S.D.
       1971 February 4; 4 p.   (Obsoleted by RFC 155)

94   Some thoughts on network graphics   (Not online) Harslem, E.; Heafner,
       J.F.   1971 February 3; 8 p.

93   Initial Connection Protocol   (Not online) McKenzie, A.M.   1971 January
       27; 1 p.

92   Not issued.

V

Resource Reference

91   Proposed User-User Protocol (Not online) Mealy, G.H. 1970 December 27; 18 p.

90   CCN as a network service center (Not online) Braden, R.T. 1971 January 15; 6 p.

89   Some historic moments in networking (Not online) Metcalfe, R.M. 1971 January 19; 12 p.

88   NETRJS: A third level protocol for Remote Job Entry (Not online) Braden, R.T.; Wolfe, S.M. 1971 January 13; 10 p. (Obsoleted by RFC 189)

87   Topic for discussion at the next Network Working Group meeting (Not online) Vezza, A. 1971 January 12; 3 p.

86   Proposal for a network standard format for a data stream to control graphics display (Not online) Crocker, S.D. 1971 January 5; 5 p. (Updated by RFC 125)

85   Network Working Group meeting (Not online) Crocker, S.D. 1970 December 28; 1 p.

84   List of NWG/RFC's 1-80 (Not online) North, J.B. 1970 December 23; 8 p.

83   Language-machine for data reconfiguration (Not online) Anderson, R.H.; Harslem, E.; Heafner, J.F. 1970 December 18; 12 p.

82   Network meeting notes (Not online) Meyer, E.W., Jr. 1970 December 9; 16 p.

81   Request for reference information (Not online) Bouknight, J. 1970 December 3; 1 p.

80   Protocols and data formats (Not online) Harslem, E.; Heafner, J.F. 1970 December 1; 9 p. (Obsoleted by RFC 123)

79   Logger Protocol error (Not online) Meyer, E.W., Jr. 1970 November 16; 1 p.

78   NCP status report: UCSB/Rand (Not online) Harslem, E.; Heafner, J.F.; White, J.E. 1970 October; 1 p.

77   Network meeting report (Not online) Postel, J.B. 1970 November 20; 9 p.

76   Connection by name: User oriented protocol (Not online) Bouknight, J.; Madden, J.; Grossman, G.R. 1970 October 28; 8 p.

75   Network meeting (Not online) Crocker, S.D. 1970 October 14; 1 p.

74   Specifications for network use of the UCSB On-Line System (Not online) White, J.E. 1970 October 16; 11 p. (Updated by RFC 217, RFC 225)

73   Response to NWG/RFC 67 (Not online) Crocker, S.D. 1970 September 25; 1 p.

Resource Reference

V

53   Official protocol mechanism (Not online) Crocker, S.D. 1970 June 9;
      1 p.

52   Updated distribution list (Not online) Postel, J.B.; Crocker, S.D.
      1970 July 1; 3 p. (Updated by RFC 69)

51   Proposal for a Network Interchange Language (Not online) Elie, M. 1970
      May 4; 19 p.

50   Comments on the Meyer proposal (Not online) Harslem, E.; Haverty, J.
      1970 April 30; 3 p.

49   Conversations with S. Crocker (UCLA) (Not online) Meyer, E.W., Jr.
      1970 April 23; 5 p.

48   Possible protocol plateau (Not online) Postel, J.B.; Crocker, S.D.
      1970 April 21; 16 p.

47   BBN's comments on NWG/RFC #33 (Not online) Crowther, W.R. 1970 April
      20; 4 p. (Updates RFC 33)

46   ARPA Network protocol notes (Not online) Meyer, E.W., Jr. 1970 April
      17; 27 p.

45   New protocol is coming (Not online) Postel, J.B.; Crocker, S.D. 1970
      April 14; 1 p.

44   Comments on NWG/RFC 33 and 36 (Not online) Shoshani, A.; Long, R.;
      Landsberg, A. 1970 April 10; 5 p. (Updates RFC 36)

43   Proposed meeting [LIL] (Not online) Nemeth, A.G. 1970 April 8; 1 p.

42   Message data types (Not online) Ancona, E. 1970 March 31; 3 p.

41   IMP-IMP teletype communication (Not online) Melvin, J.T. 1970 March
      30; 1 p.

40   More comments on the forthcoming protocol (Not online) Harslem, E.;
      Heafner, J.F. 1970 March 27; 3 p.

39   Comments on protocol re: NWG/RFC #36 (Not online) Harslem, E.; Heafner,
      J.F. 1970 March 25; 3 p. (Updates RFC 36)

38   Comments on network protocol from NWG/RFC #36 (Not online) Wolfe, S.M.
      1970 March 20; 2 p.

37   Network meeting epilogue, etc (Not online) Crocker, S.D. 1970 March
      20; 4 p.

36   Protocol notes (Not online) Crocker, S.D. 1970 March 16; 7 p.
      (Updates RFC 33; Updated by RFC 39, RFC 44)

35   Network meeting (Not online) Crocker, S.D. 1970 March 3; 1 p.

34   Some brief preliminary notes on the Augmentation Research Center clock
      (Not online) English, W.K. 1970 February 26; 1 p.

V

Resource Reference

14   Not issued.

13   [Referring to NWG/RFC 11]   (Not online) Cerf, V.G.   1969 August 20; 1 p.

12   IMP-Host interface flow diagrams   (Not online) Wingfield, M.   1969
     August 26; 5 p.

11   Implementation of the Host-Host software procedures in GORDO   (Not
     online) Deloche, G.   1969 August 1; 52 p.   (Obsoleted by RFC 33)

10   Documentation conventions. Crocker, S.D.   1969 July 29; 3 p. (Format:
     TXT=3469 bytes)   (Obsoletes RFC 3; Obsoleted by RFC 16)

9   Host software   (Not online) Deloche, G.   1969 May 1; 14 p.

8   Functional specifications for the ARPA Network   (Not online) Deloche, G.
     1969 May 5; 4 p.

7   Host-IMP interface   (Not online) Deloche, G.   1969 May; 4 p.

6   Conversation with Bob Kahn. Crocker, S.D.   1969 April 10; 1 p. (Format:
     TXT=1620 bytes)

5   Decode Encode Language. Rulifson, J.   1969 June 2; 18 p. (Format:
     TXT=27357 bytes)

4   Network timetable   (Not online) Shapiro, E.B.   1969 March 24; 5 p.

3   Documentation conventions. Crocker, S.D.   1969 April 9; 2 p. (Format:
     TXT=2403 bytes)   (Obsoleted by RFC 10)

2   Host software   (Not online) Duvall, B.   1969 April 9; 10 p.

1   Host software   (Not online) Crocker, S.D.   1969 April 7; 7 p.

FYI Index

Original Source: File /rfc/fyi-index.txt on host ftp.nisc.sri.com

```
                      FYI INDEX
                    -------------
```

This file contains citations for all FYIs in reverse numeric order.   FYI
citations appear in this format:

```
##    Title of FYI.  Author 1.; Author 2.; Author 3.    Issue date;
      ## p.  (Format: PS=xxx TXT=zzz bytes)  (Also RFC ##)
      (Obsoletes xxx; Obsoleted by xxx; Updates xxx; Updated by xxx)
```

Key to citations:

```
    ## is the FYI number; ## p. is the total number of pages.
```

The format and byte information follows the page information in parenthesis. The format, either ASCII text (TXT) or PostScript (PS) or both, is noted, followed by an equals sign and the number of bytes for that version. (PostScript is a registered trademark of Adobe Systems Incorporated.) The example (Format: PS=xxx TXT=zzz bytes) shows that the PostScript version of the FYI is xxx bytes and the ASCII text version is zzz bytes.

The (Also RFC ####) phrase gives the equivalent RFC number for each FYI document. Each FYI is also an RFC.

"Obsoletes RFC xxx" refers to other FYIs that this one replaces; "Obsoleted by RFC xxx" refers to FYIs that have replaced this one. "Updates RFC xxx" refers to other FYIs that this one merely updates (but does not replace); "Updated by RFC xxx" refers to FYIs that have been updated by this one (but not replaced). Only immediately succeeding and/or preceding FYIs are indicated, not the entire history of each related earlier or later FYI in a related series.

For example:

1   F.Y.I. on F.Y.I.: Introduction to the F.Y.I. notes. Malkin, G.S.; Reynolds, J.K. 1990 March; 4 p. (Format: TXT=7867 bytes) (Also RFC 1150)

Paper copies of all FYIs are available from SRI, either individually or as part of an RFC subscription service (for more information contact nisc@nisc.sri.com or call 1-415-859-6387). Online copies are available for anonymous FTP from ftp.nisc.sri.com as fyi/fyi##.txt or fyi/fyi##.ps (## is the FYI number without leading zeroes).

Additionally, FYIs may be requested through electronic mail from SRI's automated mail server by sending a message to mail-server@nisc.sri.com. In the body of the messaage, write "send fyi##" for text versions or "send fyi##.ps" for PostScript versions. To obtain the FYI index, your message should read "send fyi-index".

FYI INDEX

21   A Survey of Advanced Usages of X.500.Weider, C.; Wright, R. 1993 July; 18 p. (Format: TXT=34883 bytes) (Also RFC 1491)

20   FYI on "What is the Internet?".Krol, E.; Hoffman, E. 1993 May; 11 p. (Format: TXT=27811 bytes) (Also RFC 1462)

19   FYI on Introducing the Internet -- A Short Bibliography of Introductory Internetworking Readings for the Network Novice.Hoffman, E.; Jackson, L. 1993 May; 4 p. (Format: TXT=7116 bytes) (Also RFC 1463)

18   Internet Users' Glossary.Malkin, G.S.; Parker, T.L.,eds. 1993 January; 53 p. (Format: TXT=104624 bytes) (Also RFC 1392)

17   The Tao of IETF: A Guide for New Attendees of the Internet Engineering
      Task Force.Malkin, G.S. 1993 January; 19 p. (Format: TXT=23569 bytes)
      (Also RFC 1391)

16   Connecting to the Internet: What connecting institutions should
      anticipate.ACM SIGUCCS Networking Task Force 1992 August; 25 p.
      (Format: TXT=53449 bytes) (Also RFC 1359)

15   Privacy and accuracy issues in network information center databases.
      Curran, J.; Marine, A.N. 1992 August; 4 p. (Format: TXT=8858 bytes)
      (Also RFC 1355)

14   Technical overview of directory services using the X.500 protocol.
      Weider, C.; Reynolds, J.K.; Heker, S. 1992 March; 16 p. (Format:
      TXT=35694 bytes) (Also RFC 1309)

13   Executive introduction to directory services using the X.500 protocol.
      Weider, C.; Reynolds, J.K. 1992 March; 4 p. (Format: TXT=9392 bytes)
      (Also RFC 1308)

12   Building a network information services infrastructure.Sitzler, D.D.;
      Smith, P.G.; Marine, A.N. 1992 February; 13 p. (Format: TXT=29135
      bytes) (Also RFC 1302)

11   Catalog of Available X.500 Implementations.Lang, R.; Wright, R. 1991
      December; 103 p. (Format: TXT=129468 bytes) (Also RFC 1292)

10   There's Gold in them thar Networks! or Searching for Treasure in all the
      Wrong Places.Martin, J. 1993 January; 39 p. (Format: TXT=71176 bytes)
      (Also RFC 1402)   (Obsoletes RFC 1290)

9   Who's who in the Internet: Biographies of IAB, IESG and IRSG members.
      Malkin, G.S. 1992 May; 33 p. (Format: TXT=92119 bytes) (Also RFC 1336)
      (Obsoletes RFC 1251)

8   Site Security Handbook.Holbrook, J.P.; Reynolds, J.K.,eds. 1991 July;
      101 p. (Format: TXT=259129 bytes) (Also RFC 1244)

7   FYI on Questions and Answers: Answers to commonly asked "experienced
      Internet user" questions.Malkin, G.S.; Marine, A.N.; Reynolds, J.K.
      1991 February; 15 p. (Format: TXT=33385 bytes) (Also RFC 1207)

6   FYI on the X window system.Scheifler, R.W. 1991 January; 3 p. (Format:
      TXT=3629 bytes) (Also RFC 1198)

5   Choosing a name for your computer.Libes, D. 1990 August; 8 p. (Format:
      TXT=18472 bytes) (Also RFC 1178)

4   FYI on questions and answers: Answers to commonly asked "new Internet
      user" questions.Malkin, G.S.; Marine, A.N. 1992 May; 42 p. (Format:
      TXT=91884 bytes) (Also RFC 1325)   (Obsoletes RFC 1206)

3   FYI on where to start: A bibliography of internetworking information.
      Bowers, K.L.; LaQuey, T.L.; Reynolds, J.K.; Roubicek, K.; Stahl, M.K.;
      Yuan, A. 1990 August; 42 p. (Format: TXT=67330 bytes) (Also RFC 1175)

2   FYI on a Network Management Tool Catalog: Tools for Monitoring and
        Debugging TCP/IP Internets and Interconnected Devices.Enger, R.;
        Reynolds, J.K.,eds. 1993 June; 192 p. (Format: TXT=308528 bytes) (Also
        RFC 1470)   (Obsoletes RFC 1147)

1   F.Y.I. on F.Y.I.: Introduction to the F.Y.I. notes.Malkin, G.S.;
        Reynolds, J.K. 1990 March; 4 p. (Format: TXT=7867 bytes) (Also RFC
        1150)

STD Index

Original Source: File /rfc/std-index.txt on host ftp.nisc.sri.com

```
                    STD INDEX
                    -------------
```

This file contains citations for all STD RFCs in ascending numeric
order. For more information about STD RFCs, please refer to
RFC 1311, "Introduction to the STD Notes."

STD (Standard) RFC citations appear in this format:

```
##    RFC ####:  Title of RFC.  Author 1.; Author 2.  Issue date; ## p.
      (Format: PS=xxx TXT=zzz bytes)
      (This STD also includes RFC ####; RFC ####)
```

Key to citations:

    ## is the STD number. If there is no STD number to the left of a
    citation below, the previous STD number listed applies to that
    document. This is possible because the specifications of some
    standards are contained in more than one RFC document. You do not
    have the full specification of the standard if you do not have
    every RFC assigned the particular STD number for that standard.

    RFC #### is the number of the RFC which is cited as describing
    all or part of the STD.

    ## p. is the total number of pages.

    The format and byte information follows the page information in
    parenthesis. The format, either ASCII text (TXT) or PostScript
    (PS) or both, is noted, followed by an equals sign and the number
    of bytes for that version. (PostScript is a registered trademark
    of Adobe Systems Incorporated.) The example (Format: PS=xxx
    TXT=zzz bytes) shows that the PostScript version of the RFC
    is xxx bytes and the ASCII text version is zzz bytes.

    The (This STD also includes RFC ####; RFC ####) phrase refers to
    companion RFCs that are also part of the specification of the
    standard. This phrase will only appear for those STDs whose
    full specification is contained in more than one RFC.

V

Resource Reference

For example:

5   RFC 791: Internet Protocol. Postel, J.B. 1981 September; 45 p.
      (Format: TXT=97779 bytes) (This STD also includes RFC 950; RFC 919;
      RFC 922; RFC 792; RFC 1112)

This document is also RFC 791. This document is not the full specification
for STD 5. The full specification for STD 5 requires this document,
plus RFCs 950, 919, 792, and 1112 (as indicated by the "with" information).

All STDs are available online. Paper copies of all STDs are available
from SRI on a cost recovery basis (for more information contact
nisc@nisc.sri.com or call +1-415-859-6387). Online copies are
available via FTP from ftp.nisc.sri.com as rfc/rfc####.txt or
rfc/rfc####.ps (#### is the RFC number without leading zeroes).

Additionally, RFCs may be requested through electronic mail from SRI's
automated mail server by sending a message to mail-server@nisc.sri.com.
In the body of the message, indicate the RFC to be sent, e.g. "send rfcNNNN"
where NNNN is the number of the RFC. For PostScript RFCs, specify
the file extension, e.g. "send rfcNNNN.ps". Multiple requests can be sent
in a single message by specifying each request on a separate line.
The RFC Index can be requested by typing "send rfc-index"; the
STD Index can be requested by typing "send std-index".

                              * STD INDEX *

1   RFC 1410: IAB official protocol standards. Postel, J.B.,ed.
      1993 March; 35 p. (Format: TXT=76524 bytes)

2   RFC 1340: Assigned Numbers. Reynolds, J.K.; Postel, J.B. 1992
      July; 138 p. (Format: TXT=232974 bytes)

3   RFC 1123: Requirements for Internet hosts - application and support.
      Braden, R.T., ed. 1989 October; 98 p. (Format: TXT=245503 bytes)
      (This STD also includes RFC 1122)

      RFC 1122: Requirements for Internet hosts - communication
      layers. Braden, R.T., ed. 1989 October; 116 p. (Format:
      TXT=295992 bytes) (This STD also includes RFC 1123)

4   RFC 1009: Requirements for Internet gateways. Braden, R.T.; Postel,
      J.B. 1987 June; 55 p. (Format: TXT=128173 bytes)

5   RFC 791: Internet Protocol. Postel, J.B. 1981 September; 45 p.
      (Format: TXT=97779 bytes) (This STD also includes RFC 950; RFC 919;
      RFC 922; RFC 792; RFC 1112)

      RFC 950: Internet standard subnetting procedure. Mogul, J.C.;
      Postel, J.B. 1985 August; 18 p. (Format: TXT=39010 bytes) (This
      STD also includes RFC 791; RFC 919; RFC 922; RFC 792; RFC 1112)

      RFC 919: Broadcasting Internet datagrams. Mogul, J.C. 1984
      October; 8 p. (Format: TXT=16838 bytes) (This STD also includes
      RFC 791; RFC 950; RFC 922; RFC 792; RFC 1112)

RFC 922: Broadcasting Internet datagrams in the presence of
subnets. Mogul, J.C. 1984 October; 12 p. (Format: TXT=24832
bytes) (This STD also includes RFC 791; RFC 950; RFC 919; RFC
792; RFC 1112)

RFC 792: Internet Control Message Protocol. Postel, J.B. 1981
September; 21 p. (Format: TXT=30404 bytes) (This STD also
includes RFC 791; RFC 950; RFC 919; RFC 922; RFC 1112)

RFC 1112: Host extensions for IP multicasting. Deering, S.E.
1989 August; 17 p. (Format: TXT=39904 bytes) (This STD also
includes RFC 791; RFC 950; RFC 919; RFC 922; RFC 792)

6   RFC 768: User Datagram Protocol. Postel, J.B. 1980 August 28; 3 p.
        (Format: TXT=6069 bytes)

7   RFC 793: Transmission Control Protocol. Postel, J.B. 1981
        September; 85 p. (Format: TXT=177957 bytes)

8   RFC 855: Telnet option specifications. Postel, J.B.; Reynolds, J.K.
        1983 May; 4 p. (Format: TXT=6218 bytes) (This STD also includes RFC
        854)

        RFC 854: Telnet Protocol specification. Postel, J.B.; Reynolds,
        J.K. 1983 May; 15 p. (Format: TXT=39371 bytes) (This STD also
        includes RFC 855)

9   RFC 959: File Transfer Protocol. Postel, J.B.; Reynolds, J.K. 1985
        October; 69 p. (Format: TXT=151249 bytes)

10   RFC 821: Simple Mail Transfer Protocol. Postel, J.B. 1982 August;
        58 p. (Format: TXT=124482 bytes)

11   RFC 822: Standard for the format of ARPA Internet text messages.
        Crocker, D. 1982 August 13; 47 p. (Format: TXT=109200 bytes)
        (This STD also includes RFC 1049)

        RFC 1049: Content-type header field for Internet messages.
        Sirbu, M.A. 1988 March; 8 p. (Format: TXT=18923 bytes)
        (This STD also includes RFC 822)

12   RFC 1119: Network Time Protocol (version 2) specification and
        implementation. Mills, D.L. 1989 September; 64 p. (Format:
        PS=535202 bytes)

13   RFC 1035: Domain names - implementation and specification.
        Mockapetris, P.V. 1987 November; 55 p. (Format: TXT=125626
        bytes) (This STD also includes RFC 1034)

        RFC 1034: Domain names - concepts and facilities. Mockapetris,
        P.V. 1987 November; 55 p. (Format: TXT=129180 bytes)
        (This STD also includes RFC 1035)

14   RFC 974: Mail routing and the domain system. Partridge, C. 1986
        January; 7 p. (Format: TXT=18581 bytes)

V

Resource Reference

15   RFC 1157: Simple Network Management Protocol (SNMP). Case, J.D.;
      Fedor, M.; Schoffstall, M.L.; Davin, C. 1990 May; 36 p.
      (Format: TXT=74894 bytes)

16   RFC 1155: Structure and identification of management information for
      TCP/IP-based internets. Rose, M.T.; McCloghrie, K. 1990 May;
      22 p. (Format: TXT=40927 bytes) (This STD also includes RFC 1212)

      RFC 1212: Concise MIB definitions. Rose, M.T.; McCloghrie,
      K.,eds. 1991 March; 19 p. (Format: TXT=43579 bytes) (This STD
      also includes RFC 1155)

17   RFC 1213: Management Information Base for network management of
      TCP/IP-based internets: MIB-II. McCloghrie, K.; Rose, M.T.,eds.
      1991 March; 70 p. (Format: TXT=146080 bytes)

18   RFC 904: Exterior Gateway Protocol formal specification. Mills,
      D.L. 1984 April; 30 p. (Format: TXT=65226 bytes)

19   RFC 1002: Protocol standard for a NetBIOS service on a TCP/UDP
      transport: Detailed specifications. Internet Engineering Task
      Force, NetBIOS Working Group. 1987 March; 85 p. (Format:
      TXT=170262 bytes) (This STD also includes RFC 1001)

      RFC 1001: Protocol standard for a NetBIOS service on a TCP/UDP
      transport: Concepts and methods. Internet Engineering Task
      Force, NetBIOS Working Group. 1987 March; 68 p. (Format:
      TXT=158437 bytes) (This STD also includes RFC 1002)

20   RFC 862: Echo Protocol. Postel, J.B. 1983 May; 1 p. (Format:
      TXT=1294 bytes)

21   RFC 863: Discard Protocol. Postel, J.B. 1983 May; 1 p. (Format:
      TXT=1297 bytes)

22   RFC 864: Character Generator Protocol. Postel, J.B. 1983 May; 3
      p. (Format: TXT=7016 bytes)

23   RFC 865: Quote of the Day Protocol. Postel, J.B. 1983 May; 1 p.
      (Format: TXT=1734 bytes)

24   RFC 866: Active users. Postel, J.B. 1983 May; 1 p. (Format:
      TXT=2087 bytes)

25   RFC 867: Daytime Protocol. Postel, J.B. 1983 May; 2 p. (Format:
      TXT=2405 bytes)

26   RFC 868: Time Protocol. Postel, J.B.; Harrenstien, K. 1983 May; 2
      p. (Format: TXT=3140 bytes)

27   RFC 856: Telnet binary transmission. Postel, J.B.; Reynolds, J.K.
      1983 May; 4 p. (Format: TXT=9192 bytes)

28   RFC 857: Telnet echo option. Postel, J.B.; Reynolds, J.K. 1983
      May; 5 p. (Format: TXT=11143 bytes)

29   RFC 858: Telnet Suppress Go Ahead option. Postel, J.B.; Reynolds, J.K. 1983 May; 3 p. (Format: TXT=3825 bytes)

30   RFC 859: Telnet status option. Postel, J.B.; Reynolds, J.K. 1983 May; 3 p. (Format: TXT=4443 bytes)

31   RFC 860: Telnet timing mark option. Postel, J.B.; Reynolds, J.K. 1983 May; 4 p. (Format: TXT=8108 bytes)

32   RFC 861: Telnet extended options: List option. Postel, J.B.; Reynolds, J.K. 1983 May; 1 p. (Format: TXT=3181 bytes)

33   RFC 1350: TFTP protocol (revision 2). Sollins, K.R. 1992 July; 11 11 p. (Format: TXT=24599 bytes)

34   RFC 1058: Routing Information Protocol. Hedrick, C.L. 1988 June; 33 p. (Format: TXT=93285 bytes)

35   RFC 1006: ISO transport services on top of the TCP: Version 3. Rose, M.T.; Cass, D.E. 1987 May; 17 p. (Format: TXT=31935 bytes) (Obsoletes RFC 983)

V

Resource Reference

| Delete | Move | Previous | Next Item | News | Cascade |

Appendixes

ISFNET Packet Traffic

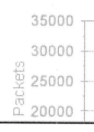

oming Mail

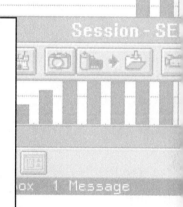

Session - SE

ox   1 Message

Call

I   MAIL INDEX   - Read mail in current folder

er

Mail in progress...

* ---- Mail Composition Editor ---- *

ftpmail@decwrl.dec.com   Edit   Done   Cancel

ile request via ftpmail server

Note: In Pine 3.0 we are encouraging folks to use the MAIL INDEX to
      mail instead of VIEW MAIL, so it is no longer on the main menu
      in the mail index, it is available as usual as the "Y" command

Help   Quit   Folders   Other
Compose   Mail Index   Addresses

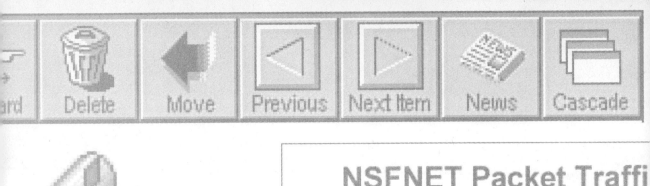

ard	Delete	Move	Previous	Next Item	News	Cascade

coming Mail

NSFNET Packet Traffi

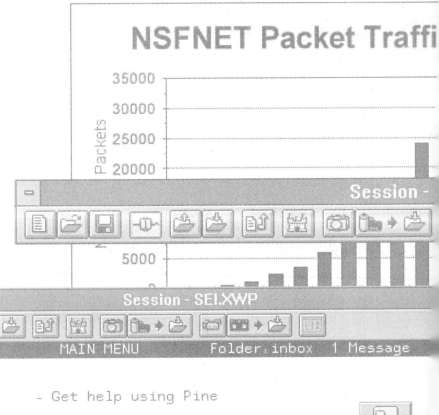

```
Packets
35000
30000
25000
20000
```

Session -

```
5000
```

Session - SEI.XWP

```
PINE 3.07          MAIN MENU          Folder.inbox  1 Message


     ?    HELP        - Get help using Pine

     C    COMPOSE     - Compose and send a message

     I    MAIL INDEX  - Read mail in current folder
```

Call

```
                                                          er
```

Mail in progress...			
* ----- Mail Composition Editor ----- *			

TO: ftpmail@decwrl.dec.com   Edit   Done   Cancel

CC:

bject: file request via ftpmail server

```
     Note. In Pine 3.0 we are encouraging folks to use the MAIL INDE
           mail instead of VIEW MAIL, so it is no longer on the main
           in the mail index, it is available as usual as the "Y" co
```

```
  ? Help      Q Quit        F Folders      O Other
  C Compose   I Mail Index  A Addresses
```

Appendix A

Using the Companion Disk

The disk that accompanies this book is designed to provide you with everything you need to get up and running on the Internet. On the disk are electronically indexed versions of the mailing list and news group lists from Chapter 20, and a copy of the Public Dialup Internet Access List (PDIAL013.TXT). By using these lists, you can quickly search for groups and lists that contain subjects that interest you, or find the closest Internet access point when you travel or relocate.

Also, Computer Witchcraft, Inc. has provided a copy of its WinNET Mail program for Windows to get you connected to the net.

The Electronically Indexed Lists

The disk contains electronic, indexed copies of three lists from the Internet:

- The list of mail lists on the Internet (MAILLIST). Use this file to search for mail lists that may interest you.

- The list of news groups on the Internet (USELIST). Use this file to search for news groups that may interest you.

> **Note**
>
> Chapter 20 contains duplicates of the mailing and news group lists.

- The list of public-access dialups into the Internet (PDIAL). Use this file to find the closest or most convenient gateway into the Internet from your present location. Helpful hints and general information about the Internet also is included in this file.

Each file has been electronically indexed so that you can search on keywords and quickly find information that interests you. If you are interested in motion pictures (movies), for example, searching USELIST yields news groups such as `alt.cult-movies` and `rec.arts.movies.reviews`; searching MAILLIST yields `sf-lovers`, a mail list for science-fiction lovers that includes sci-fi movies.

RACONTEX

The lists have been electronically indexed by a powerful textual indexing engine called RACONTEX (Rapid Contextual Search System) from Guy Software. You quickly can search text files processed by the RACONTEX system for any word that occurs in them. The searching is done by a special reader provided with RACONTEX. The reader also supports printing and exporting text in ASCII or WordPerfect document format.

> **Note**
>
> Guy Software has provided the reader for use with the lists contained on the disk in the back of this book. If you are interested in indexing your own files, see the text file README.1ST in the RACONTEX directory or the ad in the back of this book.

Installing RACONTEX and the Lists

To use the lists contained on the disk, you must install RACONTEX to your local hard drive. To install RACONTEX and the indexed lists to your hard drive, follow these steps:

1. Place the disk in your floppy drive (A or B). These instructions assume that you are using the A drive. If you are using the B drive, substitute **b:** wherever you see **a:** in the following steps.

2. At the DOS prompt, type the following:

```
a:\lists\install d:\racontex-directory
```

where *d:\racontex-directory* is the drive and directory you want to store the lists in (for example, `c:\racontex`).

> **Note**
>
> You can use any directory name you want, and the directory can be a subdirectory off the root directory or another directory (for example, C:\INTERNET\RACONTEX).

The INSTALL program is a self-extracting archive and will expand the files into the directory you specified. While it expands the files, you will see a display similar to the following:

```
LHA's SFX 2.13S (c) Yoshi, 1991

README.1ST .
MAILLIST.TXT ........
MAILLIST.DCT ..
RACONTEX.EXE .....
RACONTEX.ICO .
RACONTEX.PIF .
```

Appendixes

3. After the DOS prompt reappears, remove the floppy disk from the drive and store it in a safe place.

Starting RACONTEX

After RACONTEX is installed on your hard drive, you can use it to search the provided lists for topics of interest. **RACONTEX** supports two front-ends, DOS and Windows. The Windows front-end offers an easy way to start RACONTEX (which is a DOS-only application) from within Windows.

Starting RACONTEX from DOS

To start RACONTEX from DOS, change to the subdirectory where you installed the program and type **RACONTEX**. After a few moments, you will see the startup screen; the list of available files to search appears in a strip near the bottom of the screen, as shown in figure A.1. Use the arrow keys or the mouse to highlight the file you want to search, and then press Enter.

Fig. A.1
The RACONTEX startup screen.

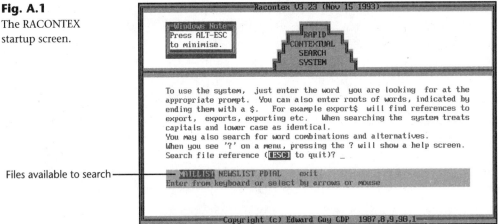

Files available to search

Note

To exit RACONTEX, highlight exit and press Enter.

After you press Enter, RACONTEX will pause and display QUE Books "Using the Internet" (see discount offer in the back of the book). Press any key to continue.

> **Note**
>
> Pressing F10 or clicking the right mouse button will shift RACONTEX into 50-line mode on monitors that support this mode.

RACONTEX next displays the license screen. After 3 seconds, press any key to move to the search screen.

> **Note**
>
> The two pauses in execution mentioned so far don't exist in the registered version of RACONTEX. See the ad in the back of this book for ordering information.

You are now ready to search the selected file, as described later in the section "Searching the Lists."

Starting RACONTEX from Windows

To start RACONTEX from Windows, first create a program icon in the program group of your choice using RCNTXWIN.EXE in the Command Line text box and the RACONTEX directory in the Working Directory text box. Then you can start RACONTEX as you would any Windows application.

> **Note**
>
> Use of the Windows front-end requires the file VBRUN100.DLL—the Visual Basic 1.0 DLL. Because of disk constraints, this file couldn't be included on the disk, but is commonly available in several locations on the Internet, bulletin boards, CompuServe, and so forth. You should place this file in your \WINDOWS or \WINDOWS\SYSTEM directory.

After starting RACONTEX, you will see the application window shown in figure A.2. The upper area of the window displays information about running RACONTEX from Windows. The lower area lets you change the default drive and subdirectory and choose the file to search.

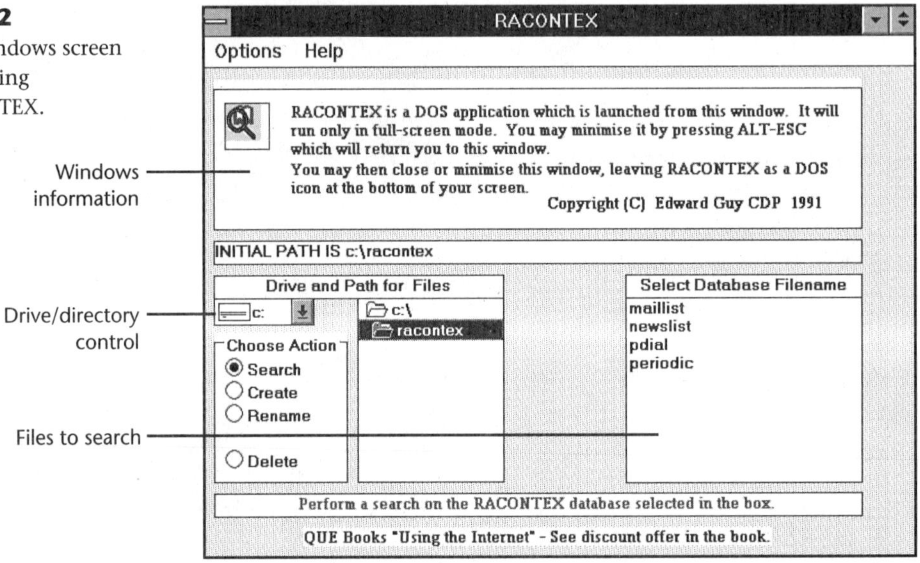

Fig. A.2

The Windows screen for starting RACONTEX.

Windows information

Drive/directory control

Files to search

> **Note**
>
> Although this window offers a Create choice in its Choose Action section, this option doesn't work with the version of RACONTEX provided with this book. The Rename and Delete options are fully functional, but shouldn't be necessary and aren't covered here.

You can use the Options pull-down menu to select the version of WordPerfect you want RACONTEX to support, or the desired screen resolution. Note that not all monitors support all screen resolutions.

Click the file you want to search from the list in the Select Database Filename section of the window. A Click to Search... button appears in the middle of the RACONTEX window. Click this button to search the selected file.

The RACONTEX Windows front-end will run the DOS RACONTEX program. The startup screen will appear, and RACONTEX will display QUE Books "Using the Internet" (see discount offer in the back of the book). Press any key to continue.

RACONTEX next displays the license screen. After 3 seconds, press any key to move to the search screen.

> **Note**
>
> The two pauses in execution don't exist in the registered version of RACONTEX. See the ad in the back of this book for ordering information.

You are now ready to search the selected file, as described later in the section "Searching the Lists."

Using the Mouse in RACONTEX

RACONTEX supports limited mouse use. In a menu of choices, you can use the mouse to make a choice. Moving the mouse right and left, for example, will select a file to search in the DOS front-end. You also can use the mouse to move a small pointer over the options listed on the status line. Click when the mouse pointer is positioned to activate the option/function.

Searching the Lists

RACONTEX indexes every word in a file so that it can quickly search the file for keywords you provide. As the startup screen explains, you can specify root words by ending your search text with a $. Specifying export$, for example, will find references to *export*, *exports*, *exporting*, and so on. RACONTEX treats the case of the text you specify as exact. Specifying Cats, for example, won't find *CATS* or *cats*.

To search for a word in the file, type the word at the Word to find? prompt (as shown in fig. A.3), and press Enter.

Tip
You also can press
Enter and then Esc
without specifying a
word to exit back to
the startup screen.

RACONTEX will search the file for the word you specified
and display the results on-screen. While you are searching
the MAILLIST file, typing `religion` would display the screen
shown in figure A.4; typing `taxidermy` would display the
screen shown in figure A.5.

Fig. A.3
Type the word you
want to find at the
prompt and press
Enter.

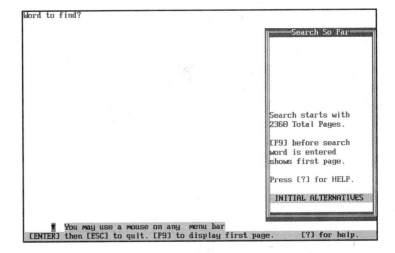

Fig. A.4
Searching for
`religion` nets 9
matches in the
MAILLIST file.

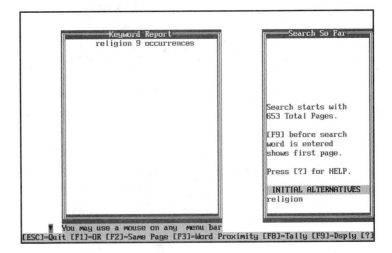

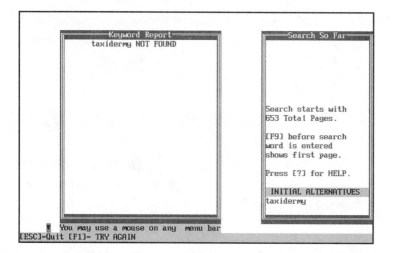

Fig. A.5
Searching for
taxidermy nets no
matches in the
MAILLIST file.

> **Note**
>
> Pressing F9 before specifying a word will display the first page of the file.

After the search results appear, you can display the results of the search, add conditions to the search, or restart the search from scratch. The available keys (and actions) are as follows:

- *Esc.* Quit back to the startup screen so that you can choose another file to search or exit RACONTEX. You are prompted to press Esc again if you really want to quit.

- *F1.* Add a word as an alternative to the first word entered so that you can build complex searches. You can search for alien OR ufo, for example, to help find all instances of UFO-related text.

> **Note**
>
> If the word you specified isn't found, RACONTEX offers you two choices: press Esc to exit back to the startup screen, or press F1 to enter another word to find.

Appendixes

■ *F2.* Specify a word that must be on the same page as the word(s) listed under INITIAL ALTERNATIVES. This way, you can find text that contains the words specified only when they appear *on the same page*.

> **Note**
>
> The MAILLIST and NEWSLIST files have been edited so that only one mail list or news group appears on each page. This way, you can use the F2 key to search only for individual lists or groups that contain several specified words.

■ *F3.* Specify a word within a set proximity to the word(s) listed under INITIAL ALTERNATIVES. This way, you can specify how many words apart the words you specify can be, thus helping eliminate results where the multiple words exist on the same page but have nothing to do with each other. After pressing F3, press the appropriate key, as listed on the status line, to specify the distance between the words.

■ *F8.* Tally the results thus far. When you add words to the search, whether through the OR, Word Proximity, or Same Page functions, only the last find is displayed. Pressing F8 will tally the results and display how many *hits* (text found that matches the criteria specified) there were. If you search NEWSLIST and specify `ufo` and then add `alien` as an OR, for example, only the number of alien hits (1) will be displayed. Pressing F8 will show you that 3 total hits matched `ufo OR alien`.

■ *F9.* Display text found. This button displays the first page of the file that matches the text specified. You then can move to the next (or previous) hit, the next page of the document, print, or export the text. See the following section, "Displaying the Search Results."

■ *?. Help.* You can press the question mark (?) key to get context-sensitive help at any screen that displays the question mark on the status line.

Displaying the Search Results

After conducting the search, you will want to display the results. From the search screen, press F9 to display the first page of the text that matches your search criteria. Figure A.6 shows the initial display screen of a ufo OR alien search.

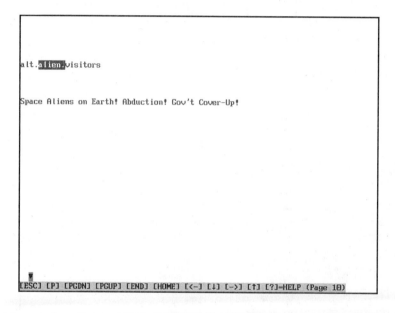

Fig. A.6
The initial display screen of the ufo OR alien search conducted on the NEWSLIST file.

Notice that the status line changes to show you the keystrokes that you can use on the display screen. Each key is described as follows:

■ *Esc.* Returns to the search screen to start a new search. Note that this button clears the search parameters completely.

■ *P.* Displays the pop-up Print menu, shown in figure A.7. You can choose to export/print the current page, all pages of the file, or only the pages that match the search criteria you specified. Press the corresponding number or click the appropriate selection. After choosing the amount of text to export, another menu appears (see fig. A.8) to give you the choice to export the text to the printer, an ASCII text file, an ASCII text file with the keywords surrounded by braces ({ and }), or a WordPerfect file. Again, press the number corresponding to the appropriate option or use the mouse.

Fig. A.7

The Print Output Selection menu for choosing the amount of text to print/export.

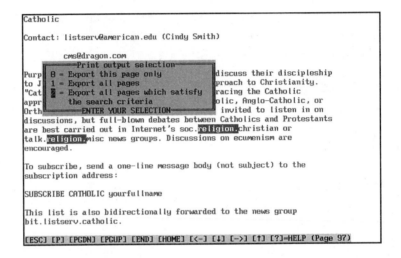

```
Catholic

Contact: listserv@american.edu (Cindy Smith)

          cms@dragon.com
         ╔═Print output selection═╗
Purp║ 0 = Export this page only      ║discuss their discipleship
to J║ 1 = Export all pages           ║proach to Christianity.
"Cat║ 2 = Export all pages which satisfy║racing the Catholic
appr║     the search criteria        ║olic, Anglo-Catholic, or
Orth╚════ENTER YOUR SELECTION════════╝ invited to listen in on
discussions, but full-blown debates between Catholics and Protestants
are best carried out in Internet's soc.religion.christian or
talk.religion.misc news groups. Discussions on ecumenism are
encouraged.

To subscribe, send a one-line message body (not subject) to the
subscription address:

SUBSCRIBE CATHOLIC yourfullname

This list is also bidirectionally forwarded to the news group
bit.listserv.catholic.

[ESC] [P] [PGDN] [PGUP] [END] [HOME] [<-] [↓] [->] [↑] [?]=HELP (Page 97)
```

Fig. A.8

The Print Output Selection menu for choosing the destination of the exported text.

```
Catholic

Contact: listserv@american.edu (Cindy Smith)

          cms@dragon.com
         ╔═Print output selection═╗
Purp║ 0 = Printer                    ║discuss their discipleship
to J║ 1 = ASCII Text file            ║proach to Christianity.
"Cat║ 2 = ASCII File with {} highlights║racing the Catholic
appr║ 3 = WordPerfect with bold highlights║olic, Anglo-Catholic, or
Orth╚════ENTER YOUR SELECTION════════╝ invited to listen in on
discussions, but full-blown debates between Catholics and Protestants
are best carried out in Internet's soc.religion.christian or
talk.religion.misc news groups. Discussions on ecumenism are
encouraged.

To subscribe, send a one-line message body (not subject) to the
subscription address:

SUBSCRIBE CATHOLIC yourfullname

This list is also bidirectionally forwarded to the news group
bit.listserv.catholic.

[ESC] [P] [PGDN] [PGUP] [END] [HOME] [<-] [↓] [->] [↑] [?]=HELP (Page 97)
```

> **Note**
>
> If you choose one of the file export options (either ASCII option, or the WordPerfect document option), you also will be prompted for a file name. Type the complete path of the file you want RACONTEX to export to, and then press Enter.
>
> The choices you make in the two print menus remain active while you continue to search the same file. Pressing the P key subsequently will output the same amount of text selected earlier to the same device you selected. Returning to the main menu will reset the choices.
>
> If you select a file export option and enter the name of a file that already exists, RACONTEX will *append* any printed output to that file.

■ *Page Up/Page Down.* Moves to the previous/next page of the file, regardless of the search criteria. You can use these keys to explore the text around the text found by the search.

■ *Home/End.* Moves to the first/last page of the file, regardless of the search criteria.

■ *Up- and down-arrow keys.* Move to the next screen of the current page. If the current page can't fit on-screen, use the up- and down-arrow keys to view the remainder of the page.

■ *Left- and right-arrow keys.* Move to the previous or next match. These arrow keys enable you to move quickly between pages that match your search criteria. The right-arrow key will display the next screen of the current page (until the last screen is displayed) before moving to the next hit.

■ *?.* Help. Displays help text relating to the display screen.

Appendixes

Exiting RACONTEX

To exit RACONTEX, press Esc to return to the startup screen, as shown earlier in figure A.1. Then choose exit from the file list or press Esc again. To exit from the search window, you may need to press Enter before pressing Esc. Look at the status line if you are unsure.

If you are running RACONTEX from the Windows front-end, you will need to exit it also. When the window is displayed, press Alt+F4 or choose Close from the window's control menu.

Helpful Hints

The indexed lists have been provided to help you find the information you need quickly. You can use Chapters 19, "USENET News Groups Index," and 20, "USENET News Groups Descriptions," in a similar manner, because they contain the same lists. If you prefer to use the book, look up topics in the index contained in Chapter 19. You can find the descriptions of the mail lists or news groups mentioned in the index in Chapter 20.

You can use the lists on disk in a similar fashion, but the disk enables you to narrow or broaden your search further. Remember the following points when using the electronic lists:

- The news groups and mail lists have been edited to place each individual group or list on one page. Use the OR feature to add additional keywords (and, hence, groups or lists) to your search, and the Word Proximity feature to limit the groups/lists found.

- Remember that the descriptions or names may not always contain the words you are looking for. Searching too narrowly can yield results that contain the word(s) you specify but aren't what you want, or may not find everything you are looking for. Use the OR and Word Proximity features frequently.

- Think generally, remember case sensitivity, search for several different words, and use the $ before giving up. Searching for camaro, camaros, and Camaro in NEWSLIST, for example, doesn't find any matches. Searching for Camaro$, however, finds F-body, the discussion of Camaro and Firebird cars.

- Search both MAILLIST and NEWSGROUP before giving up. Sometimes the descriptions in one list may not contain the words you're searching on, but the other list might.

- Use the Word Proximity feature's Adj option to build phrases to search on. For example, searching on star, then pressing F1 and selecting Adj, and then searching on trek will search for *star trek*.

WinNET Mail

This section of Appendix A provides an installation and novice user's guide for WinNET Mail. WinNET Mail is a Windows product from a company called Computer Witchcraft, which provides a nationwide, UUCP-based Internet connection service.

WinNET Mail software has been in distribution via typical shareware channels such as bulletin boards, CompuServe, and Internet archives since late 1992. Version 2.04 of WinNET Mail—used as the basis for this discussion—has been proven to be very, robust, thoughtfully designed, and easy to use.

There is no charge for the WinNET Mail software. It is freely distributed solely to support Computer Witchcraft's provider service. It has the useful feature of being able to connect to the CW host and establish your account automatically, provided you are willing to provide credit-card billing information at the time you sign up. This means that you can get connected at anytime, 24 hours a day, and begin using your account within minutes after signing up.

CW also provides an 800 number for access to its host, so that nationwide service is available with a single number. As explained in Chapter 12, although the 800 number means that your local phone company doesn't charge you for your connection time, CW does include line charges in its connect charge bill to you. The rates are usually better than normal long-distance charges, however, so you usually end up saving money by this arrangement.

WinNET Mail provides e-mail and USENET news, as well as a mail-based version of ftp.

Installing WinNET Mail

The following installation guide provides a step-by-step description of installing WinNET Mail, using a generous number of screen captures so that you can see and understand the process before having to begin.

Insert the *Using the Internet* companion disk in a floppy drive. The following procedure assumes that you are using drive A. If you are using another drive, substitute its letter instead of A.

From Windows' Program Manager, choose **F**ile, **R**un. The Run dialog box appears. In the **C**ommand Line text box, type `a:\winnet\setup.exe` and then choose OK or press Enter. After a few moments, the WinNET Mail Setup screen will appear, as shown in figure A.9.

> **Note**
>
> WinNET Mail itself takes about 2M of disk space. USENET news and e-mail messages will consume additional space.

Additional information is available in the form of detailed text files that you can view at several points during the installation process. To view these files, choose the More Information button, and a window such as that in figure A.10 will appear.

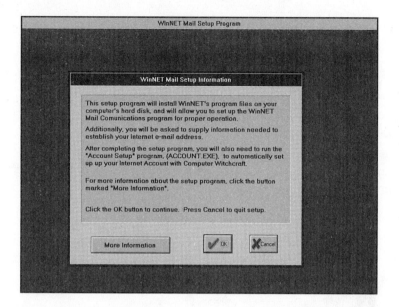

Fig. A.9
The initial setup dialog box, explaining what will occur during the installation process.

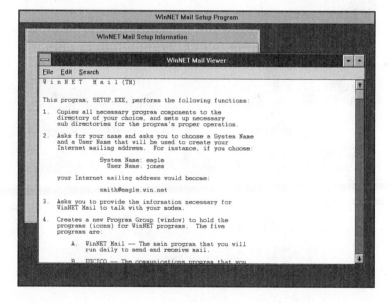

Fig. A.10
Additional information window offering further explanation at key steps during the installation process.

Choosing OK will continue the installation, which provides you an opportunity to configure the installation process in the Setup Options dialog box (see fig. A.11). First-time users should enable all portions of the installation process. After you have an account, your most common configuration will be to change modem parameters. WinNET Mail supports connections up to 57,600 bps (v.32bis with v.42bis compression and correction). Choose OK to continue.

Continuing with the installation, WinNET Mail prompts you for the disk and directory where WinNET will be installed (the default is C:\WNMAIL). Type the desired drive and path in the text box of the Select Program Directory dialog box (see fig. A.12) and press Enter.

Fig. A.11
Setup options.
First-time users of
WinNET Mail should
enable all portions of
the installation.

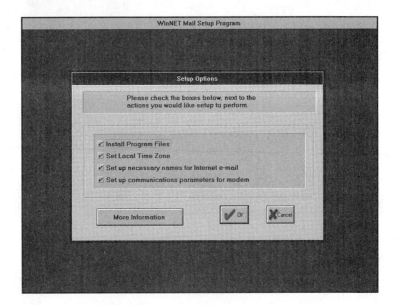

Fig. A.12
Specifying the disk
and directory where
WinNET Mail
should be installed.
C:\WNMAIL is the
default.

The Setup program then displays the Set Time Zone dialog box. For efficient use of your connection time to the host, WinNET Mail uses time stamp information to help tell whether files need to be transferred. To do so, it must adjust your local time to Universal Coordinated Time (UCT) by applying an offset that varies depending on your time zone. Select the time zone that is appropriate for you from the list given (see fig. A.13). Choose OK to continue.

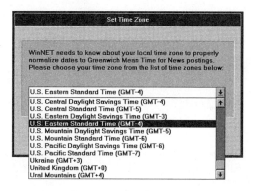

Fig. A.13
Select your time zone. WinNET Mail uses this information to determine the age of files and when new files should be transferred.

When you see the E-Mail System and User Information dialog box next (shown in fig. A.14), you need to think up a name for yourself and your system. Enter your full name as you want it to appear in the header of your e-mail messages. (It doesn't have to be your real name, if you prefer to be known by a pseudonym.) Because WinNET Mail uses UUCP for its transfer method, your machine also must have a name. After entering your full name, System Name, and E-Mail Name, choose OK. After you enter the configuration information for your address, you must specify the communication parameters that tell WinNET Mail where to find your modem, what transfer rates it can support, and so forth. This information is specified in the Communications Setup dialog box, shown in figure A.15.

Appendixes

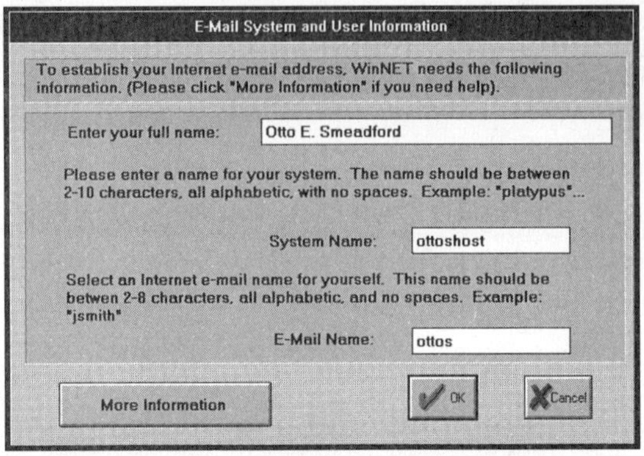

Fig. A.14
System and user
information. WinNET
Mail requires a user
name and host name
for your address.

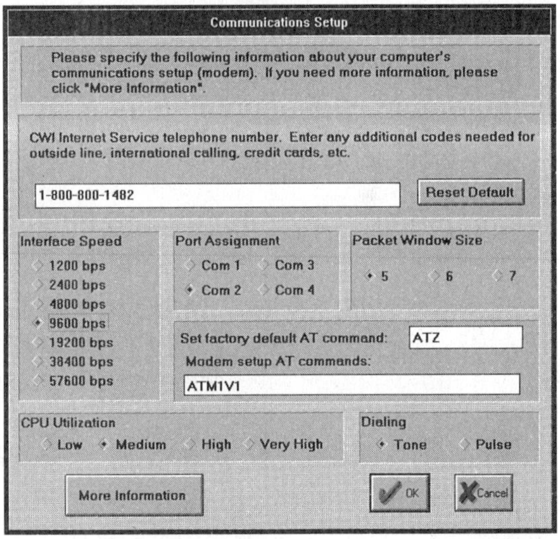

Fig. A.15
Communications
parameter selection.
WinNET Mail
supports a wide range
of connection speeds,
serial ports, and
modems.

Note

Although the default modem commands should work just fine, you may want to modify them to your needs or tastes. Consult your modem manual for guidance on specifying and using modem commands.

If you need to dial 9 (or some other prefix) to get an outside line, edit the phone number at the top of the dialog box and insert that prefix before the telephone number.

Choose OK after specifying all the communications settings.

After you specify your communications parameters, the software setup of WinNET Mail is complete, and WinNET Mail is installed on your system. A Setup Complete dialog box informs you that the installation is complete and that you need to run ACCOUNT.EXE to set up your user account (see fig. A.16). Choose OK to continue or choose Terms to read about Computer Witchcraft's Internet services.

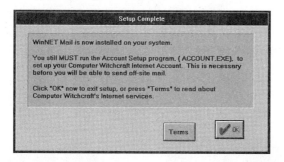

Fig. A.16
Installation is complete. The WinNET Mail software is now set up on your machine.

You now are asked whether you want a Windows group created for WinNET Mail (see fig. A.17). Because several separate programs make up WinNET Mail, you should answer "yes" to this query so that all the programs easily can be invoked.

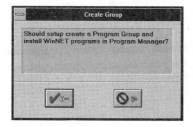

Fig. A.17
WinNET Mail can automatically create a Windows group for itself.

When the WinNET Mail group is created, SETUP.EXE completes execution, and control is returned to the Windows desktop. The WinNET Mail program group is shown in figure A.18.

Now you need to start the process of establishing an account on the CW host. From the WinNET Mail group, run Account Setup to begin the automated account creation process.

Appendixes

Fig. A.18
Example of the
group icons for
WinNET Mail.

The account setup program displays the Computer Witchcraft Internet Account Setup dialog box (see fig. A.19). Choose More Information to read about the setup process, or OK to continue. If you decide not to run the process at this time, choose Cancel.

Fig. A.19
Starting the auto-
mated account
creation process. The
entire process can take
several minutes.

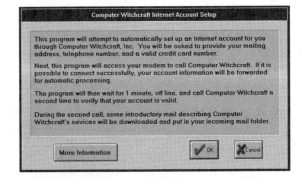

The account setup process begins by requesting mailing and billing information. Fill in the appropriate fields of the Mailing Address Information dialog box with your address, phone numbers, and so forth, and choose OK (see fig. A.20). The Account Setup program then displays the Billing Information dialog box (see fig. A.21). Just about every major credit card is accepted as a means of payment for securing your account. For detailed information regarding charges and terms of payment, click the Terms button.

After mailing and billing information is entered, choose OK. The Account Setup program is now ready to contact the CW host and establish your account. The Ready to Setup Internet Account dialog box informs you of the next step (see fig. A.22). Choose OK to continue.

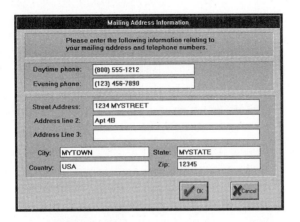

Fig. A.20
Enter your address in
the Mailing Address
Information dialog
box.

Fig. A.21
Billing information.
Automated account
sign up requires a
valid credit card.

This process can take a few minutes, and several attempts will
be made to create the account if the first tries aren't successful.
If you encounter problems, examine the TROUBLE.TXT file in
the WinNET Mail directory for common problems and possible
cures.

When your account is properly established and verified, the
Account Successfully Established dialog box will appear (see
fig. A.23). You will receive your first e-mail in the form of a welcoming message and some useful information on how to get
the most out of your connection.

Choose OK to end the Account Setup program. Congratula-
tions, you're now a member of the Internet community!

Fig. A.22
WinNET Mail is
ready to contact
the CW host and
automatically
establish your new
account.

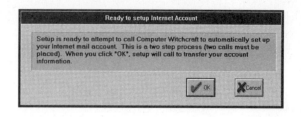

Fig. A.23
Your account has
been successfully
established with the
CW host. You also
have received
introductory mail,
welcoming you to
WinNET Mail.

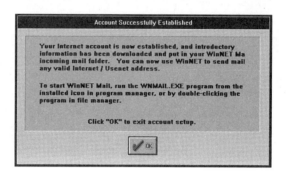

Using WinNET Mail

After you successfully install WinNET Mail and establish your
account, you're ready to begin using your connection to the
Internet. Fortunately, the user interface to WinNET Mail is quite
intuitive and easy to use, as you'll see in the figures that accom-
pany this text.

To begin, run WinNET Mail from the WinNET Mail program
group. WinNET Mail is the main program that encompasses
most of the features you will interact with on a daily basis. This
program and most others within WinNET Mail use an interface
paradigm called the Multiple Document Interface (MDI). This
approach allows the main window of the program to create
several subordinate (or *child*) windows, each of which can be
a separate entity. With this capability, you can have several
messages open at one time, for example. The operations you
select will be performed on the active MDI window, as indicated
by the color of the window title bar.

> **Note**
>
> You can use the **W**indow pull-down menu to switch between open windows in WinNET Mail. The open windows are listed at the bottom of the menu, along with a number. Press the number corresponding to the window you want to switch to.

Using the Help System

Unlike many other shareware products, WinNET Mail has a complete and very useful help facility. Don't hesitate to make use of it. Whenever you need help, choose **H**elp, **H**elp from the pull-down menus, or press F1.

Using the Toolbar

One feature that makes WinNET Mail so easy to use is its toolbar, which consists of icons that help you perform most of the functions you normally need to use. To invoke a function represented by a toolbar icon, click the desired icon once.

WinNET Mail provides the following toolbar icons:

Icon	Name	Description
Print	Print	Prints the currently selected item, such as an e-mail message.
Call	Call	Connects to the host. Initiates a UUCP exchange with the CW host to send any outgoing mail and receive any new mail.
InBox	InBox	Opens a window listing e-mail messages received.
Folders	Folders	Lists folders that have been defined.
Compose	Compose	Creates a new e-mail message.

(continues)

Icon	Name	Description
Reply	Reply	Sends a reply to the sender of the currently selected e-mail message.
Forward	Forward	Forwards the selected e-mail message to another user.
Delete	Delete	Deletes the selected item.
Move	Move	Moves the selected item to a different file.
Previous	Previous	Goes to the previous item in the list. If you have selected an e-mail message to view, for example, clicking Previous will view the previous message from the list of e-mail messages.
Next Item	Next	Proceeds to the next item in the list.
News	News	Creates a window that lists the USENET news groups subscribed to and status information showing items such as the number of messages.
Cascade	Cascade	Overlaps any open windows in a cascaded order so that you easily can bring each to the front of view.

Reviewing New Mail

 Any mail you receive is placed within the inbox folder (shown in the background of fig. A.24) and can be reviewed by clicking the InBox icon or choosing Folders, Incoming Mail from the pull-down menus. Each message in the inbox folder is listed with subject, date, and status information. The status has three values: N for new (unopened) messages, O for opened messages, and D for messages marked for deletion.

Reading Mail

Reading an e-mail message is a simple matter: double-click the line in the inbox folder message list that you would like to view, or highlight the desired message and press Enter. A new window is opened for that message, as shown in figure A.24. You can view several messages at once, if desired, and you can use the Edit menu to copy information from a message to the Clipboard for inclusion in outgoing messages or for use in other Windows applications.

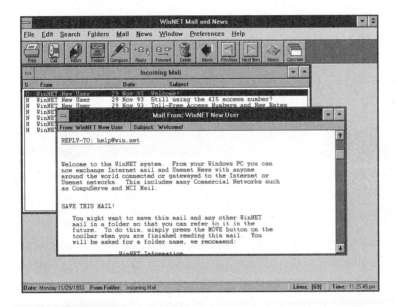

Fig. A.24
Reading an e-mail message. Double-clicking an item of the inbox list invokes the message reader.

Composing Mail

A message composition facility exists that provides address, carbon copy, and subject fields. To compose new mail, click the Compose icon or choose Mail, Compose Mail from the pull-down menus.

Fill in the TO, CC, and Subject fields and enter your message in the editing window, as shown in figure A.25. When you are finished with the body of your message, choose Done.

Fig. A.25

Composing an
e-mail message.

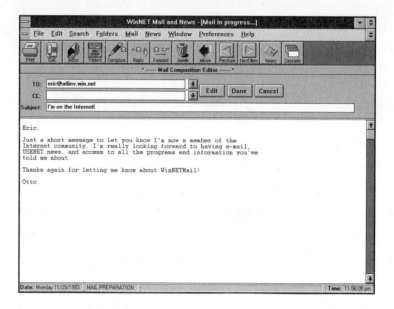

The message editor has word-wrap capability. To enable or disable
word wrap, choose **P**references, **W**ord Wrap, or press Ctrl+W.

If you have defined a signature file called PERSONAL.SIG and
placed it in the top-level WinNET Mail directory (C:\WNMAIL
by default), it automatically will be included at the end of your
messages.

Viewing the Outgoing Message Queue

After you finish composing an e-mail message, it is placed into
the outgoing message queue. The next time the CW host is
called, all the messages in the queue are transferred to the host.
You can examine this queue and modify its contents by running the Mail Queue Editor from the WinNET Mail program
group. You also can access the Queue editor (shown in fig. A.26)
from within WinNET Mail by choosing **M**ail, **Q**ueue Editor, or
pressing Ctrl+Q.

Fig. A.26
The outgoing queue
editor. You can view,
modify, or delete a
queued message,
including its header.

Connecting to the CW Host

WinNET Mail doesn't stay connected to the Internet the whole
time you use it. It connects only when you tell it to, and performs all on-line actions automatically. To send and receive
e-mail, news group messages, and perform other on-line
actions, you must connect to the CW host.

To connect to the CW host, click the Call icon or choose **M**ail,
Call **S**erver Now. WinNET will call the server and perform all
on-line actions in the background—you can continue to work
in WinNET Mail, if you want.

Note

Remember that WinNET Mail performs all on-line actions automatically, each time you call. Because you accumulate charges (phone
and Internet) each time you call, make sure that you have all your
mail written, your subscriptions active, and so on before calling the
CW server, to maximize your on-line time.

Appendixes

You also can connect to the CW host without having to use the main WinNET Mail program by running the Call WinNET program from the WinNET Mail group. This program actually performs the host communications for the main program. This method of invoking host communications provides you with a window, as shown in figure A.27, that provides a variety of statistical and status information about the host connection. The results of every session is logged in a file that you can view by clicking the Log button. You also can obtain errors and other information in a similar manner.

Fig. A.27
Connecting to the CW host. Double-clicking the Call WinNET icon produces a window with connection status information useful in optimizing and debugging.

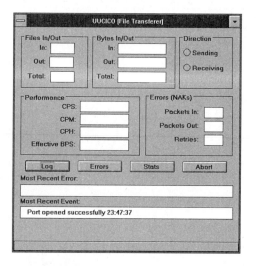

Scheduling Automatic Calls to the CW Host

One of the nicest features of WinNET Mail is that it can run in the background, transferring data to and from the host while you continue to use your PC for other tasks such as word processing. In fact, a special scheduling program called a *daemon* (pronounced "dee-mun") is provided that will automatically connect to the host once during each hour you have selected (see fig. A.28).

If you use the Scheduler daemon to call the CW server regularly, consider putting its icon in your Windows Startup group.

Fig. A.28
Scheduling automatic
calls to the CW host.
You must not close
the window, or the
daemon will cease
execution; instead,
minimize it to an
icon.

Subscribing to USENET News Groups

Subscribing to USENET news groups is also very easy in WinNET
Mail. If you already know the name of the news group you
want to subscribe to (for example, you have examined the list
in this book or the indexed file on the diskette), you can choose
News, **S**ubscription, and enter the news group's name in the
News Group Subscription Management dialog box, shown in
figure A.29.

Fig. A.29
Adding news groups
to your subscription
list. These changes—
sent to the CW host
the next time you
call—are effective
within a few minutes.

Similarly, you can remove news groups that you previously subscribed to. These changes are placed into messages that are sent
to the CW host during the next communication session. When
received by the host, these changes will be effective in a few
minutes, and you'll begin receiving an updated news feed.

Appendixes

You also can request that a message containing the list of available news groups be sent to you. As you can see in figure A.30, WinNET Mail's help facility has all the information you need to obtain an up-to-date list of the USENET news groups.

Fig. A.30

The help available through WinNET Mail for getting the list of the USENET news groups.

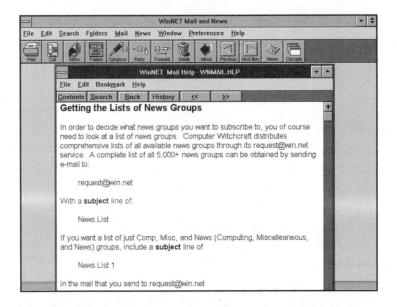

After subscribing to a news group, you will receive new articles every time you connect to the CW server. To view the new articles, choose **N**ews, News Group **L**ist. Alternatively, click the News icon or press Ctrl+Shift+L. The list of subscribed groups will appear; select the group you want to read and press Enter (or double-click its name).

You can post articles to groups by choosing **N**ews, **P**ost News.

Binary File Transfers by Mail

WinNET Mail has built-in support for uuencode and uudecode, which allows the transfer of binary information such as executable programs and data via text-based mail. To send a binary file, compose a mail message to the recipient just as you would for a textual e-mail message. You can add all the text information you want in the message. You may want to place, for example, a text header in the file that lets the recipient know the nature of the file you're including.

When you are ready to add the binary file, choose **M**ail, **A**ttach binary file; WinNET Mail handles the process of inserting it into the message (see fig. A.31). If necessary, WinNET Mail also divides a large binary file into several segments for mailing, all automatically. Similarly, if you receive a binary file, you can select **M**ail, De**t**ach binary file and specify the file name to be created with the binary data.

Tip

See the help facility within WinNET Mail for more information on binary file transfers.

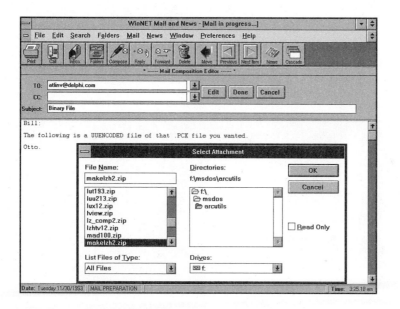

Fig. A.31
Including a binary file in a mail message. Select the file you want to send, and WinNET Mail handles converting and segmenting the file.

Other Features of WinNET Mail

WinNET Mail is a full-featured program. The preceding sections have touched only on the main points of its use, and haven't covered items such as its address book, multiple folders, and message searching capabilities.

If you have decided that a UUCP-based Internet connection is suitable for your needs, WinNET Mail provides a complete, robust, and easy-to-use product for you. It doesn't hurt that the software is free, either.

Appendixes

Appendix B

Getting On-Line with CompuServe, America Online, and Delphi

Getting connected to the Internet isn't difficult. It is much like shopping for anything else you might buy because you need to make some key decisions about the services that interest you.

Before you start shopping, however, explore the possibility that you already have access to the Internet and don't know it. Many businesses and companies provide forms of Internet connectivity for their employees. You may discover that another division in your company is already connected. Some states and other divisions of government offer services to their agencies and their employees, and, in some cases, to related businesses and services. A few colleges and universities offer Internet accesses for alumni as well as faculty, students, and staff.

Some Internet connectivity is provided over normal phone lines by community freenets and libraries. (*Community freenets* are large bulletin board systems operated by non-profit, volunteer groups.) Generally, these services are available to anyone who can reach them, but long-distance charges need to be considered if the services offer no phone number in your calling area.

If, after exploring these options, you decide that you want to get your access through a commercial provider, consider which of the following services you will want:

- *E-mail.* Some commercial bulletin board systems provide e-mail only among those who use that particular company's service, or between that service and a limited number of others. Other services provide Internet access but limit the size and number of messages you can receive or send. Still others don't allow you to receive messages from automated special-interest list servers. Rules on e-mail access frequently change—usually for the better—so check on this feature before you sign up.

- *Custom commercial databases and services.* Services such as America Online (AOL) and CompuServe offer a collection of information that they believe will be popular. This collection varies greatly in categories and depth from one service to another, and it is unlikely that they will have more information than the Internet, except in a few categories. Typically, these services are available using a menu system to make them easier to access than many Internet databases and services.

- *ftp (File Transfer Protocol).* This service enables you to log in to a remote computer on the Internet, look through its subdirectories, and download files and software that look interesting. Although this protocol will require some study and practice to master, the added access that it offers to the more than 1 million computers connected to the Internet is well worth the extra effort.

- *telnet (remote login/rlogin).* With telnet, you can connect to any computer on the Internet that has been made available to the public. You can operate many programs and services on it, just as though you were sitting at a terminal directly connected to it. Search programs such as Gopher, Veronica, Wide Area Information Server (WAIS), World Wide Web (WWW), and archie greatly expand your ability to find information. Features such as finger and WHOIS enable you to find addresses and other information about individuals who use the network, whereas IRC gives you direct, real-time contact with others on the network. Although telnet is potentially the most powerful Internet access feature, it is less often available in commercial BBS packages; when it is available, it typically adds to the cost.

Getting Connected to the Internet

Most connections to the Internet are made through large mainframe computers that are directly connected to the network through high-capacity phone lines. As a user of the Internet, you use either a terminal directly connected to this mainframe, or you communicate with the mainframe through your personal computer and modem connected to your normal phone line (as discussed in Chapter 12, "Hardware and Software").

After you sign up with a service, you can call in by using a computer, a modem, and one of several communications software packages.

Most currently available communications programs can easily handle basic Internet communications, although you should be sure that the program can transfer files in at least one of the protocols offered by the mainframe/service you are connected with. America Online, CompuServe, and Delphi have available communications software that is customized for and compatible with their systems.

Generally, you can use virtually any generic telecommunications software package to connect to the services described in the following section, unless a specific program is mentioned.

Obtaining More Information on Internet Access

The number of Internet access providers is growing, and many new services will be available. Information on other public dialup services can be found on the Internet at various ftp sites and by way of e-mail.

The anonymous ftp site at the Washington and Lee Law Library (`liberty.uc.wlu.edu`) maintains a large file called `internet.access` in the `/pub/lawlib` directory. This extensive listing of Internet access providers is updated regularly.

A listing called PDIAL, included with the disk in the back of this book, is also available by anonymous ftp and by e-mail. It outlines public dialup access with names, addresses, and contact information. It also can be obtained by ftp from `nic.merit.edu` in the `/internet` directory as a file named `pdial`, or by sending e-mail to `info-deli-server@netcom.com`, with the message **send pdial.**

Guides to On-Line Information and Services

Two popular sources of information are available on Internet services and tools. The most thorough guide to on-line information and services is *Information Sources: The Internet and Computer-Mediated Communication* by John December. This detailed guide can be obtained in a number of formats. It includes sections on the following:

The Internet and services	Communications
New-user information	Language and culture
Comprehensive guides	Education
Exploring	Government and public policy
Administrative and technical information	Miscellaneous and popular topics
Information repositories	Information services and electronic publications
Directories and documents	Discussion lists

Services and tools	Electronic journals and newsletters
Networking	Societies and organizations
Accessing networks	News groups
Information retrieval	Bibliographies

You can obtain information on retrieving this list via ftp from `ftp.rpi.edu` in the `/pub/communications` directory in the file `internet-cmc.readme`.

Scott Yanoff maintains a list of special Internet connections that describes a large variety of information resources. The list, updated every two weeks, identifies Internet resources in a broad variety of subjects, such as the following:

Agricultural information	Medical and health information
Aviation	Music information
Career information	News, weather, and sports
Educational/learning resources	Science and math information
ftp information	Software information
Games and fun	Space and astronomy
Geographical information	Stock market information
Gopher server information	User lookup services
Law-related resources	

You can obtain the list in the news group `alt.internet.services`, or by way of gopher or ftp to `csd4.csd.uwm.edu` in the `/pub` directory (file `inet.services.txt`). You also may send e-mail to `bbslist@aug3.augsburg.edu`.

Commercial BBS Access

The number of commercial Internet services is growing. Some of the mainline commercial bulletin board services are increasing their Internet services in response to subscriber interest. Subscriptions typically involve two phases: an initial sign-on, and then connecting to the service using your new login id and password.

CompuServe and America Online (AOL) are well established, very popular, and offer easy interfaces to on-line information. Delphi was the first commercial venture to offer Internet services to the public. These examples are just some of the commercial services that provide at least some access to the Internet, along with their custom collection of databases and services.

CompuServe

CompuServe has the largest number of users of all commercial on-line information bulletin board services. Currently, its Internet services are confined to full e-mail access only, but CompuServe is contemplating other services.

CompuServe offers several subscription plans that offer various groupings of services at various prices. The basic plan offers unlimited connect time for a fixed price (currently $8.95) each month. Extra fees are charged for the use of some services, however, and depending on where you live, extra communication charges may be assessed.

If you live within a local calling area served by one of CompuServe's many local access nodes, you won't have to pay extra surcharges or long-distance fees. (See the procedures mentioned later on how to find the CompuServe access numbers closest to you.) If you find that the closest number is outside your local calling area, you can use that number for your first sessions on CompuServe and type GO PHONES at any prompt to find out whether CompuServe's 800 number or access to one of the other digital networks would save you money. Check the hourly surcharge for either of these alternative connections, and then compare with what your phone company would charge for an hour connected to the CompuServe node.

> **Note**
>
> Due to the differences in intrastate and interstate regulations, in some situations you may find that calling a number outside your state is cheaper than calling the town next door.

In CompuServe's menus, you often will notice a + or a $ behind a listed item. These symbols mean that if you select this information or service, you will be billed beyond the basic monthly fee. The + items incur extra charges based on how long you use the service. The $ items have various rates, often based on how many files or database items you request.

Tip
While you are at any prompt on-line with CompuServe, type **GO RATES** for the current lists of charges.

Certificates for a free trial period often come packaged with modems or other computer equipment. You also can look through computer magazines for reduced-cost introductory offers. These offers may or may not include the custom communications program CIM (CompuServe Information Manager), but in most cases they will offer a one-month free trial and several hours of connect time for the surcharged items. Consider getting the full introductory package with the CompuServe Information Manager and the User's Guide. The combined use of the User's Guide to plan your on-line session and the CIM program to execute it will dramatically reduce any telecommunications cost or time-related surcharges.

Charges are billed monthly using either the credit card or check information that you give CompuServe at the time of signup. You can cancel your subscription at any time, on-line or by letter.

Appendixes

Getting Access to CompuServe

If you haven't already obtained signup information by one of the means mentioned in the preceding section, call Compu-Serve at (800) 635-6225 or (800) 848-8191 for information on how to obtain a starter kit.

If you plan to use your own communications software instead of the CIM package, you first need to find out what your local access phone number will be. Start by seeing your communications software documentation on how to set the following parameters needed by CompuServe: settings are 7 bits, even parity, 1 stop bit, and full duplex. Next, dial up using your communications software and modem: 1-800-346-3247. At the host prompt, type `phones`. You will be connected with a database that asks you several questions and then responds with the two nearest phone numbers.

Next, dial one of these local access numbers using your communications software. When you receive a host prompt, type `CIS`. You now should be connected directly to CompuServe, so you need only to follow the prompts to complete the full signup. Be sure to have on hand the temporary account number and password obtained by one of the methods mentioned above. Also have on hand a credit card or check from which to get account numbers and names.

If you plan to use CIM as your communications software, the procedures are substantially different. Follow these steps:

1. Insert the CIM disk labeled #1 in a floppy drive.

2. If the drive is A, type `A:INSTALL` at the DOS prompt. If the drive is B, type `B:INSTALL`.

3. After reading the welcome screen that appears, press any key and wait for the next screen.

4. Use the arrow keys to pick which hard drive you want the software installed on. Press Enter to continue.

5. You now see a screen of information about CIM's subdirectories and a question about whether you want to change

to the directory path where CIM will be located.
If you are familiar with making and using subdirectories,
changing the path will make perfect sense; if not, don't
worry, just press Enter and move to the next screen.

6. You now have the choice of abandoning this installation,
changing the path again, or continuing with the installation. Use the arrow keys to select `Continue the Installation`
and press Enter.

7. If you are already a member of CompuServe, choose `Do not`
`Copy the Signup Files`. When you first start CIM, you will
need to open the Select menu and fill in the blanks with
information about your current account name, number,
password, and access number.

If you are starting a new account with CompuServe,
choose `Copy the Signup Files` so that CIM can obtain some
of this information for you automatically.

Sit back and wait as your computer buzzes and blinks for
several minutes. The screen will show the transfers and
processing taking place.

8. You are asked whether you want to sign up for Compu-
Serve membership now. If you answer yes, the program
will connect you with CompuServe, and by answering the
questions, you will complete the signup procedure. (Have
your check or charge information in hand at this point.)

> **Note**
>
> If you can't find the modem's cord or haven't paid your phone bill,
> you can complete the signup later by typing `cd c:\cserv\doscim` at
> the DOS prompt. Press Enter, type **signup**, press Enter again, and
> answer the questions presented to you.

Installation is now complete.

Getting Connected to CompuServe

To connect to CompuServe, you can use CompuServe's CIM program or another general telecommunications package. This section covers the use of CIM only.

To run CIM, at the DOS prompt type `cd c:\cserv\doscim`, press Enter, and then type `CIM` to start the program.

Tip
CIM has context-sensitive help. When you highlight any menu item, you can find out more about it by pressing F1.

Now that CIM is up and running, double-click your mouse button when the pointer is on an item of interest in the Services menu. CIM will automatically dial and connect you with that topic or service.

You can close most information windows by clicking the small box in the upper left corner or by pressing Esc. To resize windows, hold down the mouse button when the cursor is over the arrow at the lower right corner of the window. Although many other features of CIM can be explored, you can see how easy a basic session on-line can be.

When you want to disconnect from CompuServe, press Ctrl+D. That's it. You've just had an on-line session with CompuServe.

CompuServe has a powerful search and menu system, allowing the experienced CIS user to move around swiftly by switching back and forth at will between use of the full menu system and GO commands, which skip the menus and go directly to the item of interest. A Find feature and an index of just under 900 topics also help in navigating. (Use GO INDEX to access a complete list of these topics.)

Here are a few of the topics covered:

```
Computers and Technology
        Personal Computing Forums -- Hardware
        Personal Computing Forums -- Software/Languages
        Electronic Publications
        Software Available for Download
        Vendor Support Forums for Hardware and Software
        Graphics Files and Processing Programs
```

```
Communications
      CIS Mail/Internet E-mail
      FAX
      Phone Book of 80 Million U.S. Households

News AP/Reuters/UPI
      Sports
      News
      Weather Predictions, Maps and Satellite Images

Travel Services

Shopping

Money Matters and Markets
      Industry Information
      Current Stock Quotes
      Online Brokerage Services
      Financial and Investment Forums

Business Information
      Industry and Professional Forums
      Company Profiles
      Demographics Information by Zip Code
      Government Publications

Hobbies/Lifestyle/Education
      Reference--Encyclopedia, Dictionary
      Education
      Scuba Diving, Photography, Gardening, etc.

Games and Entertainment
      Including Multi-Player
      Forums (Special Interest Discussions)
      Entertainment News
```

Sending Mail Between CompuServe and the Internet

You can send mail to and receive mail from most of the approximately 20 million users of the Internet using your CompuServe account. To send a message, get the intended recipient's normal Internet address. It might look something like `jsmith@abc.msu.edu`. Next, use normal e-mail procedures on CompuServe until you get to the prompt `Send to (Name or User Id):`; at this point, just type **INTERNET:** before the Internet address (for example, **INTERNET: jsmith@abc.mus.edu**).

Appendixes

When you join CompuServe, you receive a user identification number such as 71234,5678. This number is used for mail from other CompuServe members. Tell your Internet correspondents that your address is `account.number@compuserve.com`.

Note

Notice that a CompuServe address uses a period instead of a comma in the account number. The CompuServe account number 71234,5678, for example, would appear as `71234.5678@compuserve.com` in an Internet address.

America Online (AOL)

America Online provides its users with a point-and-click graphical user interface communications software package. This allows for a relatively easy method of navigating AOL's services. The only Internet service now provided is e-mail, but with its new Internet Center, AOL is planning to offer Gopher, WAIS, USENET, the discussion lists, and (in Expert mode) anonymous ftp.

Note

America Online offers a month of free access to its services, which includes 10 hours of connection time. You may cancel within the month and avoid all charges except any long-distance telephone charges.

Getting Access to AOL

To sign on to AOL, call (800) 827-6364. You will be given sign-on instructions, including local phone numbers. The AOL graphical interface software will be mailed to you, with information regarding installation. See the documentation provided with your AOL subscription for full instructions.

Getting Connected to AOL

AOL is one of the easiest self-explanatory, custom software packages to use. The software provided by AOL automates the sign-on procedures and the communications parameters, making for easy access. If you need help, click the help button at any time.

Click the sign-on button to initiate the sign-on procedure. Because this software has the AOL local access phone number, your password, and your screen name embedded in it, you won't need to type these items in or respond to any prompts after the software has been configured.

To navigate, click the icons and menu items of interest. To end your AOL session, just click the Close button.

Tip
When connected, you will find pull-down menus to locate services, icons, help, documentation, and more.

AOL has a Browse feature that enables users to take a look around as they make menu choices. Menu choices include the following:

```
News & Finance
People Connections
Lifestyles & Interests
Games and Entertainment
Learning & Reference
Travel & Shopping
Computing and Software
What is New and Online Support
```

To access the Internet, click the Go To pull-down menu, select the Keyword item, and then enter `Internet` at the prompt to get to the Internet Center. The Internet Center allows access to e-mail and to the icons for launching Gopher, ftp, USENET, WAIS, and mailing lists. (The actual services are limited to e-mail.)

Tip
For speedy access, the Internet Center can be added to the Go To menu.

Sending E-Mail between AOL and the Internet

Your full Internet address as an AOL member would be `screen_name@aol.com`. To send e-mail to Internet users, type their full Internet address in the `To:` field while at the mail screen.

Appendixes

Full Internet Access Providers

You can expect AOL and CompuServe to expand their Internet services beyond e-mail in the near future, but some companies, such as Delphi.com (Delphi), currently go beyond e-mail access by providing full Internet services, such as telnet (remote login) and ftp (file transfers). This discussion focuses on the Delphi service exclusively.

Tip
Delphi offers a five-hour free trial sub-scription for a month. If you sign on and decide to cancel, you pay nothing.

Delphi is a major provider of on-line services and full Internet access. Delphi maintains all the major services, e-mail, ftp, telnet, and even Internet Relay Chat (IRC), which enables you to "talk" interactively in real time with people all over the world. Delphi also provides USENET netnews, with more than 3,500 topics. Delphi provides direct access to all the powerful search tools of the Internet, such as Gopher, hytelnet, WAIS, WWW, and so on. Delphi also provides on-line help, help files, and other programs.

Delphi has an "unofficial" optional interface program called D-Lite that provides an easy-to-use interface and services assis-tance. You can download D-Lite from the Databases menu.

Getting Access to Delphi

To join Delphi, call by modem 1-800-365-4636. An interactive sign-on process will enable you to get started, and choose your on-line user name and your usage plan.

You can use any general telecommunications package on your computer to contact Delphi. The communications settings should be 8 bits, no parity, full duplex, 1 stop bit, no auto-linefeed, no carriage-return linefeed, XON-XOFF enabled, local echo off, and emulating a VT100 terminal. These settings can be set up according to the directions in your software.

Connecting to Delphi

After registering with the service and locating local telephone access, you most likely will use one of the telephone gateway networks such as Sprintnet or Tymnet for subsequent connections with Delphi. These networks are described during the signup process.

To access Delphi, dial the access number you received through the 1-800 service mentioned in the preceding section. An opening message appears, indicating that you are connected to Delphi and ending with a prompt for your user name. Enter your user name and press Enter. You are prompted for your password.

After you enter your password, you will see some announcements about interesting events, changes in the system, and so on. After this information, the main menu lists the primary categories of services. Each item leads you to submenus. Pressing Ctrl+Z will move you to previous screens. If you get lost, you can type `go main` to return to the main menu. To end the session, type `bye` at any prompt.

Forum serves as a BBS message area for communicating publicly about topics of interest. Conference takes you to an area where you can "talk" interactively with other users on-line.

Delphi's main menu lists the following options:

```
Business and Finance
Computing Groups
Conferences
Entertainment and Games
Groups and Clubs
News, Weather and Sports
Reference and Education
Shopping
Travel and Leisure
Using DELPHI
Workspace
HELP
```

On Delphi, you can find software to download, databases of useful information, and special-interest groups. Most of the software is compressed (zipped) and requires decompressing after transfer to your PC. Delphi maintains a library of decompression utilities, such as PKUNZIP, for this use.

Appendixes

Sending and Receiving E-Mail on Delphi

You can choose your user name with Delphi—provided, of course, that someone else hasn't already chosen it. Your full Internet address would be *username*@delphi.com.

To get to Delphi's e-mail service, type GO MAIL MAIL, where you can create and send a message. Internet e-mail must be addressed in the following way: at the To: prompt, type INTERNET "*userid@address.com*". Note that it must be enclosed in quotation marks.

Choosing the Mail option takes you to the area where you can choose several services. E-mail is used for sending private e-mail to remote or local users. E-mail also allows reception of the LISTSERV mailings, as well as personal messages.

Internet Services on Delphi

Internet services are found under the Internet Special Interest Group (SIG). The Internet SIG menu offers the following choices:

```
About the Internet        Help
Conference                Exit
Databases (Files)
E-mail                    FTP
Forum (Messages)          Gopher
Guides (Books)            IRC-Internet Relay Chat
Register/Cancel           Telnet
Who's Here                Utilities (finger, tracer, ping)
Workspace                 Usenet Newsgroups
```

UNIX Quick Reference

In the late 1960s, a group of programmers at AT&T Bell Labs developed the interactive operating system now known as *UNIX*. UNIX was developed in the same environment as the programming language *C* and founded on a similar programming philosophy. In the early 1970s, UNIX was almost entirely recoded in C.

After UNIX was made available in the efficient and popular C language, it could be ported to many different hardware platforms. Today UNIX has many variants, including AT&T's System V, IBM's AIX, DEC's Ultrix, and SunSoft's SunOS. UNIX (and its variants) has become the operating system of choice for multitasking, multiuser computer systems.

A system that is *multitasking* is running more than one program—considered a task or process by the operating system—at the same time. Multiuser capability indicates that more than one user can use the computer at the same time. The UNIX operating system services all users and processes and provides one or more *shells*—command-line interfaces—for each user.

Because UNIX is the operating system for many educational and research computer centers served by the Internet, most Internet explorers eventually will encounter a UNIX system in their treks. This appendix is included to give you the knowledge and confidence you need to navigate successfully in UNIX environments and to perform basic tasks. If you want to explore UNIX further, a number of UNIX references are available.

The UNIX interface is more capable and more hostile than the slick on-line menus provided by services like CompuServe, CIM, or Prodigy. UNIX and any other systems that provide the user with a command-line interface require that the user have some knowledge of the underlying operating system. This makes command-line interface systems much more difficult to learn and use than a system that provides a user an on-line menus system. On the other hand, after a user is familiar with a system, he can access the system more efficiently and all the operating system tools available.

UNIX is a very powerful and flexible operating system that allows the system administrator to configure a system in many different ways. The location, configuration, names, and availability of commands may change drastically among systems. This tends to make UNIX systems unique, further complicating learning and navigating multiple systems.

The configurations represented in this appendix are for a typical system (the examples are for a C shell under SunOS 4.1.2). In this quick reference, only the basic options for commands are given (because options may change among systems). You can use on-line help to find additional options and commands as you navigate UNIX.

Note

Be aware that subtle differences exist among the variants of UNIX. You may need to use the on-line help capabilities of UNIX to explore these differences further.

Conventions and Syntax

This appendix uses typefaces and brackets to indicate syntax requirements and options. Text that the computer displays appears in `computer type`; **`bold computer type`** represents user-entered text in displays. Variable argument names (such as a file name), which are to be replaced by text that suits you, are represented in *`italic computer type`*. Parameters that alter the action of a command are represented in `computer type`. Most of these parameters are enclosed in square brackets to indicate that they are optional.

Arguments used by commands can be required or optional. Optional arguments are enclosed by square brackets ([ ]). Groups of arguments from which you must choose one are enclosed by braces ({ }). In both cases, you don't type the brackets and braces; they are included to show syntax only. All other arguments are required. A variable-length argument list is shown ending with an ellipsis (...) to indicate the last item can be repeated as many times as necessary.

Control characters are shown in this format: Ctrl+C.

Logging In

Unlike operating systems such as MS-DOS, UNIX is *case-sensitive*. Commands and responses must be entered *exactly* as required. Typing in the user name `Phillips`, for example, isn't the same as entering the name in all lowercase letters, as in the following sample login:

```
Hawaii login: phillips
Password:
Last login: Mon Sep 20 11:18:18 on console
SunOS Release 4.1.2 (GENERIC) #2: Wed Oct 23 10:52:58 PDT 1991
Hawaii%
```

In this example, `phillips` is entered as the user name and the appropriate password is entered at the password prompt. For security reasons, the password isn't echoed back to the screen as it's entered.

Other data that typically appears each time you log in includes your last login time and the version of UNIX that is running on the system. Some systems also show a banner that indicates whose system you are logging in to and any current system messages. In the example, `Hawaii` is the hostname of the UNIX system that you are logging in to. All UNIX systems have a hostname that is often the same as the alias to its Internet node number.

The final item in the sample login script is the shell interactive command prompt. When you log in, UNIX starts a user interface shell (see the "Shells" section later in this appendix). Typically, the interface is a *C shell* or *Bourne shell*, but you can use many other shells. The default command-line prompt often enables you to identify the shell that currently is running. A `$` generally indicates a Bourne shell; a `%` usually indicates a C shell. You should check which shell is running, however, because your environment may have changed the default prompt.

A number of files in the system and in your home directory controls the initial login environment. The next section describes the process of setting up your environment.

Account Profile

User accounts have three types of profiles: *system*, *user*, and *application*. Your system profile includes administrative and security information like your password, user identification, and group identification. User and application profiles define user preferences for shells and various programs.

System Profile

Syntax: passwd [-fs]

                   chfn

                   chsh

System-level configuration of the user account is done by using the passwd command or one of its variants, chfn or chsh. These commands modify entries in the system or the network information system (NIS) password file (/etc/passwd).

Password changes are handled with the passwd command. You can change your full user name by using the chfn or passwd –f command. Your initial login shell is set using the chsh or passwd –s command. Valid initial shells are listed in the file /etc/shells (or its NIS equivalent). In the following script example, the user password, shell, and full or finger name are changed to suit the user's preferences:

```
Hawaii% passwd
Enter current password for user phillips:
Enter new password for user phillips:
Enter new password for user phillips (again):
Hawaii% chsh
Enter current password for user phillips:
Enter new shell for user phillips [/bin/sh]: /bin/csh
Hawaii% chfn
Enter current password for user phillips:
Enter new finger information for user phillips or "none" to clear
[Richard Phillips]: Richard D. Phillips
Hawaii%
```

Remember that each time the programs prompt for a password, the appropriate password is entered but not echoed to the terminal (for security reasons).

Like everything else in UNIX, the user name is really a *referenced name*. The system administrator assigns user ID and group ID numbers to each user. Even though programs utilize the user name (which can change), that user name refers to the user and group ID numbers contained in the /etc/passwd file.

> **Note**
>
> Some systems don't allow you to change your password or full name; others require you to change your password regularly. The UNIX systems administrator can control how often you must change your password (its *maturity*) and how long you must wait between changing your password (its *age*). Check with the system's administrator and watch for messages reflecting password aging and maturity.

Environment

Each time you start a shell, the shell checks for the existence of a shell initialization file (such as .profile, used by Bourne and Korn shells, or .cshrc, used by C shells). If the shell also is started by a user login, UNIX executes the .login script (if one is present in your home directory). Similarly, UNIX executes the .logout script (if one is present) when you log out. The script files are described in the following table.

File	Related Environment
.profile	Bourne and Korn shell initialization script
.cshrc	C shell initialization script
.login	Shell script executed after the initialization scripts for the first shell opened
.logout	Shell script executed during logout

You can use these script files to configure your user account, primarily by setting environment variables. The environment variables that you use to configure your environment depend on the programs you need to execute and the system configuration. The most common variables follow:

Variable	Description
HOME	User home directory
TERM	Current user terminal type (vt102, ANSI, dialup, and so on)
SHELL	Current shell (sh, csh, or ksh, for example)
USER	User name
PATH	Current search path for executable files
LOGNAME	Login name (usually the same as USER)
PWD	Present Working Directory

The following example shows how to display and modify environment variables at the command line (for a C shell):

```
Hawaii% setenv
HOME=/home/phillips
SHELL=/bin/csh
TERM=dialup
USER=phillips
PATH=.:/home/phillips:/us/ucb:/us/bin:/us/etc
LOGNAME=phillips
PWD=/home/phillips
Hawaii% setenv TERM vt102
Hawaii% setenv
HOME=/home/phillips
SHELL=/bin/csh
TERM=vt102
USER=phillips
PATH=.:/home/phillips:/us/ucb:/us/bin:/us/etc
LOGNAME=phillips
PWD=/home/phillips
Hawaii%
```

The initial **setenv** command displays the current environment variables. The second **setenv** command changes the TERM variable from type dialup to type vt102. The third **setenv** command redisplays the variables, showing the change.

This example shows C shell (csh) syntax. The syntax used to accomplish this sort of task varies, depending on the current shell in use (see the section "Shells" later in this appendix).

Appendixes

Application Profiles

Applications running under UNIX typically utilize user-defined profiles stored in your home directory. In many cases, these profiles are named using a *.namerc* naming convention. A list of some common profiles follows:

Profile	Description
.profile	Bourne shell profile
.cshrc	C shell (csh) profile
.mailrc	mail initialization
.newsrc	Internet news group (rn) initialization
.kermrc	kermit initialization
.emacs	emacs configuration

You may find that these and many other profiles show up in your directory after the initial use of various applications.

> **Note**
>
> Files with names that begin with a leading period are *hidden files*. They are listed only when you use the view all directory option (ls -a).

File System

The UNIX file system is a very flexible operating system that provides a wide variety of techniques to navigate and manipulate files. The basic element is the file, which may be of many types, including directories, links, and plain files. Directories, starting from the topmost directory / (forward slash), stores file references and attributes. References point to the physical storage of the file on the media, typically a hard disk drive.

File attributes determine the file type (set when created), file ownership, and file protections. File names are flexible, so each user may adopt his own naming convention.

You navigate and manipulate the UNIX file system using command utilities, typically found in the /bin (short for binary) and /usr/bin (user binary) directories. The next four sections cover UNIX file naming, ownership, links, and directories.

File Names

UNIX generally allows file names up to 14 characters long (some versions have different length requirements). Following UNIX convention, file names are case sensitive. File names can consist of any string of characters, but can't begin with a plus or minus sign (+ or –).

Caution

File names can even contain unprintable control characters, like Ctrl+I (tab) or Ctrl+M (carriage return). If you aren't careful, you may create a file name that can't be entered as an argument on the command line.

Unlike many operating systems, UNIX doesn't require a *name.extension* format for file names. UNIX uses a single string file name that may contain one or more period characters. UNIX users have generated file-naming conventions, however, that follow the *name.extension* format. For example, .c is often used as an extension to indicate C language program source files. Some common file types are as follows:

Extension	Type of File
.c	C language source file
.C	C++ language source file
.f	FORTRAN source file

(continues)

Appendixes

Extension	Type of File
.h	C or C++ header file
.a	Assembly language file
.o	Object file
.Z	Compressed file
.tar	tar-ed file

File Ownership

In a multiuser environment, provisions for security and privacy revolve around file ownership. Three levels of ownership are associated with each file: *owner*, *group*, and *other*. Each level of ownership provides a set of attributes that controls access to the file.

Each file has a single user as its owner, who receives *owner* access and has permission to change all the security attributes of the file. *Group* access is a second level of ownership that can be given for a file. The group is usually a restricted set of users who have a special need to access the file. Group membership is defined in the UNIX system file /etc/groups (and its NIS equivalent). If no group access is set up for a file, users other than the owner can access the file with the security privileges provided for *other*. This final level of access is available to all users except the owner and members of a group assigned to the file.

File Attributes

File attributes consist of the file type attribute and permissions. File type attributes describe files and provide UNIX with security at the file level. A file can be classified in the following ways:

Attribute	Description
d	Directory
l	Symbolic link
p	A named pipe
b	Block type special file
s	Socket
-	A plain file

The preceding list shows the file types available. The most common are directories, links, and plain files. Named pipes and sockets are used for UNIX interprocess communication streams. Each file and directory entry has read, write, and execute permissions for each of the three classes of user access. For each file, a user is classified as the owner, a member of the same group as the owner, or any other user.

File and directory permissions have slightly different meanings. File-read access enables a user to access a file's contents—to display its contents or copy it to another location, for example. File-write access enables a user to modify a file, to change its permissions, or to delete it. The file-execute permission identifies (to UNIX) files that are binary programs or shell scripts. To display the attributes for a file, use the long directory command, `ls -l` *filename*, as shown in the following example:

```
Hawaii% ls -l text.doc
-rwxrw-r-- 1 phillips    512 Sep 18 12:00 text.doc
Hawaii%
```

Directory-read access, on the other hand, allows a user access to the list of files in a directory. Directory-write access enables a user to add files, and with file-write permission, to delete a file in a directory. The directory-execute permission allows search and file access, regardless of the status of the read permission. (You can access a file, if you know its name, even if you don't have read permission.)

To move or copy a file to another directory, for example, you need read access; to overwrite or delete a file, you must have write access. For UNIX to execute a binary file or shell script, you must have execute permission.

Links

UNIX provides links to allow referenced access to files and directories, so you don't have to make multiple copies of a single file or directory. Two types of UNIX links are available: *hard* and *symbolic*. Files can use hard and symbolic links; directories can have only symbolic links.

A hard link is a new directory entry for a file, entirely separate from the original directory entry. This new entry has a new name with ownership and permissions independent from the original. This type of link is used to share the file's contents, with independent access. Both directory entries are now hard links to the file, with equal "ownership" of the file. The file will remain until all such hard links are deleted. The number of hard links to a file can be seen in the long directory listing immediately to the left of the file name. In the file attribute example earlier, the file text.doc has one hard link.

A symbolic link provides a reference to the file or directory. The file or directory maintains all ownership and permission attributes of the original. If the original file or directory is deleted, or its ownership or permissions modified, symbolic link access changes.

Directories

Like most operating systems, UNIX references files by way of a directory hierarchy that is virtually unlimited in depth (number of directory levels). Each UNIX system has a top-level directory labeled / (slash). UNIX directories follow the same name conventions as files.

> **Note**
>
> UNIX uses a forward slash (/) instead of the backslash (\) used by DOS.

Standard directories on UNIX systems include the following:

Directory	Description
/bin	Contains executable or binary files
/etc	Contains system configuration files (in most cases, these files can be modified only by the system administrator)
/home	Typically the location of user directories (named directories under /usr)
/lib	Contains standard system libraries

On-Line Help

Inexperienced UNIX users may find UNIX commands cryptic and daunting, but help is available. Four common methods of getting help are available to the user: command-line help; man or whatis (if you know the command name); and apropos (if you are looking for a command).

Command-Line Help

Many UNIX programs provide some help if you execute the command with no arguments. Just type the command name on the command line and press Enter. The following two examples (for the man and mkdir commands) show the type of command-line help you can expect:

```
Hawaii% man
Usage:  man [-t] [-P path] [-] [ section ] name ...
        man -k keyword ...
        man -f file ...
```

Tip
This type of help is good as a quick reminder of options and command formats. For more detailed help on a specific command, use the manual page command (man), discussed in the next section.

Appendixes

```
Hawaii% mkdir
Usage: mkdir directory ...
Hawaii%
```

Typical UNIX command-line help argument styles follow the basic forms used in this appendix. Optional arguments are enclosed in brackets (such as [-t] [-P path] in the man example), and required arguments are shown by their placeholder names (such as name, keyword, file, and directory in the example). When multiple argument constructions are available, they are presented (as shown in the example for man). Ellipsis (...) show when the command can accept a variable number of arguments. For example, mkdir accepts a variable number of directory arguments and creates a directory as specified by each argument.

Manual Pages

Syntax: man [-] [-t] [-M *path*] [[*section*] *title* ...] ...

The main help facility for UNIX systems is contained in the reference manual. Most established UNIX programs have an entry in the manual, called a *man page* (although some entries are more than 20 printed pages long). Users can access these pages by using the man program.

> **Note**
>
> Manual pages, typically written by the developers of the programs, often are written for other programmers. As a result, some information in manual pages can be rather cryptic for inexperienced users.

Each manual page is divided into a group of standard fields. The NAME field lists the command(s) covered by the manual page and a one-line description of the command(s). A SYNOPSIS field

shows the command format(s) with arguments. The DESCRIP-
TION field describes the operation of the command and the
meaning and format of the arguments it can take. Each manual
page usually has additional fields providing release notes and
references to related programs and files.

Describe Command

Syntax: whatis *command*

The UNIX command whatis (or man -k) is an abbreviated man
command that returns only the NAME field of the manual page.
Using whatis to describe the man command, for example, returns
a statement like the following:

```
Hawaii% whatis man
man (1)    - display reference manual pages; find
reference pages by keyword
man (7)    - macros to format Reference Manual pages
Hawaii%
```

Find Command

Syntax: apropos *keyword*

To find a command name based on a description, you can use
the command apropos. This command compares the *keyword*
you enter with the text in the NAME field of all manual pages.
The apropos command then displays the manual NAME fields
(much like the whatis command) for commands that include
the *keyword* in their description. Searching for the keyword
manual, for example, leads to the following response:

```
Hawaii% apropos manual
catman (8) - create the cat files for the manual
man (1)    - display reference manual pages; find reference pages by keyword
man (7)    - macros to format Reference Manual pages
route (8C) - manually manipulate the routing tables
whereis (1) - locate the binary, source, and manual page files for a command
Hawaii%
```

Appendixes

Basic Commands

The following sections are a brief listing of useful UNIX commands. Be aware that they don't provide a *complete* list of UNIX commands nor contain *all* the options for each command. The sections *do*, however, provide some basic commands to help you navigate on UNIX systems. You may find that different commands and/or options are used on particular UNIX systems or systems using the different variants of UNIX. To get more detailed information on additional and system-specific commands, use the on-line help facilities described in the preceding sections.

Changing the Directory

Syntax: cd [*directory_name*]

If no argument is entered, cd returns you to your home directory (as specified by the environment variable HOME).

Listing the Directory

Syntax: ls [-acglt] [*name*] ...

If *name* is a directory, ls lists the contents of that directory. If you enter a name that isn't a directory, ls lists that file(s). The *name* option provides you with a useful way to find similarly named files using wild-card characters. Wild-card characters (like ? and *) are used to expand an argument to a sorted list of file names that match the argument. The question mark (?) provides a match for any single character, and the asterisk (*) matches any number of characters (zero and more).

If you enter no name argument, ls lists the contents of the current directory. Useful options for ls include the following:

Option	Description
-a	Shows all files in the directory, including files that begin with a period (.)
-c	Sorts by last modified time, oldest first
-g	Shows group ownership of file, used with -l
-l	Shows files in the long format, including the mode, link count, owner, size (bytes), and last modified time
-t	Sorts by last modified time, most recent first

A commonly used set of switches to use together are all and long; ls -agl lists all files with file attributes and ownership.

Viewing a File

Syntax: cat *filename*

more [*filename*]

To view the contents of an ASCII text file, use the cat or more command. The cat command provides a continuous stream of text, whereas more provides one screen page worth of text. Files not containing ASCII text can also be sent to the screen, with less interesting results. Using the standard input for more is also useful to paginate output text piped in from other commands. You can view a directory listing one page at a time, for example, by entering ls -al ¦ more.

Copying Files

Syntax: cp [-ipr] *source destination*

The cp command duplicates a selected file or files (*source*), creating a new file or files (*destination*). If *destination* doesn't exist, cp creates a new file (*destination*) and copies the contents of *source* into the new file. If *destination* is an existing file, cp copies the contents of *source* into the existing file, unless the

Appendixes

-i switch is used. If *destination* is a directory, the file(s) is copied with its original (*source*) name to the destination directory. The destination file(s) reflects your ownership and protection, unless the -p switch is used.

The following describes the switches used with cp:

Switch	Description
-i	Interactively prompts for confirmation before overwriting an existing file
-p	Preserves original file attributes
-r	Recursively descends into subdirectories and copies files

Moving Files

Syntax: mv [-ir] *source destination*

The mv command duplicates (*destination*) a selected file or files and then deletes the original file(s) (*source*). If the destination is a file, or not existing, mv changes the name and path of the file to match the destination. If *destination* is a directory, the file(s) are copied with their original (*source*) names to the destination directory. The destination file(s) always maintains the ownership and protection attributes.

The mv command moves or renames a selected file or files (*source*) to a new file or files (*destination*), removing the source. If *destination* doesn't exist, mv creates a new file (*destination*) and moves the contents of *source* into the new file. If *destination* is an existing file, mv copies the contents of the source into the existing file, unless the -i switch is used. If destination is a directory, the file(s) is moved with its original (*source*) name to the destination directory. The destination file(s) reflects the original file(s) attributes. The mv switches are described as follows:

Switch	Description
-i	Interactively prompts for confirmation before overwriting an existing file
-r	Recursively descends into subdirectories and copies files

Deleting Directories

Syntax: rmdir *directory_name*

Deleting UNIX directories is done with the remove directory (rmdir) command. If the directory is not empty, it will not be removed.

Deleting Files

Syntax: rm [-fir] *name*

Deleting files is done with the remove (rm) command. The remove command removes all file(s) named without warning unless the interactive (-i) switch is set. When *name* is a directory, it is deleted only if it is empty; with the recursive (-r) switch, however, rm descends into the directory and attempts to delete all entries in that directory. rm does not delete any file without write permission, unless you are the owner and the force (-f) switch is set. The switches for rm are listed as follows:

Switch	Description
-f	Forces deletion; ignores errors and warnings
-r	Recursively descends into subdirectories and deletes files
-i	Interactively deletes files; asks before deleting each file (this option is useful for csh aliasing rm to rm -i for new or cautious users)

Appendixes

Creating Directories

Syntax: mkdir [*new_directory_path*/]*new_directory_name*

You can include a full path or just the directory name when you use the mkdir command. If the argument *new_directory_path* isn't entered, the new directory is created in your current directory.

Linking

Syntax: ln [-s] *filename* [*link*]

                ln -s *pathname directory*

Caution
Because links can cause some confusion to those not familiar with them, they should be used with care.

A *link* is a directory entry that references another file or directory. You can use the default link type—a *hard* link—only to reference a file. You can generate a symbolic link by using the -s option; this type of link can refer to a file or a directory. A symbolic link maintains the original file attributes such as size, protection, parent directory, and so on, whereas the hard link creates a second new directory entry for the file.

For linking files, the argument *filename* is the name of the original file, with a fully specified path. The optional argument *link* is the name used in the current directory to refer to the original file. If *link* isn't specified, the original file name (the last part of the *filename* path) is used as the link name.

To link a directory, you can use only a symbolic link (-s argument); the argument *directory* names the link that refers to the original directory at location *pathname*.

Changing File Ownership and Groups

Syntax: `chown [-R] newowner[.newgroup] name ...`
(to change the owner)

`chgrp [-R] newgroup name ...`
(to change the group)

You can change the ownership and group ownership of a file, or list of files, using the `chown` command. The `newowner` is the desired new owner of the file(s). You can set the new group membership of the file with the optional `chown` argument `newgroup` or by using the `chgrp` command. Both commands descend into all directories in the `name` list and update all files found when the recursive switch, `-R`, is specified. Any links found in the name list are updated, but neither command descends into linked directories when `-R` is specified.

Changing File Permission Attributes

Syntax: `chmod [-fR] mode filename ...`

File-read, write, and execute permissions are changed for each level of ownership—owner, group, and other—using the change permissions mode (`chmod`) command. The optional switches for the `chmod` command follow:

Switch	Description
`-f`	Forces `chmod` to continue, even if it fails to change the attribute of a file
`-R`	Recursively descends through directories to change the mode of all files found (symbolic links aren't traversed)

The `mode` argument may be expressed in two ways: *absolute* or *symbolic*. An absolute `mode` argument sets all file attributes at once. The absolute `mode` is represented by a set of three octal digits—one each for owner, group, and other. Each octal digit is made up of three binary digits representing the read, write, and execute flags, respectively. The binary digits follow:

4	Read permission
2	Write permission
1	Execute permission

The logical ORing (or *summation*) of the combined binary digits represents the file attributes to be given. To give owner access with read and write permission to a file called text.doc (and to view the results of your change), for example, you enter the following commands:

```
Hawaii% chmod 600 text.doc
Hawaii% ls -al text.doc
-rw------- 1 phillips     512 Sep 18 12:00 text.doc
Hawaii%
```

A symbolic *mode* argument, on the other hand, uses mnemonics to set file attributes. Symbolic arguments have the following format:

```
[who] operation permission [operation permission] ...
```

The *who* argument consists of one or more of the following:

u	User
g	Group
o	Other
a	All: User, Group, and Other

The *operation* argument is one of the following:

+	Adds permission
-	Removes permission
=	Explicitly sets permission

And the *permission* argument is one or more of the following:

r   Read

w   Write

x   Execute

The following example illustrates changing the file text.doc to add read and write privileges to group members and read access for all others:

```
Hawaii% ls -al text.doc
-rw------- 1 phillips 512 Sep 18 12:00 text.doc
Hawaii% chmod g+rw,o+r text.doc
Hawaii% ls -al text.doc
-rw-rw-r-- 1 phillips 512 Sep 18 12:00 text.doc
Hawaii%
```

Sorting

Syntax: sort[-o *outputfile*] [*inputfile*]

The sort command performs a character-by-character sort of input stream lines. The sort starts at the beginning of each line. If *inputfile* is not specified, standard input (terminal input or a command pipe from another file) is used. If *outputfile* is not specified, standard output (terminal output or a command pipe to another file) is used. For example, to sort a text file named fruit, with output to the console,

```
Hawaii# more fruit
banana
apples
pear
Hawaii# sort fruit
apples
banana
grapes
pear
Hawaii#
```

Finding User Information

Syntax: finger *user_identification*

The finger command is used to get information on a user, given one piece of user information (such as a first or last name, user name, or login name). The following is an example of a finger request and response:

```
Hawaii% finger phillips
Login name: phillips       In real life: Richard D.Phillips
Directory: /home/phillips  Shell: /bin/csh
On since Oct  3 12:43:02 on ttyb
No unread mail
No Plan.
Hawaii%
```

> **Note**
>
> In many medium- to high-security UNIX systems, finger is disabled because it bypasses some security measures to access that information.

Finding a File

Syntax: find *path* -name *filename* -print

The find command enables you to search for the existence and location of a file (*filename*). The *path* argument specifies the directory from which to begin searching. The -print option displays (to standard output) the path for each instance of *filename* found.

> **Note**
>
> The find command searches all subdirectories but doesn't traverse symbolic links.

Reading News Groups
Syntax: `rn [newsgroups]`

Internet news groups provide communication forums covering a wide range of interests and topics. Because a large number of news groups on topics exist, the `rn` command provides a subscription mechanism by which you can select only the news groups of interest to you. The news group profile, stored in `.newsrc`, holds your subscription list, the list of news bulletins you have read, and default setup information. The `rn` command creates and maintains your profile, providing an on-line method of updating your subscription list.

The `rn` command traverses the news groups and compares each news group with your news profile. New news groups (not in your `.newsrc`) are listed by name; you make a subscription choice by pressing **y** or **n**. Discontinued news groups are noted. For each news group that you subscribe to, `rn` prompts you with the name and number of unread articles:

```
******** 10 unread articles in git.ads--read now? [ynq]
```

At this prompt, press one of the following keys:

Key	Action
y	To read articles
n	To skip to next news group
q	To quit `rn`
u	To unsubscribe from this group
c	To catch up to the end of the article list (set all articles as read)

If you choose to read articles, the text is sent through the local paginator (like `more`). The c (catch-up) option is useful if many articles have accumulated and you want to get new, as yet unposted entries. Most systems limit the length of time that articles are available to users, beyond which they are marked unavailable.

For more information on news groups, see Chapter 9, "USENET."

Searching Patterns
Syntax: grep [-i] *pattern* [*filename*]

The grep command enables you to search for a pattern in the input stream indicated by *filename*, or from standard input (user terminal, or piped input). The *filename* argument can represent a single file name or a group of files (using shell wild-card search patterns such as * for any file or *.[c,h] for all C source and header files). The *pattern* argument can be a single word fragment, a group of word fragments enclosed in quotation marks, or a comma-separated group enclosed in brackets. The parameter -i enables case-insensitive matches of alphabetic characters.

For example, a case-insensitive search for the word *Apple* in all the files in the current directory (*) yields the file seen earlier in this appendix, fruit:

```
Hawaii# grep -i Apple *
fruit:apple
Hawaii#
```

Logging Out
Syntax: logout

        exit

The logout command is used to end a terminal session. When you log out, the .logout shell script (if one exists in your HOME directory) is executed. The exit command, on the other hand, terminates only the current shell. Of course, if the current shell is your initial and only login shell, exit ends the terminal session, just like logout.

Mail

UNIX electronic mail can be accessed by many programs, too numerous to mention. The most common program available to access electronic mail is the UNIX command mail, which is an interactive utility to send and receive messages. Like the rest of UNIX, mail systems can vary in configuration, but mail should always work. mail can be invoked as follows:

Syntax: mail [-eH] (to receive mail)

         mail [-F] *recipient* ... Phillips(to send mail)

Command-line arguments include the following:

Switch	Description
-e	Tests for presence of mail messages; if no messages are present, mail exits
-H	Prints header summary only
-F	Records message in a file with the recipient's name

When executed, mail initializes by using the user's local initialization file .mailrc if present, or if not, it uses system's default /usr/lib/Mail.rc file. After initialization, mail enters command mode, indicated by the ampersand (&) command prompt.

You read your mail by way of an interactive command system. If mail is present when you type the mail command, a list of messages appears that includes the header fields for each message (who the message is from, the date and time the message was received, and the subject of the message). The following is a brief listing of commands available in the command mode:

Mail command	Description
t [#]	Types current message (or the message identified by #)
d [#]	Deletes current message (or the message identified by #)

(continues)

Mail command	Description
h	Shows header list
r [#]	Replies to message
s [#] file_name	Appends message to file file_name
?	Gets help listing

Receiving mail is as simple as starting mail. If any messages exist, a list of headers is printed as shown in the following example:

```
Hawaii% mail
Mail version SMI 4.1-OWV3 Mon Sep 23 07:17:24 PDT 1991  Type ? for help.
"/us/spool/mail/phillips": 1 message 1 new
>N  1 smith        Thu Sep 30 22:01   15/380    project meeting
```

The preceding list shows that one message from smith exists with the subject project meeting. To read the mail, use the type command (t):

```
& t
Message  1:
From smith Thu Sep 30 22:01:54 1993
Date: Thu, 30 Sep 93 22:01:53 EDT
From: smith (William Smith)
To: phillips
Subject: project meeting
Our next project meeting is on Friday 1 October 1993.
Bill :)
&
```

To delete that message and quit mail, use the d and q commands as shown in the following:

```
& d
& q
Hawaii%
```

The mail facility provides a simple line editor for entering mail messages. This editor works well enough for short messages but

may be inadequate for longer mail. With the line editor, you
can enter a single line of text at a time, followed by a carriage
return. You can enter as many lines as you like. To end your
message, enter a tilde (~) as the only character on a new line.
Some useful tilde commands follow:

Command	Description
~.	Ends edit session and sends mail
~?	Displays full list of escape (tilde) commands
~h	Prompts to enter header info (To, Subject, and CC)
~x	Quits without sending mail
~r	Reads a file into message buffer

Text File Editing

UNIX is an environment rich with text processing; many UNIX
tools available are designed specifically to manipulate text in
some way. Of the available text processors, vi and emacs are
possibly the most popular, for different reasons. The appeal of
vi is its near-universal availability, but emacs is a more powerful
text processor.

Note

If you will use many different UNIX systems, you may want to learn
vi, because it is available on most UNIX systems and works on nearly
every terminal type. Editors like vi and emacs require learning a large
number of seemingly cryptic keyboard commands to use and can
take a long time to master. So you may want to concentrate on only
one editor.

Visual Editor (vi)

The most common editor used in UNIX is vi, or the *visual editor*. You can attribute its wide use to the fact that it has been included in most UNIX systems on the market, including AT&T System V.

vi was developed for programmers who want to edit quickly, using as few keystrokes as possible for each command. An extensive list of obscure commands makes vi difficult to master quickly, but you can handle a basic edit with just a few commands and an understanding of the two modes: *command mode* and *text entry mode*.

When you first enter vi, you are in command mode. Cursor movement is done using alphabetic keys and control characters (Ctrl plus a letter) on the keyboard. Many vi terminal configurations also use the keyboard cursor movement keys when they are present. The basic movement commands in command mode are the following:

Command	Direction
h	Moves left one character
j	Moves down one line
k	Moves up one line
l	Moves right one line
Ctrl+f	Scrolls down one screen (forward)
Ctrl+b	Scrolls up one screen (backward)

The basic character-movement keys are located under your right hand on a QWERTY keyboard. This placement reduces unnecessary hand movement and speeds editing.

The following are the file manipulation commands of vi:

Command	Description
x	Deletes a character
dd	Deletes a line
/	Performs a forward search
:wq	Writes and quits
:q	Quits
:q!	Forces a quit without saving changes

Enter the i command to switch to text-entry mode. After you are in text-entry mode, vi accepts any keystroke as a text entry and places that text into the file at the cursor. To exit text-entry mode, press Esc; vi returns you to command mode.

Editor Macros (emacs)

Editor macros, or emacs, is another common editor on UNIX systems. Following in the UNIX tradition, emacs is a powerful editor that is completely configurable. With the proper setup, it can be made to emulate the basic functions of any text editor.

Many users prefer emacs because it is modeless (avoiding vi's dual modes). But emacs' single mode of operation requires the use of Ctrl+key combinations, which aren't as convenient to touch typists.

The .emacs file in your home directory defines the keystrokes that invoke emacs commands; these are the emacs key bindings. emacs uses the TERM environment variable to determine compatibility with your terminal. Like most full-screen editors, emacs doesn't work with basic terminal types like dialup or

On-line help on many topics is provided by emacs. To enter the help system, you press Ctrl+h twice (Ctrl+h Ctrl+h). In help mode, emacs provides a string of single-character options at the bottom of the screen corresponding to various help topics. A third Ctrl+h calls up a description for each help topic. The most common help requested is on *key bindings* (Ctrl+h b), which informs you of the keystrokes assigned to each command. Key bindings are listed with the keystroke(s) first and then the description(s); C-key means Ctrl+key, and M-key means press Esc and then the key.

Basic emacs commands include the following:

Command	Description
Ctrl+x s	Saves the file, prompting first
Ctrl+x Ctrl+s	Saves the file without prompting
Ctrl+x f	Loads a new file
Ctrl+x i	Inserts a file at the cursor
Ctrl+x u	Undoes last edit
Ctrl+x Ctrl+c	Exits emacs, prompting unsaved files

If the keyboard editing keys aren't set up to operate in the emacs environment, use the following keystrokes for movement and editing:

Keystroke	Action
Ctrl+f	Moves right (forward)
Ctrl+b	Moves left (backward)
Ctrl+p	Moves up (previous line)
Ctrl+n	Moves down (next line)
Ctrl+v	Scrolls page down
v	Scrolls page up

Keystroke	Action
Esc >	Moves to end of file
Esc <	Moves to beginning of file
Ctrl+d	Deletes a character

> **Caution**
>
> Be careful when using the control characters over modems. Ctrl+q and Ctrl+s are particularly troublesome because they are XON/XOFF characters that can interfere with flow control.

File Transfer

Obtaining data from various sources is often the goal of Internet searching. After you locate data, you can download it to your local computer using one of many file transfer protocols. Four common protocols for downloading files are Kermit, XMODEM, YMODEM, and ZMODEM. Files are often grouped (archived) together into one file and then compressed and encoded to transfer them across the Internet.

The following sections cover sending and receiving files by Kermit and the X-, Y-, and ZMODEM protocols. File archive, compression, and encoding are also covered here because of their relevance to file transfer.

Kermit
Syntax: `kermit`

Kermit is a data transfer package commonly used with UNIX systems. Although it is primarily used for data transfer by way of modem and telephone lines, you can use Kermit for any point-to-point data transfer between two computers.

The `kermit` command starts an interactive command shell that processes Kermit transactions, checking each command-line entry for validity. Kermit provides on-line assistance by way of the `help` command. Basic Kermit commands are shown in the following table.

Command	Description
`help [command]`	Kermit provides on-line help sufficient for most users. If no *command* argument is entered, kermit displays a list of commands for which help is available.
`send filename`	Use this command to download the file *filename* to your local computer.
`receive filename`	Use this command to upload the file *filename* to the remote computer.
`set parity {even, odd, none}`	If Kermit isn't already set to the same connection parameters that you are using, set it to match your parity by selecting *even*, *odd*, or *none*.
`show`	This command displays all the current Kermit settings.

X-, Y-, and ZMODEM File Transfer

Syntax: `sz [-abknpy] filename`

           `rz [-abp] filename`

The `sz` and `rz` commands and their derivatives, `sb`/`rb` and `sx`/`rx`, are file-transfer programs that use the Z MODEM, Y MODEM, and XMODEM protocols (`sz` stands for *send ZMODEM*, for example, and `rz` stands for *receive ZMODEM*). Optional parameters for these commands include the following:

Switch	Description
-a	Converts between the UNIX \<NL\> and DOS \<CR\>/\<LF\>; this switch works for both send and receive when your local machine is a DOS machine and the remote machine is a UNIX machine.
-b	Binary file switch; transfers with no translation
-k	Sends only; uses 1,024-byte (1K) blocks
-n	Sends only; overwrites destination if source file is newer
-p	Never overwrites (protect) destination files
-y	Sends only; always overwrites destination files

tar

Syntax: `tar {-crtux}[hvwf] [tarfile] [named_files]`

tar (short for *tape archive*) is primarily an archive utility used for making backup tapes. tar combines and extracts multiple files into an archive called a tar file. A tar file can be a magnetic tape, but for this discussion it is considered any archive file.

> **Note**
>
> Because tar enables you to combine groups of files into one file (which can be compressed), the command is included in this file-transfer discussion.

When you enter a tar command, you must include one of the following parameters:

Parameter	Description
c	Creates a new tar file
r	Appends new files to an existing tar file

(continues)

Parameter	Description
t	Lists the table of contents of the tar file
u	Updates files that are newer than the ones that now exist in a tar file
x	Extracts all *named_files* from the tar file

Optional parameters for tar include the following:

Parameter	Description
h	Follows symbolic links to files. (If this parameter isn't used, symbolic links aren't traversed during tar file creation.)
v	Uses verbose reporting of status and errors. (Normally, tar works without any terminal reporting, but the verbose option reports the function and name of all files processed.)
w	Waits for user confirmation before adding or extracting each file.
f	Specifies a tar file name. (This parameter is always used when tar combines files into a *tarfile*.)

For example, to combine all the files in the current directory into a new *tarfile* called cwd.tar, use the following command:

```
tar -cvf cwd.tar *
```

To extract the files back into the current directory from the tar file, use the following command:

```
tar -xvf cwd.tar
```

File Compression

Syntax: compress [-fv] *name* (to compress a file)

         ucompress [-v] *name* (to decompress a file)

File compression is useful when you need to transfer large files across communication lines. UNIX provides a standard compression scheme using *Lempel-Ziv* coding. Compression for normal text files is typically 50 to 60 percent. The compression program assumes that you no longer need the file if you are compressing it; it removes the uncompressed file and creates a new file of the same name with a .z extension.

The following are the parameters for compress and ucompress:

Switch	Description
–f	Forces compression even if a file name with the .Z extension already exists or if the file doesn't shrink
–v	Verbose output; lists each file as it processes it, and shows the percentage reduction in size of each file

UNIX to UNIX Encoding

Syntax: uuencode [*sourcefile*] label
         (to encode a binary file)

         uudecode [*encodedfile*]
         (to decode an ASCII-encoded file)

UNIX to UNIX encoding provides a method to send binary files (8-bit data) by electronic mail systems that typically work only with ASCII (7-bit) data. UNIX to UNIX encoding strips out the eighth bit from all bytes of a binary file and encodes those striped bits into new 7-bit characters that it includes in the file. Typically, it increases the size of a file by approximately 35 percent.

Appendixes

uuencode is used to encode a binary file *sourcefile*, or a data stream from standard input (terminal input or piped input), and the output is sent to standard output (terminal output, or a piped output). The required argument label is the encoded file name used as the destination of the uudecode command. For example, to encode a file named executable to mail, you use the following command:

```
uuencode executable newexe > exe.uu
```

This creates a file named exe.uu, which is the uuencoded version of file executable.

uudecode is used to decode the encoded file *encodedfile*, or a data stream from standard input (terminal input or piped input), and the output is sent to the file specified as the label in the encoded file. uudecode strips out standard mail system headers in its decoding process. The file label retains the file attributes of the uuencode *sourcefile*. To decode the file from the previous example, you use the following command:

```
uudecode exe.uu
```

This creates a file named newexe, identical to the original file executable, in the directory that you execute the command.

Shells

The shell is the basic interface between the user and the UNIX kernel. Because many shells are available—too many to detail here!—this section discusses only the Bourne and C shells (the most commonly used).

Each shell provides the user with a method of interacting with the computer. The shell provides a command-line interface and a formal programming language that enables interaction with the UNIX kernel, files, and system resources.

The formal programming language is used to link UNIX commands and custom utilities to create other useful programs. To support this concept, many UNIX commands and programs are structured to use standard input and output for I/O. Standard input and output is usually directed to the terminal, but shell command operators can redirect standard input and output to use files or other programs as I/O.

This section is divided into three subsections, the first covering common shell syntax (showing what is common between shells) and then brief discussions of specifics for the Bourne and C shells.

Common Shell Syntax

Most UNIX command shells share some basic syntax. The Bourne and C shells share common syntax for input/output redirection, command pipes, and sequence operators. These are outlined in the following sections.

Input/Output Redirection

Syntax: *command_1 [< input_file] [{> >>} output_file]*

File redirection of standard I/O is accomplished by using the greater than (>), less than (<), and pipe (¦) operators. The < operator uses the file *input_file* as standard input. The single > operator creates a new file *output_file*, overwriting any existing file of the same name, and directs all standard output to that file. The double >> operator directs all standard output to *output_file* as well, but appends output to that file (rather than overwrites it) if the output already exists.

Command Pipes

Syntax: *command_1 [< input] [¦ command_2 [{> >>} output_file]]*

Piped commands provide a way to use the output of one command as input for a second command. The ¦ operator connects the standard output of the left operand to the standard input of the right operand. Commands operate asynchronously until the pipe provides the connection from the standard output of the `left_command` to the standard input of the `right_command`, as follows:

```
left_command¦right_command [¦right_command] ...
```

You can use this technique to chain two or more programs together. This method is very useful in UNIX because both programs run simultaneously; the `right_command` accepts the output of the `left_command` as it becomes available.

Command Sequence Operators

Syntax: `command_1 [{; & && ¦¦} command_2] ...`

Command operators provide you with a way to execute multiple shell commands, programs, or scripts with a number of interactions. You can execute commands in sequence, asynchronously, in a piped fashion, or conditionally. Operators also provide a means of redirecting input and output (see the earlier section "Input/Output Redirection").

To execute two commands sequentially, separate them with a semicolon (;) on the command line. The command to the right of the ; operator (`command_2`) is executed after the command to the left of the semicolon (`command_1`). You can execute more than two commands sequentially by using the following syntax:

```
command_1;command_2 [;command_3] ...
```

Asynchronous, or independent, commands can be placed on the command line together by using an ampersand (&). All asynchronous commands commence operation simultaneously and run in parallel:

```
command_1&command_2 [&command_3] ...
```

You can execute commands conditionally by using double ampersands (&&) or double bars (¦¦). Double-ampersand and double-bar operators provide conditional execution for the right-hand operand *command_2* when the exit status of the *command_1* is zero and non-zero, respectively. The exit status is the return code of a command, which typically indicates if it completed successfully (like a file find operation).

```
command_1&&command_2 [&&command_3]...
```

```
command_1¦¦command_2 [¦¦command_3]...
```

The Bourne Shell

The Bourne shell is the original command shell—the basic shell for all UNIX systems.

The default command prompt for the Bourne shell is the dollar sign ($). You can change your prompt by modifying the environment variable PS1.

Environment variables (or parameters) are displayed using the set command. They are modified using the following shell syntax:

```
set [variable = [value]]
```

This syntax sets an environment *variable* to *value* (or to null if no *value* is given). If no arguments are given, the set command reports all current environment variables and their values in the same format. The following are some of the most common environment variables:

Variable	Description
PS1	Interactive command prompt; the default is **$**.

(continues)

Variable	Description
HOME	Your home directory and the default argument for the command cd.
PATH	Your search path for executable commands. The path is specified as a list of directories separated by colons (:); the current working directory is specified as a null file name. The default is :/us/ucb:/bin:/us/bin, which specifies a search order beginning in the current directory (see CDPATH) and moving through /us/ucb, /bin, and /us/bin in order.
CDPATH	The current cd path.

A *shell script*, or *shell program*, is a set of shell commands and controls used to perform a function. The Bourne shell provides a basic programming language. Shell scripts are useful for repetitive operations that can be made up of one or more basic commands. This is why a large number of general-purpose UNIX utilities exists, rather than a few complex targeted programs. Bourne shell programming is an extensive topic to cover, and only the most basic topics are discussed here.

Shell scripts follow the Bourne shell syntax for command operators, input/output redirection, and piping. Three commonly used forms of control flow are given here: while looping, conditional execution, and the case statement.

While looping executes the command *evaluate*; if the *evaluate* command returns a true value (zero), it executes the *command(s)* in the do-done statement. The while syntax is shown as follows:

```
while evaluate; do command(s) done
```

A simple conditional statement executes the *command(s)* between the then and fi statements if the *evaluate* statement evaluates true as in the syntax

```
if evaluate; then command(s) fi
```

A compound conditional `if-then-else` statement allows multiple levels of conditional decision making. The Bourne shell executes the command(s) `cmd1(s)` when the `eval1` evaluates true; otherwise, it evaluates the optional `eval2`. If `eval2` then evaluates true, the shell executes `cmd2(s)`; otherwise, it executes the command(s) `cmd3(s)`. The compound conditional statement uses the following syntax:

```
if eval1; then cmd1(s) [elif eval2; then cmd2(s) [else cmd3(s)]] fi
```

The `case` conditional execution form compares an input of the form consistent to any file name to group of patterns. If the input matches any pattern, the associated code is executed. A list of conditional patterns may be logically ORed together using the vertical bar (¦). Notice that each condition is terminated with a pair of semicolons. The case syntax is shown here:

```
case input in
pattern1 [pattern2]... ) cmd1(s) ;;
[pattern3 [ ¦ pattern4]...) cmd3(s) ;;]
[*) defaultcmd(s);;]
esac;;
```

Bourne shell scripts may access any existing environment variable using the `$name` format. Temporary variables for use in the script may be defined as any other environment variable using the `name=value` commands (you should clean up temporary variables with `unset` when completed). Command-line arguments are passed to the shell script by using the following variables:

Variable	Description
$*	The entire command line used to invoke this shell
$0	The command
$1	The first argument
$2 (and so on)	The second argument (and so on)
$#	The number of arguments on the command line

Appendixes

The C Shell

The C shell (csh) was designed to provide a faster, more powerful interface (like the C language) to the user than the Bourne shell could provide.

The C shell is probably the second most common shell type available to system users. The C shell default prompt is the percent sign (%). You can change your prompt by changing the environment variable `prompt`.

The following sections detail some of the features that the C shell provides: extensive support for environment variables, command aliasing, and command history. A section also introduces shell programming, which follows a C-like syntax, designed to ease the transition to shell programming for C programmers.

Shell and Environment Variables

The C shell has two types of variables: *shell variables* and *environment variables*. Environment variables are exported (used) automatically by programs; shell variables aren't. Shell variables are displayed and modified using the shell command `set` with the following syntax:

```
set [variable [= value]]
```

Environment variables are displayed and modified using the C shell command `setenv` with the following syntax:

```
setenv [variable [value]]
```

If `set` or `setenv` are executed with arguments, `variable` is set to `value` (or to null if no `set` displays the current shell variables), and `setenv` displays environment variables.

The most common variables are listed in table C.1. Variables are listed in a tabular format to show the interaction between shell and environment variables. By default, if you update one of a shell/environment variable pair, the other is updated automatically.

Table C.1 Common C Shell Variables

Environment	Shell	Variable Description
HOME	home	Your home directory and the default argument for the command cd.
PATH	path	Your search path for executable commands. The path is specified as a list of directories separated by colons (:); the current working directory is specified as a null file name. The default is :/us/ucb: bin:/us/bin, specifying a search order that starts in the current directory (see cdpath) and then proceeds through /us/ucb, /bin, and /us/bin, in order.
PWD	cwd	Current working directory.
SHELL	shell	Current shell program - /bin/csh.
TERM	term	Terminal type; common types include vt102, ANSI, adm3a. Unknown connections by way of modem are most commonly assigned type dialup. Visual or full-screen editors need to know a specific terminal type to match cursor-movement control.
USER	user	Your user name.
	argv	Argument list for command-line entries. Arguments are accessed by way of the positional parameters $1, $2, ... and the number of arguments by way of the $#argv C shell construct.
	prompt	Interactive command prompt; the default prompt is hostname%.

Command Aliasing

Syntax: `alias` *command replacement_string*
(to add aliases)

`ualias` *string*
(to remove aliases)

The C shell provides *command aliasing*, a function that enables you to replace lengthy or repetitive command-line strings with shorter commands. The advantages of aliasing include speed (because they execute directly from memory and don't require individual executable files) and savings in disk space.

Aliases can be placed in your shell initialization script (`.cshrc` for the C shell) or entered at any time from the command prompt. To remove aliases, use the `ualias` command.

The following are some useful aliases for new users:

`alias rm 'rm -i'`   Protects against unwanted deletion

`alias cp 'cp -i'`   Notifies you before copying over a file

`alias mv 'mv -i'`   Notifies you before moving over a file

To set UNIX up to look like DOS, use the following aliases:

```
alias dir 'ls -al'
alias copy 'cp -i'
alias move 'mv -i'
alias type 'cat'
alias help 'man'
alias del 'rm -i'
alias rename 'mv -i'
```

These aliases provide DOS command names for many commonly used UNIX commands.

Command History

Syntax: `!!`

`!history_command_number`

`!history_command_string`

`^last_command_string^replacement_string^`

Command history is a shell construct that saves previous commands in a buffer. You can save keystrokes by using the contents of the history buffer to re-execute (or modify and re-execute) commands.

The history command displays the contents of the history buffer—typically, the last 80 commands. The `!!` command re-executes the last command executed; `!history_command_number` runs the history command numbered `history_command_number`. You also can execute a specific command from the buffer by using the command `!history_command_string`, replacing the variable string with enough characters of the desired command to form a unique string.

You can modify and execute the last command you entered using the `^last_command_string^replacement_string^` syntax, which finds `last_command_string` in the previous command and replaces it with `replacement_string` before executing the command again.

Wild-card substitution characters in the C shell include `*`, `?`, and `[...]`. The asterisk (`*`) is used to substitute for any number of characters; the question mark (`?`) matches any single character. The brackets provide a means for you to substitute a list of options. To use this wild-card construct to search for a group of C source and header files in the current directory, for example, enter the following command:

```
Hawaii% ls *.[c,h]
main.c    main.h    io.c    io.h    func.c    func.h
Hawaii%
```

C Shell Scripts

A *shell script*, or *shell program*, is a set of shell commands and controls used to perform a function. Shell scripts are useful for coding repetitive operations made up of one or more basic commands. For this reason, a large number of general-purpose UNIX utilities exist, rather than a few complex targeted programs.

The C shell provides a structured programming language that uses a syntax much like the C language itself. C shell programming is an extensive topic to cover, so only the most basic topics are discussed in this section.

Shell scripts follow the shell syntax for command operators, I/O redirection, and piping. Program flow follows C syntax closely, but not exactly. Three commonly used forms of flow control are `while` looping, if-then-else, and `switch`. Commands (`command(s)`) that make up the user program can be placed on separate input lines (for sequential operation), or can be grouped onto lines using command sequence operators (see the "Common Shell Syntax" section earlier in this appendix).

With `while` looping, the repetitive processing of the command or commands (`command(s)`) continues until `expression` becomes false, using the following syntax:

```
while (expression)
command(s)
end
```

A simple conditional statement executes the command if `expression` evaluates true as in the syntax:

```
if (expression) command
```

A compound conditional `if-then-else` statement allows multiple levels of conditional decision making. The C shell executes the commands between the `then` and the `else`, `elseif`, or `endif` statements when the `if` (`expression`) evaluates true. When the `if` (`expression`) evaluates false, the C shell branches to the `else` commands or the `elseif` conditional execution, or exits the `if-then-else` as indicated by `endif`. The compound conditional statement uses the following syntax:

```
if (expr1) then
true1_command(s)
[     elseif (expr2) then
true2_command(s)
[     else
false2_command(s)]] ...
endif
```

The third conditional execution form, `switch`, follows the similar C syntax format and execution. The string expression is compared with all the case labels for a match. If a match is present, the commands for that label, found between the `case` statement and the next `breaksw` statement, are executed. If no match is found, the C shell searches for an optional `default:` statement; if that statement is present, the subsequent commands up to the `endsw` statement are executed. The syntax is shown as follows:

```
switch (string)
case label:
command(s)
      breaksw
[case label:
command(s)
      breaksw
] ...
[     default:
command(s)]
      endsw
```

C shell scripts can access any existing shell or environment variable using the `$name` format. You can define temporary variables

for use in the script like any other shell or environment variable by using the `set` and `setenv` commands. (Remember to clean up temporary variables using `unset` and `unsetenv` at the end of processing.) Command-line arguments are passed to the shell script using the following variables:

Variable	Description
$*	The entire command line used to invoke this shell script
$0	The command
$1	The first argument
$2 (and so on)	The second argument (and so on)
$#	The number of arguments on the command line

Tip
You can place comments into C shell scripts by using the pound sign (#), which indicates that the rest of the current line is a comment and should be ignored during processing.

UNIX Command Summary

Command	Description	Syntax
apropos	Find command	apropos *keyword*
cat	List file	cat *filename*
cd	Change directory	cd [*directory_name*]
chfn	Change user full name	chfn
chgrp	Change file group	chgrp [-R] *new_group file_name(s)*
chmod	Change file attributes	chmod [-fR] *mode filename*
chown	Change file ownership	chown [-R] *new_owner*[.*new_group*] *file_name(s)*
chsh	Change initial shell	chsh
compress	File compression	compress [-fv] *filename* ucompress [-v] *filename*
cp	Copy file	cp *source destination*
emacs	Full-screen editor (Editor Macros)	emacs [*filename*]
find	Find file	find *path* [-name *filename*] [-print]
finger	Find information on user	finger *user_identification*
grep	Pattern search	grep [-i] *pattern* [*filename*]
ln	Create a link	ln [-s] *file* [*link*]
logout	Log out, exit shell	logout exit
ls	Directory listing	ls [-acglt] [*filename*] ...
mail	Get mail Send mail	mail [-eH] mail [-F] *recipient* ...
man	On-line help manuals	man [-] [-t] [-M *path*] [[*section*] *title* ...] ...
mkdir	Create directory	mkdir [*new_directory_path*/] *new_directory_name*

Command	Description	Syntax
more	Paginate file	more [*filename*]
mv	Move file	mv *source destination*
passwd	Change user password	passwd [-fs]
rm	Delete file	rm [-fiR] *file_name*
rmdir	Delete directory	rmdir *directory_name*
rn	Read news groups	rn [*newsgroups*]
sb or rb	YMODEM file transfer	sb [-abknpy] *filename* rb [-abp] *filename*
sort	Sort file	sort
sx or rx	XMODEM file transfer	sx [-abknpy] *filename* rx [-abp] *filename*
sz or rz	ZMODEM file transfer	sz [-abknpy] *filename* rz [-abp] *filename*
tar	Tape file generation	tar {-crtux}[hvwf] [*tarfile*] [*named_files*]
vi	Visual Editor	vi [*filename*]
whatis	Describe command	whatis *command*

Appendix D

Glossary

A

account   A user login and home directory restricted for the use of a particular person, usually password protected.

ACM   Association for Computing Machinery, a professional society for people connected with the computer industry.

address   An ASCII representation of the actual location of a computer account that lets people access that account (to send it electronic mail, or to connect to the account to transfer data).

alias   A short name to represent a more complicated one, often used for mail addresses or host domain names.

analog   Type of communications used by radio and TV, consisting of data transmitted by continuous electromagnetic waves. Any continuous wave form, as opposed to digital on/off transmissions.

archie   A tool with which you easily can search for information at anonymous ftp sites on the Internet.

archive   A repository of files available for access by the Internet community. Also, a collection of files, often a backup or files saved to tape for transfer.

ARPA   Advanced Research Projects Agency, the government agency that originally funded the ARPANET. Became DARPA (Defense Advanced Research Projects Agency) in the mid '70s.

ARPANET   The experimental network that eventually evolved into the Internet.

article   Message submitted to a USENET news group.

ASCII   Data that is limited to letters, numbers, and punctuation.

ATM   Asynchronous Transfer Mode, a developing technological advance in communications switching.

AUP   Acceptable use policy, the restrictions a network places on traffic it carries.

B

backbone   The major communication lines of a network.

bandwidth   The volume of information that can be sent over a network in a specific time period.

bang   A slang term for an exclamation point (!).

bang address   A type of computer address used to address hosts on the UUCP network. Exclamation points in the address separate hosts that communicate directly with each other.

baud   An older term for bps (bits per second), the rate at which digital information is transferred over communication lines.

BBS   Bulletin board system, a utility that allows people to connect to a computer to upload and download files and to leave messages for other users.

binary   Data that may contain non-printable characters, including graphics, programs, and sound files.

bit   The basic unit of digital communications. There are eight bits in a byte.

BITNET   Because It's Time Network, a non-TCP/IP network for small universities without Internet access.

bounce   Mail message you receive that tells you one of your mail messages wasn't delivered. Usually includes an error code and the contents of the message that wasn't delivered.

bps   Bits per second, the speed at which data is transferred between computers.

bridge   A device that connects one physical section of a network to another, often providing isolation.

BTW   By The Way, an abbreviation often used in on-line conversations.

byte   A digital storage unit large enough to contain one ASCII character.

C

CIX   Commercial Internet eXchange, a consortium of commercial providers of Internet service.

client   User of a service. Often also refers to a piece of software that gets information from a server.

compress   A program that compacts a file so that it fits into a smaller space. Also can refer to the technique of reducing the amount of space a file takes up.

CNRI   Corporation for National Research Initiatives, an organization to foster research into a national data highway.

CPSR   Computer Professionals for Social Responsibility, a group that works for socially responsible use of computers.

CREN   A joining of two educational networks of different types to enhance their capabilities.

cyberspace   A term used to refer to the entire collection of sites that can be accessed electronically. If your computer is attached to the Internet or another large network, it exists in cyberspace.

D

DARPA   Defense Advanced Research Projects Agency (originally ARPA), the government agency that funded the ARPANET. See also *ARPA*.

dedicated line   See *leased line*.

dialup   A type of connection where you dial a phone number and communicate with a computer (or the Internet) over a modem.

digest   A form of mailing list where groups of messages are sent out at one time.

digital   Type of communications used by computers, consisting of "on" and "off" pulses.

DNS   See *Domain Name System*.

DOD   Department of Defense.

domain   Highest subdivision of the Internet; usually by country or (within the United States) by type of organization (educational, commercial, and so forth).

Domain Name System   The system used to define names for Internet hosts.

dot address   The numeric (IP) Internet host address.

download   Bring a file from another computer to yours.

E

ECPA   The Electronic Communications Privacy Act, a law that governs the use and restrictions of electronic communications.

EDUCOM   An organization of educational institutions.

EFF   Electronic Frontier Foundation, an organization concerned with the legal implications of computer usage.

e-mail   An electronic message delivered from one computer to another.

emoticon   See *smiley*.

encryption   The scrambling of a message so that it can't be read by a casual observer.

ESNET   The Department of Energy's network.

EtherNet   A type of local area network hardware. Many TCP/IP networks are EtherNet-based.

expire   Remove an article from a news group after a set period.

F

FAQ   Frequently Asked Question document, which contains a list of commonly asked questions on a topic. Usually, each USENET news group has one.

FARNET   A group of networks interested in promoting research and education networking.

feed   Send USENET news groups from your site to another.

finger   A program that provides information about users on a host computer.

flame   Communicate in an abusive or absurd manner.

ftp   A program that allows you to transfer data between different computers on a network.

FWIW   For What It's Worth, an abbreviation often used in on-line conversations.

FYI   For Your Information, often an abbreviation used in on-line conversations. Also a type of Internet reference document that contains answers to basic questions about the Internet.

G

gateway   A device that interfaces two networks that use different protocols.

gigabit   Very high speed (one billion bits per second) data communications.

gigabyte   A unit of data storage approximately equal to 1 billion bytes (1,073,741,824). One gigabyte equals 1,000 megabytes.

Gopher   A utility that allows you to access publicly available information on Internet hosts that provide Gopher service.

GUI   Graphical user interface, a computer interface based on graphical symbols rather than text. PC-based window environments and Macintosh environments are GUIs.

H

headers   Lines at the beginning of a mail message that contain information about the message: its source, destination, subject, and the route it took to get there, among other things.

hosts   Individual computers connected to a network. See also *nodes*.

hypertext   An on-line document with words or graphics that contain links to other documents; usually, these links can be activated by clicking the link area.

I

IAB   Internet Architecture Board, a group of volunteers who work to maintain the Internet.

IEEE   Institute of Electrical and Electronics Engineers, the professional society for electrical and computer engineers.

IETF   Internet Engineering Task Force, a group of volunteers that helps develop Internet standards.

IMHO   In My Humble (or Honest) Opinion, an abbreviation often used in on-line conversations.

Internet   The term used to describe all the worldwide TCP/IP-based computer networks that are connected together.

InterNIC   The NSFNET manager sites on the Internet that provide information about the Internet.

IP   Internet Protocol, the communication protocol used by computers connected to the Internet.

IRC   Internet Relay Chat, a live conferencing facility available on the Internet.

ISO   International Standards Organization, which sets all types of standards to be met by organizations worldwide. ISO was working, for example, on a network protocol to replace TCP/IP (but it hasn't come into wide use).

ISOC   Internet Society, an educational organization dedicated to encouraging the use of the Internet.

K

kill file   A file that some news readers allow you to set up so that you can skip certain messages in news groups automatically (by subject, author, and so on).

knowbots   Knowledge robots, programs that automatically search a network for specified information.

L

labels   The different components of an Internet host's name.

leased line   A dedicated phone line used for network communications.

local   Pertaining to the computer that you are now using.

lurking   Observing but not participating in; often used when referring to a USENET group.

M

mailing list   A service that sends mail to everyone on a list whenever mail is sent to the service, allowing a group of people to exchange mail on a particular topic.

mail reflector   Software that automatically distributes all submitted messages to the members of a mailing list.

man   A UNIX command that gives you help on the command you specify after you enter `man`.

MBONE   Multicast backbone, an experimental network that allows live video to be sent over the Internet.

Merit   Michigan Educational Research Information Triad, the organizations that initially managed NSFNET.

MILNET   The DOD's network.

MIME   Multipurpose Internet Mail Extensions, an extension to Internet mail that allows for the inclusion of non-textual data, such as video and audio, in e-mail.

modem   An electronic device that allows digital computer data to be transmitted and received over analog phone lines.

moderator   A person who filters submissions to a mailing list or news group based on certain criteria.

Mosaic   A graphical interface to allow you to access and retrieve data from publicly accessible sites.

multimedia   Involving more that one form of communication, such as combining text, video, and sound.

N

Netfind   A service that allows you to attempt to look up an electronic address for a user.

netiquette   Network etiquette conventions used in written communications, usually referring to USENET news group posting.

netnews   A collective way of referring to the USENET news groups.

network   A number of computers physically connected to enable communication with one another.

news groups   The computer discussion groups of USENET.

NIC   Network Information Center, a service that provides administrative information about a network.

NNTP   Network News Transport Protocol, the protocol used to transmit USENET news over the Internet.

nodes   Individual computers connected to a network. See also *hosts*.

NREN   National Research and Education Network, a proposed nation-wide high-speed data network.

NSF   National Science Foundation.

NSFNET   Network funded by the National Science Foundation, now the backbone of the Internet.

NSINET   NASA's network.

O

OTOH   On The Other Hand, an abbreviation often used in on-line conversations.

P

packet   The unit of data transmission on the Internet (the information being sent along with additional overhead information).

packet switching   The communications technology on which the Internet is based, where data being sent between computers is transmitted in packets.

parallel   Means of communication in which digital data is sent multiple bits at a time, with one line per bit.

PDN   Public Data Network, a service (such as Sprintnet) that gives access to a nationwide data network through a local phone call.

poll   To check at intervals. If you poll your dialup Internet account, for example, you call it up every so often to see whether you have any e-mail or netnews.

POP   Post Office Protocol, an e-mail protocol used to retrieve your mail from an Internet provider's machine (when you don't have a dedicated Internet connection). Also means Point of Presence, which indicates the availability of a local access number to a Public Data Network.

post   Send a message to a USENET news group.

postmaster   An address to which you can send questions when you don't have a user's address at a site.

PPP   Point-to-Point Protocol, a type of communication protocol often used for serial Internet connections.

protocol   The standard that defines how computers on a network communicate with one another.

provider   Someone who sells—or gives away, in some cases—access to the Internet.

R

RARE   A consortium of European research networks.

remote   A host on the network other than the computer you now are using.

RFC   Request For Comments, documents submitted to the Internet governing board to define Internet standards.

router   Equipment that receives an Internet packet and sends it to the next machine in the destination path.

S

serial   Means of communication in which digital data is sent one bit at a time over a serial line.

server   Provider of a service. Often refers to a piece of hardware or software that provides access to information requested from it.

shell   An interactive command interpreter, usually on the UNIX operating system.

signature   A standard sign-off used by people for e-mail and news group posts, often contained in a file and automatically appended to the mail or post.

site   A group of computers under one administrative control.

SLIP   Single Line IP, a protocol used to connect a single host to an IP network over a serial line, such as a telephone line.

smiley   An ASCII drawing such as :-) (look at it sideways) used to help indicate an emotion in a message.

SMTP   Simple Mail Transport Protocol, the Internet standard protocol for e-mail transfer.

subscribe   Become a member of a mailing list or news group. Also refers to obtaining Internet provider services.

T

TCP   Transmission Control Protocol, the network protocol used by hosts on the Internet.

telnet   A program to allow remote login to another computer.

test bed   A site using an experimental version of hardware or software to test and refine it.

thread   All messages pertaining to a particular topic in a news group or mailing list.

toggle   Alternate between two possible values.

token ring   A type of local area network.

traffic   The information flowing over a network.

U

UNIX   An operating system used on many Internet hosts.

upload   Send a file from your computer to another.

USENET   A collection of computer discussion groups that are read all over the world.

username   The ID used to log in to a computer.

UUCP   UNIX-to-UNIX Copy program, an early transfer protocol for UNIX machines that required having one machine call the other one on the phone.

uudecode   A program that lets you reconstruct binary data that was uuencoded.

uuencode   A program that lets you send binary data through e-mail.

V

virus   A computer program that covertly enters a system by means of a legitimate program, usually doing damage to the system. Compare to *worm*.

VMS   An operating system used on some Internet hosts.

W

WAIS   Wide Area Information Servers, a system that lets you look up information in public databases available on the Internet.

WHOIS   A service that lets you look up information about Internet hosts and users.

wild cards   Characters such as * and ?, used when giving a command to indicate that any characters can match.

worm   A computer program that invades other computers over a network, usually non-destructively. Compare to *virus*.

WWW   World Wide Web, a hypertext-based system that allows browsing of available Internet resources.

Appendix E

Bibliography

Books

Albitz, P., and Liu, C.; *DNS and BIND in a Nutshell*; O'Reilly & Associates, Inc.; 1992.

Black, U.; *TCP/IP and Related Protocols*; McGraw-Hill, Inc.; 1992.

Comer, D.; *Internetworking with TCP/IP, Volume I: Principles, Protocols, and Architecture*; Prentice Hall, Inc.; 1991.

Comer, D., and Stevens, D.; *Internetworking with TCP/IP, Volume II: Design, Implementation, and Internals*; Prentice Hall, Inc.; 1991.

Davidson, J.; *An Introduction to TCP/IP*; Springer-Verlag New York Inc.; 1988.

Dern, D.; *The Internet Guide for New Users*; McGraw-Hill, Inc.; 1994.

Estrada, S.; *Connecting to the Internet: An O'Reilly Buyer's Guide*; O'Reilly & Associates, Inc.; 1993.

Fisher, S.; *Riding the Internet Highway*; New Riders Publishing; 1993.

Fraase, M.; *The Mac Internet Tour Guide: Cruising the Internet the Easy Way*; Ventana Press, Inc.; 1993.

Frey, D., and Adams, R.; *!%@:: A Directory of Electronic Mail Addressing and Networks*; O'Reilly & Associates, Inc.; 1993.

Hardie, E., and Neou, V., editors; *Internet: Mailing Lists*; PTR Prentice Hall, Inc.; 1993.

Hunt, C.; *TCP/IP Network Administration*; O'Reilly & Associates, Inc.; 1992.

Krol, E.; *The Whole Internet User's Guide & Catalog*; O'Reilly & Associates, Inc.; 1992.

LaQuey, T., editor; *The User's Directory of Computer Networks*; Digital Press; 1990.

LaQuey, T., with Ryer, J.; *The Internet Companion: A Beginner's Guide to Global Networking*; Addison-Wesley Publishing Company; 1993.

Lynch, D., and Rose, M., editors; *Internet System Handbook*; Addison-Wesley Publishing Company, Inc.; 1993.

Malamud, C.; *Exploring the Internet: A Technical Travelogue*; Prentice Hall, Inc.; 1993.

Marine, A., Kirkpatrick, S., Neou, V., and Ward, C.; *Internet: Getting Started*; PTR Prentice Hall, Inc.; 1993.

Quarterman, J; *The Matrix: Computer Networks and Conferencing Systems Worldwide*; Digital Press; 1990.

Ritter, D.; *The Whole Earth On-Line Almanac: Info from A to Z*; Brady Publishing; 1993.

Rose, M.; *The Internet Message: Closing the Book with Electronic Mail*; PTR Prentice Hall, Inc.; 1993.

Rose, M.; *The Little Black Book: Mail Bonding with OSI Directory Services*; Prentice Hall, Inc.; 1992.

Rose, M.; *The Open Book: A Practical Perspective on OSI*; Prentice Hall, Inc.; 1990.

Rose, M.; *The Simple Book: An Introduction to Management of TCP/IP-based Internets*; PTR Prentice Hall, Inc.; 1991.

Santifaller, M.; *TCP/IP and NFS: Internetworking in a UNIX Environment*; Addison-Wesley Publishing Company; 1991.

Smith, R., and Gibbs, M.; *Navigating the Internet*; Sams Publishing; 1993.

Sproull, L., and Kiesler, S.; *Connections: New Ways of Working in the Networked Organization*; MIT Press; Cambridge, MA; 1991.

Stoll, C.; *The Cuckoo's Egg: Tracking a Spy through the Maze of Computer Espionage*; Doubleday, New York; 1989.

Todino, G., and Dougherty, D.; *Using UUCP and Usenet*; O'Reilly & Associates, Inc.; 1991.

Periodicals

Alexander, M.; "Advocacy Group Pushes for Shift in R&D Funding"; *Computerworld*; v25; Nov. 11, 1991; p. 22.

Daviss, B.; "Knowbots"; *Discover*; v12 #4; April 1991; pp. 21-22.

Dern, D.; "The ARPANET is Twenty"; *ConneXions*; v3 #10; Oct. 1989; pp. 2-26.

Graham, E.; "Classrooms Without Walls: Advances in Telecommunications Promise to Transform Both Learning and Teaching"; *The Wall Street Journal*; May 18, 1992; p. R8.

Gruman, G.; "Safeguarding Civil Liberties in the Computer Age"; *IEEE Software*; v8; March 1991; pp. 100-101.

Higgins, K.; "Reston's Information Highway"; *Virginia Business*; v8 #2; Feb. 1993; pp. 22-23.

Laubauch, M.; "Profile: CREN—The Corporation for Research and Educational Networking"; *ConneXions*; v4 #5; May 1990; pp. 20-28.

Markoff, J.; "Building the Electronic Superhighway"; *The New York Times*; Jan. 24, 1993; p. F1, col. 2.

Marsa, L.; "Interview: Robert E. Kahn"; *OMNI*; v15 #3; Dec. 1992; pp. 83-96.

Perry, T.; "Forces for social change"; *IEEE Spectrum*; v29 #10; Oct. 1992; pp. 30-33.

Press, L.; "The Net: Progress and Opportunity"; *Communications of the ACM*; Dec. 1992; v35 #2; pp. 21-25.

Rifkin, G.; "The In-Depth Interview: Mitchell Kapor"; *Computerworld*; v25; Dec. 9, 1991; pp. 73-74.

Appendixes

Spice, B.; "Pitt supercomputer a crystal ball for weather"; *Pittsburgh Post-Gazette*; July 25, 1993; pp. B1-B2.

Weissert, R.; "TCP/IP—The Hero of Operation Desert Storm Information Systems"; *ConneXions*; v6 #5; May 1992; pp. 34-38.

On-Line References

Da Silva, S. and Von Rospach, C.; "Mailing List." Periodically posted and available on-line from the following USENET news groups: `news.lists`, `news.answers`, and `news.announce.newusers`.

Dippold, R.; "USENET newsgroup Creation Companion." Available on-line via anonymous ftp to `rtfm.mit.edu` in file `/pub/usenet/news.answers/creating-news groups/helper`.

"Internet Multicasting Service: FAQ on Internet Talk Radio"; Revised: Oct. 1, 1993. Available automatically by sending electronic mail to `info@radio.com`.

Kamens, J.; "How to become a USENET site." Available on-line via anonymous ftp to `rtfm.mit.edu` in file `/pub/usenet/news.answers/site-setup`.

Kamens, J.; "How to find people's E-mail addresses." Available on-line via anonymous ftp to `rtfm.mit.edu` in file `/pub/usenet/news.answers/finding-addresses`.

Lottor, M.; "Internet Domain Survey"; Jan. 1991. Available on-line via anonymous ftp to `ftp.nisc.sri.com` in file `/pub/zone/report-9301.doc`.

Lottor, M.; "RFC 1296:Internet Growth (1981-1991)"; Jan. 1992. Available on-line via anonymous ftp to `ftp.nisc.sri.com` in file `/rfc/rfc1296.txt`.

Lottor, M.; "RFC 1033:Domain administrators operations guide"; Nov. 1987; 22 p. Available on-line via anonymous ftp to `ftp.nisc.sri.com` in file `/rfc/rfc1033.txt`.

Malkin, G., and Marine, A.; "RFC 1206:Answers to Commonly asked 'New Internet User' Questions"; Feb. 1991. Available on-line via anonymous ftp to `ftp.nisc.sri.com` in file `/rfc/rfc1206.txt`.

Mockapetris, P.V.; "RFC 1034:Domain names - concepts and facilities"; Nov. 1987; 55 p. Available on-line via anonymous ftp to `ftp.nisc.sri.com` in file `/rfc/rfc1034.txt`.

Mockapetris, P.V.; "RFC 1035:Domain names - implementation and specification"; Nov. 1987. Available on-line via anonymous ftp to `ftp.nisc.sri.com` in file `/rfc/rfc1035.txt`.

Mockapetris, P.V.; "RFC 1101:DNS encoding of network names and other types"; April 1989. Available on-line via anonymous ftp to `ftp.nisc.sri.com` in file `/rfc/rfc1101.txt`.

"NSFNET Byte Traffic History"; available via anonymous ftp from `nic.merit.edu` in file `history.bytes`.

"NSFNET History of Usage by Service"; available via anonymous ftp from `nic.merit.edu` in file `history.ports`.

"NSFNET Network Count History"; available via anonymous ftp from `nic.merit.edu` in file `history.netcount`.

"NSFNET Networks by Country"; available via anonymous ftp from `nic.merit.edu` in file `nets.by.country`.

"NSFNET Packet Traffic History"; available via anonymous ftp from `nic.merit.edu` in file `history.packets`.

Spafford, G.; "USENET Software: History and Sources"; April 25, 1993. Available on-line via anonymous ftp to `rtfm.mit.edu` in file `/pub/usenet/news.answers/usernet-software/part1`.

Spafford, G., and Lawrence, D.; "Currently Active USENET Group List"; July 23, 1993. Periodically posted and available on-line from the following USENET news groups: `news.groups, news.announce.newusers,` and `news.announce.newgroups, news.answers`.

Appendixes

Stahl, M.K.; "RFC 1032:Domain administrators guide"; Nov. 1987. Available on-line via anonymous ftp to `ftp.nisc.sri.com` in file `/rfc/rfc1032.txt`.

Yanoff, S.; "Inter-Network Mail Guide"; Aug. 16, 1993. Available on-line via anonymous ftp to `csd4.csd.uwm.edu`.

Government Reports

"National Collaboratories: Applying Information Technology for Scientific Research"; National Academy Press, Washington, D.C., 1993.

"Review of NSFNET"; Office of Inspector General, National Science Foundation; March 23, 1993.

"The National Research and Education Network Program: A Report to Congress"; Dec. 1992.

Appendix F

Open Letter to Internet Software and Service Providers

Gentlemen:

As you are well aware, the number of products and services available for the Internet continues to grow at an incredible rate. This explosive growth makes even being aware of all the software packages and service options that exist difficult, let alone properly evaluating them for mention in a text such as this. Future editions of *Using the Internet* may be published to keep up with the latest developments in the tools, technologies, and services, but your assistance will greatly improve the chances that your product will be given the exposure it deserves.

If you want to have information on your product or service considered for inclusion in a future edition of this book, send a letter to the following address:

Acquisitions Assistant
Que Corporation, *Using the Internet*
201 W. 103rd Street, Suite 400
Indianapolis, IN 46290

Please provide a brief description of your product or service, as well as the name and phone number of whom to contact for arranging an evaluation. Every effort will be made to examine your product and include information on it in a future edition of *Using the Internet.*

All the best!

The authors

Index

magazines, *see* periodicals
Magnuson-Moss Act, 172
Mail (Microsoft), 306
mail
 addresses, 289-290
  components, 290-292
  finding, 292-300
  troubleshooting, 324
  mail delivery programs,
  e-mail, 284
 reflectors, 314, 1156
 see also e-mail
mail systems setup, 304-306
mailing search output (archie),
 517
mailing lists, 11, 50-51,
 313-314, 654, 1155
 digests, 315
 etiquette, 316-317
 finding, 315-316
 moderated, 314-315
MAILLIST, 1047
malicious use, 52
 espionage, 52
 Internet worm, 53
manual pages (UNIX),
 1110-1111
market research (commercial
 use), 251
Maryland
 BBS, 555-556
 SLIP/PPP providers, 602
 terminal servers, 589
Massachusetts
 BBS, 556-557
 dedicated access providers,
  612
 SLIP/PPP providers, 602
 terminal servers, 590
master files, 90
mathematics, 654
MBONE (Multicast Backbone),
 274-275, 1156
MCI Mail e-mail addresses, 456
mdelete command (ftp), 349
Merit (Michigan Educational
 Research Information Triad),
 36-38, 1156
Merit Network, Inc. Network
 Information Center (Merit
 NIC), 116-117
message body, e-mail, 283

messages
 distribution limitations, 18
 e-mail
  addressing, 289-300
  encrypting and privacy,
   328-330
  forging, 327-328
  header lines, 285-289
  mailing lists, 313-317
  multimedia, 318-319
  sending binary (non-text)
   data, 317-318
  troubleshooting, 322-325
  unwanted, 325-326
 error messages, *see* error
  messages
 USENET netiquette, 19-20
metamail package (AT&T Bell
 Laboratories), 319
metronet (Texas)
 SLIP/PPP providers, 605
 terminal servers, 593
mget command (ftp), 338, 346
MH mail system, 309-310
Michigan
 BBSs, 557-559
 dedicated access providers,
  613
 SLIP/PPP providers, 602
 terminal servers, 590
Michigan Educational Research
 Information Triad, *see* MERIT
michnet (Michigan)
 SLIP/PPP providers, 602
 terminal servers, 590
Microsoft Windows
 (ftp.cica.indiana.edu), 632-633
MIDnet (Nebraska) dedicated
 access providers, 613
MILNET, 33, 41, 1156
MIME (Multipurpose Internet
 Mail Extensions), 1156
mindvox (New York)
 SLIP/PPP providers, 603
 terminal servers, 591
Minnesota
 BBSs, 559
 dedicated access providers,
  613
misc hierarchy (network news),
 371
misfeasance of contract
 obligations, 181

mixcom (Wisconsin) BBS, 573
mobile computing, 276-277
mode command (telnet), 365
modem control, 471-473
modems, 15, 465-473, 1156
 configurations, 467-469
 data compression, 470-471
 flow control, 466-467
 transfer rates, 469-470
 wiring, 467-469
moderated mailing lists,
 314-315
moderator, 1156
molecular biology, 278
monthly costs, 16-25
Morris, Robert, 53
Mosaic, 1156
mput command (ftp), 347
MRNet (Minnesota) dedicated
 access providers, 613
MSen (Michigan)
 dedicated access providers,
  613
 SLIP/PPP providers, 602
 terminal servers, 590
multicasting, 83
multimedia, 1156
multimedia e-mail, 318-319
music, 654-655

N

name caches, 90
name servers, 88-89
names
 DNS (Domain Name
  System), 64
  aliases, 84-85
  IP addresses, 80-83
  labels, 65-76
  subdomain fields, 77-79
  user/account fields, 79-80
 host, 58
NAP (Network Access Point)
 managers, 42-43
NASA Mail, 457
NASA.GOV domain, 94
National Center for
 Atmospheric Research
 (NCAR), 35
National Center for
 Supercomputing Applications
 (NCSA), 35

NevadaNet (Nevada) dedicated access providers, 614
New Jersey
  BBSs, 560
  dedicated access providers, 614
  SLIP/PPP providers, 603
  terminal servers, 590
New York
  BBSs, 560-562
  SLIP/PPP providers, 603
  terminal servers, 591
news events, reporting, 54
news groups, 418
  USENET, 11
news hierarchy (network news), 371
news readers, 390-398
  common features, 390
  expired articles, 390-391
  history, 401
  PSILink, 397-398
  rn news reader, 391-393
  tin news reader, 393-394
  WinNet Mail news reader, 394-396
newsgroups, 1157
  lists, 1060-1061
  reading, 1121-1122
  subscribing to with WinNET Mail, 1077-1078
newsletters, *see* periodicals
NEXIS, 149
NIC (Network Information Center), 58-59, 1157
NICLink, 40
NNTP (Network News Transport Protocol), 1157
  history, 400
  network news, receiving, 407-413
nodes, 62, 1157
nonfeasance of contract obligations, 181
nonrecursive resolving, 91
NORDUnet, 48
North Carolina
  BBSs, 562
  SLIP/PPP providers, 603
  terminal servers, 591
NorthWestNet (Washington) dedicated access providers, 615

Notes (Lotus), 306
NREN (National Research and Education Network), 41, 137-138, 242, 1157
NSF (National Science Foundation), 1157
  management goals, 42-43
  national network development, 264
  NSF Network Service Center (NNSC), 120-121
  supercomputer centers, 34-36
NSFNET (National Science Foundation's network), 34-36, 242, 1157
  acceptable use policy, 137-138
  goals, 42-43
  growth, 56
    host, 58-59
    traffic, 56-57
  Merit management, 36-38
  network connections, 45
    CSNET, 45-47
    government, 48-49
    international, 48
  Network Information Services services, 38-39
NSINET, 41, 1157
nwnexus (Washington)
  SLIP/PPP providers, 607
  terminal servers, 594

O

Oak ftp site, 631
OARnet (Ohio) terminal servers, 592
OARnet (Ohio/West Virginia)
  dedicated access providers, 614
  SLIP/PPP providers, 604
oceanography, 278
octets, 77-78
  IP address formats, 82-83
off-line mail reading systems, 303-304
Ohio
  BBSs, 562-564
  dedicated access providers, 614

SLIP/PPP providers, 604
  terminal servers, 591-592
oldcolo (Colorado)
  SLIP/PPP providers, 601
  terminal servers, 589
on-line games, 14
on-line corporate information, 243-244
on-line databases, 267
on-line domains, 95-96
on-line license agreements, 173-174
on-line proprietary software, 481-483
  America Online, 482-483
  WinCIM (CompuServe), 481-482
on-line services, 427-429
  America Online, 443-444
  national, 586
  organizations, 585-586
open command (ftp), 342
open command (telnet), 363
OPEN service primitive, 98
operating systems (UNIX), 32
Operation Desert Storm, 54-55
oral contracts, 161
organizations, e-mail, 297
originator header lines, 287-288
OTOH (On The Other Hand), 1157

P

PACCOM (Hawaii) dedicated access providers, 612
packet switching, 30-31, 1157
packets, 1157
panix (New York)
  SLIP/PPP providers, 603
  terminal servers, 591
Paperwork Reduction Act of 1980, 226
parallel, 1157
Paris Convention, 190
Patent Cooperation Treaty (PCT), 190
patent laws, 156-160
PC-Eudora program, 305
PC-Eudora SLIP/PPP software, 497
PDIAL, 1048, 1084

Sproull, Lee, 243
SRI (Stanford Research
  Institute), 29
SRI International Network
  Information Systems Center
  (SRI NISC), 116
stacks (TCP/IP), 98-99
standards
  Internet Architecture Board
    (IAB), 107
  Internet Engineering Task
    Force (IETF), 108-109
  Internet Society (ISOC),
    105-106
  STDs (Standards), 112-113,
    1039-1043
Stanford Research Institute
  (SRI), 29
starting
  ftp (File Transfer Protocol),
    340
  telnet, 363
state laws on computer crime,
  197-202
status command
  ftp, 349-350
  telnet, 365
STATUS service primitive, 98
STDs (Standards), 112-113
  listing by number,
    1039-1043
Stock Market Reports, 660
Stoll, Clifford, 52
student interaction, 253-254
Stuffit utility, 501
subdomain fields, 77-79
  zones, 91
subscribing, 1159
subscribing to USENET groups,
  1077-1078
sugar (Texas)
  BBSs, 570
  SLIP/PPP providers, 605
  terminal servers, 593
Sun Microsystems, Inc, 628-630
supercomputer centers, NSF,
  34-36
SURAnet Network Information
  Center (SURAnet NIC), 117
surfing, net, 14
system configuration (UNIX
  accounts), 1101-1102
systems administration,
  435-436

T

tables (host), 34
tal (criteria for choosing
  service), 419-420
talk hierarchy (network news),
  371
Talk Radio, 276
tar utility, 500
tax laws, 174
  sales/use taxes, 175
  tangible/intangible items,
    174
TCP (Transmission Control
  Protocol), 1159
TCP/IP (Transmission Control
  Protocol/Internet Protocol),
  31-32, 107
  early ARPANET usage, 34
  service primitives, 98-99
  SLIP/PPP software, 494-496
  stacks, 98-99
TCP/IP Network Administration
  (book), 123-124
technologies (packet switching),
  30-31
telecommunications
  carriers
    contracts, 166
    responsibilities, 168-169
  privacy, 211-214
  responsibilities of carriers,
    168-169
telecommuting, 247
teleconferencing, 420
telerama (Pennsylvania)
  SLIP/PPP providers, 604
  terminal servers, 592
television, 660-661
Telix for DOS terminal
  emulation software, 478-479
telnet, 359-366, 1082, 1159
  archie navigator, 505-506
  criteria for choosing service,
    419
telnet command (telnet), 363
/TEMPLATES/DOMAIN-
  TEMPLATE.TXT file, 96
TERC, 258
terminal emulation, 474-480
  Gopher navigator, 520

protocols, 475
scripting, 474
software
  Crosstalk, 476
  PROCOMM PLUS, 475
  QuickLink for DOS,
    477-478
  Telix for DOS, 478-479
  Terminal for Windows,
    476-477
  WinQVT for Windows
    terminal emulation
    software, 479-480
terminal types, 475
Terminal for Windows terminal
  emulation software, 476-477
terminal servers, 427-429,
  585-595
  Australia, 594
  California, 587-588
  Canada, 595
  Colorado, 588-589
  Illinois, 589
  Maryland, 589
  Massachusetts, 590
  Michigan, 590
  New Jersey, 590
  New York, 591
  North Carolina, 591
  Ohio, 591-592
  Pennsylvania, 592
  Rhode Island, 592
  Texas, 593
  United Kingdom, 595
  Virginia, 593
  Washington, 594
terminating ftp connections,
  342
test bed, 1159
Texas
  BBSs, 567-570
  dedicated access providers,
    615
  SLIP/PPP providers, 605
  terminal servers, 593
text files, editing in UNIX,
  1125-1129
THEnet (Texas)
  dedicated access providers,
    615
  SLIP/PPP providers, 605
threads, 1159
tin news reader (USENET),
  393-394

X-Y-Z

X-Y-Z

The Internet Society

Membership

The Internet Society is a professional membership organization with voting individual members and non-voting institutional members. Contact the Internet Society office for more information about the Institutional Member Program.

The Society publishes a quarterly magazine and holds an annual meeting to which all members and other interested parties are invited. The topics of the annual meetings vary, but focus on current research in networking, Internet functionality and growth, and other interests of the Society's constituency.

Join the Internet Society

The Internet Society is the only international professional society whose focus is to facilitate, support, and promote the technical evolution and growth of the Internet as a global communications infrastructure. The Society exists to serve the interests of individuals, corporations, governments, educators, and researchers.

Membership Benefits

- Professional growth through participation in conferences, technical standards development, publications, management of the Society's business, and public service via the K-12 Committee, Technologically Emerging Countries Committee, and others.

- Automatic subscription to the quarterly *Internet Society News*.

- Discounted member rates for conferences sponsored or co-sponsored by the Internet Society. Reduced subscription rates for magazines and newsletters.

- Keep up with the evolution of the Internet.

- Meet colleagues from around the globe with interests similar to your own.

- Access on-line databases.

Join now by copying and completing the form on the following page. For further information about the Internet Society, call (703) 648-9888 or send e-mail to isoc@isoc.org.

Internet Society

APPLICATION FOR MEMBERSHIP

To: Internet Society

Please enroll me as a member of the Internet Society. I understand that membership entitles me to receive the quarterly Internet Society News, reduced fees for attendance at Internet Society conferences and other benefits. Membership privileges will be for twelve months from the receipt of payment. I am applying for

_____ regular membership at $70.00

_____ student membership at $25.00 (please send proof of status)

NAME: (Mr/Mrs/Ms) _____

POSTAL ADDRESS: _____

_____

_____

PHONE: _____ **FACSIMILE:** _____

INTERNET ADDRESS: _____

Payment Information: Payment of Internet Society annual dues may be made via check, money order, credit card or wire transfer. File headers will be accepted as signatures for e-mail transactions.

_____ Please bill me.

_____ Payment is included with this application as below.

For **credit card** payments:

____AMEX ____VISA ____MC ____DINERS ____CARTE BLANCHE

Card Number: _____

Expiration Date: _____

Signature: _____

Send **wire transfers** to:

Bank: Riggs Bank of Virginia
Merrifield Office
8315 Lee Highway
Fairfax, VA 22116 USA

Bank ABA Number: 056001260

Account Number: Internet Society
14838710

Internet Society
Suite 100
1895 Preston White Drive
Reston, VA 22091-5434 USA

Tel: +1 703 648 9888
Fax: +1 703 620 0913
e-mail: isoc@isoc.org

Racontex

RACONTEX

The lists contained on the disk in the back of this book were processed with Racontex, the file indexer from Guy Software.

Racontex functions much like FolioViews, AskSam, Zyindex, and the STAIRS mainframe product. Every word in the document is indexed so that you can quickly search and locate text by the words it contains.

Racontex is useful for legal transcript, statutes, manuals, and so forth, and is ideal for on-line software manuals.

This copy of the Racontex loading engine (reader) was provided under special license to Que Corporation for use in *Using the Internet*, Special Edition. The complete Racontex package, including the loading and indexing engines, allows you to create your own indexed documents. To order Racontex, follow the instructions provided below. The shareware copy of Racontex is also available on many on-line services and bulletin boards.

> **Note**
>
> Guy Software has extended a special 50% discount to *Using the Internet* readers! See the special coupon on the reverse side of this page, or the file README.1ST on the disk.

Racontex Pricing

Special "Registration" Price

Designed for persons running an unlicensed demonstrator version. $100 gives a license to run both the loading/indexing engine and the search engine on a single computer.

Suggested Retail Pricing

Loading/Indexing engine is licensed to run on one computer, with searching engine licensed to run on three additional computers in a single organization with no resale of searchable documents.

$350 plus $25 for each additional computer, either networked or individually running the search engine within the organization.

Wholesale

Wholesale reproduction license, available to those wanting to reproduce the instructions and disks for retail sales at the rates and on the conditions above. Royalty equal to 40% of the above rates (minimum 10).

Wholesale purchase rates: 60% of the retail rate (minimum 5).

Licenses to use the system for the production of searchable documents for sale (which would include licenses to distribute the search engine) may be negotiated.

Order Form

Mail this form, along with your payment, to:

Guy Software
1752 Duchess Avenue
West Vancouver
British Columbia
CANADA   V7V 1P9

Name: _____

Address: _____

_____

_____

_____

```
Special "Registration" package for one computer only:      @ $100     [  ]
                              or
Retail Package—Load/index for one computer;
              Search for 3 others:                         @ $350     [  ]
Retail Package—additional computers Search:    @ $25 each    $
Special Que (Using the Internet) discount (50%):            x .50
Payment Enclosed:                                          _____
```

For other options, please write supplying details of the package desired.

If you are registering after using a demonstration copy, please state its number here:

Please check appropriate box:

```
                    [ ] 5.25"  360 Kb disks
                    [ ] 5.25"  1.2 Mb disk
                    [ ] 3.5"   720 Kb disk
```

Using the Internet Companion Disk

The disk that comes with this book is a standard IBM format, 1.44M disk. This disk contains everything you need to get connected and to be productive on the Internet. The following instructions will get you started quickly with the software. Read Appendix A, "Using the Companion Disk," for detailed information on installing and using the software.

The Electronic Lists

The disk includes several electronically indexed lists of information available on the Internet. These lists were indexed with a program called RACONTEX. See Appendix A, "Using the Companion Disk," for more information on RACONTEX.

To install these lists, follow these steps:

1. Place the companion disk in your floppy drive.

> **Note**
>
> These instructions assume you are using drive A; substitute the letter of your floppy drive where appropriate.

2. At a DOS prompt, type **a:\lists\install** *d:\directory*, where *d:\directory* is the letter of your hard drive and the directory where you want the lists installed. (If the directory specified doesn't exist, INSTALL will create it. If no directory is specified, the current directory will be used.) For example, if you type **a:\lists\install c:\intlists**, the lists would be installed in the \INTLISTS directory on the C drive.

After the INSTALL program finishes installing the software, you are returned to the DOS prompt. The lists are now installed and ready to use.

WinNET Mail

The disk also contains a copy of Computer Witchcraft's WinNET Mail program to get you connected to the Internet. You will need a copy of Microsoft Windows 3.1 to run this program and a valid credit card to access Computer Witchcraft's Internet services. See Appendix A for detailed information on installing and running WinNET Mail.

To install WinNET Mail, follow these steps:

1. Start Windows.

2. Place the companion disk in your floppy drive.

> **Note**
>
> These instructions assume you are using drive A. Substitute the letter of your floppy drive where appropriate.

3. From Program Manager, choose **F**ile, **R**un. The Run dialog box appears.

4. In the **C**ommand Line text box, type `a:\winnet\setup` and press Enter or choose OK.

5. Follow the Setup program's prompts and dialog boxes. See Appendix A, "Using the Companion Disk," for more information.

When the Setup program completes, you should have a WinNET Mail program group installed in your Windows Program Manager.

Software License Agreement